BATTLEGROUND
PRUSSIA

BATTLEGROUND PRUSSIA

THE ASSAULT ON GERMANY'S
EASTERN FRONT 1944–45

PRIT BUTTAR

OSPREY
PUBLISHING

First published in Great Britain in 2010 by Osprey Publishing,
Midland House, West Way, Botley, Oxford, OX2 0PH, UK
44-02 23rd Street, Suite 219, Long Island City, NY 11101, USA

E-mail: info@ospreypublishing.com

OSPREY PUBLISHING IS PART OF THE OSPREY GROUP

A CIP catalogue record for this book is available from the British Library

ISBN: 978 1 84908 790 2

Page layout by: Myriam Bell Design, France
Index by Mike Parkin
Typeset in Adobe Caslon Pro
Originated by PPS Grasmere Ltd, Leeds, UK
Printed in China through Worldprint

12 13 14 15 16   10 9 8 7 6 5 4 3 2 1

Osprey Publishing is supporting the Woodland Trust, the UK's leading woodland
conservation charity, by funding the dedication of trees.

Front Cover: Advance of the Red Army in East Prussia, February 1945. Soviet troops seize
the town Frauenburg. (akg-images)

www.osprypublishing.com

CONTENTS

LIST OF ILLUSTRATIONS

Soviet forces near Danzig, March 1945. (akg-images)

German refugees, East Prussia, early 1945. (Bundesarchiv Bild)

German refugees, Frisches Haff, February 1945. (Topfoto)

T-34 tanks, near Königsberg, February 1945. (Topfoto)

Soviet forces, near Königsberg, February 1945. (Topfoto)

German officers march into captivity, Königsberg, April 1945. (Bundesarchiv Bild)

LIST OF MAPS

AUTHOR'S NOTE

This book was conceived from a chance conversation with an elderly lady, who told me of her life in East Prussia, and her flight from her homeland in 1945. I am indebted to Gretel Caton for introducing me to this almost forgotten episode of World War II.

The list of those who have helped me with this project is enormous. My good friend David C. Clarke was instrumental in more ways than I can list, and Tom Houlihan, John Mulholland and Euan Ferguson tirelessly read the various drafts as I produced them. Doug Nash and David Glantz encouraged me at various points along the road, for which I am grateful, as I am to Fee Rushbrooke, who gave me insights into the geography and climate of the region. Contributors to two World War II websites – the Axis History Forum and Feldgrau – were a constant source of information and encouragement. Amongst them, Jan-Hendrik Wendler and Michael Miller were especially generous to me on several occasions.

My agent, Robert Dudley, showed great patience in introducing me to the world of publishing, and the staff at Osprey, in particular Jaqueline Mitchell, Jon Jackson and Emily Holmes, helped me turn the original manuscript into something far more presentable.

And last but not least, my family put up with my obsession with this project for many years, and without their encouragement I would have given up long before the end.

PREFACE

Hear me more plainly.
I have in equal balance justly weigh'd
What wrongs our arms may do, what wrongs we suffer,
And find our griefs heavier than our offences.

– William Shakespeare[1]

This book is the story of the last months of World War II in Northeast Europe. These months saw the final death of any lingering hope that, once the war was over, the old order in the old continent would be restored. Even as one war came to an end a new Cold War began, and would dominate the world for nearly half a century. Specifically, this book describes the Soviet assault into East and West Prussia in 1944 and 1945. The fighting was as tough as any phase of the bitter conflict on the *Ostfront* (Eastern Front), and it changed the map of Europe forever. The campaigns resulted in one of the largest migrations of Europeans in history and, before the fighting was over, three of the five worst recorded losses of life at sea, which in themselves accounted for about 17,000 lives. And yet, in the English-speaking world, these campaigns and battles in what was northeast Germany remain comparatively unknown.

Western accounts of the last year of World War II in Europe describe momentous events: the invasion of Normandy in June 1944, and the bitter fighting that followed; the American breakout and the envelopment of thousands of German troops in the Falaise pocket; the jubilant liberation of Paris; and lower-key but nevertheless equally important moments as the German occupying forces were driven from other parts of France and Belgium. After the bloody failure of the Western Allies to secure a bridgehead across the Rhine at Arnhem, the narrative passes to the final German offensive in the Ardennes. Thereafter, the tale is one of an unbroken series of Allied victories – the crossing of the Rhine, the envelopment of the Ruhr and the final German collapse. If other European theatres are mentioned at all, it is usually only in the context of the Red Army's final assault on Berlin in April 1945.

Compared to the war in Western Europe, the fighting on the *Ostfront* was bitter and brutal, huge in terms of the terrain involved, the armies deployed and the destruction and bloodshed that they wreaked. Both sides treated enemy prisoners and civilians in a manner that was shocking even at the time, and completely at variance with the Western viewpoint, as exemplified by the Hague and Geneva Conventions. The *Ostfront* war was not just one of territorial ambition or strategic gain; from the very start, it was an ideological conflict, a clash between two incompatible visions of the future of mankind. The men who fought in the east, and carried out the most terrible deeds, were portrayed by their enemies as sadistic killers, further stoking the hatred and the ideological differences between the two sides. And yet, for the great majority of the ordinary soldiers this was a war like so many others. They fought because they had to, conscripted into the vast armies that battled their way back and forth over hundreds of kilometres. Many of them were driven by a love of their homeland; for the Soviet soldiers in the first half of the war in the east, and for the Germans in the second half, there was also the great motivation of wishing to protect their beloved homeland from a brutal, implacable enemy. Whilst such factors existed in the west, there was not the additional ideological edge to push the terrible inhumanity of war to the same heights as in the east. The psyche of Germany and the Soviet Union was also different from that of Western nations. Both countries had been under totalitarian rule for many years, and an entire generation of Germans, and two generations of Soviets, had grown up in systems where they were denied access to objective news reports, and were encouraged to believe that their own system was inherently superior to any other. It was inevitable that when these two cultures clashed, the result could only be the complete destruction of one or the other.

Wars are fought for many reasons. Hitler's war against Poland and the Soviet Union was to gain territory, and to destroy communism, while his war against France and Britain was to secure a free hand in the east. Stalin's war with Hitler was forced upon him by the German invasion of 1941, but there is plentiful evidence that the Soviet leader was considering a pre-emptive war against Germany. From the Soviet point of view, what started as a war of survival slowly changed to one of revenge and conquest: the suffering of the Soviet Union was so great, that there had to be some territorial gain by way of compensation, and the map of Europe would need to be redrawn in a way that would prevent any future war from devastating Soviet territory. Given Stalin's record with his own population, it is unsurprising that he spared so little thought for the millions of Poles and Germans who would be displaced as a result of this policy.

The victims of this final phase of the war in the east were the civilians of East and West Prussia, who faced a terrible ordeal either during their attempted flight in the middle of winter, or at the hands of the conquering Red Army. Whilst some of them may have been ardent Nazis, and many may have voted for the National Socialists in pre-war Germany, it would be wrong to place all of the blame for Nazi Germany's crimes at their door. They were no more guilty than the Japanese civilians who endured American air raids on Tokyo, or the atomic bombs on Hiroshima and Nagasaki. The soldiers who fought for the Wehrmacht and the Red Army witnessed, and in many cases carried out, terrible acts of violence. Determining guilt amongst them is just as difficult an issue. Those of us fortunate to grow up in democracies, with free access to information and the right to speak our minds, and constantly encouraged to question our political leaders, sometimes underestimate how tightly Germany and the Soviet Union conditioned their citizens during the 1930s. We also forget that while we condemn the racism that formed such a major part of National Socialist ideology, this was an era in which the US Army was still segregated, and the British Empire denied self-determination to much of the non-white world.

The justice that followed the end of the war has been criticized as 'victors' justice'. Many Germans were punished for the crimes they had committed, but many more guilty parties escaped. Few, if any, Soviet personnel were ever charged with crimes perpetrated during the terrible campaigns across Prussia. In the years that followed 1945, both sides would attempt to portray themselves as victims – if they acknowledged their own crimes, they placed more stress on those of their enemies.

The purpose of this book is not to allocate blame. War is truly terrible, and drives people to terrible acts. Whilst the atrocities of World War II were on a huge scale, atrocities had occurred in previous conflicts. Indeed, we have even seen them since 1945 in Europe, when Yugoslavia disintegrated in the 1990s. The aim of this book is simply to describe what happened when the Red Army reached German territory, and the desperate battles that followed. The consequences of these campaigns defined the shape of the post-war map of northeast Europe, the full significance of which has only become clear since the fall of the Iron Curtain.

OVERVIEW

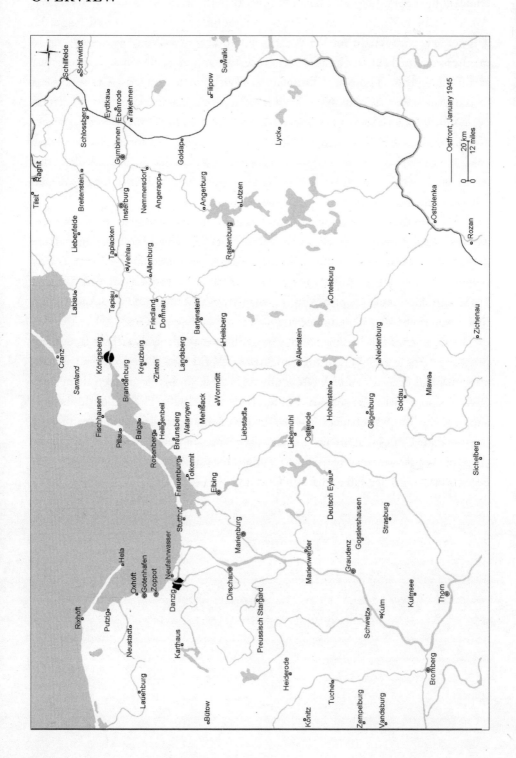

Ostfront, January 1945

0 — 20 km
0 — 12 miles

Schirwindt
Schillfelde
Eydtkau
Ebenrode
Trakehnen
Schlossberg
Filipow
Suwalki
Gumbinnen
Lyck
Goldap
Raghit
Tilsit
Breitenstein
Liebenfelde
Nemmersdorf
Instenburg
Angerapp
Angerburg
Lötzen
Ostrolenka
Tapiacken
Wehlau
Allenburg
Rastenburg
Rozan
Labiau
Tapiau
Friedland
Domnau
Bartenstein
Ortelsburg
Zichenau
Cranz
Samland
Königsberg
Brandenburg
Kreuzburg
Zinten
Lagdsberg
Heilsberg
Allenstein
Neidenburg
Fischhausen
Balga
Heiligenbeil
Braunsberg
Mehlsack
Wormditt
Liebstadt
Hohenstein
Gilgenburg
Soldau
Milawa
Sichelberg
Pillau
Rosenberg
Natangen
Liebemühl
Osterode
Brandenburg
Tolkemit
Frauenburg
Elbing
Deutsch Eylau
Hela
Stuthof
Marienburg
Marienwerder
Graudenz
Gosslershausen
Strasburg
Oxhoft
Gotenhafen
Neufahrwasser
Zoppot
Danzig
Dirschau
Schwetz
Kulm
Kulmsee
Thorn
Rixhoft
Putzig
Preussisch Stargard
Neustadt
Karthaus
Heiderode
Bromberg
Lauenburg
Bütow
Könitz
Tuchel
Zempelburg
Vandsburg

INTRODUCTION
THE SLAVS AND THE TEUTONS

Poland shall be treated as a colony; the Poles shall be the slaves of the greater German World Empire.

– Hans Frank[1]

In 1934, Gretel Dost was a young child living in the village of Friedrichstein, near Königsberg, in the German province of East Prussia. One of the most memorable days of her childhood came when Marion Dönhoff, the daughter of Graf August Karl Dönhoff, whose family had lived in their estate in Friedrichstein for centuries, visited her school. Dost was struck by the young aristocrat's beauty, and promised herself that if she ever had a daughter, she would name her child Marion. After the war, Marion Dönhoff wrote a personal account of her escape from East Prussia, and her introduction to her book paints a vibrant picture of her homeland during the early 20th century:

> This is a book about departure. Departure from the images of my youth: a vast sky, which
> arched over wide fields, modest villages, cobblestones, sunflowers in front gardens, geese
> on the roads, and everywhere those wonderful avenues that in the west were choked with
> motorized traffic. Departure from a lost world, in which the seasons still determined the
> rhythm of life: cows grazing in summer meadows, rain-clouds over empty fields of stubble,
> the cry of wild geese, heading north in the spring, the call of jays in the autumnal woods,
> the tracks of foxes in fresh snow in the forests.[2]

This idyllic picture hides certain harsh truths. The aristocratic *Junker* families who controlled much of the land (and produced such a large proportion of German officers) were traditionally conservative, and had been reluctant to embrace modernization before World War I. Consequently, their farms struggled to compete with those in the richer lands of western Germany.

As World War II drew to a close, this rural, deeply traditional land was destined to become one of the bloodiest battlefields of the entire conflict, in the depths of a bitterly cold winter. The brutality with which the Red Army would treat the Prussian

1

civilian population was shocking, but the seeds for this terrible harvest had been growing for years.

East Prussia had been a German region, in character at least, since the arrival of the Teutonic Knights in the area in 1226. Carved out of Slavic territories, the area was settled by Germans as far north as Riga. The rulers of Brandenburg and Poland variously owned the rapidly developing town of Danzig, before the Teutonic Knights seized it. Germans and Slavs continued to contest possesson of the territory, often settling these claims on the battlefield. Religious differences between the various communities – most Prussian Germans became Protestants, while the Poles remained Catholics and the Russian populations to the east remained Orthodox Christians – were strong barriers to integration, and helped preserve a sense of identity in the Prussian duchy, which was established in 1525. The Hohenzollern family inherited the dukedom in 1618, resulting in a shift in the centre of gravity for the German province. Most of the lands belonging to the Hohenzollerns lay to the west of the Vistula, and although their collective possessions were generally referred to as Prussian territory, the original Prussia was now increasingly called 'East Prussia'.

In 1701, Prussia became a kingdom. King Friedrich II, or Frederick the Great, became embroiled in fighting with the French, Russians and Swedes in the Seven Years' War (1756–63); backed by the British and the tiny resources of Hannover, he found himself facing overwhelming threats. The survival of Prussia owed much to his military skill, but by the end of 1761 it seemed that it would be only a matter of time before Prussia was crushed by its enemies. The turning point in the war came when Czarina Elizabeth of Russia died in early 1762. Her successor, Peter III, was far less hostile to Prussia, and signed a peace treaty with Frederick. The Swedes also withdrew from the anti-Prussian alliance, and Frederick turned on the Austrians, defeating them decisively at Burkersdorf in July 1762. In just a few short months, Prussia had moved from the brink of defeat to decisive victory, something that Hitler constantly held in the forefront of his mind in the dark days of 1945.

In 1806, Prussia suffered a humiliating defeat at French hands at the battles of Jena and Auerstedt, and was forced to join Napoleon's 'Continental System' against the British. A corps of Prussian troops commanded by General von Yorck formed the northern flank of Napoleon's invasion of Russia in 1812, and its commander soon received representations from Prussians fighting against Napoleon, calling on him to change sides. Von Yorck asked for advice from King Friedrich Wilhelm III, but was merely told to 'act according to circumstances'. Faced by a conflict between his orders and his own conscience, von Yorck hesitated again and again before finally turning against Napoleon. To his dying day, he remained unsure of whether he had done the right thing, a crisis of conscience that was to be all too familiar to a later generation of Prussian officers who wrestled with whether they should continue to obey orders sent to them in the name of their Führer.

In 1870, Prussia – now ruled by King Wilhelm I – was plunged into war with France. Before the war was over, Wilhelm was persuaded – somewhat against his wishes – to become Kaiser of a unified Germany. Wilhelm was a spartan figure, rarely out of uniform. If any word could sum up the character of this archetypal Prussian, it would be the almost untranslatable *Nüchternheit*, an approach to life combining sobriety, simplicity and austerity. Other strong traits, both admired and ridiculed elsewhere in Europe, were a powerful sense of duty and a willingness to accept sacrifice; the Garnisonkirche in Potsdam, the spiritual home of everything Prussian, had a glockenspiel that played a well-known song: 'Show loyalty and honesty until your dying day.'[3]

Wilhelm's son Friedrich ruled only briefly before he succumbed to cancer, and was succeeded by Wilhelm II. During his reign, most traces of the traditional Prussian virtues were swept away from the German capital in a blizzard of extravagance. It was perhaps the beginning of a rift between on the one hand the urbane world of Berlin and the heights of political power, and on the other the German Army, which remained in many respects (particularly amongst the officer corps) very Prussian in its outlook. These differences would resurface again when the Kaiser was gone, and Germany was once more preparing for war.

After the Great War of 1914–18, Poland – which had been divided between its powerful neighbours for more than a century – was re-created, at least partly because the French saw political advantages in surrounding Germany with pro-French states to guard against any future German attack on France. Immediately, problems arose concerning the borders of Poland, and the status of the different ethnic populations within those borders. The years of occupation had failed to eliminate Polish culture, but tracts of territory that would fall within the new Poland had large German, Russian and Austrian populations. The western and southern borders of Poland were decided by the victorious powers. Poland would have access to the Baltic coastline, but the key city of Danzig would be a 'free city', a designation it had enjoyed in previous centuries. The Polish response was to establish a new port immediately to the north of Danzig, named Gdynia. From humble beginnings, this grew into the busiest port in the Baltic by the mid 1930s. Danzig itself, with a stronger German identity than the countryside around it, now found itself isolated.

To the north of Poland lay East Prussia. Masuria, its southern province, was an area of lakes and woodland. It had a large ethnic Polish population, and a plebiscite was organized after the World War I in the expectation that the population would vote to join Poland, thus further weakening Germany. To the surprise of almost everyone, a large majority of Masuria's ethnic Poles voted to remain part of Germany.

The real difficulty with Poland's borders, though, lay in the east. After the surprise victory of the Poles over Lenin's armies, the Treaty of Riga in 1921 granted control of considerable parts of former Soviet and Ukrainian territory to Poland. Much of this new territory of eastern Poland had large Russian, Ukrainian and Belorussian populations, and the Poles themselves were a minority. The British Foreign Secretary, Lord Curzon, had proposed a frontier along a line that was subsequently named after him far to the west of the Riga Treaty frontier, but events passed this proposal by, leaving it to resurface at various stages, with minor but critical alterations, over the decades that followed.

The inter-war years, therefore, saw an arrangement that was unsatisfactory to all three of the major countries involved. Germany resented having had to concede what had been the province of West Prussia to Poland, and that there was no land connection between East Prussia and the rest of Germany. The Poles resented the fact that they had no control over Danzig, and the Russians resented Polish territorial gains at their expense. The city of Danzig remained strongly German in identity, though Polish inhabitants dominated the surrounding countryside. Poland also had considerable difficulties with the large non-Polish populations within its borders – about a quarter of its total population was made up of Ukrainians, Jews and Germans. In addition, there was constant tension in the Polish parts of Silesia and the former West Prussia, where large ethnic German populations resented being part of Poland.

The rapid industrialization of other parts of Europe in the first half of the 20th century had only a limited effect on the former Duchy of Prussia, perhaps because the region had few of the deposits of ore and coal that drove other regions forward. Furthermore, the isolated nature of East Prussia, which resulted in constant uncertainty about whether it would in the long term remain part of Germany, acted as a disincentive for financial investors. The cities of Königsberg and Elbing were the homes of some heavy industry, particularly in connection with shipbuilding, but the rest of East Prussian economic well-being was due to the area's agriculture and a rural lifestyle that had changed little for decades. Propped up by state subsidies, without which the agricultural economy of East Prussia would have collapsed, the landowners supported the Deutschnationale Volkspartei (DNVP; German National People's Party), with its anti-socialist policies and its support for what it called 'Christian values and German family life'. But despite Prussia's relative poverty, and the huge sense of injustice and isolation that resulted from the severance of a land connection with the rest of Germany, the rising fortunes of the National Socialists made little impact. In the May 1928 elections, the Nazi Party secured less than 1 per cent of the vote, its worst performance anywhere in Germany. The local Party organization was chaotic and poorly led, and Hitler decided something needed to be done. At the same time, the Party faced a different problem in the Ruhr, where several powerful figures were at loggerheads, seeking to undermine each other in their personal scrambles for power. To resolve both problems at the same time, Hitler ordered Erich Koch, one of the leading Party personalities in the Ruhr, to take over control of the Party in East Prussia. His removal from the Ruhr brought to an end the infighting that threatened to fragment the party, and Koch's boundless self-belief and energy provided a welcome boost for the demoralized Party officials in East Prussia.

Koch was one of four children, born in the town of Elberfeld in the Ruhr. He served in Russia during the Great War, where he spent only a brief time in the frontline before his peacetime skills with telegraphy, learned during his employment in the railways, were put to use. He spent a long spell in a military hospital suffering from illness, something that he later used to create a story of how he had been seriously wounded on active service. After the war, he was active in a number of paramilitary campaigns, including an ill-fated attempt to resist French occupation of the Saarland, an experience that left him with a conviction that the Weimar Republic was too weak to lead Germany effectively. Koch was an early adherent of the Nazi Party, though at first he didn't entirely sign up to some of Hitler's views, such as those concerning racial superiority. He was delighted to accept the role of Gauleiter of East Prussia, as it gave his political ambitions full rein and simultaneously provided him with a good income.

In East Prussia, Koch set up a Byzantine system of 'black accounts', allowing the diversion of considerable amounts of money. The precise sum is now impossible to determine, and the final disposal of this cash also remains a mystery. Part of this process involved the creation of the 'Erich Koch Institute', a vehicle ostensibly designed to help industrialization, and to organize training for young East Prussian Party members. In reality, it grew into a major commercial concern, with interests in many companies, both industrial and commercial, often with associates of Koch as their managers and beneficiaries. Some of these were acquired under dubious circumstances, sometimes after their previous owners were arrested and imprisoned for trivial offences. Whilst such practices were commonplace amongst the Party's Gauleiters, Koch earned a reputation for being particularly unscrupulous in this regard. He took advantage of the resources of the Institute for his own ends, moving to the Institute-owned Friedrichsburg estate close to Königsberg in 1938. He was careful, however, to keep his own involvement in the more questionable aspects of the Institute's affairs to a minimum, preferring to work through the Institute's manager, Bruno Dzubba.

By the early 1930s, the DNVP was a declining force, and briefly formed an alliance with the National Socialists, who rapidly eclipsed and replaced it. The other political parties in the area rarely stirred outside the larger towns. Given the extensively rural nature of East Prussian life, they therefore failed to keep in touch with a large part of the electorate, unlike Koch and his deputies, who tirelessly addressed several meetings a day in order to ensure that their message was heard widely. The citizens of East Prussia, who regarded themselves as dangerously isolated as a result of the Treaty of Versailles, welcomed the strident calls by the National Socialists for the return of Memel and the Polish Corridor to the Reich. From barely 1 per cent of the vote in 1928, the National Socialists rose to secure 47.1 per cent in 1932.

Despite subsidies for East Prussian agriculture, the economy remained fragile, not least because of the province's isolation from the rest of Germany. Unemployment remained a major problem, and the success or failure of Koch and the Nazi Party would to a large extent depend on how this problem was resolved. Fortunately for Koch, the level of unemployment in East Prussia was not as severe as elsewhere in Germany, and he was able to use his good relations with Hitler and Hermann Göring, Hitler's deputy, to ensure sufficient funds to allow several major projects to proceed, thus mopping up some of the urban unemployed in a relatively short time. Far more effective was a ruthless massaging of unemployment data, creating the illusion of almost complete employment, to the extent that East Prussia was held up as an example to the rest of Germany. Nevertheless, the narrow corridor of land that allowed Polish access to the Baltic was now increasingly a source of tension between Poland and Germany, as was Danzig itself.

Danzig was one of the last cities to endorse the Nazi Party. In the 1927 elections for the city's senate, the Party succeeded in securing only a single seat out of a total of 120. For a while, Koch attempted to have Danzig included within his realm, thus increasing his personal power, but Hitler had other plans. First, he expelled senior local officials from the Party. Göring was sent to Danzig twice in 1930 to make important speeches and to try to pull together the disparate local factions, and when he returned to Munich he advised Hitler that a new personality should be sent to Danzig. Albert Forster was the name that was suggested.

Forster was the son of a prison official from the town of Fürth, in the part of northern Bavaria known as Franconia. His early life was unremarkable; he struggled at school, spending an extra two years before completing his basic education. In a town with a large, prosperous Jewish population, the relatively impoverished Forster rapidly came to resent the successful Jewish families around him, and was an early and enthusiastic member of the Nazi Party. He proved to be a very capable organizer and public speaker, and was responsible for the rapid rise in Party fortunes across Franconia. He was therefore an ideal candidate to be sent to Danzig.

Forster arrived in Danzig in October 1930, to find a city where the main issue was unemployment, something that was of far greater local importance than the political turmoil that dominated Germany itself. Armed with a document from Hitler granting him complete power over the local Party, Forster threw himself energetically into the election campaign that was currently under way. Over the coming years, he presided over an increasingly dominant Party: in November 1930, the Party increased its standing to 12 seats in the newly restructured Danzig Volkstag of 72 seats, and became a coalition partner of the minority government; in May 1933, the Party won an absolute majority of 38 seats in Danzig; and in April 1935, 43 seats.

The reasons for the success of the Party were multiple. Other parties had been extensively undermined by violent means. Forster had also played a prominent part, as a member of the minority coalition, in creating a public works programme to find employment for the city's 40,000 unemployed. There was also a growing feeling amongst the city's German population that their best hopes for prosperity lay with reunion with the German Reich, and they saw the Nazi Party as the strongest means of achieving this goal.

The Poles grew increasingly unhappy with developments in Danzig, aware that whatever its international status Danzig was being treated more and more as if it were part of the Reich. Indeed, in October 1936, Forster declared in a speech that: 'Danzig today is already as good as German, and soon will be completely German. To be sure, people talk of treaties. But treaties are just paper, which can be torn up.'[4]

Koch and Forster were very different characters. Hermann Rauschning, who was briefly the president of the Danzig Senate before he was driven out by Forster, later wrote a book in which he compared Forster unfavourably with Koch, describing them as 'Siegfried and Hagen in the Party'.[5] He went on to suggest that while Forster was from the 'nationalist' wing of the movement, and a 'genuine Nazi', he was limited by his complete belief in everything that Hitler said, regardless of whether he understood it himself. Such subservience reduced him to the status of a 'primitive mouthpiece of Hitler'.[6] Koch, by contrast, was from the 'socialist' wing of the Party, more receptive to new ideas and genuinely able to laugh at himself. Other contemporaries paint a far less flattering picture of the East Prussian Gauleiter: 'He had not the slightest training for such an important office, but still spoke volubly on the subject. Possessed by an unparalleled need for recognition and an insatiable hunger for power, he made his way upwards, constantly seeking to be noticed by his Führer in his new actions.'[7]

At a meeting with Göring and others in May 1939, Hitler made his views about Poland clear to his subordinates. Austria and the Sudetenland had been incorporated into the Reich, and the way was now clear for a resolution with regard to Poland. Hitler told his subordinates:

Poland will always be on the side of our enemies. In spite of treaties of friendship, Poland has always had the secret intention of exploiting every opportunity to do us harm.

Danzig is not the subject of the dispute at all. It is a question of expanding our living space in the East and of securing our food supplies, of the settlement of the Baltic problem. Food supplies can be expected only from thinly populated areas. Over and above the natural fertility, thoroughgoing German exploitation will enormously increase the surplus. There is no other possibility for Europe.

Colonies: Beware of gifts of colonial territory. This does not solve the food problem. Remember – blockade.

If fate brings us into conflict with the West, the possession of extensive areas in the East will be advantageous. We shall be able to rely even less in time of war than in peace upon record harvests.

The population of non-German areas will perform no military service, and will be available as a source of labour.

The Polish problem is inseparable from conflict with the West.

Poland's internal power of resistance to Bolshevism is doubtful. Thus Poland is of doubtful value as a barrier against Russia.

It is questionable whether military success in the West can be achieved by a quick decision, questionable too is the attitude of Poland.

The Polish government will not resist pressure from Russia. Poland sees danger in a German victory in the West, and will attempt to rob us of the victory.

There is therefore no question of sparing Poland, and we are left with the decision:

To attack Poland at the first suitable opportunity.[8]

Beyond Poland, though, was the Soviet Union, the ideological enemy of National Socialist Germany. Again, Hitler had no illusions about who was the real enemy, and was frustrated by the failure of the western powers to see this, as he told his inner circle on 11 August 1939: 'Everything I undertake is directed against Russia; if the west is too stupid and blind to understand this, I will be forced to come to terms with the Russians, to strike at the west, and then after subduing it to turn against the Soviet Union with my massed forces.'[9]

Fortunately for Hitler, Stalin and the Soviets also had a low opinion of the Poles. In a letter to Vyacheslav Molotov (Stalin's Foreign Minister) in 1944, Ivan Maisky, formerly the Soviet Ambassador in London, wrote:

> The purpose of the USSR must be the creation of an independent and viable Poland: however, we are not interested in the appearance of too big and too strong a Poland. In the past, Poland was almost always Russia's enemy, and no-one can be sure that the future Poland would become a genuine friend of the USSR (at least during the lifetime of the rising generation). Many doubt it, and it is fair to say that there are serious grounds for such doubts.[10]

Whilst this letter was written as the war was coming to its close, its sentiments were not new. The Molotov–Ribbentrop Pact was announced to a stunned world on 23 August 1939. Germany and the Soviet Union agreed not to go to war with each other. Yet the most important part of the treaty was the unpublished secret additional protocol, which was not finalized until Poland had fallen. This carved up northeast Europe between the two countries; Article II of the protocol dealt specifically with Poland:

> In the event of a territorial and political rearrangement of the areas belonging to the Polish State, the spheres of influence of Germany and the USSR shall be bounded approximately by the line of the rivers Narev, Vistula and San.
>
> The question of whether the interests of both parties make desirable the maintenance of an independent Polish State and how such a state should be bounded can only be definitely determined in the course of further political developments.
>
> In any event both governments will resolve this question by means of a friendly agreement.

Neither dictator had any long-term intention to abide by the terms of the treaty, but for the moment it was in both of their interests. Within hours of signing the treaty, Stalin was telling his confidants: 'Of course, it's all a game to see who can fool whom. I know what Hitler's up to. He thinks he's outsmarted me but actually it's I who have tricked him.'[11] Molotov explained matters to the Supreme Soviet in even more detail, even as German troops flooded into Poland: 'A quick blow against Poland, first by the German Wehrmacht and then by the Red Army, and nothing more will be left of this hateful offspring of the Versailles Treaty.'[12]

The Germans invaded Poland on 1 September 1939, in what Hitler deliberately portrayed as a different kind of war. Immediately before the outbreak of war, he told a conference that 'I have ordered my Totenkopf units to the east with the order to kill without pity or mercy all men, women and children of Polish race or language.'[13] As the fighting began, he instructed his troops to be merciless: 'I have given orders – and I will have anyone who says a word of criticism shot – that the purpose of the war is not to reach a designated line, but is the physical destruction of the enemy … close your hearts to sympathy. Brutal action. Strength is right.'[14]

The first shots of World War II are claimed to have been fired in the Bay of Danzig by the elderly German battleship *Schleswig-Holstein*. The ship's four 280mm guns battered the small Polish garrison just outside Danzig at Westerplatte, and the bombardment was followed by a ground assault by a variety of German naval infantry and local SS units. To the surprise of the Germans, the tiny garrison of fewer than 200 Polish soldiers held out for a week before surrendering, despite being bombarded by land, sea and air.

Elsewhere in Danzig, Polish administrative buildings were seized without incident before dawn. Resistance was minimal, except at the Polish post office buildings in Heveliusplatz. Albert Forster, who had been declared the supreme civil authority in Poland overnight, was taken to the square in an armoured car. The frustrated commander of the police unit that had been tasked with taking the post office, Polizeioberst Willi Bethke, told Forster that he intended to blow up the building and its 50 defenders. Forster refused to allow this, for fear of damage to surrounding buildings. Instead, Bethke's men pumped petrol into the basement and set fire to it. Five men of the garrison burned to death. Six others, including a 12-year-old girl, were left badly burned, and died the following day without receiving any medical treatment.[15] It was a clear sign of the brutal nature of Hitler's new war in the East.

There were thousands of ethnic Germans on Polish territory at the beginning of the war, and in many cases their Polish neighbours turned on them. The German residents of the small corridor of land running to the Baltic coast immediately west of Danzig were rounded up by the Polish authorities in August 1939. When the war began, they were marched on foot towards Lowicz, near Warsaw. Many were badly treated en route, and those who were unable to continue were often shot. The Wehrmacht caught up with them on 9 September, bringing their ordeal to an end. In the city of Bromberg, about 10 per cent of the population of 117,000 were ethnic Germans, and this group suffered greatly until the city fell to the advancing Germans on 6 September. Somewhere between 3,500 and 5,800 ethnic Germans were killed in such incidents.[16] A report was later produced for Hitler, who rejected it out of hand, insisting that the report's findings should be increased tenfold. This action resulted in a figure of 58,000 Germans being allegedly killed by their Polish neighbours, a number that was used to justify harsh measures against the Polish population. Some ethnic German communities had organized Selbstschutz, or self-defence groups, in the brief days before the German troops arrived, and these groups were now used for 'reprisals' against the Poles. By October, the groups boasted a strength of more than 17,000 in the Danzig–West Prussia area alone, and had killed over 4,000 Poles. Anyone with a previous record of having spoken out against Germany was liable for arrest. Decisions about who should live or die were made in the most arbitrary manner, without any legal process. The Selbstschutz were formally disbanded at the end of the year, and many of their personnel were incorporated into SS units, where they continued their activities.

In addition to the Selbstschutz, several Einsatzkommandos ('task forces') were deployed in Poland. Their main task was to round up the Polish intelligentsia; it was the intention of Heinrich Himmler, head of the SS, to decapitate Polish society, leaving a pliable mass of relatively unskilled workers for German exploitation. Lists of victims had been prepared in advance, and the Einsatzkommandos acted swiftly to execute their orders, in a very real sense. Their activities were particularly intense around Danzig and what was now known as West Prussia – this area was to be cleansed completely of Poles. By the time that their activities wound down in early 1940, the Einsatzkommandos had killed between 60,000 and 80,000 people.[17] Only a few Germans raised any protests at this mass murder. Generaloberst Johannes Blaskowitz, commander of German Army units in the east, complained about the indiscriminate nature of the shootings, and made clear his strong opposition to plans to execute the entire male Polish population of certain villages. Hitler replied by deriding the childish attitude of the army leadership, adding that he had always disliked Blaskowitz, and had never trusted him. Lily Jungblut, the wife of a farmer from Hohensalza, who had been a Party member herself since 1930, wrote to Göring in his role as President of East Prussia to complain that the mass executions and arrests were surely not the will of the Führer. Göring made Himmler aware of this letter; Himmler promised to investigate. As a result, Jungblut was arrested by the Gestapo.[18]

The Soviet Union joined the attack on Poland on 17 September, when the vast bulk of the Polish Army was committed in the west. The Soviet forces claimed to be saving the Poles from fascist invaders, which must have led to some awkward moments when the Red Army and Wehrmacht held a joint victory parade in Brest-Litovsk. The result of the invasion was that Poland was again partitioned by its powerful neighbours, and the boundary between the two powers was remarkably close to the Curzon Line. All territory to the east was annexed by Stalin, though he agreed to pass part of it to Lithuania. The following year, with the consent of the Germans, Stalin absorbed Lithuania, Latvia and Estonia into the Soviet Union. The Germans took possession of the territories they had lost to Poland in 1919.

The conduct of the war in the east – against the *Untermenschen* ('subhumans') as Hitler termed the peoples there – would always be different from its conduct in the west. To their great credit, many German officers and ordinary soldiers ignored the more brutal orders that came down from above; but a great many others were only too willing to carry them out. An example of the different ways in which German authorities behaved can be seen in the case of Major Sahla. In late 1939, the major, a renowned equestrian champion, was drinking in a hotel in the town of Preussisch Stargard, a short distance south of Danzig, with the local mayor, Johnst, SS-Scharführer Schicks and a public health official called Dr Völkner. The conversation turned to the issue of removing people deemed to be 'biological inferiors'. Völkner and Schicks, who had already been involved in the execution of people infected with syphilis, commented on the large numbers of German soldiers who had acquired infections after encounters with Polish prostitutes. Johnst immediately ordered the police to round up eight women, who allegedly had sexually transmitted infections. The women were taken to the cells attached to the court in the town. At midnight, the drinking party – without Johnst – went to the cells, and selected five women, who were taken to another cell. There, Völkner attempted to strangle them with his braces. He failed, and Sahla decided to shoot the five women through the neck, claiming later that he was acting to put the suffering women out of their misery. The men left the cells, only to return later, when they discovered to their alarm that there were only four corpses present – one of the women, badly injured but not dead, had managed to escape. She was found, and taken to the prison hospital. The presence of a woman with gunshot wounds resulted in a report being written, bringing the matter to the attention of higher authorities.

When he became aware of the incident, General Fedor von Bock, the local German Army commander, immediately ordered Sahla's arrest. No action was taken against any of the Party officials involved – Johnst was a long-standing comrade of Forster, who acted quickly to protect his colleague. He even tried to intervene on Sahla's behalf, telephoning von Bock to say that he intended to discuss the matter with Hitler himself. He made light of the incident, suggesting that it was inappropriate to punish Sahla for his involvement, and even saying that he could see nothing criminal in the major's behaviour, and that Hitler would doubtless see things similarly.

Von Bock refused to be swayed by Forster. Sahla was court-martialled and found guilty, and condemned to death. Hitler promptly intervened, granting Sahla a pardon, though he was reduced to the ranks and sentenced to six years' imprisonment. He served his time in a penal battalion, and was killed on the *Ostfront* in 1942. No legal action was taken against any of the others present at the killing of the Polish women. The Reich Ministry of the Interior dismissed Johnst from his post as mayor, but within two weeks Forster had found him a new position.[19]

Koch had reluctantly ceded parts of West Prussia to Forster, but in return received substantial parts of Poland, amounting to more than 16,000 square kilometres and more than a million inhabitants, few of whom were German. The area to the east of East Prussia, around the town of Suwalki, was the scene of several mass executions and deportations as local Nazis – with the full backing of Koch – attempted to drive out the Polish majority to make way for German 'settlers'. Many of these settlers were ethnic Germans repatriated from the Baltic states; other Baltic Germans were resettled in the former Polish parts of Danzig and the surrounding territories. The area around the Polish town of Ciechanow, now renamed Zichenau by the Germans, became part of East Prussia, and was intended by Koch as a future industrial centre.

The executions of Polish 'intellectuals' in the Zichenau area reached a peak in 1940, with some 3,000 people being killed or left to die in the squalid conditions of the Soldau prison camp, 50km northwest of Zichenau. In later years, the death toll in the camp continued, but was more due to efforts to suppress the burgeoning Polish resistance movement than a continuation of the attempt to exterminate the Polish intelligentsia. Meanwhile, ordinary Poles found their lives more and more constrained. Germans were given priority in shops and restaurants, free contact between German and Polish civilians was greatly restricted and employment opportunities for Poles were reduced to those areas of work deemed most essential. Mass deportations from the annexed parts of Poland were organized from late 1940 to early 1941, with many of those deported – particularly Jews – being sent to the ghetto in Czestochowa. More deportations followed until March 1943. The impact of these executions and deportations on the population was enormous. When German troops seized the Zichenau district in 1939, it was home to about 80,000 Jews. By the summer of 1944, this number had fallen to only 350. In total, the district's population fell by 160,000 during the German occupation.

In Soviet-occupied Poland, conditions were no less harsh. More than a million Poles were dispatched to Siberia by Stalin's NKVD police organization. Several thousand Polish officers who had been taken prisoner by the Red Army were executed and buried in the forest at Katyn. When the Germans later found this mass grave, the western Allies did all they could to suppress the evidence of this atrocity committed by the Soviets, for fear of its effect on the difficult alliance with Stalin.

On 22 June 1941, Hitler unleashed his armies against the Soviet Union. It was the ultimate manifestation of his desire to see Germany expand its territories to the east.

In order to achieve this, the Slav populations of the occupied lands would have to give way to new German settlers. Many Soviet people were to be reduced to serf status, while others would simply be starved to death. From the very start, neither side showed any compunction about respecting established rules of war. Erich von Manstein, commander of the German XLVI Panzer Corps in the north, was shown the bodies of a German reconnaissance unit that had been cut off and wiped out. Many of the corpses had been deliberately mutilated.[20] Elsewhere, German units also showed no hesitation in using the most brutal measures against prisoners.

Erich Koch saw the seizure of Soviet territory as a further opportunity to increase his own powerbase, and in July 1941 he was nominated as Reichskommissar (Reich Commissioner) for the Ukraine. He then successfully lobbied Hitler to have the territory around the city of Bialystok assigned to his jurisdiction too, providing him with a continuous land corridor from the Baltic to the Black Sea. Bialystok was formerly part of Poland, handed over to the Red Army by the Wehrmacht in 1939. It was, even by Eastern European standards, a very underdeveloped area, only slightly smaller than East Prussia itself before Polish territory was added to it, with a population of 1.5 million people, most living in small farms and villages. Restrictions for non-German residents of the region were draconian – non-essential journeys, use of the telephone and postal services, even types of employment, were all banned. Movement restrictions were particularly difficult for the population in such a large rural area, resulting in widespread food shortages. The punishment for most crimes was execution, and there was a policy of collective responsibility, with entire villages being punished for the misdemeanours of individuals. The province was merely something to be exploited, with as little investment as possible; Koch stated that it was insignificant 'and entirely unimportant … if a few million foreigners' had to go hungry.[21]

Koch's greatest gain in the allocation of territories was the Ukraine. Hitler designated this area as the most important of the eastern conquests, and accordingly insisted that the person that he regarded as his best Gauleiter administer it. The area concerned was vast, some 340,000 square kilometres, with almost 17 million inhabitants, of whom about 1.5 million were Jews. Koch, consciously positioning himself close to Hitler's point of view, made clear how he intended to run the Ukraine:

If these people work ten hours a day, then eight hours of that must be for us. All sentimental thoughts must be put aside. These people must be ruled with iron force, so that they help us win the war. We have not liberated them for the good of the Ukraine, rather to provide Germany with essential *Lebensraum* and to guarantee its food supplies.[22]

As in Poland and Bialystok, local people were forbidden from living with Germans, and had their movements strictly curtailed. The Ukrainian people, who welcomed their German liberators with open arms, rapidly grew to hate the occupying forces. Given the mass starvation throughout the area in the pre-war years, anti-Soviet sentiments were strong, and the German failure to take advantage of this cost them perhaps their best opportunity to win the war in the east. Millions of tons of grain and other agricultural produce were seized and shipped off to Germany, resulting in widespread famine amongst the Ukrainian population. To make matters worse, the absence of many Ukrainian men through military service, combined with the draconian occupation policies, resulted in a huge drop in the amount of land being cultivated – compared to pre-war years, only 63 per cent as much grain was sown in 1942, and the harvest was reduced to only 39 per cent of pre-war figures. To Koch and his deputies, the only thing that mattered was that there was sufficient produce to ship to Germany – the fate of the Ukrainian population was something that was regarded with profound indifference. In a move calculated to boost his own image, Koch arranged for 'Ukraine trains' loaded with Ukrainian produce to be sent to major cities in Germany, something that was widely covered in the German press. Food parcels were also sent to soldiers from East Prussia serving at the front, and Koch used his control of the East Prussian press to paint a picture of a province in which the Ukrainians, eternally grateful to the Germans for their liberation from Bolshevism, laboured willingly for their new masters. The reality was very different.

As the war continued, partisan activity in the Ukraine, as in other territories, steadily grew. Several organizations struggled to suppress the partisans – the SS, Wehrmacht formations and even units raised by Koch and his subordinates that lay outside either regular military command. The efficacy of all of these formations as counter-insurgency forces, particularly those outside the SS and Wehrmacht, was limited, although that did not stop them from massacring thousands of people in reprisals. Yet there was almost constant disruption of rear area units, bridges and railways by partisans. Several of Koch's subordinates were themselves victims of assassinations. Although a few attempts were planned to assassinate Koch himself, he was rarely in the Ukraine, and all of these plots failed to reach fruition.

By late 1942, German authority in parts of the Ukraine barely extended beyond the edges of larger towns and cities, further reducing the available harvest. In an attempt to starve the partisans into defeat, livestock and all other sources of food were often removed from large swathes of the countryside. Coupled with the draconian movement restrictions on the local population, this measure resulted in an escalating death rate from famine and disease. The overlapping rivalries of all of the agencies involved – the

Wehrmacht commanders, the SS, and Koch and his subordinates – further undermined German efforts.

Whilst many German officers later placed the blame for the brutality of anti-partisan measures on the shoulders of the SS, there is plenty of evidence to suggest that the Wehrmacht, too, was equally guilty. On 16 July 1941, an order was sent to all Wehrmacht units:

> The leading principle in all actions and for all measures that must be resorted to is the unconditional security of the German soldier … the necessary rapid pacification of the country can be attained only if every threat on the part of the hostile civil population is ruthlessly taken care of. All pity and softness are evidence of weakness and constitute a danger.[23]

German policies could almost have been deliberately designed to alienate the people of the occupied territories. Orders stated that:

> In every instance of active opposition against the German occupation authorities, regardless of the specific circumstances, communist origin must be assumed … moreover, it must not be forgotten that in the countries in question, human life often means nothing and that intimidation can only be achieved by unusual severity. For the life of one German soldier, a death sentence of from 50 to 100 communists must be generally deemed commensurate. The means of execution must increase the deterrent effect still further.[24]

The practicalities of the ominous last sentence were that firing squads aimed below the waist, so that their victims suffered painful, drawn-out deaths, often being buried before they had actually died. Such a policy also ensured that any children amongst the hostages would also be hit, avoiding the need for officers to execute them separately.

Treatment of Soviet soldiers who surrendered was also appalling. The Soviet Union was not a signatory to the Geneva and Hague Conventions, and this, together with contempt for the *Untermenschen*, was used to justify a different regime for Soviet prisoners, when compared with British, French and American soldiers who surrendered in the west, as this account of a prison camp near Rzhev described:

> They are holding them in unheated huts, and they feed them one or two frozen potatoes each a day. The Germans threw rotten meat and some bones through the barbed wire at the prisoners… Every day 20–30 people are dying. The ones who are too ill to work are shot.[25]

The inadequate rations were allocated strictly in return for labour. At one point, an SS officer suggested that half of all Soviet prisoners should be shot immediately, in order to ensure that those who remained received something approaching adequate rations. Men who attempted to escape were summarily shot, and punishments for the most minor misdemeanours were often lethal. Some of the ways in which prisoners were tormented were completely mindless; one report told of men held near Minsk being tortured by being stripped naked, and then having alternate jugs of icy and boiling water poured on them.[26]

It wasn't long before many German officers began to see the inevitable consequences of their mistreatment of prisoners:

> Our treatment of prisoners of war cannot continue without consequences. It is no longer because of lectures from the politruks, but out of his own personal convictions that the Soviet soldier has come to expect an agonising life or death if he falls captive.[27]

More than three million Soviet prisoners of war died in German camps. The death toll amongst civilians in the occupied territories was even greater, with estimates of between seven and eight million dead, as a result of deliberate German action, famine or disease. In addition, at least three million people were sent to work in Germany as slave labour. Most of these were worked until they died.

However badly the Soviet people suffered under German occupation, things might have been even worse. In late 1941, as the prospect of the Germans taking both Moscow and Leningrad loomed closer, senior German officials made plans for how the cities should be treated. Apart from a fanciful suggestion that the residents should be driven east, most plans simply called for the civilian populations to be herded out of the cities and then left to starve. Generalmajor Walter Warlimont, a senior staff officer, drew up a discussion document in September 1941, considering the options that confronted Army Group North, which seemed poised to take Leningrad. An occupation of the city, he asserted, should be avoided, as this would carry an obligation to feed the population. Isolating the city behind an electrified fence was an option, but he feared that the starving population might become a source of epidemics that could spread to German lines. In any event, he stated, 'it is questionable whether our soldiers can be burdened with having to fire on women and children attempting to break out'. He concluded:

> We seal off Leningrad hermetically for the time being and crush the city, as far as possible, with artillery and air power (only weak aerial forces available at the time!).

As soon as the city is ripe through terror and growing hunger, a few gates are opened and the defenceless are let out. Insofar as possible they will be pushed into inner Russia, the rest will necessarily spread across the land.

The rest of the 'fortress defenders' will be left to themselves over the winter. In spring we then enter the city (if the Finns do it before us we do not object), lead those still alive to inner Russia or into captivity, wipe Leningrad from the face of the earth through demolitions and then hand over the area north of the Neva to the Finns.[28]

It is striking that this document was not the product of a Party fanatic, but a professional Wehrmacht staff officer. The population of Leningrad endured a terrible siege and intermittent bombardment. Hundreds of thousands perished, but their fate could have been far worse if the city had actually fallen under German control.

Stalin only started to consider Poland as anything other than an occupied territory after the Germans invaded Russia in 1941. He immediately recognized the Polish government-in-exile, and allowed Poles within the Soviet Union to join Polish Army formations. Characteristically, few of these new Polish formations were prepared to fight under Soviet control, and eventually transferred to the west via the Middle East. The Polish Army that fought alongside the Red Army later in the war was raised after this first group of soldiers had left the Soviet Union; this time, the Soviets took greater care to ensure the political loyalty of these new 'allies'.

In addition to recognizing the Polish government, Stalin agreed that any realignment of Poland's borders would only occur after negotiation. There were early signs of his intentions, however. For Stalin and the Soviet Union, the war started in June 1941; any talk of restoring pre-war frontiers was interpreted as returning to the status quo prior to Hitler's invasion of the Soviet Union, not to the borders of 1939. The British were alarmed when Stalin also made it clear that he had no intention of allowing the Baltic states to resume their independence. But the question of Poland remained unresolved.

In 1943, the offensive power of the Wehrmacht was irreparably broken at the battle of Kursk. From that moment on, the Red Army was able to sustain an almost continuous advance towards the west. Koch's Reichskommissariat (Reich Adminstrative Offices) in the Ukraine effectively ceased to exist in early 1944, though he and other Reichskommissars did their utmost to prevent their shrinking domains being handed back to military control. In the earlier phases of the war on the *Ostfront*, the Wehrmacht retained control of about 200km of territory behind the frontline. Yet as the Red Army advanced, every attempt by the Wehrmacht to take control of sufficiently deep rear areas was resisted, a precedent that would have fateful consequences in early 1945.

The Polish question began to grow ever more prominent, not least in the minds of the Poles themselves, as the tide of war drew closer to their borders. They were hampered by the casual mistakes made by western politicians, who loosely referred to all of the territory seized by the Germans from the Soviet Union as 'Russia', failing to make the distinction between the Soviet Union itself and territories such as eastern Poland and the Baltic states, which had been seized by Stalin prior to 1941. Stalin himself had every intention of territorial gain at the expense of both Germany and Poland, and as 1943 and 1944 increasingly showed, the Red Army had the power to deliver these gains to him. His only problem was the possible attitude of the western Allies.

After some preliminary diplomatic testing of the waters, Stalin made his decisive move at the Tehran Conference of November 1943. When the issue of Poland's borders was raised, Molotov produced a British document from 1920 proposing the Curzon Line as the eastern frontier of Poland. Embarrassed by their failure to initiate a second front in the west, Churchill and Roosevelt already felt that they were in a weak position. Churchill, without Roosevelt's knowledge, suggested that the Curzon Line might well form the basis of future discussions, provided that Poland was granted German territory in the west by way of compensation. In a private conversation with Stalin, Roosevelt made it clear that the question of Poland's border would not pose problems.

German industry had two great heartlands. The western area was centred on the Ruhr, and had been bombed heavily by Britain and the United States. By the later stages of the war, it was less important than the factories of Silesia, territory that lay to the southwest of what had once been Poland. By passing this territory to Poland, the Allies could achieve two goals: Germany would lose some of its industrial power, and Poland would receive valuable territory in exchange for what it was to lose in the east.

In 1944 the German Army experienced increasingly heavy losses in the east. Early in the year, the relentless pressure built up in 1943 in the Ukraine was continued, and the Red Army pinched off a German-held salient at Cherkassy. Although many of the trapped Germans escaped, the price they paid was heavy, with thousands of wounded men being left behind. Divisions that had fought with iron determination against 'Ivan' were badly mauled, and the Red Army ruthlessly exploited the resulting weakness when the spring campaigns began. More encirclements and breakouts followed, each one resulting in a further haemorrhage of German strength.

But the main blow fell further north, against the German Army Group Centre. Careful deceptive measures ensured that the Germans were unaware of the magnitude of the forces assembling against them, though there was awareness that a major attack was coming and some local commanders feared the worst, particularly as they knew that Hitler would refuse to countenance any withdrawal in the face of an attack. General Hans Jordan, commander of 9th Army, recorded on the eve of the battle:

> The Army believes that, even under the present conditions, it would be possible to stop the enemy offensive, but not under the present directives which require an absolutely rigid defence… If a Soviet offensive breaks out the Army will either have to go over to a mobile defence or see its front smashed.
>
> The Army considers the orders establishing *Feste Plätze* [fortresses, to be held at all costs] particularly dangerous.
>
> The Army therefore looks ahead to the coming battle with bitterness, knowing that it is bound by orders to tactical measures which it cannot in good conscience accept as correct and which in our own earlier victorious campaigns were the causes of the enemy defeats.[29]

On 22 June 1944, nearly 1.7 million men of the Red Army, backed by more than 4,000 tanks and self-propelled guns and supported by 24,000 artillery pieces and heavy mortars, launched Operation *Bagration*. This offensive, every bit as murderously efficient as any German campaign in the war, simply overwhelmed and obliterated Army Group Centre. By 4 July, the army group had effectively ceased to exist, a 400km gap in the German front had been ripped open, and 350,000 German soldiers, from generals to privates, were dead, captured or missing.

The magnitude of this defeat dwarfed even the losses at Stalingrad, as the Soviet tank armies immediately went on to exploit their success, opposed only by whatever scratch forces and transferred units the Germans could throw into the immense hole in their lines. By late July, the Red Army had advanced from Vitebsk to the Vistula and stood in the suburbs of Warsaw. On 1 August, the Polish Home Army, expecting immediate support from the Soviets, revolted in Warsaw.

The devastation in the central sector of the German line meant that both Army Group North and what had been Army Group South, now renamed Army Group North Ukraine, were vulnerable. Some 40,000 Germans were surrounded at Brody, in the northern Ukraine; a little more than half escaped. An even bigger disaster loomed in the north at the end of July, when Soviet forces drove into Army Group North's exposed flank and reached the Baltic coast to the west of Riga. The battle-hardened divisions of the Army Group North were isolated, and restoration of land contact with the rest of the German forces would require diversion of precious resources, badly needed to reinforce the paper-thin front that was gradually coalescing across Poland. Eventually, contact with Army Group North was restored, but the price was that several precious Panzer divisions were now tied up in the north.

As the end of the war approached, Stalin had already made up his mind about the shape of Eastern Europe. After all, his armies would end the war firmly in possession of the region, and whatever the Western Allies might say, they would be powerless to intervene. As for the populations of the territories that were to change hands, Stalin had no intention of leaving behind troublesome minorities, or even majorities. The Poles would have to leave their former lands east of the Curzon Line, and would be able to settle in the lands seized from Germany. The German populations of these lands would have to be removed.

Stalin was no stranger to implementing mass deportations. Millions of people had been forcibly moved within the Soviet Union, many of them dying in the wastelands of Siberia. The Poles would not represent a major problem, it was expected, as they would be receiving new land in the west. Rather more problematic was the German population that would have to leave Silesia and Pomerania to make way for the Poles, and would also have to leave East Prussia. Although the Potsdam Conference in the summer of 1945, after the fighting in Europe was over, would speak of peaceful repatriation, the realities of what a future generation would term 'ethnic cleansing' were never likely to be peaceful.

At an early stage in the war, as evidence of German atrocities in occupied parts of Europe became increasingly well known, Soviet propaganda started to issue ferocious proclamations about exacting revenge on Germany. Ilya Ehrenburg, writing in *Krasnaya Zvezda* ('Red Star'; the official newspaper of the Soviet military), was particularly vociferous:

We know all. We remember all. We have understood: the Germans are not human beings. From now on the word German means to use the most terrible oath. From now on the word German strikes us to the quick. We shall not speak any more. We shall not get excited. We shall kill. If you have not killed at least one German a day, you have wasted that day… If you cannot kill your German with a bullet, kill him with your bayonet. If there is calm on your part of the front, or if you are waiting for the fighting, kill a German in the meantime. If you leave a German alive, the German will hang a Russian and rape a Russian woman. If you kill one German, kill another – there is nothing more amusing for us than a heap of German corpses. Do not count days, do not count kilometres. Count only the number of Germans killed by you. Kill the German – that is your grandmother's request. Kill the German – that is your child's prayer. Kill the German – that is your motherland's loud request. Do not miss. Do not let up. Kill.[30]

The fact that Ehrenburg was Jewish gave added vitriol to the responses from Goebbels. Ehrenburg has – wrongly – been accused of inciting Soviet soldiers to rape German women; it should also be mentioned that the noun used for 'German' in the above piece specifically refers to male Germans. Nevertheless, Ehrenburg and many other writers stirred up a strong desire for vengeance, for which Soviet soldiers had ample justification. As they advanced across the devastated expanses of the Ukraine, Russia and Belarus, the Red Army's soldiers saw at first hand evidence of mistreatment of civilians by the German occupiers. The political officers with every unit were ordered to instil hatred of Germany in their men, and adopted a variety of means to achieve this. In many units, 'revenge scores' were established – soldiers were asked to compile lists of atrocities committed against them and their families by the Germans. It was inevitable that, when the opportunity arose, they would respond in kind.

The degree to which soldiers were incited to mistreat German civilians is contentious. There can be no doubt that officers of all positions were aware of the thirst for revenge, and that they did little or nothing to curb such a thirst – indeed, it was official policy to encourage it. Stalin would have been aware that such mistreatment was certain to encourage Germans to flee towards the west. Such an exodus would, of course, make future clearances of remaining Germans much easier to carry out.

By the beginning of October 1944, all of the pieces on the board were in place: the Wehrmacht, exhausted and struggling to find adequate supplies of fuel and ammunition, faced with a desperate defence of the homeland; behind them, a fearful population, feeding on every rumour that circulated; and before them, the Red Army, well-equipped and supplied, vastly superior to its opponent in numbers if not in quality, full of confidence after its string of victories, and bent on vengeance. All that was required was for the tragic game to commence.

CHAPTER 1
FRITZ AND IVAN

I ask you: Do you want total war? If necessary, do you want a war more total and radical than anything that we can even imagine today?

– Joseph Goebbels[1]

The armies that prepared to fight the last battles of World War II in Eastern Europe were very different from the forces that confronted each other in the summer of 1941. The early campaigns of the war – Poland in 1939, Belgium and France in 1940, and even the invasion of the Soviet Union in 1941 – created a legend of the invincible German *Blitzkrieg*. Powerful, unstoppable Panzer divisions motored effortlessly past their lumbering opponents, spreading chaos and devastation. Overhead, the Luftwaffe ruled the skies. This legend has much truth in it, but also much that is myth. From the very start, there were problems with the performance of the Wehrmacht, but it was only in the vast spaces of the Soviet Union that these problems became critical. By then, it was too late to produce remedies.

The Wehrmacht's Panzer divisions were potent formations, composed of several different arms – tanks, infantry, artillery and engineers. They also had reconnaissance and anti-tank battalions, and sufficient integrated supply and workshop units to allow them to function autonomously, often for several days at a time. They were usually deployed en masse, and operational doctrine was to use the divisions to maximize dislocation of enemy forces.

The German infantry, by contrast, was relatively unmechanized. It relied greatly on horses to pull its artillery and equipment, and its infantry went into battle in the same manner as infantry for centuries before them – on foot. The consequence of this situation was that even in favourable conditions, infantry divisions would struggle to keep up with the faster Panzer divisions. Even in Poland in 1939, the Panzer divisions rapidly outran their supporting infantry – the 4th Panzer Division was the first to reach Warsaw, and had to withdraw when it found itself unsupported. In the scything advance across Belgium in 1940, the Panzer divisions opened up a considerable gap between themselves and the infantry divisions, and the British and French attempted to restore their front by an armoured counter-attack into the rear of the Panzer divisions.

It was originally to be a two-pronged assault, with the British attacking from the north and the French from the south. Few French units were able to start their attack, however, and the British offensive was also at less than full strength. Nevertheless, it still caused much consternation and damage to Rommel's 7th Panzer Division.

This brief battle between British and German tanks revealed a second problem for the Germans. Every tank is a compromise between protection, firepower and mobility. The British and French tanks that faced the German tanks in 1940 were generally better protected, and often had better firepower. When they found themselves in action against enemy armour, German tanks were often found to be inferior. But in 1939 and 1940, these shortcomings were of no particular consequence – by the time the British and French attempted their counter-attack, the fate of the campaign had already been settled by the massive dislocating effect of the rapid German advance. On the *Ostfront*, however, the shortcomings in German armour would be magnified hugely.

In terms of its personnel, the Wehrmacht in 1941 was perhaps at the peak of its power. Most of the men who lined up along the eastern frontier in June had seen action, and were well trained. They were confident of victory, and their officers and NCOs were generally of a high calibre, tested and proven in the earlier campaigns. Equally important, Hitler had yet to interfere with the everyday conduct of operations.

At first, Operation *Barbarossa* progressed in a similar way to previous campaigns. The Luftwaffe rapidly established control of the air, while the Panzer divisions smoothly bypassed their Soviet opponents, creating huge encirclements. Immediately, though, the relatively slow rate of advance of the infantry created problems. The Panzer divisions might create pockets, but they could not seal them off and at the same time maintain the rate of advance. Some of the Soviet troops trapped within them leaked away to the east. Eventually, the Panzer divisions had to slow down while the infantry caught up.

The second deficiency of the Wehrmacht – its inferior tanks – also became increasingly significant as the campaign continued. At the beginning of the campaign, the Red Army possessed more than 1,200 T-34s, which were better armoured, better armed and faster than anything that the Germans had at their disposal, though poor training and crippling shortages of spares vastly reduced their efficacy. It would take the German tank industry more than a year to produce anything that could match the T-34. In the meantime, even after the period of great disruption when much of the Soviet Union's industry had to be moved east to escape the advancing Germans, Soviet tank production consistently outperformed German industry.

The campaigns of 1941, 1942 and 1943 brought about great changes in the Wehrmacht. Hundreds of thousands of experienced men were killed, wounded or captured. Their replacements, particularly by 1944, were poorly trained compared to their predecessors, and no longer came to the frontline with complete confidence in victory. Many of them had been combed out of rear-area units, and had little aptitude or enthusiasm for frontline service. Those who came from the homeland as new recruits brought stories of immense destruction by British and American air raids. Some were keen to do their duty; others are mentioned in commanding officers' reports as being poorly trained, with low morale.

The equipment of the Panzer divisions had also changed, as had their structure. Originally, Panzer divisions possessed a Panzer brigade, consisting of two Panzer regiments. By 1944, this structure had been reduced to a single Panzer regiment. The regiment had two battalions, one equipped with Pz. IV tanks, the other with the newer Pz. V, or Panther. The Pz. IV had been in service since the beginning of the war, and several different versions were created, each successive model having either better protection or better firepower than its predecessor. By 1944, its 75mm gun was a capable weapon, though its armour was poor by *Ostfront* standards.

The Panther was the Germans' direct response to the T-34, and was at least its equal in terms of armour, firepower and mobility. Unlike its Soviet counterpart, however, it was a complex vehicle, in need of constant maintenance. Engineering problems delayed its mass deployment in 1943, and even in 1944 it was prone to breakdowns and other faults. Yet it was popular with its crews, and its 75mm gun, more powerful than the gun carried by the Pz. IV, was capable of dealing with any tank it might encounter.

The Panzer regiment was only part of the division's fighting strength. It also had two Panzergrenadier regiments, each consisting of two battalions. By 1944, at least half of these troops were mounted in half-tracks, along with their support weapons. Casualties in these battalions were often heavy, resulting in considerable turnover of personnel. At every level, from the officers through the NCOs and down to the ordinary soldiers, there were concerns about the quality of these formations as the war progressed; the essential *esprit de corps* and close cooperation required for them to function well could not be sustained in the face of the constant attrition of manpower.

In addition to their tanks and infantry, Panzer divisions had their own integral artillery regiment, most of whose guns were self-propelled. They also had an anti-tank, or Panzerjäger, battalion. Usually, the Panzerjägers would be deployed in direct support of the division's Panzergrenadiers, but as the war continued, they were often 'loaned' to neighbouring infantry divisions to provide welcome reinforcements. This unpopular practice left the Panzer division itself weakened, often when it had most need of all its firepower.

As well as a combat engineer battalion, the Panzer division also had a reconnaissance battalion. Originally, this formation was designed to be the eyes and ears of the division, and was equipped with light armoured cars, together with a small infantry component mounted in half-tracks. As the war progressed, the armoured reconnaissance battalion, or Panzeraufklärungs-Abteilung, often found itself having to hold isolated positions for extended periods until reinforcements appeared. It therefore accumulated more and more firepower, and by 1944 it had an establishment of more than 100 vehicles, some armed with powerful 75mm anti-tank guns, and could – and often did – function as an independent battlegroup.

By the autumn of 1944, the long series of defeats had cost the Wehrmacht irreplaceable casualties and losses of equipment. It was abundantly clear to its senior officers that such a long frontline had been difficult to hold at the beginning of the year. Yet after the casualties of *Bagration* and other disasters of the east, combined with the growing need for forces to oppose the western Allies – whose victories in northern France had accounted for another 400,000 German soldiers – holding the present frontline was simply impossible. The only solution, they argued, was to withdraw Army Group North from Latvia and Lithuania, towards the borders of East Prussia. This would liberate forces that could be used to strengthen the front elsewhere.

For Hitler, though, there was no question of giving up so much territory. He had already announced, in mid July, that Germany would hold onto the Baltic states 'at all costs'. The justifications for this were, he argued, both political and strategic. First, Finland was still an ally of Germany, and withdrawal from the Baltic states could result in the Finns abandoning Germany. Second, many men from the Baltic states, particularly from Latvia, were serving in the Waffen-SS (the military wing of the SS), and their loss would seriously weaken the ability of the Germans to resist. Finally, it was vital to hold onto territory in the north, as a springboard for a future attack against the Russians. In any event, the Finns left the Axis in October, despite the presence of German forces in the Baltic states. The three Baltic SS divisions were a tiny part of German armed strength, and it was absurd to argue that the continued presence of 26 German divisions in the Baltic area could be justified by the recruitment of just three divisions. And talk of a future offensive seemed, at least to most of the senior German commanders, wishful thinking of the worst sort.

In the south, too, the Red Army continued to make progress. The German Army Groups North and South Ukraine were driven out of Soviet territory, and on 23 August Romania surrendered to the Soviet Union. Romania's capitulation was a huge blow for Germany. The country had provided considerable forces for the southern part of the *Ostfront*; much more significantly, it was also the main source of Germany's oil. Without this supply, fuel shortages rapidly became critical.

Although the front had been restored, the divisions that manned it were shadows of their former selves. The Panzer divisions still regarded themselves, with justification, as an elite, but the infantry divisions simply could not make good the catastrophic losses of the summer without consequences. A typical infantry division in late 1944 consisted of three grenadier or infantry regiments, supported by an artillery regiment. In addition, the division might have an extra infantry battalion, usually designated as a fusilier battalion, or a Panzerjäger battalion. But in terms of fighting power, these divisions were nowhere near as strong as they had been only a year before. Their ranks had been seriously depleted by the long years of warfare, and the replacement drafts that arrived were unable to endure the harshness of the *Ostfront*. The anti-tank firepower of these divisions, poor in the earlier stages of the war, was by the standards of 1944 completely inadequate. The Soviet Union had developed *Blitzkrieg* along similar lines to the Germans, though with a far greater degree of mechanization. The mobility of the Soviet forces, and the sheer number of armoured vehicles at their disposal, made defence without anti-tank firepower almost impossible.

Another event of the summer of 1944 had a profound effect on the future shape of the Wehrmacht. On 20 July, Colonel Claus Schenk von Stauffenberg placed a briefcase filled with explosives in the temporary conference room at Hitler's headquarters near Rastenburg. The usual conference room, a concrete bunker, was undergoing repairs and the conference had been moved to a wooden building. The blast from the briefcase would have been lethal within the confines of the bunker; even in the wooden building, it would have sufficed to kill Hitler had it not been moved from its original position under the conference table.

During the aftermath of the failed assassination attempt, numerous alarming facts came to light. The plotters had intended to use the Replacement Army to seize control of key locations within the Reich, and the Nazi Party moved swiftly to bring this potentially dangerous force, which had tens of thousands of armed troops throughout the Reich, under its control. Heinrich Himmler, the vastly ambitious Reichsführer-SS who was already the head of the police and SS, made sure that he was appointed commander of the Replacement Army.

One of Himmler's earliest innovations in his new role was the creation of several new Volksgrenadier divisions. These were often created around the remnants of divisions destroyed in combat, and like 'ordinary' infantry divisions they consisted of three regiments of infantry, with an artillery regiment and an additional 'fusilier' battalion. In fighting power, these formations were even weaker than infantry divisions – most of their personnel was composed of inexperienced soldiers, many of them former naval and Luftwaffe personnel. And yet, they were treated as if they were full-strength, combat-capable divisions, and were expected to hold a full segment of the front.

The experience of Hans Jürgen Pantenius was typical. After a spell of frontline service, he was serving in a training unit at the time of the failed July Plot, and was assigned to the newly created 337th Volksgrenadier Division in September 1944. The division's commander, Generalleutnant Eberhard Kinzel, greeted Pantenius and discussed the poor quality of the personnel assigned to the division. Kinzel had served as a staff officer with Army Group North during the slow, bitter retreat from Leningrad, and had a good understanding of the sort of soldiers required for successful fighting on the *Ostfront*. He readily accepted Pantenius' offer that Pantenius should return to his training unit in order to identify any good-quality officers and NCOs who could be used to bolster the new division. Although he was unable to find any officers – the only man he identified as suitable had already been assigned to another unit – he returned to 337th Volksgrenadier Division with a small group of relatively experienced NCOs. When Pantenius' 690th Grenadier Regiment was fully formed, it had 42 officers; of these, only seven were regular army officers. The rest were reservists, some of them far too old for frontline service in an infantry division.

There were also problems with the new division's weaponry. Although it received a full complement of guns, shortages of ammunition and fuel often made their use almost impossible. In addition, some of the heavy weapons were former French guns, captured in 1940, and were entirely obsolete. In particular, the division lacked sufficient anti-tank weaponry; its light Panzerschreck weapons (similar to American Bazookas) were capable of knocking out almost any tank on the battlefield, but had a maximum range of barely 200m, rendering them useless unless fighting took place in woodland or built-up areas.[2]

Pantenius was surely not alone in his conclusions about the state of the German Volksgrenadier divisions:

> In these circumstances, the question arises whether it might not have been more appropriate to replenish the old experienced frontline divisions and to restrict the practice of establishing new divisions to those occasions when total losses [of existing formations] necessitated it. At the very least, this would have allowed a whole mass of staffs and rear area units to be saved.[3]

The organization of the division into three regiments, each with only two battalions, also created its own difficulties. Traditional formations tended to follow the 'rule of threes', allowing commanders to deploy two of their formations in the frontline while holding the third in reserve. With only two battalions at their disposal, regiment commanders struggled to form any significant local reserves for counter-attacks or to strengthen endangered parts of the frontline, especially as these two-battalion regiments were still required to hold the same length of front as the old three-battalion regiments. Consequently, commanders were forced to remove a company from each of their frontline battalions in order to hold some sort of reserve; this measure made the task of these battalions, to hold huge lengths of frontline, even harder.

Another result of the failed assassination attempt against Hitler was the imposition of the Nazi salute upon the armed forces. It was a deeply unpopular move, even amongst the great majority of soldiers who had been shocked by the plot:

> The new measure proved to be a miscalculation. The soldier felt that the salute reduced him to the level of a mere Party member, for whom he had little respect, and he resented this … the new salute seemed absurd in everyday military life. From now on, whole armies carried their mess tins in their right hands in order to avoid having to give it.[4]

Long before the outbreak of war in 1939, Hitler had started to develop a parallel army under the aegis of the SS. The Waffen-SS grew steadily through the war, ensured of lavish supplies by Heinrich Himmler. When they were first used en masse in 1943, the SS divisions were highly trained, superbly equipped and devastatingly formidable. But in the months that followed, they were constantly deployed in the hottest segments of the front, resulting in high casualty rates, and it proved impossible to ensure that replacement drafts would be as well prepared as their original soldiers. The Waffen-SS also grew enormously, and by the end of the war a total of 38 divisions had been created, though many of these proved to have brief lives. Nevertheless, they resulted in a huge diversion of resources away from the Wehrmacht, particularly as the Waffen-SS had its own completely independent supply and support structure. The combat performance of these divisions was variable. Some, particularly the first-established divisions – *Leibstandarte Adolf Hitler*, *Das Reich*, *Totenkopf* and *Wiking* in particular – were amongst the toughest formations fielded by Germany throughout the war. The later divisions, frequently recruited from volunteers from occupied or allied countries, were often far less effective.

The commanders of the German armies on the Eastern Front had also changed hugely since 1941. Army Group North, responsible for the frontline from the Baltic to a point near the East Prussian frontier, was commanded by Ferdinand Schörner from late July 1944. Born in Bavaria, he served with conspicuous courage in the

German Army in the Great War, and remained an officer after the end of the war, being promoted to Oberstleutnant in 1919. He was an early supporter of the Nazis, and rose rapidly to high office. In early 1944, while commanding Army Group South in the Ukraine, he established a fearsome reputation for iron discipline, infamous for his policy of 'strength through fear'. Schörner was a physically intimidating man, and Hitler joked that he liked to have him present when foreign dignitaries visited the Führer, due to his frightening appearance. He was not, however, without imagination. When the Russians closed in on the city of Sevastopol in the Crimea, Schörner announced that any soldier who deserted his post would be shot for cowardice, but that anyone who destroyed an enemy tank would be granted three weeks' leave in the homeland. Given the desperate German position in Sevastopol, such a leave pass represented almost the last hope of escape for ordinary soldiers, and it undoubtedly inspired many men to take on the enemy tanks.

Schörner is an intriguing character. His brutal application of draconian measures seems abhorrent from a modern perspective, but many of the soldiers under his control approved of such measures – after all, they were doing their duty and continuing to fight at the front, and had little time for those who attempted to slip away to the rear areas. Schörner's insistence that rear area units be 'combed out' to raise additional rifle companies also met with general approval from frontline soldiers, who – like frontline soldiers in every army in history – had a universally low opinion of the profusion of rear-area formations. And, given the potential for chaos behind the frontline, there was always the strong possibility that the defeat of the Reich could be hastened by lack of discipline. Yet Schörner's 'drumhead courts-martial', consisting of judges accompanied by firing squads that immediately carried out sentence, were often arbitrary and repugnant. Hans von Luck, an Oberst in the 21st Panzer Division, described a typical episode that occurred in 1945, after Schörner had been transferred to take command of Army Group Centre, which by then had been driven back into Germany. Von Luck had ordered one of his best NCOs, a highly decorated soldier, to take a platoon to the division's workshops to collect vehicles that were being repaired. The NCO found that repairs would be completed overnight, so he and his platoon settled down to wait. A member of the platoon later told a horrified von Luck what happened:

> Suddenly, the door was pushed open and in rushed a staff officer with some military policemen. 'I am Chief Judge Advocate under the direct orders of Field Marshal Schörner. Why are you sitting about here while up at the front brave soldiers are risking their lives?'
>
> My platoon leader replied: 'I was ordered by my regimental commander, Oberst von Luck, to bring some armoured vehicles that are being repaired here up to the front as

quickly as possible. Work will be going on through the night. We'll be able to go back to the front tomorrow morning.'

The judge advocate: 'Where is your movement order?'

Answer: 'I had it from the commander by word of mouth.'

Advocate: 'We know about that, that's what they all say when they want to dodge things. In the name of the Führer and by the authority of the commander in chief of Army Group Centre, Field Marshal Schörner, I sentence you to death by shooting on account of proven desertion.'[5]

Despite the man's protestations, the advocate's firing squad took him outside and executed him immediately. The rest of the platoon was forced to dig his grave.

It is difficult to judge Schörner's military skills, as most of his higher commands were faced with almost impossible situations. Despite his implacable insistence on soldiers remaining at the front, however, he himself abandoned his command in the last days of the war and fled to Austria, where he was arrested by the Americans. They promptly handed him over to the Russians; he remained a Soviet prisoner until 1955, often treated harshly in captivity, and was then prosecuted and imprisoned in West Germany for ordering the execution of a soldier who had fallen asleep.

Army Group Centre, which by late 1944 was holding the frontline along the eastern borders of East Prussia and along the Vistula valley, was commanded by Georg-Hans Reinhardt. He was a former commander of 4th Panzer Division, having led it during the Polish campaign of 1939. He then went on to command 3rd Panzer Army on the Eastern Front, and was one of Germany's finest commanders. His command from August 1944 consisted of the rebuilt armies of Army Group Centre – 4th Army in the north and 2nd Army on the Vistula. Another army – 3rd Panzer Army – had temporarily been assigned to Army Group North, so that all of the front north of the East Prussian frontier could be under the control of a single army group. Whilst these armies looked strong on paper, the reality was that they consisted of a collection of bled-out divisions and a few of Himmler's new Volksgrenadier divisions.

The commanders of Reinhardt's two armies were veteran officers. Friedrich Hossbach commanded 4th Army. Like many of his generation, he served in the Kaiser's army in the Great War, briefly commanding an infantry battalion in 1918. After short-lived service with the Freikorps in 1919, he returned to the ranks of the army, holding a variety of posts during the inter-war years, including four years working at least part-time as army adjutant to the Führer. At the outbreak of World War II in 1939, Hossbach was a staff officer with first XXX Corps, then II Corps, and was appointed commander of two infantry divisions before taking command of LVI Panzer Corps in the summer of 1943. He remained with the corps (apart from a brief absence due to illness) until the following summer, when he took command of 4th Army.

Hossbach's long experience of field command made him an ideal person to command 4th Army at this critical time. He was well known for his painstaking approach to planning defensive positions, and was a master of preparing two battle positions – a forward position, and a well-camouflaged main position somewhat further back. Bitter experience on the *Ostfront* had shown the power of Soviet preparatory artillery fire, and Hossbach and others had calculated that the only way to prevent the Red Army from achieving a decisive advantage by its bombardment was to abandon the forward position at the very last moment. The Soviet bombardment would then fall on empty positions, and when the Soviet forces advanced, they would run into the true, and still intact, defensive line further back. Main defensive positions were constructed in depth, with hardened sites for artillery and anti-tank weapons. No firing from these positions was permitted, in order to prevent their locations being detected by the Soviet reconnaissance planes that were often overhead. Such a strategy required adequate time and resources to prepare, and suitable terrain in which the main positions could be prepared without their location becoming obvious to the enemy. It also required precise knowledge of the enemy's timetable, which was, of course, not always possible.

Of the 15 divisions in Hossbach's army, only seven were battle-hardened, with experience of the Eastern Front. Much would depend on these men, and on the more fragile units that formed the other divisions.

Walter Weiss had commanded 2nd Army since early 1943, and was well liked and well respected by the men under his command. His three corps had eight regular infantry divisions and a single Volksgrenadier division at their disposal; in practice, many of these divisions had little more than a regiment's fighting strength, and were holding fronts that were too long for such weak formations.

Overseeing all of these commanders was the German military hierarchy, dominated by Hitler himself. Increasingly prone to interfering with low-level decisions, in January 1945 Hitler decreed that even movements of corps and divisions could not be made without his consent. The control of the war in the east was divided between two bodies, the Oberkommando des Heeres (OKH; Army High Command), and the Oberkommando der Wehrmacht (OKW; Armed Forces High Command). The former was exclusively concerned with the *Ostfront*. OKW was responsible for the Balkans, and the entire western and Mediterranean area; it plays little part in the story of the fall of Prussia. OKH had, as its Chief of Staff, Heinz Guderian, the Prussian who had pioneered the development of the Panzer arm, and would now have to attempt to save his own homeland. Plagued by high blood pressure and heart disease, he was by this stage of the war a very different man from the impatient, determined tank commander of 1939 and 1940.

Morale amongst the German formations was variable. In his monthly reports, Clemens Betzel, commander of 4th Panzer Division, regularly contrasted the relatively high morale of his diminishing group of veterans with the apathy and defeatism of the replacement drafts.[6] This split was probably true for most divisions, and the overall mood of the division depended on what proportion of its manpower was made up of replacements. The Volksgrenadier divisions, which were almost completely 'new' formations, had the lowest morale of all. Some of their battalions were remnants of divisions shattered in *Bagration*; most of their men had never seen combat together, and had no sense of unit cohesion.

All personnel in the army, veterans and replacements alike, had a low opinion of the Luftwaffe. The power of the Luftwaffe had declined steadily through the war, with more and more fighter pilots diverted to the west to try to combat the bomber forces of the western Allies. At the same time, the Soviet Air Force's strength was growing steadily, and whilst its fighters and ground-attack aircraft – and their crews – didn't reach the high standards of their counterparts in the RAF and USAAF, they played an increasing part in the battles in the east. As manpower shortages began to bite, Hitler ordered the Luftwaffe to make men available to the army as replacements. Rather than lose personnel and prestige, Hermann Göring, head of the Luftwaffe, created a series of Luftwaffe field divisions. These first saw action on the eve of the encirclement of the German 6th Army in Stalingrad, and proved to be completely unprepared for the brutal nature of warfare on the *Ostfront*. Eventually, most of these units were incorporated into the army.

Other ground formations remained part of the Luftwaffe. Unlike their British and American equivalents, German parachute forces were part of the Luftwaffe. In common with other airborne formations, these units were regarded as elite combatants, though their quality declined through the war. Perhaps the most remarkable ground formation within the Luftwaffe was the Fallschirm-Panzerkorps *Hermann Göring* (Paratroop-Panzer Corps *Hermann Göring*). It owed its existence to the multitude of posts held by the commander of the Luftwaffe, who created a Regiment *General Göring* in 1935, based around East Prussian police officers. At the time, Göring was simultaneously commander of the Luftwaffe and Prime Minister of Prussia, as well as Minister of the Interior. The former police regiment was now part of the Luftwaffe, and slowly expanded, first into a full Panzer division and then into a corps with two divisions. The original Panzer division remained a powerful, experienced force, but 2nd Paratroop-Panzergrenadier Division *Hermann Göring* was a new formation.

It incorporated several former paratrooper formations in its ranks, but these had few veterans, and the division's senior officers had serious doubts about its fighting abilities. Despite its designation as a Panzergrenadier division, it consisted primarily of two infantry regiments, neither of which was supplied with sufficient trucks to be considered motorized, still less the half-tracks that were the preferred transport for Panzergrenadiers. Repeated requests to pull the formation out of the front to allow for intensive training were turned down. The 'paratroopers' of the division's regiments would have to learn their craft the hard way.

Behind the battered and war-weary troops that shored up the front in the second half of 1944 was East Prussia. The Nazi Party had reorganized Germany in 1934, removing the previous boundaries between provinces and replacing them with Party-defined areas. Each province, or Gau, was subdivided into districts, or Kreise. The Gauleiter of East Prussia was, of course, Erich Koch, whose eastern empires had been stripped away by late 1944. Despite the huge area for which he had been responsible, he had maintained a strong personal presence in East Prussia, spending several weeks every year touring the province and speaking at dozens of meetings, large and small. The media continued to give precedence to his optimistic outlook for final victory. The Nazi Party, Koch reasoned, had gone through hard times following Hitler's failed attempt to seize power in Munich in 1921, before finally securing power, and it was therefore logical to assume that Germany would also follow the same pattern. By 1943, the tone was changing subtly. East Prussia would be a bulwark against the east, and the only choice lay between final victory and total annihilation. The war represented a struggle between Hitler and international Jewry. Victory for the latter would result in the total destruction of Germany. If the citizens of East Prussia ever speculated about what had happened to the Jews who had formerly lived amongst them, they were careful not to do so out loud.

Koch had been nominated Reichsverteidigungskommissar (Reich Defence Commissar) as early as 1939, but until now the title had been largely honorary. Now, as the debris from Operation *Bagration* streamed back towards the west, Koch took steps to prevent retreating units from spreading demoralizing stories through his province. The eastern border of the province was strictly policed, and any military personnel attempting to cross the border without authorization were liable to be put to work on 'essential' tasks within East Prussia. In a short time, Latvian personnel attached to the Luftwaffe, several labour units of the Todt Organization and a few Soviet 'SS volunteers' had been rounded up.[7]

The personal rivalries of senior Nazi figures made the implementation of any consistent policy far more difficult than it might have been. For many years, Koch and

Goebbels had been openly hostile to each other; prior to his appointment as East Prussia's Gauleiter, Koch was implicated in the publication of a newspaper article that ridiculed Goebbels' physical handicaps. By the second half of 1944, though, the two former enemies were of one mind. Koch's success in reducing unemployment in the 1930s had been exaggerated and held up as an example to the rest of Germany, and Goebbels now foresaw another opportunity for East Prussia to set an example. On this occasion, it would show the world how Germany would defend itself against invasion, with soldiers and civilians alike uniting to hold back the Bolshevik hordes. Goebbels retreated more and more into the mythology of the Party, where unquestioning faith in the Führer and the will to triumph were the most important factors. Anyone who did not share these principles was a traitor, while anything that reinforced these views was to be welcomed uncritically.

Throughout July 1944, there were discussions about fortifying the borders of the Reich in preparation for the inevitable Allied advance. Several agencies – the Wehrmacht, Albert Speer's Ministry of Armaments and the Party itself – wrestled for the right to construct these defences, but in August Hitler assigned the task to the Gauleiters. Koch threw himself into the task with characteristic energy, directing Kurt Knuth to oversee the project. It was anticipated that the local army commanders in each district would dictate where the lines were to be constructed, and the role of the Party would be to ensure that adequate manpower and materials were available. The army was to assign an engineering officer to each of the construction teams to provide military advice. But there simply weren't enough officers available for the task, with the consequence that the fortifications were often ill positioned and of poor quality. Koch announced triumphantly that after the first four weeks of the project, he had ensured the construction of nearly 23,000km of trenches, and the excavation of more than 41 million tons of earth. Many of these trenches were too shallow, or in completely the wrong place.

In other respects, the nepotism that was such a large part of Party culture ensured that some of Koch's acolytes benefited personally:

The notorious Feuerwehrgeneral Fiedler invented a one-man shelter with a lid on top – the so-called Koch-pot – as a defence against being overrun by tanks. Herr Fiedler manufactured these 'Koch-pots' in his cement factory in Metgethen. They consisted of tight cement tubes with a concrete cover as protection against tanks. They were embedded in large numbers throughout the landscape, often in tactically unsound positions. Only one man could fit into these tubes, where he felt alone, as if in a mouse hole. There was also a substantial fragmentation effect from hits from projectiles. These 'Koch-pots' were therefore worthless. A shame about the work and materials![8]

Despite all its shortfalls, the East Prussian Defence Position was widely hailed as a great success, and Hitler declared Koch's management of the project as the standard to which all Gauleiters should aspire. Even Goebbels, Koch's old enemy, felt moved to record in his diary that Koch was undoubtedly the man of the hour.[9]

It was one thing to construct a defensive line, even a poorly designed one; it was quite another to find the troops required to man it. Plans for offensive operations in the west, and as will be seen, the steady diversion of troops to Hungary, ensured that there would be inadequate reinforcements available for Army Group Centre. Koch, however, was not at all disheartened. If the Wehrmacht was unable to furnish the troops required, then the Party would have to do the task itself. On 21 July 1944, in a telegram to Martin Bormann, the Party Secretary, Koch pushed for the creation of a new people's militia, under Party control. After General von Yorck turned against Napoleon in the 19th century, the people of Prussia rose against the French, and provided the essential manpower for the rapid expansion of the Prussian forces deployed against the French in 1813. The same thing could surely happen again, with the German people providing the manpower for a new force, led by a people's general – in which role, of course, Koch cast himself.

Plans for a militia, or home guard, had been discussed at various levels of the Party throughout the war, and the Wehrmacht staff had also considered how such a militia might be used to garrison defensive positions. On 6 September 1944, Guderian and Hitler once more discussed the matter, and the creation of this new force was officially sanctioned. Immediately, all of the rivals for power in Nazi Germany demanded the right to lead the force. Determined to prevent Himmler from securing control of this new force, Bormann was able to announce on 26 September that Hitler had entrusted the organization and leadership of the Volkssturm, as it was to be called, to the Party.

The creation of the Volkssturm, to be mobilized if the enemy crossed the German frontier, was trumpeted loudly by the German press. Immediately, it became clear that there were insufficient weapons and uniforms for the new units, and training opportunities were severely limited. Despite the propaganda, most German people could see that the Volkssturm would have little fighting power. As leaders for the new units, Koch appointed only trusted Party figures, who continued to believe in Hitler, the Party and final victory. Inevitably, almost all these figures had no military experience.

Once more Koch drew on his considerable energies, this time to seek out weapons for the East Prussian Volkssturm. Nearly 500,000 Reichsmarks were spent to purchase weapons and uniforms, many of them on the black market in Italy, where some weapons were even purchased from anti-Nazi Italian partisans.[10] Despite this, the military value of the Volkssturm remained questionable. Koch and Himmler spoke in Leipzig shortly after the creation of the Volkssturm, but were less than fulsome in the language that they used, perhaps because they did not wish the inhabitants of areas that were still some distance from the frontline to be too alarmed by the need for such desperate measures.[11]

The truth was that no part of the Reich now regarded itself as being far from the enemy. East Prussia had become temporary home to tens of thousands of Germans evacuated from bombed-out cities elsewhere in the Reich, but even here Allied bombers were now able to strike with deadly effect. Nevertheless, the approach of the Red Army created a new threat. Such an invasion had been foreseen as long ago as 1870, when it had been decided that in the event of a two-front war it would be impossible for German forces to hold East Prussia whilst heavily committed elsewhere. Plans were therefore drawn up for a phased retreat, perhaps as far as Königsberg and the Samland peninsula, until victory in the west allowed for sufficient forces to be assembled to drive the Russians out of the lost areas. This plan called for the orderly evacuation of the areas to be given up, and these plans continued to be updated regularly until Hitler came to power.

Such matters remained largely irrelevant in the early years of the war, but as the frontline approached the frontier it became clear that matters had changed greatly. First, Hitler's oft-quoted insistence on rigid defence was reiterated even more strongly – if retreat had been something that he was reluctant to consider in the occupied territories, then it was anathema for German soil to be given up. Second, there was increasing awareness in most circles not blinded by Party dogma that there would be no sudden victory in the west, allowing for an orderly and swift transfer of forces to the east.

Nevertheless, plans were still made for the evacuation of a small strip of territory close to the border. In addition, many of the refugees sent to East Prussia from bombed-out cities were now sent home, though Koch made it clear that any talk of larger evacuations was tantamount to defeatism, and would be punished accordingly. Long journeys within the Reich that might be used as an opportunity to leave the province were banned unless permission had been obtained first. A precautionary mass evacuation was out of the question. In the event of a Soviet breakthrough, the Party argued, evacuations would be organized if required. There was little consideration of how these would be accomplished, or how the required transport would be organized. The return of refugees from the west to their devastated cities, together with the limited evacuation of the most easterly parts of the province, resulted in the overall population falling from about 2.4 million in early 1944 to

1.75 million by the end of the year.[12] For those who remained in East Prussia, there was no option other than to hope that the Wehrmacht and Volkssturm would be sufficient to hold back Ivan.

* * *

The 1930s were troubled years in the Soviet Union, as an increasingly paranoid Stalin moved to eliminate possible rivals for power. Sergei Kirov, a popular man with a genuine following, was murdered by a non-entity in 1934, but there is evidence of the involvement of the Soviet security service, the NKVD, in the murder. Lev Kamanev and Gregori Zinoviev, who had helped Stalin oust Trotsky, were found guilty of conspiracy to murder Kiro and were executed in 1937. A fictitious political conspiracy to remove Stalin was used as a pretext for widespread arrests and executions of political figures, and the NKVD itself was heavily purged. But the most damaging purge of all was that inflicted on the Red Army.

By 1937, Stalin was talking openly among his inner circle of his intention to eliminate all threats. After the May Day parade of 1937, he told them: '[It is time] to finish with our enemies because they are in the staff, in the army, even in the Kremlin.'[13] Stalin's prime target was Marshal Mikhail Nikolaevich Tukhachevsky. He was the most gifted military officer of his generation, with a clear understanding of the nature of future mechanized wars. In the early 1930s, he proposed using armoured forces in deep penetrations of enemy lines, an idea that was bitterly opposed by Kliment Voroshilov and Semyon Budyonni, Stalin's military comrades from the time of the Russian Civil War. In 1936, Tukhachevsky visited Western Europe, and there were suspicions – possibly with some foundation – that he met exiled enemies of Stalin to discuss the removal of the Soviet dictator.

Shortly after Stalin's declaration to his colleagues that he was now ready to move against his enemies, Tukhachevsky and several other senior officers were arrested and charged with conspiring with Nazi Germany against the Soviet Union. Within three weeks, they were found guilty and executed. From this start, which effectively decapitated the Soviet high command, Stalin moved down through the ranks, murderously purging thousands of officers. The Military Soviet had 80 members in 1934; by late 1938, only five of them were still in post. All 11 Deputy Commissars for Defence were purged, and all commanders of military districts were executed, as were many of those who replaced them. Thirteen of 15 army commanders, 57 of 85 corps commanders, 110 of 195 division commanders and 220 of 406 brigade commanders were arrested, tried and executed. The numbers of lower-ranking officers killed were also staggering.

By 1941, when Hitler invaded the Soviet Union, the Red Army's officer corps was barely recovering from this disaster. Many officers were in their posts more because of their political loyalty than any military aptitude. The lessons of the Spanish Civil War had been imprecisely learned, with the result that Soviet tanks were dispersed throughout the army, rather than grouped together. The poor performance of the Red Army during its brief war with Finland in 1939–40 had caused much consternation, but little had changed as a result. Military training was woeful. Ammunition and equipment shortages caused severe problems, as did a lack of experienced soldiers to lead the training. Junior officers, struggling to train their often surly and uncooperative recruits, found further problems in the ever-increasing power of the political officers, who regarded it as entirely appropriate to question and obstruct any training that sounded to them to be ideologically unsound.

Nevertheless, the soldiers – and the Soviet public – had received extensive political preparation. Isaak Kobylyanskiy was born to Jewish parents in Kiev in 1923. Like many of his generation, he accepted without question the official version of history and current events:

> Being the masters of all mass media, publishing, and censorship, our rulers intended to bring up the Soviet people in the spirit of communist ideology. A huge propaganda staff was established. It unceasingly unmasked the horrors and crying injustices of the 'carrion' capitalist system, its merciless exploitation of the working masses, and its relationship with colonialism and imperialist wars. It also glorified our radiant future: communism. Political indoctrination began in elementary school. For example, the text from the ABC primer of those times taught the pupil: 'We are not slaves. Slaves are dumb.' In the reading part of the same textbook you could find a story about Lenin's childhood. A typical line from his favourite song went: 'The rich man-kulak can't sleep at night. And the man who is poor as a church mouse dances and has fun.'

> Being absolutely honest, now I can state openly: the pervasive propaganda produced its desired result, especially among the inexperienced youth and people of little education. For example, I had no doubt that everything written in our history and social science textbooks, and in the youth and 'adult' newspapers, was true. I put absolute trust in the ideological tenets that society's and the state's interests are higher than a person's; and that class solidarity is higher than patriotism... The absolute uniformity of the information published by mass media along with the absence of public disputes and polemic in the press (and all of that in conditions of mass fear of state repression) caused most of my generation to lose the ability to think critically. Probably, my parents' viewpoints, and those of other adults that I knew as well, were in conflict with the official

line, but everyone kept such information concealed. There was never any private political talk in my presence.[14]

When the purges of 1937 began, Soviet media carried dozens of reports of anti-Soviet conspiracies. Most were alleged to be instigated by foreign agencies, and readers were encouraged to help the authorities, by being vigilant for spies and saboteurs. Such activity was fostered in a variety of ways. For example, Kobylyanskiy's youth newspaper carried a serialized story of how a spy was unmasked by a Young Pioneer, the editors hoping to encourage young people to emulate the hero of the story. As the arrests spread, people started to take quiet steps to protect themselves. Kobylyanskiy's father carefully blotted out the face of a senior official in his office from a group photograph after the man was arrested, in order to ensure that he would not be tainted by appearing in the same photograph.[15]

In 1938, Sergei Eisenstein's epic film *Alexander Nevsky* was released. Although it portrayed an earlier age, the message of the triumph of Russians over their Teutonic neighbours was clear. In case there was any doubt, some of the Teutonic Knights carried shields bearing only slightly stylized swastikas. This film was followed by a more contemporary piece, entitled *If There is War Tomorrow*. The invaders of the Soviet Union were openly portrayed as Germans, though they were parodied to a comical extent. The film showed the perfidious enemy's invasion stopped in its tracks by the heroic fighters of the Soviet Union, who then went on to Berlin, where the grateful people rose up to overthrow the Nazis and to join their communist brothers.

Such films were lapped up by a generation that had come of age during communist rule. Denied the opportunity to travel, and fed a heavily censored and selective view of the outside world, Kobylyanskiy and his peers genuinely believed – despite their own austere circumstances – that they were destined to create a brave, bright future. Any force that stood in their way would simply be swept aside by historical necessity.

The Molotov–Ribbentrop Pact of August 1939 posed a difficult problem for the Soviet authorities, who had portrayed Nazism as the enemy of communism. The details of the pact were not made clear. The protocols relating to the partition of Poland and the Soviet annexation of the Baltic states were never published in the Soviet Union, appearing for the first time in 1991. The new official line that Germany was a friend of the Soviet Union was at considerable variance with what had been the case in earlier years. Wehrmacht reports were published almost without alteration, and any ideological difficulties were brushed over by the view that both National Socialism and communism called for the overthrow of capitalism. Jewish families like the Kobylyanskiys harboured doubts, especially as the anti-Jewish pogroms in Germany had received wide coverage in the Soviet Union, but they were wise enough not to say anything in public.

The realities of war with Germany were shocking, even for the higher leadership. Young men and women of the Soviet Union's cities volunteered in their thousands. In the countryside, however, there was more ambivalence. Soviet agricultural collectivization was deeply unpopular, especially in the Ukraine and occupied Poland, and many people who were hostile to the Germans were also hostile to the heavily centralized Soviet system. Nevertheless, the cumbersome Soviet mobilization machinery went into action, in the face of huge difficulties caused by enemy air superiority. Depending on how far they were from the front, new recruits found themselves in action all too soon, often with no significant training.

Stalin was devastated not only by the German attack, but by the inability of his armies to halt it. Hamstrung by shortages of the most basic equipment; many divisions lacked sufficient rifles for their men, let alone ammunition, and of the Soviet Union's 23,000 tanks, over 70 per cent were in need of maintenance or repairs, which were almost impossible to carry out due to shortages of spare parts.[16] The huge formations of the Red Army were beyond the means of their officers to control, and their communications equipment was often rudimentary, even when it was available. By the first winter of the war, almost all of the original peacetime army that had been deployed in the west was gone, many of its divisions squandered in pointless head-on attacks against the Germans, who smashed them with their superior firepower. By the end of the winter, the eastern divisions, brought west in time to save Moscow, had themselves been bled white. But the enemy had been halted, and Moscow saved. By the following winter, the hated fascists were encircled in Stalingrad, and the Red Army's confidence was growing again.

That growth was based on many factors. Soviet armaments production, badly dislocated in the first year of the war, was now in full swing, producing tanks in such numbers that Hitler simply refused to believe the figures when his intelligence officers presented them. Supplies of other kinds were flowing, too, particularly of trucks, food and fuel, via convoys from the United States and Britain. The recruits who had filled the ranks in 1941, if they were still alive, were now veterans, with enough experience to survive combat. The role of the political commissars had been reduced, allowing officers a freer hand in military affairs, and those officers themselves were far more skilful and resourceful than the men who struggled to reconcile Party-dictated doctrine with the realities of armoured warfare in 1941. The infantry formations were reduced in size, making them more manageable. Conversely, the armoured formations, often having as few as 20–40 tanks in 1941, were enlarged, allowing them to take on German Panzer divisions with a greater likelihood of success. Starting in 1942, combined-arms formations began to appear, and by 1943 the tank armies that had first been deployed the previous summer were reorganized on more standardized lines, with two tank corps, each with 168 tanks, a single mechanized corps, and other formations such as artillery and engineers.

Training had been improved, with a new emphasis on military matters rather than ideology. Evacuated to Soviet Central Asia, Kobylyanskiy joined an artillery training establishment, where the truncated training programme – reduced from two years for an artillery lieutenant to one year – was intensive and exhausting. After only two months, Kobylyanskiy and other selected cadets were told that they were being sent to a division immediately; the developing crisis at Stalingrad made previous training plans irrelevant. For those like Kobylyanskiy, who had a natural aptitude for mathematics and therefore made an ideal artilleryman, this was perfectly acceptable, as like most young men he had a strong desire to do his patriotic duty. Kobylyanskiy later estimated that only 2 per cent of those who went to the front with him returned alive after the war.

The first victories of 1942 and 1943 were analyzed, hard lessons learned, and remedial steps taken, culminating in the shattering blow that was dealt to the German Army Group Centre through *Bagration* in the summer of 1944. As the war progressed, the Red Army dealt much better with failure than the Wehrmacht; Stalin allowed officers to learn from their mistakes, rather than replacing them reflexively, as Hitler increasingly did. The Red Army quickly understood the lessons that lay behind each setback, modifying tactics accordingly, while Hitler refused to listen to good advice and fell back increasingly on a dogmatic insistence on rigid defence.

Pavel Ivanovich Batov, who was to command the Soviet 65th Army through much of the war, was assigned to this post as the battle for Stalingrad reached its peak. The evolution of 65th Army shows many of the reasons for the improvements in the Red Army as a whole. Originally raised as 28th Reserve Army in early 1942, it was prematurely committed to the disastrous attempt by Semyon Timoshenko to recapture Kharkov that spring. The German counter-attack that destroyed much of Timoshenko's forces threw 28th Army back to the Don, where its staff was ordered to hand over their units to neighbouring armies and to start the formation of 4th Tank Army in the Volga valley. When Batov arrived to take command of this army, he was astonished to discover its current tank strength amounted to only four tanks; when he raised this with his superiors, the army was renamed 65th Army.[17]

Unlike the opening months of the war, nearly all of the senior staff officers of Batov's new army were veterans with experience of staff posts and hard combat behind them. The only exception was the commander of the communications section, Captain Borissov, but his skill in maintaining communications between army headquarters and its constituent divisions earned him high praise, and the constant fighting on the flanks of the great German bulge around Stalingrad ensured that even he too soon became a veteran. When the army was thrown into the great counter-attack that encircled the German 6th Army in Stalingrad, the staff officers were experts at cooperation and coordination.

By the second half of 1944, the ubiquitous T-34s were equipped with more powerful 85mm guns, and their ranks were supported not only by western-built Sherman tanks, but by a new breed of tanks, the JS-2 and JS-3 'Josef Stalin' tanks. (Note that the Soviets regarded the Shermans as inferior to their own vehicles; due to the ease with which they could be set ablaze, they were nicknamed 'Tommy-cookers' by the Germans when they first encountered them in the west.) The JS tanks, with their immense 122mm guns, were regarded with fear by the Germans, but at least some of this fear was dispelled when they were actually encountered in battle. The 4th Panzer Division first fought them in August 1944, swiftly knocking out eight, breaking the spell cast by these 'enormous hulks, with outrageously large turrets and tree-trunk-like guns'.[18] The Germans were surprised to find that these heavy tanks had a very limited quantity of ammunition aboard, making prolonged combat impossible. In some respects, the Soviet tanks were technically inferior to their German and western counterparts – poorer gunsights and radios in particular – but their excellent armour, and simple but robust engines, provided considerable compensation. And they were present in numbers far beyond the resources of Germany.

By late 1944, some Soviet tank armies had dispensed with their mechanized corps. Nevertheless, they remained formidable forces, with more than 600 tanks and nearly 200 assault guns. The rest of the Red Army was organized into combined-arms armies, each with up to 100,000 men, 460 tanks and 200 assault guns. All Soviet armies, corps and divisions had integral artillery formations, but there were also dedicated artillery formations, organized into corps and divisions; these went a long way to offset the shortage of manpower that the Red Army faced in its infantry towards the end of the war.

The Red Army was organized into a series of Fronts, each with several armies. In the north, the three Baltic Fronts faced Courland. South of them were the three Belorussian Fronts.

General Ivan Danilovich Cherniakhovsky's 3rd Belorussian Front faced the northeast parts of East Prussia. The Front's armies fielded a total of 19 rifle divisions, three tank corps and an artillery corps. Cherniakhovsky, who commanded a tank division at the start of the war, was the youngest man to command a Front. After successfully commanding 60th Army from 1942 to 1944, he took command of 3rd Belorussian Front in time to be involved in *Bagration*, and demonstrated his ability to improvise on a major scale, recommending that 5th Guards Tank Army be committed elsewhere than its original intended deployment.

To the south of Cherniakhovsky's Front was Konstantin Konstantinovich Rokossovsky's 2nd Belorussian Front. Rokossovsky was half-Polish, and had climbed to high command via an extraordinary career. In 1937, when he was commander of a cavalry corps, he was imprisoned by Stalin during the purges that ravaged the army. He was badly treated and released in 1940, and took part in the Soviet counter-offensive at Stalingrad, which changed the course of the war. Although once more enjoying high command, he was left in no doubt that Stalin regarded the charges brought against him in 1937 as being merely in abeyance – any failure on the battlefield would result in a swift return to imprisonment. Despite this, Rokossovsky displayed great independence of thought, and was not afraid to voice unpopular ideas. During the planning phase of *Bagration*, Stalin suggested a single attack on the city of Bobruisk. Rokossovsky disagreed, insisting on a two-pronged attack, on the grounds that this would result in fewer casualties than a single bludgeoning assault. Stalin told him to go away and think things over. When Rokossovsky returned to the room, Stalin asked him if he agreed that a single thrust was best. Rokossovsky stuck to his guns. Stalin sent him out to think again. Despite the urging of Georgi Malenkov and Molotov, two of Stalin's closest political allies, Rokossovsky refused to budge. To Malenkov's and Molotov's amazement, Stalin allowed himself to be persuaded that Rokossovsky's plan was indeed superior to his own.[19]

Yet Stalin still distrusted Rokossovsky, not least due to the Soviet dictator's dislike of the Poles. Originally, Rokossovsky had been commander of 1st Belorussian Front, immediately to the south of 2nd Belorussian Front, which was earmarked as the formation that would push on to Berlin. His move north to 2nd Belorussian Front towards the end of 1944 was due to Stalin's desire for a 'proper' Russian to lead the attack on Hitler's capital.

The new commander of 1st Belorussian Front was indeed a 'proper' Russian. Georgi Konstantinovich Zhukov was born in a peasant family outside Moscow, and was conscripted into a cavalry regiment at the beginning of World War I. His military skills were clear from an early stage, as was his contempt for aristocracy, and after the revolution he rose swiftly. He was an early enthusiast for mechanized warfare, and survived Stalin's purges of the army, though he was sent to Mongolia in 1939. This proved to be a career-making move. As commander of 1st Mongolian Army Group, he smashed the Japanese forces that invaded the province. Like his British contemporary, Montgomery, he had a keen awareness of the importance of good logistics, and went to great lengths to ensure that he had assembled sufficient forces for his attack on the Japanese to be overwhelming.

In 1940, he returned to the west, and at the time of the German invasion in 1941 he was Chief of the General Staff. Stalin's refusal to allow him to order a withdrawal from Kiev led to his resigning his post, and he was sent to stabilize the defences of Leningrad. Then, he was moved to the central sector, in time to lead the defence of Moscow, before being sent south the following year to plan and execute the crushing counter-offensive at Stalingrad. The huge build-up of Soviet forces that guaranteed later success in *Bagration* was due to a large extent to Zhukov's careful planning. Now, he stood on the Vistula in command of the 1st Belorussian Front, preparing for the drive that would take his forces to Berlin.

Zhukov's long series of successes made him a popular commander, but his use of his men was often brutal. One of his few military defeats occurred in late 1942 when the Red Army tried to eliminate the Rzhev Salient, a bulge in the German frontline to the west of Moscow. The attack, codenamed *Mars*, was a disaster, with the Red Army losing between 200,000 and 500,000 men for an advance of less than 20km. He also ruthlessly enforced discipline with the use of firing squads and penal battalions, which were deployed in the most dangerous roles. Nevertheless, he achieved decisive results, and Stalin was sure that he would successfully lead the drive into the enemy heartland. This confidence in his ability was shared by his men; the catchphrase 'Where you find Zhukov, you will find victory' was widespread throughout the Red Army.

In the ranks of the Red Army, the mood by the second half of 1944 showed two conflicting trends. On the one hand, there was steadily growing confidence, fed by the momentum of the Red Army's advance. On the other hand, the veterans were increasingly war-weary. Leave from the frontline was effectively non-existent unless a soldier was wounded, and the vagaries of the field postal service were such that contact with people at home was intermittent at best. What news came often told of hardships and shortages amongst the civilians, who toiled to keep the Red Army supplied with weapons and equipment, the stories increasing the concerns of the soldiers themselves. The frontline divisions, particularly the infantry, were almost all at less than full strength. Drafts of replacements, often press-ganged in the newly 'liberated' territories, took their places uneasily alongside the surviving veterans. The poor training of these men meant that they were often used in 'human wave' attacks, as they lacked the skill to be deployed in any other way.

The year 1944 was a good one for the Red Army, and a bad one for the Wehrmacht. But the year wasn't over yet. There was still sufficient time before winter for Stalin's generals to test the resolve of the 'Fritzies' on their own soil, and to try once more to isolate Schörner's Army Group North.

CHAPTER 2
MEMEL

The Eastern border of the Memel District is an effective border between two different civilizations. It is the right border between east and west, between Europe and Asia.

– E. Hadamovsky[1]

The city known today as Klaipeda is on the Baltic coast of Lithuania. In 1944, it was the East Prussian city of Memel, at the northern extremity of East Prussian territory. At the end of the Great War, 80 per cent of the city's population was German, but most of those living in the countryside around Memel were Lithuanians – a situation analogous to that in and around Danzig. The Lithuanian delegation at the Versailles peace treaty conference requested that 'Memelland' be placed within the bounds of the new state of Lithuania, but instead the conference powers removed the area from Germany and placed it under French jurisdiction, under a League of Nations mandate. In 1923, the Lithuanian population in the enclave rose up in revolt. Lithuania's tiny army went to the aid of their fellow countrymen, and the small French garrison was withdrawn. Despite official protests, there was nothing that the League of Nations could do but accept the Lithuanian annexation of Memelland.

The German population of Memel was never reconciled with the city's new status, and unrest continued through the 1920s and 1930s. The Nazi Party established a new local branch in 1933 and met with rapid political success, resulting in the party being banned by the Lithuanian government the following year. The party's leadership was arrested and sentenced to imprisonment with hard labour, which attracted vociferous protests from Germany, especially from East Prussia, where Koch was particularly active in promoting the rights of Germans in Memel. In a series of press announcements, he spoke about the threat to the German population of Memel, and demanded that the signatories of the Treaty of Versailles enforce what had been agreed. This demand was, of course, impossible to satisfy, and formed part of an overall German policy to portray the Memelland Germans as an oppressed group who were not being helped by those who had placed them in their current state. Thus the German government paved the way for Germany to take matters into its own hands.

Plans were laid for a German seaborne invasion of Memelland in 1938, to be implemented in the event of a Lithuanian–Polish conflict. In 1939, Hitler demanded that the region be returned to German control, and in the face of the barely veiled threat of German military intervention, the Lithuanian government had no option but to agree. Nevertheless, they delayed giving their consent as long as they could, with farcical results. Hitler planned a triumphant entry into the city aboard the pocket battleship *Deutschland*. A last-minute overnight delay left him sending irritated signals to his Foreign Minister Joachim von Ribbentrop in Berlin to determine what was happening. Finally, early on the afternoon of 23 March, a seasick Hitler was able to come ashore in the city and proclaim its return to the Reich.

The following year, Lithuania, Latvia and Estonia were forcibly occupied by the Soviet Union, a consequence of the Molotov–Ribbentrop Pact that also carved up Poland. Many citizens of these countries fiercely resented the presence of the Soviets, and consequently welcomed the Germans when they invaded in 1941. Latvians and Estonians joined the SS in substantial numbers, although the Lithuanians appear to have been somewhat cooler towards the Germans, many regarding the German occupation as the lesser of evils. As General Ivan Bagramian's armies approached the Baltic in 1944, tensions began to rise.

Ivan Khristoforovich Bagramian was born the son of a railway worker in a village in what is now Azerbaijan. After serving in the Russian Army on the Turkish front during the Great War, he joined the Red Army and took part in fighting during the civil war against nationalist forces in the Caucasus. In 1941, Hitler's invasion of the Soviet Union found him appointed as Deputy Chief of Staff of the Southwest Front, based at Kiev. He was one of the few senior officers to escape the German encirclement of the city. After a brief spell as Chief of Staff to Timoshenko in 1942, he was appointed to command first 16th Army, then 11th Guards Army, before taking command of 1st Baltic Front in 1943. He executed his part of the Stavka (Soviet general headquarters) plan for the summer offensive in 1944, enveloping Vitebsk and then pressing on westwards to Polotsk, even though the losses suffered by his armies 'shook him to the core'.[2] During the exploitation that followed, though, he grew increasingly unhappy about the mass of the German Army Group North, hanging over his armies as they pushed on westwards. He asked in vain several times for permission to strike north towards Riga, in order to isolate the German divisions that were being bloodily prised out of their defensive lines east of the city. Finally, when his forces had penetrated into the heart of Lithuania, taking the town of Siauliai – Schaulen to the Germans – on 27 July, he was given permission to turn north in force. The road from Siauliai to the Baltic coast immediately west of Riga covers a distance of about 120km; Bagramian's armour travelled along this route in three days, isolating Army Group North in and to the east of Riga.

This triumph was achieved at great cost, and even greater risk. Bagramian's armies were badly over-extended, and barely able to hold their positions let alone take advantage of their gains. For a few brief days, almost all of western Latvia was undefended by the Germans, but Bagramian simply didn't have the reserves to exploit this situation. He had his hands full beating off attacks against his forces from the east, where Army Group North attempted to break out, and more significantly from the west, where several German divisions – Panzer Division *Grossdeutschland* and 4th, 5th and 7th Panzer Divisions – attempted to force their way through. Although this powerful armoured force was blocked, it was at the cost of weakness elsewhere on 1st Baltic Front's extended frontline, and an ad hoc German battlegroup was able to re-establish contact with Army Group North along the Baltic coast.

Briefly, the front stabilized, but Stavka now prepared plans for what was intended to be a final blow against Army Group North.

Starting in mid September, the three Baltic Fronts, followed a few days later by the Leningrad Front, would attack Schörner's armies on all sides. At first, Afanasii Beloborodov's 43rd Army, part of Bagramian's command, made good progress, but the attacks of the two other Baltic Fronts made little headway. The Germans were aware of the Soviet build-up, and fell back methodically from one defensive line to the next, inflicting a heavy toll on the attacking formations. It was only when the Leningrad Front joined the attack that significant headway was made. Meanwhile, the German armoured formations that had unsuccessfully attempted to break through from the southwest now attacked again. Although they once more made little headway in difficult terrain, they forced Bagramian to divert forces that he had intended to throw at Riga. It was clear that the concerted assault to eliminate Army Group North was not going to succeed.

On 24 September, therefore, Stavka issued revised instructions. Bagramian's 1st Baltic Front was to switch its line of advance from a northwards drive towards Riga, to a westwards drive towards Memel. There were several advantages in such a move. First, it would move the attack to an area where there had been no significant fighting since the original German advance in 1941; the roads and bridges over which Bagramian would advance were therefore in good shape. Second, it would allow Soviet forces to reach Reich territory, something of huge political significance. The logistical challenge of this shift of emphasis was formidable, but it was a sign of the growing skill of the Red Army that it was carried out efficiently in less than two weeks. Half a million men, 10,000 guns and mortars and more than a thousand tanks, together with thousands of tons of fuel, food and ammunition, moved west into new positions, a displacement of about 200km over poor roads, many of them already severely degraded by the earlier passage of German and Soviet armoured vehicles. Furthermore, it was carried out mainly at night, to reduce the risk of the Germans detecting the movement. By day, the troops took cover in the plentiful woods of Lithuania.

By early October, though, it was impossible to hide the growing preparations. The 3rd Panzer Army, commanded by Generaloberst Erhard Raus, had two corps

BAGRAMIAN'S DRIVE TO THE COAST, OCTOBER 1944

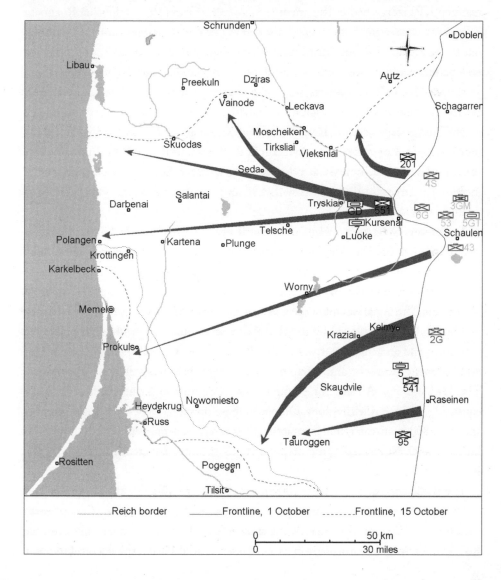

covering the frontline in front of Memel. These corps between them had only five divisions, stretched over 200km. In the north was General Hans Gollnick's XXVIII Corps, and on the eve of the Soviet attack it received welcome reinforcements in the shape of the Panzer Division *Grossdeutschland*. A shortage of fuel and railway rolling stock, however, meant that the division would arrive piecemeal.

Grossdeutschland was one of the premier formations of the Wehrmacht. Its tank regiment had, in addition to the usual two battalions of Pz. IVs and Panthers, an additional battalion of heavyweight Tiger tanks, with their lethally effective 88mm guns, and a separate battalion of assault guns. Its two armoured infantry regiments, Panzergrenadier Regiment *Grossdeutschland* and Panzer-Fusilier Regiment *Grossdeutschland*, were at this stage of the war as weakened as other similar formations, but the news on 3 October that the division's Tiger battalion, an additional attached tank battalion and the division's powerful reconnaissance battalion, were to move south to support XXVIII Corps was very welcome. Part of this force was immediately assigned to support 551st Volksgrenadier Division, in preparation for plans to eliminate enemy bridgeheads over the River Venta near Kursenai, secured by the Red Army the previous night. Long experience had taught the Germans the need to eliminate these small bridgeheads as quickly as possible, otherwise the Soviet forces would swiftly increase the strength of the units within them to a point where they could serve as springboards for an attack.

The officers of *Grossdeutschland* were swiftly brought up to date by Gollnick's staff at XXVIII Corps. Information from a variety of sources – aerial reconnaissance, radio intercepts and interrogation of deserters and prisoners – suggested that an attack was imminent. It was unlikely that *Grossdeutschland* would have sufficient time to form up all of its forces. The initial weight of the attack would fall on 551st Volksgrenadier Division.

The total force deployed by the Red Army amounted to 19 rifle divisions, three tank corps and an artillery corps. But the rifle divisions were substantially below their establishment strength, and what manpower they had was often poorly trained. The 43rd and 51st Armies, for example, were composed of a single rifle corps each, consisting of three rifle divisions. On paper, these divisions were intended to number about 11,800 men each, but in practice they rarely had more than 7,000, often as little as 3,000. Nevertheless, the preponderance of power lay greatly in favour of the Red Army.[3]

The Baltic coast was roughly a 100km west of the frontline. To the north, 2nd and 3rd Baltic Fronts continued to exert pressure, squeezing Schörner's Army Group North back through Riga into Estonia. By the standards of the great summer offensives, the Red Army's resources, particularly in terms of reserves available to exploit a breakthrough, were limited, but several opportunities presented themselves. A single-minded drive west would sever Schörner's armies from the rest of the Reich, leaving them dependent on seaborne supplies. Given the weakness of the German defences, there was also the enticing prospect that a breakthrough to the coast would open up the rear of Army Group North, allowing Bagramian's armoured forces the opportunity of perhaps rolling up the entire German front, or at least of seizing the vital port of Libau, without which the Germans would struggle to keep Schörner's two armies alive. And to the southwest, there was the possibility of exploiting a breakthrough into East Prussia itself.

Of these options, Stavka knew that the breakthrough to the coast was probably well within the Red Army's resources, but exploitation to the north or south was less likely to succeed. In both cases, significant rivers – the Venta in the north, and the Niemen, or Memel as the Germans preferred to call it, to the south – would act as major barriers to the advance. The priority, then, would be given to reaching the coast. Anything more would be a bonus.

On the German side, most of XXVIII Corps' fighting strength consisted of the arriving elements of *Grossdeutschland* and 551st Volksgrenadier Division. The remnants of 201st Security Division, which had been badly mauled during *Bagration*, held a segment of front to the north. The three grenadier regiments of Generalleutnant Siegfried Verhein's newly formed 551st Volksgrenadier Division were, on paper at least, relatively strong, but most of the men had almost no experience of infantry combat, particularly in the brutal conditions of the *Ostfront*. Furthermore, the division was responsible for an unrealistic 48km of frontline. The initial Soviet artillery bombardment appears to have been relatively ineffective, however, partly due to foggy conditions that prevented observation of fire and grounded the Soviet Air Force. When the Soviet assault began on 5 October, the German grenadiers robustly threw back the first two attacks. When a third attack was thrown at them, however, their decimated ranks gave way. In several sectors, the Red Army forces simply moved forward through deserted positions – much of 551st Volksgrenadier Division had not survived its first proper day of combat.

Grossdeutschland's armoured reconnaissance battalion was ordered to move forward in support of the shattered Volksgrenadier division. Under the command of Rittmeister Schroedter, the battalion launched itself into the flank of the Soviet regiment that was moving west. Despite having few heavy weapons, Schroedter's men swiftly scattered their opponents and pressed on to 551st Volksgrenadier Division's former positions. Here they found that the battle wasn't over; a small group of infantry had coalesced around a Hauptmann Licht, and with the help of the reconnaissance battalion, the grenadiers continued to hold the main battleline until the early hours of 6 October.

But with Soviet forces up to 15km to the rear of either flank, there was little point in holding on, and the amalgamated force withdrew towards the west.

Other armoured units were also on the move. The 7th Panzer Division was ordered south into the path of the expected Soviet attack, and some of its units were rapidly pressed into service a little further south of *Grossdeutschland*. Johann Huber was a young officer trainee who had recently joined the division, and was serving as a loader in a Pz. IV. The tank commander and gunner were both middle-ranking NCOs, but had spent most of the war in rear-area units; they had now been drafted into a frontline formation, and in their first encounter with a Soviet T-34 the inexperience of the NCOs was alarmingly apparent:

Now the black gun barrel and then the turret of a T-34 emerge from the branches. Head in, hatch closed, and a shout of 'T-34!'… Richard Braumandl [the driver] shouts over the intercom, 'Herr Feldwebel, T-34 to our front!' Now there is turmoil… Feldwebel Isecke takes another two or three seconds, then presses the trigger. The shot leaves the barrel, bitter smoke fills the turret, and as soon as the barrel has returned from its recoil, I load the second armour-piercing round and switch on the turret smoke extractor. The breech snaps closed. But Richard Braumandl shouts angrily, 'Herr Feldwebel, you have overshot, why are you firing high?' What follows, I don't hear. Isecke fires a second time.

He shoots high again. The two grumble about it. I can't see anything, I hear from Richard and Karl, who as driver and radio-operator are able to observe. 'Herr Feldwebel, he's going to fire on us, his barrel is turning towards us. Why are you shooting too high?' All I can do is load the third armour-piercing round… Then from quite close to our left, we hear the shot of one of our 75mm guns. Richard shouts, 'Now he's hit! He's burning!'

It wasn't us, Isecke overshot twice, who was it then? We would probably have copped it, as we were only 120 metres away.

It was Willi Hegen, the gunner in Oberleutnant Jakob's vehicle. Everyone is trembling inside, as it is clear that our own gunner is a twit. He failed at the critical moment. We were almost done for. I knew why he had overshot. This great bullock didn't determine the range in his *Fitzerei* [a term in the war synonymous with anxiety], and perhaps also used the high-explosive range marker instead of the armour-piercing range marker. That was the only way he could have missed.[4]

Soviet infantry were moving forward through the woods around the village. Lacking any infantry support themselves, the German tanks withdrew a few kilometres over a small river, the Shisma. Here they turned to face the advancing Soviet tanks again, and Huber's tank commander, Feldwebel Sattler, attracted the ire of the company commander, Oberleutnant Jakob, when he decided to pull back from an exposed position. This precipitate retreat nearly ended in disaster, as the rest of the company almost opened fire on Sattler in the gathering darkness. A confused night action followed. Several T-34s were shot up at close range, but in the darkness other Soviet tanks had succeeded in infiltrating into the German position. At dawn, the Germans withdrew from their positions and the Soviet advance continued.

On 6 October, Bagramian committed 5th Guards Tank Army to the battle, which was now raging across a frontage of nearly 200km. Schörner tried to extract units from the Riga front in order to send them south, but 2nd and 3rd Baltic Fronts, backed by the Leningrad Front, increased their own pressure on Riga. Several days of bloody attacks and counter-attacks around the Latvian capital resulted in little ground being gained or lost; Army Group North was effectively pinned in its defences, however, unable to move troops to counter Bagramian's thrust towards Memel and the Baltic coast.

Cloudy conditions prevailed on 7 October, with light rain, but the weather wasn't bad enough to ground the Soviet aircraft, which continued to attack every road movement they detected. *Grossdeutschland* and 7th Panzer Division, together with whatever remained of 551st Volksgrenadier Division, tried to contain the enemy breakthrough. The frontline near Tryskiai had to be abandoned, with a small group of *Grossdeutschland*'s Panther tanks providing a rearguard. Not far away, Huber and his comrades were also in action again. They took up a good hull-down position on a ridge, where they endured a brief bombardment:

The shellfire suddenly breaks off.

I get up and position myself in the loader's hatch to have a look. As far as I can see, they're not shooting at us any more, but the front rumbles away. The enemy offensive is in full swing... Over there, across the crest of the slope opposite us, the enemy appears: Russian infantry. As far as the eye can see, to left and right, they occupy the entire crest, followed by a second wave. We really didn't see them. The company commander radios: 'Hold your fire.' We couldn't do anything anyway, the range is too great, I estimate it to be about 3,000 metres.

The attack waves are about 50 metres apart. Now and then a shell flies over, but lands in front of us in the fields, to the right or left. We concentrate on counting the Red Army's attack waves. There are now seven, eight, nine, now twelve. Thousands of Russians pour forward endlessly, there must be a whole infantry division committed against us. Our eyes flicker along the horizon to left and right; no tanks, no anti-tank guns in sight.

Then we hear the 'Urrah!' The east wind carries it from the other slope to us. The first waves have already almost reached the bottom of the valley, and we can no longer see them beyond the curve of the slope. There is a continuous 'Urrah' – to the front, to the left, to the right. We are uneasy. We aren't able to shoot at what we can see. They are too far away, it would only reveal our positions. Actually, we are in a good position in our sandy hollow, with only the gun protruding forward and the turret above the top of the hollow.

Then it all begins again. The twelfth wave is the last that I see, then I pull myself back inside and quickly close the hatch. There is a further heavy firestrike by the Russian artillery. We are plastered with fire. A 172mm shell detonates a metre from the edge of our pit, hurling earth over the tank, sand flies over the cupola; Sattler has already pulled his head in. Now there's pandemonium. Just get us out of this hole. Sattler orders, 'Start the engine,' and Richard Braumandl shouts, 'Herr Feldwebel, I know!' As the tank digs itself out of the sand and moves backwards, our stern points into the air, and everyone fears that if we take an artillery hit, we may flip right over. We drive back out of the pit with our engine howling.[5]

The Red Army, too, was running out of experienced soldiers. The poorly trained replacements included many of the men from the newly liberated areas of the western Soviet Union. All that could be done with such infantry was to attack in great waves, reminiscent of World War I. It was fortunate for them that the Germans lacked sufficient artillery and infantry to smash such easy targets.

The southern flank of the German position had been turned by advancing T-34s, with two Pz. IVs lost in the fighting. A mixture of German units – the remnants of 551st Volksgrenadier Division, parts of 7th Panzer Division, and Kampfgruppe *Fabisch* (Battlegroup *Fabisch*) from the *Grossdeutschland* – now found themselves in the village of Luoke. Maximilian Fabisch's group had arrived in the village on 6 October, and beat off several enemy attacks. Huber's tank company was in position near the southern end of the town:

The Russian artillery's salvoes keep coming, four shells at a time. Right and left of us, the shells explode amongst the houses. Glancing back past the house behind us, I see our infantry running along the road beyond. They are coming from the right. Sattler sees them too, and I ask myself, who's protecting our right flank? Have we any right flank security at all? The situation isn't clear to us here, between the houses, amongst the farmers' gardens. Is 7 Company on our right? Sattler asks via the radio. The right flank is covered, comes the reply from the chief's vehicle. Two of our tanks are being sent there.

The Russian artillery fires continuously. Half-left of us, at about 11 o'clock, we can see some of our tanks moving. They are Panthers, clearly recognizable with their triangular rears, and their two exhausts visible at the top.

… There, suddenly it happens! Yellow-green tracers fly from the right, a long, poisonous flare behind it! Phosphorus ammunition: I see the shell fly and hit. One of the Panthers is hit on the side of its hull and immediately burns – and how! It blazes like a flare. That was the phosphorus. We know that such ammunition is forbidden under international law, just like explosive bullets. But the Russians use both regardless. All of us have an inner horror of it. So, we are faced by a tank unit with just such ammunition.[6]

Phosphorus ammunition was not actually used as an anti-tank weapon, more as a smoke round. Phosphorus elements were also used to create highly visible tracers for shells, and machine-gun belts with every round containing a small phosphorus tracer were used in World War I as incendiary ammunition when engaging hydrogen-filled balloons. As the use of phosphorus rounds in Iraq has demonstrated, the legal status of such ammunition remains controversial. It is likely that on this occasion, Huber was observing conventional armour-piercing rounds fitted with phosphorus tracers. The sloped frontal armour of the Panther tank was 80mm thick, but the side armour was only 45mm, and had a far less generous slope. The 85mm guns of the Soviet T-34s would have had little difficulty penetrating this side-armour. Panthers also had a bad reputation for catching fire, not least because of the poor quality of synthetic rubber that was now used in the manufacture of seals. Crews often complained of the strong smell of petrol within the fighting compartment, and in such circumstances, penetration by a round with a burning phosphorus tracer was likely to be fatal.

Huber continued to watch helplessly as two more Panthers were hit and destroyed. A short while later Jakob, the company commander, was wounded in the forehead by artillery shrapnel, and as he sagged unconscious in his seat, blood streaming from the wound, the rest of his crew feared the worst. Leutnant Müller took over command of the company, while Jakob was bandaged and, to the relief of his men, soon regained consciousness.

The Soviet artillery bombardment intensified, with Katyusha rockets now falling on the German positions. Müller ordered his tanks to pull back:

We come to a halt in the garden, from where we see the road. It is a dreadful scene. There are dozens of dead and wounded Landsers [soldiers], as I glance to the left over the turret and right to the north, I estimate at least 100, 200 seriously wounded and dead lying there. We can't drive over them, we have to look out to drive between the many living, who writhe and cry out in pain.[7]

Some of the Katyusha salvoes had struck the 7th Panzer Division's main field dressing station near the northern end of Luoke. Already overflowing with wounded, the dressing station became a charnel house, and was overrun by the advancing Soviet infantry as the tanks pulled back.

Everyone wants to pull back, the Russians have stormed the southern part of the village; a powerful tank unit must have moved in there, unnoticed by us. We feared as much. To our right, the south, we had no protection. 7 Company wasn't there to beat off the enemy in good time. Two minutes later, when we are all positioned across the road, ready finally to turn right and descend the hill that we climbed an hour before, an Unteroffizier rises up from the ground. He has been wounded in the belly with shrapnel from a Stalin organ, right through from left to right, sliced right open. He holds his spilled guts with both arms, as if holding a basket, staggers to our tank, wants to climb on, I reach for him, he cries with a pained expression, his eyes full of fear, 'Comrades, take me with you!' I want to pull him up over the turret skirting, but he can't hold on, he doesn't have the strength. He falls, with a hand to his belly, holding his entrails together, slowly keels over, sits on the road and then pulls himself halfway onto his side. His spilled intestines pour onto the sand. Dreadful. A man falls to his death, trying to reach for his last chance. I couldn't get hold of his hand, I was left grasping at empty air.

Then Richard drives on for another ten metres before halting again. The dreadful moment has passed, but there are still the living. I pull them up onto our tank, as the infantry don't know where they can climb aboard, I tug at arms, hands, necks. New, fresh clothing, recently issued, I guess they are from a Volksgrenadier division. They have the number 551 on their shoulderboards… We now have a whole group of soldiers on the back, and meanwhile heavy mortar fire continues, with ever more soldiers fleeing from the south towards us; the Russians must be really close. Now we're off, running downhill, I have to get back into the turret. From the noise of the tracks I realize we're going faster and faster. And then the fireworks start. Following the Stalin organ salvoes, the firing of the as yet unsighted T-34s and the mortars, all hell now breaks loose. Braumandl shouts, 'Russians in the open, we're driving through them, we're surrounded!'

Have the Russians bypassed us? Have we failed to notice a pincer attack? These thoughts shoot through my head. I see nothing, but Sattler taps me on the shoulder and tells me to prepare the machine-gun, and then Isecke fires like mad with the turret machine-gun towards 2 o'clock. In the front, Karl also fires one burst after another with the radio-operator's machine-gun, and outside all hell breaks loose. Then Richard Braumandl shouts, 'Herr Feldwebel, the tank in front of us, dear God!' He stamps on the brakes, we all pitch forward, and then we're off again. I am busy loading the machine-gun.

It's difficult, as the main gun is fully depressed. There is now little space above the machine-gun breech to load the belt. 'Please don't jam,' I think. But it works fine.

We drive for a long time, with ricochets clicking constantly off the armour. They're firing at us with everything they have, it must be Russian infantry! If only there aren't any anti-tank guns nearby. After a good two kilometres, Isecke, the gunner, stops shooting. He raises the main gun again and Sattler says, 'We're through now.' We must have come about two kilometres through the Russian lines. Isecke orders me, 'Go out and check the turret, it's jammed.' We drive on, but much slower. As soon as I climb out of the hatch, I catch my breath. Our tank is empty. As I climb over the turret skirting, I see that only one of our men is still there, clinging by his fingers to the grill of the engine decking and holding on. I stare for a moment, and realise that all of the infantry must have been shot off the back. None of them has survived. When I reach the Landser and try to pull him aboard, I see that he's unharmed. He is an old soldier, I reckon at least 50, if not 55. Over the noise of the tracks, I shout to him, 'Where are the others?' But he can't say a word. He just crawls forward across the engine decking and says nothing, his teeth chattering as if it were 30 degrees below zero. He's in shock. But I need to find out what's jamming the turret. That is not so easy. Finally, over on the gunner's side, I find an abandoned rifle that has jammed under the outer skirting. I have to work it back and forth to free it, and then I reckon that Isecke will be able to turn the turret.

Now we halt. Immediately, we turn the turret to 5 o'clock, so that we can shoot backwards... Now what are we to do with the soldier who lies on his side; he will have to move if we are to shoot. But he is not fit to walk, or jump off. I can see that the man has gone through hell and is the only survivor of perhaps a dozen men. Sattler agrees, we leave him up top, but he must move forward to the nose, where I secure him so that he does not place his feet on the radio-operator's machine-gun and doesn't obstruct Richard Braumandl's observation slit, which would be fatal. He still can't speak, but he understands. I can see that.

As I climb back through the hatch and don my headset, we receive new orders to take up positions either side of the road. The battle continues. The T-34s are pushing on. We are permitted 'free fire' on identified targets and are on the left of the road. Apparently, 7 Company is defending the right side.

... About 900 metres away, on the hill in front of us, we hear a shot. Rose-red tracer! Damn, T-34s. So they are already here! Nothing for it but to get back in the tank. The other vehicles in our company have already opened fire, but we can see little of the enemy tanks. Only turrets and cupolas are visible. We can't hit them beyond the ridge. Isecke also fires twice, then we give up. There's more going down to our right. 7 Company is over there. Our comrades are more involved in the tank battle than us – but I hear only their tank guns. And then the T-34s must have hit one of 7 Company. The tank burns. It isn't possible to see who's been hit. Most, or even all, have to pull back, we hear via the radio. Then we are ordered to withdraw a further two or three kilometres.

Once we are in position and evening is drawing on, Richard Braumandl begins to talk. 'Herr Feldwebel, what tank was that before us, driving in front of us, when we broke out? I wasn't able to see, as there were so many infantry in the way. You know how we drove down the hill afterwards.' The Feldwebel doesn't know. Richard asks again, 'Did you really not see him?' 'I didn't notice – there was too much happening.' 'Hmmm, what's Richard getting at?' I ask him. Then he explains. 'I only saw the tank in front of me with infantry that the Russians were shooting. But then the tank slipped into the ditch with its right track, and overran a group of our Landsers who were in the ditch taking cover from the Russians, with its right track. It was awful – arms and legs were hanging from the track, torn off by it, it drove over the soldiers for at least 30 metres, our own Landsers.' The blood drains from the three of us, Sattler says nothing, but he must have seen it too. Dreadful! The driver in front of us was responsible for the deaths of our own comrades – he simply rolled them flat when we broke out of the encirclement. Richard's words shock everyone. Nobody speaks a word, everyone thinks back about an hour and a half before when Richard shouted, 'Herr Feldwebel, the driver in front of us, dear God!' There's silence in the vehicle, with the only noise coming from the headsets, the sounds of guns firing. Death has done a dreadful business today.[8]

Both flanks of the Luoke position had been bypassed. The Soviet forces once more demonstrated their mastery of armoured warfare – avoid and bypass strong positions, and probe for weaknesses. The remaining elements of 7th Panzer Division, *Grossdeutschland* and 551st Volksgrenadier Division had no choice but to pull back; the alternative was to invite encirclement. Moving northwest from Luoke, one battalion of the *Grossdeutschland* fusilier regiment ran into enemy spearheads in Seda. As it struggled to check the Soviet advance, some of *Grossdeutschland*'s assault guns were dispatched to support it. Although the town remained in Soviet hands, a further penetration to the west was prevented, at least for the moment. A decision was then made to pull back the fragmented front to the East Prussian frontier, immediately east of Memel. In the chaos, some elements of *Grossdeutschland* found themselves cut off by the enemy. The well-armoured Tiger tanks simply held their positions until nightfall, and then broke through to the west. A Panzergrenadier battalion was isolated at Luoke, when all other formations had either fallen back or been driven away to the west. In bitter fighting, the Panzergrenadiers fought their way back to Plunge.

Just east of the old Reich frontier lay the East Prussian Defence Position, constructed with such fanfare earlier in the autumn by Knuth's labour squads. In places, it was a formidable barrier, but only if it were adequately manned. Behind this, a second line of defences had been constructed around Memel itself, following the River Minge for much of its length. It was imperative that the retreating troops hold one or other of these two positions – if they failed, the defence of the city would be right on its outskirts.

Local Party officials were of course aware of the fighting, and had been enquiring nervously of the Wehrmacht whether there would be a need to evacuate German civilians from Memelland. As early as 5 October, Schörner declared that such an evacuation was unnecessary. Whether an evacuation could actually have been carried out in an orderly manner is questionable, but the fact that it wasn't even attempted left thousands of civilians in the path of the advancing Red Army.[9]

Whatever Schörner may have believed about there being no requirement for a civilian evacuation, Raus had different views, and on his urging the Party officials along the northern borders of East Prussia finally ordered civilians to leave. The process began slowly, but soon became a panic-stricken stampede as the Red Army drew closer. Troops struggling to withdraw to the East Prussian Defence Position found the roads choked with refugees. Movements were already difficult due to constant air attacks and fuel shortages; in some cases, they now became almost impossible. Huber's tank had suffered a transmission failure, and had to be towed out of the frontline. On 8 October, Huber and the rest of the crew were towed back in the early hours through Telsche and Plunge:

> Beyond Plunge it is even harder to make progress along the congested *Rollbahn* [main road], with rear-area units, trucks and horse-drawn vehicles, all wanting to move west. There is nothing for it but to stop for hours at a time.
>
> …We pull off the congested *Rollbahn* and make no further progress. Suddenly, at about 1500, all motors are switched off and there's general silence, and we hear from the left, up front, at about 10 o'clock, a gun firing. Everyone immediately looks in that direction, from where black smoke is now rising: T-34 to the left! So since last night, when we were still defending near Luoke, the Russians have advanced at least 60 kilometres… I quickly estimate the distance to the forest edge where the T-34 is positioned. It is at least 1,400 metres, so there's no point in shooting. At that range, we would achieve nothing against a T-34's armour. Our armour-piercing rounds are only effective against this type of enemy tank at less than 800 metres. The T-34 fires again and again, and a good 1,200 metres down the *Rollbahn* there is now a black cloud – he's hit something, vehicles are burning. But then there's one of our yellow tracers going left. A hit! The T-34 immediately starts to burn. It was alone, no more are nearby.[10]

The Soviet advance showed no sign of letting up. By dawn on 8 October, Plunge had already been bypassed, as Huber and his comrades discovered. The town came under increasingly heavy attack throughout the day, but then alarming reports arrived of Soviet tanks with infantry mounted aboard, approaching the River Minge east of Krottingen, and therefore already through the East Prussian Defence Position. These were the leading formations of the Soviet 43rd Army, pressing forward almost unopposed. Elements of *Grossdeutschland* were dispatched to secure the crossings at Kartena. This reinforced company found its route from Plunge to Kartena had already been cut by the Soviet spearheads, and had to fight its way through.

Difficulties in moving supplies forward to the fighting troops were beginning to bite, and several Tiger tanks had to be abandoned due to fuel shortages. But reinforcements were also arriving: 58th Infantry Division had been moved by sea from Army Group North into Memel, and now took up defensive positions northeast of the city. Heavy fighting continued in and around Krottingen, and further north around Salantai and Polangen. *Grossdeutschland* created two battlegroups, Battlegroup *Schwarzrock* and Battlegroup *von Breese*, which pulled back in stages over the last few kilometres to Memel, while other formations raced the Soviet spearheads westwards, across the Minge and into the developing positions around the city. The division's reconnaissance battalion effectively formed a third battlegroup, and in heavy fighting alongside Battlegroup *von Breese*, it was able to hold up the pursuing Soviet forces for a few critical hours. Without this delay, 1st Baltic Front's armoured spearheads would probably have overrun several of the formations struggling to reach Memel, with serious consequences for the defence of the city. Schwarzrock's battlegroup had the furthest distance to withdraw; pulling back through Salantai, it drove through Polangen while the town was under aerial bombardment. The rubble-strewn streets hindered, but did not prevent, its withdrawal.

Memel itself had been under increasingly heavy air attack since 6 October, and most of the civilian population had now been evacuated. Von Breese's battlegroup continued to hold off the Soviet forces near Krottingen. One of its battalions found itself isolated, and during the evening of 9 October it received orders to try to break through to Memel. Despite being badly scattered by a recent encounter with a large group of T-34s, the battalion was able to concentrate its surviving vehicles and pull out, reaching Krottingen unopposed. There they found a new obstacle: the road passed over a bridge, underneath which was an ammunition train set ablaze by air attacks. The vehicles raced across one by one without mishap, and continued their withdrawal.[11]

The troops swiftly moved through the deserted streets of Memel to their assigned defensive positions. The 58th Infantry Division would hold the northern part of the bridgehead perimeter; 7th Panzer Division would hold the centre; and *Grossdeutschland* was to hold the southern part.

The Soviet 53rd Army took Polangen on 10 October, isolating Army Group North. Beloborodov's 43rd Army swept past the southern edge of Memel and pressed on to the coast, cutting off Memel from the rest of the world. The first objective of 1st Baltic Front, to isolate the German forces north of the East Prussian border, had been carried out in a mere five days. Despite repeated attempts by *Grossdeutschland* and 7th Panzer Division to re-establish a continuous frontline – at Tryskiai, Luoke, Telsche, Plunge and finally the East Prussian Defence Position – the Soviet assault troops were unstoppable.

In addition to the main drive from the Kursenai–Schaulen area, a second Soviet thrust came further south, between Kelmy and Raseinen. Here, the attacking infantry had secured a bridgehead across the River Dubrissa. On 2 October, General Karl Decker's 5th Panzer Division was ordered south from Estonia to join XL Panzer Corps in an assembly area near Kelmy, but by 5 October only small elements of the division – mainly its infantry, without any of its tanks or rear-area formations – had arrived. XL Panzer Corps' commander was General Gotthard Heinrici, a veteran of the Eastern Front who would, just a few months later, take command of the armies arrayed to defend Berlin from the final Soviet assault. His corps had originally consisted of two divisions, 201st Security Division and 548th Volksgrenadier Division, but he had been forced to transfer the former to the neighbouring XXVIII Corps. Until 5th Panzer Division arrived, his only asset was the single Volksgrenadier division. On the evening of 5 October, Braumüller, commander of 5th Panzer Division's anti-aircraft battalion, was ordered to take up positions east of Kelmy with a battery of 88mm guns, supported by one of the division's Panzergrenadier battalions and an artillery battalion. Rather than risk taking the artillery too far forward, Braumüller ordered it to deploy west of the town.

The Soviet attack was led by 2nd Guards Army, with I Tank Corps as its spearhead. On its southern flank, 39th Army – the northern wing of Cherniakhovsky's 3rd Belorussian Front – would join the attack as it developed. The assault formations simply bypassed Braumüller's position and moved west, passing either side of Kelmy. Beyond the town, they ran into the artillery battalion that Braumüller had tried to keep out of harm's way. In a confused fight, the gunners knocked out four tanks at close range, but lost ten of their guns and were swept away.

Decker prepared to mount a counter-attack. The 21st Panzer Regiment, the division's tank force, arrived during the afternoon of 6 October. Like *Grossdeutschland* and 7th Panzer Division, it had been heavily involved in fighting further north since August, and was below its establishment strength, with only 12 Pz. IVs and

15 Panthers. Nevertheless, its commander, Oberstleutnant Hans Herzog, was immediately ordered to attack, supported by the division's 14th Panzergrenadier Regiment. The battle raged all afternoon, with Herzog's battlegroup claiming 26 Russian tanks destroyed, but the gap betwen it and the next German unit to the north – an ad hoc Panzergrenadier brigade commanded by the energetic Oberst Meinrad von Lauchert – remained at least 8km. With other elements of his division being driven back to the west, Decker ordered a halt to the attack. Instead, his division would try to set up a defensive line that could link up to 548th Volksgrenadier Division on the right. The gap to the left remained wide open, and the Soviet I Tank Corps roared through it, heading west and southwest, monitored by 5th Panzer Division's armoured reconnaissance battalion. Even if 5th Panzer Division were able to link up with 548th Volksgrenadier Division on its right, this union would be of limited value.

To the south of the 548th, another Soviet assault had fallen on 95th Infantry Division. This division had been almost annihilated during the summer battles near Minsk, and had been reformed from its survivors, combined with the remnants of 197th and 256th Infantry Divisions. Although these disparate fragments had been fighting together since the summer disasters, they had yet to bed down properly as a new division. Under heavy pressure, its left flank was driven back on 7 October, sundering its link with 548th Volksgrenadier Division to the north. With much of its artillery lost and its infantry battalions taking heavy casualties, the division fell back under constant pressure.

At 3rd Panzer Army's headquarters, Raus was critical of the way that XL Panzer Corps committed the division. The corps diary includes the following entry:

6 October was marked by an attempt by 5th Panzer Division – even though it didn't have most of its armour – to deploy for a mass operation. A telephone conversation from the army reproached the corps for its 'dribbling' deployment. In the opinion of the corps, this was unfounded. The development of the situation in view of the fact that there were insufficient forces to hold both the right and left flanks of the corps, and particularly the developments in the neighbouring corps had a not insubstantial effect. A mass operation by 5th Panzer Division might well have stabilized the situation, but could not have prevented the enemy from succeeding in achieving and widening breakthroughs at other points. Crucially, the late arrival of the armoured elements of 5th Panzer Division by rail affected the conduct of operations.[12]

In addition, the supply elements of 5th Panzer Division were still far to the north; consequently, the fighting troops had to be careful about their consumption of fuel and ammunition.

Decker continued to struggle to keep his far-flung division from being swept away by the Soviet attack. Late on 7 October, he was driven back along the road from Kelmy towards Tauroggen, forced to pull back his flanks to prevent envelopment. To the south was the inexperienced 548th Volksgrenadier Division, and on 8 October a Soviet thrust by the Soviet 39th Army pierced its front and threatened to break into the rear of 5th Panzer Division. Abandoning all attempts to link up with von Lauchert's forces to the northwest, Decker sent his remaining mobile assets to deal with the most threatening Soviet penetrations on his own flanks, and with the assent of XL Panzer Corps, pulled back towards a small bridgehead north of Tilsit. The 5th Armoured Reconnaissance Battalion, the division's reconnaissance battalion, could only watch impotently as Soviet forces pushed on towards the Baltic coast.

The town of Heydekrug was overrun on 9 October, and several thousand civilians, with fragmented army formations amongst them, were trapped against the coast to the north. Using pioneer boats, army engineers laboured to evacuate them from the small town of Minge and the nearby coast. Ad hoc companies of soldiers set up a rudimentary perimeter, but for the most part the Red Army made little attempt to prevent the evacuation, which was completed on 15 October. The evacuees were landed on the Kurische Nehrung, the long sandy strip running parallel to the coast, north of Rositten. From here, they were able to withdraw south to East Prussia. Prökuls was also taken by the Red Army on 9 October. A large portion of the civilian population left it too late to attempt to leave, and those who did escape brought tales of rape and slaughter.

Pressure continued against the Tilsit bridgehead. Here, 5th Panzer Division and 548th Volksgrenadier Division, with 1st Paratroop-Panzer Division *Hermann Göring* now arriving on the western flank, beat off a series of attacks between 11 and 13 October. The 5th Panzer Division claimed to have shot up 65 Soviet tanks; whatever the true figure may have been, the Red Army was unable to break up the German bridgehead. Finally, the need for German armoured forces elsewhere necessitated the withdrawal of both Panzer divisions from the bridgehead, and it was completely evacuated by 22 October.

On the Soviet side, preparations were in hand for an assault across the Niemen on 31 October in order to seize Tilsit. The town was on high ground, dominating the northern side of the river, and an assault against prepared defences would be difficult to say the least. The 87th Guards Rifle Division was given this daunting task, and its personnel spent several days preparing wooden rafts for the crossing. There were no doubts amongst the Soviet troops about the difficulties posed by such an attack; Isaak Kobylyanskiy, serving as an artillery officer in the division, wrote a sombre letter to his girlfriend as preparations continued: 'I am on the verge of a very serious battle, and only the Lord knows what end is waiting for me. This letter might be fated to be the last one.'[13] To the relief of Kobylyanskiy and his comrades, the assault was called off on 30 October. Fighting along the Niemen valley died down as both sides took stock. General Decker left his division to take command of a Panzer corps in East Prussia and was replaced by Oberst Rolf Lippert.

It is hard to assess whether the southern flank of the drive to the Baltic coast achieved all of its objectives. On the one hand, in cooperation with 39th Army, the right-hand formation of Cherniakhovsky's 3rd Belorussian Front, 2nd Guards Army rolled the Germans back to the Niemen valley and secured a large stretch of coastline. On the other hand, the envelopment of German forces east of Tauroggen was not successfully carried out, not least due to the presence of 5th Panzer Division. Clearly, as shown by the preparations of Kobylyanskiy's division, there were plans to secure a bridgehead at Tilsit, and there is certainly some evidence that 39th Army was expected to sweep over the Niemen into the northern parts of East Prussia, but the timely withdrawal of 548th Volksgrenadier Division and 5th Panzer Division to the Tilsit bridgehead effectively prevented this movement. As was the case further north, the Soviet spearheads swiftly identified the location of the strongest German defenders, in this case 5th Panzer Division, and shifted their main points of effort to either side. One consequence was that Second Guards Army was perhaps unable to turn south sufficiently early to threaten an envelopment of the German forces pinned against the frontline. Finding a gap to the left of 5th Panzer Division, the Red Army simply surged through to the coast. Further incursions into East Prussia would have to wait for another day.

As Bagramian's main drive towards the coast near Memel developed, a tantalizing opportunity beckoned in the north. A penetration deep into the East Prussian hinterland might well be beyond the resources of the forces committed to the operation, but incursions northwards were far more inviting. Here, with the German Army Group North under heavy pressure on its eastern front, there was a chance that a swift advance could gain considerable territory, and even reach the Baltic coast at or near the port of Libau. Of the few ports on the Baltic coast of the Courland peninsula, Libau – now known as Liepaja – is the largest. If it were to be captured, the position of Army Group North would become almost impossible. Even if it were not captured, a drive northwards east of the city would cut the vital railway running inland from the city. This, too, would make it difficult for the Germans to maintain Army Group North in Estonia.

The Germans, too, were acutely aware of the danger. On 6 October, General Dietrich von Saucken's XXXIX Panzer Corps was tasked with establishing a defensive line along the Venta. Von Saucken, a former commander of 4th Panzer Division, was in many respects the archetype of the Prussian officer. Born in 1892 not far from Königsberg, he served as an officer in the Kaiser's army in the Great War, and the outbreak of World War II saw him commanding one of the Wehrmacht's few cavalry formations. In December 1941, he began his long association with 4th Panzer Division, when he took command of the exhausted division outside Moscow. The division was mainly recruited from southern Germany, but there appears to have been an instant bond between the worn-out men and their new Prussian commander. His energetic and uncompromising leadership helped restore the division's fighting ability, and he was awarded the Knight's Cross in January 1942.

After a spell commanding the Schule Für Schnelle Truppen (School for Mobile Troops), von Saucken returned to 4th Panzer Division in May 1943. He took with him many of the school's best officers, a legacy that ensured that the division would continue to prosper in the years ahead. He was therefore particularly relieved that 4th Panzer Division was available to him now, as he was tasked with securing the southern flank of Army Group North.

The 4th Panzer Division had an establishment strength of 162 tanks; at the beginning of October, it could field 92, with a further 29 undergoing repairs. In addition to the tanks of its 35th Panzer Regiment, the division had two Panzergrenadier regiments, the 12th and 33rd. In terms of manpower, these regiments were at perhaps 75 per cent of establishment strength, but they were significantly weaker than their numbers would suggest. The other combat formations of the division – its artillery regiment, engineer battalion, anti-tank battalion, reconnaissance battalion and anti-aircraft battalion – were all similarly hamstrung, to a greater or lesser extent, by a shortage of adequately experienced NCOs and junior officers.

The senior officers of the division were almost universally of the highest calibre. The current division commander was Generalmajor Clemens Betzel. Born in Bavaria in 1895, he served as an artillery officer in World War I, and remained in the army after the war until 1930. After holding a variety of army posts as a civilian, he finally left the Reichswehr (the German armed forces between 1919 and 1935) in 1933 and joined the Sturmabteilung (SA; 'Storm Detachment', a paramilitary organization of the Nazi Party). He returned to the army in 1939, and in early 1941 took command of one of 4th Panzer Division's artillery battalions. He commanded the division's artillery regiment from late 1941, and became division commander in early 1944. Within the ultra-conservative ranks of his fellow senior officers, his political affiliations of the pre-war years might have attracted suspicion and even contempt, were it not for his exemplary record with his artillery regiment. Von Saucken held him in the highest regard as a popular commander, accustomed to leading his division from the front.

The division's tank regiment, 35th Panzer Regiment, was commanded by Oberst Hans Christern. He was a younger man than his division commander, and only reached the front in the Great War in May 1918. Less than a month later, he was wounded, and was discharged from the army in 1920. He returned to the ranks in 1936, and was immediately given appointments in the new Panzer forces. He commanded a tank battalion in 1939, followed by a series of administrative posts. Christern took command of 35th Panzer Regiment in June 1944, and quickly established a strong rapport with his men. He was a cultured man, with a deep love of music; like Betzel, he regularly led from the front, sometimes resulting in hair-raising adventures for his staff. Christern was briefly absent from the division, and in his absence 35th Panzer Regiment was commanded by Major Schultz. On 6 October, Schultz led the regiment's Panther battalion, supported by an armoured car company from the division's reconnaissance battalion, 4th Armoured Reconnaissance Battalion, towards the town of Vieksniai. The rest of the division followed over the next few days, reinforced by the Tiger tanks of Schwere Panzer Abteilung 510 (510th Heavy Tank Battalion).

The Wehrmacht's heavy tank battalions were first created in the second half of 1942, and were equipped with Tiger tanks. The 510th Heavy Tank Battalion was raised in June 1944, with many of its tank crews coming from a training company stationed near Versailles. Its 57-tonne Tiger tanks, armed with a powerful 88mm gun, were more than a match for anything that they might encounter on the battlefield, and even though the battalion was under-strength, it provided valuable additional firepower for the division. The Tigers were deployed in Moscheiken, and were immediately involved in fighting as Soviet forces probed towards the town. Confused engagements followed, as Betzel's division smashed repeated probes by the Red Army across the River Venta. As the Soviet attacks died away, the Germans learned from interrogations of prisoners that they had knocked three separate infantry divisions back across the river. Slowly, the front stabilized, and 4th Panzer Division reorganized itself for a powerful drive towards the south.

During one night, a German officer and seven men crossed from the Soviet lines. They had been taken prisoner by the Red Army earlier in the war, and were now sent back to the German lines in an attempt to encourage other men to surrender. This was the second time that something like this had happened to the division, the previous occasion being in late July; on neither occasion did the attempt to induce desertions yield any results. There is no record of the fate of the returning soldiers in these two episodes, but in other such episodes these men were treated as deserters and condemned to death.

Stalin's security service, the NKVD, had set up the Nationalkomitee Freies Deutschland (NKFD; National Committee for a Free Germany) in 1943 using captured Germans who were hostile to the Nazi government, and several prominent German officers who had been taken prisoner earlier in the war, particularly at Stalingrad, had signed declarations for the Russians to use against the Wehrmacht. Generalfeldmarschall Friedrich Paulus, the commander of Sixth Army at Stalingrad, together with 29 other German generals, signed a request to Army Group North in August, appealing to the Germans to surrender to the Red Army. None of these approaches, either by high-ranking officers or by the sorts of groups sent to 4th Panzer Division, had any significant effect in terms of inducing desertions, but they caused serious consternation amongst the German hierarchy. The Gestapo examined leaflets dropped by Soviet aircraft and confirmed that the signatures on them were genuine, and Hitler ordered senior Wehrmacht officers to issue condemnations of the actions of their former comrades.

The 12th Panzer Division arrived to the west of 4th Panzer Division in the second week of October. The first part of the response to the Soviet offensive, to establish a coherent front to guard Army Group North's open flank, was effectively complete. The second part, a counter-attack into the flank of the Soviet thrust, was now possible, particularly as it was clear that the units that had been left to secure the Soviet flank were weak. On 12 and 13 October, 4th and 12th Panzer Divisions made steady progress through the difficult terrain, and with his reserves still uncommitted, Betzel was confident of further success on 14 October. More open ground lay ahead, with the possibility of faster progress. But then, orders arrived from XXXIX Panzer Corps to stop all forward movements. Attacks were to be limited to those required to straighten and improve the frontline.

The reason given for the halt was a Soviet penetration into 61st Infantry Division's sector, further west. Also, in conjunction with OKH, Army Group North was making plans for a formal counter-offensive, with its starting point much closer to the coast, aimed at reaching Memel and then pressing on to East Prussia. There were advantages in moving the counter-offensive further west. The starting point of the attack would be less than 60km from Memel, with a further 50km of ground between Memel and the frontline in East Prussia. By contrast, the frontline in 4th Panzer Division's sector was nearly twice as far from Memel. It was felt that an attack over such a long distance would carry far greater risk, vulnerable to counter-attacks against either flank. A drive down the coast to Memel, on the other hand, would at least have its western flank safeguarded by the sea.

Over the next two days, 4th Panzer Division moved to its new assembly area southeast of Libau. Autumn rains and deteriorating, narrow roads made such a mass movement slow and difficult, as did the division's diminishing fuel reserve. By the end of 15 October, the division estimated that it had sufficient petrol for only 130km, and sufficient diesel for perhaps twice this distance. These calculations were critical, as the division's combat vehicles were petrol-powered. Nevertheless, planning continued for the drive towards Memel.[14] The 4th Armoured Reconnaissance Battalion was dispatched to the front near the Baltic coast on a reconnaissance mission, but Soviet pressure on the front east of the planned starting point of the attack led to delays. The planned operation, named *Geier* ('Vulture'), involved several phases. The first phase would be a breakthrough by Army Group North's troops along the coast to Memel, followed by an attack towards Tauroggen from Memel, ultimately aimed at restoring contact with East Prussia somewhere near Tilsit – an ambitious plan, given the battered state of the units available. With precious fuel being frittered away on movements back and forth behind the frontline to guard against a possible enemy breakthrough, the likelihood of a successful attack towards Memel gradually diminished. Heavy rain set in, reducing the roads to almost impassable rivers of mud. With growing evidence of major enemy preparations for an attack against the southern flank of Army Group North, plans for *Geier* were finally shelved in the last few days of October.

Dietrich von Saucken, who had commanded XXXIX Panzer Corps for several months, was now given a new assignment. The *Grossdeutschland* Division was to be reformed in East Prussia as part of a new Panzer corps, and he was to command this new corps. He visited 4th Panzer Division on 22 October to bid farewell to his former unit. Both he and the senior officers of the division expressed the hope that they would serve together again before too long, a wish that was to be granted before the end of the war.

As with the southern flank of 1st Baltic Front's drive, the situation in the north was also stabilized. Once more, the debate about the future of Army Group North resurfaced. It was perfectly feasible for the army group to withdraw in stages towards Libau, from where it could be evacuated by sea; even at this late stage of the war, the Kriegsmarine enjoyed almost complete control of the eastern Baltic. Such a move would allow the army group's precious divisions to be distributed to other parts of the Eastern Front, which had now reached German territory. Whatever the practical difficulties of such a maritime evacuation, the main obstacle was Hitler's insistence that the Courland peninsula be held. He insisted on its being described as a 'bridgehead', to emphasize that it could serve as a springboard for a future offensive.

To the professional officers of the Wehrmacht, talk of future offensives was absurd. They had to console themselves with the thought that Army Group North – or Army Group Courland, as it became known from January 1945 – was tying down substantial

Russian forces, which would otherwise be available for use against the Reich. The soldiers of 4th Panzer Division, indeed of the entire army group, had their doubts. Who was tying down whom? Were the Germans keeping large Soviet forces busy, or were the Soviets ensuring that valuable troops that might impede the march on Berlin were contained in an increasingly irrelevant sideshow?

During the remaining months of the war, Stalin referred disparagingly to the German presence in Courland as 'the largest prison camp in the world'. But the Red Army wasn't content to leave the Germans in peace, and launched six major assaults on the bridgehead. If the Soviet leadership was genuinely happy to tie down German divisions in this increasingly irrelevant area, why was so much effort and blood spent in attempts to destroy Army Group North? The answer probably lies in the fact that the Courland bridgehead formed the last remaining piece of territory, occupied by the Germans, that Stalin regarded as Soviet terrain. When he reassured Churchill and Roosevelt with comments about wanting to restore pre-war borders, he meant the borders of 1941, not 1939 – and by that date, the Baltic states were part of the Soviet Union.

By the end of 1944, the Red Army had launched three major assaults on the southern flank of the Courland bridgehead. All of these attacks – and three similar assaults in 1945 – were repulsed, with major losses on both sides. Slowly, the Germans were driven back into their bridgehead, and as the perimeter of the bridgehead shrank, German divisions were extracted and sent back to Germany. But this trickle of soldiers could achieve little; most of them disappeared into the inferno of the frontline. If the entire pocket had been evacuated en masse, sufficient troops might have been made available to intervene decisively, but Hitler would never have agreed to such a move.

Meanwhile, as the Red Army completed its encirclement of Memel, three German divisions – 58th Infantry Division, 7th Panzer Division and *Grossdeutschland* – scrambled to take up positions around the besieged city. Rittmeister Kühn was commander of a Panzergrenadier battalion, and was ordered on 10 October to secure *Grossdeutschland*'s left wing. When he reached his assigned sector, he found none of the prepared positions he was expecting, and ordered his men to improvise as best they could:

> Scouting further north of the church I met a brave old rural police sergeant who was standing in front of his pretty white cottage in full war paint. He asked me rather timidly where our fighting troops were. When I told him that was us, he asked if he might now be allowed to withdraw to Memel, as he had received orders to fall back when the combat troops arrived. I felt sorry for the old man, and I couldn't help thinking about the fairy tale about the steadfast tin soldier.[15]

Kühn gave the old man permission to head for Memel. He then came across some border guards, whom he promptly incorporated into his battalion, much to their alarm. He needed every man he could get – even with this small additional force, he could barely manage a two-man rifle pit or machine-gun nest every 100m. He made contact with a coastal naval battery, armed with eight 128mm guns, and arrangements were made for fire support. A group of 60 Luftwaffe personnel appeared from the north, and were also incorporated into the battalion.

The Soviet 5th Guards Tank Army and 43rd Army, which had pursued the Germans to the city, launched their first assault, starting with a heavy artillery bombardment on the southern and eastern defences at dawn on 10 October. Many local civilians – invalids, the elderly and the Hitler Youth – had been mobilized in the ranks of the Volkssturm, and these inexperienced soldiers, occupying reserve positions behind those held by the regular army, endured the bombardment with varying degrees of stoicism. As daylight grew stronger, bombers also joined the assault. In the meantime, the last refugee columns from the Krottingen area struggled into Memel, picking their way through the rubble-strewn streets. The city was engulfed in a dense cloud of smoke, lit by the flashes of fresh explosions. For the refugees, it must have seemed like a vision of hell.

When the assault began, the Wehrmacht units were ready for it. As a result of the various formations that retreated into the city, there were plentiful weapons and ammunition, and despite the limited time, good preparations had been made for a coordinated defence. On *Grossdeutschland*'s left flank, Kühn and his battalion came under attack during the day.

Late in the morning the half-tracks in Dargussen reported enemy tanks approaching from the northeast. The observers in the church spire also saw about 15 tanks moving west from the direction of Grabben. At first everything remained quiet opposite the battalion's front. In the afternoon … enemy tanks attacked 1 Company's position at the church from the north. The spire was holed by shells and the artillery observers and the timberwork in which they had positioned themselves began to give way. The valiant commander of the 18-man-strong 1 Company, Feldwebel Zwillus, was almost killed by a falling rafter. He sprinted into the rectory and, standing at the window, described to me by telephone the course of the battle. He was interrupted when the tanks began firing into the house and he had to lie down on the floor. An anti-tank gun, which went into position at the last moment, knocked out the leading tank right in front of the church. The rest remained beyond the stream that ran north of the church. The only way across the stream for the tanks was a small bridge at the policeman's house, and consequently they had little opportunity to deploy.[16]

Three German assault guns arrived shortly afterwards, and the position stabilized. Elsewhere in the Panzergrenadier regiment's sector, the first wave of 'Soviet' attackers turned out to be Lithuanian civilians, collected together by the advancing Soviet forces and now ordered to charge into the German lines. Behind them were tanks, which were swiftly knocked out by naval gunners and *Grossdeutschland*'s remaining Tigers.

The Soviet infantry, with tanks in close support, repeatedly achieved penetrations into the German lines, only to be thrown back by determined counter-attacks. Off the coast, the Kriegsmarine intervened in the shape of the pocket battleship *Lützow* and the heavy cruiser *Prinz Eugen*: '[They] delivered astonishingly rapid salvoes from their enormous turrets with clearly visible effect. The physical destruction and damage to morale had as much effect on the Russian soldiers as the strength of the frontline soldiers' defensive fire.'[17]

Almost without exception, German first-hand accounts of the fighting in the closing phases of the war in the east give high praise to the fire support provided by the Kriegsmarine. The accuracy and range of the warships' guns were phenomenal, as was their striking power. The effect on morale of these ships lying off the coast was enormous. They had sufficient anti-aircraft guns to make attacks on them by Soviet planes a tough prospect, particularly as, unlike their British, German, American and Japanese counterparts, the Soviet Air Force had few formations that specialized in anti-warship operations. The failure of the Soviet Red Banner Fleet, based near Leningrad, to intervene in any way other than limited submarine operations is curious. At this stage of the war it possessed a battleship, two cruisers and 17 destroyers and torpedo boats; had the Soviet fleet made a serious attempt to disrupt German shipping, the entire course of the campaign would have been different. Although there is little hard evidence to support the hypothesis, one can speculate that this restraint was a deliberate policy – Stalin wished to drive the Germans, soldiers and civilians alike, out of East Prussia, and therefore saw no point in closing their one escape route. Furthermore, many Soviet naval personnel had been re-assigned to land-based units during the long fighting around Leningrad, and it is unlikely that all of these warships would have been operational.

The assault raged for three days. Positions changed hands several times – the estate at Paugen, just outside Memel, was lost and retaken by the Germans three times before they finally had to concede it to the Red Army. Eventually, on 12 October, the fighting died down, and the exhausted soldiers on both sides could take stock. The frontline had hardly moved. Bagramian must have hoped that a swift, powerful attack coming hard on the heels of the often chaotic German retreat to the coast would secure the city quickly; instead, the defenders made his assault formations pay a heavy price for minimal gains.

Both armies strove to resupply their frontline formations. Freighters continued to arrive at the bombed-out Memel docks, unloading precious ammunition and other supplies. The next great assault began on 14 October. The preparatory bombardment was even heavier than before, and lasted for two hours, before the infantry, supported by tanks and assault guns, moved forward. They were greeted by a tremendous tornado of fire from the defenders – artillery, tanks, coastal guns, anti-aircraft guns and the Kriegsmarine's warships all contributed. Again and again, the attackers penetrated deep into the German defences, only to face furious counter-attacks. To the north of Memel, at Karkelbeck, 58th Infantry Division faced the Soviet 179th and 235th Rifle Divisions, and was forced to concede some ground, but everywhere else, the German front held firm.

The 7th Panzer Division was involved in hard fighting to restore the frontline where Soviet forces had made deep penetrations. Willi Hegen was in one of the division's few remaining Panthers:

We set off – our tank group was led by Leutnant Müller – to the designated preparation area and waited for our deployment. At daybreak, the damned Il-2s were also constantly aloft again. Meanwhile, there were ever more attacks by enemy bombers, which dropped their loads on us. Our tank shook on its springs from the heavy artillery fire. Smoke and dirt was hurled into the air. Suddenly, the fire moved to our rear, and we knew that our foremost lines had been overrun. There soon came an order to counter-attack and, knowing the frontline positions in the Löllen–Paugen–Klausmühlen sector well from the fighting of the last few days, we ran into Russian assault guns and tanks after a few hundred metres. We were the lead vehicle and were able to deal with two assault guns in the moment of surprise. The vehicles of our battlegroup that were following were also successful, shooting up several Russian tanks.

… Slowly, guarding to either side, we rolled forward over an open meadow, of the sort that you often find in this terrain of dunes. This meadow was about a kilometre wide, bordered by a small wood. We advanced slowly over the open ground and drove the enemy from our former positions. Just before the wood, they mounted greater resistance and we drove into a firebreak. Our battlegroup still had four or five tanks, which came under increasing tank fire from the left flank. Unteroffizier Behren's tank, which was on our left flank during the attack, reported a hit, as a result of which the viewport (which was made of armoured glass in the Pz. IV) shattered into the driver's face. We were at the firebreak, under fire from the Russians, and we could not see into the firebreak clearly.

We therefore withdrew a little to one side and tried with our collective fire to pin down the enemy who was firing on us. After a while, our second tank was set ablaze. Suddenly, at about 2 o'clock to our right, next to the wood, we saw a Stalin organ that had been brought forward, firing its projectiles. The turret was swiftly turned – which was easily done with the hydraulic traverse of the Panther, and we fired a couple of high-explosive rounds at about 1,600 metres. This resulted in the rockets flying off like at a firework display.

When we turned our turret back towards the enemy who was firing at us, we saw a Pz. IV of the Waffen-SS ablaze; it had accompanied our battlegroup in our counter-attack. But we still couldn't make out the enemy tank that was firing on us from a well-camouflaged position, let alone engage it. At that moment, Leutnant Müller cried: 'Quick, there – a T-34 in the firebreak.' It was moving very carefully and slowly out of the firebreak, in order to bring its gun to bear on us. The turret was turned – and the Russian tank was barely 50 metres from us. We fired, and missed – in my haste, I had forgotten to take my foot off the turret traverse pedal. But quick as a flash, the loader inserted another round, I fired, and the T-34 exploded.

We had never before seen so clearly the law of war: 'you or me'.

There was no time for celebration. There was smoke everywhere. In front and around us were the impacts of tank rounds. We were the last tank from the counter-attack in an advanced position in this sector and our driver, Jackl Schneeberger, turned and drove away in zigzags. The turret was swiftly turned to 6 o'clock, and then there was a dreadful impact and the fighting compartment filled with flames. Our driver, radio operator and loader bailed out immediately. Leutnant Müller didn't stir, and the gunner, for whom there was no hatch in a Panther, could only get out through the commander's cupola. So I had to shove the commander, Leutnant Müller, out until I could exit myself. As I came out of the cupola, I saw Leutnant Müller, who had partly recovered from his daze and confusion, running away from the tank. I leapt from the tank in one bound and ran away from it; I had gone barely 30 metres before it exploded behind me. The cloud of debris hurled us to the ground. We found ourselves in no-man's land and sought out a little cover. Here, we found that apart from singed hair and a few small burns, none of us was wounded.[18]

Everywhere, Soviet infantry with heavy tank support pressed home its attacks. The few remaining German tanks were sent back and forth to stiffen the defensive line. Willi Friele was the driver of another of 7th Panzer Division's Panthers, and by the afternoon his tank, commanded by a Leutnant Hopfe, had already accounted for nine enemy tanks, including a Josef Stalin, which sustained no fewer than eight hits before its crew bailed out. The Panther was now assigned a new task:

At the end of this defensive action, we received an order from Hauptmann Brandes: '324 (our turret number), drive left and take up a position. There's an infantry platoon amongst the ruined houses, expecting a new armoured attack.'

We set off and came across a Feldwebel and the remnant of his platoon there. They were delighted that we were taking up position with them, as they could hear constant Russian tank engines and track noises from enemy tanks driving around. The infantry's fear of a new Russian tank attack didn't please us, though, as we had fired off almost all our armour-piercing rounds.

Late in the afternoon came the desperately awaited supplies of ammunition and fuel. When Leutnant Hopfe told the infantrymen that we had to drive off in order to refuel and take on ammunition, there was near-chaos. They were fearful that we were withdrawing and going to leave them alone. All our explanations achieved nothing, and some even threatened to lie down in front of our tracks if we tried to drive away. We stayed with the poor Landsers rather than leave them. Overjoyed, they fetched us fuel and ammunition from the supply vehicles. We remained overnight with our new friends, on guard, and the next morning, when everything remained quiet, we pulled back to our start-line at the Klemmenhof estate and then back to the Bachmann estate.[19]

The defenders reported they had destroyed a total of 66 Soviet tanks and assault guns during this latest assault, bringing the total of claimed 'kills' since the siege began to 150. As darkness fell over the ruins, the Red Army called off its attack. The toll on both armies was heavy. Swiftly, the opposing sides repaired the damage to their lines, and prepared for more fighting. The next – and last – attempt to storm Memel came on 23 October. It was the least powerful attack, and once more it was beaten off.

The fighting had exhausted the defending formations. The 7th Panzer Division was reduced to barely more than a regiment in strength, while the other two divisions, *Grossdeutschland* and 58th Infantry Division, could only field 40 per cent of their paper strength. Both sides went over to positional warfare. The Germans constructed extensive bunker positions, and improvised additional artillery from 7th Panzer Division's Panther tanks; there was a shortage of armour-piercing ammunition, but plentiful supplies of high-explosive rounds. Four tanks were positioned on a reverse slope, and fired into the Soviet-held hinterland. Sceptical artillery observers were asked to look out for the fall of shot, and were astonished by the range and accuracy of the 75mm guns. The Soviet forces came to dread them, as their muzzle velocity, far higher than that of conventional artillery, meant that there was no warning whistle of an incoming shell. This gave opportunities to use them against special targets:

From intercepted radio signals, it was possible a week later to learn that an award ceremony for decorated [Soviet] frontline soldiers had been ordered, to be held in a warehouse in front of our sector. Even the time of the ceremony was included in the message.

During the next day, the batteries fired without particularly targeting this location. The warehouse was plastered with a concentrated bombardment at the last moment. The award ceremony was ended before it even began. This example showed the results of the enemy's carelessness with radio communications.[20]

The Courland armies were entirely dependent on their maritime connection with the Reich for supplies. The loss of the Baltic islands close to Riga had effectively broken the German anti-submarine barriers that held back the Red Banner Fleet's submarines, but most attacks on German shipping were by Soviet aircraft. The pressure on German shipping, which had been minimal for much of the year, grew steadily. In the first eight months of 1944, total German shipping losses in the eastern Baltic amounted to 17 ships, totalling about 31,000 tonnes. In the remaining four months 53 ships with a total displacement of over 122,000 tonnes were sunk, mainly by air attacks.[21]

The *Füsilier* was a transport ship that relayed elements of 58th Infantry Division to Memel from Riga, and subsequently shuttled up and down the coast, bringing supplies into Memel and taking away wounded. On 19 November, the ship set off from Pillau with about 250 soldiers aboard, mainly personnel returning to the front from leave. With a single escort, the *Füsilier* made the run to Memel at night, but in poor visibility the following morning was unable to make out the entrance to the port. A soldier from Memel who happened to be aboard went to the bridge to say that, based on his knowledge and what he could see of the coast, they had already passed Memel. The captain ordered the ship to turn towards the open sea, to avoid Soviet artillery batteries that were known to be on the coast north of Memel. At almost the same moment the coast was lit up by muzzle flashes as Soviet gunners opened fire on the *Füsilier*. The steamer was rapidly left powerless, and drifted slowly north along the coast, under constant bombardment. The ship's three lifeboats took off as many men as they could, and as the remainder attempted to find lifebelts and other means of escape, Soviet aircraft attacked and inflicted further damage.

The ship swiftly sank, at which point the Soviet fighters turned their attentions to the lifeboats. One had already disappeared, and a second was now shot up and destroyed. The third survived repeated attacks, and led by the soldier from Memel its occupants sailed it through the day and following night to Libau. The ordeal of the exhausted men and two women in the lifeboat wasn't over; high waves smashed it against the pier, capsizing it. Ten perished in the freezing water, and only 13 made it to safety.[22]

Both sides began to run down their forces in and around the Memel bridgehead. The 7th Panzer Division was ordered to leave at the end of October, followed by

Grossdeutschland, which was to be reorganized as a Panzer corps. They were replaced by 95th Infantry Division, which had fought at the southern edge of the Soviet assault in early October and had been driven back through Ragnit. After the briefest of pauses for recuperation, the weary soldiers of the division were dispatched to the devastated city on the coast, taking over the northern section of the city defences, with 58th Infantry Division holding the southern perimeter. Despite fears that the Red Army would take advantage of the winter to cross the frozen waterways around the city, there was little major fighting around Memel until it was finally evacuated in January 1945.

From the Soviet point of view, the offensive on Memel gained its main objective, of isolating Army Group North. Inadequate reserves, however, prevented opportunities on both flanks from being effectively exploited; in the north, the 'aggressive defence' of Betzel's 4th Panzer Division also contributed to the rapid German stabilization. The assault on Memel itself, too, was a failure, resulting in considerable Soviet casualties. From the Soviet point of view, though, given the German setbacks during 1944, there must have been a belief that German defences would be unable to withstand a series of strong blows. The determined defence of Memel rapidly dispelled any such opinions.

CHAPTER 3
NEMMERSDORF

All of us knew very well that if the girls were German they could be raped and then shot.

— A. Solzhenitsyn[1]

Even before the fighting in Lithuania died down, it became clear to the Germans that Cherniakhovsy's 3rd Baltic Front was planning to attack East Prussia. Aerial reconnaissance detected a build-up of forces around Kovno, and provided that the weather held it was highly likely that a major assault would come before winter. Although the campaign that followed achieved few significant military gains, it laid bare the almost complete dislocation between German military and civilian authorities. And the fate of the village of Nemmersdorf, while of little military significance, came to have an enormous impact on the thinking of German civilians and soldiers alike.

The German front here was held by Reinhardt's Army Group Centre, which had – temporarily at least – lost 3rd Panzer Army to Army Group North. Opposite Kovno was General Hossbach's 4th Army, holding about 350km of frontline with five corps. Between them, these corps had seven experienced *Ostfront* infantry divisions; two security divisions that had been intended for security in the rear areas, but now found themselves in the frontline itself; six Volksgrenadier divisions; two cavalry brigades; and Police Battalion *Hannibal*, a formation made up of mobilized police units, approximately the strength of an infantry regiment. Several brigade-sized units provided small numbers of armoured vehicles, which would prove critical in the coming battle.

Throughout the autumn, a fierce argument raged in East Prussia. Hossbach, supported by Reinhardt at Army Group Centre, wanted the whole of East Prussia to be declared an operational zone. This move would immediately give the military authorities the power to have civilians evacuated. Hitler refused such a policy – indeed, even after East Prussia was finally cut off from the rest of the Reich, he still refused to grant this request. Instead, all civilian matters remained in the hands of the Party. Given the bulge occupied by 4th Army, Hossbach and Reinhardt considered that the most likely Soviet plan would be for a pincer attack, with thrusts aimed through 3rd Panzer Army towards Königsberg and through 2nd Army towards Elbing. Whilst this proved

THE GOLDAP–GUMBINNEN OPERATION, OCTOBER 1945

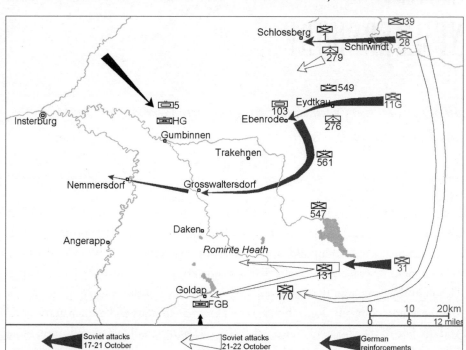

to be partly true in January 1945, it was not the case on this occasion – the attack would be far more localized, involving only Cherniakhovsky's 3rd Baltic Front.

Cherniakhovsky was given approval by Stavka for an assault into East Prussia, with the intention of exploiting along the axis Gumbinnen–Insterburg–Königsberg. It remains unclear whether there was any serious expectation of a penetration right through to the East Prussian capital, or whether the attack was intended as a means of seizing the eastern parts of the province. On the one hand, the rapid collapse of the frontline defences in Lithuania raised the tempting possibility of a swift drive into the East Prussian heartland; on the other hand, despite Hossbach's precautions, Cherniakhovsky would have been aware of the extensive work done by the defenders to prepare their positions. It seems likely that the operation was an extended probe of the strength and resolve of the defenders, with the intention of exploiting any weakness that might be revealed.

The weight of the attack would fall on two German corps, Gerhard Matzky's XXVI Corps and Hellmuth Priess' XXVII Corps. Matzky was fortunate – his corps had recently acquired the 1st Infantry Division, a veteran formation recruited mainly in East Prussia itself. The division had been fighting in the Carpathian Mountains, but was moved to Matzky's corps in August 1944. It found itself close to the same area that another Prussian 1st Infantry Division had defended against Russian armies, precisely 30 years earlier. Its arrival was most timely – Soviet forces were still pressing forward in the wake of *Bagration*, and almost immediately the division found itself struggling to restore the frontline. On the eve of the October fighting, General Ernst-Anton von Krosigk, the division's popular commander, was dispatched to take command of a corps in Courland, where he was later killed in an air raid in April 1945. His replacement in 1st Infantry Division was Generalleutnant Hans Schittnig. His experience to date had been in command of two infantry regiments, with much of his war service spent in administrative roles, and he had not served with the division before. With a Soviet offensive apparently imminent, there was understandable uncertainty about the new commander within the division.

On 5 October, 1st Infantry Division began to take up a new part of the frontline south of the Prussian town of Schirwindt and the Lithuanian town of Naumiestis, known to the Germans as Neustadt. The 28km sector of frontline lay just east of the Prussian frontier, and the division's officers and men were alarmed to find that the frontline positions were completely inadequate. Immediately, Schittnig organized work details, aided by two pioneer battalions sent to him by General Matzky. Constant Soviet harassment attacks and reconnaissance activity left no doubt about the imminence of an attack, and the soldiers laboured hard to construct both frontline positions and a second main line.

On 14 October, when Hossbach judged that Cherniakhovsky's offensive was imminent, he advised all units to move to their main battle positions. Despite the best efforts of the division's men and those of the attached pioneers, 1st Infantry Division had not completed its preparations. At 0400hrs on 16 October, East Prussia was awakened by the sound of heavy artillery fire. Hossbach's men were under attack, in a bombardment that rolled on for two hours, and many of 1st Infantry Division's troops had to endure the full weight of the Soviet bombardment in their inadequate entrenchments. Trenches and bunkers collapsed, communications wires were cut and radios knocked out. Everything was covered by dust and mud, rendering many of the heavy and automatic weapons unusable until they had been cleaned. Communications with the division's artillery were disrupted, forcing the German gunners to resort to pre-arranged fireplans rather than adapting to circumstances. The Soviet aerial bombardment was particularly heavy, striking at headquarters and artillery positions as far to the rear as the town of Gumbinnen.

The Soviet attack against 1st Infantry Division was led by 28th Army. General Schittnig's men fought back with grim determination, and by 0700hrs had driven the

Soviet attackers back. Losses were heavy, however, and perhaps one in eight of the frontline soldiers had already fallen. Coordinated defence was further hampered by the inexpert design of Koch's fortifications – deep anti-tank ditches actually did more to hinder lateral movements by the defenders than advances by the attackers. Frustrated by the German resistance, the Soviet commanders moved self-propelled guns into the frontline to open a concentrated fire on the main points of resistance. In the face of this determined onslaught, 1st Infantry Division – attacked by five rifle divisions, two tank brigades and a tank breakthrough regiment equipped with heavy tanks – had to pull back slowly, while exacting a terrible toll on the Soviet attack formations. By committing all his reserves, Schittnig managed to ensure that his division's sector suffered no fatal breakthroughs.

Further south, the front was held by 549th Volksgrenadier Division and elements of 390th Security Division. They were assaulted by General Kuzma Nikitovich Galitsky's 11th Guards Army, and fell back steadily through the day, but for the moment at least a Soviet breakthrough was prevented. Nevertheless, Hossbach and his corps commanders knew that these inexperienced units would struggle to hold back the Soviet attack, particularly once they were driven back out of their prepared positions into open ground.

Where they were supported by armour, the Germans resisted better. The Wehrmacht made extensive use of *Sturmgeschützen* (assault guns), consisting of tank chassis equipped with a fixed gun. The lack of a turret made these vehicles easier and cheaper to manufacture, and allowed them to be fitted with a larger gun, though they lacked the flexibility of tanks, as their guns had very limited lateral movement. Most of the Wehrmacht's assault guns were organized into independent brigades, which were then assigned to support individual divisions. The men of one such unit, 267th Assault Gun Brigade, had suspected for days that something was in the air; leave had been cancelled, and there had been extensive enemy aerial reconnaissance. They helped the gunners of a neighbouring artillery battery construct fake guns from timber and farm machinery to help confuse the Soviet reconnaissance pilots, and sat out the initial bombardment in their well-constructed bunker. As soon as the shelling stopped, they returned to their vehicles. The fake artillery position had been obliterated by shellfire.

Some infantry gathered around the reassuring presence of the assault guns, and a patrol was dispatched to a railway line that ran along an embankment to the north. A messenger reported back with worrying news: large numbers of Soviet troops were advancing west beyond the railway. Keeping a watchful eye to the north, the assault guns, commanded by Hauptmann Friedrich Stück and supported by the infantry, cautiously moved west, expecting contact with the enemy at any moment. After about a kilometre, they reached a broad cornfield. Stück, a veteran of the *Ostfront*, ordered his assault guns to load high-explosive shells, and to fire a single round each into the field.

> When we fired, we couldn't believe our eyes. Hundreds of Russian infantry had wanted to lead us into an ambush and annihilate us in close combat. When we began to fire into the cornfield, the Russians jumped up and began to retreat. Upon seeing that we moved our assault guns forward and fired as rapidly as we could with high explosive rounds. Our infantry immediately followed … then Hauptmann Stück gave the order to everyone: 'Forward, comrades!'
>
> We advanced through the cornfield and crushed everything that came under our tracks. The infantry played its part. Mercy was not to be expected.[2]

After an advance of about 4km, Stück and his small group pulled back; isolated and unsure of the situation on his flanks, he could not risk being cut off. He would have been very much aware that other parts of the front, with little or no armoured support, would not have fended off the Soviet assault so effectively.

First light on 17 October saw a fresh Soviet bombardment. In the north, there was a renewed attempt to drive back elements of 1st Infantry Division, which had dug in to defend the town of Schirwindt.[3] With a peacetime population of barely 1,000 inhabitants, Schirwindt was the smallest town in East Prussia. It had been extensively damaged by the Czar's armies in 1914, and was now once more a battlefield. The first assault came immediately after the initial bombardment, but was repulsed by a hail of machine-gun fire. As the day wore on, the town was outflanked to north and south. The 1st Infantry Division's anti-tank battalion, consisting of 12 Hetzer tank-hunters and six towed anti-tank guns, had taken up well-camouflaged positions and repulsed the first attempt by a battalion of T-34s to bypass the town. But pressure continued, with Schirwindt coming under increasingly heavy attack from the northwest. Fighting raged from house to house, and as darkness fell the greatly diminished ranks of the defenders were forced to abandon the town when the Soviet 27th Guards Rifle Division, supported by 113th Tank Brigade, was thrown into the battle. A second German assault gun formation, 279th Assault Gun Brigade, took up positions on either side of the Schirwindt–Schlossberg road, and its sudden intervention the following morning once more brought the Soviet attack to a standstill. A sudden air attack against the German assault guns, however, killed the brigade commander, Hauptmann Hoppe.

Further south, Soviet forces made better progress, advancing about 15km. Matzky's corps had deployed its minimal reserves, and most of its armoured assets – the two assault gun brigades – were heavily engaged. Galitzky's 11th Guards Army pressed forward against Eydtkau, storming the town in heavy fighting. From here, the main road ran east to Ebenrode, and then on to Gumbinnen, Insterburg and eventually Königsberg itself. With its southern flank torn apart, 549th Volksgrenadier Division could do little to prevent the Soviet breakthrough. Elements of the division fell back to Ebenrode, where they were overjoyed to encounter 103rd Panzer Brigade, commanded by Oberst Werner Mummert. Mummert's command consisted of a single tank battalion and a Panzergrenadier battalion, and represented the most powerful elements of XXVII Corps' reserves. They were committed to the battle immediately, bringing Galitsky's drive to an abrupt halt.

Pausing to consider his options, Galitsky found himself faced with three choices. He could continue to try to batter his way through Ebenrode, but this would cost him precious time, not to mention casualties. North of the town was broken country, where elements of 549th Volksgrenadier Division were attempting to rally amidst a series of ridges and small rivers. As with a drive through the town, this route would be difficult and costly. South of Ebenrode, there was a stretch of boggy ground. Leaving his leading elements to screen Ebenrode, Galitsky ordered the bulk of his army to pick its way south to the town of Schlossbach, beyond the bogs, from where it would be able to turn west across firmer ground.

Here was a key development in the battle. Despite their substantial losses, the German units defending the northern part of the battlefront had proved far tougher than Cherniakhovsky had hoped. Consequently, the weight of the Soviet attack began to shift further south. The terrain south of Ebenrode was critical to the success or failure of the Soviet attack. Several rivers, such as the Rominte and Angerapp, ran across the line of advance. Although these were relatively small, the river valleys often had steep sides, making the few crossings of vital importance to a swift advance. In between the valleys, the countryside was hilly, with limited lines of sight. All encounters would be at relatively close range, with plenty of opportunities for both sides for concealment and ambush. In particular, the easier approach march to Gumbinnen – from the east and northeast – was now blocked. If there was to be rapid exploitation towards Insterburg and on to Königsberg, Soviet forces would face a difficult attack against Gumbinnen from the south.

The day broke bright and sunny on 18 October, allowing the Soviet Air Force to intervene in full strength. Wherever they were still in fortified areas, the German defenders were able to hold their positions, but elsewhere the line began to give way. Galitsky's 11th Guards Army was now once more heading west, having made a wide detour south of the German strongpoint at Ebenrode. The swampy ground immediately south of Ebenrode now worked in Galitsky's favour, preventing Mummert's tanks from intervening. Soviet forces secured crossings over the Rominte at Grosswaltersdorf, and pressed on north and west into open ground between the Rominte and the Angerapp.

German alarm at the Soviet assault was widespread, and Gauleiter Koch had already issued orders for the Volkssturm in Treuburg to be mobilized. The training of the Volkssturm was non-existent and their equipment patchy, despite Koch's attempts to acquire weapons. Even worse, there were often no uniforms for them, and consequently the Soviet forces treated them as irregular formations, exempt from what passed for the normal rules regarding prisoners on the *Ostfront*. In keeping with his self-image as the people's general, Koch explicitly forbade the Volkssturm commanders from communicating officially with local military commanders, with the result that regular units had to rely on local, informal contacts to determine the exact locations and strengths of Volkssturm formations. Now, Hitler authorized a more general mobilization of the Volkssturm:

> While the enemy believes that we are approaching the end, we will make a second call on the strength of our people. We will and must succeed, as we did in 1939–1940, relying on our strength not only to defeat the destructive will of the enemy but to expel them from the Reich in such a way that the future of Germany, of our allies, and therefore of all Europe, is ensured and peace is secured.[4]

The Goldap Battalion was a typical Volkssturm formation. It numbered about 400 men, and was organized in four companies. It was fortunate in that the company commanders were reserve officers. Equipped with a mixture of Russian rifles, German light machine-guns and Panzerfaust anti-tank weapons, these men now prepared to face the feared Bolsheviks. In all, perhaps 160,000 Volkssturm were mobilized, but despite repeated requests from Reinhardt and his subordinates, Koch insisted on retaining control of these men. Only in a few locations were individual Volkssturm battalions attached to regular formations.

The 276th Assault Gun Brigade was now fighting in the Ebenrode area, near the famous Trakehnen stud farm. The brigade was equipped with the tried and tested Sturmgeschütz III, an assault gun based on the old Pz. III chassis, but armed with the same long-barrelled 75mm gun as most Pz. IVs currently in use. Against the enormous Josef Stalin tanks of the Soviet 75th Tank Breakthrough Regiment, these guns proved to be of limited value, as Alfred Regenitter found:

> In the afternoon [of 21 October], we made an attack with eight guns from Kleinschellendorf (three kilometres southeast of Hainau on the Schlossberg road to Ebenrode) to the northeast.

… then I spotted a JS-122 [Josef Stalin tank with 122mm gun] with the telescopic sight, standing empty at around 2000 metres. Every one of our AP [armour-piercing] shells hit exactly, we saw the tracer gliding slower and slower towards the target, six times – all bounced off![5]

That night, Regenitter again found himself in action against a Josef Stalin tank. He had just shot up a T-34, when he spotted one of the giant tanks in the glow of the burning vehicle:

'Same distance, armour-piercing, fire!' and – bounced off! Its tracer trail carried on, flung powerfully by the force of the ricochet in another direction. So it happened four times. Shit! All hit and no effect!… I pressed my eye to the periscope again and tried to aim at where I guessed the waist was with the point of the aiming triangle – and 'Fire!' The light tracer found the tank, hurrah, it went through! However, it did not explode. But there – a thin tongue of flame licked the underside of the hull, which I now clearly saw as a black line… Two minutes later, the Stalin blew up like a giant mushroom with a 100 metre high tongue of flame. A colossal sight! They spoke of it along the whole front in the morning.[6]

The weather deteriorated the following day, reducing Soviet air attacks. At Schlossberg, Schittnig's 1st Infantry Division held firm against all attacks by 5th Army. At Ebenrode, too, the front continued to hold. Between Schlossberg and Eydtkau, Regenitter and 276th Assault Gun Brigade fought on alongside the infantry of 549th Volksgrenadier Division, though the brigade was fast running out of vehicles. By the end of the day, an exhausted Regenitter had personally accounted for nine Soviet tanks, before his assault gun broke a track and had to be pulled out of action. He fell asleep over a bowl of chicken soup at the brigade headquarters, after having been in action for three days without any rest.

Reinforcements, in addition to the Volkssturm, were being organized. The Tilsit bridgehead was evacuated, releasing the 1st Paratroop-Panzer Division *Hermann Göring* and 5th Panzer Division. Meanwhile, the Soviet 11th Guards Army pushed on despite its growing casualties. Soviet forces that had passed through Grosswaltersdorf reached Nemmersdorf on the Angerapp on 21 October. Three battalions from the *Hermann Göring* division reached Gumbinnen on 19 October, where they were relieved to find that the division's Panther tank battalion had also arrived. On 21 October, in conjunction with some gun batteries from 18th Flak Division, the three battalions of 'paratroopers' – in reality, no more than ordinary infantry – were involved in running battles around Gumbinnen. The amalgamated forces formed themselves into five battlegroups, and by the end of the day had accounted for nine Soviet tanks, including five Josef Stalins. Their own losses, though, had been heavy, particularly when they came under air and artillery fire. Nevertheless, a swift Soviet seizure of Gumbinnen was prevented.

The local Volkssturm found themselves in the thick of the fighting. The Goldap Battalion took up defensive positions north of Goldap on 18 December, and went into action three days later, pounding advancing Soviet forces with its few mortars. The Red Army infantry pulled back, but the following day there was a heavy Soviet artillery bombardment on the entire area, inflicting considerable casualties on the Volkssturm. Now under Wehrmacht command, the battalion was ordered to withdraw to the west the following day, having lost 76 men killed or wounded out of its original 400.

On 21 October, Cherniakhovsky showed the same degree of imagination that had so impressed Stalin during the execution of *Bagration* during the summer. In a further shift of emphasis to the south, he pulled General Alexander Alexandrovich Luchinsky's powerful 28th Army out of its positions in the north, and dispatched it to the southern end of the battlefield. Despite its losses in attempting to force back 1st Infantry Division, it was still a formidable force with nine rifle divisions, and more importantly was reinforced by II Guards Tank Corps. It was ordered – in conjunction with 31st Army – to strike at Goldap. The 11th Guards Army, however, had taken heavy losses, and would struggle to make further progress.

By the end of the day, the Soviet attack had formed a salient in the German lines, with its apex formed by the leading elements of 11th Guards Army[7] around Nemmersdorf on the River Angerapp. A few artillery formations joined this small group, which now attempted to exploit westwards. Barely an hour's drive separated the Soviet spearhead from Insterburg, but such an advance invited disaster – neither flank was in contact with other Soviet forces. Galitsky was inclined to press on to Insterburg, where he hoped his units would be able to take up all-round defensive positions deep within German lines, and await the arrival of 28th and 31st Armies, but Cherniakhovsky decided the risk was too great. The spearheads were to fall back to Nemmersdorf, at least until the Soviet armies to the south could move up alongside and secure the southern flank.

To the north, obdurate resistance by elements of Panzer Division *Hermann Göring*, the flak formations and Volkssturm had prevented the Russians from penetrating to Gumbinnen. Near Gumbinnen, the arrival of 5th Panzer Division allowed Hossbach to reinforce defensive positions north of Trakehnen with part of the *Hermann Göring* division, where it came under heavy attack. Amidst heavy casualties, the German infantry were driven back, but a swift counter-attack by the division's armour restored the front. From Gumbinnen, the front ran roughly northeast through Ebenrode to Schlossberg, where 1st Infantry Division continued to beat off attacks by the Soviet 5th Army, which had taken over from 28th Army.

South of the Nemmersdorf area, the Soviet 31st Army, supported by 28th Army, advanced across the Rominte Heath to threaten Goldap. These two armies would now have to force their way through to the line of the Angerapp, so that 11th Army could either turn north to clear the main route through Gumbinnen, or advance west towards Insterburg.

To the south of the main Soviet penetration at Nemmersdorf, in the path of the Soviet 28th and 31st Armies, Hossbach had the Führer-Grenadier Brigade at his disposal. This formation was first created during the summer of 1944, and received a lavish level of equipment before being deployed near Rastenburg in early September. It possessed a Panzergrenadier regiment, consisting of three battalions – Panzer-Fusilier and Panzergrenadier battalions mounted in half-tracks, and a third battalion mounted in wheeled vehicles. It also had a Panzer regiment with three companies of Panthers, one of tank destroyers and one of assault guns. With its own artillery battalion and anti-tank battalion, the brigade had at least as much firepower as most of the run-down Panzer divisions currently in the frontline. The brigade was placed on alert on 19 October, and released to 4th Army the following day. As it moved up to the critical area of the front, it approached the Soviet salient from the south, passing through Goldap at dawn on 21 October, just hours before the town came under heavy attack. With 5th Panzer Division and the Panzer Division *Hermann Göring* able to move south from Gumbinnen, Hossbach could now plan for a pincer attack to restore the front.

The inexperience of the Führer-Grenadier Brigade became apparent almost immediately. The veterans of 5th Panzer Division arrived from the north by train in battlegroups that were already configured for action. By contrast, the different elements of the Führer-Grenadier Brigade – its two armoured infantry battalions and its Panzer regiment – arrived and were committed to the battle separately. As a result, they were unable to support each other effectively.

The leading formation of the Führer-Grenadier Brigade was the Panzergrenadier battalion's 1st Company, commanded by Leutnant Sachse. The exact whereabouts of Soviet forces in the area were unknown, and the company moved forward cautiously along Route 132 from Goldap until it reached the Daken brickworks, on high ground 800m north of the village. The rest of the battalion, commanded by Major von Courbiere, reached Daken just as Sachse deployed his company for an attack on the brickworks, and at this moment Soviet infantry moved up to attack the village.

The Germans prevailed in both actions, and the battalion took up defensive positions in Daken, with its 1st Company further north at the brickworks.

The rest of the brigade began to assemble. The Panzer-Fusilier battalion detrained west of Goldap and moved north, staying west of the main Goldap–Gumbinnen road until it was level with Grosswaltersdorf, where it was to secure the Rominte crossings. Shortly after it moved through Herzogsrode, it encountered Soviet tanks near Preussisch Nassau, and was involved in running battles until dark. Unsure of the positions of enemy and friendly forces, the battalion took up positions for all-round defence in a hollow. Further advances would have to await the arrival of the brigade's tanks.

Meanwhile, Soviet pressure on Goldap intensified. The German 131st Infantry Division had slowly been driven back to the town across the Rominte Heath. It now took up positions between Lake Goldap and the Rominte, a front of about 5km. XXVII Corps' commander, Hellmuth Priess, who had positioned his headquarters at the northern edge of Goldap, was aware of the importance of this position – if the Soviet forces were to take Goldap, they could threaten the rear of the Führer-Grenadier Brigade, and would be able to widen the salient that stretched to Nemmersdorf. Fortunately, he had available to him the guns of 279th Assault Gun Brigade, transferred south from the Schlossberg area. Hauptmann Ernst Schmid, now commanding the brigade since Hoppe's death, deployed his remaining 36 guns at the eastern edge of the town. When a powerful Soviet armoured force broke through the lines of 131st Infantry Division, Schmid was able to take it in its left flank, swiftly destroying several T-34s and JS-2 tanks. A second armoured column met a similar fate. When Schmid reported back to Priess, he found that the general had been killed by a direct hit on his half-track.

The attack against Goldap from the northeast had been severely blunted, but the Soviet 28th Army's nine rifle divisions were slowly grinding forward from the southeast. The German 170th Infantry Division was forced back, first to Goldap and then out of the town completely. The Red Army had succeeded in taking the important road junction, but the effort had cost it heavy casualties. There was little prospect of the survivors being able to threaten the Führer-Grenadier Brigade.

On the same day that the Führer-Grenadier Brigade went into action, 5th Panzer Division began its attack from the north. The division's advance elements reached Jägershagen, about 10km southeast of Gumbinnen, on 20 October, and were therefore already close to the Führer-Grenadier Brigade's objective of Grosswaltersdorf. Now, while the the Führer-Grenadier Brigade's infantry fought in and around Daken, an armoured battlegroup commanded by Hauptmann Alfred Jaedtke pushed down the east bank of the Rominte from Schweitzertal.

Jaedtke's left flank was partly covered by other elements of the division, but he was acutely aware that to his right, the west, there was almost no protection. In the circumstances, he made cautious progress in the face of initially stiff resistance, finally securing Grosswaltersdorf on 22 October.

The two German pincers were now less than 10km apart. Soviet forces assaulted Daken again, but were beaten off by the Führer-Grenadier Brigade's Panzergrenadier battalion. The hard-pressed infantrymen became aware of sounds of heavy fighting to their west, as the brigade's Panzer regiment arrived and attacked north, encountering powerful Soviet formations. The lead company was commanded by Leutnant Taaks, and his tank took a hit from an anti-tank gun on the commander's cupola. Undaunted, Taaks ordered his crew to engage and destroy the anti-tank gun, but other tanks in the company were less lucky, and were knocked out. Soviet tanks also appeared, bringing the German advance to a sudden halt. Further forward, the isolated Panzer-Fusilier battalion managed to reach Tellrode, immediately south of Grosswaltersdorf. From here, the German infantry were able to bring the bridge over the Rominte under direct fire, though they themselves became the focus of determined Soviet attacks.

Yet another attack developed against the Panzergrenadier battalion in Daken, where the Soviet XII Guards Rifle Corps moved forward with mixed groups of tanks and infantry. The advanced position at the brickworks north of the village was abandoned. Repeated air attacks destroyed the battalion's limited flak guns, and casualties mounted steadily. A group of T-34s now appeared from the west, and the defenders realized that they were surrounded. During daylight, the Soviet forces were kept at arm's length by the defenders, but it seemed likely that an assault during the night would result in the position being lost.

Just at this moment, the defenders received a welcome boost. A single Panther tank from the brigade's Panzer regiment appeared, having become lost in the fighting further west. Despite having a faulty shell-casing ejector, it was still able to fire, and it was immediately pressed into action. A T-34 that was probing the edge of the village was knocked out, and the rest of the Soviet force backed off, unsure of how many tanks they were facing.[8]

The impact of a single tank in such a battle might seem exaggerated, but it shows the uncertainty under which the Soviet forces were fighting. They would have been aware from the battle raging with the Führer-Grenadier Brigade's tanks that German armour was close by, and as this was the first time that the German brigade had seen battle, they would have been unsure of its strength. The solitary Panther might represent the first of a column of vehicles, and bitter experience had taught the Red

Army to respect the ability of their German foes to use even small armoured units to maximum effect. The incident also demonstrates the poor deployment of the Führer-Grenadier Brigade; its two infantry battalions and tank regiment were all trying to function on their own, and just as the tanks fighting a little further west would have welcomed infantry support against the Soviet anti-tank guns in their path, so the infantry welcomed the arrival of any tanks.

The southern prong of the German pincer might be decidedly battered, but its tip at Gross-Tellrode was only a few hundred metres from Jaedtke's battlegroup, and the two forces established contact on 23 October. The Germans now faced two tasks. The positions of the Führer-Grenadier Brigade would have to be reinforced; at the same time, the Soviet forces isolated to the west would have to be mopped up. Throughout 23 October, the pressure on Daken continued, and Major von Courbiere was ordered to withdraw from the village towards the end of the day. Just as his surviving men were pulling out, a counter-order was received. Von Courbiere and 30 men stayed on in the village, while the rest of the battalion fought its way west, eventually reaching Herzogswalde. In Daken itself, fighting finally died down. Further German forces filtered down from the north, with elements of Panzer Division *Hermann Göring* gradually relieving the exhausted infantry of the Führer-Grenadier Brigade in Tellrode and finally Daken, allowing von Courbiere and his small group to withdraw.

Jaedtke's battlegroup turned west, to mop up the Soviet forces that had been cut off by the successful linkup with the Führer-Grenadier Brigade, and moved through Brauersdorf towards Nemmersdorf. The German line of march was overlooked by a high ridge to the north near the village of Bismarckshöh, and Soviet forces had taken up defensive positions here – ironically, in an extensive trench system that had been dug by German civilians in the preceding weeks. Despite support from 5th Panzer Division's artillery firing from Gumbinnen, Jaedtke could make little headway until two half-tracks equipped with flamethrowers were brought to bear.[9]

Other German units approached Nemmersdorf from the west. Günter Koschorrek was a veteran Panzergrenadier from 24th Panzer Division, who was wounded in August in heavy fighting in Galicia. While recovering from surgery to remove shrapnel from his arm, he was assigned to a training company of soldiers from a variety of units – men from rear-area formations, sailors without ships – who were being reorganized as Panzergrenadiers. As a decorated frontline soldier, Koschorrek was to set an example to the inexperienced men who would soon be in the frontline. On 10 October, the company was placed on alert, and in a hastily assembled convoy of old trucks it was dispatched to the front on 21 October, as part of the ad hoc defensive line that was thrown up in the face of 11th Guards Army's advance to the Angerapp valley at Nemmersdorf.

The roads from their barracks to the new front were choked with people fleeing westwards, carrying what they could on hand-carts or horse-drawn wagons. On the afternoon of 21 October, the company began to advance towards Nemmersdorf. Some of the men remarked on the large numbers of ravens and crows gathered in the trees, but suddenly they came under fire from Soviet anti-tank guns. As darkness fell, Koschorrek and his comrades dug in on either side of the road and prepared to storm the Soviet positions the following day.

The 22 October was misty, and only faint outlines of buildings were visible to the Germans. Koschorrek's company was on the right flank of the attack, and watched other companies rush forward to their left, running into heavy machine-gun and mortar fire. When his own company attacked, the fire had slackened, and casualties were lighter than in the other companies.

When we moved through the village, we found no more Soviets. But we were greeted by grisly scenes of the people who had been caught up there, which reminded me of the atrocities suffered by Soviet villagers from their own soldiers, something I had often seen during our retreats early in 1944. Here there were German women, whose clothing had been torn from their bodies, so that they could be violated and finally mutilated in horrific ways. In one barn, we found an old man, whose throat had been pierced with a pitchfork, pinning him to the door. All of the feather mattresses in one of the bedrooms had been sliced open, and were stained with blood. Two cut-up female corpses were lying amidst the feathers, with two murdered children. The sight was so gruesome that some of our recruits fled in panic.[10]

The following day, when Jaedtke's battlegroup had finished clearing the Soviet defenders from the trenches east of Nemmersdorf, they too entered the dead village:

Apparently the Russian attack on Nemmersdorf and Brauersdorf had overrun German refugee columns; the scene that greeted us was grim. Amongst approximately 50 shot-up wagons and along the edge of the wood, about 200 metres away, were strewn everywhere the bodies of shot women and children. In Brauersdorf itself, there were many women next to the village road who had had their breasts cut off. I saw this with my own eyes. I received reports of many other atrocities from units in other areas, but particularly from Nemmersdorf.[11]

Karl Potrek was a member of a Volkssturm unit that entered Nemmersdorf:

> In the farmyard further down the road on the left stood a cart, in which were four naked women, who had been strangled. Behind the Weisser Krug towards Gumbinnen is a square with a monument to the Unknown Soldier. Beyond is another large inn, 'Roter Krug'. Near it, parallel to the road, stood a barn and to each of its two doors a naked woman was nailed through the hands, in a crucified posture.
>
> ... We found a total of seventy-two women, including children, and one old man, 74, all dead. Almost all had been murdered in a bestial manner. Amongst the dead, we even found children in diapers. In one room we found a woman, 84 years old, sitting on a sofa, she was totally blind. Her head was split in half to her throat with an axe or a spade.
>
> We carried the corpses to the village cemetery where they lay to await a foreign medical commission.
>
> ... On the fourth day the bodies were buried in two graves. Only on the following day did the medical commission arrive, and the tombs had to be reopened... This foreign commission unanimously established that all the women, as well as the girls from eight to twelve years and even the woman of 84 years had been raped.[12]

Accounts vary as to the number of victims, but about 70 murdered civilians were reported to have been found in Nemmersdorf. There were about 95 more dead in the village of Schulzenwalde, some 8km to the southeast. By the scale of German atrocities in the Soviet Union and elsewhere, this was a modest total, but the sight of German women crucified along the road into Nemmersdorf shocked Jaedtke's battle-hardened men and the other groups that retook the village. Whatever atrocities they had previously seen – or participated in – they had been perpetrated on foreigners. Jaedtke immediately reported the grim findings to his division headquarters, and word was passed up through the chain of command. Sensing a propaganda opportunity, Goebbels organized a party of reporters and observers from Switzerland and Sweden to visit Nemmersdorf, in order to see first-hand the way that Soviet soldiers had behaved on German soil. As Potrek recorded, these observers confirmed that all the female victims, from children to a blind woman in her eighties, had been raped before being killed. Newsreels of the atrocities were shown throughout Germany, with the intention of stiffening resolve to resist the Bolshevik hordes.

More recently, there have been attempts to re-examine the Nemmersdorf issue, and in particular the number of dead.[13] There is evidence to suggest that the number of dead in the village was exaggerated, and that this figure represented not only those killed in Nemmersdorf, but also those in neighbouring villages. Many of the apparent first-person accounts may in fact have been based on stories heard from others, and some accounts were written several years after the event; in these cases, it is possible that memories were coloured by the coverage that Nemmersdorf received at the time in German newspapers. Nevertheless, there can be little doubt that at least some of the village's inhabitants suffered cruelly at the hands of the Red Army.

It is not surprising that there is almost complete silence on the subject of Nemmersdorf in Soviet accounts. After their initial resistance on the outskirts of the village, most of the Soviet soldiers in Nemmersdorf slipped away into the woodland and made their way east, making it hard to determine which unit was responsible for what happened. Although Goebbels distorted Ehrenburg's statements, and the degree to which such acts were condoned or even encouraged will probably never be known, the Soviet soldiers themselves had no illusions: 'All of us knew very well that if the girls were German they could be raped and then shot.'[14]

There were many reasons for the behaviour of the Soviet forces in Nemmersdorf. In July 1944, the Red Army liberated the Maidanek extermination camp. Soviet soldiers were forced to tour the camp, to see what the Nazi regime had perpetrated, reinforcing their hatred of their enemies. News about Maidanek was widely distributed, though characteristically the Soviet media played down its significance as a camp that exterminated Jews; it was official Soviet policy that the people of the Soviet Union had suffered more than anyone else in the war, and anything that contradicted this was brushed aside. It was fortunate for the Soviet propaganda machine that Maidanek was actually not purely a Jewish extermination camp, but dealt with a variety of races. The news about Maidanek reinforced the hardening of attitudes amongst Soviet soldiers, as one testified: 'I have to say that the war has changed me a lot ... war does not make people tender. On the contrary it makes them reserved, rather coarse, and very cruel. That's a fact.'[15]

Another soldier wrote:

Our soldiers have not dealt with East Prussia any worse than the Germans did with Smolensk. We hate Germany and the Germans deeply. In one house, for example, our boys found a murdered woman and her two children. You can often see civilians lying dead in the street, too. But the Germans deserve the atrocities that they unleashed. You only have to think about Maidanek... It's certainly cruel to have killed these children, but the cold-bloodedness of the Germans at Maidanek was a thousand times worse.[16]

Given the widespread coverage across the world of the findings at Maidenek, it is unsurprising that there was little foreign reaction to the German newsreels from Nemmersdorf.

The crimes committed around Nemmersdorf were appalling by any standard, but no worse than acts carried out by Germans in the occupied territories of the Soviet Union. Indeed, Koschorrek's own account contains an interesting aside – German units retreating through the Soviet Union sometimes came across similar scenes, and were told that these were the deeds of Red Army or partisan formations that had already moved through the area. On some occasions, this was true, as the Soviets dealt harshly with anyone, civilian or military, whom they suspected of collaborating with the fascist invaders. On other occasions, though, the crimes were committed by German rear-area units, often security divisions or other units involved in the pitiless war against partisans and any deemed to be supporting them. Perhaps the most appalling feature of the Nemmersdorf incident, though, was the extreme nature of the atrocities, with apparently universal multiple rape of all female victims followed by mutilation and death, all delivered in a manner that even the battle-hardened soldiers of the Wehrmacht found shocking. Also shocking was the way that Soviet soldiers carried out these deeds effectively in the middle of a battle. This was their first foray into the territory of the hated fascists who had brought so much devastation to their own homeland, and the desire for revenge was too strong to resist. For the German soldiers who witnessed these deeds, and for others who heard the reports, the lesson to be learned was clear: Soviet incursions into German territory would result in a dreadful fate for German civilians. Whilst this may have hardened the will of many German soldiers to fight to defend their people from the wrath of the Red Army, it also left the German civilians glancing ever more fearfully towards the east. If the Red Army were to start advancing again, they would seek to flee at the earliest opportunity.

There was one organization that the German newsreels, predictably, did not blame: the Nazi Party. It would have been well within the capability of the Party to arrange a timely evacuation of the area before the Red Army arrived, but Koch had condemned all such measures as defeatist. The civilian population of Nemmersdorf and the surrounding villages paid a terrible price for his refusal. Indeed, one of the consequences of the propaganda campaign was that German people began to question why there had been no evacuation.

The fighting was not yet over. Cherniakhovsky made one more attempt to force the German positions at and north of Schlossberg. Since the battle had started, 1st Infantry Division had been driven back some 25km, but the attacking forces had paid a savage price for this ground. The defenders had accounted for nearly 130 tanks and assault guns, and their personal accounts speak of fields covered with dead Soviet infantrymen. After a short pause for reorganization, Nikolai Krylov's 5th Army made one last assault on 28 October, supported on his right by 39th Army, extending the attack as far as the Memel valley at Schillfelde, and elements of 28th Army on his left. Despite another extensive preparatory bombardment, the attack failed and the front stabilized.

For Schittnig's 1st Infantry Division, this battle was perhaps its finest hour. For 12 days it had resisted repeated assaults by superior enemy numbers, inflicting devastating casualties on the attackers. Schittnig himself had established his authority within the division with his calm leadership. But the division's losses had been high, particularly amongst the irreplaceable officers and experienced NCOs. The commander of its reconnaissance battalion was killed in running engagements with Soviet forces on the division's southern flank, and his successor, Oberleutnant Rohrbeck, fought an energetic series of actions, falling back from one strongpoint to another and launching determined, if limited, counter-attacks whenever the opportunity arose, for which he was awarded the Knight's Cross in November. It remained to be seen how well the weakened division would be able to withstand a future attack.

The Soviet attack had secured a long if fairly shallow strip of East Prussian territory, from Schillfelde in the north to Goldap in the south. Here, around Goldap, the Soviet positions formed a salient that still threatened the Angerapp valley, and Hossbach decided to reduce this bulge. The operation would be under the aegis of XLI Panzer Corps, commanded by 5th Panzer Division's former commander, Decker. Skirmishes continued around Goldap itself, which was screened off by a few ad hoc German formations. The Soviet forces in the town knew that an attack was coming, and deployed anti-tank guns and artillery pieces to reinforce the defence.

The terrain around Goldap was unfavourable for an attack, and the battle plan was changed several times. Finally, 5th Panzer Division, with the Führer-Grenadier Brigade's Panzergrenadier battalion, was positioned to attack towards Goldap from the north, while 50th Infantry Division, reinforced with the Führer-Grenadier Brigade's Panzer-Fusilier battalion, attacked from the south. The constant fighting in Lithuania and south of Gumbinnen had taken a toll on 5th Panzer Division; on 1 November, it had only 12 Pz. IVs, 21 Panthers and 87 half-tracks available.

On the evening of 2 November, 5th Panzer Division moved into position northwest of Goldap. German officers and NCOs had reconnoitred the area a couple of days before, but heavy snow made it hard to recognize terrain features, and there was much confusion. By midnight, everything was ready. There was no preparatory artillery bombardment, partly in an attempt to ensure surprise, but difficulties in moving artillery into position, and securing sufficient ammunition, probably also played a part. Nevertheless, the assault began at 0010hrs on 3 November, with the attack formations improvising their own preparatory fire:

After substantial fire magic from our guns and those around us, we set off, firing like mad in front of us, as it was not possible to make out targets in the snow. The first tanks and half-tracks drove onto mines. But we reached the first Russian trenches, which they appeared to have abandoned hastily. As we advanced, we penetrated into a trench system, where in places the Russians mounted a stiff defence. In one such trench, Oberleutnant Kröcher … found himself encircled by the Russians, but in close-quarter fighting he was able to bring his half-track out. Oberleutnant Meissner, commanding 3 Company, ran over a mine and suffered a serious foot wound. During the night, the snow showers eased and we were able to orient ourselves and reorganize the muddled companies. The Russians mounted only isolated resistance. After reaching Lake Goldap, we pushed on south towards Goldap. As 3 November dawned, we saw Goldap some two kilometres away. To our left on the edge of the wood, we hastily deployed some tanks for defence and drove on to Goldap with the bulk of our forces. Shortly before we reached the bridge over the River Goldap, which here ran from the west to the east across the northern edge of the town, there was a powerful detonation. The Russians blew up the bridge right under our noses. Under covering fire from the tanks and half-tracks, the grenadiers set off and stormed into Goldap over the remains of the bridge. Later, we were able to cross the bridge, which was torn up on the right, with half-tracks and tanks, after Hauptmann Pilch's pioneers had secured it and later rebuilt it. Goldap quickly fell into our hands. Some of the Russians were still asleep in the beautiful houses, some of them drunk senseless.[17]

The northern part of the German assault was an outstanding success. Further south, the Führer-Grenadier Brigade's Panzer-Fusilier battalion attacked towards prominent high ground in front of Goldap, while Generalmajor Georg Haus' 50th Infantry Division advanced towards the southern side of the town. Immediately, the Panzer-Fusiliers came under heavy fire. The terrain was swampy and unsuitable for such an assault; the Germans had hoped that the winter weather would freeze the ground, but the going remained very heavy. Amidst mounting casualties, the battalion's officers and NCOs strove in vain to get the half-tracks moving forward again.

The soldiers of 50th Infantry Division had an easier time. Supported by an armoured train, they were able to overcome the Soviet defences, and swiftly established contact with 5th Panzer Division east of Goldap. Here, they set up defensive positions, and for two days beat off repeated attempts by the Red Army to break through to the forces trapped in Goldap itself. The division had already won praise for its resolute defence at Ossowiec in Poland, and in the snowy terrain east of Goldap it now accounted for another 42 Soviet tanks.

The isolated Soviet forces in and around Goldap were finally mopped up by the end of 5 November. By then, the picturesque town had been reduced to ruins. Gradually, the German armoured elements were withdrawn to reserve areas to allow them to recover, and were replaced by infantry. It was the last time that Decker and his former division served together. Decker was assigned to the command of an infantry corps on the Western Front, and did not survive the war; when his corps was surrounded in the Ruhr pocket, he preferred suicide to surrender.

The fighting along the East Prussian frontier gave both sides a clear indication of what lay ahead. For the Germans, there was satisfaction in the way that the Soviet assault had been repulsed, tempered by horror of what occurred in Nemmersdorf, Schulzenwalde and Brauersdorf. There was also concern at how the German Army had performed. The veteran formations such as 5th Panzer Division and 1st and 50th Infantry Divisions had all fought well, but had suffered serious casualties. The Führer-Grenadier Brigade had fought less effectively, and paid a huge price in terms of its invaluable officers and NCOs. For Cherniakhovsky, the battles must have had a chastening effect. In the west, as German forces stabilized their frontline after the disasters in France, Montgomery tried to achieve a quick victory with the airborne assault on Arnhem, but determined German resistance showed that the days of rapid advances were over. Now, in the east, Cherniakhovsky learned the same lesson. Where the Germans had been able to retreat to their well-concealed main battle positions, his assault forces made almost no impression, and even in the areas where the initial artillery bombardment caught the Wehrmacht in the frontline, success was not guaranteed, particularly against veteran formations such as 1st Infantry Division.

It is intriguing to consider what might have been possible if Cherniakhovsky had coordinated his attack with Bagramian's drive to Memel, as two of the divisions used by the Germans– 5th Panzer Division and Panzer Division *Hermann Göring* – were used in both battles, and a simultaneous Soviet attack would have prevented this. Yet such coordination may well have been beyond the logistic resources available, and would either have required Cherniakhovsky to bring forward his timetable, or for Bagramian to delay his attack. The former might have resulted in Charniakhovsky's armies going into action with inadequate preparation, while the latter would have risked worsening weather in Lithuania. The long pursuit of the retreating Germans after *Bagration* was over. Any future Soviet assault on East Prussia would be resisted fiercely.

CHAPTER 4
THE LAST CHRISTMAS

The Ostfront *must help itself and make do with what it's got.*

– Adolf Hitler[1]

Fighting died down along the East Prussian front as autumn turned to winter. Both sides were exhausted by the battles that had moved the frontline hundreds of kilometres west, from the heart of Belarus and Ukraine onto German soil. Only in Hungary, and in the north around the embattled Courland pocket, did fighting continue at high intensity.

Stalin only agreed to a downturn in Soviet attacks with reluctance. He was keen to continue offensive operations, but Zhukov was adamantly opposed, and his advice prevailed. In November 1944, 1st Belorussian Front and Ivan Konev's 1st Ukrainian Front to its south were designated as the main forces for the coming offensive. They would exploit along the 'Warsaw–Berlin axis' in order to deal a decisive blow to German forces in the east. To prepare for this, Zhukov insisted that his battered units needed time to reorganize, incorporate new drafts, repair damaged equipment and to prepare for what should be the decisive battle.

In most respects, it had been a stunningly successful year for the Soviet Union. The prospect of final victory now lay ahead, and the disjointed nature of the fighting on the *Ostfront* increased the likelihood of Soviet success. The battles in Courland and Hungary tied down German forces some distance from the critical sector of the front, the main axis for the Soviet offensive. Such matters were first discussed in detail in early November. Zhukov's and Konev's fronts would receive massive armoured reinforcements in preparation for their key role. Their northern flank posed considerable concerns for the Soviet planners: as Zhukov's forces moved west, they would skirt the southern side of the heavily fortified German line in East Prussia. Isolation of East Prussia and its elimination, therefore, would be critical for the main Soviet drive into the heart of the Reich.

Meanwhile, German units were redeploying. The *Grossdeutschland* Division was withdrawn from Memel and began to reform in East Prussia. In conjunction with the recently created Panzergrenadier Division *Brandenburg*, it was to form a new *Grossdeutschland* Corps. The 83rd Infantry Division, which had an illustrious record of service on the *Ostfront*, was transferred from Courland and dispatched to Thorn, where it received reinforcements. The fighting in Courland had reduced the division to about 7,000 men; the division medical officer reported to Generalleutnant Wilhelm Heun, the division commander, that at least 10 per cent of replacement drafts were simply not fit for frontline service, and should be discharged immediately.[2]

Towards the end of November, 7th Panzer Division was withdrawn from the Memel bridgehead, and Huber and his comrades sailed south aboard a freighter called the *Volta*. The ship made the overnight run down the coast of the Samland peninsula to Pillau, and from there continued up the channel to Königsberg, where the crews and tanks of 7th Panzer Division's 25th Panzer Regiment were unloaded. From the docks, the men travelled the short distance to the nearby barracks, where they were to spend the night:

> We are all shocked during our short drive through the inner part of Königsberg. There are only ruins there. Rubble and empty darkness lie to left and right. There must have been a heavy air raid on the city in recent times. The bombers have reduced everything to soot and ashes. Beautiful Königsberg! The strong smell of smoke surrounds us as we drive through the streets. Everyone thinks of his own folk at home. Does it look the same as this? They have written to us so often about the bombing attacks – although we haven't had to face this at the front, we are nevertheless familiar with the problem.[3]

Apart from some minimal bombing by a few Soviet aircraft in 1941, Königsberg had survived unscathed until August 1944. On the night of 26–27 August, 174 RAF Lancasters – allegedly violating the airspace of neutral Sweden – struck the city, followed by a heavier raid three nights later. This second raid by 189 Lancasters could only deliver 487 tonnes of bombs, as the aircraft were operating at maximum range, but the damage was considerable. The planes delivered a lethal mix of high-explosive and incendiaries, striking the historic city centre and reducing the Teutonic castle, the cathedral, the university and many other famous landmarks to rubble. About 3,500 people were killed, and many more were left with their homes at least partially damaged. Alerted by the previous raid, in which four Lancasters were shot down by flak, the defenders put up better resistance, destroying 15 bombers.

In anticipation of possible attacks, some of the city's residents had been evacuated to the countryside. Gretel Dost, the girl from Friedrichstein who had been overawed by Marion Dönhoff's visit to her school, was now a nurse working in a private clinic in the city, and in midsummer the clinic was relocated from Königsberg to Fischhausen, a small town to the west of the Prussian capital. Dost and her colleagues were delighted with the move, because they found themselves next to a military hospital, with plenty of time to fraternize with the army personnel. Erika Morgenstern, who had been born in 1939, was sent to a farm in the village of Almenhausen with her mother and younger sister:

> On a wonderful summer's day, when there was nothing to suggest death or suffering – at least not in Almenhausen – a few women were standing in the village street with their children in their arms or holding their hands. It was between breakfast and midday, the sun was high in the sky and this gathering was an unusual sight at this time of day. My mother too joined the group of women with we children. Silent and saddened, everyone stared in one direction, in which normally there was nothing to see but fields. But on this day, there was something else. A large part of the sky from the horizon upwards was deep, dark red. A grisly image, as if blood was rising into the sky. A woman said, 'Königsberg is burning.'[4]

Air raids struck other parts of East Prussia, too. Tilsit was bombed several times by Soviet planes, as were other towns along the frontier. For much of the war, the citizens of East Prussia had been envied by their fellow Germans who lived further west, within range of British and American bombers; now, the long arm of the Allies' air fleets could reach even to here, and Soviet aircraft were close enough to threaten air attacks at any time.

Despite this, East Prussia at the end of 1944 was still relatively untouched by the war, compared to other parts of Germany. Its farms continued to work productively, albeit relying on workers from prisoner of war camps. In some cases, these prisoners had been captives since the opening months of the war, and some had worked on the same farms for years. Many were regarded almost as family by the German women who struggled to keep their farms functioning while their men were away at the front. The Party issued strict orders that the Poles and others were to be kept in isolation from the German population, but the realities of farm life were such that most farmers simply ignored such instructions, as one such farmer related to a girl sent to work on his farm:

> Jan is not allowed to go to the next village, not even to church. He is not supposed to listen to the radio or read a newspaper. He must not sleep under the same roof as us and should take his meals in the shed where he lives. They told us not to get too chummy with him; there are hefty penalties for that sort of thing. But I say 'bullshit'. He's more like a member of the family; out here a man is as good as his work and I will not have a man treated like an animal on my property. Mind you, when Herr Stiller is here – he's

the rural inspector, a Party man, a real Hitler fanatic they say; you know, 'Heil Hitler' here, 'Heil Hitler' there – I shout a bit at Jan to make Herr Stiller think I'm keeping Jan on a tight rein![5]

The East Prussian farms were a vital part of the Reich's ability to continue to function, with an annual productivity of several million tonnes of agricultural produce – the farms produced more food than all of Holland. Meat, dairy products and fish (from the productive fleets of small boats operating from the Baltic ports) ensured that even with widespread rationing the people of East Prussia continued to be comparatively well fed.

The mood of the German people at this time is difficult to assess, particularly by those who have never had the misfortune to live in a totalitarian state where all forms of communication are firmly under government control. People had abundant evidence of the perilous state of German fortunes – cities right across the Reich had been bombed repeatedly, and every family had lost men on the various fronts. The eastern edge of East Prussia itself was now occupied by the Red Army, and of course everyone knew about Nemmersdorf, and feared further advances by the Bolsheviks. In Berlin, a city that had never enthusiastically embraced Nazism, the grim joke in circulation this Christmas revolved around the eternal question of what to buy as a Christmas present: 'Be practical,' suggested the wags, 'send a coffin.' Others, such as the dissident Marion Dönhoff, could see only one outcome, but how freely they were able to discuss such matters is open to question. The ever-increasing death toll of the war, though, left few unscathed:

Frau Duttke was … a self-confident, but at the same time modest, outstanding woman. She looked after the pigs and was proud that she hadn't missed a day's work for many years. She and her husband had simply worked all their lives so that their children should have something better. The younger son was killed in France, and the older was an NCO – a magnificent, straightforward, reliable chap, that any army in the world would have regarded with pride: he was certain to become an officer one day, and then all the drudgery would be worthwhile.

But this day didn't come; instead, a day came in autumn 1944, when I saw Frau Duttke crossing the estate yard, a bucket in each hand. The handsome woman looked old, absent-minded, a ghost of her former self. 'In God's name, Frau Duttke, what's happened?' She looked at me with staring, dead eyes, put down the buckets – and suddenly threw her arms around my neck, and cried and cried: 'Karl is dead, the news came today. Now everything is at an end. Everything was for nothing – our whole lives.'[6]

Many soldiers in the frontline, too, were under little illusion about what lay ahead:

> It was therefore not surprising that confidence in military leadership ... from the front to the highest levels of the Wehrmacht, was deeply shaken, given the completely false evaluation of the facts by these leaders. All that remained now was to save innocent victims of the senseless war from the retaliation of the Red Army, driven on by the revengeful Soviet demagogues.[7]

To speak publicly of such things was to invite court-martial for defeatism, so most soldiers remained cautious, even when discussing matters amongst themselves. Some, though, while aware that things looked grim, continued to hope for a favourable outcome:

> We receive a startling report on 18 December. Our forces on the Western Front, in the Ardennes, have launched a counter-offensive. Strong army formations and tank units have hurled back the Americans. We hope for a decisive victory by our side on the Western Front. Our own morale rises. That must be why we have received so few supplies and have had to give up so much ground on the *Ostfront* – the units in the west were being prepared for an attack!
>
> Days later, the radio reports the success of the Luftwaffe. Six hundred enemy aircraft were shot down yesterday! So, the fortunes of war are turning.[8]

The Ardennes offensive broke as an enormous surprise for both the Allies and most of Germany. In a final burst of productivity, German armaments production reached record levels in the autumn of 1944, and several divisions were completely re-equipped and prepared for action. Guderian and others wanted these divisions deployed in the east to shore up the fragile front, but Hitler gambled on a last offensive in the west. Under heavy skies, which grounded the Allied air forces, the German assault formations made good initial progress, but from the earliest stage stubborn pockets of American resistance delayed them. Ultimately, the offensive came to a standstill some distance short of the River Meuse, the first major objective, and as the skies cleared, Allied air power was brought to bear with lethal effect. The offensive cost the Germans 80,000 casualties for no tangible gains.

The Luftwaffe attack on New Year's Day, 1945, was also far from a great triumph. A secret airstrike was planned against Allied airfields, with the intention of destroying as many planes as possible on the ground. Most German aircrews were unaware of the exact mission until the morning of the attack. The German pilots struck shortly after dawn, and appeared to be devastatingly successful; more than 460 Allied aircraft were destroyed or damaged. But the flak defences of the airfields were stronger than anticipated, and British and American fighter patrols inflicted heavy losses on the German fighters as they flew home. Even worse, the mission had been prepared in such secrecy that the German flak defences had not been alerted. Seeing large numbers of planes flying out of the west, they opened fire on their own pilots, adding to their casualties. The Germans lost more than 270 planes, but most importantly 211 pilots were killed. The Allies, on the other hand, suffered serious material losses, but their aircrews escaped almost unscathed. Once replacement aircraft were brought forward, albeit over several weeks, they were able to resume operations without difficulty. The Luftwaffe, by contrast, suffered irreplaceable losses of experienced pilots. It would never mount an operation on this scale again.

In his New Year message to the German nation, Hitler characteristically showed no sign of doubt:

> Millions of Germans of all callings and backgrounds, men and women, youths and girls, right down to the children, have laboured with spades and shovels. Thousands of Volkssturm battalions have been raised or are being formed. Divisions have been re-equipped. People's artillery corps, rocket brigades and assault gun brigades as well as armoured formations have been deployed, fighter squadrons once more refreshed and supplied with new machines, and above all the German factories have through the efforts of their male and female workers achieved singular results. In this way, whatever our enemies destroy has been restored with superhuman diligence and heroic courage, and this will continue until one day our enemies will find their end. That, my fellow countrymen, will be regarded as the wonder of the 20th century! A people, who labour so endlessly at the front and in the homeland, who endure so much ill fortune, will never be ground down. They will come out of this furnace tested and stronger than ever before in their history.[9]

To some extent at least, Hitler spoke the truth. Tank production peaked in December 1944, with 1,854 tanks and assault guns being completed, equivalent to almost half the entire production of 1941, sufficient to re-equip several Panzer divisions. But this was the last surge of production, and Hitler's armaments minister, Albert Speer, was well aware that raw materials were running out. There was no longer sufficient brass to manufacture the huge quantities of cartridges required, and in some cases steel was being used. These steel cartridges were more prone to jamming, causing additional problems. There was also a shortage of tungsten, resulting in armour-piercing ammunition being of a poorer quality, and sometimes not even available.

Everywhere, German soldiers and civilians held on in the hope of the promised *Wunderwaffen* ('Wonder Weapons') – the miraculous new weapons that would turn the tide of the war. New assault rifles were now in widespread circulation, and official reports had made much of the advent of new Luftwaffe aircraft, particularly the jet-powered Me 262 and rocket-powered Me 163. Large parts of London had felt the power of V-1 and V-2 missile bombardments, and there were constant hints that other, even more potent weaponry would soon be available. But would it come in time?

All along the *Ostfront*, senior officers used what little time they had available, organizing training for their new drafts, preparing defensive positions and contemplating a grim future. Günter Emanuel Baltuttis was a member of a replacement draft sent to bring the former 16th Parachute Regiment, now renamed 3rd Regiment, of the Paratroop-Panzergrenadier Division *Hermann Göring* back to something approaching full strength. The draft consisted of a number of former airmen as well as new recruits like Baltuttis. When they assembled near Insterburg, they were surprised by the greeting they were given by a stony-faced Oberleutnant: 'Take note, I will not hesitate to drag any laggard or coward before a court martial!'[10]

Baltuttis and his comrades were sent straight into the frontline, where they endured muddy, rainswept conditions – in order to keep their loads to a minimum, they had been sent forward in summer clothing, with the assurance that winter uniforms would follow in due course. These garments didn't actually appear for two months. Within days, Baltuttis had developed a form of trench foot from constant immersion in water and damp earth.

Baltuttis' regiment was holding the frontline in the area where the Führer-Grenadier Brigade had run into Soviet armour, west of Daken, and the landscape was dotted with burnt-out wrecks. From time to time, the soldiers came across the corpses of men who had fallen in the fighting, and had been left to sink slowly into the mud. Desertions to the enemy were a regular feature. Soldiers faced draconian punishments for other misdemeanours. Baltuttis' company commander, Leutnant Saul, was assigned to a court-martial, and recounted the story to Baltuttis when he returned to the company:

An 18-year-old soldier, whose father was an Oberst in our corps, was condemned to death for the capital offence of plundering, because he had taken an abandoned wristwatch that he found in some ruins during a counter-attack. Leutnant Saul objected to the case being brought, and finally refused to take part, forcing an adjournment, probably saving the life of the accused. The chairman accused Leutnant Saul of 'refusing to follow orders', and reported the events to the regiment commander, resulting in an immediate summons for Leutnant Saul. But contrary to expectations, the commander, Oberstleutnant Rebholz, issued not the slightest rebuke, but just gently shook his head, and made it clear that he regarded the procedure as unnecessary and pointless. Leutnant Saul escaped any punishment.[11]

During the winter, Baltuttis' company suffered a steady stream of casualties. These included two suicides, two executions (one for desertion, one for self-wounding) and two deaths as a result of attempts at self-wounding that went badly wrong. Baltuttis noted that all of the casualties, including those from enemy snipers, involved new drafts rather than the company's small number of veterans.[12] Alarmed by the poor performance of new recruits, both the division and corps commanders recommended that the division be pulled out of line and allowed to undergo intensive training; the almost non-existent reserves available on the front effectively precluded any such action.

The German soldiers worked hard to improve their bunkers, which served as homes as well as fortifications. They would need all the protection they could get; German intelligence made force estimates that gave the Red Army an advantage of 11:1 in infantry, 7:1 in tanks and 20:1 in artillery. Hitler dismissed these estimates, deriding them as 'the greatest bluff since the time of Genghis Khan'. For the moment, though, Hitler had other concerns in the east than Army Group Centre.

August 1944 was a bad month for the Reich in the Balkans. Bulgaria first declared itself neutral, and then – under pressure from the Soviet Union – declared war on Germany. Bulgarian contributions to the Reich's war effort had always been modest, but the political impact of Bulgaria's defection was considerable. Romania also defected, in a much more dramatic manner. After secret negotiations with the Soviet Union, Romania switched sides and the two armies guarding the flanks of the German 6th Army allowed the Red Army unrestricted passage. In 1942, the failure of Romanian armies guarding the German flanks at Stalingrad had resulted in the envelopment of the 6th Army, and now the same result ensued, with the remnants of no fewer than 20 divisions being encircled near Kishinev. Few men succeeded in breaking out of the envelopment. In October, as Hungary's government was finalizing secret arrangements to surrender to the approaching Red Army, Germany engineered a coup, putting the Crossed Arrows Party, the nearest Hungarian equivalent to the Nazi Party, into power. Most of the last remaining Jews in Hungary, about 70,000 individuals in and around Budapest, were gathered together into an area of about 0.3 square kilometres and were force-marched to the Austrian border during November and December. Many perished in the cold.

The 337th Volksgrenadier Division was ordered on 16 October to take over a sector of the front from the Hungarian 5th Reserve Division, near Warsaw. The Hungarians were to be disarmed, a task that Hans Jürgen Pantenius and his fellow officers found deeply distasteful, as they had established very close relations with the Hungarian division:

Without any major fanfare, I travelled to Natolin, and explained the situation and my mission to the [Hungarian] commander, and asked him for his pistol, not out of any sense of danger to my own person, but because I wanted to prevent a suicide attempt. The commander was completely helpless, tears filled his eyes, and he could not and did not want to issue orders; he handed his weapon to me silently. The adjutant … issued the orders I wished, concerning the replacement, disarmament, and internment. Due to previous discussions about replacement and the positional maps that had been prepared, the action was carried out comparatively swiftly and without difficulty. Naturally, the Hungarians could see no reason for their disarmament and like their commander were concerned and agitated. This did not prevent the officers and NCOs from taking care to list what weapons and equipment they handed over.

I never found out who at army, corps or division level actually issued the order for the disarmament of the Hungarian reserve division. Did those in higher commands really think that the division would desert to the Poles? If they had asked the 'frontline', in other words our general or 337th Volksgrenadier Division's regimental commanders, for our advice beforehand, we would have told them that we never doubted the camaraderie of the Hungarians. But the views of subordinates were not sought. But the very same day came a counter-order. The Hungarian division was to be given back its weapons immediately, the internment was to be stopped, and the division was to prepare for transport to Hungary the next day. The whole affair was a mess. I was now tasked to make my 'colleagues' who remained in Natolin aware of the new situation and to return their weapons to them with expressions of regret. The Hungarians were delighted with the prospect of returning to their homes in Hungary … our general was almost speechless with anger.[13]

Meanwhile, the Red Army was approaching Hungary from the east. Stalin may have agreed to a pause in offensive operations into Poland and Prussia, but he urged the powerful Ukrainian Fronts forward towards Budapest. His Front commanders asked in vain for an opportunity to pause and gather their strength, but the disjointed nature of their attacks actually proved to their advantage. A single, well-organized thrust at Budapest would probably have been successful, and Hitler would have been forced to accept the inevitable, but the succession of drives against the Hungarian capital resulted in a steady transfer of German forces to this sector, stripping Poland and East Prussia of vital armoured reserves. By mid December, the Hungarian capital lay in a salient, with both its flanks threatened. The SS Dirlewanger Brigade, which had acquired a grim reputation for its part in the suppression of the Warsaw Rising, was routed north of the city. As the diminishing defenders were frantically reshuffled to restore the front, the pincers of 2nd and 3rd Ukrainian Fronts turned towards each other.

On 26 December, they met at Esztergom, northeast of Budapest. The Hungarian capital, containing about 188,000 German troops, was surrounded. Refusing to accept the loss of the city, Hitler ordered the garrison to continue to resist, and IV SS-Panzer Corps, currently deployed as armoured reserve in Poland, was sent south. Much of the *Ostfront* had already been denuded to shore up the defences, and this latest move left the critical Warsaw–Berlin axis dangerously weak.

Worse was to come in January. After the Ardennes offensive was abandoned, the SS divisions that might have provided a vital reserve for Army Group Centre were sent to launch another relief attempt in Hungary. For the moment, though, the diversion of IV SS-Panzer Corps left Reinhardt's Army Group Centre only one Panzer division and two Panzergrenadier divisions as armoured reserves. To make matters worse, the army group's frontline, which bulged dangerously to the east, inviting strikes against either flank, was rendered less defensible as the winter frosts froze the marshy land around the Narew and Bobr, terrain that had previously been impassable to Soviet tanks. Hossbach found that the Masurian Lakes to his rear were now ideal landing areas for airborne troops, and his engineers had to improvise obstacles, using farm machinery and tree trunks embedded vertically into the frozen surface of the lakes.

The fighting around Goldap and Gumbinnen had been complicated by the inability, or unwillingness, of the Wehrmacht and the local Party officials to cooperate and arrange a timely evacuation of civilians, and to arrange appropriate deployment of the Volkssturm. Now, there was a third entity, raising the possibility that matters would become even more complex. General Otto Lasch had been appointed as commander of Wehrkreis I (Defence District I), the military administrative authority that oversaw most of East Prussia. Rather than being subordinate to Reinhardt's army group, Lasch was answerable to Heinrich Himmler in his role as commander of the Replacement Army. Lasch was from Silesia, but was married to an East Prussian, and had spent most of his life in the province, serving as a police officer in Lyck and Sensburg before rejoining the army in 1935. He was serving in France, about to take command of LXIV Corps, when he received the news over the telephone that he was to go to East Prussia:

'Why me, a frontline solder?'
'Precisely because of that, things are now hotting up in East Prussia.'

I had the gravest misgivings, particularly with respect to Gauleiter Koch, with whom I had had few personal dealings, but about whom I had unpleasant memories as a fanatical National Socialist from the years of peace. I also was aware that two Wehrkreis commanders had already been replaced at his insistence, as he did not regard them to be working in a sufficiently National Socialist manner. Whether I would be able to succeed in my military role in the face of the inconsiderate interference of someone who unfortunately was so well connected seemed more than questionable.[14]

He found the civilian population of the city of Königsberg in low spirits, constantly and fearfully looking east. The Nazi repression of dissent was at its peak. The Gestapo, for example, incarcerated an Allenstein couple for several weeks merely because their housekeeper reported them for making adverse comments about Hitler. Lasch tried in vain to get the couple released. They were still in the Gestapo cells when Allenstein fell to the Red Army.[15]

Struggling to act as some sort of 'honest broker' between Reinhardt and Gauleiter Koch, Lasch found his life further complicated by the deep-seated hostility between Koch and Himmler. Fortunately for Lasch, Himmler had so many responsibilities at this stage of the war that he had little time to meddle in East Prussian affairs. At times, the beleaguered Lasch felt himself almost completely without support, and was at least grateful that he had as his Chief of Staff Oberst Freiherr von Süsskind-Schwendi, who had served with Lasch in 217th Infantry Division when Lasch commanded the division for much of 1943.

One of Lasch's main tasks was finding replacements for the frontline divisions. He had barely three or four weeks to turn men released by the Luftwaffe and other agencies into men capable of serving in combat. He was acutely aware of the inadequacy of their preparation: 'It was with heavy hearts that we had to send half-trained young soldiers to the front.'[16]

In order to try to improve the quality of these soldiers, additional training was organized at the level of the frontline armies. *Waffenschulen* ('Weapons Schools') were established to train men in the use of support weapons; one such unit would find itself in the thick of the fighting in the new year. Meanwhile, other soldiers were allowed to return home on leave. Friedrich Stück, who commanded elements of 276th Assault Gun Brigade during the fighting northeast of Gumbinnen, was one such individual:

By this stage of the war, the days far away from the front weren't very restful for the majority of leave-takers; frequently they were more depressing than comforting: bomber attacks day and night, craters everywhere, bad news from the front, many relatives and acquaintances were dead, wounded or missing![17]

Back at the front, attempts were made to disrupt Soviet preparations for their offensive. One such operation was codenamed *Schneeflocke* ('Snowflake'), and was carried out on 5 and 6 January 1945. Part of 5th Panzer Division, supported by 367th Infantry

Division, was to attack near the old East Prussian frontier to shorten the front near Lake Rospuda. It was also known that Soviet armoured reserves were stationed somewhere in the area, and the attack would hopefully force them to be committed, revealing their location and in turn providing a clue to future Soviet intentions. The main attack would be made by one of 5th Panzer Division's Panzergrenadier regiments, supported by the Panther tank battalion and a force of tank destroyers. They were to push forward from Hill 227 to Sapiene at the northern tip of Lake Rospuda, from where the Panthers, with the rest of the division's armoured battlegroup, would continue the attack southeast.

The initial assault on 5 January took the Soviet defenders by surprise. The rugged snow-covered terrain, amply sowed with anti-tank mines, proved more of a hindrance than Soviet resistance, but half the distance to the lake was swiftly covered. At this point, the division committed the armoured battlegroup, which struggled against increasing enemy resistance and terrain that was completely unsuitable for armoured vehicles. The battlegroup reached Wolka, at the southern end of Lake Rospuda, shortly before dusk, where it ran into heavy anti-tank fire. A large group of Soviet tanks was spotted to the south, moving west from Filipow; just in time, the division's Panthers arrived, having completed their mission to help the Panzergrenadiers reach the lake, and were able to break into the rear of the Soviet armoured group, disrupting its movement.

The armoured battlegroup now found itself at the tip of a salient projecting southeast, with increasing Soviet forces to the east and south. An attempt to widen the salient to the west failed when the battlegroup ran into a dense minefield. A group of damaged half-tracks was sent to the rear while the battlegroup sought permission to withdraw. When permission was granted, the battlegroup commander ordered the Panther battalion and a battalion of Panzergrenadiers to pull out, leaving the Panzer regiment's Pz. IVs and a second battalion of Panzergrenadiers as a rearguard. Meanwhile, Soviet infantry had infiltrated into the rear of the battlegroup, and there was confused fighting in the hilly countryside as the Germans withdrew. In some cases, damaged vehicles were towed by intact ones, only cast loose when combat was unavoidable.[18]

Kleine and his regiment from 367th Infantry Division were also involved in *Schneeflocke*. He describes the final moments of the operation:

> The tanks and half-tracks of 5th Panzer Division drove back, some loaded with the dead
> and seriously wounded. Soviet ground-attack aircraft flew back and forth, attacking the
> retreating troops and tanks with their weapons. Sometimes, they also dropped small high-

explosive bombs, in such quantities that they looked like swarms of bees from a distance, falling from the sky. The losses in men and materiel were not light, as the Russians were very strong. But this 'reconnaissance mission' was over.

I should mention that the battalion commander of 1st Battalion, Oberstleutnant von Prinz, was killed in this attack. His battalion had to take a hill which was held by the Russians with machine-guns and mortars. Oberstleutnant von Prinz was unable to bombard the enemy strongpoint with our mortars and artillery. As his battalion advanced across open ground into range of the Russian mortars and machine-guns, it suddenly came under heavy fire, apparently taking heavy losses. As a result, the attack on this position had to be called off and the battalion pulled back. Apparently, Oberstleutnant von Prinz found this failure and its attendant consequences for his battalion unbearable. He took up an assault rifle and, in his bright green leather coat, set off towards the Russian lines, until he was hit by a Russian bullet and fell. It was not possible to recover his body.[19]

Early in January, Heinz Guderian, Chief of Staff at OKH, set off on a tour of the *Ostfront*. He had endured a dispiriting Christmas. On 24 December, his latest suggestion that Courland and Norway be evacuated had been rejected, and the following day Hitler ordered IV SS-Panzer Corps south from Poland to try to relieve Budapest. No replacement formation was sent to Poland. Now, on 5 January, Guderian learned from Generalfeldmarschall Otto Wöhler at the headquarters of Army Group South that the attack to relieve Budapest had failed. Renowned for his cool-headedness, even Wöhler couldn't hide his gloom. General Herbert-Otto Gille, commander of IV SS-Panzer Corps, had a long association with SS-Panzer Division (formerly Panzergrenadier division) *Wiking*, and was widely respected by his men. He had led his division with distinction through some of the toughest fighting in the Ukraine, particularly during the retreat after Kursk and the Cherkassy pocket battles of early 1944. The first attempt to reach Budapest had cost his corps more than 3,000 casualties. He was normally a self-confident optimist, but he responded to Guderian's questions about the failed attack with a phlegmatic shrug of his shoulders: 'We no longer have the material of 1940. I now need three men where before I could have made do with two, or even one.'[20]

From this depressing conference, Guderian travelled north to General Josef Harpe, commander of Army Group A, in Cracow. Harpe and his chief of staff, Generalleutnant Wolfdietrich von Xylander, had devised an operation codenamed *Schlittenfahrt* ('Sleighride'), which would see the front withdrawn about 20km from the Vistula to a defensive line that was about 100km shorter. Von Xylander was confident that, as a result of this adjustment, the army group would be able to stop any Soviet offensive short of the Silesian border: 'That is the extent of what we may do by such means. However, the Upper Silesian industrial region will remain in production, the enemy will be held away from German soil, and the higher leadership of the Reich will gain time to turn the military situation, as created by us, to advantage by political negotiations.'[21]

Fully aware of what 'higher leadership' would think of the suggestion of negotiations, Guderian promised to raise the matter with Hitler, but warned Harpe that he shouldn't expect too much.' "He should cashier me then," replied Harpe quietly, "I am only doing my duty."'[22]

The same evening, Guderian telephoned Reinhardt at the headquarters of Army Group Centre in Wartenburg, near Allenstein. Reinhardt, too, proposed an orderly withdrawal to a shorter line, particularly for Hossbach's 4th Army. He also urged intervention by Hitler to force Koch into allowing evacuation of civilians. The news from the Luftwaffe was no better. The greatly diminished Luftwaffe assets in East Prussia were organized as Generaloberst Ritter von Greim's Luftflotte 6 (Air Fleet 6). In the face of growing Soviet air power, he told Guderian, he could do no more than try to protect the main roads and railways.

After a long discussion with Generalfeldmarschall Gerd von Runstedt, the German commander on the Western Front, Guderian presented a grim summary of the situation to Hitler at Ziegenberg on 9 January. The meeting was as stormy as Guderian had anticipated, Hitler flatly refused to accept what he was being told, and flew into a rage when Guderian doggedly raised once more the subject of a timely evacuation of Norway and Courland in order to free up troops. At the end of the conference, Hitler declared that: ' "The *Ostfront* has never before possessed such a strong reserve as now. This is your doing, and I thank you for it." I replied, "The *Ostfront* is like a house of cards. If the front is broken through at one point, all the rest will collapse."'[23] Hitler's concluding remarks show a rare acceptance of reality: 'The *Ostfront* must help itself and make do with what it's got.'[24]

The German policy of withdrawing at the last moment to a well-prepared main battle position was now in widespread use, but it required the main battle position to be sufficiently far back to escape degradation in the initial Soviet bombardment. Reserves had to be held even further back, so that they could come to the assistance of hard-pressed areas without first having to endure the fury of the Red Army's opening salvoes. Unfortunately for the fought-out soldiers along the *Ostfront*, Hitler insisted that the gaps between the frontline, the main battle position and the reserves deployed to the rear should not amount to any more than 15km. This would not allow for any freedom of manoeuvre when the inevitable Soviet attack came.

By this stage of the war, General Reinhard Gehlen's Fremde Heere Ost (Foreign Armies East) – the branch of German military intelligence responsible for the *Ostfront* – was struggling to make meaningful assessments of Soviet capabilities and intentions. Intelligence evaluations were primarily based on three different sources of information: prisoner interrogations, interception of radio traffic, and aerial reconnaissance. Whilst prisoners continued to be taken, their interrogation took time, and this source of information was by its nature unreliable. In any event, Soviet commanders at regimental and battalion level were often informed of plans only two days before the operation was to commence, and rarely had knowledge of higher plans. Their soldiers therefore knew even less. Generally, every Soviet commander only had an understanding of the parent formation's task – a company commander would know the battalion's mission, the battalion commander in turn would know the regiment's mission – and this further restricted the value of prisoner interrogations.

Since the start of successful Soviet offensive operations at Stalingrad, the Red Army had adopted an increasingly rigorous policy regarding radio traffic, with strict orders governing the use of transmitters powerful enough to be detected from German lines. Indeed, the Red Army now deliberately used radio messages to mislead the Germans. Whenever a unit was withdrawn from the frontline, its replacement unit was then assigned the same radio call signs, to prevent German listeners from detecting the change of unit. On other occasions, radio traffic was faked to give the impression of troop concentrations.

Given the steady decline of the Luftwaffe, aerial reconnaissance was also of diminishing value. Even though the likelihood of German reconnaissance flights was now greatly reduced, the Soviet forces continued to place enormous importance on camouflage, so that even if a German aircraft did appear, it was less likely to see anything. Lieutenant B. Tartakovsky here explains some of the camouflage measures: 'The bridgehead was small and there were a lot of units there. The tanks were parked three or four metres apart. First off, we painted them white. Then we covered them with nets. Then we used branches to obliterate tracks in the snow where the tanks had driven.'[25]

Soviet officers went to great lengths to check the quality of their units' camouflage:

We moved the tanks from the east to the west bank of the Vistula, to the bridgehead, only at night, spread out over time and in individual subgroups. At that time as well, the artillery fired and aircraft flew in order to hide the noise of the tanks. Then, I recall, when the brigade was almost formed up, the corps chief of staff called me in, introduced me to an aviator, and said, 'Head for the airfield, board a plane, overfly your brigade, its positions, and see how it looks from above, and take immediate camouflage measures.' I must admit that this was my first aeroplane flight, over the Sandomierz bridgehead. So, what else could I do?... I examined the entire brigade disposition and saw how the troops had prepared the camouflage compared to what we had instructed them to do. It was poor. From above, it was possible to count all the tanks.[26]

Nevertheless, what intelligence was available to the Germans showed that the Red Army possessed considerable reserves, which would soon be thrown into battle against the *Ostfront*. Gehlen had been predicting an attempt by the Red Army to isolate East Prussia by a drive to the lower Vistula since October, and on 5 January 1945, he reported that the long-awaited assault would begin in mid January. There would be a thrust into Silesia, and a second towards Graudenz and Thorn. The objectives for the attack would be in depth, and the only way of dealing with this onslaught was to have strong German operational reserves available.[27] The nature of the front – mainly along large rivers, with several Soviet bridgeheads of varying sizes – made predicting the points of attack relatively easy. An assault crossing of a major river, even when it was frozen, was unlikely, so the assaults would emerge from the bridgeheads. Yet the Germans remained unaware of the exact details of which Soviet forces were in which bridgehead, and could therefore only guess at how strong each attack would be.

However grim a picture was painted by Fremde Heere Ost, the reality was actually even worse. The Germans consistently underestimated Soviet armaments production. During 1944, the Soviet Union produced a staggering 29,000 tanks and assault guns. In addition, the Soviet Union had received more than 400,000 trucks and jeeps from the USA, giving its infantry a degree of mobility that the Germans couldn't match. The main thrust of the new assault would be made through Poland by 1st Belorussian and 1st Ukrainian Fronts, operating on the Warsaw–Berlin axis and aiming for the Oder valley and ultimately Berlin. The northern flank of this thrust would be protected by 2nd and 3rd Belorussian Fronts, which would complete the conquest of West and East Prussia respectively. Rokossovsky's 2nd Belorussian Front was required to isolate East Prussia by a drive along its southern border, and then north along the Vistula to the Baltic coast; the Front would then form the northern part of the push to the lower Oder by Zhukov's 1st Belorussian Front.

Preparation was meticulous. Fuel and ammunition were organized for resupply of the advancing formations. The contents of about 1,200 freight trains were massed behind the front, stockpiled in precise packets for specific formations. Sufficient fuel and ammunition were provided to give each fighting vehicle 2.5 loads. The engineering support for the armoured formations had also been reorganized and streamlined, with recovery crews right behind the attacking forces. Disabled vehicles would be taken to damaged vehicle assembly points for repair, so that those that could be fixed easily would be returned to the frontline in as short a time as possible.

The political preparation of the troops for the assault was also thorough. Ehrenburg's diatribes against the Germans continued apace, and achieved almost holy status; his articles in newspapers were never used to make cigarettes, unlike almost every other scrap of paper. As we have seen, his more extreme proclamations have often been quoted as being what lay behind the horrors of Nemmersdorf and other such incidents:

> Kill! Kill! In the German race there is nothing but evil; not one among the living, not one among the yet unborn is anything but evil! Follow the precepts of Comrade Stalin. Stamp out the fascist beast once and for all in its lair! Use force and break the racial pride of these German women. Take them as your lawful booty. Kill! As you storm onward, kill, you gallant soldiers of the Red Army.[28]

Whilst there were undoubtedly other perhaps more important factors involved, these proclamations – which must have been authorized at a high level – did much to fuel the desire of Soviet soldiers to kill and rape. The editor of *Krasnaya Zvezda*, in which most of Ehrenburg's articles appeared, became involved in a wrangle with the writer about some of the articles, but Stalin swiftly intervened, telling the editor that 'There is no need to edit Ehrenburg. Let him write as he pleases.'

One phrase resurfaced again and again in proclamations issued to the troops, regarding the issue of justice: 'The soldier's rage in battle must be terrible. He does not merely seek to fight; he must also be the embodiment of the court of his people's justice.'[29] Many soldiers had no doubt that they were in Germany to exact justice for the crimes of Germans in the Soviet Union:

> I've already written to you that I'm in Germany. You said that we should do the same things in Germany as the Germans did to us. The court has begun already; they are going to remember this march by our army over German territory for a long, long time.[30]

Whilst many, perhaps most Soviet soldiers believed that theirs was a campaign of liberation to free the enslaved people of Europe from Nazi tyranny, the overall mood was one of revenge. In a final proclamation to his troops, Cherniakhovsky declared: 'There is no question of honour. The land of the fascists must be laid waste.'[31]

The plans about the exact timing of the Soviet operation remain controversial. Originally, it seems that the offensive was planned for about 20 January, but Soviet sources later claimed that it was brought forward in order to reduce the pressure on the western Allies in the Ardennes. This seems improbable, as the Ardennes campaign had turned decisively in favour of the western allies by this stage. It seems far more likely that the timing was determined by two factors. The first was the weather. On 4 January, a high-pressure system developed over Finland. Temperatures in northeast Europe plummeted as the wind swung around to the northeast. The ground hardened, creating the sorts of conditions in which the Soviet forces revelled. The second factor was the coming Allied conference in Yalta in February. Stalin wanted to be sure that his preferred solution for Poland, Prussia, Pomerania and Silesia was already in place before he met Churchill and Roosevelt.

CHAPTER 5

THE HOUSE OF CARDS – THE GREAT JANUARY OFFENSIVE

You only have to kick the door in and the whole rotten structure will come crashing down.

– Adolf Hitler[1]

The climate in Poland and East Prussia varies considerably during the winter. If the prevailing wind remains in the west or southwest, the weather tends to be wet, though relatively mild. If it swings to the north or northeast, the temperature plummets rapidly. The cold weather that descended on northeast Europe in January rapidly froze the ground. Snow fell, heavily in places, and lakes and rivers that had begun to thaw now froze again. Conditions were perfect for an armoured offensive. The terrain was relatively flat, with few naturally defensible positions. The iron-hard ground could not be dug easily to create defensive fortifications, and the frozen rivers would not be obstacles for infantry. Once the initial German defences were overcome, there was every prospect of a rapid advance.

The *Ostfront* ran along a series of river lines. In the north, 3rd Panzer Army faced 1st Baltic Front across the Niemen on either side of Tilsit, and then south along the Ostfluss to Schillfelde. From there, the frontline ran across country, with 3rd Belorussian Front replacing 1st Baltic Front, into the gentle bulge that was all that remained of Cherniakhovsky's October offensive, facing Gumbinnen and Goldap. Raus' 3rd Panzer Army had minimal reserves available – its only significant armoured formation, 5th Panzer Division, was concentrated in the upper Inster valley with 68 operational tanks and another 23 undergoing repairs. In addition, the division had 36 new Jagdpanzer IV (Jg.Pz. IV) tank-destroyers, with the long-barrelled 75mm gun that armed the Panther tank but in a fixed, turretless mount. These vehicles were a mixed success. On the one hand, they were armed with a powerful gun; on the other hand, they carried a very limited amount of ammunition, and the long barrel that stretched far in front of the vehicle made it difficult to manoeuvre amongst trees and buildings.

There were also recurring problems with its mechanical reliability, though the reason for this is not clear. The chassis and engine were the same as the Pz. IV, which had been in service for the entire war and had a good reliability record. It seems that the quality of German vehicles built in the last months of the war may have been lower than in previous years. Crews also constantly complained about the poor quality of engine oil, which would have accounted for at least some of the mechanical problems experienced.

Near Gumbinnen, responsibility for the German frontline passed to 4th Army, with the front returning to waterways, this time the Rospuda and Bobr. Hossbach too had minimal reserves available to him. In the north, Hans-Horst von Necker's 1st Paratroop-Panzer Division *Hermann Göring* was about 15km behind the front. This division had 80 combat-ready tanks, with a further 65 in the workshops. Further south, between the Masurian Lakes and the front, Hossbach had two divisions held behind the lines, the Panzergrenadier Division *Brandenburg* and 18th Panzergrenadier Division. The former was a newly created division, formed around the disparate regiments of the *Brandenburg* division. The Brandenburgers had never before served as a single division, usually being deployed in battalion strength, often in raiding, anti-partisan or 'special forces' roles. They were now to form part of the newly enlarged Panzer Corps *Grossdeutschland*, but even before this corps had assembled properly it was ordered to disperse. There was a need for a division to be sent a little further south to the Willenberg–Chorzele area, and in the circumstances the only battle-ready part of the corps – the original *Grossdeutschland* Division – was ordered to move. This left only the Brandenburgers in the original assembly area, and they, too, were ordered to depart – on 13 January, they received orders to proceed to Angerburg for entrainment to Lodz, in view of the deteriorating situation in the south. In the increasingly chaotic circumstances that prevailed, sufficient trains were not available to complete the move until 19 January, and for six critical days, the division was unable to take part in combat in either its old area or its new area. To make matters worse, as will be seen, Hitler bizarrely dispatched another Panzer division in almost exactly the opposite direction, resulting in two of the few armoured formations available on the *Ostfront* being out of action at the beginning of the Soviet offensive. In an attempt to ensure that the *Grossdeutschland* Panzer Corps would have sufficient forces in its new operations in the Lodz area, 1st Paratroop-Panzer Division *Hermann Göring* was also moved to Lodz, at almost exactly the same time. Like Panzergrenadier Division *Brandenburg*, it spent critical days being transported by train, and in any event arrived too late to do anything other than be caught up in the retreat across southern Poland. Army Group Centre was thus deprived of two of its precious armoured divisions, which arrived in the south too late to be of any significant help to Army Group A.

The 18th Panzergrenadier Division, the other reserve formation of 4th Army, was almost completely destroyed during the disasters of summer 1944, and was reformed in September 1944. In January 1945 it was still far from being a cohesive, well-organized division. Its Panzer battalion had no tanks, but did have 31 assault guns, with a similar number under repair. For Josef Rauch, the commander, this was his first divisional command.

Another formation, 23rd Infantry Division, was in reserve just west of the Masurian Lakes. This division had suffered heavy losses in the offshore Baltic islands in the autumn of 1944, and was still reforming. Officially, it had not been handed back to the army by General Lasch's Wehrkreis I, and was barely at regimental strength.

Just south of the boundary between the German 4th and 2nd Armies, the Soviet 2nd Belorussian Front occupied a small bridgehead over the Bobr at Rozan. A second smaller bridgehead was a little further south, with the town of Pultusk separating them. The Wehrmacht watched as the Red Army steadily built up its forces in both bridgeheads through the winter. It was inevitable that they would be launch pads for a major attack. The only question was when the attack would come. Facing the bridgeheads was Weiss' 2nd Army, with two significant formations in reserve. Panzergrenadier Division *Grossdeutschland* was in the process of transferring south to an area astride the Polish–Prussian frontier. It remained a formidable formation, with 84 tanks, including 19 Tigers. Another 73 tanks were being repaired, and the division's tank-destroyer battalion had 38 of the excellent Hetzer turretless tank destroyers at its disposal; unfortunately, more than a third of these were unserviceable.

A little further south, Huber and his comrades in 7th Panzer Division had gathered around Zichenau. Huber's company was in a small village outside the town, billeted with Polish families:

They don't want to know anything about the Soviets – they have heard the reports of the many atrocities committed by the Russian soldiers and they know that they can't expect any good from the Russians if they come here. Such friendly thoughts amongst the civilian population naturally divert us from thinking about the end of the war. The Poles – and, secretly, ourselves too – have great doubts that we can achieve final victory and that the supply situation will be any better soon. You can see that the people are anxious that things might turn out differently from what we tell them. And there's so much that you can't say – it's dangerous to say what you think.[2]

It is hard to judge whether such a friendly relationship between the Poles and their German occupiers was widespread. In some parts of Poland, there appears to have been considerable fraternization between the two nationalities, but in others there was implacable hostility. The 7th Panzer Division had 66 tanks operational, but like all German armoured formations, it faced shortages of spare parts, and many of its vehicles were in the hands of the workshops.

These seven divisions – 5th Panzer Division, 1st Paratroop-Panzer Division *Hermann Göring*, Panzergenadier Division *Brandenburg*, 18th Panzergenadier Division, 23rd Infantry Division, Panzergrenadier Division *Grossdeutschland* and 7th Panzer Division – formed the entire reserve available to Army Group Centre. Even if they had been at full strength, they would hardly have constituted the major reserves that Gehlen and Fremde Heere Ost had recommended be placed in readiness for the coming Soviet assault. In their weakened state, even before two of them were transferred elsewhere, there was little prospect of them doing more than temporarily slowing down the Red Army.

The Red Army had made a huge effort to mislead German intelligence about the troops in the various bridgeheads along the *Ostfront*, and Glantz provides a thorough discussion of this effort.[3] In the north, the Germans successfully identified 43rd Army from the 1st Baltic Front along the Niemen valley. The 3rd Belorussian Front was assessed to have seven armies deployed.[4] This assessment was fairly accurate, and reflects the recent fighting in this sector – the units had clashed many times with their German counterparts, and were therefore well known to each other. However, German intelligence failed to detect the presence of I Tank Corps, believing that this formation was far to the north, near Riga.

Further south, the Germans had detected five armies from 2nd Belorussian Front,[5] and one from 1st Belorussian Front.[6] They were also aware of 2nd Shock Army and I Guards Tank Corps, held slightly behind the front. Yet Rokossovsky had inserted 70th Army on his left flank, without this being detected. Far more important, the Germans were unaware of the presence of the powerful 5th Guards Tank Army in its preparation areas behind the front.

The coming campaign would to a large extent be dictated by the terrain. In the north, the East Prussian defences would make any major Soviet penetration very costly, as Cherniakhovsky had discovered in October 1944, and the hills of the Pregel valley, and of the Masurian Lakes area a little further south, were ideally suited to defensive fighting. Across Poland, however, with the exception of some high ground just north of the Sandomierz bridgehead, the terrain was flat and open. The partisan-infested forests northwest of Warsaw would serve to hinder German lateral movements, and would therefore assist the Red Army.

The Soviet offensive had a staggered start, with different Fronts launching their attacks on different days. This was a deliberate policy – the Germans would either have to commit their reserves before they knew the full scale and shape of the Soviet assault, or would have to delay their deployment until the overall situation became clearer, by which time it might be too late. The original start date of the offensive, 20 January, was brought forward in early January. The official reason remained a desire to aid the western Allies, though the true cause remains a controversial issue, and as already discussed considerations about weather conditions probably played a large part in the final timing.

The first blow fell on 12 January in the south, where Konev's 1st Ukrainian Front smashed its way out of the Sandomierz bridgehead, about 180km south of Warsaw. The commander of Konev's artillery, Ivan Semenovich Varennikov, had enormous resources at his disposal, with up to 300 barrels of fuel per kilometre of front and plentiful ammunition. The 1st Ukrainian Front had packed a huge force into the bridgehead, and after one of the most intensive bombardments of the war, which inflicted 25 per cent casualties amongst the frontline troops, Konev's forces erupted through the German lines. By the end of the first day, the breach in the German front was at least 50km wide. General Walter Nehring's XXIV Panzer Corps managed to concentrate some of its units in Kielce; bypassed by the Soviet torrent, Nehring held on until 16 January, when he ordered his command to withdraw towards the northwest. Unsure of the location of any other German units, the 'wandering cauldron' began an epic march, moving mainly by night and trying to avoid contact with Soviet units.

Zhukov's 1st Belorussian Front's initial attack was less spectacular, but just as effective. The one-hour barrage that preceded the attack fell on fog-shrouded German lines, and as the fog began to clear, smoke and dust rose into the cold sky to obscure the vision of both attackers and defenders. By the end of 14 January, Soviet forces on the northern side of the Magnuszew bridgehead had secured crossings over the River Pilica, despite determined resistance from the staff of the Urban Warfare School that Pantenius' 337th Volksgrenadier Division had established in Warsaw during the autumn. North of Warsaw, the Soviet artillery bombardment rapidly disrupted all communications between the frontline and rear areas. A battalion of 73rd Infantry Division found itself isolated, but still managed to beat off the initial Soviet probes, taking several prisoners. The account of the fighting records that there was nowhere to hold these prisoners, who were herded into a potato cellar, but remains silent about their fate.[7] Unable to make contact with other units, the battalion commander ordered his men to fight their way back to German lines. A small group from battalion headquarters eventually managed to escape.

Pantenius and his regiment from 337th Volksgrenadier Division withdrew on foot to the town of Tarczyn, some 25km south of Warsaw. They came across other retreating German units, including a battery of heavy howitzers, a flak unit and two companies of 88mm anti-tank guns, stranded in the town by fuel shortages. When the town came under threat on 16 January, Pantenius and the artillery commanders had no choice but to destroy the valuable guns, as there were no means for moving them.[8] His regiment now set out on foot, heading northwest, aware that Soviet tanks were already operating further west. While his exhausted men rested in a small wood, Pantenius had a lucky encounter with four assault guns that had become separated from 251st Infantry Division. Near Chylice, a Soviet reconnaissance unit crossed in front of Pantenius, moving northeast. Pantenius promptly dispatched the four assault guns, supported by an infantry company, to attack the Russian column from the rear, while the rest of his regiment continued its retreat.[9] Shortly after, he linked up with the Urban Warfare School, and then ran into Soviet armour:

> I was with the last battalion in my Volkswagen when we heard loud noises of combat, the firing and impact of tank shells, and soon we could also see the group of T-34s that had caught us. The tanks were apparently from a tank battalion that had been summoned to help the ambushed reconnaissance detachment. They had overrun the anti-tank defences of the Urban Warfare School and were now thrusting towards us. The frozen terrain favoured both sides. The men immediately scattered, and the vehicles too tried to drive past on all sides. As the Russian tanks had no turret stabilization at that time and were firing on the move, they hit little of significance, but the impact on morale was immediately apparent, as the retreat now turned to flight; there was no cover, the few bushes and trees barely obscuring sight, and the anti-tank troops tried to score a few hits with their 'stovepipes' [Panzerschrek anti-tank weapons], but had little success. Attempts to assemble the scattered soldiers … were only partially successful. Although my Volkswagen represented a large target, we were not hit, the driver Peper turning tightly to right and left – the open terrain meant that the tank that was aiming at us could not line us up. Then, completely unexpectedly, a company of Hetzers appeared as our saviour angels, and immediately went into action against the T-34s. They were so quick and agile that the enemy tanks couldn't match them. The marksmanship of the Hetzers was markedly better than that of the Russians, a few T-34s were hit, and most turned around and were not seen again. Such were the last-gasp fortunes of war.[10]

Accompanied by the Hetzers, Pantenius and the rest of his column continued their retreat to the northwest. Other units were less fortunate, and were overwhelmed or scattered by the freely-ranging Soviet armoured forces.

Further south, Nehring's 'wandering cauldron' slowly made its escape. Fortunately for the German group, the weather was in their favour, with light snowfalls and mist.

In addition, substantial gaps were opening up between the Soviet armoured forces pouring west and the infantry that was following, and it was possible to move in this small breathing space. After about 36 hours, Nehring discovered strong enemy units in his path, about 40km north of Kielce. He now turned west, receiving welcome reinforcements in the shape of the remnants of Hermann Recknagel's XLII Corps; Recknagel had ordered his men to destroy their heavy equipment and to set off on foot. Of his five divisions, only 342nd Infantry Division retained any significant fighting capability.

Another huge bonus for Nehring was the discovery of an intact army supply depot at Odrowaz, and here the fuel tanks of the remaining vehicles were topped up, eliminating at least one concern. Nehring received a further boost on the night of 18–19 January, when he was finally able to establish brief radio contact with the rest of the world, speaking to Luftwaffe General Hans Seidemann in Poznan. Seidemann was unable to advise Nehring of the exact locations of Soviet forces, but was at least able to make other German units aware of the existence of Nehring's group.[11] The 'wandering cauldron' continued to move at night and hid by day in whatever cover was available, stretched out over at least 50km of roads.

The crisis was spreading along the front. The main routes heading west from Warsaw were now severed by 2nd Guards Tank Army. German forces around the Polish capital, under the aegis of XLVI Panzer Corps, attempted to pull back to the second line of positions on 16 January, with the intention of strengthening the line currently held by the weak 391st Security Division. There was a conflict between the need to keep open lines of retreat, and the requirement to destroy bridges over the River Szura before they fell into Soviet hands. Fuel shortages plagued the retreating German columns, and part of 337th Volksgrenadier Division's artillery regiment was overtaken by Soviet forces near Warsaw and overwhelmed.[12] Meanwhile, as soon as he became aware of 9th Army's plans to pull back, Hitler sent a direct order to the commander of the Warsaw 'fortress', Generalleutnant Friedrich Weber, to hold the city at all costs. Fortunately for Weber and his men, the order arrived too late to be put into effect. The garrison had already destroyed much of its equipment that it was unable to carry, including most of its anti-tank guns. Hitler's fury fell on the frontline generals. Smilo Freiherr von Lüttwitz, the commander of Ninth Army, was recalled from the frontline, with General Theodore Busse replacing him; General Walter Fries, commander of XLVI Panzer Corps, and Generalleutnant Weber were arrested and court-martialled. Fries was ably defended by General Otto von Knobelsdorff, and was acquitted, but Weber was found guilty of negligence, in that he failed to ask for clarification even though the orders he received were completely out of date. Despite vindictive instructions from Berlin, he escaped the death penalty.

Confused orders continued to arrive at the frontline from Berlin, hopelessly out of touch with the pace of events on the ground. Eventually, most of XLVI Panzer Corps struggled back to the line of the Szura, but Zhukov's armour had already seized bridgeheads, rendering the line untenable. Soviet forces pressed the retreating Germans back towards the Vistula, forcing them to cross and attempt to move west along the northern bank, with the intention of reaching Plock before the enemy. The town came under heavy pressure from Soviet forces, and on 20 January, 337th Volksgrenadier Division was forced to pull back to the northern bank of the Vistula.

Von Saucken arrived with elements of his *Grossdeutschland* corps in the Lodz area on 16 January. Panzergrenadier Division *Brandenburg* was deployed piecemeal as it arrived, under the mistaken belief that there were other German units to the east. The advancing Soviet spearheads roared through the Brandenburgers' positions that night, scattering them in minutes. Von Saucken himself arrived in Lodz on 18 January. He was aware that his two divisions were still in the process of arriving, and that they were too scattered to be able to achieve very much. His main force, Panzergrenadier Division *Brandenburg*, had already lost nearly half its infantry. He was also aware that Nehring's group was still struggling towards him, and briefly considered trying to drive east to link up with with the formation; however, news that a Soviet force was threatening Sieradz, some distance to the southwest of Lodz, forced a decision. All elements of the *Brandenburg* and *Hermann Göring* divisions were to assemble south of Lodz, and then fall back to the Warthe valley around Sieradz, where they would hold on until Nehring reached them. With his own flanks completely bypassed, von Saucken retreated as slowly as he dared, and 22 January Hauptmann Friedrich Müller-Rochholz, commander of the *Brandenburg* armoured combat engineer battalion, made contact with the leading elements of Nehring's cauldron in Marcenin.[13]

It would take several days for all of Nehring's command, including its long tail of stragglers, to cross the river. But their ordeal was not yet over. Von Saucken's position had in turn been bypassed by the swift Soviet advance, and a further long retreat lay ahead. The combined force finally reached the Oder crossings at Glogau on 26 January. As they approached the river, Nehring's men passed a refugee column that had been overrun by Soviet tanks. The roadside was littered with wrecked and crushed vehicles and carts, and strewn with dead civilians.[14]

By the end of January, Konev's and Zhukov's Fronts had completed their decisive breakout from the Vistula bridgeheads, aided enormously by Hitler's insistence that all German forces remained concentrated close to the frontline, well within range of the initial Soviet bombardment. Although some German forces – the Nehring and von Saucken groups were merely the largest and best-known – succeeded in fighting their way west, they were able to offer little resistance. Zhukov's armies erupted across central Poland, enveloped their goal of Poznan, and pressed on to the middle reaches of the Oder. To the south, Konev reached the upper Oder within 12 days, considerably faster than had originally been planned, hindered more by his lengthening supply lines than German opposition.

Further north, Cherniakhovsky's 3rd Belorussian Front had spent much of the winter preparing for another attempt to break into East Prussia, and launched its assault a day after Konev's troops ripped apart 4th Panzer Army far to the south. Army Group Centre had lost key divisions – Panzer Division *Hermann Göring* and Panzergrenadier Division *Brandenburg* – on the eve of the Soviet attack. By way of replacements, it was to receive 24th Panzer Division, which spent the winter in heavy fighting east of Budapest. This formation had a striking lineage. It originated from the Prussian 1st Cavalry Brigade, subsequently enlarged to 1st Cavalry Division. At every stage of its evolution, the formation prided itself on its close family atmosphere – most of its officers and senior NCOs were recruited from East Prussia, and their remarkable closeness was successfully nurtured and preserved by the division's commanders throughout the war. In 1941, the division found itself unable to find sufficient fodder in the Soviet Union for its horses, and its officers were asked for their opinions about what should happen to the division – surely a unique exercise. In October 1941, the troops bade farewell to their surviving horses, and were shipped west by train for equipment and training as a Panzer division. They were back in the Soviet Union in early 1942, where they became involved in the ill-fated drive to the Volga; most of the division was destroyed in Stalingrad.

Using elements of the division that had been outside the Stalingrad encirclement, 24th Panzer Division was rebuilt, returning to the *Ostfront* in 1943. On 10 January 1945, the division began to hand over its vehicles and heavy equipment to 23rd Panzer Division, and the first trainload of personnel headed for East Prussia two days later, arriving in East Prussia almost exactly as Cherniakhovsky's assault began. The division was intended to receive fresh equipment on its arrival in East Prussia, and it was inevitable, given the prevailing state of affairs, that it was impossible to re-equip the division completely. Indeed, it was remarkable that any vehicles could be found at all. For the men of 24th Panzer Division, most of whom were East Prussians, this was a homecoming of mixed emotions. After their years in the depths of the Soviet Union and the Balkans, glimpses of their homeland through the train windows must have raised terrible fears: the war had come to their own hearths.

The redeployment of German divisions at such a critical moment was disastrous. The two divisions dispatched to southern Poland arrived too late and too piecemeal to make a difference, and whilst it is unlikely that their presence in East Prussia would have altered the final result of the coming campaign, they would have been able to check the Soviet advance rather more effectively than they did in and around Lodz. The 24th Panzer Division, which could have reached the Lodz area more quickly than the divisions from the north, arrived in East Prussia with no heavy equipment, and was able to contribute little more than a battlegroup to the coming fighting. Valuable trains and rolling stock were deployed in moving the formations in almost reverse directions.

The reasons for these movements are hard to fathom with any certainty. They originated with Hitler, who – increasingly towards the end of the war – seems to have believed that German soldiers would fight more effectively if they were defending the area of Germany from where they originated. It is almost impossible to find any other justification for these troop movements.

On the evening of 12 January, as news began to arrive of Konev's assault out of the Sandomierz bridgehead, Soviet deserters alerted the Germans manning 4th Army's defences of an imminent attack. As was the case further south, Soviet commanders deployed their forces to guarantee maximum advantage. The most northerly army of Cherniakhovsky's Front, 39th Army, left just one formation covering much of its frontage, so that the bulk of the army could concentrate at the southern extreme of the army's area. South of Goldap, 31st Army held an extended frontline, where it was probably outnumbered in places by the German divisions facing it; this allowed Cherniakhovsky to achieve far higher concentrations of troops facing Gumbinnen and Schlossberg.

The Soviet plan was to launch two major attacks against East Prussia. The first would see Cherniakhovsky's Front batter its way into the Inster valley, and thence to Königsberg. Despite its heavy defences, this route remained the traditional invasion path into East Prussia, and had the advantage of avoiding the lakes and swamps further south. More importantly, the attack would ensure that valuable German divisions were tied down in heavy combat, and would thus not be available for mobile operations elsewhere. The second blow directed against East Prussia was more powerful, with Rokossovsky's 2nd Belorussian Front thrusting out of the Narew bridgeheads and driving northwest to the lower Vistula valley, ultimately aiming to capture the city of Danzig and isolate East Prussia from the rest of the Reich. Aware that he faced strongly fortified positions, Cherniakhovsky ensured that his three assault groups[15] were tightly concentrated. Behind them were the exploitation forces, waiting to be committed after a breakthrough was achieved.[16]

In the south, Rokossovsky concentrated his forces in the two bridgeheads either side of Pultusk. North of Pultusk were 3rd, 48th and 2nd Shock Armies, facing 129th

3RD BELORUSSIAN FRONT, JANUARY 1945

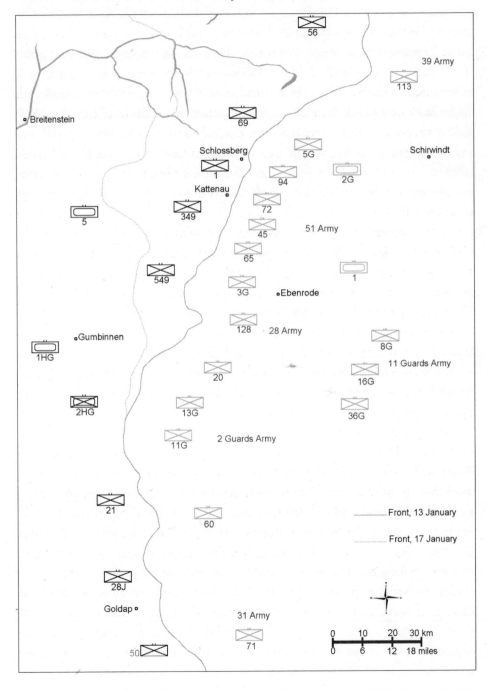

and 299th Infantry Divisions, and part of 5th Jäger Division. The rest of this last formation extended the German line south of Pultusk, where it was linked to 35th Infantry Division. Beyond this lay 232nd Infantry and 592nd Volksgrenadier Divisions. South of Pultusk, Rokossovsky had massed 65th and 70th Armies, with 5th Guards Tank Army close behind. Each of Rokossovsky's frontline armies had a tank, mechanized or cavalry corps, which would be held back until the second day of the battle. 5th Guards Tank Army would not enter the battle until the fifth day, by which time it was expected that all major resistance would have been overcome. It would then exploit westward, aiming to capture the string of large towns along the Vistula, ultimately reaching the Baltic coast in the Danzig area. East Prussia, and the German forces within it, would thus be cut off from the Reich. This would prevent any concentration of German forces developing north of Zhukov's 1st Belorussian Front – vital if a drive on towards Berlin was to be made at an early date.

Alerted by deserters, 3rd Panzer Army and 4th Army quietly moved out of their frontline positions late on 12 January and into their main battle positions. When the two-hour Soviet bombardment fell on their lines, it struck mainly empty trenches. The thunder of shellfire was audible more than 30km away. The men of 5th Panzer Division, billeted in and around Breitenstein, were awakened by the noise and, even before they received any orders, made preparations to redeploy.

At first light, on a misty morning, Soviet infantry felt their way forward. German guns bombarded their forming-up areas with good effect, and Soviet gains during the day were minimal; the only penetrations occurred in areas where the Germans had deliberately abandoned untenable positions. As in the autumn battles, Schlossberg was the scene of bitter fighting. A battalion of 1st Infantry Division's 22nd Fusilier Regiment held on grimly amidst the ruins, mounting a counter-attack to recapture the southern edge of the town when Soviet forces threatened to break through. Further south, though, where 549th Volksgrenadier Division was deployed northeast of Gumbinnen, the Soviet III Guards Rifle Corps made some headway near Kattenau. The German 61st Infantry Division, defending the approaches to Gumbinnen, found its northern flank exposed, and was forced to realign its front.

General Matzky, commander of XXVI Corps, immediately committed his only corps-level reserves – a single fusilier battalion – to a counter-attack to restore the front. Commanded by Hauptmann Schröder, the battalion carried out a difficult approach march under repeated air attack. In the face of heavy Soviet artillery bombardment, its attack made little headway. Matzky now requested further help from 3rd Panzer Army headquarters, and Raus had no alternative but to commit his only reserve formation, 5th Panzer Division.

Early on 14 January, the division attacked in two battlegroups. The left battlegroup retook Kattenau, despite constant Soviet shelling that made all movements difficult. The right battlegroup, moving southeast towards Altpreussenfelde, a small village a little to the south of Kattenau, made good progress at first, but was brought to a standstill when Soviet tanks emerged from Neutrakhenen on its open flank. The division's tank-hunter battalion was assigned to the hard-pressed 349th Volksgrenadier Division, immediately to the north. Although the deployment of 5th Panzer Division allowed Matzky to restore his front, 3rd Panzer Army now had no reserves available to cover its entire front. Meanwhile, the fighting around Schlossberg raged on. The Soviet XCIV Rifle Corps took Blumenfeld, immediately southwest of Schlossberg. The 22nd Fusilier Regiment launched a counter-attack, retaking the village in bloody fighting late in the evening. Two days of combat had cost both sides heavy losses, but for the Germans these casualties were irreplaceable.

The 14th of January was also the start date for Rokossovsky's offensive further south. The Soviet infantry, following another heavy bombardment of German positions, made the initial assault. General Sokolsky, Rokossovsky's artillery commander, had 240 guns and mortars per kilometre of front. As was the case the previous day, Soviet deserters had warned the Germans of the coming attack, and most units were safely in their main battle positions. German artillery struck back against known Soviet concentrations, but there weren't enough guns with enough ammunition to achieve more than a nuisance effect. Fog and snow prevented Soviet aircraft from being used, and in some areas the German defences held up well. In the bridgehead north of Pultusk, around Rozan, the Soviet XXXV Rifle Corps made good progress, pushing deep through the snowstorms into the positions of the German 129th Infantry Division. Just to the south, 48th Army and 2nd Shock Army pushed back the German 7th Infantry Division, only to trigger an immediate counter-attack by 507th Heavy Tank Battalion, which ran into a Soviet tank battalion equipped with JS-2 tanks. The superior guns of the Soviet tanks – 122mm compared with the 88mm guns of the German Tiger tanks – were critically disadvantaged by their slower rate of fire. Fighting in the foggy landscape, the Tigers knocked out 22 JS-2s at almost point-blank range, without losing a single vehicle.

The southern attack by Rokossovsky's 65th and 70th Armies, from the bridgehead south of Pultusk, fell on three German divisions of XXVII Corps, now commanded by General Maximilian Felzmann. Batov, commander of 65th Army, described the opening phase of the battle in his memoirs:

Our artillery preparation lasted an hour and a half. Thirty minutes of this was sufficient for us to shoot up the most forward German defensive lines, and it was so effective that the

THE ROZAN–SEROCK BRIDGEHEADS, JANUARY 1945

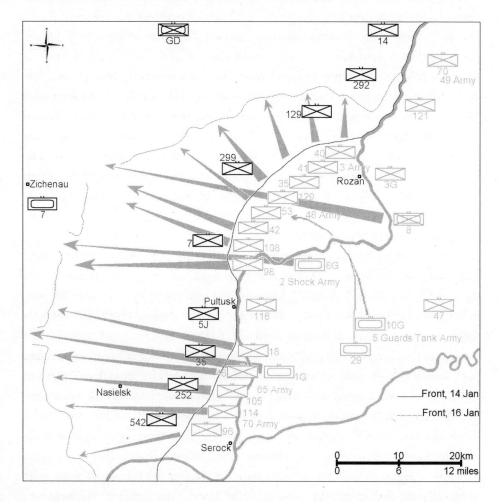

enemy was unable to respond for some considerable time. The infantry advanced behind
a wall of fire, which extended to a depth of between one and a half and two kilometres.
In front of the rifle divisions, the army's two tank regiments operated on the main attack
axis with our heavy self-propelled guns, destroying any remaining machine-gun positions
and field guns. Our artillery fire provided constant support for the infantry. Guns from
regiments, divisions and corps had three or four 'basic loads' of ammunition, with a further
seven held at army group level. 'You can have as many shells as you can transport,' General
Sokolsky had said when discussing the artillery fire plan… This unprecedentedly heavy
artillery bombardment was a particular hallmark of our January offensive, for which we
used a special artillery corps as well as nine independent gun regiments and brigades, not
including anti-aircraft guns. The coordination of such a mass of artillery required a

widespread communications system, which Borissov had masterfully organized: 1,188 radio sets were in use in the ranks of our army. The artillery swiftly received fire mission requests from corps, divisions, regiments, and even battalion commanders.[17]

Dmitri Fedorovich Alexeyev's CV Rifle Corps advanced swiftly towards Nasielsk. As his men approached the town, they reported a counter-attack by German armour. This attack was by Major Wilhelm Kröhne's 190th Assault Gun Brigade, and posed little real threat to the Soviet division. Alexeyev took no chances, however, deploying his anti-tank reserves in response. As the German attack faded away, 44th Guards Rifle Division moved into Nasielsk, securing the town before nightfall. To the north of Alexeyev's corps was XLVI Rifle Corps, which also advanced steadily, picking its way through the first line of German defences by the end of the day.

All three German divisions in the path of 65th Army's attack – 35th Infantry Division in the north, 252nd Infantry Division in the centre and 542nd Volksgrenadier Division in the south – were driven back a few kilometres, but the German front remained intact. Local reserves, like 190th Assault Gun Brigade, were committed to the battleline, providing desperately needed anti-tank firepower for the infantry. Overall, Rokossovsky had made modest progress, compared with the shattering blows that Zhukov and Konev had dealt the German frontline further south. Nevertheless, he had reason to be satisfied. Many of his armoured formations were now moving into the bridgeheads, ready to exploit the previous day's successes. Behind the Narew valley, he still had 5th Guards Tank Army, waiting to be committed. Given that his opponents had no further reserves available, a breakthrough was only a matter of time.

Walter Weiss' 2nd Army had two armoured formations in reserve – the *Grossdeutschland* Division, moved south from its original position, and 7th Panzer Division near Zichenau. Both were now ordered into action, though to the frustration of both division commanders they were unable to deploy their divisions as a single formation. Instead, they were forced to 'loan' armour and anti-tank units to the hard-pressed infantry, greatly reducing the strike power of the rest of the division. But without this armoured support, there was no prospect of the infantry divisions being able to hold on in the face of powerful attacks by the better-equipped all-arms Soviet units facing them. From its holding area on the old Prussian frontier, *Grossdeutschland* was ordered south to deal with the deep penetration in 129th Infantry Division's sector. The attack by the division's Panzer-Fusilier Regiment ran into Soviet forces moving in the opposite direction, and only the commitment of the division's Tiger tanks allowed the German attack to make any progress. Eventually, after making a little ground, the combined group was forced back, its remaining tanks almost out of fuel. The Panzergrenadier regiment, supported by the division's Panther tank battalion, also made some progress, but once more at the cost of heavy casualties. Both battlegroups found themselves tied down in the frontline.

Meanwhile, the absurd game of rearranging divisions continued. At 0300hrs on 16 January, 2nd Army Headquarters received a telephone call from General Walther Wenck, Guderian's Chief of Staff. He told Otto Heidkämper, Army Group Centre's Chief of Staff, that the order to move *Brandenburg* also applied to *Grossdeutschland*; the division was to be pulled out of line immediately and transferred to Army Group A. Heidkämper was aghast, and protested that this would deprive his army group of most of its armoured reserves. Given the current deployment of *Grossdeutschland*, it would also create a hole in the German lines. Wenck responded that a major enemy breakthrough had occurred in southern Poland, and troops were urgently required to remedy the situation there. In any case, he pointed out glumly, this redeployment order came directly from Hitler, so there was little point in arguing about it.

The withdrawal order gradually trickled down the chain of command to the hard-pressed battalions of *Grossdeutschland*. In many cases, they were already falling back under Soviet pressure, and suffered further losses as they withdrew beyond the Orzyc river line. Any prospect of extracting the entire division was remote, and the order was soon forgotten in the continuing turmoil.

The 7th Panzer Division was also in action. During the night of 14–15 December, the division's two tank battalions slowly edged forward. The Panther battalion had a sharp encounter with a Soviet division, which fell back after a brisk firefight. The two battalions assembled together in a field shortly before dawn and refuelled, while the regiment commander, Oberstleutnant Graf Pückler, carefully surveyed the terrain through his binoculars.

Pückler was an unlucky and sometimes tactless commander. The Gestapo arrested him after the failed July plot against Hitler, and many of his family and close friends remained in custody after he was released. Pückler was serving in a staff post at the time, and he wrote to his commanding officer to protest about this. The letter was forwarded to Guderian, who realized that even to write such a letter was to invite a death sentence. He summoned Pückler to him, and placed him under arrest for two weeks on an administrative charge, to prevent him from falling into the hands of the Gestapo; when he was released, Pückler was sent to 25th Panzer Regiment. Unfortunately for both Pückler and the regiment, he had no experience of handling groups of armoured vehicles.

Pückler had been in his new post only two months, and the junior officers of the regiment grew increasingly nervous as the sky lightened. There had been a warning that there might be German-laid minefields and anti-tank ditches in the open ground across which the regiment was to attack, and Pückler naturally wished to clarify this. Due to the haste with which the counter-attack was organized, there had been insufficient time to obtain maps showing all of the defensive positions created since the autumn. A motorcycle rider, dispatched to division headquarters for confirmation, failed to return. Finally, after receiving the required assurances over the radio, Pückler gave the order to advance: the Panther battalion would move forward on the right, the Pz. IV battalion on the left. As it turned out, Pückler's caution was justified. There was indeed a German minefield, which resulted in one Panther being lost.

Although there was still widespread mist and poor visibility, the delay in beginning the attack had cost the Germans any chance of surprising their opponents, who had spent the night reinforcing their forward positions. As they moved forward through the morning mist, Huber and the other tank crews of 7th Panzer Division could barely make out trees to their front and either side. There was no sign of the enemy. Twice during the morning advance, Huber's tank stalled, and he and the driver had to strip the carburettor to remove ice, a sign of water contamination in the tank's fuel. Slowly, the Germans probed forward about 2km.

General Ivan Fediuninsky, commander of 2nd Second Shock Army, had spent the night of 14–15 January trying in vain to obtain information about the exact positions of his leading formations. The weather had grounded his air assets, and the assault by 7th Panzer Division's tank regiment struck, by chance, at the exact seam between his two leading rifle corps. It was an unpleasant shock for Fediuninsky, who had been advised by his superiors that 7th Panzer Division had been transferred elsewhere along the front. Just in time, he rushed forward part of 60th Anti-Tank Division and 94th Heavy Tank Battalion.[18]

When the leading German tanks were almost in sight of the Narew, Soviet anti-tank guns hidden along the edges of the woods on either flank suddenly opened fire. Within moments, several German tanks were hit, while the rest attempted to withdraw. Huber's tank plunged into an anti-tank ditch, hidden in the deep snow, and its engine finally gave up the struggle. Another Pz. IV came to its aid, and towed it back to the regiment's starting position. In just a few minutes, Huber's company lost six of its 13 tanks. The regiment's other companies had suffered similar losses. Still under tow, Huber and his comrades withdrew along the same road that they had used for their approach march. The rest of the regiment regrouped and prepared for another attack. A confused night action followed between the German tanks and Soviet infantry.

Rokossovsky's armies were now making good progress, as their armoured elements entered the battle. The I Guards Tank Corps was committed in 65th Army's sector, south of Pultusk, and swiftly broke through the German 35th Infantry Division near Nasielsk, though the remaining assault guns of 190th Assault Gun Brigade continued to put up stiff resistance, knocking out 25 Soviet tanks during the day. One of I Guards Tank Corps' brigades drove off the last of the German assault guns, and Rokossovsky now ordered Batov to send the tank corps west with all speed to capture Thorn, on the middle Vistula. Batov had mixed feelings about this – on the one hand, the main German defences had been ruptured, but on the other hand, the departure of the tank corps would leave his army with far fewer tanks. Several small rivers lay across his line of advance, and Batov was aware that the Germans would attempt to rally their retreating units along each line. Without the firepower of the tank corps, 65th Army would rely on the weight of its artillery, and the pace of its advance, to prevent a new German frontline from coalescing.

With both of its flanks threatened, particularly to the north where the Soviet VIII Guards Tank Corps went into action, 5th Jäger Division was forced to abandon Pultusk, allowing the two Soviet bridgeheads to coalesce. Yet another powerful Soviet formation, VIII Mechanized Corps, moved across the Narew into 48th Army's sector, and in the northern part of the bridgehead, III Guards Cavalry Corps prepared to burst through the hard-pressed frontline still tenuously held by *Grossdeutschland* and 129th Infantry Division. By contrast, the German 2nd Army had no more reserves to deploy.

After a wild night action on 15–16 January, 7th Panzer Division's remaining tanks and other armoured vehicles concentrated for another desperate counter-attack. A reconnaissance group had moved forward before dawn, but as a bitterly cold morning light spread across the battlefield, Pückler was unable to establish radio contact with the spearhead. Oberleutnant Jakob, Huber's dour company commander, was towards the right of the battlegroup, where he noticed movement on the flank – a group of T-34s was outflanking the German armour to the south. Despite this alarming development, Pückler still refused to move, and Major Brandes, one of the battalion commanders, ran over to his tank to urge him into action. Finally, as mortar shells began to fall on the assembled vehicles – one shell landed in the interior of a half-track, resulting in several casualties – Pückler finally ordered a withdrawal. Several tanks were hit and knocked out as they pulled back, including Jakob's vehicle. When they paused to regroup, the survivors found they had been reduced to only ten vehicles.

The outflanking movement was carried out by part of General Panov's I Guards Tank Corps, which now pressed on westwards, having smashed 7th Panzer Division's assembled forces without losing a single tank. The remnants of 7th Panzer Division pulled back towards Zichenau. Schmitz, the commander of the missing reconnaissance detachment, had actually passed right through the Soviet lines, and managed to rejoin the division after a circuitous journey.

In the north, Cherniakhovsky continued to make little headway against the tough German defences on 15 January. The Soviet exploitation forces had still not entered the battle, mainly because the German line continued to hold firm, though Kattenau was now back in Soviet hands. German losses were becoming increasingly serious; 549th Volksgrenadier Division had to shorten its front, handing over responsibility of an extended sector to 5th Panzer Division. Whilst this allowed the frontline to be held, it further prevented any possibility of 5th Panzer Division – 3rd Panzer Army's only mobile force – from being pulled back into reserve. The battle for Schlossberg was also coming to an end. During the night of 15–16 January, the exhausted defenders were ordered to withdraw before they were completely encircled, and carrying their wounded with them they retreated towards the west.

The 549th Volksgrenadier Division remained under heavy pressure on 16 and 17 January, needing assistance from 5th Panzer Division to deal with several Soviet penetrations. There was another major Soviet penetration a little to the north, along the seam between 349th Volksgrenadier Division and 1st Infantry Division, and 5th Panzer Division had to dispatch an armoured battlegroup to restore the front. During the afternoon, 349th Volksgrenadier Division came under pressure again, and once more the armoured battlegroup went into action. It was increasingly clear that the German infantry was nearing the end of its strength.

The frontline in the Gumbinnen–Schlossberg sector was slowly being levered back towards the west, and as a result of this General Raus requested permission to withdraw the divisions of his northern corps from their positions along the Niemen, particularly at the eastern end of their sector, where they were in danger of being enveloped. Hitler refused. Raus quietly started to transfer the forces anyway. The first formation to be moved out of the endangered salient was a battalion of 56th Infantry Division, which was immediately deployed to help 349th Volksgrenadier Division.

Meanwhile, Rokossovsky's offensive was unfolding comparatively smoothly. With *Grossdeutschland* and 7th Panzer Division tied down, Soviet armoured forces were able to dictate the course of the battle. VIII Guards Tank Corps and VIII Mechanized Corps pushed forward through the depleted German lines towards Zichenau, while General Vasily Volsky's 5th Guards Tank Army now moved towards the frontline, ready to erupt through to the west. Only the weak 18th Panzergrenadier Division lay in its way.

By the end of 17 January, the German frontline had effectively burst apart either side of Zichenau, and 5th Guards Tank Army motored through the gap. General Semen

Nikolaevich Borshchev, commander of 46th Rifle Division, recorded that just in the area facing his corps German losses amounted to 160 tanks, 48 half-tracks and about 4,000 dead, with more than 2,000 prisoners.[19] The remnants of 7th Panzer Division fell back through Plonsk, where three Pz. IVs under Jakob's command guarded the Modlin road all night, even though they were completely out of ammunition.[20] From there, the division retreated westwards in several fragments; 25th Panzer Regiment, near Sierpe, had only five Pz. IVs available for combat. Supported by a few half-tracks and self-propelled guns, Püchler led this little battlegroup forward early on 19 January in another hopeless counter-attack. As the five tanks advanced, they came to a snowy field, bordered by woodland. Püchler ordered the leading tank to advance. Its commander protested that he thought the enemy occupied the woods ahead, and that if he advanced he would probably be shot up. Püchler insisted, and the advance continued. After moving forward only 40m, the lead tank was hit. Fortunately for the crew, the round bounced off. Seconds later, there was a second hit, knocking the turret from the vehicle. Miraculously, the occupants of the turret were only lightly wounded. To his astonishment, the driver found that the turretless tank was still mobile, and turned back. Meanwhile, other Soviet armour deployed along the edge of a wood to the right engaged the small group. Püchler's tank was also hit on the turret, killing the regimental commander, and Leutnant Preiss, one of the crew, was badly wounded. The rest of the crew pulled their wounded comrade from the stricken tank and carried him to a nearby half-track, which took him to the rear. They feared they would never see him again, but Preiss made a full recovery and returned to the regiment just days before the end of the war.[21]

Reinhardt, commander of Army Group Centre, telephoned Hitler on 17 January. His Chief of Staff, Otto Heidkämper, recorded in his diary:

In the evening, there was a one-hour telephone conversation between the Führer and the OB [Reinhardt]. 'You must excuse my difficulty in understanding you,' began the Führer, 'You know, Generaloberst, that my hearing has been bad since 20 July. As a result, I'm handing over the receiver to General Burgdorf.' The OB described the situation ... he requested permission for 4th Army to pull back from its advanced positions in the Nowogrod–Gehlenburg line, to Goldap, in order to release three divisions as a reserve for 2nd Army. He had no other means of reinforcing 2nd Army. The enemy would otherwise break through, threatening the rear areas. Burgdorf [replied]: 'As a result of five years' experience, the Führer is convinced that every retreat results in no release of forces. These retreats lead only to a break-up of the front and have always brought catastrophe to the front.' The OB persisted in his request. But General Burgdorf answered that the Führer was not going to change his mind. I had the impression that Burgdorf conveyed only those words from the OB to the Führer that reinforced his impressions.[22]

Reinhardt didn't even bother to respond to Hitler's final suggestion, that he use the Volkssturm to reinforce 2nd Army.

In any event, it was too late. The rupture of 2nd Army's lines resulted in the Germans falling back along two axes. North of the breakthrough, German units pulled back into East Prussia, while south of the breakthrough German divisions were swept west, struggling to stay ahead of Rokossovsky's forces to their north and Zhukov's forces to their south. The 18th Panzergrenadier Division could do little more than delay the Soviet drive towards the northwest. Further south, Major Kröhne and his indefatigable assault guns claimed to have shot up another 20 Soviet tanks, but nothing could disguise the magnitude of the Soviet breakthrough.

Cherniakhovsky, by contrast, continued to struggle. On 17 January, he committed II Guards Tank Corps to the fighting. Supported by the 250 tanks of the corps, the Soviet infantry of 5th Army managed to push forward a few kilometres into the lines of 349th Volksgrenadier Division, but at a heavy price, and a breakthrough continued to elude them. Meanwhile, belated permission arrived for Raus to start withdrawing troops from his most northeasterly positions, something that was already underway. The rest of 56th Infantry Division pulled out, but as its southern neighbour, 69th Infantry Division, began to withdraw, it came under heavy attack. In confused fighting, the division headquarters was overrun and broken up. Nevertheless, it was an opportunity for 3rd Panzer Army to pull back to a shorter line. Despite this, other than the battalions of 56th Infantry Division, which were immediately fed into line to support 349th Volksgrenadier Division, there were no reserves available.

Cherniakhovsky, by contrast, still had most of his exploitation forces waiting to be committed. General Vasily Vasilevich Butkov's I Tank Corps had already moved north from its previous holding area, and Cherniakhovsky now became aware of the shift of the German 56th Infantry Division. In a move reminiscent of his imaginative improvisation during *Bagration* and the Goldap–Gumbinnen battles of the previous year, he ordered the entire 11th Guards Army to deploy in the north. If the main German defences on the Insterberg–Königsberg axis were too tough, he would bypass them. II Guards Tank Corps, considerably weakened by its futile assault on 349th Volksgrenadier Division and by the determined counter-attacks of 5th Panzer Division's armoured battlegroup, was also pulled out of line and sent north.

I Tank Corps launched its attack on 18 January, and made swift progress through the disorganized lines of 6th Infantry Division and secured crossings over the Inster.

The following day, as 11th Guards Army and II Guards Tank Corps also began to make ground, the German divisions holding the line north of the heavily contested battlefield of the preceding days (69th Infantry Division and 549th and 561st Volksgrenadier Divisions) were swept away. Soviet forces were now across the Inster either side of Breitenstein, about 30km northeast of Insterburg, and pushing west and southwest.

The 5th Panzer Division was ordered out of its frontline positions and dispatched to the new crisis in a final desperate attempt to restore the front. In reality, only part of the division – its armoured battlegroup and a single battalion from its artillery regiment – could be extracted. Delayed by Soviet air attacks, this force thrust north towards Breitenstein late on 19 January, but ran into powerful Soviet anti-tank defences. On 20 January, under heavy pressure, the battlegroup struggled west together with elements of 1st Infantry Division and 349th Volksgrenadier Division, reaching the area north of Insterburg during the day. The northern flank of the defensive positions that had held back 3rd Belorussian Front for a week had been turned.

Guderian's 'house of cards' – the weak, overextended *Ostfront* – had now completely collapsed, exactly as he had predicted. In the north, Cherniakhovsky had expected heavy fighting on the main axis of advance, and German resistance had proved to be robust. Indeed, 3rd Belorussian Front incurred the great bulk of Soviet casualties along the entire *Ostfront* during the great January offensive. But this obdurate defence was only possible at the cost of weakening the front further north, and as soon as Cherniakhovsky became aware of this, 3rd Panzer Army's fate was sealed. A little to the south, Rokossovsky was able to unfold his operation almost exactly according to his plans, and the huge hammer blows dealt to the front further south, by Zhukov and Konev, opened the way for a swift advance towards Berlin.

Several factors stand out in this operation. First, Soviet deception measures were very effective, making it impossible for the Germans to come to accurate conclusions about Soviet intentions. Second, the deliberately staggered start of the offensive, with Konev's massive blow in the south leading the way, resulted in catastrophic orders for German reserves to be dispatched from one part of the front to another, only to find new crises erupting in the very areas they had just vacated. The overall weakness of the German line – under-strength infantry divisions holding absurd lengths of front with inadequate anti-tank firepower, and far too few armoured formations available to launch counter-attacks – was only ever going to result in one outcome. By being forced to hold such extended frontlines, the infantry divisions were unable to hold back any of their own forces as local reserves, and consequently when they came under heavy pressure they immediately called for help. Once the limited help that was available had been committed, the overwhelming superiority of the Red Army, with its comparatively enormous reserves, made the final collapse of the German defences inevitable.

Only the middle segment of Army Group Centre's front, from south of Goldap to the area just north of Rokossovsky's breakout, remained relatively quiet. Here, 4th Army became increasingly threatened with encirclement, but despite constant telephone calls from Reinhardt and his Chief of Staff, Heidkämper, to both Guderian and Hitler himself, permission for a timely withdrawal was constantly refused. Finally, on 20 January, Hitler promised to transfer forces from Courland and Denmark to reinforce the collapsing positions in East Prussia. Such a move had been requested by Guderian before the Soviet offensive broke, and Hitler had flatly rejected the suggestion. Now, it was far too late. The Red Army was able to advance in strength on either flank of 4th Army, and had the mobility and firepower to overwhelm any attempt at resistance. And in the path of the triumphant spearheads lay the East Prussian population, still unaware of the critical danger.

CHAPTER 6
CHERNIAKHOVSKY AND THE PREGEL VALLEY

There is no question of honour. The land of the fascists must be laid waste.

– K. Cherniakhovsky[1]

The perilous state of the *Ostfront* was clear to everyone before the onset of the great Soviet offensive. The commanders in East Prussia – Raus, Hossbach and Weiss in their army headquarters, Reinhardt at Army Group Centre – and those in higher posts – Guderian and Gehlen, to name but two – were only too aware that the forces arrayed along the frontline would not be able to withstand the coming blow. In the face of Hitler's intransigence, nothing was done to warn the civilian population, still less evacuate them in a timely manner. Caught up in their fantasy world where the will to win was sufficient to ensure victory, and trapped within a Party system where personal prestige was of paramount importance, Hitler and Koch refused to allow East Prussia to fall under military jurisdiction, something that would have allowed Reinhardt to take appropriate steps without any delay. Instead, matters pertaining to the civilian population remained within the remit of the Party.

Whilst Koch remained completely committed to the Führer's vision of final victory, and ensured only those Party members who shared this view were appointed to high office, even some diehard Party officials realized what lay ahead. Many quietly began to move their possessions and families to places of greater safety, though in many cases it was hard to see where in the Reich could be regarded as 'safe' – almost every city had been struck by air raids, and all the frontiers of the Reich were threatened. Some civilians with contacts in appropriate places also left East Prussia, despite strict orders that no evacuation was to occur – such an act was deemed to be defeatist. If one knew the right people, it was still possible to obtain permission for such journeys, despite Koch's ban on movements by civilians out of the province.

An overview of the Soviet advance into East Prussia reveals several distinct themes. In the north, 3rd Panzer Army was driven back along the Insterburg–Königsberg axis by Cherniakhovsky's 3rd Belorussian Front. In the south, Rokossovsky tore a huge hole in 2nd Army, and sent his forces surging west, covering the northern flank of Zhukov's 1st Belorussian Front. In the centre, between these two Soviet thrusts, the German 4th Army was left almost untouched, occupying an increasingly vulnerable salient as both its flanks came under threat. Ultimately, the presence of such a large group of German forces resulted in a change of direction for Rokossovsky's armies, with most of his forces being diverted onto a more northerly axis in order to isolate and break up 4th Army. This, in turn, had enormous consequences for the drive to the west by Zhukov's armies, which now found that the protection they needed on their northern flank had disappeared. The next three chapters look at these themes in turn.

Driven back towards Insterburg, 5th Panzer Division continued to try to press into the southern flank of the Soviet breakthrough on 20 January. The division's armoured battlegroup was now acting independently from the rest of the division, under the direct command of Matzky's XXVI Corps. Hauptmann Jaedtke kept a detailed account of events as he tried to drive north:

After refuelling [in Insterburg] we set off. There was constant refugee traffic along the road in the opposite direction. They came from the villages around and north of Breitenstein. They could tell us nothing about Russian units.

In Mittel-Warkau (15 kilometres north of Insterburg) I set up HQ in a manor house. We had only elements of 2/14 [i.e. part of a Panzergrenadier company] and the staff with us. Most of I/14 and II/31 [I Battalion, 14th Panzergrenadier Regiment and II Battalion, 31st Panzer Regiment] were still somewhere behind us, unable to push through the refugee traffic.

With a few half-tracks, we probed northeast towards Mohlen [about 4km to the east]. We saw smoke rising there, but heard no sounds of fighting. It was growing dark by the time the rest of the group arrived. Hauptmann Ellmers was immediately dispatched to Aulenbach [4km north of Mittel-Warkau] with a mixed company.

I called the post office in Aulenbach by telephone from an office in the manor. A woman answered. In reply to my question about what was happening in Aulenbach, she said, 'I was on night duty, but this morning nobody has arrived to replace me. So I've stayed here, as the phone keeps ringing. Russian tanks drove through the village tonight, and now there are German soldiers here.' I asked her to fetch a German officer to the telephone. It could only be Hauptmann Ellmers. A second attempt to phone Aulenbach failed. The line was dead. Nevertheless, credit to a woman conscious of her duty.

Shortly after, there was a radio message from Ellmers: 'In heavy combat against enemy tanks in the centre of Aulenbach.' After II/31 had fully arrived, we guarded towards the northeast at Mittel-Warkau with a few tanks and half-tracks. Everything else was dispatched in haste to Aulenbach. We succeeded in pushing through to the heart of the village and blocking all roads. Six to eight Russian tanks were shot up in the village. The flames from these set a few houses alight. Ground-attack aircraft attacked us constantly with bombs and fixed weapons. We were amazed that the Russians had established no guards at the southern edge of Aulenbach, which was such an important junction. They apparently felt completely secure.

In the first hours of darkness, Russian tanks and infantry attacked from the north and from the railway to the west; somewhat later, from the east too. These forces were apparently thrown together in haste, in an attempt to clear the advance routes. It grew increasingly unpleasant in Aulenbach.

When we then came under attack from the southwest and thus were threatened with encirclement, we decided to pull back behind the Prawe to a good position at the southern edge of the village. We had some prospect of being able to hold this until early on 21 January. The young woman from the post office was in one of Ellmers' half-tracks.

The centre of Aulenbach was almost impassable due to the shot-up Russian tanks and the spreading fires. Nevertheless, the Russians thrust into it with ten to 15 tanks, and then advanced swiftly while Russian ground-attack planes bombed the village. As a result, they bypassed our left flank to the southwest. In addition, the enemy thrust into Papuschein Forest, ten kilometres north of Norkitten. During the night, the enemy also reached Markthausen, eight kilometres west of Aulenbach.[2]

North of Aulenbach, the German line effectively disappeared completely. There was a gap at least 70km wide, through which 11th Guards Army was now advancing. The breakthrough at Breitenstein had finally unhinged the German defences, and the exhausted infantry divisions, with their very limited mobility, disintegrated once the phase of positional warfare ended. A composite battlegroup formed from several different formations held on north of Insterburg, and elements of 50th Infantry Division were still holding the original frontline near Gumbinnen, but there were only isolated fragments of 61st Infantry Division between the two. The Inster valley ran northeast from Insterburg to Breitenstein, and east of this lay the Eichwald Forest. Scattered elements of 349th and 549th Volksgrenadier Divisions attempted in vain to re-establish a defensive line here on 20 January. Local Volkssturm units from Goldap, Angerburg and Insterburg were then committed to the battle. With almost no heavy weapons, their undoubted courage and resolve to defend their own homes was of no avail – the three rifle corps of 5th Army brushed them aside. A small group of German assault guns launched a local counter-attack, but the forest line was untenable, and the defenders fell back to the Inster and Insterburg itself.

In principle, the Inster should have been defendable. The winding river ran through swampy terrain, with only one small bridge over the river between Insterburg and the Soviet bridgehead at Breitenstein. The northwest bank was higher than the southeast bank, which should have permitted the defenders to fight effectively, if they had been present in sufficient numbers. But the heavy winter frosts and snow had frozen the Inster and the swampy ground on its banks, and it posed no obstacle to the advancing Soviet infantry. Reinforced by armour filtering down from Breitenstein, the Red Army swiftly bypassed the scattered German positions along the river.

Cherniakhovsky was trying to make up for lost time. The 11th Guards Army, with the two tank corps attached, turned its line of advance to the southwest, and pressed towards the Pregel valley west of Insterburg. Matzky continued to struggle to restore his frontline; the two Volksgrenadier divisions were tasked with holding back the Soviet forces immediately northeast of Insterburg, and 56th Infantry Division took up positions to their west, broadly where Jaedtke and his battlegroup had tried in vain to push north through and beyond Aulenbach. The 1st Infantry Division, pulled out of the front in the east, attempted to take up positions west of 56th Infantry Division, while 5th Panzer Division gathered together its dwindling armoured forces for a further counter-attack on 1st Infantry Division's left flank. In short, Matzky desperately shuffled his forces westwards to keep up with the rapidly advancing Soviet forces.

Unfortunately for the hard-pressed German corps commander, his formations lacked the mobility to keep up with the Red Army. The 561st Volksgrenadier Division came under heavy pressure from the Soviet 39th Army, which also drove back 69th Infantry Division, opening a breach northwest of the Insterburg positions. XXXVI Guards Rifle Corps, the most easterly unit of 11th Guards Army, drove through Aulenbach during the early hours of 21 January, after Jaedtke had pulled back, and pushed on 10km to Gutfliess, reaching the village at midday. From there, the Soviet infantrymen, with tanks in close support, turned south and thrust through the Papuscheiner Forest, which lay northwest of Insterburg. They reached Saalau – barely 3km from the Pregel, and 15km west of Insterburg – by the evening. Jaedtke's battlegroup launched a vigorous counter-attack as darkness fell, retaking the town. Much of 5th Panzer Division crossed the Pregel bridge south of Saalau at Norkitten to the south bank during the night.

The civilian population of this part of East Prussia finally awoke to its danger. Often far too late, local Party officials issued orders for evacuation; usually, civilians were simply exhorted to flee by retreating German soldiers. Along roads choked with snow and military traffic, the refugee columns, mostly reliant on horse-drawn vehicles, struggled westwards through Insterburg. Most strove to cross the Pregel to the southern bank, either in Insterburg, or via the bridges at Norkitten and Bubainen, held open by 5th Panzer Division:

The terrain was ideal for a bridgehead, as south of Saalau there was a former bed of the Pregel. In front of the bridge – it was an old iron construction – which crossed the river about ten metres above the water on a number of supports, there were many refugee vehicles, stragglers and supply vehicles from different divisions. Most of our division had already crossed during the night. Under the close-packed, heavily loaded vehicles, the bridge swayed visibly. The pioneer company attached to the armoured group by the division took over control of the traffic and prepared the bridge for demolition. All vehicles had to cross the bridge with large distances between them. Wehrmacht personnel, apart from the wounded, were gathered together in the bridgehead to create *Alarmeinheiten* [alarm units]; reconnaissance troops scouted to the north.

There was a constant stream of refugee traffic. They reported that the Russians were pressing on to the west and towards Wehlau. A reconnaissance troop from west of Taplacken gave the same report. The refugee flood didn't want to stop. Their columns contained almost only women and children, barely any old men. They waited patiently until they could cross the bridge. They gathered around their heavily laden wagons and fed the horses in the grim cold, with snowstorms and icy roads. Russian air attacks rolled on overhead along the refugee columns. It reminded one of the dreadful scenes from Nemmersdorf. I learned from Oberstleutnant Herzog [acting commander of 5th Panzer Division] that I had to hold the bridgehead until the last refugee vehicle had crossed.

Reconnaissance towards Insterburg reported chaotic scenes on Reichsstrasse 1. The Russians had broken into Insterburg. We were still able to recover many things from the burning supply dump. I took a half-track company and a tank company east to secure Reichsstrasse 1. The armoured group remained in this position until the morning of 23 January.

Ever more vehicles carrying refugees came from Insterburg, interspersed with stragglers who, in the absence of any other orders, were incorporated into the battalion. These soldiers were happy with this. They received food for the first time in days, and no longer needed to run. They could regard themselves as part of an organized unit, and fought well in the battles that followed.

After the last units had crossed the bridge at 0300 on 23 January, the bridge was blown. Unfortunately, it was not completely destroyed, and infantry could still cross.[3]

Once south of the river, many of the refugees sought cover in the Kranichbruch Forest, southwest of Insterburg. Leaderless, they struggled west as best they could, their arrival in villages and towns often triggering further refugee columns.

Wehlau, roughly midway between Insterburg and Königsberg, was full of refugees from the east. In vain, the population waited for an evacuation order from the local Party officials. On 20 January, the local mayor, Landrat von Bredow, took matters into his own hands, telling people to take to the roads. The following day, with Soviet forces approaching rapidly, permission for an official evacuation was finally given. The army had insisted that Reichsstrasse 1, the main road running west towards Königsberg, should be reserved for military use, meaning that the refugees had to flee southwest towards Friedland. A freight train was commandeered late in the day, but could only take a limited number of people. The rest joined the turmoil of people struggling south. Progress was dreadfully slow, as little as 1km per hour.

Insterburg was lost on 21 January. The following day, 39th Army continued to exploit its breakthrough, driving 69th Infantry Division back to Tapiau and seizing Wehlau. The 5th Panzer Division was ordered to restore the front. The River Alle flowed north through Wehlau to the Pregel, and most of the town was on the east bank of the Alle; as Jaedtke's battlegroup arrived, it found the local Volkssturm was still in control of the western parts of the town. Jaedtke swiftly pushed the Soviet infantrymen back across the river. An attack to clear the eastern parts of Wehlau was unfeasible – Jaedtke lacked the infantry for such an operation. In any event, he had orders to secure a large segment of frontline, and all he could do was blow the bridges across the Alle. South of Wehlau, in the town of Allenburg, the men of 5th Panzer Division found a tuberculosis clinic. There were still 40 patients, mostly women, in the clinic, under the care of a female doctor and two nurses. The division medical officer, Dr Bureck, managed to find transport for 25 patients. The rest were left behind, with their medical attendants, to face an uncertain future.

Soviet forces continued to cross the Pregel at Wehlau, and 5th Panzer Division desperately fought to hold the line of the Alle. The Red Army made constant forays across the frozen river, but the ice was not thick enough to support tanks. Exploiting their success in Insterburg and at Wehlau, the Soviet 5th Army and 11th Guards Army secured the entire southern bank of the Pregel between the two towns on 23 January and pushed southwest towards Allenburg. Further east, the German 50th and 61st Infantry Divisions continued to hold their front south of Insterburg, but the surge of 11th Guards Army and 5th Army across the river to their west once more unhinged the line, and a breach rapidly opened between the most westerly elements of 61st Infantry Division and the remnants of 349th Volksgrenadier Division, struggling to hold the line before Allenburg.

Refugees converged on Königsberg in growing numbers. Hans Graf von Lehndorff, a surgeon who had himself fled to the city from Insterburg, was assigned work near the main railway station, and was struck by how unperturbed many of the refugees were. He asked one woman where she intended to go next:

> She didn't know, she just wanted to reach somewhere in the Reich. And then, she suddenly said, 'The Führer won't let us fall into the Russians' hands, he would rather gas us all.' I stole a quick glance around, but nobody appeared to have found anything remarkable in this statement. Dear God! I thought, you have such confidence even in these times![4]

From briefings he had received, von Lehndorff knew that the Soviet spearheads were now close to the city, but the civilian population appeared to be unaware – cinemas were still open, and the trams continued to run as normal.

Eva Kuckuck was working in Königsberg, and she travelled to her parents' house in Allenburg on a regularly timetabled train in order to help with the evacuation. Her parents had moved to Berlin, but she wanted to see if some of their possessions could be saved. The local mayor was a retired Oberst who made repeated, fruitless telephone calls to the offices of the Wehlau Kreisleiter for permission to begin the evacuation; he was told that there was no immediate threat to the area. Kuckuck spoke to a secretary in Wehlau, and was alarmed to learn that Soviet forces had already been sighted close to the town. Late on 21 January, a neighbour informed her that the mayor had decided to order an immediate evacuation of the town. No trains were available, and the only transport provided by the authorities was reserved for the most elderly. Everyone else was to proceed on foot to Friedland to seek further evacuation from there.

Kuckuck telephoned Oberst von Weiss, the mayor, who knew nothing about any such evacuation. After making further enquiries, he told Kuckuck that permission had been given to prepare for evacuation, but that nobody was to depart yet. The required order was finally given early on 22 January, and Kuckuck joined the group leaving Oberst von Weiss' village:

> A whole village left its homeland and fled into the unknown. As it was no longer possible for us to proceed along the planned route, we had to hit the narrow country lanes. As a result of a thaw, we were only able to move at a walking pace. It took us 11 hours to travel ten kilometres down the road. We spent the night in a guesthouse … that was so crowded that we could only take turns to sit two at a time on a stool. At first light, we set off again. As we left the woods at dawn, we saw as far as the eye could reach that every road was choked with refugee wagons, wandering people, and

animals running free. The most hopeless picture of a nation driven forth seared itself into my memory. Many wagons had tipped over and had strewn the last possessions saved from home and hearth into the watery ditches. These poor people had to continue their journeys on foot.

Almost all day long we were accompanied by the thunder of artillery fire, and we had no way of knowing whether German or Russian guns were making this noise.

Thankfully, we were spared direct contact with Russian troops, and aircraft didn't attack us either.[5]

Von Weiss managed to secure transport for his people in army trucks heading west, but many of the estate workers chose to continue with their wagons, rather than lose their last possessions. The army trucks safely reached Königsberg, but Kuckuck never discovered what became of those left behind on the choked roads.

Once in Königsberg, the small party managed to secure passage aboard a small steamer, the 900-tonne *Consul Cords*, which was undergoing repairs in the dockyards. Some 1,000 refugees crowded into the ship:

Although, as we discovered, the ship was not fully repaired, the captain was ordered to leave immediately with the refugees who were aboard. All his objections that the steamer was simply not seaworthy yet, and that he must therefore decline any responsibility for the refugees, went unanswered. Perhaps the unseaworthiness of the ship explained why there were no Party officials or NSV [Nationalsozialistische Volksfürsorge, the Party's welfare organization] people aboard. But nor were there doctors or nurses on board the completely overcrowded ship. The captain was helpless and turned to Oberst von Weiss and asked whether he would assume charge of the refugees, as far as he could. Herr von Weiss said he was willing to do so, without knowing how this would work out.

After leaving Harbour Basin One, we set course for Pillau, finally reaching there during the night. We were lying in the coalbunker of the ship on straw. It was so dark in this bunker that you couldn't see your neighbour, even if you could see anything at all. It was only when a small petroleum lamp was lit that we no longer felt as if we were in a prison.

As far as I could determine, the *Consul Cords* moved only at a snail's pace. The captain certainly didn't want to take any risks. We didn't have any idea where we were headed after we left Pillau.

At midday the following day, Kapitän Fretwurst called Herr von Weiss over. He told him that the ship would only stay afloat for another hour or two, as there were serious mechanical problems. The captain explained that all calls for help to Gotenhafen had been unanswered. None of the 1,200 people on board knew of the danger in which we all were. Herr von Weiss advised the captain to steer for Hela and urged him to press on with all his courage, advice that Kapitän Fretwurst followed.

And it was successful; we reached Hela and seemed to be saved. As soon as we reached the Hela roads, a pilot boat came out to the *Consul Cords* to take the ship's helmsman and Herr von Weiss to the Hela commandant. The captain remained aboard the ship. The Hela commandant immediately decided that all the refugees aboard should come ashore until the steamer was once more seaworthy.[6]

On 30 January, the refugees boarded the *Consul Cords* again, and the little steamer slowly sailed to Kolberg, reaching its destination on 1 February. Like many of the refugees, Eva Kuckuck swore that should she be forced to flee from Kolberg, she would do so by road or rail, and never aboard a small ship like the *Consul Cords*.

Back in the Pregel valley, Jaedtke found himself operating alongside a Volkssturm battalion, just south of Wehlau:

Braunsberg [on the East Prussian coast, southwest of Königsberg] was my last peacetime posting. The battalion leader was the secondary school teacher Krause, whom I knew from peacetime as an efficient, energetic man, who had lost his right arm in the First World War.

He now reported that the battalion had no field kitchens, signals equipment, medical support or supply vehicles. It was armed with rifles, mainly captured ones of differing calibres. This 'wooden leg' was a hindrance for us, as we relied on our mobility for our strength.

The battalion was deployed on the right flank of the armoured group, at the junction with other parts of the division. There were several farms there between Paterswalde and Richau, so that the elderly gentlemen could at least take turns at warming themselves up, as it was still bitterly cold, down to minus 15 degrees at night. In order to make the Volkssturm battalion commander mobile and to ensure better communications with the armoured group, we gave him a half-track with an experienced Feldwebel. Nevertheless, the use of this battalion was irresponsible.

... Shortly after dusk (23 January) the Russians attacked along the entire division front, against the armoured group in Wehlau and Allenberg [not to be confused with the nearby Allenburg] and east of Paterswalde. We generally held our positions, but the Russians infiltrated everywhere through the large gaps in the front. As a result, they ran rampage in the hinterland. At midnight, the Volkssturm battalion was also attacked on its left flank, and later its entire front. The men fired ammunition from their assorted weapons – about 20 rounds per man – and then pulled out to the southwest. Oberstleutnant Herzog sent the battalion home.[7]

Dietrich von Saucken, pictured here in 1943, last commander of German forces in Prussia. He went into captivity with his men, and remained a Soviet prisoner until 1955.

Erich Koch, Gauleiter of East Prussia. At the height of his influence, the region under his control ran from the Baltic to the Black Sea. He was blamed by many East Prussians for the lack of preparations for civilian evacuation.

Walter Weiss (second from left) and Friedrich Hossbach (fourth from left), photographed in the summer of 1944 at a gathering of officers of Army Group Centre shortly before the onset of *Bagration*.

Karl Mauss, commander of 7th Panzer Division, photographed shortly before he was wounded outside Gotenhafen in 1945. He recovered from his wounds to resume his peacetime career as a dentist.

Karl Lorenz, commander of the *Grossdeutschland* division, photographed here in the Ukraine in January 1944.

Ivan Khristoforovich Bagramian, commander of 1st Belorussian Front, photographed on the eve of Operation *Bagration*, summer 1944.

Konstantin Konstantinovich Rokossovsky (left), speaking to Georgi Konstantinovich Zhukov in Poland in late 1944, at about the time that the latter replaced the former as commander of 1st Belorussian Front.

Members of the military council of the 3rd Belorussian Front; Vasilii Emelianovich Makorov (left), Alexander Mikhailovich Vasilevsky (centre) and Ivan Danilovich Chernyakhovsky (right), in the autumn of 1944.

The *Prinz Eugen* in Copenhagen harbour, where she arrived on 20 April 1945. Lack of fuel prevented the ship sailing again, and after the war, she was handed over to the USA and was sunk during atomic bomb tests in 1946.

The *Admiral Scheer*, one of several vessels that provided invaluable fire support to the Wehrmacht in 1945. The *Scheer* fired so many rounds that the rifling in her main gun barrels was burned out, and on 9 April 1945, the ship was sunk in Kiel during an RAF raid.

The *Wilhelm Gustloff* on her maiden voyage, 1938. The ship was the first vessel built for the KdF, to provide holidays for ordinary German workers. At the outset of the war, she was designated 'Hospital Ship D', and became a floating barracks from 1940 until shortly before she was sunk.

The *Steuben*, pictured here in 1925 when she was still named *München*.

The Pz. IV. Although poorly armoured in comparison to many other tanks in 1944–45, the Pz. IV remained a capable fighting vehicle in experienced hands. In its various forms, the Pz. IV remained in production throughout the war.

Panther tanks entraining for the front, December 1944. Although complex, requiring extensive maintenance, and prone to breakdowns, Panthers were hugely popular with their crews, due to their excellent frontal armour and powerful gun.

The heavyweight Tiger, more than a match for any Soviet tanks. By 1945, many Tiger battalions had been re-equipped with the King Tiger, but the original Tiger, shown here, remained in widespread service to the end of the war.

Jg.Pz. IVs moving up to the front, pictured here in Hungary, 1944. These vehicles were produced in remarkably large numbers towards the end of the war, and despite the limitations of not having a turret, they proved to be a match for the Soviet T-34.

A Jagdpanther similar to the vehicle used with such good effect by Bix outside Preussisch Stargard, photographed here in France in the summer of 1944. With excellent armour, a lethal gun, and good cross-country performance, the Jagdpanther was one of the most advanced armoured vehicles used by any nation during the war.

On either side of the Pregel, the Soviet I Tank Corps and II Guards Tank Corps continued to lead the advancing elements of 11th Guards Army westwards. They took the town of Tapiau, west of Wehlau, late on 23 January, and most importantly seized the Pregel crossings intact. They could now send armoured units into the rear of the German units that were still holding the line of the Alle, south of Wehlau.

Such a threat could not be ignored, and 5th Panzer Division was ordered out of its positions along the Alle. It was to proceed through the Frisching Forest, and then strike against the Soviet bridgehead at Tapiau. In addition, it was also required to continue holding a large segment of east-facing frontline –a stretch of at least 24km. Even if the division had been at full strength, this would have been a formidable task, given the strength of Soviet forces facing the division, but in its weakened state it was a hopeless one.

Jaedtke and his armoured battlegroup made their weary way to a rendezvous at Bieberswalde, south of Tapiau, with Gruppe Knebel. Knebel had taken command of soldiers attending 3rd Panzer Army's weapons school, one of the institutions established the previous year to improve the level of training of new recruits, and had used the school's personnel to create an ad hoc formation. His command struggled to hold back the Soviet forces in their bridgehead, and early on 25 January Soviet tanks pushed back Knebel's left flank, along the southern shore of the Pregel at Pregelswalde. This Soviet force threatened to push west along the river road towards Königsberg, and Jaedtke's battlegroup immediately counter-attacked into the Soviet southern flank. About 15 Soviet tanks were destroyed, either by Jaedtke's force or Knebel's anti-tank guns, and the remaining Soviet forces pulled back to Tapiau. But Jaedtke's own attack towards Tapiau ran into powerful anti-tank defences, and was unable to make any progress. A day of confused, hard fighting followed, along the edge of the Frisching Forest. By midnight, Jaedtke's exhausted men were in Gross Lindenau, about 10km west of Tapiau, after sweeping through the northern edge of the forest, encountering and destroying several small Soviet groups along the way.

After a brief rest, Jaedtke pushed north the following morning, reaching the Pregel valley. Although the tangle of vegetation along the river made it impossible for armoured forces to move freely, it was good terrain for infantry, who could also cross the frozen river without difficulty. Further attacks by the armoured battlegroup were unlikely to achieve any success, and Herzog ordered the scattered units of his division to adopt a defensive stance.

The 5th Panzer Division, together with the remnants of 61st Infantry Division and elements of 2nd Paratroop-Panzergrenadier Division *Hermann Göring*, was now trying to hold back almost all of 11th Guards Army. During 26 January, the southern flank of the division came under intense pressure, and 13th Panzergrenadier Regiment was split in two, falling back to positions west of Jaedtke's battlegroup. With his southern flank exposed, Herzog ordered the armoured battlegroup to pull back towards Löwenhagen. As they prepared to withdraw, Jaedke's men heard sounds of fighting to the east:

> At 2000, there were loud noises of fighting east of the railway station at Lindenau. There was anti-tank and tank fire. In the last six months, we had often seen occasions when isolated German troops fought their way back to our lines at night. We therefore assumed that this was such a situation and fired our 'green starburst' flares, which the Russians didn't yet have. The improvised obstacles with anti-tank mines on the road were cleared. We were too weak to make an attack of our own. After a time, the first tank came towards us along the road, driving fast. As a result of the many flares, it was as bright as day. We could see clearly that it was a Hetzer of our tank destroyer battalion, which was commanded by Major von Ramin. We were overjoyed! On the Hetzer, there were several grenadiers from Gruppe Knebel. Major von Ramin had been assigned on the evening of 26 January to leave our division to reinforce Gruppe Knebel. After Gruppe Knebel was overrun during 26 January, they decided to fight their way out to the west.[8]

There was no rest for von Ramin and his tank-destroyers; they were dispatched to join 5th Panzer Division's combat engineers on the division's exposed southern flank, where the remnants of 13th Panzergrenadier Regiment fought on, despite having almost no ammunition for their heavy weapons.

Throughout 27 January, the division's various elements managed to hold their positions in the face of repeated air attacks. By the evening, Soviet incursions down the Pregel valley necessitated a further withdrawal, to a line covering the immediate southeast approach to Königsberg. Almost immediately, the designated positions in the village of Steinbeck were outflanked, and Jaedtke's battlegroup pulled back almost to the edge of the city. The proximity of Königsberg was not without its advantages; the division's workshops had been operating in the city for several days, and were now able to return repaired vehicles to the combat formations swiftly. The tank strength of the division, despite daily losses, continued to hover at about 30 vehicles, many of which had been through the workshop on several occasions. The armoured battlegroup claimed to have destroyed 250 Soviet tanks since the beginning of the battle, though many of these, too, would have been repaired and returned to action.

Jaedtke's experience of the defensive positions constructed on the orders of the Reich Defence Commissar are revealing:

Early on 28 January, the Russians reached the trenches at the northern end of the village, which Gauleiter Koch had had dug by women and schoolchildren for defence. Since the beginning of the fighting in East Prussia, these damned trenches had hindered us more than helped us. As a Panzer division – weak in infantry – we couldn't use the trenches ourselves. But once the Russians were in them, it was hard for us to drive them out.[9]

Königsberg had been under artillery fire since late on 26 January, something that completely changed the complacent mood amongst the civilians. Refugees had been slowly shuffling along the road towards Pillau, even though there was no news yet of any evacuation. Those who remained in the city had no idea whether they would be caught up in a battle, or if Königsberg would simply pass into Soviet hands. The shelling stopped abruptly during the afternoon of 27 January, but only so that Soviet aircraft could attack. That evening, von Lehndorff's hospital received instructions that all female medical personnel should attempt to leave the city during the hours of darkness. Von Lehndorff's nurses asked if they could ignore the order and remain with the wounded, something he greeted with relief. As the reality of their plight dawned on them, many civilians despaired. The parents of one of von Lehndorff's colleagues, unable to bear the thought of abandoning the house that had been their home for 30 years, took cyanide capsules, which seemed to be freely available.[10]

The 5th Panzer Division's new positions in Gutenfeld came under pressure on 28 January, but all attacks were repulsed. Jaedtke was wounded by a shell splinter and sent back to Königsberg. He was to be evacuated from the city with other wounded men, but refused, preferring to remain with the division's medical team. Although his battlegroup continued to hold its positions, the Soviet II Guards Tank Corps drove in the southern flank of the division, finally pushing aside 13th Panzergrenadier Regiment. At dusk, Soviet spearheads reached the coast, southwest of Königsberg. The 3rd Panzer Army was cut off from the rest of the Reich. The 5th Panzer Division, together with elements of 1st, 56th and 69th Infantry Divisions, was now responsible for the southern perimeter of Königsberg itself.

In Königsberg, General Lasch found his role as commander of Wehrkreis I was increasingly redundant, as the territory overseen by him was lost to the Red Army. Many of the headquarters personnel of the Wehrkreis and Replacement Army officers left the city on 22 January. Generaloberst Raus, commander of 3rd Panzer Army, moved into the city, and a few days later relocated further west to Fischhausen, taking control of Königsberg and much of the surrounding area. The local Party leadership was also moving; Lasch learned indirectly that Gauleiter Koch had hastily moved his possessions to Friedrichsburg, just to the west of the city. Civilian refugees and stragglers from Wehrmacht formations, both frontline and rear-area units, streamed into Königsberg, where the absence of a combat commandant left a vacuum. But Lasch's criticism was directed mainly at the Party: 'The Party failed completely with regard to proper support and guidance of the stream of refugees, since its prominent leaders with few exceptions thought only of their own welfare.'[11]

With the arrival of General Schittnig and the staff of 1st Infantry Division in the city on 25 January, some order was established. This was also the date that the German army groups in the east were renamed. Army Group North became Army Group Courland; Army Group Centre became Army Group North; and Army Group A became Army Group Centre. Lasch travelled to the port of Pillau to discuss the possibility of seaborne evacuation of civilians with the naval commandant. When he attempted to return to the city on 27 January, he found it almost impossible to travel the 40km. A flood of refugees streamed west into the Samland peninsula along the frozen roads. It took Lasch almost all day to make the journey:

> When I finally reached my headquarters in Moditten during the night hours, my chief of staff was waiting with a message that the Gauleiter urgently wanted to speak to me – he was leaving Friedrichsberg and had important news for me. When I found Koch amidst mad confusion in Friedrichsberg, he told me that during the day, the Führer had personally called him, something that had only ever happened two or three times before. He [Hitler] had asked him about my suitability and reliability as a commander of troops, as he had an important task for me.[12]

Lasch was unimpressed that his reliability was being discussed in such a manner, and could guess the task that Hitler had in mind. The following morning, he received a signal that confirmed his suspicions: he was appointed commander of the newly designated 'Fortress Königsberg'. In a telephone discussion with Guderian, Lasch pointed out that the overlapping responsibilities of Raus' 3rd Panzer Army and the new fortress commandant made the role of the latter unclear. Lasch then attempted to contact Reinhardt, only to learn that the army group commander had been dismissed, and was to be replaced by Generaloberst Lothar Rendulic, summoned from Courland. Rendulic, a lawyer from Austria, was an early adherent of the Nazi Party. Before the war was over, he would establish a reputation for standing courts-martial to rival that of Schörner, and spent several years in prison after being convicted of conducting a scorched earth policy in Finland and Norway in 1944 and for crimes against civilians in Yugoslavia. Whatever his reputation, Lasch and the other commanders were dismayed to have lost their trusted superior.

Rendulic swiftly confirmed Lasch's appointment as fortress commander. Lasch contacted the frontline units, and discovered that the Red Army was on the outskirts of the city to the south, east and northeast. From a point almost due north of the city, the front ran north across the Samland peninsula towards Cranz. The Soviet 11th Guards Army faced the southern perimeter of Königsberg, and 39th Army was closing from the east and northeast. 43rd Army completed the Soviet line as far as the coast near Cranz. The two armoured formations – I Tank Corps and II Guards Tank Corps – were advancing north and south of the Prussian capital. II Guards Tank Corps had already reached the coast, and the advancing Soviet tanks north of Königsberg now threatening to envelop the city. Facing the Red Army were several German formations. 5th Panzer Division and 69th Infantry Division formed most of the southern perimeter. The eastern approaches were held by fragments of several divisions – 548th Volksgrenadier Division, 1st Infantry Division and 367th Infantry Division, the latter diverted here from further south. North of the city, 551st Volksgrenadier Division struggled to hold back the onrushing forces of 39th Army. Nearer Cranz, the front stabilized. The two divisions of XXVIII Corps in Memel – 58th and 95th Infantry Divisions – had been ordered to evacuate the ruins on 22 January. In three phases, the garrison withdrew during the freezing nights, leaving only elements of 58th Infantry Division as a rearguard. These finally pulled out before dawn on 28 January. The two divisions thus released helped shore up the line near Cranz; since Bagramian's attempts to storm Memel in the autumn, they had enjoyed relative peace, and had been able to replenish their ranks. They now provided welcome reinforcements for 3rd Panzer Army.

Isaak Kobylyanskiy, the artillery officer from Kiev, was now advancing towards Königsberg with 43rd Army. In a village not far from the East Prussian capital, he encountered some civilians:

I visited a few empty houses before I entered one where I found a group of elderly women sitting in the basement. Two of them were sitting in wheelchairs. During a short conversation with the group I understood [why they were hiding]: they were mortally frightened and were expecting some terrible Russian punishment.

In the house next door to this one, I found a couple in their late forties. They were amazed by my good knowledge of the German language… After perhaps deciding that this 'Russian' would do no harm to them, they asked me if they should hide their fourteen-year-old daughter from the Soviet soldiers. Before answering them, I asked them to show me the girl. Then an awkward, long-legged girl crawled out from under the bed. She wasn't shaped like a real teenager yet, although she was quite tall. As for me, the girl had no sex appeal, but my advice was to hide her more carefully.[13]

Turmoil spread to the Samland peninsula. Erika Morgenstern, the small girl who watched Königsberg burn after the August raids, had spent Christmas with her mother and younger sister, staying at her grandparents' house in Hindenburg, close to Labiau in the northeast part of the Samland peninsula:

28 January 1945 came, a day that I would not forget for all of my life… I was standing by the window behind the long, white curtains daydreaming as I looked out at the beautiful world, and had completely forgotten the war. The garden … and its surrounding fence, the roofs of the barn and stable, all were covered in a thick blanket of snow. Even the house and all the roads were covered by this thick, white, frosty layer. The sun shone down on this winter splendour, giving it a magical appearance. Exactly as if all the stars in the heavens had fallen to earth. Everything glittered and sparkled, as far as I could see, and I felt as if there could be nothing so beautiful in all the world.

My thoughts were interrupted at this point. A dark, moving spot in the distance, clearly visible against the endless whiteness, broke into my dreams. The spot grew larger, coming closer, and soon it could be seen that it was a man, running towards my grandparents' house. He took very large strides, wanting to go faster, trying sometimes to run, slipping, opening his mouth to shout something, but nothing could be heard. He waved both arms in the air, like someone trying to gesticulate. As fast as he could, he came closer, giving the impression that death and the devil were at his heels. And it wasn't a wrong impression! Shouting loudly, he reached the farm, but the adults still hadn't noticed him – only me. Out of breath, eyes and mouth open wide, he entered the room we were in, and spoke the fateful phrase that changed the world: 'We must flee!'[14]

In this disorganized manner, word spread through the area. A wagon was loaded in haste – some items were eminently sensible, such as food and fodder for the horses, while other items, such as valuables and keepsakes, would later be abandoned. When they set off, Erika Morgenstern's mother and grandparents found that there was only sufficient space left on the wagon for the children. As they left the farm, they saw men emerge from the nearby woods, and open fire. Immediately, there was pandemonium, wagons overturned and horses broke free. The refugees struggled slowly down roads choked with crowds and snow. They hadn't travelled far before they came to a complete standstill: Soviet forces had bypassed them and turned north to reach the coast. They were cut off.

Haunted by the images of Nemmersdorf, many of the refugees decided that they would attempt to slip past the Soviet forces by venturing onto the frozen Kurisches Haff, the lagoon between the mainland and the Kurische Nehrung:

The large zinc tub filled with furniture was removed from the wagon and abandoned at the roadside. Slowly, in a strained silence, leading the horses, one wagon after another ventured out onto the ice. We children too had to dismount from the wagons and run along beside them. My grandfather held the horses' bridles and walked along with his head close to theirs. As they walked onto the ice, they grew unsettled and nervous. But my grandfather stroked them, spoke quiet words, and these smart animals quickly learned to take short steps, just like the humans with them. Nobody spoke a word… Suddenly, the ice cracked under the wagon's wheels. My heart leapt to my throat, and I held my breath, as if that would have been of any use if we had fallen through. There – sudden chilling cries behind us! Two wagons were driving too close to each other. The ice broke and in seconds, the icy, gurgling water swallowed everything. In such a situation, there was nothing that could be done to help. The next wagon made a large detour around the hole and sought out a hopefully stronger road across the ice.[15]

Eventually, the refugees made it back to land, and continued their slow progress.

The Soviet onslaught continued throughout these days. Whilst the southern and eastern approaches of Königsberg were well defended, 551st Volksgrenadier Division couldn't hold its positions. The Cranz road was cut on 27 January. A thrust towards the northeastern part of the city was beaten off by a mixture of units, including a Volkssturm formation commanded by Kreisleiter Wagner, who earned himself the Iron Cross for his actions. Later, in a characteristically petty gesture, Gauleiter Koch censured him for accepting his decoration from the Wehrmacht, instead of allowing Koch to present it to him.

Hastily deployed elements of 367th Infantry Division's 974th Grenadier Regiment, commanded by Major Schaper, supported by an anti-tank detachment, went into action to defend the road that ran south to Königsberg from Cranz:

The approach march was greatly hindered by a helpless tangle of traffic on the Königsberg–Cranz road… I had to abandon my car, as it was only possible to get through on foot. In addition, there was artillery fire at the edge of the city, and enemy aircraft fired on the refugee columns without hindrance.

The two battalions being used – as far as I can remember, I Battalion on the right and the division's fusilier battalion on the left – succeeded in reaching the positions about one or two hours before the Russians, literally at the last moment.

Russian attacks started at midday on 27 January, and were beaten off.

The fusilier battalion was in the thick of the fighting, and received good support on its right from one or two 88mm flak batteries. During the afternoon a crisis developed on the left flank, where ... the remnants of 3rd Panzer Army's formations had retreated into Samland. Further attacks were halted with the help of the flak. Twenty-eight to 30 tanks were shot up, two or three of them by the fusiliers with Panzerfausts. Thereupon the Russians stopped their attacks on these positions and marched west through the Fritzen Forest with powerful units without meeting significant resistance, in order to close their pincer around Königsberg. At dusk, I reported to the division that at least a complete Russian division had marched past.

Then, during the afternoon of 28 January, the Russians began to drive in the front of the fusilier battalion from the north; its flank had had to be pulled back the previous day... Late in the afternoon, 367th Artillery Regiment's 2nd Battalion was belatedly deployed behind the open left flank of the fusilier battalion, despite my warnings. Even as the battalion deployed in unprotected positions, it was smashed by the attacking Russians. There were no reserves anywhere. Attacked on its flank and in its rear, the fusilier battalion streamed back ... 1st Battalion was not affected by this development. The remnants of the fusilier battalion reached the high ground near the regimental headquarters just to the east of Stiegehnen and about 150 metres west of the Königsberg–Cranz road, facing north, but still with an open left flank... Throughout the evening of 28 January, the situation remained very threatening, with loud tank noises suggesting that an attack was coming. At my urging, the division finally placed the assault gun battalion at my disposal. It would not be able to reach us until later that night.

... Between 2300 and midnight, then, the anticipated armoured thrust either side of the Cranz road appeared. Tanks and enemy infantry advanced in large numbers to within 200 metres, and then pressed forward. The crisis had arrived, not only for us but for Königsberg. We fired with all barrels. If no help came, the situation was untenable.

Then – as if sent from heaven – the assault guns arrived. Rolling down the road towards Cranz, they engaged the advancing Russian tanks by the light of flares. Five or six assault guns skilfully took up positions in low ground and in an instant shot up six to eight Russian tanks, including some 'Stalins'. The entire landscape was lit up as bright as day by the exploding and burning tanks.

That was the turning point. Even today, I can see the look of relief in the eyes of the solders after the dreadful events of the previous tough days with their ceaseless fighting and hard exertions. The Russian infantry that had followed their tanks in dense crowds and were now fleeing were cut down with assault rifles, machine-guns and the two anti-tank guns of 14th Company. For once, it was a proud triumph. On this night, the few assault guns of 367th Infantry Division, behind which there were no combat-ready reserves, saved the city of Königsberg from being seized. The Russians were apparently unaware of their actual superiority.[16]

The forces that had bypassed Schaper's battalions pressed on, turning southwest to complete the envelopment of the city. Kurt Dieckert, a major in the reserves, tried to track down Luftwaffe personnel who were meant to be withdrawing from Seerappen, west of Königsberg, in order to organize them into an ad hoc infantry unit:

I … drove with the increasing flood of refugees through Gross Heydekrug, Widitten and Elenskrug about as far as the railway crossing east of Bludau. I pulled aside at a fork in the road and let the refugees stream past me. An endless procession of suffering greeted my eyes. The women with small children who had to push their prams through the snow seemed particularly grim. Many must have become stuck on the roads. An officer from Fischhausen later told me that his unit found about 20 children frozen to death along the edge of the road.

Finally, I saw two Luftwaffe officers in a truck, and halted them. One of them was a Hauptmann Hey – commander of a flak battery from Goldschmiede. He explained that he had destroyed his 12 88mm flak guns as ordered, to prevent them being used by the enemy. He had no information about the personnel from Seerappen airfield. As there was no further point in my waiting and I wanted to return to Königsberg before dark, I set off. The refugee stream had grown considerably weaker, and contrary to my expectation we made good progress. In Vierbrüderkrug, I saw a few Luftwaffe officers with about 20 men, who wanted to leave for Fischhausen. Despite their protests, I led them to Oberst Häfker [another officer trying to organize ad hoc units] and on his orders, they took up positions along the edge of the forest south of Metgethen, facing north.

As I drove back, I had a singular experience. The frontline created by Oberst Häfker ran along the road to Moditten, consisting of a few foxholes. As I drove past, I noticed that whole groups were abandoning their foxholes and running away. I immediately tried to halt them, leaping out of the vehicle and asking an agitated NCO what was happening. He merely waved with his arm and, clearly distressed, stammered, 'The Russians are coming!' In the gathering darkness, I could actually see a row of dark brown shapes, running towards the road on a broad front. Looking back, I saw that they were raising their hands. They were actually conscripted Ukrainians who came from a work camp at Metgethen and did not want to fall into the hands of the Russians. I sent the fleeing men back and restored order here. This episode showed the value of *Alarmeinheiten* in which nobody knew each other. It was striking that nobody had fired a single shot against the presumed enemy.[17]

During the night of 30–31 January, the Soviet I Tank Corps completed its drive to the coast east of Königsberg. The Prussian capital was encircled, cut off both from the south and the west. Inside the city, its population swollen by refugees, Lasch struggled to maintain order and to organize defenders for the 12 ageing forts around Königsberg. General Hans Mikosch, formerly commander of all fortifications in East Prussia, cobbled together an improvised division to defend the western approaches. Elsewhere, in addition to the few regular units that had retreated into the city, the defenders consisted of the infamous 'ear' and 'stomach' battalions. These were composed of men who had previously been excused military duty due to medical problems, but who were now organized into units where all the personnel had the same medical condition, in the hope that they could thus receive whatever treatment was required for them to remain in the frontline.

Lasch was gratified to discover that he had plenty of artillery, but there was a severe ammunition shortage. Throughout 30 and 31 January, he and his staff awaited a decisive Soviet strike against the paper-thin defences to the west and northwest; to their surprise, the only attack came when 11th Guards Army attempted an armoured thrust against the positions of 5th Panzer Division. The German tank crews beat off the first attack with some ease, and were astonished as the Soviet tanks attacked in two more waves, each following almost in the tracks of the previous assault. After sustaining heavy losses, 11th Guards Army gave up and settled back to lick its wounds.

Cherniakhovsky's forces had suffered heavy casualties in their advance across northern Prussia, and their first attacks on the northern and eastern outskirts of Königsberg had been robustly thrown back. It seems likely that there was considerable concern at the probable cost of attacking such a large urban centre, particularly given the experiences the previous year in Memel. Whatever the reason, Lasch was grateful for the pause, which allowed him to organize his forces and to start rebuilding the battered divisions that had been able to retreat into the city. In addition to the crowds of civilians in the encircled city, there were thousands of soldiers from every conceivable type of unit. Lasch and his staff set to work with these men, organizing them into independent battalions, or sending them to reinforce the divisions in the city. There were justifiable concerns about the ability of units assembled from men who did not know each other to hold together under fire, but ultimately Lasch estimated that these reorganization efforts managed to return about 30,000 soldiers to frontline duty.

The imminent arrival of Soviet troops had been consistently hidden from German civilians. Working in her seaside hospital, Gretel Dost was shocked to hear from the neighbouring military hospital that all military units were being evacuated immediately. The soldiers urged her and her fellow nurses to leave as soon as they could. On a freezing night, Dost and her friends waited outside the town with the last of the military personnel; an army truck was to collect them and take them on the first stage of their journey down the coast to Danzig. After several hours, just as they were giving up hope, the truck appeared. The driver told them that the road was cut and there was no way out over land. Other refugees were already heading for Pillau, and Dost joined the weary columns heading for the port.

North of Königsberg, Erika Morgenstern and her family, together with thousands of other refugees, struggled along congested roads. Overhead, Soviet aircraft repeatedly strafed the columns. The refugees could see the smoke and hear the noise of the fighting towards Königsberg, and were constantly redirected by military police at major road junctions. After days of travel, Erika's grandfather realized that they were passing a place they had already passed – they were moving in circles, surrounded on all sides by the Red Army.

Exhausted by the ordeal, Erika's mother made a desperate decision:

She left her parents and the refugees, in order to pass through the raging hell to Königsberg, where she would be able to get us warm clothing. It would have been wiser in this situation to remain in the protective warmth of the wagon rather than run into the arms of death. But the mistake of a second can result in a lifetime of anxiety ... my mother took my three-year-old sister by the arm and took a small case in her other hand. As she had no hand left for me, I trotted along next to her, holding a one-litre milk tin that my grandmother had filled with food. We hadn't been underway for long when a dreadful snowstorm broke. The bombardment steadily grew worse. We found ourselves on the edge of Königsberg, and thus directly in the frontline. A truck full of German soldiers came towards us and halted, and the driver asked my mother, 'Where are you trying to go, Madam?' When they heard that my mother wanted to return to her home, the soldiers said, 'Go back, there's no other choice, that's drumfire, come with us.' The men must have thought my mother was tired of life when she didn't take their advice and pressed on.

It was exactly as the soldiers had described. The whole city seemed to be engulfed by fire and smoke and there were dead everywhere. Shots and shrapnel constantly flew over our heads, making a whistling noise ... we had to press on carefully from house to house, always on the lookout for cover. The air was so full of smoke and foul smells that it was often difficult to breathe. Every house around us seemed to be burning. At one stage, we thought we were fortunate to find a house that was still standing and appeared undamaged. We quickly rushed inside, but it was almost overflowing with people. We had only just gone in, thinking ourselves safe and secure, when there was a loud crash and I can still remember clearly ... how the corridor walls visibly swayed. A voice called out, 'We must get out.' Everyone immediately ran out into the burning, smoky, stinking, whistling hell. At the very moment that we were all outside, there was an ear-splitting noise. I ducked down low, thinking that it was all over, I would die now. Half bent over, I looked up and saw the house in which we had been standing collapse. It would have become our grave.

Collapsed houses blocked the roads. We had to clamber over these mounds of rubble, which for me meant struggling on three limbs, as I still held my milk can in one hand. My mother didn't have a free hand to help me.[18]

In this manner, the Morgensterns, like dozens of other refugees, made their desperate way through the frontline into Königsberg. How many perished attempting the same journey is impossible to calculate.

Further hard fighting lay ahead in the north. For the moment, though, Cherniakhovsky's armies could look back on the campaign with satisfaction. They had reached the Baltic coast in a little over two weeks, despite spending the first week battering their way through the tough German defences. Casualties had been heavy, but Königsberg – the capital of East Prussia – was encircled, and 3rd Panzer Army was broken into fragments. As the slower pace of siege warfare established itself, there was time for rest, and to collect loot.

On many occasions, the first encounters between German civilians and the advancing Soviet forces were remarkably civil. Those Soviet soldiers, often members of the fast-moving tank corps that were a day or more ahead of the following infantry, warned the Germans to be careful. Many of the Soviet second-echelon units had a grim reputation, which events would show was fully justified. Men like Lev Kopolev, who was both a Soviet officer and an active member of the Communist Party, were rare:

Millions of people have been brutalised and corrupted by the war and by our propaganda – bellicose, jingoistic and false. I had believed such propaganda necessary on the eve of war, and all the more so for the war's duration. I still believed it, but I had also come to understand that from seeds like these came poisoned fruit.[19]

Part of the problem was that the casualties suffered by the Red Army during its long war had left its divisions short of manpower. Throughout the war, even in these last months, Soviet casualties were generally heavier than those of their German opponents. The poorly trained replacement drafts often suffered terrible casualties when they went into action. Those who survived were perhaps more inclined to give vent to their wrath on the civilian population, particularly as many – perhaps most – of the soldiers were often drunk. The civilians who had not escaped before the arrival of the Red Army faced an horrific future:

Women, mothers and their children lie to the right and left along the route, and in front of each of them stands a raucous armada of men with their trousers down. The women who are bleeding or losing consciousness are shoved to one side and our men shoot the ones who try to save their children.[20]

In many cases, officers stood by and watched, often actively encouraging their men. It was a pattern to be seen in other theatres, and in other conflicts – every man was pressured into taking part, to share the collective guilt. Kopolev continued to find examples as his unit moved through Insterburg, Neidenburg and Allenstein. Females of all ages were repeatedly raped, and many were killed and mutilated with a brutality that almost defies belief. When he continued to protest to higher authorities about the impunity with which these crimes were committed – officially, the punishment for rape or looting was death – Kopolev found himself charged with 'bourgeois humanitarianism' and 'sympathy for the enemy'. Although his initial court-martial, in 1946, acquitted him, he was re-arrested, and ultimately served ten years' hard labour in Siberia. Few, if any, Soviet soldiers were ever punished for rape or murder in the first two months of 1945, when the atrocities were at their peak. Later, there were cases of executions to deter further crimes, but such executions, sometimes carried out in front of the convicted soldiers' units, often failed to have the desired effect: 'Some officers will shoot their own men over a German bitch.'[21]

Officially, the Soviet Union never acknowledged the atrocities that undoubtedly occurred on German soil. Rokossovsky's memoirs contain the following section:

Long before entering German territory, the Front's Military Council had discussed the question of our people's behaviour on German soil. The Nazi occupation forces had inflicted so much suffering on Soviet people, they had perpetrated such terrible crimes that our soldiers were filled with a legitimate and understandably fierce hatred for the enemy. However, it was our duty to prevent this legitimate hatred from degenerating into blind rage against the whole German nation. Our war was with Hitler's army, not the civilian population of Germany. And when our troops crossed the German frontier the Front Military Council issued an Order of the Day congratulating our men and commanders on this portentous event and reminding them that we were entering Germany, too, as liberators. The Red Army had come to help the German people get rid of the Nazi clique and its poisonous propaganda. The Military Council called upon all our officers and men to maintain the highest discipline and uphold the honour of the Soviet soldier.

The line and political officers, all Party and Komsomol activists continuously explained to the men the essence of the Soviet Army's mission of liberation, its responsibility for the destinies of Germany, and for the fate of all the other countries we would liberate from the Nazi yolk.

I must say that on German soil our people displayed human kindness and magnanimity.[22]

Murder and rape were not the only crimes. Compared to any other area reached by the Red Army, East Prussia was a rich land. The Red Army allowed soldiers to send regular parcels home from the frontline, ranging from 5kg per month for soldiers to 16kg for generals. Aware of the shortages at home, soldiers sent food and clothing, as well as tools, nails and even typewriters, even though these captured typewriters – with their non-Cyrillic keyboards – would be almost useless in the Soviet Union. Tens of thousands of railway wagons carried this loot east, where enormous piles of undistributed parcels gradually formed. Some contained bizarre items – on at least one occasion, a Soviet officer sent home a porcelain toilet, even though there were no means of plumbing it into his rural house.

Some of the finds were baffling to the Soviet soldiers, accustomed to the austere conditions of life in the Soviet Union:

Stepan Volynkin was our wagon driver in his late forties. Everybody in the battery knew him as a person whose thirst to scavenge and scrounge anything useful from our surrounding neighbourhood was unquenchable.

In early March 1945 our regiment was encamped in a forest, and we were all living in dugouts. Once Volynkin entreated Alexey Nemukhin [the battery sergeant major's assistant] to let him go for a short drive… He returned with a mysterious find: a 100-litre metal cask lay in Volynkin's wagon.

The cask was filled with a mysterious light yellow, odourless, fatty substance that resembled congealed melted butter. After exploring the find, Nemukhin asked me to take a look at the unknown substance. By sight it reminded me of a type of Soviet technical grease. Being overcautious, I hesitated to reach a firm decision even about using it as a lubricant for our weapon: what if the substance had an acid admixture? So Alexey received no advice from me.[23]

Nemukhin discovered that the strange substance could be used as fuel for simple lamps, but Volynkin wasn't satisfied:

Three days passed, and Volynkin unexpectedly entered my dugout. He held a mess kit covered by a clean piece of white fabric. While smiling slyly, Stepan uncovered the kit and said, 'I brought you a couple of warm "oladyas" [soft, thick pancakes fried in fat] to taste.'

The pancakes turned out to be fat and extremely delicious, and I looked at Volynkin approvingly and at the same time questioningly. With this unspoken prompt, Stepan continued:

'From now on, my find will be of real benefit to us all. To tell you the truth, I was dissatisfied with Nemukhin's decision on how to use the "substance". From the day when we first opened the cask, I felt that the stuff had to be edible. However, having heard plenty of rumours about poisoned food, I had patiently restrained my desire to try it for two days. Then, remembering that a man can die but once, I yielded to temptation. To avoid doing much harm to anyone else, I decided first to test the substance on myself. I did it yesterday evening. After I awoke this morning alive and feeling fine, I shared everything regarding my find with Bezuglov, the cook. Then we fried a lot of pancakes and stuffed ourselves up to the neck.'

When Volynkin finished his monologue, I went to Nemukhin to try the substance out for myself. I scooped a little of the substance up with a spoon and, without hesitation, directed it into my mouth for the final tasting... After a few seconds, I decided, but without real confidence, that the substance was probably margarine. I wasn't quite certain because I knew about it just from hearsay during the prewar years.[24]

A recurrent theme in Soviet letters from this time is incomprehension that such a wealthy nation could have chosen to invade the comparatively poor Soviet Union. In some cases, this resulted in even more hatred of the fascists, and a further escalation in the orgy of rape and destruction. It also posed political problems – within the Soviet Union, the Communist Party had indoctrinated people into believing that they were far better off than the wage-slaves of the capitalist world, but now the soldiers could see the reality for themselves. As the weeks drew on, the commissars were increasingly busy dealing with the fallout. But Königsberg and western Samland remained unconquered. Further hard fighting lay ahead.

CHAPTER 7
ROKOSSOVSKY REACHES THE COAST

If we go much further north, we'll be in Sweden!

– Driver of one of the first Soviet tanks to reach Elbing[1]

Further south, near the former Polish-East Prussian frontier, 7th Panzer Division's scattered battlegroups struggled west, hamstrung by crippling fuel shortages. In many cases, small formations were aware that they had already been passed by Soviet spearheads, but managed to remain in radio contact with forces further west and tried their best to break through.

Huber and his comrades had moved back towards the rear with their crippled tank. His crew was in Zichenau just before the town fell to the advancing Red Army, and witnessed an air attack. Huber took refuge in a snow-filled crater in the railway yard until the attack was over. When he approached the stricken train, he was horrified to find that it had been full of refugees:

Another couple of Landsers stand shuddering there. I want to go away, when the one standing next to me cries, 'Dear God!' He bends and in front of us, and from half under the wagon's threshold, he pulls out a white padded cushion with a baby. We stare. Everyone chokes. The baby is dead. The cushion springs protrude from the side of the cushion; it's been split open by shrapnel. And there's a small hole in the baby's temple. A small amount of blood, quite fresh, runs over its back. I let my glove fall and take hold of its little hand. It is still warm. I say to my unnamed Wehrmacht comrades, 'Leave it, it's dead too.' The suction from the explosion near the wagon must have pulled it out. I have to go. I can't bear this. Dead, wounded comrades, I've seen all that before, but this dead baby – no. What else will happen in this dreadful war?[2]

The effectiveness of Soviet air attacks is controversial. On the one hand, many German accounts are disparaging about the poor training and accuracy of Soviet pilots. On the other hand, there is no question that the free-ranging fighter-bombers made movements, particularly of logistics in the rear, very difficult. There was little of the close cooperation between ground forces and aircraft that the Germans themselves had achieved earlier in the war, or was increasingly the case in the west, but attacks on supply columns undoubtedly exacerbated the pre-existing fuel and ammunition shortages.

The train carrying Huber's tank moved on to Soldau, where they were nearly overrun by the advancing Soviet forces:

We remain outside in the cold on the platform, when suddenly at about 1400, from the right, we hear tank shots from the town. The explosions follow immediately after, telling us that they are landing close to us. Everyone is electrified and knows what it means. 'T-34s are in the town, the Russians are there.' The reaction follows a few seconds later: the Landsers start running... Whole crowds run away, fleeing in panic. We decide to prepare our tank for combat. This is urgently necessary, as we have draped blankets over the turret ring to try to keep relatively warm, and these now have to disappear quickly, or we won't be able to turn the turret. We clear the gun and I turn the turret as a precaution to 2 o'clock, the direction from where the T-34 shots came. At least we can try to sell ourselves as dearly as possible. If we wait and the T-34s come directly towards us and the railway station, we reckon, we can shoot up a few of them from the wagon. Two, three armour-piercing rounds are prepared, in case we need them quickly. We have a free field of fire. We now sit ready for combat in the turret, Karl Fritsche and Schütz remain outside, as we don't need them – there's no need for a driver and radio operator.

After a while, when there have been a couple more shots from the T-34s and the confusion amongst the soldiers has increased, a locomotive approaches, links up with us, and pulls us out of the station. I quickly have to turn the turret back to 12 o'clock, in view of the nearby telegraph poles. Just in time, before the enemy has properly penetrated into the town, we leave the railway station... We drive through Lauenburg and Strasburg towards the north, first to Gosslershausen, and then we continue on towards the northeast, towards Deutsch-Eylau. That takes the afternoon and through the evening, with halts on the line and in stations, well into the night. We sleep another night in the cold in our tank.[3]

On 21 January, as Party officials organized a train for civilians to be evacuated, Huber and his comrades waited for their own departure:

It's become frighteningly quiet, with no sound to be heard other than the steam pistons of our locomotive up at the front of the train. It seems to me that danger is likely to come from the 1 o'clock direction, as that's the direction of open ground near the railway station. If the Russians head for the lake via the town, there will be shooting in the streets first.

Only ten minutes pass before we hear them. A first tank shot, and straight afterwards the explosion of a high-explosive round... Meanwhile, it's grown quite dark.

The temperature has also fallen to about 25°C below zero. We keep our eyes open. But all we can see of the T-34s approaching from the south are their muzzle flashes. We can't make out any of them. They appear to be firing high-explosive rounds into the first houses along the edge of Rosenberg, along the lake shore. Schorsch loaded an armour-piercing round a while back, but it is risky to fire it, as the train hasn't set off yet. If we miss, we'll be presented as a target high on our train, as if on a platter.

There's a short peep from the locomotive. Departure! Weitz quickly orders 'Free to fire' and I fire immediately. I have already aimed at the muzzle flashes. But I know that I won't hit anything, as they are about 1,500 metres away and in darkness, I've lost the horizon against the snow in the gunsight. However, we have shown them we know where they are, and they will show more caution on the road. We are already rolling, and I fire another round, as there's no return fire, and then another. There's no chance of hitting, as the wagon is wobbling too much to make a well-aimed shot possible. The train makes good speed running north into the night. I raise the gun and turn the turret. We have left Rosenberg.[4]

From there, the train rolled north, and as they passed the historic town of Marienburg they were shocked to see that it was already ablaze.

That day, as Soviet forces continued to exploit their breakthroughs, both in the south and towards Königsberg in the north, Reinhardt made yet another telephone call to Hitler. He had discussed the desperate situation with his chief of staff, and resolved to force Hitler to accept the necessity for 4th Army's withdrawal from its increasingly threatened position. The discussion with Hitler followed familiar paths – retreat would result in demoralization, argued Hitler, and reinforcements were already en route. Reinhardt reiterated the perilous position of his army group, with mobile Soviet forces advancing freely towards the coast on either flank. Finally, Hitler acquiesced: 4th Army could abandon its positions in the east and withdraw to the coast. The following day, 22 January, Hitler approved the evacuation of the two divisions of XXVIII Corps from Memel.

Soviet planners had predicted a withdrawal by Hossbach's 4th Army, and the day before Rokossovsky issued fresh orders to Ivan Boldin's 50th Army, facing most of the German 4th Army. To date, Boldin's command had been very passive, and Rokossovsky urged his subordinate to take a more aggressive role in order to pin the German forces in their positions. Boldin continued to hesitate, and when a reconnaissance unit finally moved forward on 22 January, it found that most of the German forces had already withdrawn. Rokossovsky immediately sacked Boldin, and ordered Fedor Petrovich Ozerov, the Chief of Staff of 50th Army, to take command.

Not all the units facing Boldin's army had a completely quiet time. Baltuttis, who was serving with Paratroop-Panzergrenadier Division *Hermann Göring*, found that his company had been completely outflanked by a Soviet raiding party, and that their position looked as if it would simply be rolled up, but the expected attack failed to materialize. Nevertheless, the company's strength continued to diminish through a mixture of casualties and men simply slipping away. The regiment's commander visited the position later in the day, to find that the company's fighting strength had dropped to only 26 men, despite incorporating stragglers from other units. A heavy machine-gun team, inadvertently left behind when the rest of the battalion withdrew, fought on alone until it was silenced by shellfire, but it succeeded in preventing the Soviet forces from following up their successful assault on Baltuttis' company.[5]

There was almost no fighting for several days after. When orders came for Baltuttis and his comrades to withdraw late on 21 January, they did so with no interference from the Red Army. Yet as the Landsers trudged back through the darkness to a footbridge over the River Angerapp, the small body of pioneers at the bridge warned them that Soviet forces were reported to be probing forward to the north:

Immediately after we crossed, they blew the bridge. We cursed their haste. Feldwebel Ewald collapsed and lay motionless on the road. We feared that a splinter of wood or iron had struck him. We examined him, and found he wasn't injured; he explained that he wanted to be left lying there, because he lacked the strength to march on. After he failed to respond to our good advice, I hauled him to his feet and supported him as we continued. Feldwebel Ewald was a small, exhausted man. I had noticed his sad eyes in November 1944. At the time, I had thought that he must have experienced many terrible things. After a short time, he thanked me and said that he wanted to continue alone. Several times, I looked for him and saw him at the end of our column. Twenty minutes later, he disappeared without trace. He apparently decided to curl up somewhere. His family would never know where he lay. I reproached myself for not looking after him better.[6]

At the same time, Stavka became aware that the substantial German forces now withdrawing in an orderly manner in front of Boldin's army posed a considerable threat to the northeastern flank of Rokossovsky's spearheads. Originally, 2nd Belorussian Front was tasked with covering the northern flank of Zhukov's 1st Belorussian Front; now, Rokossovsky's main mission changed. Only 65th and 70th Armies would continue to advance on the Vistula. The rest of his Front[7] was ordered to turn north first to isolate, then to break up, the German forces in East Prussia.

One of the striking features of the last year of the war on the *Ostfront* was the growing operational flexibility shown by the Red Army. Both in the preparation and execution of *Bagration*, plans were changed at short notice, and the same pattern was seen in later campaigns. All of the higher command levels, from the Front commanders to Stavka, showed great willingness to re-think previous plans, and the Red Army's staff now had the skill to put these changes into effect with the minimum of fuss. Bagramian's redeployment prior to the drive on Memel, Cherniakhovsky's flexible use of 11th Guards Army, and now the speed with which Rokossovsky changed the axis of advance of his Front, all demonstrate flexibility of the sort that characterized some of the Wehrmacht's early victories. Indeed, as the war continued, German higher commands became less and less flexible, due to the dead hand of Hitler's interference, at the same time that the Red Army learned that operational rigidity almost always resulted in failure.

As Hitler had said to Reinhardt, German reinforcements were finally en route. Far to the north, in Courland, 4th Panzer Division had been pulled out of line for rest and replenishment, and on 17 January was ordered to proceed to the port of Libau as quickly as possible for transport by sea to Germany. Like 24th Panzer Division, it was to leave behind its heavy equipment, and would be re-equipped on arrival; only the division's reconnaissance battalion, 4th Armoured Reconnaissance Battalion, took its vehicles with it. The first elements sailed aboard the troopship *Preussen* on 19 January, reaching the Bay of Danzig two days later. After a brief spell in the seaside resort of Zoppot, the advance party headed south by train towards the army training area at Gruppe, northeast of Graudenz:

For the first time, we saw German people fleeing. Our hearts bled at the sight. Prams, pushed by brave young mothers, or by nuns or Red Cross nurses; horse-drawn wagons with the sick and old; women, women, women, wounded and ever more wounded; misery upon misery!

And they all beseeched us silently, here and there with reproachful glances, to keep the Soviets from them, and not to leave them in the lurch.

Fought-out, exhausted German soldiers sometimes passed us, shaking their fists: 'You idiots! You're just prolonging the war!'

And we, too, began to have doubts about whether we were right, when in view of the hopeless situation we once more placed ourselves in the path of the Soviets. Sometimes we passed small German battlegroups, trying to set up defensive positions by the roads with their remaining strength.

And then once more we saw the columns of misery, the children, women, the elderly, wounded, with helpless, pleading eyes, obliging us to risk everything.

The villages further south were deserted. Nobody wanted to fall into the hands of the Soviets. All wanted to be protected by the German troops.

Unsuspecting, we had come by sea from Courland into this raging storm, and now fought our way against the flood of fleeing people, knowing that we wanted to, should, must protect their escape and shield them to give them time to escape.

… Further south we could see signs of burning villages in the ghostly half-dusk of the winter nights. Smoke and soot fell from the snowy skies by day. Distant shots rang out from the east beyond the Vistula.

A few German soldiers wandered here and there in the area, leaderless and without purpose, their faces full of fear and uncertainty. They were therefore glad to be able to join us, even if [we] were heading in the wrong direction. And ever more comrades, hobbling, with blood-crusted bandages.[8]

Arriving in the training depot near Gruppe on 22 January, 4th Panzer Division's advance party found that there was little preparation for them. Betzel (who had been promoted to Generalleutnant at the beginning of the year) and his staff were alarmed to find that their division was to receive only a partial re-equipment, and had been allocated 32 Pz. IVs, 14 assault guns and 145 half-tracks. Of these latter vehicles, vital for the mobility of the Panzergrenadiers, fewer than 80 were immediately available. Betzel promptly made the first of several requests that the Panther tanks the division had left behind in Courland should be transported to Danzig.

A Stabsfeldwebel and a few ancient Obergefreiters 'administered' and conscientiously guarded the fighting vehicles and heavy weapons, which had been authorized by a whole group of directors, technical inspectors and quartermasters. But the 'fine people' of the higher pay grades had long departed the area.

This must be stated quite clearly: the relationship between the frontline troops and the rear-area authorities was badly disrupted during the great retreat from Russia. While the fronts were held ever more thinly, the cities along the supply routes overflowed with supply formations, administrative staff, Party offices, special commands and other administrations that then all took to their heels when they heard the sounds of battle. Over time, this had embittered the men of the front. They thus had no love for these people of the 'JWD' ['janz weit dahinten', or 'much further back'] who regarded themselves as so terribly important.

We took possession of all the weapons and vehicles that we could take, all without much formality. The old warriors gladly wanted to complete their last tasks of this war with our blessings and signatures.

Problem after problem! Not a single tank had a complete radio set. Others who had organized things for us had messed up. All the radio batteries and transformers were missing. The ones we found in the air raid shelters, used for lighting, were useless. And there wasn't a drop of fuel in the tanks. This had all been siphoned off, according to the arsenal Obergefreiters, to permit the administrative staff to escape from the danger zone. There wasn't a drop of petrol to be found to allow the fighting vehicles to be driven to their positions.

Three cheers, therefore, for our Hauptmann Bruno Schalmat, Chief of Staff of the tank workshops! In the blink of an eye, he brought sufficient fuel forward to give us sufficient mobility to travel about 30 kilometres. How the crews were able to get this fuel remains a mystery to me to this very day.

Only a few hours after our arrival in Gruppe, the thunder of 300-PS engines resounded across the area, though there were no radios. Only the two company commanders' vehicles had complete sets. The tanks didn't have far to drive. The Soviet T-34s did us a favour in that in their haste for victory, they drove directly into our gunsights. They had a sudden shock. Soon after the first clash, 14 T-34s had been left in flames.[9]

Most of Rokossovsky's forces might have been diverted north, but sizeable numbers were still heading for the Vistula valley. The 4th Panzer Division and other units being thrown hastily into the breach would soon have their hands full.

Meanwhile, on 22 January, Rokossovsky's change of direction was already having serious consequences. His initial assault had ripped open 2nd Army's front, and his forces had poured through the gap; German units driven to the northern side of the breach had nevertheless managed to maintain a semi-continuous front. Now, as his most powerful forces turned north, they tore a hole in this line, and it became clear to Hossbach and Reinhardt that swift action would be required to prevent a rapid Soviet drive to the coast at Elbing.

The 5th Company of 7th Panzer Division's Panzer regiment, without any remaining tanks, had reached Strasburg on 20 January, where it found 17 brand-new Jg.Pz. IV tank-destroyers on a train; these vehicles had been intended for 24th Panzer Division, but there was now no prospect of their reaching their intended users. Instead, the crews of 5/25 took possession, delighted to find that they were fully armed and fuelled. They were now deployed for a counter-attack towards Deutsch-Eylau. The 372nd Rifle Division, a leading formation of 2nd Shock Army, seized the town on 20 January, while neighbouring towns were overrun by other elements of CVIII Rifle Corps. At this stage, the leading Soviet forces, the armoured formations of 5th Guards Tank Army, were already more than 20km ahead of the following infantry divisions.

The 7th Panzer Division's new vehicles had been hastily whitened to provide some degree of winter camouflage, and the gunners had spent a few hours adjusting the gunsights – the vehicles were so new, they hadn't even been 'fired in'. The company drove through the night and by midday had reached Bischofswerder. Several vehicles broke down en route:

The other 11 vehicles, which formed the bulk of the company, were supported by 25 half-tracks of our rifle regiment and drove on during the morning. They ran into the spearheads of the attacking Russian troops in front of Deutsch-Eylau. After a tank battle, the company broke off contact, to find that it had already been encircled. It pulled back and during the night drove back through a forest along the railway line from Deutsch-Eylau towards Gosslershausen, so that they were hopefully hidden from Ivan's sight. As only 400 litres of fuel per vehicle were available in Strasburg at the outset and each vehicle used about four litres of fuel per kilometre, fuel ran out for one vehicle after another. These vehicles were then taken in tow.

Oberfeldwebel Hönniger with his Pz. IV … was driving at point. After driving along the railway line for about three kilometres through the wood, they reached the edge of the wood and found a suitable crossing of the railway line, and drove on across open ground. Hönniger spotted a T-34 in the darkness shortly afterwards, only 30 metres to his right at the same height, and driving in the same direction. The T-34 halted and turned its gun on him. Hönniger also stopped immediately and likewise turned his gun to the left to deceive the Russian, in other words away from him. The T-34 commander was deceived, turned his turret back and drove on. Hönniger let Renner drive on too. They went on another 400 metres, until the T-34 once more became suspicious, halted again and turned its turret back again. Hönniger dispassionately repeated the trick, turning his gun to the left again. The Russian tank crew fell for it a second time and were misled in the darkness, turning their turret back to the front.

But now, Hönniger allowed Hans Kalb to turn the turret right back and fired at the Russian, who was still visible in the darkness, at close range. In this precarious situation, the cold-blooded Hönniger gave his crew the advantage that the Russians had previously had: the first shot at close range.

… 5th Company escaped the enemy encirclement. They drove on across country until dawn, travelling a further ten kilometres, reaching an isolated country estate warehouse at 0900, exhausted by the night march. Meanwhile, the critical fuel shortage had resulted in six tanks being towed. Oberleutnant Jakob did not want to risk any further losses, and ordered the towing column to form up in the estate and positioned the four remaining operational vehicles outside the manor facing the forest, from where the enemy attack was expected. The others were to 'take a break' and await the desperately needed supplies; Major Brandes was procuring fuel.

Braumandl, who also had a Panzerjäger in tow, was part of Oberfeldwebel Lechler's crew (with Unteroffizier Renz as gunner and Michel Heidenreiter as loader/radio-operator). The towed vehicles were not unhooked, which would prove to be very significant in what followed. Lechler did not position himself in the estate, but in the cover of a large canteen building. The towed crew were behind them, attached by a cable. The crew went indoors to get something to eat.

Shortly after Hönniger had halted his tank at the warehouse, five or six 8-wheeler armoured cars drove down the road, vehicles captured by the Russians and used by them. The armoured cars stopped, drew up and fired a few rounds with their 20mm guns at the warehouse, but then promptly withdrew.

Oberfeldwebel Hönniger, who as an old hare wasn't bothered by this incident, said to the crew, 'There'll be more,' and drove with his tank from the manor and took up a position some 50 metres away in a garden, between bushes and low trees. He had only three armour-piercing rounds.

Events now unfolded quickly.

The others had hardly begun to eat their bread when the Russians attacked. Next, some nine or ten enemy T-34 tanks emerged from the wood about two kilometres away with a large group of infantry and attacked the warehouse across the open fields. At the same time, Russian artillery laid down a heavy bombardment. There was tremendous confusion. The crews of the towed tanks were partly taking cover from the artillery fire in the buildings, while the four tanks standing guard under Oberleutnant Jakob's command went into direct action against the attacking T-34s. There was wild shooting. Lechler ordered his people back into the tank as soon as the attack began and started his engine.

Hönniger's crew also went into action promptly and shot up the first two T-34s. As they had fired their last armour-piercing round, they gunned their engine and drove back. They hadn't come far when after about 250 metres they slipped sideways into a ditch and the engine stalled. They had run out of fuel, and the engine was dry. As they could see crowds of Russian infantry about 1.5 kilometres away attacking across the open fields, Hönniger ordered the tank to be destroyed. He himself ran to the manor. Fritz Renner, Kalb, the radio operator and the loader ran back, zigzagging to avoid the enemy infantry.

Soon, the limited ammunition of the other guarding tanks was used up (the Panzerjäger 39/IV carried only 55 rounds). They had to withdraw, as the Russians were already dangerously close.

The previously dismounted crews were in the hallway of the large canteen building, driven there by the heavy artillery fire, and by tanks firing high-explosive shells.

Another crew wanted to make a quick escape in its tank, which had been driven into a garage area, and one of the crew who was standing behind the vehicle was crushed against a wall in the confusion. Others, such as the freshly arrived Oberfeldwebel Hönniger, and also Oberfeldwebel Meier and Feldwebel Schütz, ran into the garden with other company personnel and tried to find protection amongst the trees, which were being shredded by high-explosive rounds fired by the tanks.

Meanwhile, Braumandl's crew were in their tank, and their engine was running, but Braumandl was unable to drive off, as the other tank was still hitched up by a cable and its crew were taking cover in the buildings – a fatal misunderstanding.

Lechler's crew waited for these comrades, but in vain. Barely two minutes later, two T-34s appeared from the left at the corner of the building, driving in high gear. They had to negotiate the narrow entrance to the manor, some 30 metres from Braumandl. Trying to do this at high speed, both T-34s shed their tracks and came to a standstill. Their crews bailed out and sought cover in the snow.

Braumandl waited for an order from Lechler over the intercom. Then, through the vision slit, he saw about 15 metres away one of the Russians from the tank crews under cover behind a pillar in the garden, preparing to throw a hand grenade at the tank's open hatch. It landed next to them and exploded outside. Richard looked around and realized that the tank was empty, and that Lechler, Renz and Michl had already bailed out. Braumandl had no choice but to get out, and ripped off his microphone and headset. As he jumped out of the tank, he saw Unteroffizier Renz, who had returned the previous day to the company from home leave; he was lying next to the tank, with both legs blown off by the hand grenade. He barely showed any signs of life. Braumandl had to get away before a second hand grenade was thrown. He pulled up a fencepost, quickly crept through a gap into the garden, and then ran towards the Feldwebel. Richard saw the Russian behind a tree, throwing a couple of hand grenades through the hatch. The tank exploded. Now it was definitely time to get away, through the garden, then over the adjacent snow-covered cattle meadows. He fled under fire from enemy tanks over a stream.

At the same time, Braumandl also saw the attempt by the other three guarding tanks, which had fired off all their ammunition, to escape. In quick succession, all three vehicles were shot up by the T-34s. Oberleutnant Jakob and his crew, Unteroffizier Kühn, Moritz and the gunner, were hit as they tried to drive up a small incline. None of them came out, they were all killed.

… Fritz Renner and Hans Kalb had made a large detour during their escape, to avoid the enemy infantry. After about two kilometres, they reached a village in which the V-Company [supply unit] was waiting in vain for the Kampfgruppe with ammunition and fuel.

… Braumandl and the other six or seven men in the garden who had joined him soon ran into Major Brandes, our Abteilung commander, who happened along in his Kübelwagen. Brandes asked, 'What are you doing here, men?' They reported what had happened. Brandes was shaken and only said, 'The main thing is you're still alive!' Completely exhausted, Braumandl and his fleeing comrades boarded a truck a short time later and were taken further back. Braumandl reported that many had been left behind in the manor.

On this day, 5th Company lost all its tanks.[10]

The following day, 7th Panzer Division's remaining Panther tanks were also in action. Led by Major von Petersdorf-Campen, who had commanded 25th Panzer Regiment since the death of Pückler, a mixed force of tanks and half-tracks found itself a little to the east of Bischofswerder, desperately short of fuel and ammunition. A group of about 20 Sherman tanks attacked at midday, and apparently took the Germans by surprise, in an almost exact replica of the battle that destroyed 5th Company. In moments, the half-dozen remaining Panthers were all shot up, and the regimental commander was killed. Few of the troops escaped back to German lines. In its daily report to corps and army headquarters, 7th Panzer Division recorded that on this day it had no operational tanks left in the field.

Marion Dönhoff, the aristocrat from Friedrichstein who was briefly detained by the Gestapo after the 20 July attempt on Hitler's life, had spent the winter in the village of Quittainen, 30km southeast of Elbing. She had watched as refugees straggled into the area over the previous months – first a few farmers from Belarus, then Lithuanians, then Memellanders and finally the brief surge of those fleeing from Gumbinnen, Goldap and Nemmersdorf. She was struck by how inadequate the wagons used by the refugees were, with little protection against the weather, and advised all of the farms in the area to prepare roofs made of straw and latticework for their wagons. This brought a visit by a representative of the local Kreisleiter, who told her that such measures were defeatist and that unless she desisted, she would feel the full weight of the law.[11] She continued with her preparations, though with more circumspection.

On 20 January, all able-bodied men in the area were summoned for service in the Volkssturm, rather undermining the assurances given by Party officials just a day earlier that there was no cause for concern. A couple of days later, Dönhoff telephoned the Kreisleiter's office in Preussisch Holland to request a rail ticket so that she could travel to Königsberg, and thence to Friedrichstein. To her astonishment, the official on the telephone replied, 'But don't you know that the area must be evacuated by midnight?'[12] Swiftly, she informed the locals, many of whom refused to believe that the Führer's promise of final victory, and that not a yard of German soil would be yielded, had proved to be worthless. Urging them all to leave and meet at a nearby crossroads, she rode back to Quittainen through the bitterly cold night. The village had been home since the previous autumn to about 400 refugees who had fled from Goldap, and this increase in population had put a strain on local food reserves. Even while the sound of gunfire could be heard growing louder in the east, Party officials ordered the menfolk from Goldap to collect together their horses and return to Goldap – some 250km to the east – in order to collect fodder and food. The result of this was that the women and children from Goldap were left with neither their menfolk nor their horses, at the very moment that they would need them most.

Dönhoff had drawn up a detailed plan for the evacuation of the area, including several copies of maps with all roads clearly marked. In the chaos that now ensued, these plans were simply ignored. Dönhoff and her Oberinspektor exhorted the farmers to take only what was clearly necessary, in vain. Nor was it possible to coordinate with other local farms as she had originally planned. She made her own preparations, packing a change of clothes and a few other essentials, while her staff did likewise:

> Fräulein Markowski, the older [of the two secretaries], a very efficient woman, was one of the Führer's most devoted followers, and had rejoiced at every special bulletin for years – now she was very still, but I was startled when she asked herself whether the 'unbelievers' and traitors should not nevertheless be held responsible.[13]

At midnight, Dönhoff and her staff left the house for the last time to join the column that was forming up outside. She saddled her toughest, most experienced horse. The first leg of the journey, to the town of Preussisch Holland, was about 11km, which should have taken about an hour. On the crowded, frozen roads, it took six hours. After being stationary for two hours just outside the town, Dönhoff rode ahead to see what was happening. She found the town gridlocked with refugees, and the local Party offices abandoned. A farmer informed her that the Party officials had been the first to depart. She returned to her fellow refugees, who were shivering in temperatures of -20°C. Some had already decided that if they were to be overrun by the Red Army, they would prefer to be in the warmth of their own homes when it happened, rather than freezing here in the open. They had also come to a conclusion about Dönhoff: they urged her to flee on horseback, as she would be able to bypass the clogged roads. If she should fall into Soviet hands, they reasoned, she would be in danger of being shot out of hand, purely because she was an aristocrat. Accompanied by a soldier on horseback who had been separated from his unit, she rode westwards, past scenes that seared into her memory:

We rode all day, constantly feeling as if we were in a great queue: in front of us, behind us, alongside us were people, horses, and wagons. Here and there one saw a familiar face or read the name of a familiar place on a small sign hanging from a wagon. Beyond the small town of Preussisch Holland, we encountered people from smallholdings and shopkeepers who had set out with small handcarts loaded with their grandmother, or with their possessions heaped onto them. My God, what images. And where were these people actually trying to go? Did they want to travel in this manner for hundreds, perhaps thousands of kilometres?[14]

At a road junction, an officer on the lookout for stragglers took her companion away, leaving Dönhoff with two horses. At that moment, a small group from Quittainen hailed her. They rested in a farmhouse, but left when they heard that the Russians were barely 3km away. Along roads choked with fleeing civilians and the jetsam of dozens of Wehrmacht formations, Dönhoff and Georg, the 15-year-old son of one of her estate foresters from Quittainen, reached the Nogat:

In front of me lay the long railway bridge over the Nogat. Old-fashioned high iron bracings, with a solitary hanging lamp blowing in the wind weakly casting grotesque shadows. For a moment, I reined in my horse, and before its hooves clattering on the boards of the bridge drowned out all other noise, I heard a strange, rhythmic, short knocking, as if something was labouring awkwardly on three legs or with a crutch over the resonating boards. At first, I couldn't make it out, but soon I saw three figures before me in uniform, silently and slowly dragging themselves across the bridge. One was on crutches, one had a stick, and the third wore a large bandage on his head, and the left arm of his coat hung empty.

All of the occupants of the military hospital had been given permission to leave and advised to save themselves by their own strength, they said, but out of about a thousand wounded, only these three had the required 'strength'; all the others, after days in unheated trains without food or medical care, were too worn down or listless to follow this desperate advice. Advice? Their own strength? The Russian tanks were at most only thirty kilometres, perhaps only twenty kilometres from us; these three could put no more than two kilometres behind them in an hour. And the temperature was between 20 and 25 degrees below zero – how long would it therefore take until the frost had taken hold in their open wounds? … for me this was the end of East Prussia: three desperately ill soldiers, dragging themselves over the Nogat bridge into West Prussia. And a woman on horseback, whose ancestors had travelled east from the west six hundred years before through the wilderness on either side of this river – six hundred years of history dissipated.[15]

Rokossovsky's main effort to isolate and break up 4th Army continued. The German 299th Infantry Division and 18th Panzergrenadier Division were driven back from Hohenstein, though *Grossdeutschland* continued to hold up the 3rd Soviet Army near Passenheim. Between these two German concentrations, the Soviet III Guards Cavalry Corps was beginning to make its presence felt, pressing forward towards Allenstein. But the most startling development came further to the west. Late on 22 January, Captain Mikhail Diatchenko of XXIX Tank Corps, part of 5th Guards Tank Army, received orders to lead his group of nine T-34s in a drive north towards the Baltic coast. The Soviet spearheads were 70km from the coastline, and the purpose of this raid was to push as far as possible until resistance was encountered.

Diatchenko set off early on 23 January, and his nine tanks covered the first 20km without encountering any resistance. The Soviet tank crews were under strict orders not to open fire unless absolutely necessary, and they carefully picked their way through constant refugee traffic, which frequently yielded passage only with the greatest reluctance. Twice, the T-34s encountered German military traffic, which simply moved to one side and allowed them to pass; it seems that all the exhausted people on the road, civilians and soldiers alike, simply assumed that the tanks were German vehicles, and didn't examine them too closely in the bitter cold.

By midday, the tanks had reached Preussisch Holland. Carefully, the Soviet drivers made their way through the roads, which were choked with refugees. One tank crashed into a two-wheeled cart, but even now they weren't recognized as enemies.

Just north of Preussisch Holland, Diatchenko halted to take stock. He was alarmed to discover that two of his tanks were missing, apparently stranded in traffic in the town. There was a sudden burst of firing, with shells landing in the fields on either side. The civilians along the road scattered in terror, but the firing stopped as quickly as it had started, whether out of fear of hitting the civilians, or because the gunners were still not sure if the tanks were Wehrmacht or Red Army vehicles. Diatchenko and his remaining crews pressed on. By 1600hrs, the remaining seven tanks had reached Grunau, only 8km from Elbing. Here, they found themselves in a great tangle of vehicles, all trying to cross the only southern route across the anti-tank ditches that had been dug around Elbing. Patiently, they waited their turn, and finally crossed the ditches, and motored into the city itself.

Diatchenko found himself driving along a city street behind a fully loaded tramcar. Pedestrians passed by on either side, either going home after work or visiting the shops that lined the street. At the same moment, the tanks were finally recognized as enemies and came under fire from the nearby Gallwitz barracks. Diatchenko gave the order to open fire, and the tanks careered through the swiftly emptying streets. Two were rapidly knocked out, but the others moved on north of Elbing, trading shots with infantry who pursued them with Panzerfausts. Two more were destroyed, and a fifth disabled on the northern edge of the city. The survivors moved on some 7km and they took up defensive positions to await the arrival of their comrades.

The raid caused widespread panic in Elbing. The Party leadership suddenly ordered 'level three evacuation', requiring all civilians to leave the city. For the military garrison, this was doubly wrong: it resulted in enormous traffic on the roads, and simultaneously led to the departure of vital civilians, such as medical personnel. By the time the order was rescinded later that night, it was already too late to prevent chaos. Refugees continued to stream out of Elbing throughout 24 January, struggling over the bridges of the city and along the frozen roads towards Danzig. Faced by constant delays on the roads, many refugees were unable to endure the constant cold and abandoned their attempts to leave, returning to the city.

As with so many German towns in the path of the Soviet tide, the local commandant, Oberst Eberhard Schöppfer, was forced to improvise the best defence he could. No complete division fought in the defence of Elbing; fragments of several formations were variously commandeered or retreated into the city. The replacement battalions of Panzer Division *Feldherrnhalle*, responsible for training new recruits for the division, were based in Elbing, and they provided Schöppfer with the core of his defensive force, which ultimately amounted to about 10,000 men. Officers were dispatched to the roads leaving Elbing to extract any soldiers attempting to leave, so that they could be incorporated into the defending units. Troops returning to the front from the Reich, who were now unable to continue further east, were taken under command. Major Kühnek, the fortress artillery commander, took advantage of guns being manufactured at the Schichau dockyards to improvise five artillery batteries.

The first test of the defenders came on 24 January, when Soviet tanks once more threatened the outskirts. The Soviet XXIX Tank Corps, advancing from the south, probed the German perimeter, while X Guards Tank Corps drove northwards to the east of Elbing. This latter move cemented the rupture between Elbing and East Prussia, cutting the last road and rail links running to the east. The personnel of 561st Volksgrenadier Division's 1142nd Grenadier Regiment, without any of their heavy weapons, repelled the attack by XXIX Tank Corps, but Schöppfer could do nothing about the gap between his garrison and 4th Army to the east. The city was surrounded by about 12km of defences, laboriously dug by civilian labour. Schöppfer and his staff estimated that these defences would require about three divisions to be manned properly, and the forces available were too few. A tighter perimeter would have to be improvised.

The following day, the left flank of the Soviet 48th Army[16] passed through Preussisch Holland, reaching a point barely 20km south of Elbing. Parts of Generalleutnant Karl Mauss' 7th Panzer Division were close by. Mauss had volunteered for service as a fighter pilot in the Great War; he was injured in a crash in 1918, ending his career as an aviator. In 1929, he qualified as a dentist, but five years later he was back in uniform as an infantry officer. After time with an infantry regiment in 20th Motorized Infantry Division, he commanded one of 4th Panzer Division's Panzergrenadier regiments before taking command of 7th Panzer Division in early 1944, a post he retained with three short breaks until almost the end of the war. Swept northwest with the debris of his division, Mauss made no attempt to hide his anger and contempt for those who had brought Germany to this dire position, as his radio operator recorded:

In this phase of the war, the division commander revealed an almost bottomless hatred of the 'brown regime', particularly against Goebbels and his clique. He curtly dismissed any opinions and comments made by National Socialist officers. He frequently spoke with us, the crew of his command vehicle, about the inability of higher army command and the wicked intention of Hitler to leave Army Group North to its fate in Courland, even though with their men and weapons, this force might have provided sufficient strength for Army Group Vistula to maintain contact with the west.

For Dr Mauss, the final straw was when he was ordered to report to Dirschau, after Himmler had taken over Army Group Vistula. On the road there, bodies of men and women, some very young, hung from gallows in the trees, each bearing a placard on their chests: 'I refused to work for Greater Germany', or 'I am a deserter', etc. From this moment on, the commander's plans and deeds were only to help as many German people as possible to be saved from the advancing Red Army and to be taken west over the Baltic.[17]

The retreating men of the division witnessed many harrowing scenes as they fell back:

Morning dawns, with a grey sky and an ice-cold east wind. The fine snow is blown from the fields over the roads and onto us, and you can hardly see the ground. On the left side of the road, there are horse-drawn vehicles – refugees. They have apparently stayed there all night. Thick icicles hang from the horses' nostrils, bridles and legs. They stand with their heads bowed in the snowstorm. Between the horse-drawn wagons is a civilian truck in the refugee column, a wood-powered vehicle. We have to halt here again, and once more I see a dreadful scene: the tail flap of the truck is hinged back, and at the end of the loading deck amongst the bundles of refugee property huddle two shapes, already thickly covered with snow. They are women. One, on the left, rouses herself and pushes the snow from her shoulders, making it easier to see her. The woman has a small baby in her arms, dead and blue with the cold. She seems to me so hopelessly sad with her eyes red from crying – and she clutches the frozen baby to her chest, as if to warm it even in death. As she does so, the snow falls from the little bundle, the woman shakes herself and draws forward the blanket that she has draped over her shoulders to cover the dead child. It's just as well that the N-Staffel [signals section] vehicle moves on and we drive onward. Will at least the mother make it? Today it's at least 20–25°C below zero and as before, my felt boots are frozen stone hard on my feet. I keep seeing the woman with the dead child in front of my eyes as we drive on.[18]

Two partly constructed torpedo boats in the Elbing dockyards were towed to the port of Pillau on 25 January along a channel created by an icebreaker. When news spread of the imminent departure of the vessels, and that they were prepared to take refugees with them, there was further chaos in Elbing. Thousands rushed to the dockyards, where they came under Soviet artillery fire. About 400 refugees were taken onto the torpedo boats before they left.[19]

Around Elbing itself, pressure developed steadily. XXIX Tank Corps sealed off the eastern side of the town, while part of 2nd Shock Army [20] pressured the defences from the south, threatening to push on to the Baltic to the west of Elbing. General Batov's 65th Army, meanwhile, continued to advance along Rokossovsky's original axis towards the Vistula bend:

The hardest moment of the operation for us was the establishment of a bridgehead across the Vistula, which was about four hundred metres wide and up to seven metres deep. The weather constantly interfered. At first, it became warm. Melting snow and rain saturated the ground. Our troops could only advance slowly, as they were forced to stick to the roads. We planned to establish a pontoon across a strip of ice-free water. Our combat engineers, who were following the leading infantry elements in long columns, were already moving up, when a sharp frost intervened. At night, the thermometer fell to -25°C. The asphalt roads became ribbons of ice, and the trucks slipped into the roadside ditches or became stuck. Everything ground to a halt. The Vistula froze too, but the ice was too weak, particularly for the transfer of combat materiel. Consequently, we had to consider an alternative means of crossing, to strengthen the ice and build ice roads.

On 26 January, the Soviet 354th Rifle Division reached the Vistula, the first [of 65th Army's divisions] to do so.[21]

Two days later, Soviet engineers were able to reinforce the ice with a layer of logs, but the amount of weight this could take was still limited. On 29 January, the engineers blew a channel in the ice, and built a pontoon bridge across the open water. Nevertheless, the rate at which Batov could reinforce 354th Rifle Division on the west bank of the Vistula was limited by German resistance around Graudenz. Batov discussed the problems with Rokossovsky when the Front commander visited 65th Army's headquarters on 30 January. Rokossovosky ordered him to detach the weak 37th Guards Rifle Division to 2nd Shock Army, which would use it in conjunction with its own forces to contain the Graudenz garrison. This would allow Batov to concentrate on his bridgehead west of the Vistula.[22]

Rokossovsky's 2nd Belorussian Front thus completed its modified mission with alacrity. All along the Vistula, the various armies of the Front drove back the scattered German defenders, while on Rokossovsky's southern flank the forces tasked with continuing the original line of attack continued to make progress. The German units in their path were a mixture of the original frontline divisions, now battered and weakened by their retreat, and a scattering of small units that suddenly found themselves in the thick of the fighting. The town of Hohensalza, a few kilometres southwest of Thorn, was the objective of elements of General Berzarin's 5th Shock Army. As the remnants of XLVI Panzer Corps fell back through the town, a staff officer informed the local commander, Sturmbannführer Baron von Foelkersam, that he was to defend the town to the last man, with his garrison of only 500 men.

The first attack came on 18 January, as the Soviet 220th Tank Brigade and XXVI Guards Rifle Corps enveloped Hohensalza. Von Foelkersam had only one radio contact with the outside world, a link to the headquarters of Otto Skorzeny, the renowned German special forces commander, who was now in a headquarters north of Berlin. The fighting in Hohensalza continued until 21 January, when von Foelkersam contacted Skorzeny and reported that the situation was untenable, and asked if he should attempt a breakout. Skorzeny agreed that he should, but that evening a last signal from the town reported that von Foelkersam had been badly wounded and was unconscious. Nevertheless, a breakout was attempted that night.

Two months later, two officers and 13 men from the Hohensalza garrison reached German lines after a march of more than 340km. They reported that the surviving 200 men of the garrison had broken through the encircling Soviet forces in two groups, with their unconscious commander in a half-track. The vehicle disappeared in the confused fighting during the night, and the two groups rapidly became fragmented. The 15 men were the only known survivors.[23]

There was a yawning gap between the new Army Group Centre – formerly Army Group A – and Reinhardt's battered armies along the middle Vistula and in East Prussia, and in order to fill this gap a new Army Group Vistula was created. It was essential that the commander of this new army group should be someone with experience, energy and great skill. Guderian's nomination for the post was Generalfeldmarschall Maximilian von Weichs, who had recently distinguished himself when commanding an army group in Greece and the Balkans. Generaloberst Alfred Jodl, the OKW Chief of Staff, agreed that von Weichs was the ideal man for the post. When the matter was discussed on 22 January, Hitler rejected this advice, saying that he regarded von Weichs as too old and too tired for the post. To Guderian's disappointment and irritation, Jodl made a remark about von Weichs' deep religious convictions, and that appeared to seal the matter. Instead, Hitler announced that the commander would be Reichsführer-SS Heinrich Himmler. The defence of parts of West Prussia, and all of Pomerania, would be in the hands of a man with no field experience, who insisted on adhering to a strict daily regime that allowed him less than five hours' work a day, and who remained in his luxurious personal train instead of visiting the field units assigned to him.

This astonishing appointment owed much to Hitler's continuing distrust of senior Wehrmacht figures after the July plot. Himmler had briefly served as Befehlshaber Oberrhein in the west in 1944, a post that involved him in very little serious work, as most decisions were made by von Runstedt and his staff. Nevertheless, he left behind him a very negative impression. Once he arrived in the east, he did little to impress the professional soldiers around him, as one later recorded:

> When it came to an operational overview of the entire situation, he simply wasn't up to the task. He just averted his gaze from the large gap that he had to close. He saw the advance of the Russians south of the Netze towards Posen as a unique opportunity … to thrust into their flank, thus attacking and destroying them. He constantly used the words 'assault' and 'thrust in the flank'. He did not recognize that the Russians were in a position to turn the flank of the hard-pressed 2nd Army.[24]

Even within the ranks of the SS, there was a low opinion of Himmler's abilities: 'Himmler had no authority as a military leader … he was also unaware that he lacked military experience and knowledge … it was a tragedy – no, a crime, to entrust this army group to Himmler in this most desperate situation.'[25]

Meanwhile, on the northeast side of the Vistula, the Soviet 70th Army was bearing down on the city of Thorn. The city, which was established by German settlers in 1231, lay mainly on the right bank of the Vistula. It had a mixed Polish and German population, having been part of Prussia and Poland at different stages of its history, and had been extensively fortified after the Franco-Prussian War to create what was regarded as a formidable fortress in the Kaiser's Germany, second only to Metz.

In 1939, the city was known as Torun and was part of Poland; it fell almost without a fight to the advancing Germans, and its antiquated defences were not put to the test. In 1944, the defences were renovated and improved, with fields of fire cleared and anti-tank ditches dug. On 23 January 1945, General der Pioniere Otto Lüdecke was appointed as fortress commander. Two days later, he was able to report that he had some 32,000 men in his garrison; these troops were of limited value, however. They included the remnants of the Warsaw garrison, and the personnel of the Fahnenjunkerschule IV (Officer Candidate School IV), which was based in the city. What remained of 31st Volksgrenadier Division had also retreated to Thorn. The city defences had been intended for a force of five divisions, and the available units amounted to less than half this. Furthermore, there was only sufficient heavy weapons ammunition for about three days of intense fighting, though food and munitions for light weapons were adequate for several weeks.

Most of Thorn's German population had already left, but perhaps half of the city's 24,000 Poles stayed on in expectation of liberation from the Germans. As a vital communications hub on the middle Vistula, the capture of the city would allow Rokossovsky and Zhukov to establish a further link between their Fronts. For the Germans, the orders were the same as for every location declared a fortress: it was to be defended to the bitter end.

Thorn came under attack on 24 January, when small infantry units with armoured support probed the perimeter. The following day, Generalmajor Franz Schlieper's 73rd Division, retreating from Modlin, was able to break through the thin Soviet perimeter and reached the city with 7,000 troops. Schlieper's division had lost much of its heavy equipment when it was forced to retreat from north of Warsaw, but it was still in comparatively good shape, and without it even the most rudimentary defence of Thorn would have been impossible.

The original reasoning behind the development of Thorn as a German fortress in the late 19th century was to provide a bulwark against which attacks from the east could be broken up and held at arm's length, until German forces were able to win a decisive victory in the west and could then be used for a counter-attack in the east. It was clear in January 1945 that such a strategy was out of the question, and as soon as he arrived in Thorn, Generalmajor Schlieper contacted Lüdecke to suggest an immediate breakout; the only purpose that could be served by continuing to hold Thorn was to tie up Soviet forces and prevent their being used elsewhere. Aware of Hitler's likely response to such a development, particularly after the Warsaw garrison abandoned their 'fortress' without permission, Lüdecke decided to hold firm for the moment. As a precaution, however, he ordered three squads of reconnaissance officers to position themselves in nearby woodland, with a view to scouting out possible escape routes. The Red Army discovered all three squads, and only one man survived as a prisoner.[26]

Although the Red Army vastly outnumbered the Wehrmacht, the diversion of most of Rokossovsky's strength from its originally intended axis resulted in fewer forces being available than had previously been anticipated. At first, Vasily Popov's 70th Army could only spare a single under-strength division to attempt an envelopment of Thorn, and a full-scale assault on the defences was impossible. It could not, therefore, be argued that the garrison was tying down significant Soviet forces, and under constant pressure from Guderian, Hitler astonished everyone by agreeing on 29 January that there was little to be gained by continuing to hold the fortress, and permission for a breakout was granted. The order was passed through the chain of command, reaching Lüdecke the following day.

By this point, the frontline had moved 40km beyond Thorn – the Red Army had continued its drive to the northwest. In addition to closing with the Vistula along its banks from Fordon to Kulm, the right flank of Popov's army [27] advanced on Kulm and the Vistula as far as Graudenz. In an attempt to hold up this drive, Pantenius was ordered to deploy his regiment from 337th Volksgrenadier Division near the village of Kulmisch Pfaffendorf, about 8km northwest of Kulmsee. Like the rest of the division, Pantenius' 690th Volksgrenadier Regiment had lost much of its heavy equipment during its long retreat from Warsaw. As it arrived in the village, it found that most of the residents, Poles and Germans alike, had already fled. The relatively flat countryside, with its surface still firmly frozen by nocturnal temperatures of -12°C, seemed ideal for a swift armoured advance. Pantenius' attempts to establish contact with his neighbours – 542nd Volksgrenadier Division to the northeast and 251st Infantry Division to the west – were fruitless. Communications with higher commands were also muddled, and Pantenius was not to know that both his flanking formations had already pulled back towards Kulm and the Vistula, leaving his regiment dangerously exposed.

Pantenius organized his men as best as he could, without any supporting anti-tank weapons or artillery available to him – the only weapons capable of stopping a tank were the Panzerschrecks and Panzerfausts carried by the infantry themselves. The advancing Soviet 162nd Rifle Division attacked the village on 25 January, though to Pantenius' relief little attempt was made to bypass his exposed flanks. With radio contact lost, Pantenius decided to hold on at least until nightfall, to give the defences of Kulm time to prepare. Fighting raged in the village all day, with Soviet infantry stubbornly pressing against the infantry positions without trying to outflank them. A few Soviet tanks appeared, but warily kept their distance. During the afternoon, the hard-pressed defenders fell back to the northern edge of Kulmisch Pfaffendorf. Here they were surprised by the sudden appearance of a half-track accompanied by four assault guns. The half-track contained Generalmajor Werner Heucke, commander of 251st Infantry Division, who ordered the assault guns into immediate action, repulsing the Soviet attackers. Pantenius was ordered to withdraw to Kulm, and was able to disengage from the battle while the assault guns provided covering fire. With a heavy heart, he had to leave behind many of his wounded men; after the war, attempts by the Red Cross to determine the fate of these men were in vain, and it appears that they were shot out of hand by the advancing elements of 162nd Rifle Division.

The retreating regiment came under constant pressure from the advancing Soviet forces. One of the two battalion commanders had been wounded and was missing within Kulmisch Pfaffendorf, and the other now became a casualty. With Soviet forces in hot pursuit, Pantenius gathered together what men he could to assemble some sort of rearguard for his retreating regiment. They withdrew through the night to the Vistula, and crossed via one of the remaining ice bridges. Out of his original 850 men, Pantenius had lost 400 dead, wounded or missing. Stragglers continued to arrive for several days.[28]

On 26 January, leading elements of the Soviet I Guards Tank Corps had passed the Thorn encirclement and pressed on to the great bend in the Vistula between Thorn and Bromberg. The bridge over the river near Fordon was held by 300 men from 2nd Army's weapons school, but the sudden appearance of the Soviet force put them to flight before the bridge could be blown. Leaving just a single company to hold the bridge, the small Soviet group pressed on towards the northwest, and late on 27 January the Germans who had retreated to Fordon made a surprise counter-attack, seizing the bridge and destroying it, after which they set off northwards, reaching German lines three days later.[29]

Although this small force might have felt that it had reprieved itself by recapturing and destroying the bridge, their action would have serious consequences for the Thorn garrison. The Fordon bridge represented the only crossing over the Vistula downstream from Thorn until Graudenz; although there was a ferry at Kulm, this had already been destroyed to prevent it falling into Soviet hands. Nevertheless, the destruction of the Fordon bridge hindered the movement of 70th Army's troops, and in particular its supplies, across the Vistula.

Meanwhile, Bromberg too had been isolated on 25 January. The city, which for much of its history has been known by its Polish name of Bydgoszcz, had been the scene of the infamous 'Bromberg Bloody Sunday massacre' of September 1939, which was used as justification for much of the suppression of the Poles in the early weeks of the German occupation. Unwilling to wait for instructions from Danzig, Rampf, the local Party Kreisleiter, ordered all civilians to leave on 21 January. A few days later, a proclamation appeared in Berlin under the title 'Death and punishment for dereliction of duty':

> Reichsführer-SS Heinrich Himmler has decreed the severest punishments for certain neglectful officials who have shown themselves to be unworthy in the last few days.
>
> The former SS-Standartenführer and Chief of Police in Bromberg, von Salisch, was demoted and shot for cowardice and dereliction of duty.
>
> The former Regierungspräsident of Bromberg, Kühn, and the former Bürgermeister of Bromberg, Ernst, are stripped of their decorations and posts, demoted, and ordered to serve as probationer soldiers in a probation battalion, after witnessing the execution of von Salisch.
>
> The former Kreisleiter of Bromberg, Rampf, who has been expelled from the Party and demoted on the orders of the Party Chancellery, is likewise ordered to a probation battalion, where like Kühn and Ernst he will be assigned arduous and dangerous tasks.[30]

The commander of the cavalry school, Oberstleutnant von Arnim, took command of the small garrison of Bromberg. The most powerful unit available to him was a Panzergrenadier battalion from 4th Panzer Division, and when this battalion was recalled to the Graudenz area von Arnim tried to contact Danzig to request permission to break out to the north. After failing to receive a reply, he decided to act on his own initiative.

Early on 26 January, 4th Panzer Division's Panzergrenadiers, mounted in half-tracks, led the way north out of Bromberg. The various units of the garrison – flak, the personnel of the cavalry school and police – followed them. A small body of infantry reinforced by combat engineers formed the rearguard. In snow and fog, they succeeded in breaking through the encircling ring, which was only lightly manned (after surrounding the town, the Soviet 103rd Tank Brigade and 234th Rifle Division had marched north, leaving only small units behind).

The German column reached the village of Maxtal without encountering resistance. At midday, the vanguard ran into Soviet forces near Klahrheim. Bitter fighting erupted, and it took until nightfall for von Arnim's forces to secure the nearby railway station. Attempts to push northwest towards the village itself ran into further Soviet forces, and a decision was made to continue northeast towards Prust, where it was hoped that the

Germans would encounter friendly forces. The 33rd Panzergrenadier Regiment, from 4th Panzer Division, was driving south towards Prust in conjunction with Pantenius' 690th Volksgrenadier Regiment. These forces succeeded in taking Prust on 27 January, and in three columns the Bromberg garrison reached the town late that day. Eventually, in groups of varying sizes, perhaps three-quarters of the Bromberg garrison succeeded in reaching German lines.[31]

Popov's 70th Army was now facing difficulties. Its headlong advance had resulted in many of its formations becoming strung out along the line of march, and supply problems were developing. Indeed, one of the factors that saved Pantenius' regiment in the fighting south of Kulm was a lack of artillery support for the attacking Soviet forces, something that Pantenius presumed to be due to difficulties in bringing forward sufficient artillery ammunition. The overall plan for Popov's divisions was to transfer them to the west bank of the Vistula, from where they would be able to drive north and northwest, but the isolated towns left in their wake now caused significant problems. Furthermore, the arrival of 4th Panzer Division in the Gruppe area provided the German XLVI Panzer Corps with some welcome muscle, and a new German defensive line was rapidly forming to the south and west of Schwetz. The casualties of the long advance were also taking their toll on Popov's forces.

Weiss' 2nd Army also had serious problems. The left flank of the army, deployed mainly along the Vistula, was solid enough, particularly as rising temperatures made ice bridges across the river far more hazardous. The sector in and around Schwetz, too, was now fairly firm, but further to the west 2nd Army's right flank was still hanging in the air. Although Weiss had two armoured divisions at his disposal – 4th Panzer Division and 7th Panzer Division – both were effectively tied down in the frontline, and even if they could be freed for mobile operations, fuel and ammunition shortages greatly reduced their efficacy. In common with other senior officers, Weiss suggested the evacuation of Courland, and even of East Prussia, to provide sufficient forces to allow for a continuous frontline to be restored. When this was refused, Weiss requested that the city of Graudenz be abandoned, so that its troops could be made available to his army to reinforce the frontline, and in particular to form a counter-attack group that might be able to strike east across the lower Vistula to restore contact with 4th Army. This request, too, was refused. Weiss could do little but watch his exposed right flank with growing concern, aware that the Soviet forces before him were steadily shifting their point of effort to the west.

The arrival of elements of 1st Belorussian Front on Popov's left flank, in particular II Guards Cavalry Corps, followed by their swift advance to the north, forced the German units still consolidating the new frontline around Prust to consider a withdrawal in order to prevent their open western flank being turned. Popov could now concentrate his 70th Army on a tighter front, with its axis of advance more to the north than the northwest, and he accordingly brought the powerful I Guards Tank Corps across the Vistula and up into position south of Prust. Faced with growing pressure to his front and the threat of being outflanked, General Martin Gareis, commander of XLVI Panzer Corps around Prust, ordered 4th Panzer Division to move northwest towards Tuchel. The immediate consequence of this was that the weakened 337th Volksgrenadier Division was left on its own to face the Soviet forces at Prust. On 28 January, Popov began to press north along the west bank of the Vistula towards Schwetz, and as 251st Infantry Division and 542nd Volksgrenadier Division were slowly driven back, 337th Volksgrenadier Division was forced to extend its front to the east. Under constant pressure from the Soviet 16th Rifle Division, the Volksgrenadiers fell back over the next two days, until they were level with Schwetz. The arrival of a company from 4th Panzer Division's 35th Panzer Regiment, with 14 assault guns, provided some welcome reinforcements on 29 January.

The Thorn garrison began its breakout early on 31 January. The route of 80km that it would have to take was far longer than the path followed by the Bromberg garrison, with complete uncertainty of how to cross the Vistula at the end of the journey. Inevitably, most of the garrison's heavy weapons would have to be abandoned, though attempts were made to improvise transport to allow the wounded to be taken with the retreating troops. The garrison formed up in three groups – 73rd Infantry Division on the right, 31st Volksgrenadier Division on the left and the other units gathered together as Kampfgruppe von Rhaden in the centre – and set off from Thorn, blowing the city's bridges before they left.

With most of their personnel on foot, the three groups made slow progress through the heavy snow. By the evening of the first day, they had covered 20km. The Germans soon realized that the Red Army had left minimal forces around the city, and that the Thorn garrison was now in a clear area behind Popov's frontline. Indeed, most of the casualties suffered on the first day were from air attacks rather than fighting on the ground. Nevertheless, the small units in their path, combined with the snow-covered terrain, would ensure that the breakout would not be easy.

The first serious ground fighting erupted on 1 February, as elements of 73rd Infantry Division ran into the Soviet 136th Rifle Division near the town of Siemon. On the left flank, close to the frozen Vistula, 31st Volksgrenadier Division also encountered tough resistance, this time from parts of the Soviet 162nd Rifle Regiment. Once this was overcome, the division pressed on along the eastern bank of the Vistula, while engineers considered the practicalities of building an ice bridge across the river.

THE BREAKOUTS FROM THORN AND BROMBERG

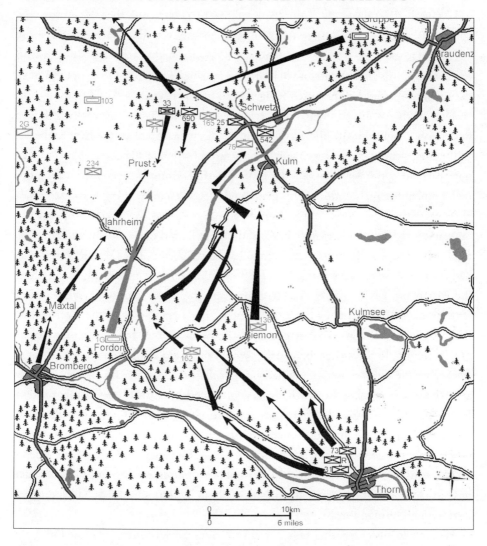

The other two columns converged with 31st Volksgrenadier Division, and early on 3 February the first elements of 73rd Infantry Division crossed the river about 5km south of Kulm, probably at the same point that Pantenius' regiment had crossed. Radio contact between the different columns had become increasingly fragmented, and Schlieper had to make a decision on how to proceed without being able to consult the other commanders. He decided to press on; a morning of confused fighting followed, before the first elements of the division managed to link up with the main German frontline held by 542nd Volksgrenadier Division near Schwetz. Most of the division followed over the next 24 hours.

This success was not without consequences. The 73rd Infantry Division had been tasked with defending the right flank of the breakout, and this flank was now dangerously exposed as Battlegroup von Rhaden and 31st Volksgrenadier Division attempted to cross the Vistula on 4 February. The wind had shifted to the west, with a resultant slight rise in temperature to just above freezing. The ice was not strong enough to support the weight of the buses being used to transport wounded, and precious time was lost as the wounded men were transferred onto sleighs for the crossing. Soviet forces now caught up with the garrison, and artillery fire shattered the river ice before all the troops could cross. Oberst von Rhaden led those who had succeeded in crossing northeast along the west bank, under sporadic artillery fire; he was killed during one such bombardment, but most of his command succeeded in reaching Schwetz.

News of the Thorn breakout had resulted in Batov's 65th Army transferring some of its infantry back to the eastern bank of the Vistula, and these units now reinforced the Soviet troops surrounding the remnants of the garrison. The German forces that had been unable to cross the ice bridge formed a long, shallow bridgehead along the east bank. Major Ernst-Albert Grote was the most senior surviving officer with perhaps 15,000 men, who had the increasingly fragile ice of the river behind their backs, and the growing strength of the Soviet forces before them. German meteorologists forecast that the weather would turn cold again, allowing the river to freeze, but the thermometer remained stubbornly just above freezing. Popov's troops attacked the bridgehead on 6 February, preceded by an artillery bombardment. Fighting raged on until 9 February, when the surviving 11,000 German soldiers laid down their arms. About 2,000 died within a few days, some from their wounds, others from the cold weather, but many were casually executed, perhaps as a reprisal for the refusal of the garrison to take prisoners as it attempted to fight its way back to German lines. Of the original garrison of about 32,000, about half had succeeded in reaching German lines.

Meanwhile, bitter fighting raged around Elbing. Soviet forces continued to try to isolate the town from the rest of Weiss' command, but a composite group formed from elements of 7th Infantry Division and a few of 7th Panzer Division's tanks, just released by the division's workshops, managed to intercept the Soviet advance and keep a tenuous connection open. These units then established a shuttle to try to evacuate civilians from Elbing, fighting their way in and out of the town every night. Some of Huber's comrades were involved in the operation:

Three times, the battlegroup succeeded in breaking through the Russian encircling ring. Each time, a few thousand refugees were brought out in columns of trucks. On the fourth occasion – which took place at night – the Russians had closed in on the Tiegenhof–Elbing road. The enemy was waiting at the approaches to Elbing.

… The enemy had taken a family house adjacent to the road and positioned anti-tank guns in the house. Either the Russians had broken through the walls or the anti-tank guns were dismantled and carried into the house. The first armour-piercing shot – despite the darkness – at a range of only 50–80 metres struck the right front of the tank. The shot went through the sloping armour and struck Fritsche [one of the crew] on the right upper arm, ripping it off and leaving it attached only by a little skin and the uniform sleeve. Despite this, he was able, along with the other three, to bail out. He tumbled over the right side of the deck and fell into the snow.

But that was the enemy side, on which the Russian infantry were already quite close. So first he had to work behind the tank and take cover on the other side. Then he ran back to the others, away from the tank, and came upon Paul Korte. Fritsche wanted him to bandage his arm quickly. Korte had weak nerves and fainted – right in the frontline. Fritsche had no belt, but had tied a rope around his trousers. This he now took off and tied around his arm, tying it with his teeth and his left hand.

Under fire from the Russians – Korte soon regained consciousness – they ran back together and after a short while they came across the other two members of their crew. Feldwebel Schroers took command of a truck from their battlegroup, loaded Fritsche aboard and ordered the driver to take him immediately to the field hospital. Fritsche soon lost consciousness in the truck, but after about a two-hour drive reached Dirschau.[32]

After undergoing surgery, Fritsche waited in vain to be evacuated further west. Finally, he set out under his own steam, hitching rides on passing vehicles and eventually reaching safety in Mecklenburg.

On 27 January, Soviet infantry and tanks penetrated into the northern parts of Elbing from the northeast. Generalleutnant Fritz-Georg von Rappard was forced to commit parts of his 7th Infantry Division to the defence of the town, particularly as it now became clear that 4th Army, trapped against the coast to the east, was about to attempt to break out towards Elbing. Essential personnel, including the director of the town's electricity works, took advantage of 7th Panzer Division's activity to return to Elbing, and to everyone's astonishment succeeded in restoring electrical supplies on 28 January, triggering a furious bombardment from the Soviet besiegers, who were now able to identify their targets. Schöppfer dispatched messengers to the electricity works to order that the supply be discontinued.

On 30 January, Soviet forces pushed down the western bank of the Elbing Canal, effectively isolating the garrison. Oberbürgermeister Leser, the local Party chief, had long since discarded his brown Party uniform, preferring his military Hauptmann uniform, which he wore as a reserve officer. Despite the wildly optimistic messages from higher commands, which described how Himmler was organizing a restoration of the front with 'new' Panzer divisions, Leser and Schöppfer had no doubts that the end was coming closer. Life within the town grew ever harder. Alice Bendig, who worked as an army telephonist, had dispatched her children to the Frische Nehrung the day that Diatchenko's tanks roared through Elbing. No longer required to operate a switchboard, she worked with an army surgeon, Dr Kretzchmar, to care for wounded soldiers and civilians, even venturing out into the dangerous streets to recover wounded men until a Soviet sniper forced her to take cover in a nearby cellar.[33]

In early February, Soviet aircraft joined the attacks, leaving much of the town ablaze or in ruins. Support for the defenders came from two outside sources. A small group of Luftwaffe dive-bombers attacked Soviet concentrations repeatedly, with little interference from Soviet fighters – the speed of Rokossovsky's advance had outstripped his fighter cover, and even his ground-attack planes were operating at maximum range. Attempts to improvise airstrips closer to the front were hampered by the changeable weather. The second source of support came in the shape of the Kriegsmarine. The heavy cruiser *Prinz Eugen* and the pocket battleship *Lützow* were constantly close by, adding their powerful and accurate salvoes to Major Kühneck's improvised artillery batteries. Nevertheless, it became increasingly clear that Elbing would soon be overrun, and on 9 February Himmler reluctantly gave Schöppfer permission to break out. He was ordered, however, to ensure that a bridgehead across the Elbing Canal continued to be held. When Weiss passed these instructions to Schöppfer, it was clear to both men that such a bridgehead was impossible.

The breakout took place that evening. Elements of 7th Panzer Division, led personally by Generalleutnant Mauss operating a machine-gun, led the way as 3,200 defenders, accompanied by 850 wounded and several hundred civilians, fought their way out of the ruins. At the same time, other parts of 7th Panzer Division attacked towards Elbing, in order to link up with the escaping garrison. Unteroffizier Schwalbe was in one such group:

> ... He ran into a group of four Hitler Youths, aged 15 or 16, without firearms, equipped only with Panzerfausts. He asked what they were up to.
>
> 'We are the last of our company. We were led by a marine soldier and were to attack the Russians who are beyond the dyke. The soldiers told us we should use weapons captured from the Russians.'

Schwalbe asked them, 'What do you want to do with your Panzerfausts? Do you actually know how to fire them?'

They answered, 'Actually, they don't work, as we have no fuses!'

He then spoke harshly to the Hitler Youths: 'Throw the things away and go home. That's an order!'[34]

Alice Bendig was with a group of soldiers accompanying Schöppfer during the breakout. All through the night, she helped a wounded Hauptmann struggle to the canal, and then to cross it. Combat engineers manned punts to ferry personnel across the water until Soviet artillery fire brought operations to a halt at dawn. Meanwhile, those who succeeded in crossing were subjected to a brief bombardment by German artillery, which mistook them for attacking Soviet troops. When the refugees reached Danzig later that day, scenes of almost unreal normality greeted them. Trams were still running, shops were open and cinemas were still operating. But the streets were thronged with refugees, who had gathered in the city for many weeks. Bendig was awarded the Iron Cross for her service during the fighting in Elbing, and then dispatched to Hungary for further service as an army telephonist. She was not reunited with her children until long after the war.

More than 1,000 civilians were left behind in Elbing, most because they did not wish to leave. Most of the men – who were almost exclusively either youths or elderly – were deported to the Soviet Union as forced labour. Few returned. The women were subjected to repeated rapes, which continued for a week until 2nd Shock Army was redeployed against the lower Vistula.

Further south, fighting raged on near Graudenz. One consequence of the breakout from Thorn was that Popov delayed the commitment of I Guards Tank Corps, choosing to hold it in reserve near Fordon, from where it could rapidly be transferred east, should it be required to stop the Thorn garrison. Despite this diversion of forces, the pressure continued to grow on 337th Volksgrenadier Division. Pantenius had been replaced as commander of his regiment, and was no longer with the division on 31 January when it came under massive attack. Its three regiments were completely overrun, and the momentary illusion of a solid German front disappeared. As the fragments of the division fell back, 4th Panzer Division was forced to make a counter-attack to the southeast in an attempt to restore the front. On 1 February, Betzel's division fought its way as far as Blondmin, and took the village the following morning in the teeth of tough resistance:

Outside, it was a drizzly night. I was in the headquarters of Hauptmann Küspert, who commanded the tanks of 35th Panzer Regiment. A reconnaissance troop had been sent towards the Blondmin cemetery. It had discovered a Soviet raiding party, without being spotted. Carefully, the men of 12th Panzergrenadier Regiment made their way back and were able to alert our outposts. We jumped into our hatches. Far and wide, not a sound could be heard. The Soviet soldiers worked their way carefully forwards. Suddenly, there was a burst of noise from half-left. One could clearly hear the hollow hammering of heavy Russian machine-guns. An anti-tank gun barked between bursts, and mortars hurtled down. There was wild shooting for five minutes, then everything was once more deathly quiet. A breathless messenger arrived at headquarters: 'Enemy raiding party repulsed, one prisoner.' The Red Army soldier was brought to Hauptmann Küspert. He was wounded and first we bandaged his wounds properly. He was hungry, we gave him bread, a cigarette and a cup of schnapps. He then became more lively and loquacious, but we couldn't understand a word. He was dispatched to regiment HQ with a vehicle that had brought us warm coffee.

A pair of wounded from 12th Panzergrenadier Regiment hobbled up. Last of all was a very young lad, who was leaning heavily on a stick. In the light of a few Hindenburg lamps, he let himself fall heavily to the straw. He clamped together his teeth and pulled off his trousers, which were soaked with blood. Carefully, we helped him remove them. In his right thigh, just under the groin, there was a gaping hole, in which one could easily put a fist: a pulsing wound. He must have lost a great deal of blood, but he was astonishingly brave. While the others bandaged him, I held his head and spoke to him, in order to distract him. He was only just 18 years old and this was his first battle.

'It all happened so quickly, I'd never have believed it. I've barely seen anything of war!' That seemed to be his biggest worry. He asked me if the wound was bad and he wanted to see it. We distracted him, because the wound in his flesh looked too ghastly. He would surely have been distraught.

When he was bandaged, he complained of pain in his left leg. We examined him again and found a second deep wound in the left side of his lower leg, but it too didn't appear to be life threatening. There was only a piece of skin missing. Despite all his misfortune, he was damned lucky. And we said to him to give our best wishes to the Homeland. He was from Ingolstadt.

Then I slept for a while … I was still so tired that I missed the return of Hauptmann Küspert and only woke when everyone went outside. It was already beginning to grow light. In half an hour, the attack would start.

I reported to Hauptmann Küspert as the war diarist and asked him if I could travel with him on his command tank, an old Pz. IV with a rigid turret and fake gun. I felt really unwell and with the best will I couldn't have eaten a thing.

Slowly, the tanks moved through the gardens into their preparatory positions. On the stroke of 0800, the fighting vehicles that had moved into the edge of the wood by the railway line during the night burst forward towards Blondmin, bounding forward over the snow-covered fields. Heavy defensive fire erupted from the village. From our position behind a hedge, we observed the attack through our binoculars.

Hauptmann Küspert sat on the edge of the turret and issued fire orders via radio, because we could clearly see the anti-tank positions from their muzzle-flashes. Our tanks were also firing like mad into the village, where several positions were now ablaze. Black spots appeared next to each other on the open fields. They were the blasts of Soviet shells, sprinkling the snow with black soot.

And sooty smoke lay like a low cloud over the fields and meadows, through which the bright red muzzle flashes flickered. The Panzergrenadiers followed the advancing tanks in thin lines. Here and there, one would see one or two men leap up, scamper forward a few steps and then fall once more into the snow. Some of them didn't rise again.

When the extreme left flank reached the village, Hauptmann Küspert gave the attack order for our right flank. The tanks advanced out of their cover, the grenadiers accompanied them.

… Our vehicle, on whose rear I was standing, snorted and shuffled to the foremost row of bushes. Behind us was a small church. We now came under heavy fire. One could clearly hear the crack of anti-tank guns, as they shot at us or other targets. Heavy mortars crashed into the houses behind us, sending bricks flying and covering everything in a red dust.

One of our tanks, about 50 metres from us, took a hit in its side. Then there was an ear-splitting crack. I had been crouching behind the turret for some time, flattening myself on its back like a bug. Hauptmann Küspert, whose upper body was sticking up out of the turret, disappeared like lightning. Only one arm remained raised outside. For a moment, everything went dark around me. Clumps of snow and earth rained down on me. Splinters clattered against the steel hull. One splinter sliced through my glove a millimetre from my forefinger. A 122mm shell had exploded half a metre from our right drive sprocket.

We pulled back and took up a position next to the church. There was another shrill blast, a sizzling and rumbling. Ten metres away, an explosion in the church. I was bombarded with red brick fragments. The adjutant now stood in the turret. Hauptmann Küspert was wounded. Although he had moved quickly, his arm was still outside and had been hit by some shrapnel.

Our tanks rolled further forwards. The left flank was already embroiled in heavy street fighting. The Soviets fired from all the houses. The right flank also drew ever closer to the village through the furious fire. Flames gushed out of roofs, black clouds of smoke hung over the village.

Our command vehicle followed the tanks. In quick time, we swept through the cemetery, which had been devastated by shellfire. None of our tank tracks ran into any ditch. This was remarkable, as the land was widely criss-crossed with icy tracks.

The artillery fire suddenly began to diminish. The Soviet battery at the exit from the village became silent. Only a few guns from further back still fired. Fire control appeared to be rather haphazard, with shells landing randomly across the landscape.

Then we reached the Blondmin road. The first of our tanks appeared beyond the village. One could see the abandoned Soviet guns with one's bare eyes: anti-tank and infantry guns.

We drove right up to such a position. Our tanks had done well. The ground around the position was cratered from shellfire, the trees badly splintered. Many dead lay in the snow and the guns were all shot up. Not far from the position were the ammunition trucks, all American Studebakers.

In the village, the sounds of fighting faded away. We advanced a short distance until we could overlook the Ebensee. From there, a heavy shell flew over, a heavyweight 'Josef Stalin' tank, which our Pz. IVs could not engage.

The Red Army soldiers tried to flee. They abandoned the supply trucks and guns that they could no longer use in the snow. The Soviets tumbled across the open fields, on foot and with handcarts, appearing as dark points on the white snow.

Three of our tanks, which were standing by the forestry house on the road, also attacked, rolling through the wood. At 1100, the important crossroads 20 kilometres northwest of Schwetz was attacked and taken. We were unable to watch the action from our position. So we drove back, once more passing through the cemetery, and entered the village.

The Panzergrenadiers had already made away with a couple of the Russian/American trucks, and were siphoning valuable fuel from the rest. But we drove on into the village. There was a lot of loot there, loads of good things that the Soviets had been forced to leave behind. Most of it was looted German market goods. There were heaps of canned fruit, packets of fish, tinned meat, smoking goods, all your heart could desire.

… Outside, the fires crackled, and we sat with steaming dishes and ate until we were full. It didn't bother us that from a corner nearby came the stink of the Russians' latrine.

After this period of 'marking time', we drove back with our tanks on the main road and searched through the wood in slow time towards the crossroads. We soon came across the foremost fighting vehicle. Two farms burned to the left. The Soviets had once more taken up positions there and greeted our tanks with powerful fire. We saw the wrecks of two T-34s and an assault gun, gushing thick black smoke.

Hauptmann Küspert received instructions about the overall situation from his commander, and issued his orders for a further attack. From the left, a group of tanks advanced, while the vehicles with us watched the edge of the wood and provided fire support wherever they saw the flicker of defensive fire. The tanks advanced swiftly as if on a training exercise. They fired as they advanced. When they overran the road to Ebensee, they swung in a wide arc to the right towards the burning farms. We watched as the grenadiers dismounted and searched through the buildings, while the tanks slowly followed, crushing bushes and fences. We overran the crossroads and pushed past the other vehicles into the strip of forest, which was not occupied by the enemy. Here we established a security line for the night.[35]

From here, it was possible to press on as far as Kraupen, but Popov's I Guards Tank Corps was now deploying, and in the face of heavy anti-tank fire, 4th Panzer Division fell back to Blondmin.[36]

With 4th Panzer Division unable to restore the front, and 337th Volksgrenadier Division in full flight, it seemed that XLVI Panzer Corps' positions might collapse, but at that moment reinforcements arrived in the form of 227th Infantry Division, shipped back to the Reich from Courland. Whilst it would take several days to assemble around Dirschau, its presence at least compensated for the disintegration of 337th Volksgrenadier Division, whose fragments were withdrawn to Heiderode to re-form. Although fighting continued west of the Vistula, the intensity slowly reduced as Popov and Rokossovsky abandoned their hopes of an early and swift advance on Danzig. Time would now be spent on a redeployment of forces for the next decisive thrust. The Soviet high command was also aware that troops were arriving in Himmler's new command in a steady stream. There was therefore the threat of a thrust south into the gap between Rokossovsky's armies – whose westward advance had been greatly delayed by the requirement to divert forces north against Elbing and the German forces in East Prussia – and Zhukov's 1st Belorussian Front, which had reached the Oder. Any thought of pressing on immediately towards Berlin became increasingly questionable. The German forces assembling north of Zhukov, and those trapped within East Prussia, would have to be reduced first.

CHAPTER 8
ENCIRCLED IN EAST PRUSSIA

The plight of the East Prussian population in the coming weeks was clearly grim enough, but it occurred behind an intact front. It would have been insupportable if this last dam had also been breached.

– K. Tippelskirch[1]

Memories of Nemmersdorf were indelibly engraved on the minds of everyone in Germany, and as the Prussian population became aware of their perilous position, few were prepared to take their chances and stay. On the Seythen estate near Osterode, Inspektor Romalm, the estate manager, was alerted to the Red Army's imminent arrival by a messenger, who arrived early on 19 January. The messenger came from the local Party hierarchy, and ordered Romalm to dispatch his Volkssturm unit to positions in the nearby village of Osterschau. To Romalm's consternation, he added that the Red Army was not far away. Immediately, Romalm awoke his platoon of 20 elderly men and youths and sent them marching down the road to Osterschau. He himself remained behind, with an elderly man – he was reluctant to leave the estate, where 35 Russian and 14 French prisoners of war provided much of the workforce.

For the moment, Romalm remained calm; he had heard reports of increasing partisan activity on the other side of the Polish frontier, a mere 20km away, and he assumed that something of this kind had perhaps spilled into East Prussia. But barely an hour later, still before dawn, the messenger was back. The Party had ordered the civilian population to prepare for departure, though nobody was to leave until further orders were issued. Romalm wasted no time. The Russian prisoners were marched to Hohenstein, where an assembly camp had been prepared for them, while the Frenchmen were assigned tasks as wagon drivers for the evacuation column. There was general chaos as people argued about what to take and what to leave behind. It was only when a group of six Soviet fighter-bombers roared past and fired on the estate – without causing any casualties – that the reality of their peril struck the estate population.[2]

After its failed counter-attack near the original frontline, *Grossdeutschland* was driven back across the East Prussian frontier just to the east of the Seythen estate, near Neidenburg. A battlegroup commanded by Major Maximilian Fabisch of the division's

Panzer-Fusilier regiment found itself cut off by Soviet forces south of Neidenburg, and tried to break through. Despite suffering heavy losses, Fabisch's group made little progress, and was forced to turn west. Leaving a trail of abandoned vehicles along its path, the group then turned north across country, and finally reached Neidenburg after a long, hard march in the bitter cold. Immediately, they had to take up defensive positions, and before they could recover from their exertions, they came under attack by heavy Soviet armour. Prolonged defence was impossible, given the battlegroup's casualties and lost equipment, and the Germans were driven north on 19 January, the same day that Soviet aircraft caused so much alarm in Seythen.

Romalm's refugee column of 18 wagons from Seythen was still waiting for an evacuation order. Finally, at midday on 20 January, he dispatched a messenger to Osterschau to find out what was happening. The man returned within an hour. The local Party chief, on whose evacuation order everyone was waiting, had left Osterschau with his family by train that morning. Angrily, Romalm got his column underway. With considerable foresight, he had decided to travel to Osterode along side roads, to avoid the inevitable congestion on major routes, but progress through the snow was slow. In an attempt to speed up movement, Romalm insisted that heavy items such as furniture and sewing machines should be discarded. This was achieved in the teeth of protests and resistance, but at least the wagons were able to make better speed across the snowy hills.

When they reached Osterode, Romalm and his fellow travellers rested in a brickyard. At that moment, a column of Soviet tanks and trucks roared towards the town. As Soviet soldiers dismounted and headed for the brickyard, Romalm fled, accompanied by his employer's wife and two other women, together with their children. They sheltered in a group of trees in a small ravine, and at dusk considered what to do. Romalm and his employer's wife, together with her daughter, decided to try to reach Mohrungen to the northwest on foot. The other two women, aware that their small children could not endure such a journey, headed back to the brickyard. The local Volkssturm and some of the soldiers in the town beat off the Soviet column, which was merely the tip of the Soviet spearhead.

There was chaos and confusion everywhere. The Party officials who had insisted on retaining control, rather than allowing all of East Prussia to fall under the remit of Reinhardt and his staff, almost without exception took no steps to evacuate civilians in a timely manner. When the arrival of the Red Army was imminent, their first thought was often for their own safety. Many refugee columns from the southern parts of East Prussia were caught up in the spearheads of Rokossovsky's armour, which frequently fired on the refugees merely to drive them off the roads before continuing their own advance. A group of refugees from Seemen was heading for the town of Saalfeld. When they received news that the Red Army had already reached the town, they turned around, but then encountered a Soviet armoured column. There was wild firing by several Soviet armoured cars, which disappeared as quickly as they had appeared. Darkness was falling, and through increasing snow showers the refugees struggled on towards Preussisch Holland. Along the road, they were overtaken by a rider who warned them that the Red Army was close behind. The first tanks appeared moments later, motoring past the column of refugees. With the tanks were infantry in trucks; the Soviet soldiers waved at the German civilians, calling out in bad German, 'How far to Berlin, comrades?'

The Soviet vehicles disappeared down the road, but soldiers on foot were close behind. The column was looted, the women subjected to multiple rapes. Anyone who attempted to intervene was shot. The refugee column then turned and wearily headed for home – there was no point in continuing to flee, now that they had been overtaken. They were stopped in Maldeuten, and forced to endure a night in the open, during which there were more rapes and what few possessions had escaped earlier searches were rifled again. The following day, the small number of men with the refugee column – in the main, the elderly and infirm, as everyone else was either serving at the front or as Volkssturm – were taken away. At first, the women refused to continue on their homeward journey without their men, but the Soviet soldiers drove them off at gunpoint. They never discovered what happened to their menfolk.[3]

Many refugees attempted to flee by train. Huge crowds gathered at the railway stations, and the Reichsbahn tried heroically to keep trains running until the last minute. More than 2,000 people gathered at the railway station at Hohenstein early on 21 January. In the absence of any orders from above, the local Party leader took it upon himself to assemble an improvised train of some 30 mixed passenger carriages and goods wagons. An elderly locomotive was hitched to the train, and it departed late in the evening. Without encountering any Soviet units, it succeeded in escaping to the west. The last train from Osterode left at about 0100hrs the same day, when the town was already under fire from Soviet artillery. Every conceivable space in the train was crammed with people, with others clinging to the outside. The train travelled to Dirschau and crossed the Vistula heading west, but was then directed into a small station a little to the south, where it stayed for five days. People were afraid to leave the train in case it were to depart again, and conditions in the tiny station deteriorated steadily, only the bitter cold keeping the stench of the improvised latrines in check. Eventually, the train returned to Dirschau, where it stayed for another two days. After the long period with little water and no heating, 14 of the passengers, mainly children, were dead.

Another train was meant to leave Mohrungen, 25km north of Osterode, on 21 January, but actually departed the previous day, leaving hundreds waiting in vain. Finally, a goods train arrived in the town. It was a very long train, and the waiting crowds trudged aboard. When the train tried to leave, the railwaymen found that it was now too heavy for the locomotive, so they unhitched half the train and left with the first half. Fortunately for those left behind, a locomotive appeared in the evening, crewed by four exhausted men; they had left Zichenau even as the town fell to the Red Army, and had travelled without rest for four days. Now, their locomotive was hitched to the stranded wagons, and set off for Dirschau. Slowly the train moved on, often stopping while the ageing locomotive struggled to create sufficient steam pressure with its supply of poor-quality coal. Eventually, in the middle of the night of 22–23 January, the exhausted railwaymen fell asleep. The train slowly lost speed as its steam pressure failed, and its drivers were awoken by a sudden crash: they had ploughed into the rear of a stationary hospital train. Despite having slowed considerably due to its reduced steam pressure, the locomotive still crushed the last two carriages of the hospital train.

An engineering locomotive arrived from the nearby Grünhagen station and towed both trains into the town. The refugees were forced to disembark, and waited in the station for a new train to take them to safety. Suddenly, a Soviet column arrived and stormed into the station. There were bursts of firing, and then the men were separated from the women. Both groups were systematically stripped of valuables, and the women and children were then herded south on foot, back towards their homes.[4]

After Rokossovsky changed direction on 20 January, the long southern flank of the German bulge came under even greater pressure. *Grossdeutschland*'s disparate battalions continued to resist when they could. A single company was sent to secure Passenheim, between Ortelsburg and Allenstein. The company made good use of abandoned equipment to obtain spares and replenish its meagre stock of fuel and ammunition, but when it came under attack on 22 January the small group of soldiers simply lacked the firepower to hold back the Red Army. By the end of the day, Passenheim had been lost, as well as Scheufelsdorf. The capture of the latter opened the road for the Soviet armoured spearheads towards Allenstein. The main threat to Allenstein, though, came from further west. The Soviet III Guards Cavalry Corps was now in action in full strength, and operating on the very western flank of *Grossdeutschland*'s area. Even if the division had not been hamstrung by fuel shortages, it would have lacked the strength to intercept this powerful force, which continued to drive north, threatening constantly to outflank *Grossdeutschland* on its open western flank.

By early 21 January, III Guards Cavalry Corps was barely 7km from Allenstein. Several Party officials gathered for a meeting and tried to contact Königsberg in order to get permission to order an evacuation. To their alarm, they were told in blunt terms by Gauleiter Koch's office that such an evacuation was not necessary. They tried again during the afternoon, and finally permission was granted. After much searching, the officials managed to locate a goods train, and directed it to the railway station. The train was mobbed by the desperate refugees, and departed in the early evening. A second train arrived at about 2000hrs. By this time, the railway station was once more full, not only with those who had not been able to squeeze onto the earlier train, but also with newcomers from the outlying villages. This train, also hideously crammed with refugees, left two hours later.

The first shells landed on Allenstein shortly after. Karl Becker was one of those who had not been able to board a train. He was an *Ostfront* veteran, having lost an arm two years before. When the incoming rounds exploded, he recognized them as mortars, and knew that Soviet troops were therefore very close. He and his wife fled north on foot; they were fortunate to encounter an empty ammunition truck heading in that direction, and were given a lift to Heiligenbeil. Hildegard Aminde, a woman who had to care for her elderly parents, managed to get her mother onto a goods train. Her father disappeared in the confusion. Just as the train was about to leave, a young woman thrust three small children onto the train. Unable to join them, she gestured helplessly from the platform. 'I'll follow you!' she called forlornly to her children.[5]

Allenstein was the capital of the district of Southern Prussia, and President Karl Schmidt had done little to aid his juniors in their attempts to secure permission for evacuation. Instead, he spent his time tracking down Assistant Gauleiter Dargel in order to get approval for the move of Schmidt's office from Allenstein to Seeburg, 35km to the northeast. Once this approval was granted, he boarded a car with five of his officials and drove off to the north. They reached the coast near Braunsberg the following day, many days before any other inhabitants of Allenstein. Friedrich Schidat, the mayor of Allenstein since 1933, showed more devotion to duty. He led a column of refugees north out of Allenstein on foot. Many dropped out along the road, either turning back in despair or stopping in one of the villages they passed, but many survived the long march across the snow-covered roads to the coast.

Amongst the refugees were the inmates of the women's prison in Allenstein, whose crimes ranged from black marketeering, through seditious behaviour (usually disparaging remarks about the Party that had been reported by the ubiquitous informants) to a few who had been arrested as part of the round-up that followed the failed July 1944 plot. As soon as they were away from the town, their guards disappeared into the crowds of refugees. Many of the former prisoners took the opportunity to return to Allenstein, to take their chances with the advancing Red Army.

Together with those who had stayed behind, had turned back or had been overrun by the advancing Soviet forces, they were segregated – men from women, old from young. Over the days that followed, many were forced to march on foot to the east, to Zichenau. From here, they were placed on trains, and spent long years working as forced labourers in coal mines in the Donetz basin of the Ukraine.

Elements of *Grossdeutschland*'s Panzer-Fusilier regiment fought bitterly around Allenstein throughout 22 January, but were soon forced to abandon their defences and move north. Here, *Grossdeutschland*'s retreat slowed; the country was heavily wooded, and favoured the Germans. Additionally, the Red Army was intent on exploiting its drive towards Elbing, and for the moment was content merely to contain *Grossdeutschland* and the other German forces in East Prussia. Nikolai Oslikovsky's III Guards Cavalry Corps had actually sustained considerable losses in its assault on Allenstein, and paused to lick its wounds. Rokossovsky's increasing exasperation, however, was not caused by Oslikovsky; 50th Army still did little to hinder the orderly withdrawal of Hossbach's 4th Army.

Hossbach's first units had pulled back late on 21 January, and more followed. Hossbach, a native East Prussian, had no intention of sitting passively while the fate of his army was the subject of endless arguments between Reinhardt and Hitler. His aim was to withdraw sufficient forces to assemble a concentration of troops facing west, with which he would then seek to drive into the flank of the Soviet forces advancing on Elbing. On 22 January, he held a conference with his corps commanders and made them aware of his plan. Horst Grossmann's VI Corps would form up around Guttstadt and aim to reach the lower Vistula. General Matzky's XXVI Corps, primarily 28th Jäger Division, would protect the northern flank of the attack, while General Mortimer von Kessel's VII Panzer Corps protected the southern flank. VI Corps, as the main striking force, was the strongest, with 131st and 170th Infantry Divisions earmarked for the initial assault. There would be a second echelon, consisting of 547th and 558th Volksgrenadier Divisions and part of 299th Infantry Division. Although none of the Panzer divisions in East Prussia were available for the attack, Hossbach had identified two assault gun battalions and two tank-destroyer battalions as armoured support. The following day, he informed Reinhardt of his plan.

Reinhardt had independently come to the same conclusion as Hossbach: it was impossible to continue to hold East Prussia with the forces at hand. The only hope now lay in an attack towards the west. But this attack would not merely be to disrupt Rokossovsky's advance: it was seen as the first stage of an orderly movement to the west. The whole of Reinhardt's army group, with hundreds of thousands of civilians accompanying it, would follow the attack formations as a vast 'roving cauldron', aiming to reach the lower Vistula in the Elbing area. Such an operation would, of course, necessitate the evacuation and abandonment of Königsberg, Samland and indeed all that remained of East Prussia. The probability of Hitler giving approval for this was negligible, and Hossbach and Reinhardt, like other German generals before them on the *Ostfront*, could do little more than hope that matters would become so fluid that Hitler would be unable to keep up with events, and would therefore be unable to intervene. It was a vastly ambitious endeavour, but neither Reinhardt nor Hossbach could see any realistic alternative. The dreadful weather, the fuel shortage and the unguided flight of the civilian population made matters worse. Military police struggled to hold the main roads open for military traffic – a request from Reinhardt to Gauleiter Koch for Party assistance with traffic control went unanswered. Preparation for the operation would be difficult; a large shipment of fuel that had been destined for use by the strike force was stuck in Marienburg, southwest of Elbing. The soldiers required for the breakout would have to reach their forming-up areas on foot.

One of the German divisions that withdrew unmolested from the perilous eastern tip of the German salient was Bodo Kleine's 367th Infantry Division, some of which managed to reach Königsberg before the city was encircled. The line of retreat was from Riemannswalde, where the division had remained in its frontline positions since the end of *Schneeflocke* the previous month, through Angerburg at the northern end of the Mauernsee, and on to Rastenburg:

> As we moved through Stobben, we came across two elderly women, sitting on the pavement in front of a house. When I advised them to come with us, as we were the last troops and the Russians were close behind, they replied that they wanted to stay, because they did not know where they should go.
>
> We therefore had to let them stay and face their fate.[6]

Baltuttis and his comrades of the Panzergrenadier Division *Hermann Göring*, forming their regiment's rearguard, were also struggling westwards:

> The East Prussian sky was crystal clear and seemed endless. We often moved off the road and through snow-covered fields. The villages were deserted, and we found the nocturnal stillness pleasant. The cursed war seemed to be far away. We enjoyed the winter landscape, which for once we didn't regard as 'terrain'. The soldiers chatted with each other, and everyone said they would come back here one day. We were in a romantic mood, which seemed to fit with our youthfulness. I thought of some poetry by Eichendorff: 'And my soul stretched wide its wings, and flew over the still land, as if flying home.'

Sadly, grim reality soon returned to us. Our soldiers began to show signs of fatigue. They limped, and complained of cramps in their legs. Leutnant Saul ordered me to march at the end of the column to make sure that nobody dropped out. But it was no pleasure being 'tail end Charlie', with a constantly changing rate of travel accelerating the onset of fatigue. Those who I regarded as having the lowest stamina I would recommend be moved further forward, so that they could keep up with Leutnant Saul's march pace – as a national-standard athlete, he knew how to conserve energy, something that I constantly rediscovered. On the road, we found four brand new trucks and six field howitzers, in impeccable condition. Apparently, they had had to be abandoned due to a shortage of fuel. But I did not understand why the equipment was not destroyed. That annoyed us! A little later we came upon a store of Panzerfausts and machine-gun ammunition. We took some with us, but couldn't carry much. At midnight on 22–23 January, two villages behind us went up in flames... Leutnant Saul called a short halt in order to orient himself. He ordered an absolute prohibition on sleeping. Using his map, he determined that we had passed our turning, because we had depended upon the roadsigns, without realizing that they had all been altered to point in the wrong directions, in order to confuse the Soviets. We were now in a critical situation, as the Soviets were right on our heels. Our suspicions were confirmed when two enemy tanks approached us, but then turned away to carry out their reconnaissance in another direction. When we set off again, we were missing six soldiers, who couldn't be found. We had to assume that they had crept into the stables or barns in order finally to get some sleep. Our need for sleep clouded our awareness of danger. It was too late for a thorough search. Later, the company commander spoke to Gefreiter S, asking him where his machine-gun was. S, who was popular with his comrades, had to admit that he had thrown the weapon away. Leutnant Saul took his name for disciplinary action. A little later, S also disappeared without trace. The roads stretched on endlessly. An Obergefreiter fainted and collapsed. The column came to a halt. When we were ordered to march on, there was open dissent. But Leutnant Saul inexorably prevailed. I knew how hard the decision was for him. We pressed on, and I too began to have serious misgivings, because it did not fit into my concept of camaraderie to abandon a collapsed comrade without any help. At the same time, I knew that we no longer had the strength to carry him with us.

... A soldier I didn't know stayed silently with the comrade who was unable to march on. Leutnant Saul, who was very pale, raised no objections. I saw how the two tried slowly to follow us, with one more carrying than supporting the other. I lost sight of them at a turn in the road. I will never forget that sight.

At 0500, we were missing a total of 14 soldiers. Our task as rearguard was turning into a catastrophe with an unknown outcome. I was almost grateful that the missing had disappeared unnoticed, sparing us further difficult conflicts. The soles of my boots had worn away. The 'foot-cloths' in my boots were soaked in blood. I was only aware of my surroundings as if through a fog. Trees, houses and roads receded into a vague distance. When I cut myself a piece of bread, I managed to slice deeply into my hand, as I had lost fine control of my hand movements... Our group was now tightly drawn in, and everyone was in close contact. For the first time, I really understood what the real meaning of close contact was. Those who had held together so far, would reach our destination.[7]

Along frozen roads, often through biting snowstorms, the men of 131st and 170th Infantry Divisions struggled to their start line. Meanwhile, the pressure on Raus' 3rd Panzer Army on the Königsberg approaches now became critical. There would be no point in mounting an attack towards the west if the rear of the 'roving cauldron' were to collapse. Reluctantly, Hossbach released 547th Volksgrenadier Division to be sent north to bolster the front against Cherniakhovsky's armies. There were also concerns in the south. VII Panzer Corps lacked significant forces to protect the southern flank of the planned attack, and 558th Volksgrenadier Division was now assigned to this role. The second echelon of the attack force was thus dissipated even before the attack began. The 24th Panzer Division, which had been sent to East Prussia without any of its equipment, had meanwhile formed up as best it could. Its Panther tank battalion had for many months been serving elsewhere on the front, separate from the rest of the division; although the original intention had been to reunite it with the division in East Prussia, 5th Guards Tank Army's drive to the coast ensured that this would never happen. Other elements of the division, including all of the signals battalion, also failed to reach East Prussia before the rail link was lost. Indeed, Generalmajor Gustav-Adolf von Nostitz-Wallwitz, the division commander, was aboard the last train to reach the division. Only about 40 Pz. IVs and half-tracks were available for re-equipment, with which it was possible to form an armoured force under the command of Oberst Hans-Egon von Einem, commander of the division's 21st Panzergrenadier Regiment. Unfortunately for this battlegroup, its strike power was constantly overestimated, and it was often treated as if it was comprised of the entire division. Moreover, it was deployed as soon as it had formed up, and before its men had had sufficient time to organize themselves properly, resulting in heavier losses than might otherwise have been the case. The battlegroup was dispatched to Willenburg on 22 January, and was constantly involved in the fighting there and at Ortelsburg. As the only significant armoured formation in the area, it shuttled to and fro to deal with crises as they developed, and men and equipment were lost at an alarming rate. The remnants of 18th Panzergrenadier Division, in almost constant action since the start of the great Soviet offensive, were now assigned to 24th Panzer Division. These reinforcements amounted to little more than a signals company and a weakened Panzergrenadier regiment.

Parts of 23rd Infantry Division, gathered together as 9th Grenadier Regiment, were also added to 24th Panzer Division. The men seem to have won the confidence of 24th Panzer Division almost immediately, and fought well with the division through the weeks that followed. There were good reasons for this friendship. Before the war, the precursor of 9th Grenadier Regiment was 9th Infantry Regiment, which was widely known throughout the Wehrmacht as Graf-9, on account of the large number of aristocratic names associated with it. Competition to enter the regiment was fierce, and despite the years of casualties and replacement drafts, the 9th Grenadier Regiment still retained much of its old character. Its officers, therefore, felt an immediate kinship with their fellow East Prussians in 24th Panzer Division, many of whom were also from long-established aristocratic families.

On 23 January, 24th Panzer Division was ordered to mount a counter-thrust through Wartenburg towards Allenstein. With one of his Panzergrenadier regiments and all his tanks already in operation with Group *Einem*, von Nostitz-Wallwitz had only Major Höhne's 26th Panzergrenadier Regiment, and the division's 24th Panzer Reconnaissance Battalion, commanded by Major Blume, available for this attack, together with the attached formations from 18th Panzergrenadier Division and 23rd Infantry Division. Before an attack could be launched, Soviet formations from 3rd Army pushed through Wartenburg and threatened to drive on to the northeast. They were halted at Gronau, just to the north of Wartenburg. The assembled elements of 24th Panzer Division remained in a defensive line here for nearly a week.

At last, the Soviet 50th Army began to chase the retreating Germans. Fighting erupted east of Lötzen on 24 January, and continued for several days. Kleine's 367th Infantry Division was now heavily engaged. After passing through Stobben, Kleine's regiment continued southwest to Rosengarten on about 25 January and found the village full of refugees. Soviet forces were reported close behind, and Kleine's regiment commander ordered him to head back to the Stobben railway station and the nearby crossroads with about 50 men, and to hold off the Soviet pursuers until the refugees and rear area units could withdraw to safety from Rosengarten:

> As we reached the crossroads, we suddenly came across three German assault guns coming from the direction of Taberlack, and wanting to move on to Rosengarten. I halted them and explained my mission to the first assault gun, and asked them to accompany us in our attack, advancing alongside the road. They turned around and set off with us towards Stobben. We now came across Russian soldiers in their brown uniforms everywhere in the

deep snow, who took to their heels at the first sight of the assault guns across the fields. There were more and more of them. A great crowd of between 100 and 150 of them fled back along the road. These Russians had apparently been stricken by 'Panzer fright'. The assault guns now fired on this retreating group, and we joined in as best we could. I had taken an MG-42 from a Landser, as I – as a Leutnant and leader of this counter-attack – had to lead from the front. So I set up my MG-42 and fired on the retreating Russian group... When most of the Russians had disappeared behind the houses of Stobben, the assault guns halted and withdrew.

So, as ordered, we had cleared the railway station of Russians. We had even taken a prisoner, who had been stuck in the snow. What were we to do with him – it wasn't possible for us to take him with us. I therefore locked the Russian in the cellar of a house at the crossroads, after giving him half a loaf of bread that I had in my pack. Meanwhile, my Schwimmwagen ... had reached the crossroads, and I used it to send back a soldier with leg wounds.[8]

Kleine was aware that he would be in trouble if it was discovered that he had left the Soviet prisoner where he would be able to return to his own side, but fortunately none of his soldiers spoke a word about the incident. When the tangle of traffic in Rosengarten had eased, Kleine's little command was able to resume its retreat. He continued to come across civilians; in one house he found several women, who were too exhausted by their march through the bitter cold to continue, despite Kleine's urging. On another occasion, he advised a young woman to leave her house, as his unit was the last German formation:

When I told her that the Russians were coming behind us and that she could ride in the Schwimmwagen, she asked if she could bring her pickling jars, which she had in a large box. When I explained to her that there wasn't space, she told me, to my incomprehension, that she wouldn't come with me. People risked their lives and well-being for such trivial matters.[9]

Baltuttis found himself in a village near Domnau, where some – but not all – of the civilian population had left:

Smoke rose into the wintry sky from the chimney of a small, solitary house about 100 metres from us. Cautiously, we approached and knocked on the door, which was opened by a girl of about 12, with a tear-streaked face. What we saw shocked us: we found a mother with seven small children. The youngest had only been born two days before. The father was fighting in an East Prussian infantry division. The woman told us that a

Soviet reconnaissance troop had stopped at her house the previous night. The soldiers had been very friendly, but had urged her to flee immediately with her children, as 'very bad men' were coming behind them. We looked for a solution, but could find no way out, as we had no transport. As we left, full of concern, the family wept. I felt our helpless situation as a matter of personal guilt, even later when I told myself that there was nothing that we could have done any differently. We were completely thwarted and more or less irrelevant. The thought of what our comrade, their father, fighting on the *Ostfront* would have to say, was unbearable.[10]

Not long after, Baltuttis' company was ordered to retreat once more, this time to Braunsberg, and Baltuttis became separated from his comrades. For a while he travelled with a refugee column, but was aware that if he was caught by the military police, he might be treated as a deserter and be hanged on the spot. Pressing on alone, he experienced harrowing scenes:

At one point, I found an empty house in a village, with four dead babies laid out on a table. Every child was carefully covered with a blanket, as if to keep them warm. I sat with them and stared at them for a long time. How many life plans were lost with their deaths? The senselessness of this war dragged me down. Later, I came across an elderly couple, who reminded me of Philemon and Baucis from the Greek myths. The old couple laboured along with their little fully laden handcart behind them. They stopped again and again, every few metres of their difficult journey, to rest. Completely exhausted, they dragged themselves on through the snowstorm, but there was nobody there to help them. I asked a man with an almost empty wagon to take the two with him, but the fellow callously refused.[11]

Lötzen was another of Hitler's so-called fortresses, though on this occasion there was some justification for the title. It was located at the eastern end of a narrow land bridge separating two large lakes. In principle, a comparatively small force should have been able to hold the town for a considerable time, but it was swiftly outflanked. The frozen lakes posed no obstacle to the advancing Soviet infantry, and the Soviet advance through Stobben towards Rosengarten meant that one flank had already been turned, and the southern flank was forced on 25 January. The following day, Soviet infantry swept into Lötzen from all directions. Most of the garrison had already withdrawn; a few small elements that remained fought on for several hours before succumbing.

News of the loss of Lötzen, almost without a fight, came as a huge blow to the high command in Berlin. Guderian was deeply shocked, and Hitler was furious: he had specifically ordered that the town be held unless he personally authorized a retreat. He demanded explanations, but instead received a further alarming communiqué. The pressure on Königsberg was such that 4th Army would have to continue its retreat further, abandoning all of East Prussia to the east of the River Alle. There was another long telephone conversation between Reinhardt and Hitler, in which Reinhardt repeatedly tried to impress upon the Führer the necessity of such a retreat. Characteristically, Hitler could not bring himself to accept something he found unpalatable, and he promised to call Reinhardt back with a decision by 1700hrs. The deadline came and went without a call, and Reinhardt made several fruitless attempts to contact Hitler. Finally, at 1900hrs, he signalled OKH that, in the absence of any orders, he was pulling his forces back to the Heilsberg–Friedland line along the Alle, as he had previously suggested. Two hours later, the teleprinter chattered into life, and Reinhardt learned that he and his chief of staff, Heidkämper, had been dismissed.

For Reinhardt, who had led 4th Panzer Division to the gates of Warsaw in the heady days of September 1939, this was the end of a long career. Officially, he was replaced because of wounds, and played no further part in the war. He became a prisoner of war after the final surrender, and was prosecuted for a variety of war crimes, including authorizing the execution of prisoners and partisans in the east, as well as forcing civilians to dig fortifications in the occupied parts of the Soviet Union. In 1948, he was sentenced to 15 years' imprisonment, but was released in 1952.

On the same day that Reinhardt was dismissed, Hossbach's divisions completed their approach march of up to 250km and immediately deployed for an attack. In order to maximize surprise and reduce Soviet numerical and aerial superiority to a minimum, the start time for the assault was 1900hrs. The snow showers that had continued throughout the day had ceased, and the German infantry attacked by the light of an almost full moon. A Soviet artillery unit was surprised and swiftly overwhelmed, the gunners abandoning their weapons and taking to their heels; 170th Infantry Division captured 96 artillery pieces.

The full blow of the attack fell on LIII Rifle Corps, part of 48th Army. The following day, as 28th Jäger Division arrived and joined the northern flank of the German attack, the neighbouring XLII Rifle Corps came under pressure too. For Rokossovsky, this attack came at a singularly awkward time. The 5th Guards Tank Army was to the east of Elbing, holding a strip of coastline, and 2nd Shock Army, in addition to covering the lower Vistula, was attempting to establish a perimeter around the south of Elbing. The troops of 48th Army were urgently needed to complete the envelopment of the city, and to take over from 5th Guards Tank Army, so that the mobile forces could be released for action elsewhere. Instead, 48th Army now found

HOSSBACH'S BREAKOUT ATTEMPT

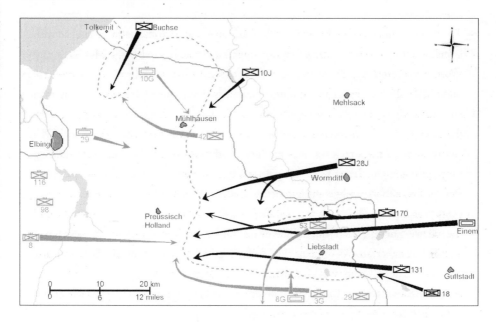

itself involved in an increasingly bitter battle. Near Wormditt, 28th Jäger Division enveloped two Soviet divisions (17th and 96th Rifle Divisions) and two others (194th and 399th Rifle Divisions) were driven to the rear. Further south, 17th Rifle Division was also encircled, this time by advancing elements of 170th Infantry Division. But the German forces lacked the numbers, or the firepower, to reduce the enveloped formations. All they could do was encircle them and press on, through villages that had been only briefly occupied by the Red Army. Here, they found further examples of the treatment meted out to civilians by Soviet soldiers.

Despite the gravity of the crisis, Rokossovsky had plenty of forces available. The 2nd Shock Army's XCVIII Rifle Corps had been moving towards Marienburg, but was now sent east, to form a second line of defence against the German attack. It deployed a division in line south of Elbing, facing east, while it kept its other two divisions in reserve. Volsky's 5th Guards Tank Army was ordered to counter-attack against the northern part of the German assault, with two tank corps pitted against 28th Jäger Division and whatever forces could be found by Hossbach to reinforce the hard-fighting infantry. Three other powerful formations – VIII Guards Tank Corps, VIII Mechanized Corps and III Guards Cavalry Corps – were ordered into position against the central and southern parts of the German attack. In short, a massive force of five tank, mechanized or cavalry corps, with a rifle corps forming a second line of defence behind them, rushed to the aid of 48th Army.

Group *Einem* found itself deployed at the southern side of the German attack:

The tanks, commanded by Rittmeister Fischer, moved along roads that were choked with hopeless refugees and burning supply vehicles, through Heilsberg, Mehlsack and Wormditt. From here, they were deployed as ordered for a breakthrough attack on the night of 27–28 January. In a determined night attack, the enemy defences were overrun and an advance of ten kilometres was made to the village of Krikehnen, with the destruction of numerous mortars and guns. There … as the necessary force for the continuation of the attack was lacking, further advances had to be postponed. During the following night, the tanks set off again and this time were able to reach the crossroads west of Behlenhof, barely eight kilometres east of Preussisch Holland. Here, there was considerable resistance… Due to a fuel shortage, the enterprise had to be abandoned until the following night. As a result, the enemy had time to bring up sufficient defensive forces and make further attacks difficult. The following night – a daytime attack was clearly pointless – a new attempt was made with about 20 tanks and after very heavy fighting the village of Karwitten was taken, but it became clear that with the forces available at this point, no further successes could be expected.

… Despite the constant urging of all local commanders for an attempt at a breakthrough at other points, the outcome was different. The tanks were moved constantly back and forth on the following days on firefighting tasks, and if these operations were particularly successful, the feeling that a great opportunity had passed by could not be dispelled, as we knew that we had come within ten kilometres of forces moving towards us from the west.[12]

The crisis for the Germans came on 29 January, as the advance slowed to a crawl. Here was the moment for Hossbach's second echelon to be thrown into battle, now that the exhausted men of the first echelon were within 10km of Elbing. But the second echelon divisions had all been diverted elsewhere, and there were no other reserves available. Elements of 7th Panzer Division attacked eastwards from Elbing in a desperate attempt to help Hossbach, but were swiftly brought to a standstill. A single battalion of 83rd Jäger Regiment, the 'Hirschberger Jägers', part of 28th Jäger Division, marched straight through the confusion and into Elbing. For a tantalizing moment, a link-up between Hossbach and the Elbing garrison, and from there to the lower Vistula, was achieved, but the door closed as swiftly as it had opened. The escape from the Soviet encirclement by the battalion of Hirschbergers was very short-lived. The battalion was transferred to the west; at Swinemünde, it was put aboard ships and sent back to rejoin the rest of its division.

The entire operation had been mounted on Hossbach's initiative, with the support of Reinhardt. Berlin had deliberately been kept in the dark, in the hope that by the time it became clear to Hitler what was happening, it would be too late for him to insist that Königsberg and other areas should continue to be held. Guderian and Hitler followed news of the progress of the attack anxiously, but – in Hitler's case – with increasing suspicion. At this point, Gauleiter Koch made a crucial intervention. As the situation around Königsberg worsened, he moved to a prepared bunker at Neutief, on the Frische Nehrung. From there, he now sent a message to Hitler: '4th Army is fleeing towards the Reich. It is cravenly trying to escape to the west. I am continuing to defend East Prussia with the Volkssturm!'[13]

The existence of this telegram has recently been disputed.[14] The telegram itself has not survived, and Koch later denied ever having sent it. Regardless of the truth in this matter, news of developments in East Prussia proved to be the factor that tipped Hitler's distrust of Hossbach into action. The Prussian general was dismissed on 30 January.

Hossbach flew back to Berlin, to report to OKH. From there, he went to Göttingen, in Saxony. While he was being treated in hospital for an ear problem, local Party officials attempted to arrest him on charges of ordering an unauthorized breakout from East Prussia. He successfully resisted arrest by drawing his pistol and threatening to shoot them. His replacement in East Prussia was General Friedrich Wilhelm Müller, a stolid, unimaginative officer with a record of personal bravery but little or no ability to improvise. From Hitler's perspective, he was a 'reliable' appointment, who had once said: 'I am a good NCO and I know how to carry out orders, but strategy and tactics are quite beyond me. Just tell me what I ought to do!'[15]

Müller was ordered to continue the attack towards the west, but East Prussia was to be held. In any event, the German attack was coming to an end. The assault formations were at the limits of their strength, and no reinforcements were available. Rokossovsky's preparations were complete, and his forces now counter-attacked, driving the exhausted German infantry back over the hard-won ground. If Hossbach's originally planned second echelon had been available, it seems likely that a breakthrough to the west might have been achieved, but given Rokossovsky's overwhelming resources such a breakthrough would only have resulted in a temporary reprieve, certainly not sufficient to organize the evacuation of all of East Prussia. For such an operation to have succeeded, a large armoured force would have been required to counter the tank strength of 2nd Belorussian Front.

The tragedy for East Prussia was that such an armoured force could have been available. It had been clear since early January that the Ardennes offensive was not going to succeed, and although the SS Panzer divisions of 6th Panzer Army had been mauled in the fighting, they remained a formidable force. Guderian had tried in vain on several occasions to have them transferred to Prussia, where they could have been deployed to good effect – for example, their intervention along the lower Vistula at the same time as Hossbach's attempted breakout would have vastly increased the chances of success. But the deployment of 6th Panzer Army in support of Hossbach's breakout would have implied that the rest of Hossbach's plan – a complete evacuation of East Prussia – should follow, and Hitler would never have agreed to this. In any event, Hitler had other plans for the SS armour. As early as 20 January, he was discussing further attacks in Hungary to relieve Budapest. The small oilfields near Lake Balaton provided almost all of the Reich's non-synthetic fuel, and Hitler remained obsessed with ensuring the security of this tiny supply. The 6th Panzer Army was dispatched in its entirety to Hungary, where it launched an attack towards Budapest in March. The attack was a failure.

It is arguable that it would have taken too long for 6th Panzer Army to be moved to the lower Vistula. Whilst it is certainly true that the entire army would indeed have required a substantial number of trains, and therefore time, for such a move, it would have been possible for some of the divisions to have shifted to the Vistula in time – after all, it proved possible to move the *Brandenburg* and *Hermann Göring* divisions out of East Prussia even after the Soviet attack had started. If even these two divisions had remained in East Prussia, it seems likely that they would have been able to provide Hossbach with much-needed armour and firepower during the breakout attempt.

One of the most remarkable aspects of the entire operation is how it was conducted without any reference to higher authorities. Hossbach and Reinhardt took it upon themselves to plan and execute the operation without even going through the motions of securing permission from Hitler. Such independence, at such a high level, must be unique in the history of the difficult relationship between Hitler and the Wehrmacht.

Rokossovsky's counter-attack was bitterly resisted by 4th Army, whose casualties steadily increased. The 5th Guards Tank Army pressed east from the Elbing area, while 48th Army struck back from the southwest, reinforced by III Guards Cavalry Corps. The encircled Soviet divisions that had been bypassed by Hossbach's men were relieved on 31 January, and though 170th Infantry Division clung to its positions near Preussisch Holland, this was the tip of an increasingly threatened salient. The 4th Army was now trapped with its back to the Frisches Haff, in what was to become known as the Heiligenbeil pocket. (The Frisches Haff is a strip of water that extends from the Nogat–Vistula estuary in the west to Königsberg in the north, a distance of nearly 100km.)

Elsewhere around 4th Army's perimeter, pressure grew steadily. The 24th Panzer Division was ordered to take up positions in fortifications that formed part of a defensive system known as the Heilsberg Triangle; these had been built before the war, and were of limited use, not having been designed for the weapons currently in use. The fields of fire from the gun emplacements were inadequate, and had not been cleared of vegetation. In any case, the order was impossible to fulfil: the bunkers of the Heilsberg Triangle were all locked, and in the chaos the keys could not be found. The division was forced to take up defensive positions further north. On 5 February, Group *Einem* was thrown into a counter-attack south of Landsberg:

As planned, the tanks moved out of their forming-up area near Finken at 0800 and moved across country like in the old days, in this, the last major tank battle that this war would bring to the battalion. By incorporating assault gun units, the princely total of 35 vehicles was achieved and this picture, not seen for a long time, gave every tanker a feeling of pride in their weapons. The first points of resistance were swiftly cleared and then, without any roads or tracks and only the compass for guidance, the advance continued to the east without any pause for breath. Strong anti-tank defences were overrun near Glandau and thus the occupation of the village by the grenadiers was facilitated. We were already deep in the enemy's hinterland and were once more working our way through supply and rear-area units, as there were particularly rich pickings around Grünwalde. An enemy division staff had set up camp here, unaware of our approach. There was active traffic on the Landsberg–Heilsberg road, through which the tanks swept like a tempest and rampaged like wild boar. A large number of refugees, who had been in the hands of the Russians for days, were freed and their thanks were the only incentive needed for us to give all we had to give. Despite bitter defence by the Russians, Grünwalde was taken and in the evening the tanks stood either side of the Landsberg–Heilsberg railway.

Continuation of the attack was not possible, as our infantry were insufficient to clear and occupy the ground that had been won. Despite this, a crucial success was achieved and this sector now became quiet. Although the enemy attempted to drive back the German attack group the following day with a counter-attack, supported by a considerable amount of artillery, he was unable to achieve any success. During the following night, the battalion was pulled back and now moved to the hard-pressed division sector southeast of Mehlsack.[16]

By word of mouth some of the civilian population of East Prussia became aware of 4th Army's attempt to break out to the west, but many – perhaps even most – remained oblivious. Emil Mischke was a farmer from near the town of Friedland, and also a local

Party official. He watched troop convoys heading west from 23 January, and correctly guessed that a counter-attack was being planned. The organized columns of soldiers were gradually replaced by signs of retreat – rear-area units, wounded and stragglers, all mixed together. Friedland was soon full of the debris of war. Mischke was also the commander of a Volkssturm company, and was assigned to guard a railway bridge and the nearby railway station. After deploying his two platoons as best he could, he encountered two soldiers who seemed determined to flee:

'Don't you want to defend the Homeland?' he demanded of them.

'You call this our Homeland? Our Homeland is in the hands of the English and the Americans. And we're going there too,' one of them replied. Mischke was so astonished that he let them pass.[17]

Mischke had decided not to evacuate his wife and ten-year-old son until an official order reached him – he regarded anything else as improper conduct, given his Party responsibilities. Others were less dutiful. By 25 January, 15 of his Volkssturm company had slipped away, trying to reach their homes and flee with their families. News now reached Mischke that his wife and son had left their farm and were going to try to reach Königsberg. Mischke knew that the Red Army had already effectively cut off the city, but he could do nothing. During the evening, hundreds of refugees arrived from Allenburg. They had been assured by the Party that there was no danger, only to be told less than an hour later by the Wehrmacht that they should leave immediately. Their anger with the Party was clear, and Mischke quietly threw away his Party uniform jacket.

When Mischke held a roll call of his company the following morning, he found that he had only 40 men. The railway bridge had been demolished, and as the day progressed there were further signs of imminent fighting. The sounds of combat grew ever louder, and Mischke and his men were startled when a nearby artillery battery was blown up to prevent it falling into enemy hands. Mischke's wife and son left aboard a horse-drawn sled, accompanied by their Russian worker, Michel.

The fate of former Soviet citizens who were in German hands was little better than the fate of the Germans themselves; Stalin had decided in 1941 that Soviet citizens who had been detained outside the Soviet Union, whether as prisoners of war or as conscripted labour, had been politically contaminated, and on their return to Soviet hands would be imprisoned. It seems unlikely that this was common knowledge amongst people like Michel in 1945, but many Soviet prisoners and workers, knowing only too well the way that Stalin had behaved in the pre-war years, were keen to take their chances of escape with their German captors, rather than allow themselves to fall into the hands of the Red Army. By nightfall, they had made slow progress along the rutted road, and Frau Mischke decided to seek shelter in a small village. Michel was desperate to put more distance between himself and the Red Army, and chose to continue on foot. After a freezing, sleepless night. Frau Mischke decided to return to her house. The village of Böttschersdorf, where the Mischkes lived, was deserted, and after tending to her horses she set off westward again, joined by the French prisoner of war who had worked nearby for several years, helping look after a neighbour's cattle.

Meanwhile, in Friedland, Mischke and his fellow Volkssturm were hiding in cellars from Soviet artillery fire. After a brief trip to report to Hauptmann Böhm, the commandant of the tiny garrison, Mischke returned to his company to find that it had shrunk to only six men, the others having slipped away. The remaining men now decided that there was little point in staying, especially as an abandoned train in the nearby railway station was thought to be loaded with ammunition – if it were hit by incoming rounds, the entire area would probably be flattened. The seven men made their precarious way on bicycles through the snow and ice to Postehnen, just to the west of Friedland. After spending the night there, they continued on to Domnau, where Mischke was able to find his battalion commander, Hauptmann Laza. Laza discharged them, telling them to seek out their families. Mischke went in search of anyone from Böttschersdorf who might be able to give him firm news about his wife. Learning that refugees from Böttschersdorf had passed through Domnau on their way to Preussisch Eylau, Mischke took to the frozen roads again on his rickety bicycle, struggling past slow-moving wagons carrying refugees from dozens of towns and villages. Eventually, he found someone who told him that his wife was further ahead in the column, and he was able to rejoin her.

The refugees followed each other along the roads and tracks, gradually losing their sense of direction. The general trend was first west or southwest, in the direction of Hossbach's attempted breakout; when this failed, they stumbled north and northeast. Those who still had energy to spare, speculated on the nature of the *Wunderwaffen* that Goebbels had constantly promised, the miracle weapons that would give Germany final victory. Would they be aircraft, or submarines, or something completely new? Incredible as it may seem, large numbers of Germans, civilians and soldiers alike, remained confident that the tide would turn in their favour, even though the reality of defeat stared them in the face.

Grossdeutschland, meanwhile, had pulled out of the shortened frontline, and moved northeast in stages. Battlegroup Fabisch, reinforced by the reconnaissance battalion, was dispatched in an attempt to revive the flagging breakout attempt, but by the end of

29 January much of the division had withdrawn to Kreuzburg, to the south of Königsberg. Two attacks were now launched in an attempt to restore contact with Königsberg, which had been cut off since the drive by the Soviet II Guards Tank Corps reached the coast to the south of the city. In its last major attack, the division's Panzer regiment gathered together its remaining tanks – perhaps 25, mainly Tigers and Panthers – and used these to drive through to Maulen, halfway to Königsberg. A further push towards Wundlaken and Warthen, just a short distance to the north, failed in the face of anti-tank fire. In bitter fighting, *Grossdeutschland*'s infantry reached Jäskeim, but could go no further. During the night of 31 January–1 February, Generalmajor Karl Lorenz concentrated his fast-diminishing division's strength along the coast road, and in a short, determined attack *Grossdeutschland* was able to break through to Königsberg. Lasch and the rest of the garrison were no longer isolated, even though their only contact was with 4th Army, which was itself trapped within the Heiligenbeil pocket.

Contact remained tenuous, though, with the road constantly under Soviet fire. On 4 February, a second attack was launched towards Königsberg in an attempt to improve matters. The village of Warthen, which had proved impossible to take in the initial assault, was swiftly captured. This achievement removed the immediate pressure on the coast road, but it remained a dangerous route, and the movement of supplies was only possible at night. Fighting continued along this narrow neck of land, with the Soviet XVI and XXXVI Guards Rifle Corps launching repeated attempts to isolate Königsberg, without success. Casualties piled up on both sides, for no significant gain or loss.

Baltuttis' company had been replenished with stragglers and rear-area personnel, and was deployed for the defence of Kreuzburg. Several unusual events – encounters with unknown German officers, the deaths of a platoon of infantry, shot apparently without putting up any resistance – led Baltuttis and his comrades to believe that the NKFD was active in the area, something that became much more obvious one evening:

> At about midnight, we heard some terribly loud music, which sounded as if it came from the foremost house of the cluster facing us. After a German military march, the speaker announced himself as a member of the Nationalkomitee Freies Deutschland. He gave an intelligent, objective and striking report of the military and political situation, showing how hopeless things were. It was clear that he was probably an officer of the general staff. Then, another voice called to us, telling us to lay down our weapons and desert. We were promised good treatment for the duration of our Russian captivity, and a swift repatriation after the end of the war. Unfortunately, this brought other thoughts to mind, and at the end there was a demand for us to choose between death or life in the coming hours, or to face our destruction.[18]

Another episode occurred, the following night:

> An hour later, piercing cries for help disturbed our sleep. I rushed out of company headquarters to the front. I felt awful – my mouth and tongue felt coated, and my injured ear ached down to my neck. A man called out in an apparently desperate voice: 'Comrade, pull me back! Comrades, I'm wounded, help me! Don't leave me here! Help!' The pitiful cries continued on, fraying at our nerves. Experience had taught us much – this wasn't the first time we had been in such a situation. Using such traps, the Russians would try to lure us forward in order to capture us. But on the other hand, the play-acting left us with mixed feelings, as we couldn't be sure that it wasn't actually a wounded comrade. Covered by several soldiers, I carefully crept towards the village and called, 'Comrade, where are you?' After a short delay there was an answer, but from a different direction and further away. It was clear to us what was going on. We went back. It was the last time I was going to play this game.[19]

Far to the west, Zhukov's spearheads rested on the middle Oder, almost within range of Berlin. But both their flanks were exposed. To the south, Konev was faced with a bitter battle for Silesia, and to the north the diversion of Rokossovsky's armies towards Elbing, almost perpendicular to the direction of advance of Zhukov's armies, allowed the Wehrmacht to assemble Army Group Vistula in the lower Vistula valley and Pomerania. Even though the 'Vistula–Oder operation', as it became known in Soviet accounts, had been a resounding success, Stavka remained concerned that Zhukov's spearheads were dangerously isolated. This concern gained strength when German forces launched an attack from the north. The attack, codenamed *Sonnenwende* ('Solstice'), was of only marginal importance to the fighting in Prussia; it was the northern part of what was originally intended to be a pincer attack to isolate and destroy the Soviet armour along the middle Oder. Although it made little progress, it highlighted the danger to the Soviet forces from the north, and Stavka duly resolved to eliminate this danger. The reduction of all forces trapped in East Prussia – in Samland, Königsberg and the Heiligenbeil pocket – would be carried out under the control of Cherniakhovsky's 3rd Belorussian Front. Rokossovsky would concentrate on overrunning the rest of the Vistula valley and the eastern parts of Pomerania, while Zhukov drove into western Pomerania. This final success would then allow the Red Army to concentrate on its ultimate objective: Berlin.

CHAPTER 9
HANNIBAL – THE BALTIC EVACUATION BEGINS

Six hundred years of history dissipated.

– Marion Dönhoff[1]

The flood of German refugees streaming back to the coast began to cause serious concern for the German authorities. The most easterly port to attract large numbers was Pillau, at the tip of the Samland peninsula. From 1941, Pillau was the home of 1st U-boat Training Division, and several large ships – the 16,600-tonne *Pretoria*, the 27,200-tonne *Robert Ley* and the 9,500-tonne *Ubena* – were moved to Pillau to serve as accommodation. Further down the coast, the 2nd U-boat Training Division was stationed at Gotenhafen, and it too had several large ships that were used as floating barracks. With commendable foresight, the Kriegsmarine had started preparations for the possibility of a maritime evacuation of Prussia as soon as the Soviet offensive began in January. Responsibility for these plans rested with the 46-year-old Konteradmiral Conrad Engelhardt.

Engelhardt served in the German Navy in World War I, and remained in service for most of the inter-war years. He held several land-based posts after a brief time as gunnery officer aboard the pocket battleship *Admiral Scheer* in 1937–38, and in early 1944 became Seetransportchef der Wehrmacht (Sea Transport Chief of the Wehrmacht). He oversaw the evacuation of German troops from Finland after the Finns withdrew from the war, and after the fall of Riga he anticipated that as the Red Army advanced the other German ports on the Baltic coast – Libau, Pillau, Danzig and Gotenhafen – would all come under pressure. Consequently, he took it upon himself to start drawing up plans. On 15 January, even as the Soviet offensive was starting, Engelhardt received a telephone call from Grossadmiral Karl Dönitz, commander of the Kriegsmarine. He was now officially to begin planning for a maritime evacuation of civilians and military personnel from the eastern Baltic.[2]

Engelhardt had a detailed list of all the shipping available. He now distributed this list and other plans to his staff, but although officers in the eastern Baltic ports were notified, no order was yet given for an evacuation to begin. Engelhardt could not commence the evacuation without permission from Dönitz, and Dönitz knew that Hitler would never countenance such a thing.

The first refugees arrived in Pillau on 19 January, followed by hundreds of thousands who squeezed into western Samland. The half-empty naval and flak barracks were swiftly made available, and local Party officials attempted to provide rations for the helpless refugees. Other Party officials, however, continued to interfere. In his role as Reich Defence Commissar, Koch ordered the ships of the 1st U-boat Training Division to leave port immediately. They were not to take any refugees with them – ever the fanatic, Koch still held onto the hope of final victory, and additionally was aware of the effect that a civilian evacuation would have upon his own standing in Berlin. This order, Koch insisted, had been agreed with Dönitz. Kapitän zur See Fritz Poske, commander of the training division, was unimpressed; he regarded himself as answerable to the naval chain of command, not to Koch. The following morning, he contacted naval headquarters in Kiel. Admiral Hans-Georg von Friedeburg, commander of Germany's submarine forces, confirmed what Poske had already suspected: this order had nothing to do with the Kriegsmarine, and there had been no discussion between Koch and Dönitz. Poske and von Friedeburg agreed that the ships would only leave port on receipt of the codeword *Hannibal* from Kiel, and would take as many wounded and refugees with them as possible.[3] This codeword would also trigger the plans being put in place by Engelhardt's team.

Meanwhile, the Party continued to work in its accustomed manner. Despite official insistence that an evacuation was not necessary, local Party officials in Pillau received an order on 23 January that a train of 500 refugees would arrive shortly, and were to be embarked aboard the *Pretoria*. The train contained the families of prominent Party members in Königsberg.[4]

On 21 January, Dönitz decided that he could wait no longer. The previous evening he had had a long telephone discussion with Engelhardt. The latter had made his superior aware of the growing crowds of refugees in Danzig, Gotenhafen and Pillau, and had stressed that matters would only get worse in the coming days and weeks. Without waiting for approval from Hitler, Dönitz used his own authority to authorize the commencement of *Hannibal*.

Officially, this operation concerned the orderly evacuation of the two U-boat training divisions from the eastern Baltic, but the reality was that this would also begin the evacuation of the thousands of civilians who were gathering around the ports.

In addition to all of the staff and equipment of the submarine personnel, as many refugees as possible – those designated 'not fit for combat' – as well as wounded soldiers, were to be taken west by sea. It was estimated that the departure of the large ships used by the U-boat training divisions as barracks would allow for up to 20,000 refugees to be taken to safety. Engelhardt had emphasized to Dönitz that in Gotenhafen alone there were about 100,000 refugees waiting for evacuation. The removal of 20,000 would be merely the first step.[5]

Many of the large ships in the Baltic ports had been in port for several years, and their crews, a mixture of civilian and naval personnel, worked feverishly to make their vessels ready for their new tasks. Meanwhile, Party officials began the impossible task of deciding who was 'not fit for combat'. Passes were swiftly printed and allocated to women, children and the elderly, but inevitably there were bitter arguments about whether 15-year-old boys or men in their sixties should be classed as fit or unfit for combat. The first civilians began to board the ships on 23 January.

The first convoy left Pillau the same day. Two small steamers arrived in port the following day, carrying ammunition and military supplies. To help unload them, a group of about 20 concentration camp prisoners was dispatched to the docks. These prisoners were held in a small compound near the old Pillau fortress, and had originally been inmates of the large camp at Stutthof, in the Vistula estuary. Once their duties as labourers were complete, their SS guards executed them.[6]

At 1800hrs on 25 January, the *Pretoria* left Pillau, followed by the other large vessels. Protected by the small ships of the Kriegsmarine's 9th Security Division, the convoy made its way to Swinemünde, carrying some 22,000 refugees. Koch was furious that civilians had been taken aboard in direct opposition to his 'orders', and tried in vain to have Poske court-martialled.[7] Shortly after the ships left Pillau, there was a huge explosion – the marine arsenal at Forst Stiehle had been blown up. It had been prepared for demolition, but the charges were not due to be detonated for several days. It was fortunate that the refugee ships had left, as they had reduced the numbers of people within reach of the explosion; nevertheless, the blast killed about 300, and wounded another 600. Equally importantly, the blast damaged electric pumps needed for the water works, resulting in a loss of running water to much of the town.[8]

On 5 February, the Soviet Air Force made its first major attack on Pillau. On a cold, sunny winter's day, about 60 bombers attacked in the early afternoon. Most of the bombs landed in the water of the port, but there were 54 fatalities. A small steamer, a ferry and two minesweepers were sunk, and the raid also dealt a final blow to the town's water works. Electricity supplies remained precarious, relying on the generating power of a disabled U-boat in the port.[9]

An early innovation of the Nazi government in the years before the war was the creation of an organization named Kraft durch Freude, or 'Strength through Joy.' This was part of the Deutsche Arbeits Front (DAF; German Labour Front), and was intended to allow working-class Germans access to leisure opportunities that had hitherto been reserved for the middle classes. This facility was aimed at keeping the workers content by giving them a taste of luxury, while allowing industrial output to concentrate on military production instead of consumer goods. Several large cruise ships were built to take German workers on holidays, particularly to the Norwegian fjords.

One such ship, launched in 1937 at the Blohm und Voss shipyard in Hamburg, was the *Wilhelm Gustloff*, with a displacement of a little over 25,000 tonnes. In peacetime she carried almost 2,000 passengers in comfortable surroundings, travelling as far afield as the Mediterranean and North Atlantic. In September 1939, the *Gustloff* became *Hospital Ship D*, and after serving in the Danzig area during the Polish campaign the ship took part in the German invasion of Norway. By late 1940, her voyaging days appeared, temporarily at least, to be over. She was moored in Gotenhafen and used as floating accommodation for the personnel of the 2nd U-boat Training Division. Her distinctive white paint, with a green band around the hull and the red crosses on her funnels that marked her unmistakably as a hospital ship, was replaced by navy grey.

The ship's captain was Friedrich Petersen, who had captained her for a single peacetime voyage. He was captured by the British and held at the beginning of the war, but then repatriated to Germany because he was aged 66, on condition that he did not command a ship again. When he was assigned to the *Gustloff* in early 1944, the prospect of the ship leaving port during the war must have seemed remote, and there was therefore no apparent question of his breaching his parole. But in mid January he received orders to make the ship ready to set sail again. Once the crew completed preparations for the voyage on 23 January, there was at first an orderly influx of passengers. The first to be granted passage were over a thousand naval personnel, including 373 female naval auxiliaries. Some 162 wounded soldiers were also taken aboard.

The 21,000-tonne *Hansa* was another ship used by the U-boat personnel, and it was also to be used to move people to safety from Gotenhafen. The *Hansa* was to transport the officers of the 2nd U-boat Training Division, together with all of their training material, to Lübeck, but both the *Hansa* and the *Wilhelm Gustloff* received an additional order that they were to take with them as many refugees as possible. Unlike the *Gustloff*, the *Hansa* had little provision for medical care, particularly for children, and the port authorities tried to direct anyone with small children to the *Gustloff*, resulting in many families being separated and divided between the two ships. The ships would leave Gotenhafen together, so the separation would, it was anticipated, be a short one.

Responsibility for organizing convoys in the eastern Baltic lay with the 9th Security Division, commanded by Fregattenkapitän Adalbert von Blanc. For two days he delayed the departure of the large ships, as he was unable to provide adequate escorts. By contrast, the senior officers of the U-boat training division were anxious to leave as soon as possible, and pressured von Blanc's local deputy, Korvettenkapitän Leonhardt, for immediate departure. In the absence of vessels of the 9th Security Division, they insisted, the U-boat training division would provide its own escorts. The submariners planned to leave Gotenhafen on 29 January, but a large contingent of wounded men arrived by train in the port that morning, and many were loaded aboard the already crowded *Wilhelm Gustloff*. Departure would now take place the following morning, with escorting torpedo boats provided by the 2nd U-boat Training Division.

On 30 January, there were further delays. The long wait for departure meant that provisions aboard were running low, and additional supplies had to be loaded. Some of the ship's officers brought their families aboard; the First Officer, Louis Reese, declined to take advantage of the opportunity to move his loved ones to safety. He had a bad feeling about this voyage, he explained to the other officers. Schlichting, the Oberbürgermeister of Gotenhafen, put 13 members of his family into one of the last cabins still available aboard the ship. He went back ashore himself, telling his family that he had to stay and do his duty. He remained in the city to the very end, and died during the final Soviet assault. By that time, his family had already been dead for two months.

The *Wilhelm Gustloff* left the Gotenhafen pier shortly after midday. Refugees had boarded her right up to the last moment, and the system of boarding passes had broken down completely. It will therefore never be known how many people were aboard, but it far exceeded the 4,000 refugees that had been mentioned in the orders issued as part of *Hannibal*. The true figure was probably at least 7,000. Even as the tugboats edged the liner away from the shore, a small steamer came alongside. The *Reval* had travelled overnight from Pillau, with about 600 refugees crammed aboard. Most had endured a night in the open, and they now pleaded to be taken aboard the *Gustloff*. Walkways were lowered to the *Reval*, and the frozen refugees were helped to climb them. Finally, under her own steam for the first time since 1941, the *Wilhelm Gustloff* set off.

The weather was poor, with constant flurries of snow. Ice floes were reported in the Baltic, but the voyage would be a short one – it was anticipated that the ship would reach northern Germany the following morning. For everyone aboard the ship, the bad weather was most welcome – it would help reduce the risk of air attacks. As the *Wilhelm Gustloff* approached Hela, the *Hansa* came into sight. The two ships stopped within hailing distance and awaited their escorts, which were still refuelling in

Gotenhafen. The wait dragged on, and then came news that the *Hansa* had engine problems. No sooner had these been fixed than a new problem arose. The *Hansa's* rudder suddenly stopped responding, and the strong wind blew the helpless ship towards the wreck of the old battleship *Schleswig-Holstein*, sunk by an air raid in late 1944. A collision was avoided, but the *Hansa* would require repairs before she could make the voyage west.

Back in Gotenhafen, Korvettenkapitän Leonhardt received this news with relief. He assumed that both ships would now return to port – the *Wilhelm Gustloff* under her own steam, the *Hansa* towed by harbour tugs – and that departure would be delayed by a day. He was confident that the 9th Security Division would be able to put together sufficient escort vessels given a further 24 hours. However, alarming news followed almost immediately: the senior officers of the U-boat training division insisted that the *Wilhelm Gustloff* leave immediately, accompanied by two torpedo boats.

On the bridge of the former KdF ship, all was not well. In addition to the elderly Petersen, there were three other senior officers aboard. Kapitänleutnant Wilhelm Zahn, who had commanded the U-boat personnel billeted aboard the ship, made no attempt to hide his exasperation with Petersen. Two merchant marine captains, Köhler and Weller, were also on the bridge, adding to the profusion of opinions and suggestions. Most of these centred on the course the ship should follow, and whether it should take a zigzag course to reduce the risk of submarine attack. The ship's First Officer, Reese, wanted to pursue a course close to shore, so that in the event of any mishap the ship could be run aground. The other officers voted against this, on the grounds that the coastal channel might be mined. Reese protested in vain that there was no evidence that it was mined, and that the same could be said about any course that was selected. There were also differences of opinion regarding the ship's speed. Zahn, an experienced submariner, knew that British liners had used their speed to outrun U-boats in the Atlantic, and felt that if the *Gustloff* were to travel at a speed of at least 15 knots, this would reduce the danger of attack. The ship had been damaged in an air raid in 1944, however, and although the damage had been repaired, Petersen was not convinced that the repairs would stand up to such a speed. He insisted on the speed not exceeding 12 knots.

At about 1800hrs, the ship received a signal that a minesweeper convoy was in the area, heading in the opposite direction, and a new dispute began on the bridge: should the *Gustloff* turn on its navigation lights to avoid a collision? Again, there was much argument, with several officers arguing that the risk of collision was slight, and that small blue lights would suffice. Petersen was adamant: the main red and green lights would be switched on, and would remain on until the minesweepers had safely been passed.

Amongst the passengers, there was a widespread feeling that they were already safe, despite the strong headwind resulting in many people suffering from seasickness. Dr Helmut Richter was the senior medical officer of the 2nd U-boat Training Division, and now found himself acting as ship's medical officer aboard the *Gustloff*. Before the ship left Gotenhafen, he and his team had already assisted four women give birth, and two more were now in labour. The medical staff took great pleasure in drawing up birth certificates, recording the exact coordinates of the ship when the child came into the world. Such records, they were sure, would be significant historical documents in years to come.

Peter Schiller, a member of the crew, found time to talk to an elderly refugee, whose heartbreaking account could serve as a testament for many millions of refugees of all nations who had been forced to leave their homes during the war:

'The evacuation order was announced two weeks ago, we were to leave our beautiful East Prussian village within 48 hours.

'We had lived there for over six decades, and had been married for 32 years. Our two sons were at rest, one in Russia, one in a plane over England. So we sat there on our own. All alone. I am a pastor, and we had a nice little house right next to our church.

'We didn't have much to pack, and I wanted to be the last to leave the village. At the edge of the village, I stopped one last time and looked back.'

He gazed for a while at the pale disc of the porthole and then continued quietly:

'Yes – and then it was out along the icy roads, with thousand of others, together in a seemingly endless trek. We older folk soon felt that we would not be able to endure the hardships for long. The cold and the storm made it hard for us to go on. My wife was particularly hard pressed. Her legs soon failed her. We often had to stop to rest, but the great stream always swept us on.

'Everywhere we looked, there was only suffering and despair.

'Then I found a place for my wife on a horse-drawn cart, a wagon covered with just a canvas. I marched behind with many others. When we stopped, I climbed aboard to speak to my wife. I noticed from day to day that she was getting weaker and weaker. She didn't want to make a fuss and was determined to pull through, but it was all too much for her...'

His voice had grown quieter in these last sentences, until it was no more than a whisper.

'Then – yes, then came the most dreadful day of my life.

'We had stopped again for rest, somewhere by the side of the road. We ate a piece of bread, and my wife cried quietly to herself. I tried to encourage her, but when I looked into her eyes, I knew that she was gone.

'We sat for a while next to each other...'

His chest heaved with a long sigh.

Peter Schiller, sitting opposite him, didn't know where to look. The old pastor had his head in his hands and stared out with empty eyes.

Schiller didn't dare to break the silence.

'We took my wife from the wagon and laid her down at the side of the road. It was about midday,' continued the pastor after a while. 'I don't know how long I sat next to my wife. Those walking past could well have thought that I too was no longer amongst the living. Later, I fetched a pickaxe and shovel from the next house. She shouldn't be left by the side of the road, like so many others!'

'And where do you want to go now?' Peter Schiller forced himself to ask after a few painful minutes.

'Where? I don't know. I have nobody on this earth who is waiting for me. But all our lives are in God's hands!' And then, after a while: 'I have a feeling that I will soon be with Him.'[10]

Meanwhile, the *Gustloff*'s nemesis was lying in wait. The Soviet submarine *S-13*, commanded by Alexander Marinesko, had left Turku in Finland on 13 January, and after failing to find any prey in the Memel area, continued down the coast to the Bay of Danzig. From there, Marinesko moved west towards the Stolpe Bank. Here, at 2000hrs, he sighted the *Gustloff*'s navigation lights. Through snow flurries, he made out the shape of the large liner. Visibility was still poor, and the low silhouette of the submarine was undetectable against the waves. No Soviet submarine had succeeded in sinking a large target, and Marinesko intended to be the first. He ordered his crew to move into an attack position, without submerging. Andrei Pichut, one of the sailors in the torpedo room, had written slogans on the four loaded torpedoes: 'For the Motherland', 'For Stalin', 'For the Soviet people', and 'For Leningrad'. He now looked forward to firing them.

Conditions aboard the ship had steadily deteriorated. Petersen had ordered everyone to wear lifejackets throughout the crossing, but many discarded them as the temperature and humidity in the crowded interior increased. Many people had never been issued with a lifejacket in the first place, particularly amongst those who boarded in the last chaotic stages of preparations for departure.

The poor weather might have made aerial attack unlikely, but it also interfered with wireless communications. Only broken messages reached the *Gustloff*, and her escort, the torpedo boat *Löwe*, was only monitoring U-boat frequencies; the torpedo boat, part of the U-boat training division, was not tuned into the radio frequencies of the 9th Security Division, where warnings about possible Soviet submarine sightings had been broadcast at least an hour earlier. In any event, a build-up of ice made the *Löwe*'s submarine detection equipment inoperable.

Marinesko and his officers remained uncertain about whether the ship they were approaching was a merchant or a warship. They knew it was a large target, and given its location it had to be an enemy ship. The *S-13* inexorably caught up with the *Gustloff*, taking up a firing position a kilometre south of the liner, between it and the coast. Marinesko launched his attack at about 2100hrs, firing four torpedoes. One – 'For Stalin' – became lodged in its launching tube, causing much alarm aboard the submarine before it was made safe. The other three raced through the water and struck the *Gustloff*. The first struck her bows, the second impacted amidships opposite the drained swimming pool, in which the female naval auxiliaries were attempting to sleep. The third struck nearer the stern.

Inside the ship, there was pandemonium. The explosion amidships hurled ceramic fragments from the swimming pool through the large area, causing many dreadful wounds. Only a handful of the naval auxiliaries escaped from their part of the ship, seven metres below the waterline. Swiftly, the *Gustloff* began to list to port. The strike astern knocked out her engines, and for a few moments, before emergency lighting was activated, the ship was in complete darkness. The ship's watertight doors closed automatically – one consequence was that most of the off-duty crew, who were vital for an evacuation of the ship, found themselves trapped in the forecastle. None of them escaped. It was not possible to use the main radio transmitter to call for help; the emergency set had a limited range, but was at least able to transmit to the *Löwe*.

As red distress flares soared into the bitterly cold night sky, the escort ship hurried to the aid of the stricken liner, retransmitting the distress call. When she reached the *Gustloff*, the scenes were dreadful. It was almost impossible to stay upright on the icy, listing deck, and people constantly slid into the freezing water. Some lifeboats were swamped, others launched with only a few occupants. After just an hour, the *Gustloff* sank beneath the Baltic. She left behind her a sea full of dead and dying. For the rescuers, some of the most harrowing scenes related to children, who had often been thrown overboard with lifejackets hastily fitted. The lifejackets, designed for adults, adopted their maximally buoyant positions, which with such small occupants resulted in the children floating upside down.

Some of the *Wilhelm Gustloff*'s lifeboats had been used in Gotenhafen to carry smoke-pots, to create smokescreens when the port came under aerial attack. Several cutters and rafts, and hundreds of lifejackets, had been brought aboard prior to departure. In the chaos of the last minutes prior to sinking, however, it simply wasn't possible to launch all the boats and rafts, especially as so many of the crew were trapped behind the watertight doors of the forecastle.

The first help to reach the area came in the form of another torpedo boat, escorting the German heavy cruiser *Admiral Hipper*. The cruiser had left Gotenhafen after the *Wilhelm Gustloff*, and with its higher speed expected to pass the refugee ship at about midnight. Kapitän zur See Hans Henigst, commander of the *Hipper*, was worried about the threat of a submarine attack on his cruiser, and in any case the *Hipper* was also carrying about 1,500 refugees. The safety of these refugees, and of one of the Kriegsmarine's last remaining major warships, was Henigst's highest priority. Nevertheless, he ordered his ship to take on board as many survivors as possible. Even as the ship slowly moved through the gaggle of lifeboats, rafts and lifejacketed figures, the cruiser's escort reported that it had picked up the sounds of a submarine engine. Worried that another torpedo attack was imminent, Henigst ordered his ship to resume its course at full speed. As the Hipper surged away, its wake overturned a lifeboat and swamped many of those still struggling in the icy waters. Yet the *T 36*, the torpedo boat accompanying the *Hipper*, stayed to rescue survivors. The small vessel, with a displacement of only 1,300 tons, was already carrying 250 refugees, and now took aboard 564 people from the lifeboats and out of the water. In the middle of the rescue operation, engine noises were once more detected, and the *T 36* was forced to take evasive action as two torpedoes were fired at it. Despite the danger to those still in the water, the commander of the *T 36*, Kapitänleutnant Hering, ordered a depth-charge attack to drive off the submarine. Throughout the night and the following morning, various ships launched depth-charges, often at random; Vladimir Krylov, the political officer aboard the *S-13*, kept a count of the number of explosions, which finally stopped at a total of 234.[11] The *Löwe* took aboard 472 survivors, including both Dr Richter and the 21-year-old woman from Elbing who had gone into labour shortly before the *Gustloff* was hit. Her son was delivered aboard the torpedo boat, and she named him Leo in honour of the ship that had saved her life.

There were delays in getting additional help to the scene, because the *Löwe* was operating on U-boat radio frequencies, and precious minutes were lost before the officers of the 9th Security Division became aware of what was happening. Slowly, other vessels responded to the distress call, but the icy conditions proved fatal for most of those who were not rescued within the first hour, though a few individuals were saved even as late as seven hours after the sinking – a baby, still alive, wrapped in woollen blankets and squeezed between corpses, was recovered from a drifting lifeboat by the crew of a small patrol vessel. Apart from the abortive arrival of the *Hipper*, the first major vessel to reach the scene was the *Göttingen*, carrying some 2,436 wounded and 1,190 refugees from Pillau. Still constantly alert for the presence of a Soviet submarine, the *Göttingen* and the smaller ships in her convoy did what they could to retrieve those still in the water.[12]

A little more than 1,200 people were saved from the disaster. The number of dead will never be known with any certainty, but it seems likely that more than 6,000 people – more than 9,000 according to some estimates – died in the Baltic that night, making the loss of the *Wilhelm Gustloff* one of the two most costly maritime disasters in history, about six times worse than the *Titanic*. Despite this, the incident remains comparatively unknown outside Germany. Hitler was informed of the catastrophe by Dönitz the following day, and the conversation seems to have centred on the limited capabilities of the Kriegsmarine when it came to submarine hunting. At no stage did Hitler enquire about the number killed.[13]

In total, the Germans lost 11 large vessels in the Baltic during January 1945, with only the *Wilhelm Gustloff* being sunk by torpedoes. Although *Hannibal* had been in operation for only a few days, the numbers brought to safety were already impressive: 4,213 from Libau, in Courland; 19,437 from Memel; 25,019 from Königsberg; 106,429 from Pillau; 21,770 from Danzig; 58,229 from Gotenhafen; 850 from Hela; and 4,812 from Elbing – more than 240,000 people in total. Despite the loss of the *Gustloff*, the operation had to be regarded as a success to date.

In Pillau, refugees waited desperately for the return of another ship, which had already made two runs west with several thousand refugees. The ship had started life as the *München*, and was badly damaged in a fire in 1930 while in New York. She managed to return to Bremerhaven, where she was rebuilt as an oil-powered liner, and renamed *General von Steuben*. With her large dining halls and ballroom, and with almost every room having its own bathroom or shower, she was a popular ship, and was soon known as the 'beautiful white *Steuben*'. In 1938, her name was shortened to *Steuben* – the Nazi authorities decided that it was unsuitable for the ship to bear such a close link to a man who had achieved fame fighting for the Republican forces in the American War of Independence, not least because von Steuben had been forced to leave Prussia after being accused of homosexuality.

After serving as floating accommodation for much of the war, the *Steuben* was designated as a 'wounded transport ship' at the end of July 1944. This was a peculiar classification, not covered by the Geneva Convention as a hospital ship. With a modest number of anti-aircraft guns for protection, the *Steuben* made 18 voyages in the eastern Baltic in 1944, carrying more than 26,000 wounded soldiers and over 6,600 refugees to safety.

In late December 1944, the *Steuben* was once more assigned as floating accommodation, but this proved to be a short-term role; on 23 January 1945 she was again brought into service as a wounded transport ship. She left Danzig the same day for Pillau, where she took aboard 2,800 wounded and 1,000 refugees, as well as a Luftwaffe medical unit. Fourteen wounded men died during the short run to Swinemünde, from where the ship returned to Pillau on 31 January. A further 3,000 wounded and 370 refugees came aboard, and were carried safely to Swinemünde. The crowds of refugees in Pillau were relieved when the *Steuben* returned to the port on 8 February to take on board her third complement of wounded and refugees.[14] One of the wounded was a Luftwaffe officer, Hauptmann Franz Huber:

On 3 February 1945, I was badly wounded twice in the face and the back of the head by mortar fire in Fischhausen, near Pillau. At the time I was wounded, I was sitting in a motorcycle sidecar, and due to the mortar fire the driver drove into a tree at about 80 kilometres per hour. As a result, I sustained an additional large bruise to the abdomen. I was brought to the field hospital in Pillau with these wounds and first received medical treatment there.

… Early on 9 February 1945, I was assigned for transport to Germany. A few hours later, an ambulance carried me over tremendously bumpy roads through Pillau to the port. As a result of my six-day-old wounds, I had a high fever and was in almost unbearable pain. The journey to Pillau harbour, where I was to be loaded aboard a ship, seemed an eternity to me. But finally, we were taken aboard the *Steuben*.

As I was from Bavaria, I had had no opportunity to learn about ships before. As a result, the *Steuben*'s bulk seemed to me to be like a small town, which it certainly was, with so many people aboard.

I was taken into the interior of the ship and heard from other comrades that I was in the *Steuben*'s former tearoom. The mattresses lay on the floor, very close next to each other, in order to make space for as many wounded to be brought aboard the *Steuben* as possible.[15]

Another of the wounded was Obergefreiter Alfred Burgner, who was wounded in the right arm in a hopeless counter-attack south of Rastenburg on 27 January. He eventually reached Heiligenbeil:

Then, we were taken by boat to Pillau, along a channel made by an icebreaker. Here, we were first put in a large barracks, and we were told that we would be sent to Swinemünde on the next hospital ship to leave Pillau. We greeted this with enthusiasm. But when we heard a few days later of the sinking of the *Gustloff*, when some of the dead were brought to Pillau and buried here, we became aware that our seaborne transport to the west was not without danger as we had at first believed, and that escape across the Baltic on a large ship had its risks, too. But as there was no other escape route, my comrades and I put our faith in God and our own good fortune, and we were delighted on the morning of 9 February 1945 to be taken aboard the *Steuben*.

When I saw the ship alongside the pier, I resolved to spend the entire voyage on the upper deck, so that in the event of misfortune I would be in the open, near to a boat. But after almost all of the wounded had been taken into the ship and only refugees were sent to the upper deck, I was spotted on the upper deck by a medic and taken into the ship. The medic followed a couple of paces behind me and I found myself in a gangway, right next to a toilet door, where a mattress and blanket was assigned to me. All places in the cabins and gangways were already occupied, as I was one of the last to come aboard the *Steuben*.[16]

There were nearly 4,300 people aboard the *Steuben*, including 2,800 wounded and 800 refugees. At 1230hrs on 9 February, the ship left Pillau. Several thousand refugees who were left behind watched the 'beautiful white *Steuben*' slowly move away, and consoled themselves that even if they had been left behind, the ship would be back in a few days.

Near Hela, the *Steuben* was joined by two escorts, the *T 196* and the *TF 10*, the former carrying a further 200 refugees. Both the escorts were elderly vessels, and they did nothing to inspire confidence in the officers of the *Steuben*. Two Soviet aircraft put in a sudden appearance, but their bombs narrowly missed the *T 196*, and they disappeared swiftly into the clouds. After this scare, the little convoy set off for the west at a speed of 12 knots.

Marinesko and the *S-13* were still in the area. After the attack on the *Wilhelm Gustloff*, the submarine remained submerged as long as it could, finally surfacing late on 31 January with her batteries almost exhausted. Marinesko immediately signalled his superiors in Kronstadt, reporting that he had sunk a ship of about 20,000 tonnes displacement. His claim was greeted with scepticism. In October 1944, he had claimed to have sunk a 5,000-tonne steamer in the Bay of Danzig, but it had then transpired that his victim was the tiny *Siegfried*, a coaster of only 563 tonnes. In any event, Marinesko decided to remain on station, narrowly missing collision in fog with a German submarine heading on an opposite bearing on 6 February. Now, late on 9 February, the Soviet submarine's lookouts spotted the faint light of sparks in the smoke of one of the *Steuben*'s escorts, the sparks standing out against the cold, clear night sky. Purely by chance, the escort was headed straight for the *S-13*, and Marinesko immediately ordered his submarine to dive. When he surfaced 30 minutes later, he and his officers could see the three German ships silhouetted against the sky 4km away. Tentatively, they identified the largest ship as a German cruiser of the *Emden* class, and submerged again to prepare for their attack. Just before 0100hrs on 10 February, Marinesko ordered two torpedoes to be fired from his rear tubes.

Both torpedoes struck the starboard side of the *Steuben*. At first, the ship appeared to be able to remain afloat, but about 15 minutes after the explosions she gave a sudden lurch and began to settle lower in the water, listing first to one side, then the other. Immediately, there was a rush for the lifeboats. For the wounded men in the interior of the ship, there was no prospect of escape, and as the water flooded into the ship many shot themselves. One of the last to escape from the sinking ship was Hauptmann Huber, the wounded Luftwaffe officer:

I awoke from a deep sleep to a dreadful din. The entire ship shuddered, and at first one had the feeling that it would burst apart at any moment. Everyone in the neighbouring rooms was screaming and shouting, the medics and nurses were standing at the doors, the ship lurched powerfully hither and thither, probably deciding on which side it would roll over and sink. The wounded who could stand were on their feet, but were thrown against whichever wall the ship was inclined towards. The other wounded in their beds tumbled together against the wall, and we crushed each other, injuring ourselves even more than we had been in the first place.

As a first step, the medics told us to help each other into our lifejackets. This was done. I pulled my jacket on over my lifejacket, and a comrade standing next to me helped me to fasten it … in a panic, my comrades and I tried to reach the steps to the upper decks. Unfortunately, this wasn't possible at this time, as the ship was listing against us. We waited a few moments until the ship had rolled to the other side, and then tried to reach the steps. We had learned that the ship had been hit by two torpedoes, but that the bulkheads could still be closed. Despite the hits, one hoped that the ship would still be able to continue under its own power.

It was now possible for us to reach the upper deck barefoot, and I stood at first with my feet on the iron deck and noted how shockingly cold it was outside. The night was pitch black, and the ship constantly rolled from side to side.

I saw hundreds of wounded, doctors, personnel and nurses jump into the sea from the deck. I tried to reach the highest point of the ship in the hope that this would be the last part to be submerged.

I sat there alone in the darkness for some time and heard screams from the sinking ship. I heard them calling to our Lord in a manner that one seldom if ever heard in one's entire life. I heard cries from the water and saw that the ship was burning in places, creating shadows on the water... I continued to wait, not really knowing why and for what I was waiting, until I heard a voice close by:

'We have to jump now before it is too late and we get sucked down!'

This advice persuaded me, and I jumped from a height of about 20 metres. I think I lost consciousness in the air, perhaps partly through anxiety, and only came back to my senses when I was deep in the water.

I reached the surface with much effort, but I was right next to the sinking ship and it listed ever more toward me, and I thought that it would roll over me at any moment.

I made the greatest efforts to swim as far as possible away from the ship, until I thought I would no longer be sucked down with it... As the water then surged through the sinking ship's hull and gurgled and crashed, those still alive began to cry out dreadfully, far worse than before. It was an overwhelming, terrible spectacle, which I will never forget. Everyone who was still alive cried out for help. The dead and wounded, women and children, who were still aboard were tipped from the deck and swam in the water. As I swam forwards, my hands struck the bodies of the dead and the living.[17]

Obergefreiter Alfred Burgner had also escaped from the sinking ship, on one of its lifeboats. Thirty minutes after she was hit, the *Steuben* gave another lurch and finally sank. Those in the water and in the lifeboats endured the freezing night as best they could. Many died before the two escort vessels could reach them; Burgner was one of those taken aboard the *T 196*.

Struggling to stay afloat in the icy water, Hauptmann Huber came across a nurse. They vowed that they would either survive or drown together, and shortly afterwards they saw a lifeboat. The boat was already overcrowded, and many of its occupants fought off any attempts by those still in the water to try to struggle aboard. Just as he was giving up hope, Huber's hand encountered a rope. He pulled on it, and found that it was attached to an empty lifeboat.

Huber and the nurse now found that the icy water had robbed them of the strength to get into the lifeboat. Another man in the water floundered onto the boat, but then collapsed and didn't respond to Huber and the nurse when they called to him to help them aboard. Eventually, Huber was able to haul himself in, but he found it impossible to help the nurse into the boat. Then, a wounded Obergefreiter who had escaped from the *Steuben* – losing two fingers when machinery on deck fell onto him – swam over. He managed to climb in, and with his help, Huber was able to get the nurse aboard too.

Unlike the night of the sinking of the *Wilhelm Gustloff*, there was almost no wind, though the temperature was close to freezing. Huber advised the others that they should huddle together to share their body warmth. The man who had first clambered aboard but had then remained silent – a Feldwebel – now spoke up, saying he wanted to remain where he was in the bottom of the boat, but a few sharp words from Huber were enough to make him cooperate. They sat together, and saw searchlights appear towards the eastern horizon:

> The Feldwebel, who had been so silent until now, tried to stir us up:
>
> 'That's a Russian submarine, it's going to take us away to Siberia, to imprisonment beyond the Urals!'
>
> 'Complete rubbish,' I said, and told him to keep his mouth shut. The last thing we needed in our situation was pessimism.
>
> The ship's searchlights came closer to us, but didn't light us up. We wanted to call out, but had no more strength. Then we tried to use the whistles attached to our lifejackets, but we couldn't get a note out of them.
>
> The lights and the ship went away, apparently still searching for survivors in the water. This happened three or four times, the searchlights coming ever closer but not close enough. It shredded our nerves, hoping again and again but not being spotted.
>
> Then, finally, it happened: the searchlight caught our lifeboat full in its beam. Now we four once more found our strength, and we called out together:
>
> 'Help – help – wounded!'
>
> And then we heard the words that allayed our fears called out over the sea:
>
> 'We're coming!'[18]

At 0530hrs, the four survivors, the last to be rescued alive, were taken aboard the *T 196*. The two escort vessels, heavily laden with survivors, headed for Kolberg. The *Steuben* had been carrying about 4,200 people; only 659 were saved.

Admiral Engelhardt was not slow to draw conclusions from the losses of the *Wilhelm Gustloff* and the *Steuben*. Both ships had been travelling with inadequate escorts – on both occasions the 'convoys' had been organized by the U-boat arm of the navy, and not by the 9th Security Division. Such unilateral acts by the U-boat officers, Engelhardt decided, had to stop with immediate effect. There were also problems with the destination ports for the evacuation voyages – Swinemünde, Warnemünde and Sassnitz could no longer cope with the thousands of people arriving in their ports. In early February, Hitler issued an edict that evacuees would, if possible, be taken to Copenhagen. Although this would reduce pressure on the north German ports, the increased duration of the voyage would require additional food and fuel, and would leave ships in danger of air and sea attack for a longer period. This order was also significant in that it made mention of 'compatriots who had temporarily been evacuated' rather than refugees – Hitler still couldn't bring himself to acknowledge the true nature of what was happening in East Prussia.

There has been controversy over the years about whether the *Wilhelm Gustloff* and the *Steuben* were legitimate targets, or whether Marinesko's attacks constituted war crimes. In the case of the *Gustloff*, the ship was armed, albeit with just two quad anti-aircraft guns, and was carrying a large number of naval personnel. She was not painted in the distinctive livery of hospital ships, and given that this was her first voyage since 1940, Marinesko could not be expected to recognize her, especially on a dark night with frequent snow showers. However tragic her loss may be, it seems that she was a legitimate target for a submarine attack. Similarly, the *Steuben* was also armed, and was designated as a 'wounded transport ship' rather than as a hospital ship. Again, in the darkness of a winter's night, accurate identification of the ship was impossible. In any event, the Soviet Union had made clear as early as July 1941 that it regarded hospital ships as legitimate targets, and made no attempt to avoid attacks on them.

When Marinesko notified his superiors that he had sunk a second large vessel, they were already aware that his previous claim was actually accurate. Soviet naval intelligence swiftly confirmed that his second victim was not a light cruiser, but was in fact the *Steuben*. Full of pride at having sunk more shipping than any other submarine officer in the Soviet fleet, Marinesko headed for home, confident that both he and his ship would be honoured for their achievements. The *S-13*'s arrival in the port of Turku was marked by a dinner in honour of its crew, but the expected awards did not follow. Marinesko was already under suspicion due to a number of disciplinary offences, and was dishonourably discharged from the navy in October 1945. Later, he was accused of stealing state property after arguing with the manager of a state institution where he had been able to get work, and spent several years in a labour camp in Siberia. Ultimately, he was rehabilitated, and in October 1963 he was finally given the award that traditionally awaited a submarine captain at the end of a successful voyage. In 1990, he was posthumously awarded the title 'Hero of the Soviet Union'.

News of these losses was suppressed within Germany – the Party had no intention of allowing such demoralizing news to circulate. Nevertheless, people became aware of the disasters through a variety of sources – those in the ports where the bodies recovered from the sea were brought ashore rapidly learned what had happened, and word spread quickly. Many people, including military signals units, regularly listened to foreign radio stations, despite the risk of severe punishment if they were caught, and the sinkings were prominently reported, particularly by Scandinavian stations. The Allies also produced a German-language newspaper, *Nachrichten für die Truppe*

(News for the Troops), which was dropped by air over German frontlines, and the story of the sinking of the *Gustloff* was a front-page item.

The ports receiving the refugees in the west – Warnenemünde, Swinemünde and Sassnitz – were completely swamped with arrivals. Both towns had limited rail connections with the hinterland, and accommodation for the refugees was soon exhausted. Ships that arrived often waited several days before they could unload their passengers – in the case of Sassnitz, the port was too small for the largest vessels, and smaller ships acted as ferries. Supplies of food, fresh water and fuel were also almost exhausted, resulting in ships waiting several days before they could head west again to collect more refugees. Inevitably, such a collection of shipping attracted the attention of RAF and USAAF aerial reconnaissance. Late on 6 March, five Mosquito fighter-bombers from the RAF's 5 Group appeared over Sassnitz, triggering air raid warnings. Such alerts were not new, as RAF bombers on their way to Berlin often passed over the port, but on this occasion the Mosquitoes released parachute flares. A force of 150 Lancaster bombers followed them, dropping their loads on northern Sassnitz. A second group of 41 bombers dropped magnetic mines into the port, trapping the ships waiting there. More than 490 tonnes of bombs fell on the town, inflicting terrible casualties in the crowded streets and destroying the single rail line. One Lancaster bomber was lost. Two ships – the destroyer *Z 38* and the hospital ship *Robert Möhring* – were hit and sunk. The following morning, the 21,600-tonne *Hamburg*, which had finished unloading her passengers and was awaiting supplies before heading east, struck two mines while attempting to manoeuvre in the approaches to Sassnitz and swiftly sank.

Worse was to come. Swinemünde was a larger port, with a peacetime population of about 22,000. Marshal Sergei Aleksandrovich Khudiakov, the Soviet Air Force's Chief of Staff, made an urgent request to the western Allies for the port to be bombed, in order to disrupt the maritime line of supply for the German forces fighting around Königsberg and Danzig. In response to this request, the USAAF 8th Air Force dispatched a force of 227 B-24s and 450 B-17s, with a fighter escort of about 450 aircraft, to bombard Swinemünde. The attack occurred in overcast conditions, but had a devastating effect on the overcrowded town. Seven ships were sunk, including the freighter *Andros*, struck by bombs while tied up at the pier – 570 refugees died on board. The exact toll of those killed in Swinemünde is unknown, but has been estimated at 23,000. Almost all of those killed were refugees from the east.

CHAPTER 10
THE RIVIERA OF HADES AND THE FALL OF POMERANIA

The bear belongs to me – after all, I killed it.

– Josef Stalin[1]

Even as the Red Army in the east and the Anglo-American forces in the west violated the frontiers of the Reich, Hitler remained defiant. An alliance of such contradictory interests, he doggedly maintained, could not endure. This was not the first time that the German people had been beset by enemies, he constantly reminded his entourage. During the Seven Years' War, the coalition of France, Austria and Russia seemed on the verge of destroying Friedrich II's Prussia, but after the sudden death of Czarina Elizabeth of Russia the anti-Prussian alliance disintegrated, allowing Friedrich to emerge triumphant. Such an event would happen again, Hitler believed.

The Allies, too, were aware that they were united by little more than a common enemy. As early as 1941, when he was criticized for embracing Stalin as an ally against Germany, Churchill retorted that he 'would sup with the devil himself' if he were fighting Hitler. In the earlier years of the war, with an Allied victory far from certain, there had been little reason to dwell on the differences between the 'Big Three' – Britain, the United States and the Soviet Union. Now, as thoughts turned to a post-war future, these differences loomed ever larger, threatening to rupture the alliance in exactly the manner that Hitler had predicted.

In 1943, the leaders of the Big Three met in Tehran, where it became clear that the Soviet Union would accept nothing less than a border with Poland that approximated to the frontier achieved by the Moltov–Ribbentrop Pact. Embarrassed by their inability to establish a second front in the west, the British and Americans were in little position to object. The best that Churchill could manage was an acceptance that by way of compensation, Poland would receive German territories in the west.

At the beginning of February 1945, Churchill and President Roosevelt met in Malta prior to travelling to meet Stalin at Yalta, in the Crimea. Churchill had sent Roosevelt a signal as early as 5 January, stating: 'This may well be a fateful conference, coming at a time when the Great Allies are so divided and the shadow of the war lengthens out before us.'[2] When the two leaders met on 2 February aboard the USS *Quincy*, there was little time for the extensive preparation that Churchill felt was vital. The meeting was clouded by disagreements between the two western leaders, relating both to the conduct of the war and to the shape of the world after the war. The prickly relationship between Dwight D. Eisenhower, the supreme Allied commander in the west, and Bernard Montgomery, commander of British forces, had been difficult since long before D-Day. Now, with the Anglo-American armies poised along the Rhine frontier, disagreements centred on the shape of the coming assault across the river.

There was little time for detailed discussions. Anthony Eden, Churchill's loyal lieutenant and foreign secretary, anxiously enquired about American attitudes to Poland. He was gratified to learn of US hostility to the puppet government, the 'Lublin Committee', that Stalin had already installed in Warsaw. But it was also clear that US concerns centred primarily on their proposed World Organization, which would eventually be transformed into the United Nations. Eden feared that Roosevelt regarded Soviet cooperation with these plans as far more important than the fate of Poland.

The journey from Malta to Yalta was by air. Two aircraft carried the British and American leaders east during the night of 2–3 February. They landed at the airfield at Saki the following day, and from there travelled to Yalta itself, through a landscape that still bore the vivid scars of fighting; the peninsula had been liberated by the Red Army only ten months before. The population had then been heavily purged, with most of the Crimean Tatar population deported to Uzbekistan as punishment for the existence of a Tatar legion in the German Army. Most of the personnel of the legion were actually recruited from the Volga Tatars, but their Crimean cousins joined them in exile. Then, as the Yalta conference approached, Stalin's NKVD descended again on the peninsula. Some 74,000 inhabitants of the neighbourhood were screened, and nearly a thousand arrested. Surveying the shattered, empty streets of Yalta, Churchill dubbed the seaside town 'the Riviera of Hades'.[3]

Stalin arrived by train on 4 February. He met Churchill and Roosevelt separately, dealing with each man in a different way – to Churchill, he expressed great satisfaction about the Soviet successes in Poland and Prussia, whereas with Roosevelt he emphasized the difficulties faced by the Red Army. Roosevelt made little attempt to hide differences of opinion between the British and Americans about the proposed Rhine crossing, and then joined Stalin in expressing doubts about British intentions to re-establish France as a significant European power. It was clear that Hitler's contemptuous view of the unity of the Allies was far from incorrect.

That afternoon, the conference started with a presentation by General Alexei Innokentovich Antonov, head of the Red Army Operations Directorate. He described the scale and success of the recent Soviet advance, and the damage done to the German Army: he estimated that some 45 divisions had been destroyed or rendered no longer functional. German casualties were placed at 400,000. Now, though, the Soviet armies were forced to pause for breath. Zhukov and Konev, who had appeared to be poised to thrust on over the Oder and Neisse, even to Berlin itself, were stalled. They were hamstrung by the casualties suffered during the advance, by the extended supply lines, by threats to their flanks and by a sudden change in the weather – higher temperatures resulted in a melting of the frozen waterways, and turned the grass fields used as forward airfields by the Soviet Air Force into quagmires.

There was also serious concern about the numbers of German divisions being redirected to the Oder front. Antonov estimated that between 35 and 40 divisions – some from the Western Front, some from Italy, some from Norway and others held in reserve within Germany – might be available to the Wehrmacht. In these circumstances, he stressed, it was vital that the western Allies increased pressure to tie down as many divisions as possible.

General George Marshall, the Chief of Staff of the US Army, then spoke on behalf of the Western Allies. The Ardennes fighting was now over, and preparations were in hand for the assault across the Rhine. There were ongoing supply problems due mainly to German rocket attacks on Antwerp, an assertion that Stalin dismissed on the grounds that such attacks were rarely accurate enough to be effective. Marshall retaliated by pointing out that Allied air raids had reduced German synthetic oil production by 80 per cent, and had devastated rail movements.

It was the beginning of a series of prickly exchanges, increasingly exposing the differences between the Big Three. Marshall estimated that the Germans had 79 divisions facing 78 Allied divisions in the west, and that the only superiority enjoyed by the Allies was in the air. This was disingenuous, to say the least. The German divisions in the west and in Italy were often as under-strength as those on the *Ostfront*, and faced severe supply shortages. The British, American and Canadian divisions that faced them were relatively strong, with fuel and ammunition available in quantities that were now far beyond the Wehrmacht. They also enjoyed a far greater degree of mechanization.

By the end of the session, a veneer of good relations had been restored, with Stalin promising to look at the possibility of a rapid capture of Danzig in order to hamstring U-boat production and training. The following morning, there were further military discussions. Both sides wanted the other to tie down as many Germans as possible.

There was little progress in the discussions, leaving Antonov with the clear impression that Soviet forces attempting to advance into Germany could expect to face German forces reinforced by men from other fronts. He also received confirmation that British and American intelligence expected 6th Panzer Army to move from the Ardennes to Hungary, where fighting around Budapest was reaching a climax.

By the end of the day, discussion had moved to the shape of post-war Germany. Zones of occupation had already been drawn up, but were now complicated by a British request for the French to have their own zone. Such discussions had first started in Tehran in 1943, and had been developed further by a conference in Moscow in October 1944, but Stalin now wanted detailed planning. Dismemberment of Germany was, he insisted, an essential part of the terms of surrender, and in the face of Churchill's resistance, he won the day with Roosevelt's support. The French issue now took centre stage. Stalin expressed doubts about British proposals for France to be allocated an occupation zone, asking if this would lead to other nations claiming the same right. He was assured that this would not happen, and that Britain saw an important role for a strong France as a bulwark against a future Germany. Britain, explained Churchill, may need to face a German threat in the future without the presence of American troops. Roosevelt agreed with him, and then stunned Churchill by stating that he expected American troops to withdraw from Europe within two years of the war coming to an end.

Stalin then raised the subject of reparations. He wanted a defeated Germany to pay the Soviet Union ten annual payments, as well as allowing the Soviets to dismantle and take away factories. Churchill had little problem with reparations in principle, but was concerned about a possible recurrence of the problems with reparations that followed World War I. The Big Three agreed to establish a Reparations Commission, with the details to be worked out by their Foreign Ministers. Eventually, this Reparations Commission formalized what had already been agreed, including the right of the victors to force Germans to work in their countries on reconstruction.

Roosevelt's prime concern of the entire conference was the proposed World Organization, and this dominated the agenda on 6 February. Stalin carefully examined the convoluted matter of voting within the proposed Security Council, and then dismayed the Americans by requesting that all of the constituent republics of the Soviet Union be given a separate vote. When the matter of Poland was raised, there was even less agreement. In almost every respect that mattered, Stalin held all the cards: his army was in control in Poland and his nominated government, the Lublin Committee, was already in Warsaw. Whatever the western Allies might say, he was in a position to dictate terms. There was no possibility of a return to the 1939 frontier – Stalin wanted the Curzon Line, or something close to it, and was in a position to insist.

The following day, there was time to return to the issue of the new World Organization. Stalin announced that he was happy with the proposed voting arrangements, and dropped his claim to large numbers of votes, requesting only that two or three Soviet republics would require a vote. Despite this latter point, the relief of the Americans was palpable. Soviet proposals for Poland were thus presented in the wake of this relief: there were minor alterations to the Curzon Line, and a few democratic leaders from Polish leaders from outside Poland would be included in the provisional government, pending elections. Churchill attempted to return to the question of Poland's frontiers, expressing concern that the transfer of large parts of Germany, particularly Silesia and Pomerania, to Polish control might lead to the result that 'the Polish goose dies of German indigestion'.[4]

Stalin dismissed this concern without any fuss. Huge columns of refugees, he stated, were fleeing before the advancing Red Army. At the previous meeting of the Big Three in Tehran, Stalin had shocked Churchill by suggesting that a lasting peace would require the execution of 50,000 German officers. Roosevelt had tried to make light of it, assuring Churchill that it might be necessary to execute only 49,000. Eventually Stalin dismissed the matter as a joke, but at this stage Churchill and Roosevelt must have been aware of the massacre of 16,000 Polish officers by the Soviet Union at Katyn. There was, therefore, every possibility that Stalin meant exactly what he said. In addition, there was an understanding that substantial transfers of territory between Germany, Poland and the Soviet Union would result in major movements of civilians. Now it became clear that this was already being carried out, in a way that from a 21st-century viewpoint could be viewed as forcible ethnic cleansing on a massive and brutal scale. Sitting in the Crimea, still bearing the scars of the most savage war in history, it is perhaps understandable that the Big Three saw matters in a rather different manner.

The conference continued for a short time, addressing issues such as the Soviet Union's participation in the war with Japan, but the salient issues had been settled. Stalin had effectively achieved everything that he had wanted, and joked about it later:

Churchill, Roosevelt and Stalin went hunting. They finally killed their bear. Churchill said, 'I'll take the bearskin, let Roosevelt and Stalin divide the meat.' Roosevelt said, 'No, I'll take the skin. Let Churchill and Stalin divide the meat.' Stalin remained silent so Churchill and Roosevelt asked him: 'Mister Stalin, what do you say?' Stalin simply replied, 'The bear belongs to me – after all, I killed it.'[5]

Meanwhile, events on the battlefield continued to unfold. The encircled German and Hungarian troops in Budapest finally surrendered on 10 February, an event that

POMERANIA, FEBRUARY–MARCH 1945

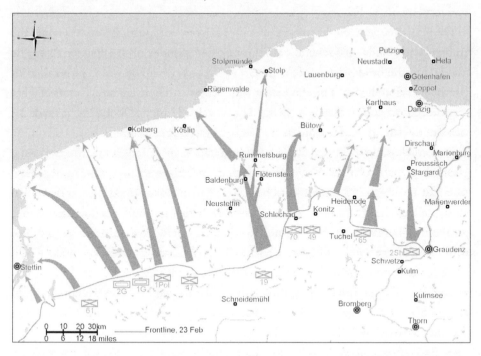

heralded another outbreak of rape and slaughter by the Red Army. Once again, after the exhausted frontline troops had marched on, the Soviet second echelon forces roamed the devastated city. An estimated 50,000 rapes occurred, adding to the trauma suffered by the civilian population during the siege.

Despite the final capture of Budapest, 6th Panzer Army continued to assemble in the Lake Balaton area, and was duly launched in yet another German counter-attack. The terrain selected for the attack was completely unsuitable, especially for the heavyweight King Tiger tanks of the SS, which found it impossible to manoeuvre in the swampy ground. Vital forces that might have made a difference further north were squandered for no gain.

Zhukov's 1st Belorussian Front was at the tip of a huge salient that stretched across Poland and parts of eastern Germany. On the south of the salient, Dietrich von Saucken was ordered to organize his Panzer Corps *Grossdeutschland* and what remained of Nehring's divisions into a counter-attack against Soviet forces that had secured a bridgehead across the Oder north of Steinau. Several days of confused fighting followed, and von Saucken's assault formations found themselves isolated, then surrounded when permission to withdraw was granted far too late. At great personal risk, von Saucken drove through Soviet lines to reach the trapped men, and led them to safety late on 11 February.

Despite this, von Saucken was dismissed from his post. After receiving the embarrassed thanks of General Fritz Gräser, commander of 4th Panzer Army, he travelled to the headquarters of Army Group Centre, where he was kept waiting for four hours before he had a brief meeting with Schörner. There are no accounts of what was said, but when von Saucken emerged he was clearly angry. Doubtless, he made his views of the stupidity of the orders he had been given very clear.[6]

Nevertheless, these limited attacks concentrated Soviet minds on the threats to the great salient, particularly as Pomerania remained in German hands to the north. These facts had already forced Zhukov to conclude that, with Rokossovsky's Front tied down far to the east, he would have to clear his flanks before he could resume the advance on Berlin. Plans were quickly formulated. Konev would drive into Silesia and deal with the southern flank, while forces released by both Zhukov and Rokossovsky would be sent north to overrun Pomerania, where Himmler's Army Group Vistula was assembling. The elimination of this 'Baltic balcony' would allow Rokossovsky to assemble his armies along the lower Oder, from where they would be able to assist in the final drive on Berlin.

A detailed account of the fighting in Pomerania is beyond the scope of this book. By the end of January, Rokossovsky had extracted several of his armies from the heavy fighting against 2nd and 4th Armies in Prussia, and regrouped them in the Graudenz–Bromberg area. Here, he now assembled a formidable force. On the left was Popov's 70th Army, with 49th Army (Grischkin), 65th Army (Batov) and 2nd Shock Army (Fediuninsky) forming up to its right. III Guards Cavalry Corps, available now that Hossbach's breakout attempt was over, was the Front's main reserve formation. On 8 February, Stavka drew up orders for an offensive by Rokossovsky to eliminate German forces in Pomerania. He was to continue his advance to the Vistula estuary and secure a line from there, running through Dirschau, Bütow and Rummelsburg to Neustettin by 20 February. At this stage, reserves would be committed to launch a major assault against Army Group Vistula, driving to the Oder estuary and Stettin, and to eliminate German forces isolated around Danzig. The intention was to complete these operations by early March, allowing for forces to be moved west to concentrate for the final assault on Berlin.

On 10 February, Rokossovsky was ordered to transfer 3rd, 48th and 50th Armies and 5th Guards Tank Army to Cherniakhovsky's 3rd Belorussian Front, so that the forces arrayed against the German pockets trapped in East Prussia would be under a single unified command. Despite being deprived of such powerful formations,

Rokossovsky and his Chief of Staff, Aleksandr Nikolaevich Bogoliubov, continued preparations for the drive into Pomerania, while simultaneously maintaining offensive operations along the Vistula valley. The 49th Army was transferred across the Vistula on 4 February, and further reinforcements were sent to 70th Army. Formations known as 'fortified regions' were used to replace divisions of 2nd Shock Army on the east bank of the Vistula, allowing the divisions themselves to be transferred across the river south of Graudenz. This in turn allowed other formations to be shifted further west.

Artillery assets were moved to Rokossovsky's left flank, and the Front's engineers, commanded by Mikhail Lvovich Cherniavsky, returned impressive numbers of damaged vehicles to frontline formations. As supply lines lengthened, the efficacy of the repair crews declined, but compared with previous Soviet campaigns the ability of the Red Army to recover and repair damaged vehicles had improved greatly, and played a major role in the capability of frontline formations to sustain offensive operations. An analysis of the number of tanks recorded as knocked out, the number repaired and the number still running at the end of the campaign, shows that many vehicles were repaired several times. German repair teams were equally effective, but even on the occasions that these teams were available, the Red Army usually ended the day controlling the battlefield, and therefore in possession of most of the damaged vehicles. Consequently, most German vehicles recorded as hit were effectively lost, while many Soviet vehicles were simply handed over to the repair teams.

Engineers also worked to construct bridges over the Vistula, a task complicated by the broken river ice slowly floating downstream, and to lay or repair hundreds of kilometres of telegraph wires. Two pipelines were established over the river for fuel to be brought swiftly to truck depots, from where it could be distributed to frontline formations – and all of this while offensive operations continued along the Vistula valley. Soviet logistical skills had indeed come a very long way.

Political preparation, too, continued. The commissars worked to ensure that soldiers remained committed to fighting, and that the natural tendency of soldiers towards the end of a war, to start thinking about avoiding risks so that they are not needlessly killed, did not result in a slackening of their fighting spirit. Units were encouraged to produce proclamations stating their resolve, such as this one from the 207th Tank Destroyer Battalion:

> On behalf of all soldiers and NCOs, I declare that the power of the Soviet State is great, and we will take complete revenge upon the fascists for their crimes. The defeated fascist soldiers have already repeatedly tried to avoid retribution. But the cries of the Hitlerites

are useless. We have already entered Germany and let us now pay back the fascists. We will destroy the fascist order so that the fascists will never again be able to raise weapons against our native land.[7]

As was the case before the January offensive, the importance of taking revenge upon the hated enemy played a major part in the preparation of the soldiers. Communist Party officials had correctly calculated that this was a powerful means of overcoming combat fatigue. At a conference of senior commissars, the importance of using division and corps newspapers to eulogize the heroic exploits of individual soldiers was also stressed. Post-war accounts also speak of the role of Party officials in ensuring that the 'liberated' Poles were treated well by the Red Army, and that Soviet soldiers were called upon to conduct themselves in ways that were worthy of their great mission of liberation. The Poles had been very harshly treated by their German occupiers; the fact that many chose to flee with the Germans as the Red Army advanced suggests that the message of benevolence towards the Poles was not universally embraced by the advancing Soviet forces.

On land, fighting continued. The town of Schneidemühl saw the first major battle in Pomerania as Soviet forces turned north to deal with the Baltic balcony. Fighting reached the outskirts of the town on 28 January; the garrison held on until late on 13 February, when it attempted to escape to the north. Only a few men escaped. Now Zhukov moved more forces north to add to those of Rokossovsky. Semen Bogdanov's 2nd Guards Tank Army joined Pavel Alexeyevich Belov's 61st Army, Frants Iosivovich Perkhorovich's 47th Army and Stanislav Poplavsky's 1st Polish Army along a line running from Landsberg to Schneidemühl. 1st Guards Tank Army (Mikhail Efimovich Katukov) and 3rd Shock Army (Nikolai Pavlovich Simoniak) would follow later.

Soviet preparations for an attack into Pomerania were now almost ready; in some areas, Rokossovsky continued to grind forward, attempting to move up to the start line that was to run from the Vistula estuary to Neustettin. The 4th Panzer Division, still hamstrung by inadequate replacements for the tanks and other vehicles it had left behind in Courland, continued to dispatch small battlegroups to neighbouring divisions in attempts to restore the situation. The petrol shortage was particularly pernicious; there was plenty of diesel fuel, however, and a delivery of eight-wheeled diesel-powered armoured cars to the division's reconnaissance battalion was greeted with a mixture of relief and enthusiasm. There then came welcome news: the division's Panther tanks, left behind in Courland, would be transported to join it, but for the moment Betzel's men had to make do with whatever was available. Just south of Tuchel, a small battlegroup probed forward:

We move through Tuchel heading south. A road-sign states that we have reached Liebenau. Tired, fought-out soldiers of a Luftwaffe unit occupy trenches in the streets. They wave to us, they know that without our attack, they would be Russian prisoners of war.

We drive under a railway bridge. Immediately, we see the red tracer of a Russian anti-tank round coming our way. 6 Company deploys by platoons and takes up hull-down positions. Only the vehicle commanders can see over the cover. The platoon commander orders that we are to fire only on his command. Soon, the first three Russian tanks appear at the railway bridge. A KV-2, unmistakable with its massive turret, leads the way. We suddenly open fire at 50 metres. The three Russians are soon burning. The crews bale out. The following tanks turn rapidly, but are caught by flank fire from another platoon. In panic, they disappear back into the village. We receive orders to push into the village and to take it. A Tiger is assigned to us, and soon arrives. Where it came from, I have no idea. Now it's with us, and stays with us.

First, we attempt a frontal attack, but this doesn't succeed, as we come under fire from all sides. So we drive around the village and attack from the side. The Tiger does good work for us, shooting up the Russian tanks at 2,000 metres range with its 88mm gun. But when we press into the village, again we don't succeed, as the enemy swiftly concentrates the fire of all his weapons on us. So we pull back again, and try again from the south. Meanwhile, however, it's growing dark. The even white surface proves to be treacherous. Suddenly, the ground under my tank gives way. We have broken through the ice over a stream. Water pours through the engine compartment. We nearly tilt over. Only luck and cunning allows me to work free. But our Tiger – our pride and joy – is hopelessly stuck as a result of its huge weight.

Our hearts bleed when we are ordered to return to our starting positions and to blow up the Tiger.[8]

The Tiger was one of the remaining vehicles of 507th Heavy Tank Battalion, now subordinated to 4th Panzer Division. After its involvement in the original Soviet assault, this unit had slowly retreated across Poland, losing 17 of its Tigers, though only six due to enemy action – the rest were abandoned due to breakdowns and fuel shortages. The remaining 13 vehicles now provided 4th Panzer Division with some much-needed additional firepower. Tuchel itself became the centre of a bitter battle. Short of fuel, the German forces in the area struggled to hold the town and its railway station. Casualties in 4th Panzer Division had been heavy – on 11 February, one battalion of Panzergrenadiers, which had been assigned a 12km section of frontline, reported that it had only 12 exhausted men available for duty.[9]

Late on 14 February, Generalleutnant Betzel accepted the inevitable and pulled 4th Panzer Division out to a new line north of Tuchel. In the preceding four days, his division had recorded that it had accounted for 99 enemy tanks, 12 assault guns, 2 armoured cars and 41 anti-tank guns.[10] Even after allowing for the inevitable exaggeration of combat reports, and the fact that many of these 'kills' would have represented vehicles merely disabled rather than destroyed, the numbers give an indication of the intensity of the fighting. Four days later, Hauptmann Kästner, who had been dispatched to Courland, arrived in Danzig with the division's 27 Panther tanks. Another 23 were en route from factories in the Reich. Provided they all reached the division, it would once more become a powerful striking force – if sufficient fuel and ammunition were also available.

On 12 February, the surplus tank crews of 507th Heavy Tank Battalion boarded a train in the town of Bütow. They took with them almost all the women and children who had gathered at the railway station, and left for the west. For the veterans of the formation, this was an end to two long years on the *Ostfront*. Their train took them to Paderborn, where they were re-equipped with heavyweight King Tiger tanks. Some ended the war fighting against the Americans in the Harz Mountains; the rest of the battalion attempted to break through to the west in order to surrender to the Americans at the end of the war, but was forced to surrender to the Red Army.

Rokossovsky, meanwhile, had received notification of the reinforcements that would be required for the second phase of the planned operation, in the shape of III Guards Tank Corps and the comparatively fresh 19th Army, newly arrived from the Finnish front. These two formations would be committed once the Vistula estuary–Neustettin start line had been reached, and would drive through to the Baltic coast, breaking the German forces in Pomerania in two. The reinforcements were most welcome: 70th, 49th, 65th and 2nd Shock Armies had all been in constant action, and were severely below strength. The 45th Rifle Division had fewer than 4,000 men.[11] Nevertheless, the Red Army continued to move north, and 47th Army attacked Konitz in mid February. The town was defended by 4th Panzer Division's reconnaissance battalion, armed with a mixture of Lynx light tanks, its new armoured cars, and half-tracks that carried formidable 20mm and 75mm guns. However, they were hamstrung by fuel and ammunition shortages, and were also forced to defend a large stretch of ground either side of Konitz. The men of 4th Armoured Reconnaissance Battalion were relieved to be able finally to hand over the town and the surrounding area to 7th Panzer Division on 16 February.

The 7th Panzer Division, most of which had gathered west of the town of Marienburg, had been pulled into reserve. Johann Huber and his comrades in 7th Panzer Division were re-equipped with Jg.Pz. IVs. On 30 January, Huber listened to

Hitler's radio broadcast; speeches from the Führer on the anniversary of his acquisition of power were now something of a tradition:

So we listen attentively. Hitler speaks with a changed voice, and we can barely recognize him. 'The situation in which the German Reich finds itself today resembles the situation of internal political affairs in 1933.' What does he mean? And then he goes on. The Führer demands that the German troops on the *Ostfront* don't concede a single metre of German soil, that they throw back the enemies on all fronts, and drive them back over the German frontiers. I have inner doubts that this can be done in the face of Russian superiority. And then comes the salient sentence: 'I have to say to the German people: we have no *Wunderwaffen*; the belief in our *Wunderwaffen* is a belief in our greater Germany.' We look at each other, stunned. So no *Wunderwaffen* – we're really going to lose this war! And then comes another salient sentence: 'A people can do no more than work and fight, and if this does not bring victory, then that is our fate!' Everyone looks at each other; Hitler has finished, and the transmission ceases.[12]

Not all the news was bad. Pauli Schütze, who was something of a joker in Huber's company, returned to the frontline after a period of leave, wearing an Iron Cross. He then regaled his comrades with the story of how he won it:

In September of last year, our Quartermaster Jeck asked for volunteers to train as 'sabotage commandos' behind the enemy lines and Pauli, who volunteered, was actually selected. Nobody believed that Pauli Schütze had any chance, and everyone laughed about it.

So he tells me with much humour, that he only volunteered to get away from the endless hassles within 5 Company. In this special unit, he was first given a new uniform and then promptly assigned to a training unit to learn Russian. After six weeks of the best rations and special training in the unit, he told me, 'they realized that I couldn't do anything!' I think to myself, that was smart of him, stupid but still clever. But when they realized, he told me, that they could do nothing with him, they ordered him to be transferred to a field replacement battalion for the infantry. 'There, I was of course much better off, you see, Huber, after my training in 5 Company!' He continues in a lively way to tell me that after weapons training and other deployments, he made such an impression that he was swiftly made commander of his group. The unit was then deployed in East Prussia in the Rominte Heath near Gumbinnen. 'There, the company commander made me a messenger.'

I ask him curiously what happened next, and delighted with my interest, he tells me that every day, he had to carry orders forward from the company HQ, about 1.5km behind the lines, to the platoon commander, and bring back reports. 'And then I shot down a plane! There I was marching forward one morning, and then a Russian biplane appeared, really low, you see!' Pauli explains to me that he unslung his rifle from his shoulder and said to his comrade, 'We have to shoot at it like we were shown in training!' But his comrade took off after uttering the Götz von Berlichingen. [When called upon to surrender by the bishop of Bamberg, the robber baron Götz von Berlichingen famously replied, 'He can lick my arse!'] And then, as Pauli related to me, 'I took my rifle, aimed at the pilot, and you see, like we were trained, aimed three aircraft lengths ahead and fired! And the plane was hit and crashed.' And then with particular emphasis: 'A head-shot!' And then, 'we walked over to where the biplane was lying on the field and saw that he was dead'. By now, I had figured out that it was a UvD [*Unteroffizier vom Dienst*, or 'duty NCO', the nickname given by German soldiers to the Polykarpov biplanes that turned up unexpectedly on nuisance raids]. Then Pauli was very smart and took the dead pilot's papers. These he took straight back to company HQ and discovered that it was a courier flight with the most important documents. The pilot, a commissar, had lost his way.

And then Pauli concludes: 'And then the company commander promoted me to Gefreiter, and I was awarded the Iron Cross, Class II, which I would never have got in 5 Company!'

And with the air of a conjuror, he produces his leave pass and tells me, 'And then I was awarded three weeks' home leave for courage in the face of the enemy. You understand, that's important, courage in the face of the enemy, it's written here!' I listen patiently to this story from Pauli, our company twit, veering from amazement to laughter.[13]

On 14 February, 7th Panzer Division set off for Konitz, where a 20km gap yawned between 32nd Infantry Division and 4th Panzer Division. The leading battlegroup of 7th Panzer Division, formed around ten tanks led by the division's Panzer regiment commander, Major Ernst Brandes, motored into Konitz and was greeted by cheering civilians. The tanks took up positions in the square in the middle of the town, which was choked with refugee wagons and an assortment of military vehicles.

On 16 February, Popov's 70th Army swept through the positions of the exhausted 15th SS Waffen-Grenadier Division. This formation had originally been a Latvian volunteer legion. Its troops, still mainly Latvians, had been in almost continuous combat against Rokossovsky's advancing forces since January, and the division's commanding officer, Brigadeführer Herbert von Obwurzer, was killed in action on 26 January. Weiss, the commander of the German 2nd Army, was acutely aware that the division was fast approaching the end of its strength, and toyed with the notion of reinforcing it with 7th Panzer Division. Yet the gap in the lines at Konitz remained open, and he had to decide where to send his only mobile reserves. By opting to close the gap at Konitz, he effectively sealed the fate of the Latvians.

The Soviet I Guards Tank Corps and XCVI Rifle Corps attacked towards Konitz from the south. The spearhead, commanded by Major Kryakhov, consisting of three assault guns with infantry support, found that the route to the town led through dense woodland. A river ran across the Soviet line of advance, but the single bridge was still intact. A swift attack on 15 February secured the vital crossing before it could be destroyed, and the Soviet forces rushed forward to reach the outskirts of Konitz itself.[14]

As the German screen outside Konitz was driven back, 7th Panzer Division's battlegroup continued to assemble in the town. There was sporadic sniper fire from some of the buildings, and it became clear that Soviet forces were infiltrating through the buildings. Soviet heavy weapons followed, as Hufnagel, one of the division's soldiers, later recalled:

> Our battlegroup took up positions around the large square, with our Pz. IV near the red cemetery wall, with the turret turned to six o'clock, and after a short time we were shot up. The shell struck the rear, in the engine, which immediately started to burn. We therefore baled out, apart from the driver, who couldn't exit from his hatch because unfortunately the turret locker was overhead. Thank God the fire soon went out.
>
> The tank commander, Unteroffizier Schiessl, wanted to rescue our driver from this awkward situation, but every time we climbed onto our tank to climb in and turn the turret, the tank took another hit from the Russian gun; this happened three or four times. We also did not know whether it was an anti-tank gun or a tank that was firing at us. As Schiessl was determined to help our trapped driver, Obergefreiter Kleinhempel, he sent me to the tank of the commander, Major Brandes, which was about 40 metres away, to ask for help, particularly for covering fire. The commander was positioned with his engine towards the enemy and, like us, had turned his turret to six o'clock.
>
> Major Brandes considered for some time whether he should leave his position with his Panther. His tank was somewhat in cover behind a roadblock, which had been set up at the entrance to another road that he was covering. In order to take cover from the enemy, I stood near the front of his tank and waited.
>
> Finally, the regiment commander decided to help us free our driver by providing covering fire. Major Brandes stood up in the turret and nodded to me.
>
> He ordered his driver to drive backwards. He probably wanted to drive past on the right side of the roadblock. The turret remained in the six o'clock position.

The Panther had barely come any distance when the Russians immediately opened fire on it, but too high, and thus struck Major Brandes' head from his shoulders. Brandes' body fell into the turret.[15]

Brandes was a popular officer in the division, and had won the Knight's Cross in Memel just a few months before. Within moments, Hufnagel learned of the fatal wounding of another popular officer:

We were there [near their Pz. IV, whose driver had finally managed to escape] for a short time when infantrymen carried our Leutnant von Rohr and his gunner back; both had been severely wounded. Leutnant von Rohr had left his vehicle and intended to shoot up an enemy tank at close range with a Panzerfaust, and was badly wounded by the backblast of his own Panzerfaust.[16]

Another battlegroup of 7th Panzer Division, led by Oberleutnant Völkel, moved into Konitz and tried to continue the defence of the town:

They drove into the town at night in pouring rain. It was Leutnant Freikamp's platoon, and Oberleutnant Völkel commanded the battlegroup. We took up positions at 0800 in a large, open plaza, apparently the marketplace. This was at the eastern edge of the town centre. The Russian attack was expected from the west. There, the main road ended about 500 metres further away where another road crossed it. It was a cold and foggy day, with poor visibility in the town. It was completely silent at this time. No civilians, no infantry, no enemy to be seen. With their new Jg.Pz. IV (crewed by Feldwebel Iseke, Michl Weber, von Egloffstein, Klotz) they guarded this main road, part of Reichsstrasse 1, in the centre of Konitz, facing west.

South of the main road the marketplace was bordered by a wall, behind which was a school. This school had been designated as a field hospital, and there were still 200–300 wounded soldiers there.

At about 0900 there were the sounds of tracks: tanks! First the crew saw only a gun barrel and the muzzle-brake of an enemy tank. There were certainly others behind it. They wanted to cross the main road guarded by Feldwebel Iseke's tank, from right to left. They were Stalin tanks … Egloffstein fired on the second, but in the new Jg.Pz. IV, which was still unfamiliar, the fighting cabin ventilation system struggled to cope with the smoke after each shot and the smoke from the barrel formed a cloud in front of the tank, making vision for the gunner difficult. Our trusty Pz. IV had a muzzle brake that diverted most of the barrel gases to the sides; the barrel of the light Jg.Pz. had no muzzle brake, and as a consequence most of the barrel gas simply went forward and obscured vision after the shot. Through the powder smoke, Egloffstein caught sight of four or five Stalins crossing the road at high speed, and the closeness of the corner house made an aimed shot impossible.

… About 20 minutes later, Russian snipers appeared. From the upper parts of a house on the eastern side of the marketplace, one shot smashed the mirror on the open hatch behind the commander. The marksman was aiming for Iseke's head. He was struck in the neck by some splinters from the shattered mirror. He bled heavily and had to be bandaged quickly, but remained with the crew. Then they changed position to the other side of the marketplace, where other tanks of the company were in position.

… The Russians were isolated in the houses, but couldn't be driven out. Feldwebel Iseke now warned Oberleutnant Völkel, who frequently dismounted and moved around in the open, about the snipers. At 1100, the chief was wounded in the arm while in the open, outside his tank.

Leutnant Freikamp thus took over command of the battlegroup. But because of interference from the buildings around the marketplace, Iseke's tank was the only one with radio contact with the battalion headquarters, and Iseke had to take over radio communications. It was also impossible to establish direct radio contact with the Panthers, as they were on a different frequency.

At 1200, the tanks were ordered: 'Establish contact with the battle commander and prepare for a breakout at dusk.' They passed this message on to Leutnant Freikamp, who sought out and found the local commander. Apparently, the hopeless situation with the Russians encircling the town had overwhelmed him. He had turned to alcohol and was roaring drunk. The major could only babble.

Leutnant Freikamp was very downcast by this and went to Iseke's tank and said, 'Iseke, what should I do, the local commander is completely drunk. What should I do?' Iseke then sent an elegant signal to battalion headquarters: 'Local commander not fit for duty, preparing for breakout.' – to which the battalion replied, 'Order for breakout still stands.' Iseke then said earnestly to Leutnant Freikamp: 'Herr Leutnant, go to your tank, the air is full of steel, and you'll end up a casualty too.'

At about 1500 proper streetfighting began against the Red Army troops, who had penetrated into the upper parts of the nearby houses. Some of our infantry (they were from another unit) remained in the cellars all day and did not dare come out, meaning that our tanks and the two half-tracks with the Panzergrenadiers were caught up in a wild infantry battle. The tanks joined in the streetfighting, using high-explosive rounds against the snipers and machine-gun nests in the houses.

Another battlegroup with infantry had entrenched in the cemetery that lay to the east of the marketplace and from there fired on the Russians in the houses opposite.

This infantry battle was a new experience for the men in the Jg.Pz. IV. Due to the gunshield of the loader's machine-gun (MG-42), it was not possible to fire the machine-gun upwards, as the available elevation was minimal. The Red Army soldiers though were everywhere in the upper parts of the houses (the German Landsers were in the cellars) so that the loader/radio operator had to dismount the MG-42 and use its bipod on the edge of the open hatch to shoot upwards.

Then dusk fell and everyone received the radio order they were hoping for: 'Break out with the infantry at dusk,' i.e. between 1630 and 1700. The battlegroup prepared itself for the breakout, with a Panther as spearhead, then a half-track, then Freikamp, then two more half-tracks, then Iseke, then the second Panther with its turret turned to 6 o'clock. Egloffstein recorded that at the outset, his tank threw a track. Michl Weber noticed the change in resistance and swiftly brought the vehicle to a halt.

Together with him, the experienced driver, and Klotz, they quickly levered the faulty return roller with a crowbar back over the track teeth, and Michl jumped back into the tank and selected reverse gear; the others simultaneously used the crowbar to push the track back into place. They paid no regard to the powerful bombardment.

Meanwhile the heavy radio traffic had seriously drained the batteries of their tanks, and the starter would not turn the engine. Berthold von Egloffstein and Klotz, the loader/radio operator, had to get out again to turn the engine over with the crank. At this point, they were fired on by the Russians, and Klotz was seriously wounded by an explosive bullet. Klotz fell down next to the tank. Berthold leaped through the nearest open house entrance and pulled Klotz in with the help of an infantryman in order to dress his wounds. Meanwhile, in response to the signalled breakout attempt, a huge crowd of soldiers poured out of the houses lining the main road and the marketplace (the other half of the town of Konitz appeared already to be completely in the hands of the Russians), but also civilians, women and children, all rushing up to the battlegroup's tanks. It seemed to Bert that there was more than a complete infantry company. They wanted to be taken along.

By now, it had already grown dark, and time was pressing. Bert and Michl Weber together swung the engine crank, and the engine started. Then Bert asked the infantrymen gathered at the house entrance in preparation for a breakout whether there was anyone with anti-tank training, to serve as a replacement for the seriously wounded loader. An Obergefreiter came forward and made himself known. With him, Bert first loaded the badly wounded Klotz – he had a large flesh wound – onto the engine decking. Then women and children were also helped onto the engine decking, and a couple of infantrymen sat on top of Iseke's tank. The other vehicles were already fully loaded. Some of the infantrymen, who couldn't find places on the tanks, followed alongside, using them as cover.

It was now quite dark, with visibility reduced to 30–50 metres. The breakout began. At moderate speed, in view of the accompanying infantry and the darkness, with the wounded loaded into one of the half-tracks, they drove, barrels lowered and without stopping, through the town in this formation. Soon they heard shots. A short time later they found themselves beyond the houses in an avenue.

Suddenly directly in front of them was a bright flash, followed by an unholy loud crash: the half-track with the wounded aboard had been hit and flew apart like a shoebox, bursting apart on all sides – Bert saw this through the optics. Everyone who was in the half-track must have been killed instantly.

But Iseke and Weber shouted: fire, fire, fire! Michl had already turned the tank a little to the right. But Bert could only see the spearhead Panther through the gunsights and shouted back, 'I have a Panther in my sights, I can't fire on a Panther!'

Then Michl Weber turned the Jg.Pz. IV further to the right. Now Bert saw his target in the darkness: a large, red Soviet star on the turret of a Stalin close by. Bert ... aimed at the lower part of the turret and fired.

But the gun didn't fire! The Obergefreiter from the infantry, who had only trained with an anti-tank gun and not a tank gun, didn't understand the electric firing mechanism and hadn't secured it! Bert had to reach over the breech, secure it, and then – the Stalin had almost turned its turret onto him – finally fired. The cupola hatch flew off the Stalin tank, a sheet of flame shot out, and the Russian burst into flames.

But there wasn't just this tank in the field to the right – there were six or seven. In the firelight of the burning enemy tank and the explosions of its ammunition, they saw the others sitting there, either not ready for action or not crewed. Apparently, the Russians were busy plundering the nearby houses. The infantry and civilians sitting on Iseke's vehicle leaped off it as soon as it fired. With their Panzerfausts, they now moved on the other Stalin tanks. The enemy tanks were formed up close to each other as if in a circle, so that after a few were knocked out, Bert couldn't tell in the confusion exactly how many were left.

... The first line had been broken. The breakout had to continue quickly, the infantry and civilians sat down on the vehicles again and the column drove on. After about a quarter of an hour, they reached our outposts. It was the crew of a half-track from our unit that first met the approaching battlegroup.

Now the comrades of 5 Company learned that Oberleutnant Völkel, our wounded company commander, had been in the half-track that was hit and exploded. Berthold said that they were very downcast by this news, but were still pleased that the loader/radio operator Klotz had been able to get out on the engine decking. He was sent to the west in a hospital train.

The Russians now plundered Konitz.[17]

The Soviet 76th Guards Rifle Division, part of CXIV Rifle Corps, attempted to cut the roads to the east of Konitz before the Germans could pull out, but in confused fighting the garrison withdrew. To the east of CXIV Rifle Corps, 385th Rifle Division took up positions outside Konitz, and immediately had to endure several German counter-attacks. As casualties mounted, the Soviet division's 237th Rifle Regiment assaulted the village of Johannisburg from the southeast, supported by a battalion of assault guns. A three-hour battle raged around the ruins of the village, and finally the surviving German forces pulled back a short distance.[18]

The 7th Panzer Division retreated to the east of Konitz and took up defensive positions. In the division's sector, the Soviet forces tried to renew their drive, but were beaten off without major difficulty. Rokossovsky's men made better progress on either flank of 7th Panzer Division's position, and by the end of 21 February were threatening to envelop the German defenders. Slowly, 7th Panzer Division was levered back, withdrawing perhaps 15km over the next three days.

The 4th and 7th Panzer Divisions continued to put up stern resistance, fully justifying their status as elite formations, but the infantry divisions that formed the bulk of the German line were increasingly brittle. Their experienced cadres had almost disappeared, and the replacement drafts, made up of a mixture of rear-area troops, barely recovered wounded and stragglers from other formations, lacked the training and cohesion to put up strong resistance. Struggling to hold his army together, Weiss had no armoured reserves available other than the two Panzer divisions – only two of the assault gun brigades that had been created for this role were in 2nd Army's area, and they had only a few vehicles left. Although many divisions now had a complement of anti-tank guns, including Hetzer tank-hunters, the frontage defended by each division was so large that these weapons, where available, were never present in sufficient numbers. Consequently, to prevent 2nd Army's exhausted infantry divisions from being overrun, Weiss had to order the Panzer divisions to 'loan' small packages of armour to support the infantry, in the face of bitter protests from Generalleutnant Betzel. These packages, often only a couple of tanks, were sometimes overwhelmed before they could even engage the enemy. On other occasions, the Panzer divisions received requests for help faster than they could respond.

The Germans now realized that Rokossovsky's attack had two main points of effort. To the east, 2nd Shock Army attempted to push up the west bank of the Vistula, while to the west the drive towards and through Konitz rapidly became a major threat. Should these two assaults break through the German lines, there was the prospect of Weiss' battered infantry divisions being surrounded and destroyed in the area of the Tuchel Heath, between the two Soviet thrusts. What mobile forces were available to the Germans would have to be used to their utmost effectiveness to prevent this.

On 19 February, just as it seemed that the German line might collapse, Rokossovsky was forced to halt the drive by his left wing towards the Baltic coast. Supply problems for his armies had steadily worsened, and he badly needed a pause to regroup and bring forward reinforcements. As planned, 19th Army and III Guards Tank Corps were intended to take forward the drive, and were ordered to their forming-up areas, with instructions to be ready to renew the advance in 48 hours. But Soviet planners continued to overestimate the strength of German forces facing them. Intelligence estimates put the strength of Weiss' battered 2nd Army at two Panzer divisions, 14 infantry divisions, four independent infantry brigades, two independent Kampfgruppen, four independent infantry regiments and 15 independent infantry battalions, with a total strength of about 230,000 men and 341 tanks and assault guns, supported by over 200 combat aircraft.[19] Weiss would have been glad to have had anything approaching this at his disposal. In addition, Soviet intelligence reports predicted that five infantry divisions would be moved from Courland to reinforce German units in Pomerania. One of the divisions listed was actually already trapped in the Samland peninsula, in East Prussia, and the others remained in Courland until the end of the war. The 11th Army, deployed in western Pomerania, was believed to have an additional 200,000 men and 700 tanks; Rokossovsky may have had doubts about these numbers, but he intended to take no chances.

Soviet thinking remained focused on reaching Berlin as quickly as possible. Stalin was haunted by the possibility that, despite their public pronouncements, Roosevelt and Churchill might be persuaded by Hitler to make peace in the west, allowing Germany to switch all its military assets to the east. A drive on Berlin was out of the question while Soviet intelligence estimates reported such powerful forces threatening the northern flank. Stavka therefore continued to place great importance on the clearance of the Baltic coast, and issued further orders to this effect. Rokossovsky in turn passed on the orders to his subordinates. The fresh forces of 19th Army, reinforced by III Guards Tank Corps, would thrust towards the Baltic coast near Köslin, before sending units east to roll up the German lines towards the Bay of Danzig. On the opposite flank of his front, 2nd Shock Army would drive to Preussisch Stargard and onwards to Danzig from the south. The armies in between would keep up constant pressure on the German line.

This pressure was having significant effects. On 20 February, 4th Panzer Division was ordered to launch a counter-attack to restore the front in the sector held by 251st Infantry Division. Yet on the evening of the same day, long before the front had been restored, the division was turned 180 degrees and sent west to help 227th and 73rd Infantry Divisions; the latter was one of the two divisions that had escaped from

Thorn, and had been in continuous action since it was first encircled there. After completing this task on 21 February, Betzel had to dispatch his reconnaissance battalion back to 251st Infantry Division's sector on 22 February to deal with another Soviet penetration, but the following day 227th Infantry Division was once more in difficulties and required further support. Despite this, the division continued to report relatively large numbers of combat-ready vehicles. On 24 February, for example, it had 17 Pz. IVs, nine assault guns and 28 Panthers available, with another 21 Pz. IVs, 13 assault guns and 33 Panthers undergoing repairs.[20] This account by Oberleutnant Ulrich Sachse, serving with the division's reconnaissance battalion, gives a flavour of these firefighting missions:

> Bitter defensive fighting north of Heiderode, around Long and the Schwarzwasser stream. An enemy coup-de-main at a bridge is bloodily dealt with in the blink of an eye after a rapid redeployment. Long is lost. Leutnant Gsell makes a futile thrust at Long during the night. The plucky Leutnant is fatally wounded. Then the reserve Reconnaissance Battalion *München* attacks the enemy. Counter-attacks and more counter-attacks. We assist the bravely fighting infantry. The general commanding 83rd Infantry Division stands with his men holding a rifle. His eyes bulge when we arrive – our tanks? Are such things still available?... We dismount and stand with them. Another counter-thrust! Leutnant Stöhr falls, Unteroffizier Flurschütz falls – losses, ever more losses. Battalion HQ is 'Tree 17' somewhere in the wood.
>
> No artillery support, no fuel for the ammunition transports. A couple of shells here and there, carried to the guns by hurrying horses with trembling flanks through the sand of the endless heathland. Enemy tanks approaching! We too still have tanks! But the Panther battalion has been sent some way to the north to the Dramburg–Bütow area, where an enemy breakthrough is approaching the Baltic. The little Count Moltke is still with us, with his solitary Pz. IV. He is everywhere, wherever he is needed. With thundering exhausts, he drives back and forth, day and night. His trusty, lame wagon roars for the entire battalion.[21]

In an attempt to extract 4th Panzer Division from the frontline, so that at least parts of it could be available for counter-attacks against Soviet penetrations, Weiss moved infantry formations away from the defences along the lower Vistula. Now that the river ice was breaking up, it could be argued that the defences could safely be weakened, but Weiss was aware of the great speed with which the Red Army had built bridgeheads over the huge rivers in the Soviet Union during the Wehrmacht's long retreat. This strategy, forced on him by events, carried its own risks.

Ever since the creation of Germany, German military planners had regarded the Vistula as a natural defensive line in the event of an attack from the east. Fortresses such as Thorn, Graudenz and Marienburg, most of which had played a role in the turbulent history of the region for centuries, had been modernized in the late 19th and early 20th centuries. Although warfare had evolved in the intervening years, these fortresses still represented formidable strongpoints. Marienburg was the home of the Teutonic Knights until it fell to Poland in 1460. Its most effective fortifications dated from the 1870s. The intention was for the fortress to defend the crossings over the lower Vistula and Nogat. These crossings, at Dirschau and Marienburg respectively, were foreseen as essential for the withdrawal of German forces pulling back from East Prussia; they would also provide a route for an eventual counter-attack towards the east. However, the General Staff survey of 1911 made it clear that Marienburg could only function as a fortress if a German field army were available west of the Nogat and Vistula. By 1945, the two roles of the fortress were effectively redundant: Rokossovsky's thrust to Elbing had isolated the German forces in East Prussia, and there was no prospect of their retreating back to the river crossings. Nor was there any prospect of a drive towards the east by German forces.

Marienburg was in a bend in the Nogat, with the river protecting the town to the west and north. In late 1944, the civilian population helped dig additional trenches and anti-tank ditches to defend the town from the south and east. These fortifications would require about a division of infantry to be held properly, but by December 1944, the only forces allocated to Marienburg were four artillery batteries, equipped with Italian and captured Russian guns, two battalions of replacement personnel, and a single battalion of Volkssturm. The fortress commandant, Oberst von Koeller, raised doubts about the ability of these forces to hold the town, but the only result of this was his dismissal.

On 25 January, leading elements of VIII Mechanized Corps, part of Fediuninsky's 2nd Shock Army, attempted to rush the defences. There was bitter streetfighting over the next two days. Armed with Panzerfausts, the defending Germans inflicted a heavy toll, claiming to have destroyed 50 Soviet tanks on 25 and 26 January. Fediuninsky now pulled VIII Mechanized Corps out of the firing line, leaving the reduction of the town to the infantry divisions of CVIII Rifle Corps. Further to the northeast, a division from CXVI Rifle Corps crossed the frozen Nogat in an attempt to outflank the defenders, but ran into elements of the German 7th Infantry Division, and was driven back with heavy losses. Within Marienburg itself, fighting died down at the end of January, with only the old Teutonic fortress and the older part of the town still in German hands. Aware that there was no prospect of a swift capture of the river crossings, Fediuninsky steadily withdrew forces from the area, moving them south to cross the Vistula in preparation for Rokossovsky's drive along the west bank of the river, thus eliminating the need to capture the crossings. Eventually, on 9 March, the remaining German defenders withdrew, destroying the bridge behind them.

Further upstream, the city of Graudenz had been intended to serve a similar function in the German defensive plans for the Vistula. The old fortifications formed a horseshoe, protecting the city from the east, and it had been envisaged that Graudenz would be held by four divisions, three in the horseshoe defences and one held back on the west bank. Unlike Marienburg, Graudenz had received substantial supplies in late 1944, with the result that it was estimated there was sufficient ammunition and food within the defences to supply a 30,000-man garrison for up to three months.

Yet as was the case elsewhere, the required numbers of defenders did not materialize. The 354th Rifle Division, the leading element of 65th Army, attacked the city on 25 January and the fortress commandant, Generalmajor Ludwig Fricke, had only a mixture of replacement drafts, a fortress battalion and rear-area units, plus an artillery battalion equipped with a mixture of Italian and Russian guns. Elements of 35th and 252nd Infantry Divisions prevented a swift collapse of the defences, however, and further reinforcements were on their way.

Generalleutnant Wilhelm Heun's 83rd Infantry Division had been brought by sea from Courland in January, and originally sent to Thorn for replenishment and re-equipment. The division had left most of its anti-tank battalion's guns in Courland, and replacements were not forthcoming. When the Soviet onslaught against East Prussia was imminent, the division was ordered to move east to provide reserves for 4th Army, but almost immediately the order was cancelled and the division was ordered back to the Thorn area. Unfortunately, most of its artillery had already been dispatched to East Prussia, and in the chaos that followed the beginning of the Soviet assault, these batteries were unable to return to their parent division. On 20 January, Heun deployed the forces that had been able to regroup around the town of Sichelberg, but was ordered to hand over the sector to another unit and withdraw. One of the division's infantry battalions was unable to disengage from the advancing Soviet forces, and lost contact with the rest of the division. It was reassigned to another unit, and ultimately destroyed in combat with Rokossovsky's spearheads. The rest of Heun's division now took up defensive positions at Strasburg, where one of his battalions was badly mauled on 22 January. From here, the division fell back towards the northwest, its right flank completely open and exposed to attack. A Soviet reconnaissance sweep revealed no German units for at least 13km to the west, and Soviet armour swiftly took advantage of this gap to penetrate into the division's remaining artillery positions; a battery was forced to destroy its guns to avoid their capture.

XXVII Corps, under whose aegis 83rd Infantry Division was operating, ordered Heun to launch an attack to the northwest to establish contact with his neighbouring division. Heun lacked the forces to mount such an operation, and now faced a dilemma. If he attempted an attack, it would certainly fail, and his outflanked division would be trapped and destroyed in the open. But if he fell back towards Gosslershausen without permission, he risked the wrath of Berlin for abandoning defensive positions without permission. Contact with his corps commander was lost on 23 January, and in the absence of any opportunity to discuss matters with his superiors, Heun ordered a retreat to Gosslershausen. The withdrawal was carried out without difficulty, and by the morning of 24 January a new defensive line had been established south of the town. From here, Heun was able to strike to the west and establish contact with 252nd Infantry Division, thus closing the gap on his right flank.

Despite this success, Heun's unauthorized withdrawal had not gone unnoticed. A representative of a military court appeared in 83rd Division's headquarters on 24 January to investigate the circumstances of the move. Heun refrained from arguing with him, and merely submitted a report. Ten days later, Weiss issued a brief statement: 'The leadership of 83rd Infantry Division on 23 January 1945 was faultless. There are no grounds for military legal involvement.'[22] It seems extraordinary that such time and effort could be spent on this legal effort, when the Wehrmacht was literally fighting for its life.

The line at Gosslershausen was untenable, and Heun was ordered to fall back towards Graudenz. Despite the losses his division had suffered, its arrival in the city on 26 January provided welcome reinforcements for the garrison. The following day, a replacement battalion originally destined for 1st Paratroop-Panzer Division *Hermann Göring* also appeared.

As with other fortresses, the Red Army did not waste huge resources in attempting to storm Graudenz. From the German perspective, there was awareness that the garrison – particularly 83rd Infantry Division – represented troops that were desperately needed elsewhere, and Weiss requested permission to abandon the city. The 2nd Army was now part of Army Group Vistula, and Himmler curtly forbade such a withdrawal. The city, he decreed, would be held to the last man and the last bullet, as it represented a launching point for a future counter-offensive towards the east.

The effect of such fantasies on Weiss' staff can be imagined. Nevertheless, they issued instructions for 83rd Infantry Division and elements of the *Hermann Göring* division's forces to withdraw to the west bank of the Vistula, to reinforce defences in that area. On 14 February, Heun led his division across the bridge and thence to Schwetz, where it almost immediately went into action. Despite his strong protests, Heun was ordered to leave one of his regiments within the city. Fighting alongside 252nd Infantry Division, 83rd Infantry Division was slowly driven back, and on 17 February the advancing elements of the Soviet CV Rifle Corps cut off Graudenz from the rest of the front.

The diminished garrison withdrew into the city itself. The besieging forces were now from 2nd Shock Army, mainly Major-General Anisimov's XCVIII Rifle Corps. Aware that the defenders' number had been reduced, the Red Army commenced a major bombardment on 17 February, supported by aerial attacks and followed by a general assault. The 37th Guards Rifle Division attacked the German perimeter from the east, while elements of 142nd Rifle Division attempted to drive north along the eastern shore of the Vistula. Despite the extensive preparation, the advance made limited headway, at the cost of heavy casualties on both sides. Platoon-size combat groups of 37th Guards Rifle Division, supported by assault guns and light field guns, battered their way through the city blocks, and the defenders pulled back to their inner defences over the following days, until fighting died down on 20 February. The 142nd Rifle Division had rather more success, cutting the garrison off from the last crossing points over the Vistula. Casualties here, too, were heavy; the Soviet attackers had to use all the skills they had learned in their long advance, as this account of one of 946th Rifle Regiment's assault groups shows:

> The assault team seized part of a house in one of the blocks in Graudenz. Attempts by other units to clear the enemy from the remaining houses in the block were not successful.
>
> The regiment commander who controlled combat operations in this section reinforced the assault team with five man-portable flamethrowers and ordered the assault team commander to use the flamethrowers to set fire to those houses where the enemy continued to offer resistance, and to use smokescreens to cover the deployment of the flamethrower teams.
>
> In all, three smokescreens were created, not simultaneously but one after another, with small intervals in between. The setting of smokescreens in this manner was a deliberate tactic. Its purpose lay in the fact that the first two smokescreens drew the enemy's fire; it was intended to make an attack with infantry and flamethrower teams under cover of the third smokescreen, to complete the mission.
>
> When the first and second smokescreens were laid, our marksmen and the mortars conducted intensive fire and imitated an attack with shouts of 'Hurrah!'
>
> Assuming that our infantry would begin their assault on the buildings under the cover of the smokescreen, the enemy opened strong fire, attempting to repulse our attacks.
>
> When the third smokescreen was laid and our rifle teams opened a heavy fire, the enemy, suspecting this was another fake attack, barely reacted. Our flamethrower teams

used this opportunity to approach their objective. They rapidly created five fires, and the assault team, attacking those enemy in those buildings that were not engulfed in the flames, rapidly completed the crushing defeat of the enemy and mastered the entire block.[23]

At this stage, Major Bernhard Bechler appeared on the scene. Bechler had served with the Wehrmacht, and was taken prisoner at Stalingrad; some sources suggest that he had actually deserted to the Soviet side.[24] Together with Leutnant Heinrich Graf von Einsiedel, a former Luftwaffe pilot, he called upon the defenders to surrender. As was usually the case, he and his fellow members of the NKFD promised them good treatment, and swift repatriation after the war. Again, as was usually the case, these calls fell on deaf ears.

On 1 March, the commander of the remaining *Hermann Göring* units in the city, Oberst Meyer-Schewe, went to the garrison commander and suggested an immediate breakout. Generalmajor Fricke was despondent about the situation, and suggested instead that the garrison should surrender. Meyer-Schewe's staff immediately started making their own plans, dispatching two patrols north to investigate whether vital bridges across the Ossa were in enemy hands. Late on 5 March, the breakout attempt began. Some 120 Soviet prisoners of war asked to accompany the attempt, having decided that their fate if they fell into the hands of the advancing Red Army was likely to be a grim one. Their request was turned down.

The leading elements of the breakout reached the bridge over the Ossa at Burg Belchau early on 6 March, and successfully drove off the small Soviet force holding it. Attempting to press on northwards, the Germans ran into Soviet infantry a few kilometres north in wooded terrain and were rapidly dispersed. Only a few individuals managed to make their way back to German lines.

Of those who remained in Graudenz, some surrendered after a further approach by representatives of the NKFD. The rest laid down their weapons shortly after. Despite all assurances, those who surrendered to the NKFD were treated exactly like all other German prisoners of war. Few of them were able to return to Germany for several years. Members of the Volkssturm were gathered together in the inner courtyard of the Courbiere Fortress, which had formed the heart of the defences, and were shot.[25]

The 2nd Shock Army continued to grind forward to the west of the Vistula. On several occasions, Fediuninsky's spearheads achieved deep penetrations, but a decisive breakthrough eluded them. Immediately to the west of the river, the German line was held by 35th Infantry Division, with 252nd Infantry Division and 542nd Volksgrenadier Division to the west. The 251st Infantry Division, with what remained of 83rd Infantry Division, formed the next link, with 227th and 289th Infantry Divisions completing the line. The 7th Panzer Division remained to the north and east of Konitz, and 4th Panzer Division struggled to provide support for this long line. On the Soviet side, CVIII Rifle Corps stood closest to the Vistula, with XCVIII, CV, XLVI and XVIII Rifle Corps to its west. The three regiments of Pantenius' 337th Volksgrenadier Division, which had been replenished after its near-destruction in the fighting in the Tuchel Heath, had been dispersed amongst the other infantry divisions struggling to hold back the Red Army. As 2nd Army's line was slowly driven back, Pantenius led his regiment out of its positions near the Vistula, to avoid being bypassed and surrounded. As they fell back, the Landsers witnessed a tank duel:

> The weather was ideal for our purposes, sunshine and clear visibility. For the first three kilometres towards Königswalde, there was nothing to be seen for some distance, no evidence of the enemy, no tanks, no infantry. After Hill 70, 600 metres west of Pehskerfelde, we spotted the enemy 1,200 metres to the southwest in a tree-line, about 12 T-34 tanks that had apparently bunched together, making use of every bit of cover, and without infantry. Opposite them, about 800 metres away, were four German assault guns – apparently from 83rd Infantry Division (we had no assault guns in our division, only Hetzers). The accompanying infantry had dismounted and were taking cover behind a crest. There followed a duel between the Russian tanks and the assault guns with astonishingly little success on either side. The Russians were clearly in better cover, but their shooting was very poor. The assault guns were almost presented on a platter, and as a result took a few hits, but apparently no penetrating strikes, in any event no tanks burst into flames or exploded.[26]

Pantenius continued to Gogeln, close to the town of Mewe, where his regiment took up defensive positions. As the German line continued to withdraw, the remnants of infantry divisions were re-arranged. Pantenius' regiment was now attached to 23rd Infantry Division, as part of XXIII Corps. Confusingly, the staff of 337th Volksgrenadier Division took over what remained of 23rd Infantry Division, with the latter formation now effectively disappearing. As casualties continued to mount, officers took desperate steps to try to keep their formations up to strength. Pantenius was annoyed when the unit to his left incorporated one of his companies into its ranks, and only returned it to his command after strenuous protests.

The soldiers of Pantenius' regiment were relieved to find that they had plentiful support in the form of mortars and field guns, and even a heavy flak battery to provide some welcome anti-tank firepower. However, all the artillery was desperately short of ammunition. Opposing Pantenius' regiment was the Soviet XCVIII Rifle Corps, which attacked on 21 February and with increasing intensity in the following days. To prevent 2nd Shock Army driving through to Danzig from the south, 4th SS-Polizei Panzergrenadier Division, which had been in action further west in Pomerania, was dispatched by train to Dirschau to reinforce the front, and 215th Infantry Division was recalled from Courland as additional reinforcements – yet another division extracted from the pocket of troops far to the north. If these units had been brought back to Germany en masse, they might have had a decisive effect, but arriving in a trickle they disappeared into the raging front with almost no effect.

On the opposite wing of 2nd Belorussian Front, the Soviet 19th Army slowly moved into its forming-up areas, hindered by destroyed bridges and railway lines, and by widespread muddy conditions as the weather slowly warmed. Further delays were brought about by attempts to restrict major troop movements to the hours of darkness, in order to keep the Germans guessing about Soviet intentions. The plan for attack would see two of 19th Army's three rifle corps being deployed in a front of 10km, achieving troop strengths of seven rifle battalions per kilometre of front, with commensurately powerful artillery concentrations.[27]

On 24 February, after a 40-minute artillery barrage, the offensive began. Bitter fighting raged around Schlochau, where a German counter-attack was beaten off with heavy casualties on both sides. By the end of the day, Soviet forces had advanced about 10km, and in an attempt to accelerate matters, III Guards Tank Corps – originally to be held back in reserve until the German line had been breached – was ordered to move forward and provide armoured support for the struggling infantry. At 1100hrs on 25 February, 3rd and 18th Guards Tank Brigades entered the battle, and immediately achieved deep penetrations, thrusting forward 40km. The leading Soviet spearheads reached Baldenburg that evening, and the leading tank, commanded by a Lieutenant Makarenkov, roared through the town at full speed. As the startled defenders attempted to fire at it with light anti-tank guns and Panzerfausts, the following tanks and their mounted infantry moved in to clear out the German positions, which had now been revealed. By the following morning, the capture of the town was complete.[28]

The Soviet breakthrough was now unstoppable, but the infantry of Lieutenant-General G.K. Kozlov's 19th Army continued to lag behind the swiftly advancing armour. The 19th Army might be comparatively strong in numbers, but it lacked the experience of the hard fighting that had characterized the campaign, particularly when the Germans had found time to establish their defences. Losing patience with General Kozlov, Rokossovsky sacked him and replaced him with General Vladimir Zakharovich Romanovsky, the commander of 67th Army.

Rokossovsky now wanted to reinforce the left flank of 2nd Belorussian Front, but found that he had no reserves left, something he had never experienced before as a Front commander. He was also increasingly anxious about what lay beyond his left flank:

As our units advanced to the north, our left flank was being exposed, since the 1st Belorussian Front had so far not budged. More and more frequently the enemy struck at the flanks and rear of our advancing units. We looked with apprehension at Neustettin. The city, to the west of our Front's boundary line, was swarming with enemy forces which might launch an attack against our exposed flank at any moment. I reported this to GHQ. A little later I was called to the telephone by the Supreme Commander. I reported the situation on our Front in general, and on the left wing in particular.

'You mean Zhukov is up to something?' Stalin said.

I said that I did not think he was up to anything, but the fact remained that his troops were not advancing, thereby creating a danger to my exposed flank. I had no forces with which to protect it as my reserves were used up. Therefore I requested that either the Front should be reinforced or the 1st Belorussian Front instructed to assume the offensive as quickly as possible. I also outlined the situation in the Neustettin area.

'Could you take Neustettin with your own forces?' Stalin asked. 'If you do, we'll fire a salute in your honour.'

I replied that we could try, but this would not markedly improve the situation. Stalin said that he would hasten the 1st Belorussian Front and rang off. Judging by his voice, he was pleased with the way events were developing.[29]

It is hard to imagine what the ever-paranoid Stalin feared about Zhukov's intentions; most probably, he wondered whether 1st Belorussian Front held back in the hope of still being able to resume its drive on Berlin. Neustettin fell to a pincer attack by III Guards Cavalry Corps – either Rokossovsky's intelligence was wrong, or he was deliberately exaggerating the strength of German forces in the town. No attempt had been made to evacuate the civilian population, and 300 civilians were killed. Some took their own lives; most of the women were raped and then killed. On this occasion, at least, Soviet forces did not live up to the exhortations of their commissars to conduct themselves as honourable liberators.

Elements of 7th Panzer Division had been rushed west in the anticipated path of the Soviet advance, and reached the town of Flötenstein early on 27 February. Soviet forces were moving to attack the town from the east and south, as Rokossovsky attempted to widen the breach he had made; he had been relieved to hear that Lieutenant-General Nikolai Sergeevich Oslikovsky's III Guards Cavalry Corps had encountered elements of

1st Belorussian Front's II Guards Cavalry Corps near Neustettin, which at least meant that his left flank wasn't as exposed as he had feared. A group of Sherman tanks attacked Flötenstein shortly after the arrival of 7th Panzer Division's battlegroup, but were driven off. Huber's Jg.Pz. IV took a hit on the frontal armour, which to the enormous relief of the crew failed to penetrate. During the night, Huber and his comrades heard Soviet infantry infiltrating forwards, and fought them off by the light of flares. The following day, the tank crews became increasingly concerned about their left flank. According to radio messages from battalion headquarters, another unit was meant to be deployed there, but there was no sign of it. During the morning a frontal attack was repulsed, but in the afternoon Soviet forces moved around the left flank of the German position, through the empty space where there was in fact no flank cover, necessitating a rapid withdrawal:

We can only move slowly through the difficult ground, as the ground has really thawed in the afternoon sunshine and the tracks sink deep, and the engine roars and struggles.

There, about 900 metres away, to our left, at 11 o'clock, there is a Russian assault gun taking up position. It's a 152mm gun on a Stalin chassis. I see its muzzle flash, and then a couple of seconds later its shot howls in and strikes in front of us, hitting the ground we've just driven over. It was damned close. Chunks of earth fly up over the tank and rain down on us. We need to get out of here. Bruno drives our Jg.Pz. IV in a curve as Bach orders him to turn to the right. By the time the Russian has loaded, aimed and fired again, we have driven on a bit further. As soon as we see the muzzle flash, our driver immediately turns in the other direction, and the shot passes to one side… When I estimate the range to be 1,500 metres, the assault gun gives up. We had no chance to stop and fire back. By the time we would have aimed at the enemy, he would already have fired, and his shot would have been before ours.

At the end of the run, in the heavy, difficult ploughed-up land, our engine cuts out. The long drive at full throttle was too much for it. The engine oil we've received during the war is simply not good enough. We drive right over the high ground behind us, see the assault gun disappear from view, and then there's a crunch in the engine compartment. The engine stops abruptly and won't make another sound. We are only just out of danger, but our tank is immobile. Bruno says laconically, 'Time to stretch our legs.' He means that the piston rod has broken through the cylinder head and the crankcase has broken.

The other tanks of our company are a further 500 metres away and in position, guarding towards us. They see us coming. Oberfeldwebel Sattler's tank contacts us by radio. He drives up to us, while we prepare our towing hawser, and then he tows us back. Over the thawed-out road, lit up by the late afternoon sunshine, Sattler slowly pulls us back towards the northeast.[30]

Huber and his crippled vehicle were sent east to the division's workshops. They must have escaped being captured by Rokossovsky's advancing spearheads by just a few hours. The only German forces available to intercept the advancing Soviet armour were a few battlegroups of the severely damaged SS-Division *Charlemagne* and SS-Polizei Panzergrenadier Division. The latter unit was ordered west from its assembly area around Dirschau, almost a reverse of the journey it had made in an attempt to shore up the front near the Vistula. Neither of these two SS formations left a positive impression on 7th Panzer Division when it encountered them:

> During the afternoon we came upon SS units; we hadn't been aware that our 2nd Army also had Waffen-SS units. We guessed from this meeting that we were on the western flank of our army.
>
> We chatted with the SS personnel, or at least, we wanted to. It turned out that they were Wallonian volunteers. They were well-disciplined, but very low in morale. They only spoke a little broken German. Their homeland was occupied by the Western Allies, and they were now regarded as traitors. The war was turning out disastrously. We were left feeling bad, as we ourselves didn't know how it would end for us either.
>
> The following day, 26 February, we ran into a group of German SS [from the SS-Polizei Division]. The fellows were drunk and shooting wildly, smashing windows and deliberately scaring the population.
>
> A woman called: 'Help, help us!'
>
> Our NCOs, gathered around Oberfeldwebel Hönniger, advanced on the SS with drawn pistols.
>
> Hönniger muttered to us: 'Stay back, we'll deal with this!'
>
> And then, cuttingly, he called out, 'Because of you, we're losing the war! You bunch of pigs, I'll bring you to your senses! Put your weapons down!'
>
> His comrades gathered together the weapons.
>
> I had never seen anything like it during the war.[31]

It should be pointed out that SS-Polizei had a good combat record. The *Charlemagne* division was another newly created formation; until February 1945, it had been a brigade, and the training of many of its personnel was rudimentary at best. Inadequately equipped with heavy weapons and radios, the regiments of the division were swiftly engulfed by the advancing Red Army north of Schlochau. Their remnants withdrew on foot to the coast, marching 80km along frozen roads, carrying what equipment they had been able to salvage.

One of the problems faced by the Germans was that only a minority of the divisions defending Pomerania were actually German. The others – SS formations of Latvians,

French, Wallonians and Scandinavians – had large numbers of personnel who came from territories already overrun by the enemies of the Reich. At this stage of the war, they can have had few illusions about what awaited them on their eventual return home, should they survive the fighting.

On 1 March, Zhukov's armies finally joined the attack, making swift progress; the Germans had expected the concentrated forces to move west over the Oder, and were completely unprepared for a push towards the north. The following day, Alexei Pavlovich Panfilov's III Guards Tank Corps, the leading formation of Rokossovsky's forces, reached the coast to the east of Köslin. Panfilov considered waiting for 19th Army's infantry to arrive, but then decided to take Köslin by an all-round attack, giving the task of storming and clearing the town to 2nd Guards Mechanized Brigade, reinforced by the motorized rifle battalions of his tank brigades. The 3rd and 18th Guards Tank Brigades would cut off the town from the west.

At 1700hrs on 3 March, the corps moved into its starting positions. After a ten-minute artillery bombardment, the attack began. The 3rd Guards Tank Brigade's units completed the encirclement of Köslin within three hours. The 18th Guards Tank Brigade was involved in tough fighting all night, but by the following morning it had cut off all German lines of retreat to the south and southwest.

Bitter fighting raged in the streets of Köslin as the Soviet mechanized units battered their way into the town. The garrison consisted of barely trained replacement drafts, parts of SS-Division *Nederland*, SS-Regiment *Jütland*, Grenadier Brigade *Karl der Grosse*, one Panzerjäger battalion and an artillery replacement battalion.[32] Despite being encircled, they hindered the advance of the Soviet units, who were hamstrung by having few infantry with them. At this stage, elements of 19th Army's 272nd Rifle Division arrived. A small German Volkssturm garrison briefly held up the Soviet infantry at Gross-Tychow, but on 4 March 272nd Rifle Division reached the outskirts of Köslin.

The 1065th Rifle Regiment immediately carried out a reconnaissance sweep around the edge of Köslin and reported that the German garrison was attempting to infiltrate between the tank units and retreat to Kolberg. A motorized rifle battalion was swiftly dispatched to cut the road to Kolberg, while within Köslin itself the Soviet armour renewed its attacks. Faced with certain annihilation, the garrison commander, Generalmajor von Zühlow, ordered his surviving men to surrender on 5 March.[33]

A second major blow fell two days later, when 1st Guards Tank Army, part of Zhukov's 1st Belorussian Front, reached the Baltic a little further west. Rokossovsky learned about Panfilov's success when he received an unexpected gift:

A messenger arrived at the Front HQ with three bottles of a clear liquid, a gift from Panfilov's tankmen to the Front Military Council. Curious, we tasted it. It was water, brackish water smelling of seaweed. Water from the Baltic Sea! We heartily thanked the men for their fine symbolic gift.[34]

Similar gestures were attributed to the commanders of Zhukov's spearheads. Regardless of this, 2nd Army was now isolated in West Prussia, along with hundreds of thousands of refugees. Many of those who had trekked along frozen East Prussian roads, had endured the crossing of the frozen Frisches Haff, and had finally reached the Vistula estuary, had then set off westwards across Pomerania. They now fled back to the east, and the population of Danzig and Gotenhafen soared.

One of the destinations of the refugees was the small port of Stolpmünde. Already struggling to cope with the demand for shipping to evacuate the eastern Baltic ports, Konteradmiral Engelhardt now had to find resources for the refugees herded towards the Pomeranian coast. Fregattenkapitän Kolbe was dispatched to handle matters, and arrived in Stolpmünde on 6 March. The town had a pre-war population of less than 5,000, but now contained several times this number. Kolbe immediately had the port area secured by whatever units were available, and summoned ships to the endangered town. Fourteen vessels, the largest with a displacement of only 1,500 tonnes, arrived over the next day, and immediately began to take on refugees. Naval vessels, mainly small gunboats and ferries, also gathered to help. The weather deteriorated, with a storm from the northeast hammering the coast late on 7 March. With Soviet forces at the edge of the town, the ships began to leave early on 8 March. A fleet of fishing boats and military ferries accompanied them, all heavily laden. One ferry was swamped in the heavy seas as it left the safety of the port, and the civilians crammed onto the decks of the other ships could only watch helplessly as the waves claimed the lives of those aboard.

The fleet left, carrying a total of more than 20,000 refugees to the west, Fregattenkapitän Kolbe boarded *U-J 120*, a small submarine hunter, and departed from Stolpmünde. About 3,000 people were left behind. Many chose not to risk a voyage across the waters of the Baltic; some continued to believe the Party's promises of final victory.

Surging up to the town, Soviet troops surprised a small retreating column of German troops. In seconds, a solitary German tank was knocked out, and one of its accompanying half-tracks left burning in the middle of the road. The rest of the small force was swiftly overwhelmed. At about the same time, a German U-boat arrived in the port, unaware that Stolpmünde had been given up to the Red Army. Fortunately for the submariners, a small body of Kriegsmarine officers, who had been left behind and were preparing for an almost hopeless attempt to escape to the west over land, saw the submarine and rushed aboard. The U-boat escaped before it could be spotted by the advancing Soviet soldiers of III Guards Tank Corps.

The 7th Panzer Division's redeployment further west had left the frontline near Konitz dangerously weakened. The Soviet 70th Army deployed five rifle divisions, reinforced by VIII Guards Mechanized Corps, to exploit this opportunity, but the rate of advance was too slow for Rokossovsky. VIII Guards Mechanized Corps was ordered to drive forward swiftly to Bütow, but in the face of unexpectedly tough resistance it made limited headway. On 3 March, a frustrated Rokossovsky ordered 70th Army, and the neighbouring 49th Army, to pause their advance and regroup.

The arrival of SS-Polizei Panzergrenadier Division created an additional problem for Rokossovsky. As the SS unit began to disembark from its trains in Rummelsburg, it was spotted by Soviet reconnaissance aircraft; indeed, its rail journey to its new deployment had been delayed by constant air attacks. The division's artillery regiment was forced to detrain at Bütow and continue by road. Its Panzergrenadier regiments found that the station in Rummelsburg was already under Soviet artillery fire when they arrived, and hastily took up positions. With 7th Panzer Division on their eastern flank, they were to attack the advancing Soviet forces, aiming to close the gap that had been torn in the German front. Ultimately, Army Group Vistula optimistically stated, the attack would 'isolate and encircle' the Soviet mobile forces.[35] However unrealistic these plans were, the presence of an armoured formation here, menacing the right flank of 19th Army and III Guards Tank Corps, could not be ignored. General Vladimir Zakharovich Romanovsky, 19th Army's new commander, ordered XL Guards Rifle Corps to attack Rummelsburg. XVIII Guards Tank Corps was dispatched to the area, and III Guards Tank Corps was ordered temporarily to halt its advance. In addition, VIII Mechanized Corps would drive north from its assembly area around Konitz, drawing away the units of 7th Panzer Division.

The SS-Polizei Division's artillery regiment finally arrived in Rummelsburg on 1 March. The two Panzergrenadier regiments attacked to the south and west; neither made significant progress. More and more Soviet forces were fed into the battle, and after two days of stiff fighting, Lieutenant-General Khariton Alekseevich Khudalov, commander of 10th Guards Rifle Division, sensed that SS-Polizei was approaching exhaustion. Early on 3 March, before dawn, his reconnaissance units penetrated into the rear of the village of Klein-Wolz, a strongpoint just outside Rummelsburg. Most of the garrison was made up of ill-equipped Volkssturm, and they were swiftly routed or captured. As it grew light, Khudalov's artillery began to bombard Rummelsburg itself. Under cover of this bombardment, one of 10th Guards Rifle Division's regiments used a deep drainage ditch to infiltrate close to the southeast corner of the town, and then rushed the defenders. By the afternoon, Rummelsburg was in Soviet hands. The remaining regiment from SS-Polizei fell back along the road running north, trying to delay the Red Army as long as possible to allow the civilian population to escape.[36]

The situation now became very fluid. One SS battalion, whose depleted ranks could barely form two rifle companies and a support company, fell back and approached the village of Turzig, some 16km north of Rummelsburg. The village was in Soviet hands, but the Germans could see a large number of vehicles from their division, apparently captured when the Soviet advance caught them by surprise. The battalion was ordered to retake the village, and did so in a sudden frontal attack. Despite this, the Germans were still surrounded, and a further long night march lay ahead before they made good their escape. Having failed to break through to the infantry in Turzig, SS-Polizei's tank battalion also found itself surrounded, and had to break through the encircling ring twice before it was able to escape.[37] Meanwhile, 7th Panzer Division's 7th Armoured Reconnaissance Battalion was subordinated to SS-Polizei, and allowed Stadartenführer Walter Harzer, commander of the SS division, to keep his scattered units more or less in contact.

The Wehrmacht abandoned Rügenwalde on 6 March, but there was insufficient shipping available to evacuate the civilian population, which was left to its fate. Two days later, Major Jass, designated commander of the makeshift garrison at Stolp, realized that his forces, mainly made up of the remnants of one of SS-Polizei's Panzergrenadier regiments, would be unable to do more than delay the Soviet forces. Ignoring the town's Kreisleiter, he ordered all civilians to leave. Most fled east to the Bay of Danzig. Fighting an almost continuous rearguard action, the SS Panzergrenadiers fell back through Stolp and retreated towards Neustadt. A large party of rear-area troops from SS-Polizei, commanded by Hauptsturmführer Blattner, found its route to Neustadt blocked by four T-34s at a vital crossroads. Reconnaissance suggested that the ground beyond the crossroads was still free of Soviet forces. Blattner sent a party of 40 men to the south, from where they noisily attacked towards the crossroads. The T-34s promptly drove south to beat off this 'attack', and Blattner and his men were able to pass through the crossroads and onwards to Neustadt.[38] Other units were not so fortunate, and were either shot up and scattered by the advancing Soviet spearheads, or surrendered.

The Soviet 2nd Shock Army continued to make progress along the western shore of the Vistula, and in late February the commitment of VIII Guards Tank Corps and an independent assault gun brigade provided additional weight and firepower. Now that SS-Polizei Panzergrenadier Division had been moved west, there was an urgent need for armoured reinforcements for the hard-pressed German infantry, and a detachment of 4th Panzer Division was dispatched to the area. Hermann Bix had been with the division since the start of the war, and had led its spearheads in the drive towards Moscow in 1941. His company should have been re-equipped with Panther tanks, but instead received Jagdpanthers:

The hulls did not have a swivelling turret; one had to aim the whole vehicle roughly at the target, and then one had a little leeway for accurate aiming. But on the other hand, the poorly constructed steel colossus had at its disposal an 88mm gun of enormous penetrating power as main armament, a whopping range, and good general protection. So we quickly forgot our unfamiliarity with the Jagdpanther and made strenuous efforts to learn about its benefits. We had very little time to get to grips with them properly.

... With three such Jagdpanthers, I was stationed south of Preussisch Stargard, protecting the grenadiers' positions and providing security for the construction of a new defence line. Everyone had pulled back, and only snowflakes remained on the dark mounds of earth – the abandoned German field positions. I was with my Jagdpanther in a small settlement behind a big muck-heap, so that I could barely look over it with either my eyes or the gun. The flat upper structure of our tanks only protruded slightly above the cover of the muck-heap.

Behind me was Oberfeldwebel Dehm in another Jagdpanther. The two of us didn't have much ammunition. I had only one load of shells. I ordered the gun loaded. As the mist slowly lifted, two Soviet tanks cautiously appeared on the heights in front of us and edged slowly closer. When they were 1,200 metres away, I was able to determine that they were neither T-34s nor KV-1s, but American-built tanks. I knew from experience that they would be easy to crack at this range. We opened fire together – and for a while, Ivan didn't dare put his nose out again.

The village was held by a group of tankers, crews who had lost their vehicles. I was safe from being surprised from right or left.

... Roughly half an hour after the two shots I heard the sound of a tank about 1,000 metres to the right and soon saw two Soviet tanks, which were heading for our village. At this range, my 88mm cannon couldn't miss. In short order, these tanks were burning too.

It was clear to us that the Soviets were looking for a weak point through which they could thrust. It was therefore important to remain watchful along the entire front, and I was alone in this area. The two other Jagdpanthers moved away with my agreement, as they had already run out of ammunition. My gunner told me that we had five high-explosive and 20 armour-piercing rounds.

My company commander, Leutnant Tautorus, was stationed somewhere with his Panther. I reported to him by radio about my position and shortage of ammunition, and received the order to hold off the Soviets as long as possible, as the infantry hadn't finished preparing their positions.

In the meantime, the tank's close protection had to withdraw, to keep in contact with other units. As a result, I no longer had a clear idea what was happening to my right and left. The Soviets could therefore have marched in, formed up in three ranks, and nobody would have seen them coming.

I carefully studied the slope before me, and saw that the Soviets had positioned two anti-tank guns there without hindrance. Were they trying to collar me? I loaded a high-explosive shell, aimed the gun, and – bang! We watched chunks of wood and clumps of stuff fly into the air. The fellows had tricked us and set up a couple of mock-ups, in order to draw our fire, and we idiots had promptly done what they wanted. I didn't fall for the joke again. I decided to save my precious shells.

We were as quiet as a mouse, and rolled our tank back just a little so that it couldn't be seen from the front. When I stuck my head out of the hatch, I could still look out across the cover.

I could hardly believe my eyes: I could see a long column of armour coming directly towards me, the leading tank about 1,200 metres away, with supply vehicles close behind the tanks.

As a precaution, I had already determined the range to fixed landmarks before me. I therefore knew that I could open fire on the leading tank with an armour-piercing round when it had passed the 800-metre point.

I don't know why, but my excellent gunner missed the tank with his first shot, and hit a huge tree next to the road. The trunk split in the middle, and the crown and branches fell onto the leading tank. Suddenly unable to see where he was going, he slipped and tumbled into the ditch by the road, and was left unable to move.

The following tanks drove up and continued, but they didn't see me. They all turned their turrets to the right and opened fire on the dark mounds of the abandoned infantry positions.

… So, I opened fire on a tank in the middle of the column, and it burst into flames with the first shot. The next one came up. Bang, it too was burning. After that, we fired easily at the row, which stood before us like a shooting gallery.

In ten minutes, we shot up 11 Soviet tanks in the column. The rest in their panic tried to turn into the ditch, where they were concealed by the flames and smoke of the row of burning tanks.[39]

Almost out of ammunition, Bix decided that it was time to withdraw, but the heavy Jagdpanther became bogged down. Another Soviet tank appeared to one side, but it too became stuck in the soft ground; Bix was able to knock it out with his last round before it could fire. For this day's work, Bix was awarded the Knight's Cross, having taken his personal tally of Soviet tanks to 75.

The area of Preussisch Stargard had a German population of about 65,000 in 1939. During the war, this number grew as refugees arrived from bombed-out cities in the west, particularly Hamburg, and the town was designated as a reception area for the inhabitants of the Rosenberg area of East Prussia. The first refugees fleeing the Soviet advance reached the town on 20 January, not only from Rosenberg but also from Lodz, Dirschau, Mewe and Neuenburg. The local authorities did their best to keep the refugees moving westwards, but these long columns of exhausted, frozen civilians greatly hindered military traffic. It was therefore critically important for the German line to hold as long as possible, to give the refugees every opportunity to escape to the ports along the coast. Many despaired and found they couldn't face leaving their homeland. The Oberbauernführer (head of the local rural civilian authority) of Gross Montau organized the people of his village into a column, saw them set off, and then shot his wife, daughter and grandchild before taking his own life. The owner of a farm just to the east of the Vistula accompanied his tenants and their workers as far as the Vistula crossings, before turning back to his home with his family. Once they returned to their farm, he shot his three daughters, aged between 17 and 21, and his wife, and then himself. Another Party official from Rosenort escorted his refugee column as far as the Vistula estuary before he and his wife took poison.[40]

In an attempt to free up some reserves, 337th Volksgrenadier Division was to be pulled out of line south of Preussisch Stargard, but constant Soviet pressure made this impossible. Despite the heroics of Bix and others, Soviet tanks and infantry from CXVIII Rifle Corps penetrated into Preussisch Stargard on 6 March. Desperate counter-attacks made no impression and the Soviet advance continued, threatening Dirschau two days later. A little to the west, the German XXVII Corps came under heavy pressure as elements of 65th Army, backed by the tanks of I Guards Tank Corps, threatened to shatter the lines of the exhausted German infantry. Already, the Soviet penetration to the coast had turned Weiss' western flank, and now, a breach developed southeast of Berent, creating the very real possibility of 2nd Army being broken in two – one element would be driven back along the Vistula and Nogat to the coast near Danzig, while the western element, rendered almost immobile by catastrophic fuel shortages, would be left stranded and encircled. With his limited armoured forces desperately needed to prevent 2nd Army's open western flank from being rolled up, Weiss had no option but to order the entire southern line to pull back and close ranks.

The withdrawal order came just in time for elements of 83rd Infantry Division fighting on Hill 107 near Preussisch Stargard on 8 March. The men had been in almost continuous combat since their withdrawal from Graudenz:

> Ground-attack aircraft flew over the battling troops, pouring heavy fire onto the open landscape. Reports from there were catastrophic. One bit of bad news followed another. Then came the order: Hill 107 was to be recaptured. Shaken, the commander replied: the regiment's fighting strength was only 20 men and a single operational machine-gun. He did not want to commit his last command to such a senseless operation. General Heun himself came forward, looked over the situation, and ordered a withdrawal. The regiment that had arrived in Thorn with over 1,000 men had been almost completely destroyed. The commander, well known and highly regarded throughout the division, was at the end of his strength. He was invalided out. Major Müller took command of the 251st Regiment.[41]

What remained of Heun's division withdrew from the frontline. Its personnel received reinforcements, many of dubious quality, before it was dispatched towards Gotenhafen by train.

To the west of Rokossovsky's Front, the full weight of Zhukov's armies was far more than the skeleton forces opposing them could face. Only Kolberg, on the coast, continued to hold out. The town's peacetime population of about 30,000 had more than tripled due to an influx of refugees and retreating soldiers, and Oberst Fritz Fullriede, the garrison commander, knew that his ragtag collection of stragglers, Hitler Youth and Volkssturm could not possibly endure in the face of enemy attacks, particularly as almost no preparations had been made for the town's defence. He requested permission to attempt a breakout, but was ordered to remain where he was. Nor was he given permission to dispatch the many refugee trains that had gathered in the town towards the west: the exact location of the advancing Soviet forces made such a journey risky, and possibly fatal for the civilians aboard the trains.

Fullriede had at his disposal a fortress regiment, an infantry regiment and an artillery regiment, as well as a full regiment of Volkssturm. The torpedo school in the town provided the personnel for a marine infantry battalion, and the stragglers in the town were used to reinforce these units, and to create additional infantry and artillery formations. Four Pz. IV tanks that were undergoing repairs in the town were also commandeered, as was an armoured train.

Eva Kuckuck, the refugee from Allenburg, and the retired Oberst von Weiss and his wife were still in Kolberg, where they had come ashore from the *Consul Cords*. On 15 February, after failing to secure passage to the west on a train, they and many other refugees had to face the prospect of another voyage, despite Kuckuck's previous vow that she would never venture forth upon the sea again. The *Consul Cords* was in the port, with a cargo of aircraft engines and grain. Consequently, the little vessel was unable to take on as many refugees as she had during the escape from Königsberg, and left port on 17 February with a total of 155 people aboard.

Late on 18 February, Kapitän Fretwurst received a radio message ordering him to heave to and await an escort – RAF aircraft had been seen dropping mines into the approaches to Swinemünde and Warnemünde, and it would be best to await minesweepers before the ship approached port. Fretwurst advised his passengers that he intended to press on without waiting, as he didn't have enough coal aboard for a prolonged delay. At midday on 19 February, about two hours from Warnemünde, the *Consul Cords* struck a mine. Kuckuck was sleeping in a bunk at the time, but managed to get off the ship before it broke up. She and 48 others were rescued, and taken to Warnemünde.[42]

The siege of Kolberg began on 4 March. Two days later, the garrison launched a surprise attack on Polish forces advancing from the southwest. Fullriede's intention was to try to clear the railway and road running west to allow an evacuation of the town, but despite initial successes, the attack was abandoned when it ran into a battalion of JS-2 tanks. The garrison withdrew to its defences; any evacuation would be by sea.

The Soviet 47th Army and 1st Polish Army began their formal assault on the town on 7 March. Artillery fire set much of Kolberg ablaze, and the attackers made slow but steady progress through the ruins. The defenders made good use of the River Persante, running northwest through the town, and by destroying all its crossings were able to keep General Stanislav Poplavsky's Poles at arm's length. The main threat now came from 47th Army, advancing from the southeast.

Following his successful evacuation of Stolpmünde, Fregattenkapitän Kolbe arrived in Kolberg on 9 March. Once more, ships of all sizes were summoned, with the larger vessels staying outside the port while smaller boats and ships ferried passengers to them. A soon as they had taken aboard a full load, the ships headed west, the first leaving on 11 March. Normally, refugees boarded the ships during daylight, so that the vessels could make their run west during the night. Despite Engelhardt's concerns about ships travelling without escorts, the majority of journeys were made by single vessels, relying on the shortness of the voyage to Swinemünde and the protecting darkness. By 16 March, nearly 70,000 people had been evacuated. The garrison, reduced to barely 2,000 men, now held a strip that was less than 2km long and only 400m deep.

After the last evacuation ship had left Kolberg, about 1,200 refugees remained in the town. Kolbe summoned the destroyer *Z 34* into the port, and the last civilians were taken aboard. With her decks heavily overcrowded, the destroyer headed west, its sailors struggling to ensure that the area around each gun turret was kept free, in case the ship had to go into action. All that remained now was the garrison, and the destroyer *Z 43* and torpedo boat *T 33*, which had been providing fire support for the defenders, were tasked with taking aboard these last men. All but 400 of the defenders were withdrawn before the town fell early on 18 March. Oberst Fullriede and the last platoon left the port aboard the *Z 43*'s motorboat, under fire from the advancing Soviet troops. Kolbe left even later, escaping aboard a small vessel with ten other men.

The Party turned the story of the defence of Kolberg into a propaganda epic, praising the heroic defenders who held off a Soviet army and four Polish divisions. They were aided in this respect by the role Kolberg had played in history – it endured a long siege by French forces in 1807, and an film had been made about this historic siege. Goebbels commissioned the film in the dark days after the surrender at Stalingrad, and the film enjoyed its premier only a few days before Kolberg was engulfed in fighting. It is certainly true that Fullriede made very skilful use of the limited forces at his disposal, and that the terrain – particularly the broad river that blocked the advance of the Poles – did much to nullify the Red Army's numerical superiority. But the attacking formations, particularly those of Perkhorovich's 47th Army, were very under-strength as a result of the losses they had suffered in their long advance to the Baltic coast. It is probable that the besiegers were in no hurry to take the town. In both political and military respects, it suited the purposes of the besiegers for German civilians to leave. More than 130,000 refugees were evacuated from various locations along the coast; they left behind devastated towns, looted first by the advancing Soviet troops, then by the Poles. Eventually, the civilians who had remained behind would be forced from their homes.

CHAPTER 11
HEILIGENBEIL - BETWEEN THE DEVIL AND THE DEEP BLUE SEA

All that remained now was to save innocent victims of the senseless war from the retaliation of the Red Army.

– H. Schäufler[1]

The beginning of February found the three German armies of Reinhardt's former command effectively isolated from each other. Walter Weiss' 2nd Army, now part of Himmler's Army Group Vistula, fought to hold on in the lower Vistula valley and Elbing. In the north, the divisions of Raus' 3rd Panzer Army, renamed Armee Abteilung Samland (Army Detachment Samland), had been smashed by Cherniakhovsky and herded into the Samland peninsula; several formations were besieged in Königsberg. Between these two was 4th Army, commanded by Friedrich Müller, its back to the frozen Frisches Haff, with the most tenuous connection with Königsberg.

Numerous pockets formed along the *Ostfront* as it collapsed, most of them around large urban centres – Königsberg, the fortress cities of the middle Vistula, and at Danzig, Breslau and Posen. In addition to providing the refugees and defending troops with protection, the cities within these pockets were valuable sources of industrial output. In Breslau, the city garrison continued to hold on right to the end of the war, using the city's industrial workshops to improvise weapons, including the hazardous business of extracting high explosive from Soviet bombs that had failed to explode. In Königsberg, engineers made good use of the large number of wrecked vehicles that had been brought to the city prior to its encirclement to cobble together replacements for 5th Panzer Division. But for 4th Army's troops surrounded in the Natangen district, in what became known as the Heiligenbeil pocket, there was no such resource. The towns of the coastal strip were too small to provide more than minimal protection, and completely lacking in industrial capability. This is one of the reasons why this pocket was the first of the major encirclements to be reduced.

THE HEILIGENBEIL POCKET

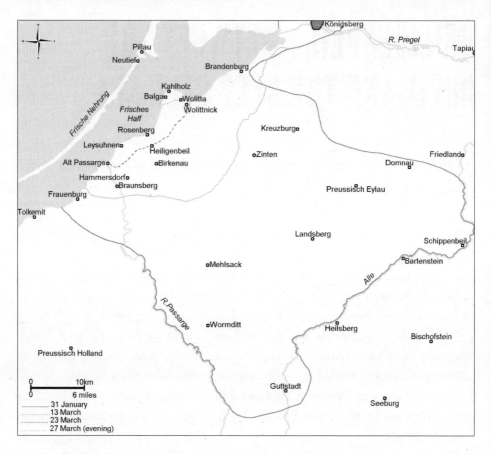

The events that unfolded around Heiligenbeil, Königsberg and Danzig are to some extent contemporaneous, but to provide a coherent narrative, the destruction of each pocket is described individually, over the next three chapters.

In this small area that stretched for less than 70km along the coast and slightly less inland, the shattered remnants of 24 German divisions gathered together, organized into seven corps, with hundreds of thousands of refugees from all over East Prussia. The task of the troops, as dictated by Hitler, was to defend every square metre of East Prussian soil to the last drop of blood. Repeated requests for a breakout, either north along the coast towards Königsberg or south towards Elbing, were rejected. Such a breakout would only have been possible if 4th Army had been allowed to gather together its fast-waning strength, immediately necessitating the sacrifice of considerable territory. Even in those circumstances, success would not have been guaranteed. But in any event, no attempt was made. Now that he had restored his control of 4th Army via the stolid and unimaginative Müller, Hitler had no intention of releasing his grip. Even local tactical withdrawals, without express permission, were prohibited.

In reality, the task of 4th Army's soldiers was to buy sufficient time for the civilians to be evacuated. There was also the hope that by tying down troops here in East Prussia, 4th Army was buying time for a new front to be established further west. Zhukov, Konev and Rokossovsky actually had far more forces available than they required to break down Germany's last defences, but the troops of 4th Army clung to this hope, that their sacrifice might not be in vain.

By the end of January, the perimeter of the Heiligenbeil pocket ran from near Tolkemit on the shores of the Frisches Haff, along the Passarge valley, to a salient centred on Guttstadt. From here, it extended northeast along the Alle through Heilsberg, Bartenstein and Schippenbeil, before turning first north, then northwest, returning to the coast near Brandenburg, where there remained a fragile connection with Königsberg.

Now that the huge drive across Poland and East Prussia was over, Cherniakhovsky's intention was to reduce each of the main challenges facing him – 4th Army in Heiligenbeil, Königsberg and finally Army Detachment Samland – one by one. The Heiligenbeil pocket would be the first. The 48th Army, now recovered from the shock of Hossbach's attempted breakout, remained along the western edge of the pocket, with 3rd Army on its right flank. Beyond 3rd Army was 50th Army, under its new commander, Fedor Ozerov, who had replaced the ineffective Boldin. Then came the armies of Cherniakhovsky's 3rd Belorussian Front: 31st Army, 2nd Guards Army and 28th Army. The 5th Army, supported by 11th Guards Army, faced both the northern tip of the pocket and the southern part of the Königsberg perimeter.

The Heiligenbeil pocket had formed along the shores of the Frisches Haff. The Baltic coast is characterized by gently shelving sea beds, with modest tidal flows. Millennia of wind and wave action has ground the coastal rocks into a fine silty sand, and the relatively small tidal flows have deposited much of this sand a short distance off the coast in the form of a series of sand bars. One such line of dunes, known at that time as the Frische Nehrung, separates the Frisches Haff from the Baltic itself. This strip is connected with the mainland at its southwest end, and is separated from Pillau at its northeast end by a narrow channel. At its narrowest, the Frisches Haff is about 7km wide. The waters of this lagoon are not deep, reaching a maximum depth of only a few metres, and usually freeze during the winter. The winter of 1944/45, one of the coldest on record, resulted in the ice on the lagoon being thicker and stronger than usual. By the time that the Wehrmacht and the East Prussian refugees were driven back to it, the ice was easily thick enough to bear the weight of vehicles. The local residents had a healthy respect for the Frisches Haff. The ice, often more than a metre thick, would move and crack during the winter, with plates riding over each other when storm winds blew. On other days, a thick fog would lie over the ice, and it was easy to lose all sense of direction.

As the fighting around the pocket raged on, attempts were made to evacuate the refugees across the ice. If they could reach the Frische Nehrung, they would be able to travel along the narrow road along the dunes, heading southwest towards Danzig. Alternatively, they could move northeast, and cross the small channel to reach Pillau. In either case, they would then be in a port capable of taking ocean-going vessels. An additional complication for the refugees resulted from the rescue of the three half-completed torpedo boats from Elbing in the last week of January. In order to take these vessels to Pillau, an icebreaker had cut a channel in the ice, leaving a 30m obstacle of freezing water close to the Frische Nehrung.

The first refugees crossed the ice on 23 January. Jakob Klein, a fisherman from the village of Cadinen, had been urged for several days by an army NCO who was billeted with him to make preparations to flee. At first, Klein wanted to stay in his home, but late on 23 January, when the sounds of gunfire could be heard coming closer, he departed with his 14-year-old daughter aboard a sled fitted with a sail. Other such vessels also set off, and they all reached the channel left in the ice by the icebreakers at about the same time. There they found two small vessels waiting. Abandoning their sleds, the refugees were ferried across the channel, and reached the dunes of the Frische Nehrung shortly afterwards.[2]

The largest gathering of refugees was in Heiligenbeil itself, and the nearby port of Rosenberg. The latter was the headquarters of 4th Army, with its attendant rear-area units and hospitals. Tens of thousands of refugees flooded into this area, many of them brought by the last trains to leave the inland towns of East Prussia. Hildegard Aminde, who had boarded the last train from Allenstein with her elderly mother, was herded from her train in Heiligenbeil, after a journey that lasted several days, during which there was almost no food, water or heating. Several of the refugees were dead, and they were laid on either side of the tracks. Those who were able to walk formed up spontaneously into a column, and set off across the frozen fields. Finally, they were led to a school, which was already occupied by refugees.[3]

Emil Mischke, the farmer and Party official from Friedland, reached Frauenburg, where he managed to secure a pass that assigned him to XX Corps in Danzig. He was fortunate; other able-bodied men were pulled out of the refugee columns and conscripted into Volkssturm units. Lying at the western tip of the pocket, Frauenburg soon came under Soviet artillery fire. At first without any direction, then guided by army engineers, the refugees began to stream across the ice of the Frisches Haff. Eventually, six roads were created across the Haff, their course marked by poles embedded in the ice. Lights illuminated the routes at night, and inevitably they attracted the attention of Soviet artillery and aircraft – the roads were in use for the movement of ammunition into the pocket, as well as for the evacuation of refugees and wounded. In places, bridges were erected across the channel left by the icebreakers, and elsewhere army ferries shuttled back and forth. As a result, refugees now poured across to the Frische Nehrung, where the small road running along the dunes proved hopelessly inadequate. General Ritter von Heigl, Army Group North's senior engineering officer, was given responsibility for bringing order. Some 30,000 refugees were diverted to Pillau, where they joined the tens of thousands driven into Samland, all waiting for a ship to the west. General Schönfelder, another engineering officer, organized work parties of military and civilian engineers to improve the Nehrung road, which in places ran across dykes that threatened to collapse under the constant traffic. A second road was created along the ice of the Frisches Haff, some 400m to the east of the Nehrung, and many refugees were diverted onto this and hurried on their way to the southwest.

Military police tried to ensure that refugee wagons maintained a distance between each other, to reduce the weight on the ice. On the night that Mischke and his family crossed, snowstorms swept the Haff, driven by a southwesterly wind, and as the refugees turned southwest along the ice road that ran parallel to the Nehrung, the snowflakes were driven into their faces. As morning dawned, the snow stopped. To the south, across the Haff, Mischke and the other refugees could see the town of Tolkemit, where fighting raged on. Looking back, they could see that the battle had also engulfed Frauenburg, the town they had left just hours ago. Finally, the refugees reached Kahlberg, near the southern end of the Nehrung. Here, they found every building was already full, but at least there was the semblance of order – a Wehrmacht kitchen had been set up, supplying the exhausted people with hot soup. Amongst the refugees sheltering in the village church were Inspektor Romalm and his employer's wife; after their narrow escape from the Red Army in the Osterode brickworks, they had escaped through Mohrungen to the coast, and had then crossed to Kahlberg.[4]

Refugees from Herzogswalde were caught by Soviet air attacks. Paul Kosche was in the first of two wagons with his sister; the second wagon, driven by a French prisoner of war, contained Kosche's wife Anna and their two children. As a formation of Soviet aircraft swept towards them, the children leaped from their wagon and ran. Bombs fell, raising great spouts of ice and water, and Kosche and his sister were hurled from their wagon. The second wagon narrowly missed a crater, and then the attack was over.

Anna Kosche ran across the ice, searching amongst the wreckage of other wagons until she found her daughter, lying unconscious. The 15-year-old had a chest wound, and died the following day. Her husband and his sister, too, were dead. She never saw her son again.[5]

Meanwhile, the perimeter of the Heiligenbeil pocket was slowly being driven in. Stalin issued an order on 9 February requiring Cherniakhovsky to overcome all German forces still active in East Prussia – those in the Heiligenbeil pocket, the Königsberg garrison and Army Detachment Samland – by 25 February. Cherniakhovsky rejected this as unrealistic, and chose to concentrate on 4th Army in the Heiligenbeil pocket first. The town of Kreuzburg was assaulted on 7 February, and Baltuttis' company came under heavy shellfire. When the bombardment stopped, the survivors gathered together, and under a hail of automatic weapon fire, they fell back from their shattered trenches. A counter-attack was ordered for the following morning to retake Kreuzburg, something that all ranks, from the battalion commanders down to the infantrymen, knew was a futile mission. At the very last moment, Hauptmann Kuhlwilm, the battalion commander, took it upon himself to abandon the attack. Shortly after, both Baltuttis and his friend and company commander, Leutnant Saul, were wounded, and evacuated from the frontline.[6]

Frauenburg, at the western tip, fell to the Red Army on 8 February. The 28th Jäger Division was ordered to retake the town, but despite fire support of the warships *Lützow* and *Admiral Scheer*, the attack failed. Inland from Frauenburg, the frontline along the winding Passarge valley was too long for 28th Jäger Division and 131st Infantry Division to occupy continuously, and Soviet troops constantly infiltrated during the long nights, necessitating costly German counter-attacks the following day. It was only due to the difficulties faced by the Red Army in bringing tanks across the frozen river that the Germans were able to prevent a breakthrough, but nevertheless they were gradually levered back.

Wormditt, just a few kilometres east of the Passarge valley, now became the centre of fierce fighting. The 131st Infantry Division managed to repulse all Soviet attacks, culminating in battles on 8 February that were enormously costly to both sides. For a few days, Soviet pressure ceased. The 48th Army's infantry divisions were reorganized and replaced by fresher units. The Germans had no such luxury. Instead, they quietly arranged for Wormditt to be abandoned. The remaining residents were at first reluctant to leave, and had to be urged by the army to depart. As the evacuation was carried out, the troops made an extraordinary discovery. In the railway station, they found a goods train loaded with a dismantled timber mill. This proved to be the property of the brother of Gauleiter Koch. The Gauleiter, in the middle of the crisis and at a time when he should have been organizing the evacuation of civilian refugees, had diverted an entire train to help his brother transport the dismantled mill out of East Prussia. The train was left in the sidings, and presumably became part of the booty secured by the Red Army. Another surprise came when the retreating troops pulled back through the nearby Luftwaffe airfield. Here, they found a large number of aerial bombs; a Luftwaffe unit had abandoned them, and had failed to notify the army of their presence. The bombs, which would have been useful to the army for demolition purposes, had to be destroyed to prevent their falling into Soviet hands.

At the other end of the salient, Bodo Kleine's 975th Infantry Regiment, part of 367th Infantry Division, was deployed along the coast. The division's other two regiments had been able to reach Königsberg before the city was first cut off. Soviet pressure on the narrow connection continued. Both sides constantly sought to gain an advantage. On one occasion, Kleine and his men found that the Soviet troops had succeeded in bringing a tank into their frontline and had dug it in, up to its turret. This tank caused considerable annoyance to the Germans, as it was able to fire on almost anything that moved, but was too far away to be knocked out by Panzerfausts, which were the only anti-tank weapons available. Another sign of Soviet impunity was the presence of tethered observation balloons for artillery spotters; the Luftwaffe had been absent for so long, these relics of a previous war were able to provide Soviet gunners with valuable targeting information.[7]

Grossdeutschland made another attempt to improve the link with Königsberg. The earlier battles between *Grossdeutschland* and 11th Guards Army's XVI Guards Rifle Corps had done more than secure the fragile coastal road to Königsberg; they had also prevented the Red Army from its original intention to thrust down into the northern part of the German pocket. On 6 February, Generalmajor Lorenz planned to attack with what remained of his division, reinforced by Kleine's regiment from 376th Infantry Division, to recapture the railway line from Kobbelbude to the southern perimeter of the besieged city. A preliminary night attack suffered a disastrous start when German combat engineers fired flares that illuminated the attacking force. Soviet guns immediately opened fire, destroying two of the few remaining Panthers. The main attack by the Panzergrenadier regiment also suffered an ominous blow at the outset when a sudden Soviet mortar barrage killed the regiment's commander, Oberst Wolfgang Heesemann. The attack made minimal progress, and was eventually abandoned.[8]

Elements of *Grossdeutschland* now found themselves deployed almost everywhere in the pocket, providing support for the hard-pressed defenders. Fighting raged along almost the entire front of the pocket throughout February, and the perimeter slowly shrank. In an attempt to comply with Hitler's insistence that there should be no voluntary retreat, almost every division adopted the policy of deploying only the lightest of screens in unfavourable areas. These were swiftly driven back as soon as the Red Army attacked, but the attack would then encounter the main line of resistance where it could be brought to a halt. The pretence of holding territory and only conceding it when driven back was thus maintained.

Away from the frontline, German rear-area units struggled to provide care for the wounded, and to move supplies to the combat formations. Baltuttis and his company commander, Leutnant Saul, were in a train that had been converted into a makeshift hospital. The less seriously wounded contributed to the care of those in a worse state:

Our wagon was loaded with 18 wounded men, for whom there were clean beds, laid out as bunks, allowing for a restful stay. Our seriously wounded were in single beds, laid out next to each other.

… To their credit, the medics worked for us in an exemplary manner. Amongst the wounded were three comrades who had gunshot wounds to the lung. One of them, an infantry Feldwebel, had applied a field dressing, which had to be secured in an airtight manner to the wound, and had then made his way back on foot over 30 kilometres of ice and snow. In a moment of carelessness, I tipped a bowl of soup on him, all over his face. Thank God that there was no harm done! But I was very worried and consequently spent a lot of time with him. A young Gefreiter had lost his eyesight from shrapnel. He had to be fed like a small child when we were given hot meals. Filled with a great restlessness, he constantly felt his way around the wagon, as if hoping that by feeling things, he might be able to recover his sight. None of us was able to offer him any helpful words to bring him closer to us. So he remained in the darkness that surrounded him. A major and a Gefreiter had been badly wounded with abdominal wounds. The major, an infantry Knight's Cross holder, spoke not a word, didn't cry out, and showed no expression in his face. Only his snow-white face showed that he was suffering. The Gefreiter, called 'Hänschen' by everyone, groaned and called out constantly for water, but was not allowed to drink. He had a high fever, and his tongue was swollen. If he didn't get intravenous fluids soon, he would die of dehydration… In the third night, the Gefreiter fell silent. In the morning, the medic confirmed that he was dead. Nobody wanted to remark on whether this death had been painful, as a bottle of Lysol, which had been drunk, was found next to him. How he managed to get hold of the disinfectant during the night remained unclear.[9]

On 11 February, the train moved to Heiligenbeil, where the wounded were unloaded. From there, the walking wounded were dispatched across the frozen waters of the Frisches Haff from Rosenberg:

Shortly after we set out across the ice, a swarm of Russian bombers flew overhead. People scattered in panic, running wildly hither and thither. The flak that had taken up positions on a rear slope on the coast near Rosenberg opened up a rapid fire with its quad guns. Tracers flashed through the crowd of machines, but none of them came down. Unbothered, they continued their course towards the northwest and the open sea. They had other objectives than us. There was aerial combat high above us. We saw condensation trails and heard the hammering of guns. We did not know what units were involved… After several hours of marching, a sympathetic woman let me sit on the driving seat of her wagon. I gladly accepted her invitation. We had a pleasant conversation. Her husband was a major in 111th Infantry Division. She was intelligent and very nonchalant, which impressed me greatly as an 18-year-old. She complained bitterly about the officials of the Party, who took good care of themselves but made no provision for refugee columns, as a result of which countless East Prussians fell into the hands of the murderous Soviets. My companion had experienced gruesome events, but had come through unhurt. Her account struck a chord with me, as it reminded me of my grandfather, who was tormented for years by the Gestapo because he refused to stop holding church services in Lithuanian. Well-meaning Party members protected him from being sent to a camp by making statements that he was an old man seized by 'religious delusions'. At the time, he said to me repeatedly that we Germans would have to pay dreadfully for our conduct. I knew that these words required no prophetic abilities. During our conversation, there was a sudden surprise attack on our wagon by a Russian attack aircraft. It was flying about 15 metres above the ice. I could clearly see the head of the pilot and thought, 'Now we're for it.' But immediately before opening fire, the pilot turned his machine sharply to the right and fired past us at the open ice. We were sure that he deliberately missed us. I hope he survived the war!

We reached the Nehrung at Narmeln. Relieved and thankful, we parted. A pioneer reckoned that we had been lucky, as this day had been the quietest for a long time.[10]

Despite constant pressure on the pocket, Cherniakhovsky failed to achieve a breakthrough anywhere. In view of this, Stalin issued new orders. Samland now became the concern of Bagramian's 1st Baltic Front. Cherniakhovsky would concentrate first on the Heiligenbeil pocket, and then on Königsberg. On 18 February, while he was being driven to his frontline headquarters, there was a sudden explosion behind the vehicle. Shrapnel tore through the back seat and went straight through Cherniakhovsky's chest before wounding the driver and embedding itself in the dashboard. The general died within minutes.

There have been suggestions that the explosion that killed Cherniakhovsky was caused by a mine, possibly laid by the Red Army itself, but the most likely explanation is that he was killed by random German artillery fire. Whatever the cause, the Red Army lost its youngest senior commander, a man who was popular with both his fellow commanders and those he led. He was buried in Vilnius; in 1990, following Lithuanian independence, his remains were exhumed and moved to Novodevichy Cemetery in Moscow.

Aleksandr Mikhailovich Vassilevsky was now appointed as commander of 3rd Belorussian Front. Cherniakhovsky had already made extensive preparations for a decisive assault on the Heiligenbeil pocket, and Vassilevsky, who also inherited command of Bagramian's 1st Baltic Front, continued to bring forward ammunition and supplies. When he advised Stalin that preparations would need almost three weeks to be completed, there was no reaction. Stalin seemed to have reconciled himself to a far slower pace of progress.

Around the pocket, the end of February saw a few days of relative peace, punctuated by sudden artillery bombardments and constant loudspeaker broadcasts, urging the defenders to surrender. Despite the hopelessness of the situation, few German soldiers took this route. Soviet intelligence reported that morale within the German forces was low, but discipline remained strong.

As well as *Grossdeutschland*, 24th Panzer Division was also extensively used in a 'firefighting' role within the pocket. The 26th Panzergrenadier Regiment formed a battlegroup that was involved in heavy fighting around Guttstadt. Slowly, the battlegroup was driven back to the Freimark Heath, suffering heavy losses. These were replaced by tank crews who no longer had tanks, soldiers from other divisions, even Volkssturm. Despite the often rudimentary training of these replacement drafts, the battlegroup was able to maintain its line, and prevent a breakthrough. The division's Battlegroup Einem was involved in bloody fighting near Zinten, where the battle centred on a barracks complex that had previously housed armoured troops. A counter-attack by von Einem's group, supported by units from three infantry divisions, caught the Soviet 5th Army by surprise on 11 February, retaking ground either side of the town, but despite costly assaults the barracks remained in Soviet hands. Casualties amongst the division's senior officers were heavy. Oberst Baron von Holtey, commander of the division's tank regiment, was badly wounded, and Major Höhne and Rittmeister Hahn, commanders of 26th Panzergrenadier Regiment and the regiment's 2nd Battalion respectively, were both killed in the Zinten battles.

On 12 February, battlegroup Einem was dispatched to defend the southern part of the perimeter, where Soviet forces were attempting to drive up the main highway towards Braunsberg. Gradually, other elements of the division arrived, and the Soviet thrust was brought to a halt. By 26 February, the division claimed to have destroyed 209 tanks since its arrival in East Prussia. Meanwhile, the division's rear-area units had congregated in a narrow wooded ravine near Heiligenbeil. This location became known as the division's 'support village', with a network of well-camouflaged bunkers where the medical, engineering and supply personnel continued to sustain the division. It was also a place where stragglers were gathered together and organized into replacement drafts for the division's battlegroups.[11]

The weather grew warmer towards the end of February. The ice of the Haff became increasingly unreliable, but most of those who wished to cross had already made the perilous journey. One estimate put the number of refugees who crossed the ice at 450,000.[12] Finally, early on 4 March, the ice melted completely. For those who remained within the pocket, the only escape was now by boat. Those who had crossed the Haff congregated at either end of the Nehrung, either in Pillau and its immediate hinterland in the north, or the Vistula–Nogat estuary and the Danzig–Gotenhafen area in the south, awaiting ships to the west. Yet after the success of the first convoy from Pillau, the tragedies of the *Wilhelm Gustloff* and *Steuben* made many reluctant to risk the short sea journey to northern Germany or Denmark.

Eventually, by early March, almost all civilians had left the Heiligenbeil pocket. Only the battered but unbroken remnants of army divisions remained; many of these divisions, such as 18th Panzergrenadier Division, had taken such heavy losses that they were disbanded and their men transferred to other formations. Division and corps commanders repeatedly enquired about evacuation plans for the troops, but in vain – Hitler had decided that 4th Army was to continue to hold its positions, even though there was now not the slightest reason, tactical, strategic or humanitarian, for it to do so. Despite constant disciplinary measures, stragglers began to congregate in the small ports along the coast.

Meanwhile, the Red Army's preparations continued. The 48th and 3rd Armies, facing the southern parts of the pocket, had taken heavy losses, and this sector now grew quiet. The main effort would be made directly opposite Heiligenbeil, and further north against the link with Königsberg. The slowly shrinking perimeter of the pocket also created difficulties, as the Soviet forces found themselves compressed closer and closer, often lacking room to deploy or manoeuvre effectively. In an attempt to reduce congestion, Vassilevsky pulled 2nd Guards Army out of the line, to allow it to recuperate prior to the anticipated reduction of Königsberg and the Samland peninsula.

On 12 March, Army Group North's commander, Generaloberst Lothar Rendulic, was dispatched to take command of Army Group Courland. In his place came Walther Weiss, who had commanded 2nd Army. Weiss' home town of Tilsit now lay far behind Soviet lines; he was perhaps another example of Hitler moving officers and men into areas where personal loyalties might encourage them to fight harder. The following day, the gathering storm broke. The initial bombardment of the German lines was the heaviest since the January offensives. Despite this, the defences repulsed the first Soviet assaults. The men were now fighting in positions right in front of their supporting heavy weapons, which often served as rallying points. Attacks were followed by counter-attacks, and no breakthrough occurred. Nevertheless, it was impossible not to concede ground, particularly in the northern parts of the pocket. Here, *Grossdeutschland* tried in vain to fend off the massed forces of 11th Guards Army, and was slowly driven back to the coast, which was reached on 16 March, finally severing the link with Königsberg. Brandenburg was abandoned the following day. A large ammunition dump on the outskirts had to be destroyed, as there was insufficient fuel or transport to move it.

On 14 March, the southern part of the perimeter came under intense pressure. The 24th Panzer Division's left flank was turned when what remained of 131st Infantry Division and 541st Volksgrenadier Division were driven back, as the Soviet 48th Army thrust towards Heiligenbeil. The entire southern perimeter was now withdrawn to a line running from Alt Passarge, through Hammersdorf, to Birkenau, and Volsky's 5th Guards Tank Army pushed closer to Braunsberg. For a while, Soviet attempts to encircle the town were hindered by the winding Passarge, and 28th Jäger Division was able to put up a tough defence. Soviet engineer units succeeded on 17 March in throwing a bridge across the river between Braunsberg and the Frisches Haff. Swiftly, 5th Guards Tank Army's forces surged through the shattered ranks of 14th Infantry Division and reached Wermten, barely 2km south of Heiligenbeil. To the southeast of Braunsberg, though, it proved almost impossible for Volsky's units to make such rapid progress, and it was only after Braunsberg itself was taken on 20 March that supplies could be brought forward to replenish the spearheads.

Elsewhere, 24th Panzer Division found that Soviet forces were still deep behind its left flank, necessitating further withdrawals. Bitter fighting raged around the railway line between Heiligenbeil and Braunsberg; 24th Panzer Division's last three tanks accounted for more than 20 Soviet tanks, and for the moment the line was held. Heiligenbeil itself, however, became the focus of the next major attack. The 21st of March was, in the words of one of the combatants, 'a day of fighting of the first order'.[13] A deep Soviet penetration towards the town could not be cleared by counter-attack, and it became clear that not only was the pocket shrinking, but would soon start to break up.

To date, only a few rear-area units had been allowed to transfer across the Haff to the Nehrung. Late on 21 January, General Grossmann, commander of VI Corps, dispatched his Chief of Staff, Oberst Freiherr von Ledebur, with a ninth request for permission to withdraw. At this stage, the little port of Rosenberg was still open, albeit under artillery fire, and an evacuation of sorts was still possible – if permission could be obtained. Inevitably, Hitler refused.

Heiligenbeil had become the central point for the collection of wounded throughout the pocket. Peter Bamm, an army surgeon, had set up an 80-bed hospital in a disused factory in Heiligenbeil. He kept a record of casualties treated by his unit, and after the war he calculated that his teams cared for more than 13,000 wounded; between 200 and 400 new cases passed through their hands every day. As a result of this flow of traffic, Bamm found that his unit was constantly short of blankets, which were taken away with every wounded man. In an attempt to deal with this, Bamm had to send some of his precious men with each seaborne transport from Rosenberg to Pillau, with orders to reclaim the blankets from the wounded and bring them back to Heiligenbeil. Sometimes the flood of wounded exceeded the numbers evacuated. By the time that Heiligenbeil was under artillery fire, Bamm had 1,200 wounded crammed into his hospital. The resourceful medics recruited help wherever they could – a group of French prisoners of war agreed to help in the hospital, together with some Russian women. Other medical units were absorbed into the field hospital, and five military buses were commandeered to provide transport to Rosenberg. Other casualties, particularly those with head wounds, would not be likely to survive the long journey – first to Rosenberg, then by sea to Pillau, and from there by ship to Germany. There was an airfield next to Bamm's hospital, but as the town came under increasing fire it proved difficult to persuade pilots of transport planes to stay on the ground long enough to arrange for casualties to be taken from the hospital. Bamm's quartermaster came up with the solution:

In a little place near Heiligenbeil he had discovered a sugar factory in which there were still several hundred sacks of sugar weighing a hundredweight each. He confiscated them and offered the air authorities one hundredweight of sugar for every batch of casualties they took back. The pilots had families in Germany who hadn't enough to eat; and if the airfield didn't happen to be under fire at the time, for a hundredweight of sugar it was worth taking the risk that it might not come under fire for a further ten minutes. Thus our ambulances which drove to the airfield always contained four stretchers, three head injuries and the fourth with a sack of sugar. In this way we managed to get the cranial casualties evacuated to Germany until the field hospital completely ceased to function.[14]

As the end grew closer, Bamm and other senior medical personnel were called together. They were now informed that the chances of Heiligenbeil being held long enough for an evacuation were non-existent, and that they would have to surrender to the Red

Army. Bamm and his energetic staff had worked hard to move the wounded out, and by now the hospital had only 20 casualties left within its battered factory. He returned to his staff with the bad news. To everyone's surprise, however, the first Soviet assault on Heiligenbeil was beaten off, and the line continued to hold. It seems that the Soviet forces had suffered devastating losses too. Two precious days were bought at a terrible cost in blood, allowing the last of the wounded to be moved.

Early on 24 March, the day that Heiligenbeil was finally lost, Bamm received permission to move his remaining personnel to Rosenberg for evacuation. When he attempted to board a ferry with his French helpers, a military policeman stopped him – the French prisoners of war were to be left behind. Bamm couldn't face the thought of abandoning any of his helpers, but at that moment, a fight erupted nearby. While the MP dealt with it, Bamm hurried his people, including the female Russian helpers, into the ferry. Moments later, he was joined by his faithful NCO, nicknamed 'Moccasin', who had deliberately started the fight to distract the MP.[15]

The loss of Heiligenbeil brought the end of the pocket closer. The remains of *Grossdeutschland*, 28th Jäger Division, 562nd Volksgrenadier Division and 2nd Paratroop-Panzergrenadier Division *Hermann Göring* were driven back into the small Balga peninsula, while Grossmann's VI Corps retreated to the area around Leysuhnen. Soviet forces now pressed forward from Heiligenbeil to the coast, separating these two areas. In VI Corps' sector, all contact with other commands was lost, as the remnants of 24th Panzer Division, 131st Infantry Division and 61st and 541st Volksgrenadier Divisions found themselves with their backs to the Frisches Haff. It seemed that they would have to defend their tiny bridgehead while a maritime evacuation was organized. They were indeed in a good defensive position – the terrain was favourable, and the Leysuhnen area contained plentiful supplies. But then an order arrived, by a circuitous route, directing them to attempt a breakout along the coast to the Balga peninsula. This order was drawn up by General Müller at 4th Army headquarters on 23 March, before the loss of Heiligenbeil and before the subsequent Soviet advance to the sea. Unable to reach VI Corps headquarters due to the fighting in Heiligenbeil, the messenger carrying the orders made his way to the coast, where he found a rowing boat and was able to reach Leysuhnen. Here, he delivered the order to Grossmann.

The order was out of date, and the loss of Heiligenbeil plus the subsequent Soviet drive to the coast made execution of the orders almost impossible. All of the division commanders pressed for the order to be ignored, but Grossmann issued instructions to prepare for a breakout on the night of 24–25 March. Grimly, the soldiers made their preparations, destroying the few heavy weapons that were still functional.

At midnight, they set off. At first, the march made good progress along coastal tracks to Rosenberg. Then they encountered Soviet forces, and any organized movement disintegrated. Casualties were enormous. Barely 500 men of 24th Panzer Division succeeded in reaching the Balga peninsula. The rest were killed, taken prisoner or scattered. Small groups of stragglers continued to appear for several days. Sheltering in a foxhole near Rosenberg, Generalmajor von Nostitz-Wallwitz, the commander of 24th Panzer Division, presented the Knight's Cross with Oak Leaves to Oberstleutnant Rudolf Trittel, the commander of 23rd Infantry Division's 9th Infantry Regiment, which had been attached to the Panzer division since the start of the campaign. Within a day, they were both severely wounded by Soviet shelling.[16]

The devotion to duty of the messenger carrying the order to VI Corps thus resulted in the destruction of the entire corps. This is an extraordinary incident; Grossmann, the corps commander, had helped organize and carry out Hossbach's attempted breakout in January, and was therefore no stranger to doing what he believed to be right. On this occasion, particularly after his conference with his division commanders, he must have known that the entire venture was certain to fail, yet he ordered an attempt to be made. It is possible that, in the absence of any means of communicating with 4th Army headquarters, he feared that no naval evacuation of his command would come. Another factor is that he no longer had the like-minded Hossbach as his superior, but the rigid and inflexible Müller. It is perhaps significant that in the account of the campaign that he co-authored after the war, Grossmann makes no mention of this episode; this account is based on the unit history of 24th Panzer Division.

Within the Balga pensinsula, many of the new arrivals were incorporated into the ranks of the defenders, while others joined the apathetic, exhausted throngs of men desperately seeking an escape route across the Haff. The 24th Panzer Division's personnel, armed only with rifles, pistols and a few machine-guns, fought to defend the road from Hoppenbruch to Balga; following the wounding of von Nostitz-Wallwitz, command passed to Oberst von Einem, who was immediately wounded himself, and then to Major Rudolf von Knebel-Doeberitz. On 27 March, the small group, now barely 300 strong, caught a Soviet force in a surprise flanking attack and prevented a breakthrough.[17]

Grossdeutschland reached the Balga peninsula from the north, fighting its way back through the Soviet spearheads. The remnants of the division's Panzer-Fusilier regiment, together with a hotchpotch of rear-area personnel, fought desperately around Wolittnick before falling back to Wolitta, buying valuable time for others to reach the precarious safety of the peninsula. The division's last two Tiger tanks were lost here. Slowly, the defenders were compressed into a smaller area. To their rear, the last of the wounded were successfully evacuated from Balga and Kahlholz. On 28 March, orders arrived from 4th Army headquarters: all remaining forces in the peninsula were subordinated to *Grossdeutschland*, and the peninsula was to be held. *Grossdeutschland*'s commander, Generalmajor Lorenz, sent a signal back that the peninsula could be held until dawn on 29 March at best. Later on 28 March, Müller bowed to the reality of the situation and gave permission for *Grossdeutschland* and the last remaining German troops to be evacuated.

Generalmajor Henke, one of the engineering officers who had laboured to provide the civilians trapped within the pocket with an escape route, had improvised a vessel to take troops from the Balga peninsula to Pillau. Nicknamed the *Sea Snake*, the vessel consisted of several landing boats lashed together in a train about 65m long, with flak-armed motorboats attached to either side to provide both propulsion and protection. Late on 28 March, the exhausted German troops waited on the coast for their rescue. At first, there was no sign of the *Sea Snake*. Finally, a rowing boat was sent out into the night, and located the *Sea Snake*, whose crew had been unable to find the Kahlholz jetty. As the sailors brought their cumbersome vessel into the tiny port, a thick fog settled over the coastal area. Lorenz stood on the pier, waving the survivors of *Grossdeutschland* aboard. Finally, there was nobody left, and he went aboard himself. The overloaded *Sea Snake* sailed away from the coast, reaching Pillau just before dawn. Behind them, there was a final burst of gunfire; the remnants of Oberst Hufenbach's 62nd Volksgrenadier Division had been unable to withdraw to the coast, and were overwhelmed near Balga. The Heiligenbeil pocket had ceased to exist.

It is impossible to assess the casualties suffered by the two sides in the battles that raged in February and March around the pocket. *Grossdeutschland* alone recorded more than 5,600 casualties from the beginning of the Soviet assault on 13 March to the last day of the pocket. The number of civilians who died in the pocket, or out on the ice of the Haff, will also never be known. Soviet estimates of German losses from the beginning of the final assault were of the order of 93,000 killed and more than 46,000 prisoners.[18] One estimate records that during the last 12 days of the pocket's existence, some 60,286 wounded, 10,169 soldiers, 4,838 civilians and even a tank were evacuated by sea.[19] Nor is it possible to obtain accurate estimates of Soviet losses, but they must have been at least as heavy as the German casualties, particularly once the final assault began. Many of those who took part in the fighting described it as tough and as brutal as any previous battle in the long, grim history of the *Ostfront*. But the battle for the Natangen district was over. In the smashed towns and villages, the remnants of the civilian population, many already brutally treated by the Soviet occupiers, awaited their uncertain future.

CHAPTER 12
KÖNIGSBERG

Everyone lived and laboured in the hope of continuing to hold
Königsberg until freedom came, either in the shape of the often-promised
relief from outside or through the end of the war.

– Otto Lasch[1]

Cherniakhovsky's exhausted spearheads completed the encirclement of Königsberg as January 1945 drew to a close. For a short time – perhaps as much as two days – the defences of the city were too disorganized to put up any significant resistance, but Cherniakhovsky appears to have been wary about sending his troops, tired and depleted after their hard fighting at the outset of the campaign, into a potentially protracted urban battle. Equally surprising, for the defenders, was the reluctance of the besiegers to take stronger measures to break the tenuous connection that was achieved between the garrison and the Heiligenbeil pocket. Lasch and his fellow officers used the breathing space well, reorganizing the men at their disposal, drawing on the crowds of stragglers that had retreated into Königsberg. Oberstleutnant Wurdig took charge of all combat-worthy officers and men, and after only eight days had formed eight new infantry battalions, fully equipped from the plentiful supplies within the garrison arsenals. The only thing lacking was time to train the men to work effectively together.[2]

Explosives acquired from the torpedo stores in Peyse and Pillau before the city was encircled were used to create thousands of mines, though it often proved difficult to deploy them in the frozen ground around the city. Shells were manufactured, with fuses flown in from the Reich. Meanwhile, despite the perilous overall situation, Lasch enjoyed the chance to deal with the problems that he faced with little interference from above, particularly Gauleiter Koch, who continued to sit in his bunker in Neutief. 'The entire population was delighted that the pressure of the Party had gone. With the return of a degree of order, morale also began to rise.'[3]

Party officials who remained in the city – many had followed Koch's example and had fled to the coast before the encirclement was complete – now worked closely, and remarkably effectively, with the military authorities. Oberbürgermeister Dr Will cooperated with Lasch and his officers, ensuring that civilian matters were dealt with in ways that were consistent with the wishes of the army. Kreisleiter Wagner, dispatched to Königsberg by Koch late on 27 January, also proved to be a valuable and reliable figure, and ultimately died in the city. Obergruppenführer Heinrich Schöne had worked alongside Koch in Ukraine during the German occupation, in charge of one of the six districts of the Reichskommissariat; he chose to remain in the city rather than join his leader in Neutief, and fought as a soldier in the frontline, where he met his death.

Some Party elements, however, continued to exert their malign influence. In an attempt to raise civilian morale, Lasch announced that he would initiate a postal service from Königsberg to the rest of Germany. Postcards could be deposited at the main post office, and would be delivered when an opportunity arose. A former senior Party official took advantage of this and wrote to his family in western Germany, telling them how grim things were in Königsberg, and that the Party – particularly Koch – had abandoned their posts. Unfortunately, the postcard fell into the hands of a standing court dealing with civilian matters. Several Party officials were members of this court, and they sentenced their former official to death for spreading rumours that were detrimental to the defence of the city and to the Party. Lasch, however, who had the final say in any death sentences passed within the city, was able to prevent a needless tragedy.[4]

Suicide was an option chosen by many. Hans von Lehndorff commented in his diary that cyanide capsules seemed to be in plentiful supply, and the matter was discussed openly, as if it were a trivial thing. Shortly after the siege began, von Lehndorff and his fellow surgeon, known under the pseudonym 'Doktora', found a newly arrived field hospital, struggling to cope with wounded soldiers, and volunteered to help:

> We applied ourselves to our work. On the first floor, where the light was best, some of the wounded had already been arranged in rows. Two junior doctors and some medics were changing their bandages, which were no more than lumps of fabric hanging from shattered arms and legs. We kneeled on the floor and tried to immobilize their limbs with splints. They were running with pus. Each of them needed at least an hour to be tended properly; here, we could allow only five minutes, as hundreds were waiting. Many were still in uniform, as they had come straight from the trenches, and nobody had yet seen to their wounds. While we worked, our helpers plied us with coffee and the best tinned produce. Doktora and her sister were the first women, and we were the first civilians, who worked with this field hospital.[5]

While shells landed constantly outside, von Lehndorff joined the field hospital's surgeon in a makeshift operating theatre, and they worked through the night and the following day in shifts. Slowly, order was restored; outside, the orderlies stacked the dead like timber. Army officers visited the hospitals regularly, seeking out any men who could conceivably be returned to duty.

Even the Hitler Youth were dispatched to frontline units. Hauptmann Schröder, commander of 1st Fusilier Battalion, recorded the arrival of such a draft:

> At the beginning of February, the battalion received between 60 and 80 Hitler Youth, aged between 14 and 15, as recruits for replenishment of our ranks. With some consternation, all ranks took to these half-grown children. They were sworn in with suitable solemnity and formality on the tennis courts at the Tiergarten. These boys threw themselves into training with eagerness. Most could not be issued with steel helmets, as these were too big and fell over their eyes when they shot their rifles. Only partial remedies were possible. In view of their youth, they received no alcohol or cigarettes in their rations, but sweets and chocolate.[6]

Of the units trapped in the city, the most powerful was 5th Panzer Division. Shortly after the encirclement, it reported that it had only 17 tanks available; in addition, it had seven Jg.Pz. IVs, with a similar number undergoing repairs. Replacement tanks soon appeared – wrecked vehicles had been brought to Königsberg from all over 3rd Panzer Army's sector prior to the encirclement, and the workshop teams now laboured to cannibalize and repair them. Nevertheless, there was a worrying shortage of anti-tank ammunition. The Jg.Pz. IV was also a particular concern for the division's anti-tank battalion:

> The highly mobile combat operations of the last weeks have revealed that the Jagdpanzer IV is in no way up to the required standard. Just the requirements of mobility result in most vehicles falling out with reduction gear, transmission and engine problems. The few towing vehicles available to the battalion are inadequate to recover broken down vehicles and haul them along the refugee-choked roads. Of the 14 total losses suffered by the battalion, only three were in combat or the result of enemy action. The other 11 had to be blown up to prevent them falling into enemy hands, as there was no means to tow them.[7]

Despite their mechanical shortcomings, the small number of operational Jg.Pz. IVs claimed 87 Soviet tanks and 43 anti-tank guns destroyed prior to the encirclement of Königsberg.

Fuel shortages had plagued German efforts to defend East Prussia since the outset of the Soviet offensive. A synthetic fuel plant in the Königsberg docks produced about

5,000 litres of petrol every day, enough to refuel about 20 tanks. Priority was given to 5th Panzer Division's vehicles. Lasch knew that their strike power represented the garrison's best hope, and it was with reluctance that he had to accept the division's use in a 'firefighting' role, preventing Soviet incursions into the city's defences.

General Raus and 3rd Panzer Army's staff departed for Pomerania, and the remnants of Raus' former command, gathered in the western part of the Samland peninsula, was now designated Army Detachment Samland. Immediately after the encirclement of Königsberg, there was brief discussion of the possibility of an immediate counter-attack. The two divisions of General Gollnick's XXVIII Corps, newly withdrawn from Memel, were gathered around Cranz, 30km north of the city, facing the exposed flank of the Soviet forces that had surged west into Samland. The 95th Infantry Division actually launched a local attack towards the southeast from Cranz, supported by the guns of the heavy cruiser *Prinz Eugen*, and its success hinted at further, larger gains. Was it possible for these divisions to strike south, and link up with the Königsberg garrison? Such an operation could only succeed if Lasch attacked north at the same time, and given the precarious state of the city's defences Lasch was against the operation. The 3rd Panzer Army sided with him, and vetoed it. Instead, Gollnick's corps was ordered to fight its way southwest to link up with the rest of the troops in Samland. This task was completed on 7 February, but the severity of the fighting suggests that Gollnick's proposal for an attack in conjunction with the Königsberg garrison would have been a hazardous undertaking – it may have been possible to cut off the Soviet forces within Samland, but their reduction would have proved extremely difficult.

Now, on 17 February, Lasch received orders from Gollnick, who had been appointed commander of Army Detachment Samland: 'On 19 February, the Samland divisions will attack to relieve Fortress Königsberg. To this end, Fortress Königsberg is to mount a breakout towards the attacking Samland divisions. It is to use parts of 5th Panzer Division and 1st Infantry Division for this purpose.'[8]

Lasch had naturally spent much time contemplating a breakout, and his view was that the forces deployed in Samland were unlikely to make much progress. If a breakout was to succeed, the garrison of the city would have to cover most of the ground, not least because none of the attacking formations had any significant armoured assets. Just as the defenders of Königsberg had put the intervening weeks to good use, it was likely that the Soviet forces around the city would also have been busy, and the breakout would therefore face much hard fighting. For a successful attack, the two divisions within Königsberg nominated for the operation would not be sufficient, and Lasch decided to use 561st Volksgrenadier Division too. Of the divisions he would need, only

1st Infantry Division was currently not deployed in defence of Königsberg. The other two divisions would have to be extracted from the frontline, and replaced by a mixture of police and Volkssturm formations. Lasch was aware that this would weaken the defences of the city, and that it therefore represented a huge risk. He concluded, however, that this was the last, best hope for the garrison, and was therefore a risk he would have to take.

Radio intercepts showed that the Red Army was aware of the possibility of a German breakout. On 15 February, Soviet forces to the west of Königsberg were warned to be ready to defend against a German attack, and received reinforcements. The main forces present were the three rifle divisions of CXIII Rifle Corps, part of 39th Army. Yet discipline in the divisions had broken down badly, with many of their officers and men more concerned with accumulating loot from the Prussian hinterland than with their duties. Alcohol consumption rendered many men incapable, and vehicles were heavily laden with plunder. On 7 February, Lieutenant-Colonel Landsov, 950th Rifle Regiment's Operations Officer, was convicted of drunkenness and sentenced to five days' house arrest and a fine that amounted to half his salary. His regiment's commander, Lieutenant-Colonel Zubchenkov, was also reprimanded.[9]

Lasch discussed the planned operation with Gollnick, and was told on 18 February that his proposed deployment of all – not just part – of 5th Panzer Division, as well as 561st Volksgrenadier Division, was contrary to the opinions of Army Detachment Samland and Army Group North. Consequently, their use was Lasch's sole responsibility, something that Lasch willingly accepted.

Orders had started reaching the formations designated for the attack, codenamed *Westwind*, the previous day, when 5th Panzer Division's operations officer briefed senior officers. An hour before dawn, 1st Infantry Division's Regiment *Singer* would advance either side of the road and railway that ran to the eastern edge of Metgethen. Once they arrived there, they would signal 5th Panzer Division, which would then advance. It was particularly important for the men of the Panzer division that the infantry took the ground as far as Metgethen first, as much of the road from Königsberg to Metgethen ran across swampy land, where deployment of tanks off the road would be impossible. Should this attack be held up in any way, 5th Panzer Division would seek to advance to Friedrichsberg before turning towards Metgethen.

The division's tank regiment was now in good shape. It had incorporated the remnants of 505th Heavy Tank Battalion into its ranks, and had about 80 tanks available. Fuel was sufficient if not abundant, but ammunition remained limited. The Panzergrenadier regiments had received replacement drafts, but there remained serious concerns about their fighting potential. The division had been commanded by

THE BREAKOUT FROM KÖNIGSBERG, FEBRUARY 1945

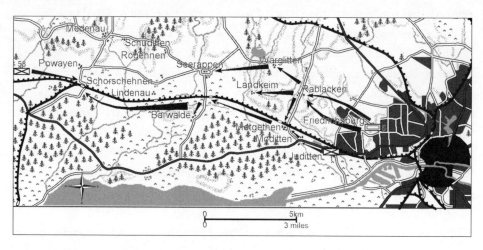

Oberstleutnant Herzog since the last days of January, and now, on the eve of the breakout, Generalmajor Günther Hoffmann-Schönborn arrived by plane to take over. In the circumstances, he decided to wait until the operation was over before taking command.

Jaedtke had recovered from his wounds sufficiently to return to the division, and was in command of the group that was to follow 1st Infantry Division from Juditten to Metgethen. He commanded the division's first battlegroup, consisting of 14th Panzergrenadier Regiment, most of 31st Panzer Regiment, and some of the division's combat engineers. The 13th Panzergrenadier Regiment, with the rest of 31st Panzer Regiment and the remaining combat engineers, formed a second battlegroup. The first battlegroup would be the main attacking force, while the second battlegroup protected its right flank. The division's 5th Armoured Reconnaissance Battalion would cover the left flank, particularly the Kobbelbude Forest. Lasch had deliberately set tight limits to the first day's gains; one of his fears was that 5th Panzer Division would burst right through the Soviet lines, only for the lines to reform behind it.

Jaedtke and his men moved into position late on 18 February, and watched 1st Infantry Division's infantry set off at 0430hrs. They then waited for the call that would tell them that the foot-soldiers had reached Metgethen.

> The call came surprisingly early. It was Oberstleutnant Herzog: 'Jaedtkus, the infantry have taken Metgethen. On you go!'
>
> The first Panthers and half-tracks set off immediately... Suddenly, while we were still on the dyke, we came to a halt. The leading tanks and half-tracks were firing to the left.

The leading Panther burst into flames, the crew bailed out and ran back. The Feldwebel reported that he had been shot up from the left at short range. It was not going to be possible to advance past the brightly burning tank, whose ammunition was exploding. The ground to left and right of the road was impassable bog. So, 'phase two', as foreseen in the planning. In the roadside ditch, I came across the commander of the attacking infantry, and in the midst of the firefight, he told me: 'We made a mistake, we haven't reached the eastern edge of Metgethen yet, we're still in Moditten.' The villages there have all grown into each other, so it's not a remarkable mistake. I called to him: 'Try to press on, we're attacking through Friedrichsberg!' Turning around on the narrow road caused great difficulties. Back at our starting point, I advised Oberstleutnant Herzog of developments.[10]

The second battlegroup, deployed a little to the north, now became the leading unit. Accompanied by Jaedtke's men, it advanced either side of Friedrichsberg, bypassing a small Soviet unit in the estate. The lead vehicles came under fire from anti-tank guns in the Moditten brickyard, and as they attempted to outflank the Soviet position to the north, they ran into Soviet tanks. There was a brisk exchange of fire, after which the Soviet tanks withdrew. After several more sharp actions, Jaedtke secured Rablacken and Landkeim, and then entered Metgethen from the north. At the same time Hauptmann Schröder, with 1st Infantry Division's fusilier battalion, advanced down the Juditten road:

The battalion was ready in the frontline by 2300. On the front and right was 1st Squadron, commanded by Rittmeister von Saucken, on the left was 2nd Squadron under Oberleutnant von Lüttwitz. 3rd Squadron was held ready as a reserve near Headquarters and was earmarked for deployment against the dense woodland on the left flank to prevent a surprise attack from there.

As soon as the bombardment began, 1st Squadron was to deploy along a stream, and break into a trench system immediately south of the girls' school, trying to roll up the positions around the girls' school from the flank. After crossing the stream, a mine clearance troop was to be assigned to it. 2nd Squadron was tasked with crossing the relatively open terrain, dotted with a few ruined houses, in the southeast part of Metgethen and breaking into the Russian trenches; with its southern flank protected, it would secure the fire station as the first objective.

The heavy 4th Squadron was to support the attack by firing on known targets, and to be prepared to move forward in stages after a successful penetration. The heavy mortars had already been successfully 'fired in' on 17 and 18 February. Apart from heavy harassing fire on 1st Squadron's preparation area, which caused a few casualties, everything went smoothly and quietly, contrary to expectations.

There were fierce sounds of fighting in the area held by the neighbouring unit, attacking on the left, 15 minutes before the attack began, but fortunately Russian readiness was only minimal... After a rapid deployment from the preparation areas, 1st Squadron was particularly successful, after tough fighting, in penetrating the first trenches of the Russians' deep defensive system. Large numbers of anti-tank guns and automatic flamethrowers as well as the fiercest defence from the girls' school threatened to fragment the attack. But through the skilful command of the assembled forces, one point of resistance after another was overcome, and in the toughest of fighting, with heavy casualties, the defensive system was penetrated and the Russians expelled.

The attack by 22nd Fusilier Regiment's battlegroup, commanded by Hauptmann Malotka, was able to advance faster, thanks to the mass of tanks committed on its right flank. In a swift advance through the residential part of the town, the battalion reached and secured the western edge of Metgethen after its open left flank was secured by 3rd Squadron.[11]

The tanks that allowed Malotka to make such rapid progress were from Jaedtke's battlegroup. Now that 1st Infantry Division was able to secure Metgethen, his men had a chance to regroup, and look around Metgethen:

The inhabitants had been surprised during the night by the Russian attack on 29–30 January. There were few men in the houses, mainly women and children, with their bloodstained heads smashed in, most of them in their nightclothes, lying in their beds where they were raped, or on the floor... Even though the Russians had been in the village for two weeks, nobody had been buried, nothing had been cleared up. It was worse than in Nemmersdorf!

After these shocking discoveries, there was no longer any doubt that the attack had to succeed, in order to open the way for about 100,000 women and children to escape from Königsberg. Soldiers wrote 'Revenge for Metgethen!' on their vehicles.

The first elements of the second battlegroup now arrived and took over the task of guarding our right flank. All of the first battlegroup could now push on westwards. The main thrust of the attack was either side of the railway and along the road to Seerappen. The terrain was favourable, as the area between the Kobbelbude Forest in the south and the high ground to the north (at 111 metres, the highest point in Samland), was an area, eight to ten kilometres wide, of open ground. In radiant sunshine and clear visibility, the attack group made a good target for the enemy against the snow-covered landscape. He had plenty of opportunity to observe us from the high ground. The enemy artillery fire grew more accurate and heavier.

… Early in the afternoon of 19 February, Seerappen railway station was taken, and shortly afterwards, the village itself, two kilometres to the north, was in our hands. We had reached the attack objective for the day, as elements pushing south from the railway station would soon be able to take Bärwalde. We reported to Division and asked if we could continue the attack. Oberstleutnant Herzog came forward from HQ, congratulated us on our achievements, and ordered that first 13th Panzergrenadier Regiment 13 and Panzerjäger Abteilung 53 [53rd Tank-Hunter Battalion] had to take over protection of the north flank before the attack could continue.

… We stayed at the southern edge of Warglitten on the high ground, as the village was being attacked by about 20 Russian tanks. The attack was beaten off with heavy Russian losses, with about ten tanks being shot up… Shortly after, there was a new Russian attack, this time from the north against Seerappen. Again, there were about 20 enemy tanks… The enemy suffered the same fate as at Warglitten. He persisted in his old tank tactics and attacked only in individual battalions – thank God!

From the battlegroup's headquarters, in a farm about a kilometre east of Seerappen railway station, Oberstleutnant Herzog gave the fortress commander a situation report. He asked for permission to continue the attack after the successful deployment of 13th Panzergrenadier Regiment. It would not suit us at all if permission was not given, as we would then not be able to advance and in the morning would face a freshly rebuilt Russian front.

Oberstleutnant Herzog did, however, approve energetic reconnaissance, so that we would be able to interfere with Russian movements during the night.

During the late afternoon, the Russian artillery fire became increasingly effective, making movements only possible in armoured vehicles. So we waited for darkness until the division's second battlegroup could finally relieve us on our right flank at Seerappen. The southern flank was also taken over by arriving infantry. At about 2000, the Russians attacked strongly from the southeast against Bärwalde, shortly after the infantry had taken over the sector. The attack was beaten off by our tanks and half-tracks, which had just been withdrawn. At 2300, the division intercepted a Russian radio message. During the night, a new line of resistance was to be set up east of the villages of Lindenau, Schorschehnen and Rogehnen. We had to prevent this, but the renewal of the attack was ordered for first light. People in higher positions were getting cold feet and were fearful that the division would be cut off in Seerappen.

We succeeded in interfering with Russian plans between Lindenau and Rogehnen during the night with our combat-strength tank and half-track raiding parties. Fortunately, parts of the second battlegroup were able to hand over the Friedrichsberg estate and the area north of Metgethen to 561st Volksgrenadier Division.[12]

There was now fierce debate on how to continue the operation. Lasch had two choices. He could use 561st Volksgrenadier Division to clear the Kobbelbude Forest, or alternatively use it to relieve 5th Panzer Division, freeing up the armour for a further drive. The latter option was what had originally been intended, but Lasch was deeply concerned that considerable Soviet forces had retreated into the forest, from where they could strike into the exposed flank of 5th Panzer Division as it pushed forward. While the argument continued, help came in the unexpected form of a radio intercept: a Soviet division commander was ordered to withdraw his headquarters to Kondehnen. Confident that the Soviet CXIII Rifle Corps was not planning a counter-attack, Lasch agreed to release 5th Panzer Division for a further advance.

Once more, Jaedtke was in the forefront of the advance:

On the morning of 20 February, at 0300, we finally received approval for further operations. Shortly before first light, Battlegroup 1 set off. At about the same time, the Russians also attacked from the north and northwest with tanks and infantry. Battlegroup 2 held onto the village of Seerappen. But the Russian attack fell right on the right flank of the attack. As a result, it was held back, while the attack south of the railway line prospered.

I/31 remained at Seerappen railway station with a half-track company to shield towards the northwest. Most of the first battlegroup now attacked south of the railway line. Despite unfavourable ground, the attack made progress. Everywhere, the Russians mounted considerable resistance and they must have had a lot of anti-tank guns, even though few enemy tanks appeared. The Russians attempted a counter-attack here out of the Kobbelbude Forest into our left flank. They were beaten off. Parts of our 5th Reconnaissance Battalion pushed forward quickly here and took over flank protection until they were replaced by infantry.

Division then arranged for the second battlegroup to take over Seerappen railway station. So, at midday, I/31 and its half-track company became available. During the afternoon, we heard loud sounds of battle from the west. Before nightfall, our leading units established contact with 58th Infantry Division, which was attacking from Samland, at Powayen railway station. There was great joy at the success of the operation. Several Russian divisions had to be trapped in the Kobbelbude Forest. This was a result of the failure of the Russian attempts to smash our spearhead with attacks from the north and south.

Already during the advances of 20 February, the second battlegroup had to beat off strong Russian attacks from the north against Warglitten and Seerappen. The village of Seerappen was lost again.

Now, the Russians also attacked the first battlegroup from the north, from Medenau. The old story – lots of Russian infantry with about 20 tanks. In any event, we had already pushed north with some elements once we had established contact in the west. Now, all our tanks and a half-track company were deployed against this enemy, while II/14 guarded the Kobbelbude Forest with a half-track company. Our tanks found good positions behind the railway embankment and let the Russians approach. South of Schuditten, most of the Russian tanks were shot up. A few fleeing tanks were claimed by the assault guns of our infantry, which now attacked from the village of Powayen. At least 12 enemy tanks were destroyed.

In the evening, we were holding both a northern and southern front. Shortly before darkness, we were able to take the village of Lindenau on our right flank. This was useful, as it meant that the men could warm themselves during the icy night hours.

Throughout the night to 21 February, the Russians launched attacks along the entire northern front of the division with strong infantry formations backed by tanks, while at the same time making attempts to break out from the south, particularly at Bärwalde.

This night was very critical. The corridor that we had fought to gain was only narrow.[13]

At the same time, 1st Infantry Division, supported by the Division *Mikosch*, set about clearing the Kobbelbude Forest.

Lasch's concerns about the ability of the Samland divisions to advance towards Königsberg were fully justified. Three divisions had been earmarked for the attack. The 93rd Infantry Division was deployed in the north, 58th Infantry Division in the centre and 548th Volksgrenadier Division, reinforced with an ad hoc battalion of former U-boat trainees, in the south. Despite supporting fire from the guns of the Kriegsmarine, the attack made slow progress in the face of strong Soviet defences. On the first day, they gained only 3–4km of ground, with the high ground around Galtgarben changing hands several times in bitter fighting. If Lasch hadn't had 561st Volksgrenadier Division available, and if only part of 5th Panzer Division had been used in the breakout, it seems likely that the operation would have failed. The risk that Lasch had taken in stripping the city's defences had been brilliantly vindicated, particularly by the energetic execution of the attack of 5th Panzer Division. General Gollnick, commander of Army Detachment Samland, graciously acknowledged in an order of the day that the success of the breakout was entirely due to the initiative of the fortress commandant, who had acted contrary to the wishes of higher authorities. Now that the operation was over, Herzog handed over command of 5th Panzer Division to Hoffmann-Schönborn. Herzog himself was now promoted to Oberst, and summoned to Berlin to receive the Oak Leaves to the Knight's Cross for his part in *Westwind*.

Attempts were now made to exploit the breakout and to widen the connection between Königsberg and the forces in Samland. Supported by the guns of German warships off the coast, 5th Panzer Division, with supporting infantry from 58th and 93rd Infantry Divisions, attacked towards the high ground around Galtgarben – 'Hill 111.4'. At first, the attack made progress, but determined resistance by the Soviet defenders resulted in increasing casualties.

Amongst the ranks of the Soviet forces in this phase of the battle was Isaak Kobylyanskiy. The infantry companies that his battery of 76mm guns was supporting were deployed around the base of the hill itself:

> The flat top of the hill, somewhat smaller than a soccer ground, was crowned with a tall structure built in the style of a medieval fortress tower... In case we were forced to retreat, our combat engineers had mined the tower with a substantial amount of explosives and established round-the-clock duty beside it. About 30 metres below the top of the hill, in a two-metre-deep ditch, many shelters and dugouts housed the command post with a squad of guards and two regimental battery commanders with their orderlies. There were about 30 of us there.
>
> During the daytime, our companies supported by my battery's guns managed to repel two or three German infantry attempts to approach the hill. As it grew dark, the shooting faded away. All of us relaxed, and after a late supper with '100 grams' of vodka we fell into deep sleep.
>
> But the night turned out to be full of unexpected events. In the middle of the night a low sound of a flare, fired from the top of the hill, woke us up. We heard distinctly strange voices from upslope: they were Germans, who had reached the top of the hill by some miracle. One more flare soared into the sky. Naturally, it was a signal to their command that the infiltrators had seized the hill. All our telephones were silent; evidently the uninvited 'guests' had cut our telephone wires on their silent climb to the top. None of us knew the size of the party of infiltrators. The fate of the two combat engineers, who were on duty near the tower, was unknown as well.[14]

Here was a serious development. If the Germans were to recapture this prominent hill, they would force the Red Army to pull back a considerable distance, as artillery observers on the hill would have a commanding field of vision, and would be able to direct the guns of the Kriegsmarine with devastating effect. Unsure of the overall situation and unable to contact any other unit, Kobylyanskiy and his comrades discussed what they should do next. Shortly after dawn, the explosive charges around the tower on the hill were detonated. Trying to take advantage of this, the Soviet soldiers made two attempts to storm the hilltop, but were driven back. Kobylyanskiy then contacted his battery commander, requesting artillery support:

In 20 minutes or so we heard the familiar howling sounds of two Katyushas, and right after that, the threatening rustle of wind over our heads before some three dozen shells exploded on the hilltop. When the thundering roar stopped, we went into the attack for the third time.

This time, the Germans couldn't withstand our 'Hurrah!' and fled downhill at the sound of our cheers. We gave chase, and almost all of the runaways were caught.[15]

Although the German attacks towards Galtgarben and Hill 111.4 made only modest gains, one notable success was achieved: the Red Army was driven back far enough to allow trains to run at night between Königsberg and Pillau. It was now possible for refugees to leave the city. But throughout the regained territory, the Germans found further evidence of the Soviet thirst for revenge for the suffering inflicted on the Soviet Union during the years of German occupation:

The scenes that confronted us in the re-won area were dreadful. The Russians had murdered the people en masse in the villages. I saw women who still had around their necks the cords with which they had been strangled. Many were often tied up next to each other. I saw women with their heads in ditches, their underwear showing the clear signs of their bestial mistreatment. All women between 14 and 65 had been raped, often those who were even younger or older.[16]

Now that contact with the outside world was restored, Lasch hoped and expected that the Party would arrange for an evacuation of the tens of thousands of refugees in Königsberg. To his disappointment, no such instructions were forthcoming. Despite the best efforts of Engelhardt and his staff, the number of ships available to take refugees from Pillau could barely cope with the number of refugees awaiting evacuation, and in any event the disasters of the *Wilhelm Gustloff* and the *Steuben* were now well enough known to deter many from attempting the crossing. Eventually, a transit camp was set up in Peyse, but it was chaotically organized, with illness and hunger adding to the cold conditions to plunge the unfortunate evacuees into further misery. Many of the women and children chose to return to Königsberg. Despite the dangers of Soviet artillery and air bombardments, they felt safer there, and at least they could find food and adequate shelter. To the irritation of the military authorities, Koch announced towards the end of March that he and his Party officials had to date arranged for the evacuation of almost a million civilians. This evacuation was entirely due to the efforts of the Kriegsmarine and merchant shipping authorities, acting under Engelhardt's directions. Without the help of prisoners of war – mainly a mixture of

Poles, Belgians, French and even Russians – far fewer East Prussian women, children and elderly would have escaped. The Party's contribution was almost entirely negative.

Koch did not restrict himself to vainglorious announcements. Diversion of resources to rebuild Koch's personal estate at Friedrichsberg was an annoyance, little more. But acting on the Gauleiter's orders, Party officials began the construction of dozens of barricades within the city. Houses in the city centre were levelled to create a makeshift airstrip, despite Lasch's objections that there were no aircraft available to use such a strip. Only on one occasion, though, did the Reich Defence Commissar venture back into Königsberg, returning for a short visit during the hours of darkness.

In Königsberg itself, a strange normality resumed. Shops, cinemas and businesses opened once more, and newspapers were published. From a military point of view, affairs took a dangerous path. General Gollnick had concluded that the next Soviet assault would be against Samland, intended to isolate Königsberg again and to drive the rest of Gollnick's command back into the peninsula. To prevent this, Gollnick ordered Lasch's two best formations – 1st Infantry Division and 5th Panzer Division – to be moved out of the city and deployed to face the expected Soviet attack. In return, Lasch was given 548th Volksgrenadier Division. Even if this division had not been under-strength, it was a poor replacement for the two divisions that Lasch and his staff had spent so much energy returning to decent fighting power. Equally serious was the removal of more than 70 anti-aircraft guns from the city, together with a variety of small units. A large portion of the city garrison's artillery ammunition, much of it laboriously manufactured during the siege, was shipped to 4th Army, which was about to begin its last battle around Heiligenbeil. By the end of March, a despairing Lasch contacted Weiss, now commander of Army Group North, to request that he be discharged from his post as fortress commandant; his role was effectively over, now that the city was in contact with the rest of the German forces in Samland. Weiss was sympathetic, but his requests to higher authorities for such a change went unanswered, and in any event, Weiss was himself about to be moved from his post.

The reduction of the Heiligenbeil pocket had consequences for the German chain of command. The headquarters of Army Group North now seemed superfluous given that its forces were so reduced – 2nd Army had been transferred to Army Group Vistula, 4th Army had ceased to exist as a fighting force and what remained of 3rd Panzer Army in Samland amounted to no more than a corps. Consequently, Weiss and his staff were withdrawn, and their role taken up by General Müller and his staff from 4th Army.

For Königsberg, the first consequence of the end of the Heiligenbeil pocket was the arrival of 10,000 wounded. Lasch questioned the wisdom of this move, and was assured that as soon as they had recovered, these men would be a welcome boost for the garrison. Shortly before the final fighting began, Lasch ordered the wounded to be evacuated to Pillau.

Volkssturm also came to the city from Pillau, amongst them Heinz Kroll, originally from Wehlau. He had not seen service in the army, as he had had a leg amputated above the knee, but now served as an administration clerk. He owned a small apartment in Königsberg, and was delighted to find that it was completely intact. His only problem was his badly damaged artificial limb, held together with tape and string. He had ordered a new one from an orthopaedic supplier in Königsberg, and now took advantage of his return to the city to visit the supplier. To his disappointment, the premises were deserted. A woman in a neighbouring house told him that the workshop had moved to a school, and Kroll spent the next four afternoons limping from school to school after he had finished his clerical duties. Finally, he found a wrecked school in which there were stacks of orthopaedic supplies; the workshop had been moved here, only to suffer a direct hit from artillery shells. After a few hours' rummaging around in the deserted building, he discovered a package bearing his name: it was his replacement leg. He returned to his apartment with great joy.[17]

Bodo Kleine, who had fought with elements of 367th Infantry Division on the Brandenburg–Königsberg road, was now in the city itself. One of the many consequences of the failed July plot against Hitler was the creation of a German equivalent of the Soviet commissar. The post, named Nationalsozialistische Führungsoffizier (NSFO; National Socialist Leadership Officer), was put in place at every level from the regiment upwards, and Kleine had been appointed in this role for his regiment. One of his duties was to tour the frontline and read passages from the new Party news sheet designed for the Wehrmacht, the *Panzerfaust*. Kleine was aware that the articles bore little relation to reality, and he also had no illusions about the scepticism of the troops he addressed. After his regiment joined the rest of the division in the northeast part of the Königsberg perimeter, he continued this unwelcome duty, though he found time to visit the increasingly derelict city on 2 April, Easter Monday.

Helplessly, the men of the Königsberg garrison watched the Soviet forces facing them grow stronger, as troops used to crush the Heiligenbeil pocket were redeployed. Aware of the Wehrmacht's ammunition shortages, Soviet forces moved about openly by day, and with exposed headlights at night. The forces facing the defenders were formidable. After the war, Lasch estimated that perhaps a third of the entire Soviet Air Force was deployed in his area. To oppose this, the Germans had only their anti-aircraft guns, hamstrung by ammunition shortages. No help could be expected from the Luftwaffe. The artillery estimated that it had sufficient ammunition for only one day of fighting. In terms of manpower, Lasch had no more than 35,000 defenders. The number of Soviet forces encircling the city has been put as high as 250,000, but this estimate includes a variety of transport and rear-area units which would not go into action. Nevertheless, despite all Soviet formations being under-strength, they easily outnumbered the defenders. After the withdrawal of 5th Panzer Division, the Red Army's superiority in armour was also colossal – Lasch had only a single company of assault guns at his disposal. The true superiority of the Red Army only became apparent later:

> During the march into imprisonment through the hinterland, the degree of overwhelming force, which previously one could only estimate, became visibly apparent. Gun after gun stood in the encirclement around Königsberg, with huge stores of unused ammunition … every village was stuffed full of troops.[18]

A regimental commander had a similar experience:

> I had never seen such an assemblage of artillery. Gun after gun, one battery behind another, all calibres, with masses of ammunition. There were rows of tanks and Stalin Organs. Most of these weapons had hardly been used. There were constant columns of all sorts of weapons along all the roads, heading forward towards Königsberg. Every road junction was controlled by female traffic police, who directed traffic in a masterful fashion. There were Russian roadsigns, directions, unit insignia on all the signposts. Even the smallest copse, every farm, every village was occupied. Wherever we went, the Russian military was everywhere.[19]

Vassilevsky was under pressure from Stalin to start the assault on Königsberg no later than 28 March, but insisted that such a timetable was impossible. It would take several days after the elimination of the Heiligenbeil pocket, he argued, before artillery and aircraft could be deployed around the East Prussian capital. In contrast to Hitler's reaction whenever his generals contradicted him, Stalin listened and agreed to a short delay, and even allocated additional staff resources to help Vassilevsky.

On 2 April, General Müller visited Lasch in Königsberg, as Lasch remembers:

> Despite his experiences in Heiligenbeil, he was astonishingly still full of illusions and could not comprehend my pessimistic view of the situation. He demanded the

summoning of all commanders of divisions and independent units, and particularly Party leaders. In the cellar of the university, he gave them a forceful, highly optimistic speech about his conviction in final victory. All he could offer to send us in Königsberg was a new battlegroup of soldiers who had been salvaged from the last battles of 4th Army, equipped with a few handguns. From the city, a new great offensive would be launched, which would drive the Russians from East Prussia. When I pointed out that it would require at least four or five battle-worthy divisions for any significant success, he was unable to say where these troops could be found. But, he maintained, everything would be fine.

Afterwards, he told me that I would be replaced shortly. There was an impression that I no longer had sufficient faith in the defensive abilities of the fortress, and that only a completely fresh commander would suffice. When I asked when I could expect to be relieved of duty, he told me that there were still a few difficulties to be overcome, as the previous senior commander [Weiss] had given such a good report about me that nothing could be done immediately. However, he would use the great reach of his influence to request the Führer to bring about my replacement.[20]

Reconnaissance activity continued on both sides. The Red Army made constant attempts to infiltrate the city with spies, some of them former German soldiers who attempted to pass themselves off as escaped prisoners of war. A large group of soldiers appeared in the trenches of 561st Volksgrenadier Division north of Metgethen at the end of March, asking to be led to company headquarters. When they arrived there, they opened fire, and then returned to Soviet lines, taking about 20 prisoners with them. Elsewhere, raids were made in a more conventional way, allowing the Soviet forces to secure better positions for a future attack, and it became clear that the final assault was only days away.

So confident were the Soviet commanders of success, they made no attempt to hide their plans, and even announced them to the Germans. The troops in the southern part of the city perimeter listened to a loudspeaker broadcast that informed them that the attack would start on 6 April. The speaker was Generalleutnant Vincenz Müller, who had been the commander of XII Corps, and was taken prisoner by the Red Army during *Bagration* in July 1944, when his surviving men surrendered in Minsk. After his capture, Müller agreed to make broadcasts to German soldiers calling on them to surrender. After the war, he rose to high rank in Eastern Germany, and for a time was Chief of Staff to the army. He went to considerable lengths to ensure that this new army was trained along Wehrmacht lines, and encouraged several other former Wehrmacht officers to be involved.

The massive Soviet superiority in armour and artillery, and complete control of the air, did much to offset the weakness of their infantry formations. Furthermore, Vassilevsky was able to use the same technique applied to such good effect in January: as the attacker, he could choose to concentrate his forces wherever he wished, leaving large parts of the frontline held by forces that were barely equivalent to the German units facing them. Nearly half the city perimeter, to the east and northeast, was held by a single corps, allowing 43rd Army to mass five corps against the northern part of Königsberg. The 39th Army had an additional three corps poised to sever the connection between Lasch and the German forces in Samland, while 11th Guards Army gathered its strength for a powerful thrust against the southern part of the perimeter. At a lower level, special assault units had been organized, consisting of a single battalion of infantry, a company of combat engineers, a section of 76mm guns, a flamethrower platoon, a mortar platoon and a group of tanks and assault guns. Unable to carry out aerial reconnaissance, Lasch and his senior officers could do little more than sit and wait for events to take their course.

On 6 April, with a bombardment heavier than any so far experienced on the *Ostfront*, 3rd Belorussian Front began its attack. Over the previous two days, Soviet guns had been in action, but heavy cloud and driving rain had prevented Soviet aircraft from adding their power. Now, under clearing skies, artillery salvoes and bombers crisscrossed the entire city. Communications between the German frontline and headquarters formations were swiftly obliterated, and everyone – soldiers and civilians alike – cowered in the city's cellars. The first ground attack, by 43rd Army, fell on 548th and 561st Volksgrenadier Divisions, to the northwest of the city. A single regiment of 548th Volksgrenadier Division was available as a reserve, and was immediately committed in a counter-attack, to no avail. In places, the German lines held up well to the assault, especially around the massive Friedrich Wilhelm III and Lehndorf forts – despite their positions being hit by more than 500 artillery rounds of the heaviest calibre, the defenders continued to resist all day. But elsewhere, the attacking Soviet forces made swift headway, and isolation of Königsberg from Samland looked inevitable.

Isaak Kobylyanskiy's 87th Guards Rifle Division was part of 43rd Army's assault on the northwest perimeter of the city:

Our attack began late in the morning of 6 April 1945… At noon we reached the Fort 5a Lehndorf. But it was not our job to capture the fort. We bypassed it to the west and continued moving forward, while it was the 2nd Rifle Battalion's mission to encircle the fort and force its garrison to surrender.

KÖNIGSBERG, APRIL 1945

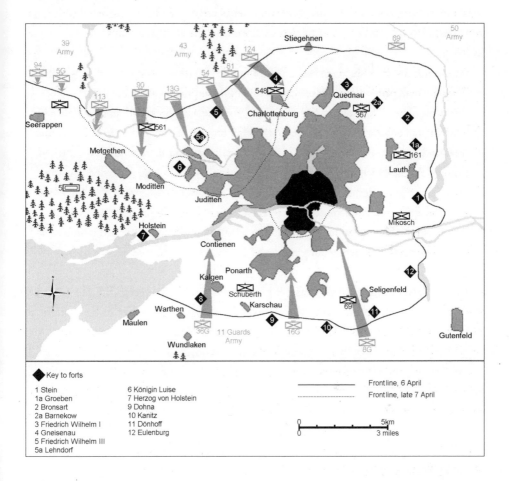

Key to forts

1 Stein	6 Königin Luise
1a Groeben	7 Herzog von Holstein
2 Bronsart	9 Dohna
2a Barnekow	10 Kanitz
3 Friedrich Wilhelm I	11 Dönhoff
4 Gneisenau	12 Eulenburg
5 Friedrich Wilhelm III	
5a Lehndorf	

Frontline, 6 April
Frontline, late 7 April

0   5km
0   3 miles

Overcoming German resistance, we continued our advance. Before sunset we approached the narrow Landgraben Canal that flowed along the outskirts of the city. Soin's troop was halted close to a bridge across the canal by heavy-calibre machine gun fire. My battery fired a few shells at the enemy in return, but the machine gun seemingly had changed its position and continued to fire.

At dawn the next day, both SU-76s [self-propelled guns] crossed the canal, the rest of the troop following closely behind them. Hard street fighting went on all day long.[21]

With no more reserves available, Lasch requested 5th Panzer Division's deployment in an attack from Samland to restore 548th Volksgrenadier Division's positions. Meanwhile, 11th Guards Army rapidly pressed into the southern parts of Königsberg, aiming to reach the Pregel from the south and thus link up with the northern pincer.

Elsewhere the front remained quiet, apart from artillery fire. Gun commander Dröger was a member of one of the anti-tank regiments created from the assorted units that retreated into Königsberg, and he was deployed on the southern front:

After a furious drumfire, there was a massed infantry attack at 1200, supported by tanks. The anti-tank platoon near Prappeln was caught by surprise, and one of our guns took a direct hit. About 200 metres left of Kalgen, the Russians broke through to Ponarth. The anti-tank obstacles from Kalgen to the Haff brought the attack to a halt. The entire infantry line from Prappeln to the Haff was torn apart, and those who survived taken prisoner. As the attack continued in a series of waves, a few Russians succeeded in getting close to the guns; despite this, we were able to extract ourselves from the dangerous situation with a few hand grenades. Several tanks were shot up by us, a few pulled back… As we had used up our ammunition and our left flank was hanging, we had to pull back that evening, after rendering our guns unusable. I had been wounded in both hands.[22]

On 7 April, there was another massive bombardment. Compared to the previous day, the weather was better, allowing the full weight of Soviet air power to be brought to bear. Air Chief Marshal Aleksandr Aleksandrovich Novikov, Commander-in-Chief of the Soviet Air Force, was closely involved in coordinating attacks with those of ground forces, and now ordered Alexander Evgenevich Golovanov's 18th Air Army to commit its long-range bombers in an unprecedented daylight attack. Golovanov protested in vain that his aircrews had little experience of daylight operations, and would be vulnerable to German fighters. Novikov brusquely overruled him, promising him massive fighter support. The resulting rain of bombs added further devastation to the already shattered city.[23]

To the west, 5th Panzer Division prepared to launch its counter-attack, but a further Soviet drive by 39th Army against 1st Infantry Division, deployed west of Königsberg to protect the direct approaches to Peyse, Fischhausen and ultimately Pillau, necessitated a change of plan. Battlegroups from 5th Panzer Division were committed to prevent the line west of Königsberg collapsing entirely. Feldwebel Will of 14th Panzergrenadier Regiment was in one such group:

Behind the railway embankment (7 April), on the stretch to Pillau, we prepared to attack towards Landkeim. After a brief, powerful preparatory fire, we stormed forward over the fields. We succeeded in occupying the estate and setting up a position immediately beyond it. But the success was a costly one. This day cost my company four dead and 28 wounded. Leutnant Hagen, who had taken over the company a few days before, was one of the fallen. By dusk ... there was no company commander any more, and most of the platoon commanders were wounded. After a few hours' sleep in the estate cellar I was back on my feet. In a trip around the positions, I checked to ensure that the teams were all in contact with each other. When I returned to my company HQ platoon, the magic kicked off again. The Russians fired on our thinly held position with countless guns. Shortly before 1000, a shell landed right behind me in the trench. I felt a blow on my elbow and my ribs and felt blood streaming out. I had no time for bandaging. Unteroffizier Paul was screaming right in front of me. I jumped over to him and pulled him into our trench. I could see both of his shoulder blades exposed. As he could still run, the two of us luckily reached a sunken road where we were protected from direct fire. A glance over the embankment told me that the Russians were advancing against our abandoned positions with many tanks. We reached battalion HQ, where I made a brief report to Hauptmann Wiesmann, who was also wounded later. The commander then had us taken to the doctor in a two-wheeled wagon for treatment of our wounds.[24]

The fighting in support of 561st Volksgrenadier Division resulted in the loss of almost all of Will's battalion. In the face of the furious Soviet onslaught, there was no prospect of any significant counter-attack towards Königsberg. Late on 7 April, 11th Guards Army's southern thrust into Königsberg reached the Pregel, and during the night, Soviet infantrymen crossed to the northern bank. Elsewhere in the southern part of the city, parts of the German 69th Infantry Division fought a bitter battle for the main railway station. Dröger and his comrades were also in action in the same area:

The remnants of our force fought in Spandienen during the night, and by early 7 April were in Schönbusch. As the enemy was pushing into Schönbusch from Ponarth, we could only retreat to Nassen Garten. The meadows either side of the road were flooded and under Russian fire. Sheltering behind the road embankment and some of the time in the water itself, we fortunately got through. A few stragglers who tried to swim through the water came under Russian machine-gun fire. Some units were already in position in Nassen Garten, including two anti-tank guns.

The rest of the company also went into position by the truck garages of the Linger Barracks. Several Russian 120mm guns took up positions on the Schönbusch road, but these were struck again and again by well-aimed shots from our anti-tank guns. The infantry gathering on either side of the road were also shot up... Then the Russians came against us with four T-34s. Our Leutnant was killed. Aircraft attacked us until dusk. As the road back to the main railway station was already in enemy hands, we had to pull back to the Schichau works. From there, we went further along the Pregel. At dusk – in constant contact with the Russians – we crossed the railway bridge, which was blown up shortly after our crossing.[25]

Kleine's regiment from 367th Infantry Division was now in the massive Fort Quednau, one of the fortifications built prior to World War I. Despite its antiquity, the fortress still provided considerable protection from Soviet shelling. Outside the fortress was one of 367th Infantry Division's last assault guns:

The assault gun commander was an Oberfeldwebel, and he drove off towards the Russians as far as a predetermined road junction. Russian T-34s had come from there, and did not appear to want to come further along the relatively intact streets, as they feared they would be shot up by German infantry using Panzerfausts from the cellars. Every time he returned to take on more ammunition, the assault gun commander reported that he had shot up one or two Russian tanks. So he went off several times on these 'tank hunts', but after the fourth or fifth time he didn't return. Apparently, he too had been shot up by the Russian tanks. Meanwhile, Russian infantry armed with flamethrowers had also worked their way forward, and now poured streams of flames into the cellar windows. Some of these cellars were still occupied by civilians.[26]

Police units fought alongside the Wehrmacht in the south of the city. One such formation was Battlegroup Schuberth, the remnants of a police formation that had retreated into the city in January and had then been brought up to strength with personnel from the city's police and SS personnel in Königsberg. Elements of the battlegroup were caught in Ponarth and almost wiped out.

Soviet forces swiftly infiltrated east and west after reaching the Pregel, attempting to trap parts of the city's garrison south of the river. The city centre, reduced to rubble, was now the main battlefield as the remnants of the southern defenders attempted to hold their last bridgeheads across the Pregel. By the end of 8 April, there were insufficient troops left to continue the defence, and Lasch ordered the survivors to withdraw to the northern shore. The whole of Königsberg south of the river was now in Soviet hands. What remained of the police battalions and 69th Infantry Division took up positions along the northern bank:

At dawn [9 April], the enemy strengthened his artillery fire on the northern parts of the city that were still held by us. Aerial bombs rained down almost continuously on headquarters, gun positions and strongpoints… After the artillery and aerial preparation the enemy launched a concentrated attack on the northern part of the city centre, roughly the university area. There was constant streetfighting all day between advancing enemy units and the garrisons of the German strongpoints. One strongpoint after another was lost as a result of the enemy's superiority.

… Battlegroup Schuberth held its positions until late in the afternoon. The enemy's attempt to cross the river in the battlegroup's sector was nipped in the bud. The battlegroup's position was endangered as the enemy, advancing towards Königstor and Sackheim, pushed close to the Rossgarten Market … in order to halt this enemy attack, 31st Regiment's left flank was pulled back to the New Market and extended along Landhofmeisterstrasse as far as Königsstrasse. Retreating troops of other units were rounded up and deployed as reinforcements. Early in the afternoon, the enemy worked his way close to the city centre from all directions. There was streetfighting and house-to-house fighting everywhere. The civilians in the cellars despaired and cried out, but their cries were lost in the sounds of fighting. The frontline was not clear, indeed, it was muddled. Nobody knew precisely what parts were in our hands or the enemy's hands. Communications between battlegroup commanders and regiments had been destroyed long ago. Likewise, contact with the garrison command and neighbouring units had been lost. Organized combat was no longer possible. The strongpoint garrisons were on their own.

In this situation, I received instructions from my commander, Generalmajor Schuberth, to break through to the garrison commander's headquarters at Paradeplatz with two reliable men in order to make the commandant aware of the situation with the battlegroup, to find out what was happening elsewhere, particularly with our neighbours, to clarify the question of ammunition supplies, and to collect some Iron Crosses Class I for immediate award to brave combatants.

Unfortunately, I was unable to get back to battlegroup headquarters after this task, as I was wounded in the right thigh by shrapnel as I left the commandant's bunker and was no longer able to walk.[27]

On 7 April, while there was still contact with the German forces in Samland, Lasch made an urgent request for permission to organize a breakout. Such a breakout to the west would necessitate abandonment of the city, and Lasch can hardly have been surprised when Müller refused permission. By the end of 7 April, the last road to Pillau had been cut. Under massive bombardment, the defenders tried to shuffle their fast-disappearing forces. What remained of 61st Infantry Division, barely three battalions, was sent to shore up the defences along the Pregel. Delayed by bombardment, they arrived too late to prevent Soviet forces securing footholds on the northern bank. Early on 8 April, these footholds erupted northwest, linking up with the Soviet forces that had cut the Pillau road from the north.

Kobylyanskiy's division was also pressing into the city from the north on 8 April:

It wasn't easy to get our bearings in the central part of Königsberg. Besides, other assault detachments were operating on adjacent streets, and we stopped at almost every intersection to get more specific information on our current position, the enemy's position, and the overall situation.

During one of these halts, the signboard of a small hotel attracted my attention. Out of curiosity, I opened the entrance door and entered a spacious lobby. It was crowded with elderly women. There were at least five infirm persons sitting in wheelchairs among them. Two of them also suffered from hand tremors. Everybody looked terrified.

At the far end of the hall, there was some loud commotion. An elderly German was standing in the centre of a group of four or five Soviet soldiers, who did not seem to be from our unit. The short and grey-haired German was wearing a dark blue uniform with gilt buttons, lace, and shoulder straps. The soldiers, evidently taking the German for an important military officer, were trying to drag him toward the exit. The old man resisted with all his might, shouting over and over again 'Ich bin der Portier!' ('I'm the doorman'). I couldn't remain indifferent to the situation, while understanding what the man was shouting. I intervened, explaining what the man was saying and why he was wearing this uniform (at the time, most of my compatriots were from rural areas and had never seen a doorman before). Then I advised the German to change out of his uniform immediately.

My translator's mission didn't stop yet, though. Just after the incident with the doorman was over, I heard from the corner of the lobby a loud female voice pronouncing in German, 'Leave me alone, please. I'm fifty and I'm old enough to be your mother...' Then I saw an unfamiliar Soviet soldier, who was embracing the resisting woman. I asked the solder if he understood what she had just said and, without waiting for his answer, I translated her words. This soldier, who was in his mid-twenties, momentarily grew angry, stepped away from the woman, cursed in Russian at the top of his voice, and headed for the exit.

We continued to advance, and at noon our assault detachment approached the bridge across the River Pregel in the central part of the city. From this vantage point, we could see the outlines of two large buildings. Later I learned that these were the Royal Castle and the Königsberg Cathedral. They were prominent works of old architecture, but both now showed heavy damage caused by the Royal Air Force bombing raids in late August 1944 and Soviet bombardments prior to our final assault.

Soon we encountered guardsmen of Colonel Tolstikov's 1st Guards Rifle Division, part of the 11th Guards Army that was advancing from the opposite side of the river. That meeting was one of the crucial events foreseen in the general plan for the battle.[28]

The city was now completely encircled. The 561st Volksgrenadier Division was ripped apart, with most of its survivors left outside the encirclement. Lasch now received a deputation from senior Party officials, requesting radio communication with their absent Gauleiter to organize a breakout. Koch passed their request to Müller, who now modified his instructions to Lasch. The city was to be held at all costs, but weak forces could be used to achieve a breakout to the west.

Lasch then personally contacted Müller and pointed out the unfeasible nature of such instructions. Only a breakout by the remaining forces in the city en masse would have any chance of success. Müller remained obdurate: 'Fortress' Königsberg was to be held to the last man. Weak forces were to restore contact with 561st Volskgrenadier Division, which would attack with parts of 5th Panzer Division. These attacking formations were to proceed no further east than Juditten, out of concerns that they might find themselves trapped in the city if the Red Army counter-attacked.

Lasch now took matters in his own hands and gathered together the strongest force he could, aware that it would in any event be almost impossible to move the remnants of his garrison under the massive bombardment of the Red Army. Generalleutnant Rudolf Sperl, commander of 61st Infantry Division, was to gather what battalions could be spared from his division, together with parts of 548th Volksgrenadier Division and the artillery of 367th Infantry Division. Additional support would come from what remained of the fortress artillery units. It would be the Party's responsibility to assemble and guide the civilians.

Under constant fire, the combat elements struggled to reach their forming-up areas. Meanwhile, the Party ordered civilians to assemble at 0030hrs on 9 April on the western exits from the city without any attempt at coordination with military movements, and without even notifying Lasch that such an order was being given. This mass movement not only blocked the roads needed by Lasch's combat forces, it also gave the Soviet forces advance notice that a breakout was imminent. Massive artillery fire was concentrated on the area, with devastating casualties amongst the massed civilians.

Major Lewinski, commander of one of 61st Infantry Division's regiments, received orders early on 8 April to withdraw his regiment from the frontline and to stand ready to break out towards Pillau from the Rossgarten Market, supported by a battalion of his division's artillery. With constant Soviet fire and probing attacks, such an order was impossible to execute, as the Red Army would have detected the move immediately and would have taken advantage of the regiment's withdrawal to burst through the perimeter. That evening, new orders finally arrived: the remnants of 548th Volksgrenadier Division, 561st Volksgrenadier Division and 61st Infantry Division were to attack south of the Königsberg–Pillau road, break through and secure the road for civilian evacuation, under the overall command of Generalmajor Erich Sudau, commander of 548th Volksgrenadier Division. At the same time, a small force of assault guns and self-propelled flak would attempt to force a way through along the main Pillau road. Five hours after the attempt began at 2300hrs, 5th Panzer Division would attempt to push east from outside the pocket to try to link up with the men trying to break out.

Before the attempt could begin, 561st Volksgrenadier Division's commander, Generalleutnant Sperl, was badly wounded by shellfire. Nevertheless, Lewinski's 192nd Grenadier Regiment, supported by the artillery battalion, was to lead 61st Infantry Division's attack, and made its way under constant fire to the comparative safety of an orphanage next to the Sackheim Tower, one of the old fortifications within the city:

Every battalion had leaders who knew the terrain, but later we discovered that they were useless, as no knowledge was of help in the inferno that central Königsberg had become. There were ghostly moonscapes where large roads had run through the city. Routes that had been reconnoitred were impassable an hour later. The detonations of bombs, mortars and heavy rockets crashed again and again, tumbling the remaining building frontages into the streets and leaving huge craters. Rear-area units, trucks, artillery and assault guns came into this hell from north and south, until they were so tightly wedged together that they could neither move back nor forward. The regiment had to work its way through this inferno, constantly seeking routes, constantly turning back from anti-tank barriers and gigantic craters. Our artillery and support column was in a short time completely stuck, wedged in between trucks of all kinds, its route blocked by new craters and rubble. At 0035, the regimental staff finally reached the ghostly forest that had previously been the Botanical Gardens. Here too, there was a dreadful landscape of craters with shattered and splintered trees… Parts of 548th and 561st Volksgrenadier Divisions were to have set off at midnight from the northern railway station and post office. It wasn't possible to find out whether they had been successful. The Sternwarte bastion lay before us, an old fortification of the inner ring of defences, and immediately to its west was the trench from which we were to make our leap into the unknown. We were greeted with scenes of complete gloom in the bastion. Hundreds of soldiers and officers had gathered in its rooms and passageways, in order to wait for daylight. Here, we came across Hauptmann Berthold, who was nearby with the remnants of 171st Grenadier Regiment and wanted to join up with us. He had only about 150 men left with him.

Meanwhile, the first companies had set off. But it was almost 0200 before most of the regiment reached its start line, and even then whole companies were missing. Major Hartmann from 367th Artillery Regiment had assembled a handful of men, perhaps 30;

his guns were stuck in the city centre. The 61st Infantry Division's Chief of Staff repeatedly pushed for a start, and time too was pressing if we were to break through to Samland under cover of darkness. At about 0200, we set off with the reinforced 1st Battalion on the right and what remained of 171st Regiment on the left. There was a deep railway cutting in front of our trench, the line from the main railway station to the northern station, and we had to cross it. The first Russian lines were swiftly overrun, and we pushed on into the cemeteries that lay behind. Here we encountered the first difficulties. There was flank fire from all sides, with salvoes of Stalin Organs landing on the cemeteries. It was almost impossible to keep a sense of direction in the overgrown landscape with its barbed wire entanglements and only a few paths. The only landmark was a Russian loudspeaker vehicle somewhat to our right, which constantly broadcast its propaganda into the night. The regimental staff was right behind the battalion with an assault company. We encountered only isolated resistance, which we overcame with our assault rifles. Half-right from the regimental staff, one infantry battalion was held up in a heavy firefight. Apparently, the 1st Battalion was too far to the right and had ventured into the housing along the old Pillau road. Messengers that were dispatched did not return, and it seemed that the second wave, which should have been following close behind, had not yet set off. We halted after we had crossed the high wall around the cemetery on our left. Here, we separated from Major Hartmann, who pushed on a little further with his gunners. Shortly after, he found it impossible to advance in this direction and returned to Königsberg with his men.

We had no more contact with the 171st Regiment on our left, only a few submachine-guns chattering here and there, and it wasn't possible to work out where they were. We crossed the railway line, where we came under heavy fire from both sides and had to pull back, even though we originally wanted to press on from there. Our guide, Oberleutnant Dr Käser, was completely lost. So we pushed into a completely devastated factory area, where the enemy's tanks were meant to be forming up, without encountering any opposition.

Suddenly and unexpectedly, we found ourselves on the Holsteiner Damm and the shore of the Pregel. It was already growing light, but we had no choice: on we went along the Holsteiner Damm, heading west. We were now a group of between 40 and 50 men. We had already lost a lot of men in the cemetery. We managed to pass several houses occupied by the Russians without being noticed, until our vanguard came under fire near the grain silo. In a few moments, all hell broke loose. We came under fire from every window, and even from the opposite bank. Shot at from all sides, we managed to reach the end of the row of silos. There, we turned right. We were not able to press on along the Holsteiner Damm, as everyone in the area was now alerted and there was no prospect of us getting through. It was already 0500, and in the misty morning light there was already good visibility.

Finally, we penetrated the flooded swampy ground between Moditten and Gross-Holstein during the following night, after spending the entire day halted in the swamps. Nearby, there was a group of about 20 men with some officers from 171st Regiment, and also a few people from 548th Volksgrenadier Division who had set off before us. The breakout failed, with only a few small groups and a couple of assault guns succeeding in getting through. Shortly after the beginning of the attack, Generalmajor Sudau was killed near the Luisenkirche.[29]

Command and control broke down completely during the confused night as troops and civilians streamed back into the city to escape the hammering shellfire. For a moment, the western defences of the city were completely open, and it was only with difficulty that some semblance of a defensive line was restored.

Kleine and some of his comrades from 367th Infantry Division were also close to the city cemetery, where he almost ran into a Soviet anti-aircraft position. Under heavy fire from the soldiers around the Soviet guns, the Germans made a hasty retreat. Reunited with the staff from his regiment's headquarters, Kleine set off again. Although the shelling had eased a little, it was still dangerous, and Oberst Kassner, Kleine's commander, was hit in the arm by shrapnel. Kleine and his comrades took him to the finance ministry, where a field hospital had been set up. Leaving him there, they made their way to the Dohnaturm, another of the city's old fortresses, now the last headquarters of 367th Infantry Division's 974th Grenadier Regiment 974.[30]

Some groups of Germans attempted to escape from the city in small ad hoc groups. Kobylyanskiy's unit, now based in the ruins of a hospital, came across two soldiers who described such an attempt to their captors:

Their force was a motley group: the remnants of a few combat detachments, plus a few small groups and some individuals who had strayed from their units for a variety of reasons. By the time evening fell, approximately 300 people had gathered there, including several civilians and three women.

Some high-ranking officers took charge of the group. They decided to try and escape by taking the group back through the city by night in order to reach the main road that stretched westward along the bay. They planned to avoid combat and hoped to slip thorough our lines quietly, counting upon traditional Soviet carelessness and our soldiers' deep sleep.

A slowly moving 'Tiger' [Soviet accounts frequently describe all German tanks as 'Tigers', so this should not be taken literally] led the group; a few cars followed it, after which the pedestrians walked in column. At first things went well. They passed our hospital, not even noticing the foxhole where our sentries were sleeping peacefully. Then they passed the location of the regimental headquarters, and had continued on about 300 metres, when the lead tank suddenly fell into a deep bomb crater. The entire column stopped.

Unfortunately for the fleeing group, at that very moment two Soviet artillerymen were making their way to a field gun, which was standing among some shrubs fencing a front yard. They were moving to relieve the sleeping guard. Just as they reached the gun, they saw a car and several German soldiers standing around it some 15 metres away. The two relief sentries quickly woke up the sleeping artillerymen, and the crew of four prepared the gun and fired a shot directly at the car. Panic-stricken Germans broke into a run, and the artillerymen started firing at them with submachine guns. Looking for some cover from the fire, some Germans vaulted fences and ran into yards and houses. Others pressed themselves tightly against a fence, while the majority simply fled. Only a few of the Germans returned fire. The sudden sound of battle woke up many sleeping Soviet soldiers, who joined the artillery crew and opened fire on the disintegrating German column. The Germans retreated back into the forest, leaving behind at least ten corpses in the street.[31]

Kobylyanskiy decided to send the two captured Germans back to their group to persuade them all to surrender, and to return the following morning at 0630hrs, and settled back to enjoy his supper with a plentiful allotment of vodka. At precisely the agreed time, the Germans reappeared, accompanied by about 100 other soldiers. None of them were wearing officers' insignia, though it is possible that officers had removed their rank badges before surrendering.[32]

By dawn on 9 April, Lasch knew that his frontline was disintegrating. His situation map showed how hopeless things were. At the western edge of central Königsberg, what remained of 61st Infantry Division held barely a kilometre of frontline around the Sternwarte bastion. Mikosch's improvised division was in position to the southeast of 61st Infantry Division blocking the way into Steindamm and Lizent, with Schuberth's battered formations continuing the front east along the Pregel. A mixture of Volkssturm and ad hoc groups clung to the rubble around the Lithuanian Tower. In the northeast, much of 367th Infantry Division continued to hold the old but formidable fortifications of the Grolman bastion, with elements of 69th Infantry Division and a hotchpotch of other formations forming the northern perimeter of the city. In the northwest, there was once again no distinct unit, merely an uncoordinated scatter of broken groups.

Before long, fighting degenerated into individual actions; it was pointless to attempt to withdraw to the final inner ring of prepared fortified buildings, as the roads were hopelessly choked with rubble and abandoned vehicles. Wherever strongpoints were able to put up significant resistance, they were simply bypassed, the Soviet soldiers using the ruins as cover. Now it was mainly an infantry battle, with Panzerfaust-equipped defenders also taking advantage of the plentiful cover to get close to attacking Soviet tanks. Nevertheless, there could only be one victor. As the morning drew on, Lasch decided once more to act unilaterally.

Cut off from higher authority and with the fate of the surviving troops, not to mention tens of thousands of civilians, resting heavy on his conscience, Lasch conferred with his staff. Ammunition stocks were exhausted, and there was no possibility of distributing any stores that remained. There was no prospect of outside help. The last news from the outside world had confirmed that Pomerania, Silesia and Brandenburg were in Soviet hands, while Anglo-American forces were across the Rhine and threatening Hannover. Further loss of life was pointless. The division commanders who had managed to reach his headquarters agreed, and Oberstleutnant Kerwien, commander of the troops defending the nearby frontline, was ordered to deliver a written message to the Soviet forces facing him, requesting that they contact their high command to arrange a ceasefire. A radio message was also sent to OKH.

Meanwhile, fighting raged on. Hans Gerlach, a reservist officer, was in the old castle in the heart of the city, and he retreated into the cellars with a band of diehards. Completely isolated and unaware of any ceasefire arrangements, they fought on. Two officers attempted to make a dash out of the rubble to find out what was happening elsewhere, and disappeared without trace into the hail of Soviet fire. Finally, at 0100hrs on 10 April, the remaining defenders surrendered.

In the south, resistance by the remnants of Schuberth's police battalions was also coming to an end. Oberführer Horst Böhme, the commander of the East Prussian Sicherheitsdienst (SD; Security Service, the intelligence arm of the police and SS), was now the commander of an ad-hoc SS regiment. When he learned that Lasch had ordered a surrender, he announced that the fortress commander was immediately removed from his post. Generalmajor Schuberth was now declared the new fortress commandant. Schuberth was not enthusiastic about this new development, and told his staff that he regarded himself as unsuited for this role. He nominated the commander of 31st Police Regiment, Major Voigt, as fortress commandant, and subordinated himself to the major.

Voigt accepted the nomination and ordered the remaining troops of the battlegroup to continue fighting. As Soviet forces continued to press on, bypassing some strongpoints, overwhelming others, Voigt ordered a withdrawal by all forces to the castle, where they would mount a last stand. Soviet infantry had already moved into the streets between the survivors of the police battlegroup and the castle, and the retreating groups now had to fight their way through. In small groups, perhaps 150 men managed to reach the castle, carrying only their personal weapons, which were almost out of ammunition. The attacking Soviet forces were also aware that the castle might be used as a final point of resistance, and they now hammered it with artillery. As losses mounted, Voigt decided to abandon the castle, and at midnight the remaining combatants set off in small groups, hoping to infiltrate their way through Soviet lines to reach German lines in Samland. This was a hopeless attempt, and none of the groups succeeded. Voigt himself disappeared into the devastated city without trace, presumably killed. Oberführer Böhme, the SD commander, tried to cross the Pregel in a boat, was shot, fell into the water, and drowned.

Schuberth, together with the police Chief of Staff, Oberstleutnant Peschke, the police operations officer, Major Denninghaus, and a few other members of the staff managed to reach some bunkers near Juditten, where they took cover and paused to consider what to do next. Suddenly, they heard Soviet soldiers approaching. The occupants of one of the bunkers were called upon to surrender or be killed, and the men emerged, their hands raised. Schuberth, Peschke and Denninghaus were in a second bunker. They, too, were ordered to come out. There was no response, and the waiting Soviet soldiers hurled hand grenades into the bunker. Schuberth had previously made it clear that he had no intention of allowing himself to be taken prisoner. The bunker entrance was firmly barricaded and it wasn't possible for the Soviet infantrymen to force their way in. Whether the German officers had already left the bunker, or whether they died in the hail of shrapnel from the exploding grenades, cannot be determined. None of them were seen again.

From his position west of the city, Major Lewinski, whose group had succeeded in slipping through the lines of the Soviet encirclement, watched the end of the siege:

Now it was day, we saw behind us the dying city. Covered in its mantle of smoke and fire, it was lit up by the flashes of heavy shells that were still landing. At 1700, the firing died down. There were still occasional bursts of machine-gun fire from a few positions, but eventually even these last signs of fighting died away. As dusk fell, the black clouds of smoke, lit by the unholy red glow of numerous fires, covered the dead city.[33]

One by one, the remaining pockets of resistance laid down their weapons, or were overwhelmed. In some cases, isolated garrisons disagreed about what to do. The remnants of Major Vollmer's East Prussian Technical Police Battalion were the last defenders of the 'Pregel Bastion'. The junior officers wanted to continue resistance, but their commander could see no point in further fighting, and ordered a surrender.

Late in the evening, Oberstleutnant Kerwien, who had been ordered to contact the Soviet forces, returned to Lasch's headquarters with a group of Soviet officers. They explained that they had come to agree terms of surrender, which were in keeping with previous announcements. Those who laid down their weapons would be assured that they would receive adequate supplies; there would be medical treatment for the wounded and aid for civilians; and there would be a speedy return home after the end of the war. Lasch accepted these terms willingly. He later wrote that he had no inkling that these terms would not be honoured, which seems remarkable given the way that both the Germans and their Soviet enemies had treated prisoners throughout the war.

The first sign of what lay ahead came as Lasch and his staff marched away from their headquarters. Almost immediately, Soviet soldiers attempted to rob them of their watches and other possessions. The Red Army officers accompanying the German prisoners did little or nothing to intervene. The same occurred wherever German soldiers were taken prisoner. Now the fighting was over, other Soviet soldiers took advantage of the official permission granted to them to spend two days plundering the devastated city, even as their erstwhile foes were led away:

The houses burned and smoked. Soft furnishings, musical instruments, cooking utensils, paintings, china – all were thrown out of the houses. Smashed vehicles stood between burning tanks, clothing, equipment lay everywhere. Amongst this danced drunken Russians, shooting wildly, searching for bicycles to ride, falling over and lying by the kerbstones with bloody injuries. Weeping girls and women were dragged into the houses despite their resistance. Children cried out for their parents. It was unbearable. We marched on. We saw scenes that cannot be described. The ditches by the sides of the streets were full of corpses, many of them clearly showing signs of unbelievable maltreatment and rape. Dead children lay around in great numbers, bodies hung from the trees, their watches cut off. Staring-eyed German women were led in all directions, drunken Russians flogged a German nun, an elderly woman sat by the side of the road, both of her legs having been crushed by vehicles. Farmsteads burned, the household belongings lying in the roads, cows ran across the countryside, and were indiscriminately shot and left lying. Cries for help from German people came to us constantly. We could not help. Women came out of the houses, hands raised beseechingly – the Russians chased them back and shot them if they didn't hurry. It was dreadful. We had never imagined such things.

Nobody had boots any more, many were barefoot. The untended wounded groaned with pain. Hunger and thirst were the greatest torments. Russian soldiers assailed the platoon from all sides. They took away coats from some, caps from others, the odd briefcase with its meagre contents. Everyone wanted something. 'Watches, watches,' they called, and we were left defenceless against this banditry.[34]

When the German 6th Army surrendered in Stalingrad in early 1943, buildings used as collecting centres for wounded – the encircled Germans had long since run out of sufficient medical supplies to justify the title of 'hospital' for such buildings – were unceremoniously set on fire by the Red Army. Similar events occurred in Königsberg. Those who managed to stagger from the buildings were often simply shot.

Bodo Kleine found himself stripped of his officer insignia, his boots and even his socks. His watch had been given to him by his godmother on the occasion of his confirmation; rather than allow one of the looting Soviet soldiers to get it, he removed it and hurled it to one of the Russian women who watched as he and his comrades marched past. Fortunately, another soldier had a spare pair of poor-quality shoes, which he now gave to Kleine. Shortly after being taken prisoner, he was led away from the main column and found himself in a building with four or five other officers. Their guards loaded their guns and prepared to shoot, but a Red Army officer intervened at the last moment to prevent their execution.[35]

When he learned that the prisoners were being systematically robbed, Lasch made urgent representations to Vassilevsky, who to his credit tried to have their belongings restored to them. Such an attempt proved to be little more than a gesture. Vassilevsky may have felt that the officially sanctioned looting of the city was a different matter from robbing prisoners of war, but such fine distinctions were lost on his troops. They descended on their victims with a mixture of relief at their own survival and anger at their losses, fuelled by plentiful alcohol and the ongoing effects of Soviet propaganda.

On the first morning of the Soviet occupation of Königsberg, von Lehndorff visited the wounded in the cellar of the building where he had been working. Soviet soldiers had already visited, taking watches and beating up a Russian woman who helped in the hospital. Matters slowly worsened:

In the ambulance, the young nurses defended themselves against a few particularly intrusive individuals. I didn't dare imagine what would happen when they grew more confident. Now, they were still clearly in haste and concerned with loot. Particularly striking were our storage buildings. I stood speechless before the heaps of foodstuffs there, which had been withheld from us during the months of siege, and thought back in anger at my naivety, at how we and our patients had gone hungry the whole time. Now there was a wild, howling mess, as the finest tinned produce and supplies, which could have kept hundreds alive for a whole year, were destroyed in a few hours.

Doktora was in the operating theatre, bandaging patients. A swarm of nurses had fled here and eagerly pretended to help. In the background, the Russians moved through the wounded soldiers, searching for watches and usable boots. One of them, a young chap, suddenly burst into tears, because he had still not found a watch. He held up three fingers: he would shoot three men unless he was given a watch immediately ... finally a watch appeared from somewhere, with which he disappeared, beaming with joy.

The appearance of the first officers destroyed my last hopes of a bearable outcome. All attempts to speak to them were completely in vain. For them, too, we were no more than dressed clothes dummies with pockets. They only saw me from the shoulders down. A couple of nurses who were in their path were seized and dragged along behind them, and before they could comprehend what was going on, they were released, completely dishevelled. They wandered around the passageways aimlessly. There was nowhere to hide. And new trouble came upon them constantly.[36]

Many German accounts – particularly those inspired by Goebbels – spoke of the terror unleashed upon German civilians, especially women, by Soviet soldiers from the eastern parts of the Soviet Union, the so-called 'Mongols'. Von Lehndorff recorded in his diary that these soldiers were actually better disciplined than those from the western provinces of the Soviet Union, but his best hope for protecting his staff came when a Red Army major appeared in the operating theatre and demanded that a tiny wart be excised from his face. At gunpoint, von Lehndorff carried out the operation, to the delight of the major, who then provided protection for the terrified nurses and wounded through the night. The following day, however, as alcohol began to flow, matters took a darker turn. At first, there were screams from neighbouring buildings as Soviet soldiers hunted down women; there were even cries of 'Shoot me!' from the desperate victims of multiple rapes. But as the ordeal continued, von Lehndorff recorded that it was as if something died in the souls of the victims as their strength to resist was exhausted, and the screams were replaced by hysterical laughter. Doktora, who had intervened repeatedly to protect her nurses, was raped in the operating theatre.

Erika Morgenstern, her mother and her younger sister had endured the siege in a cellar, like so many others in Königsberg. As the fighting died down and was replaced by an eerie silence, she slowly made her way to the entrance to the cellar:

Just when I had reached the heavy iron door, it was opened by a hefty kick and crashed against the cellar wall. What now happened, both in thought and events, took just a few seconds. Before me was a figure, the likes of which I had never seen before, pointing a machine-gun at me. A monster from the darkest fairy tale, I thought, and for the first time began to scream in terror for my life. I had simply never seen anything like this: the unfamiliar headdress (which all soldiers who drove in tanks wore), the stitched jacket, all quite filthy, and finally the face that glared at me with hate-filled eyes. I screamed and trembled. The Russian soldier then … spoke calming words: 'Nix Angst, nix Angst', and the look from his still hostile eyes became milder.

Later, I often thought back to this first encounter. With what fear must the soldier have kicked open the cellar door? He must have assumed that behind it were German soldiers, partisans, everything that would have meant death to him. And instead, what did he have before his machine-gun? An innocent blonde girl, whom he had scared to death. He could have opened fire on us and killed us all, but he didn't.[37]

It is estimated that between 30,000 and 35,000 German soldiers, 15,000 foreign workers and more than 100,000 civilians were in the city when it surrendered.[38] About 42,000 died during the Soviet assault, most as a result of the tremendous aerial and artillery bombardment. The number of Soviet casualties is difficult to determine. Many German accounts give an estimate of about 60,000 dead and wounded, but this seems a huge number, given the German shortage of ammunition. The total number of Soviet tanks and assault guns damaged or destroyed was put at 195.[39] A post-war memorial erected in honour of the dead of 11th Guards Army in the fighting for the southern part of the city commemorated 1,200 dead, and General Belobodorov estimated the losses of his 43rd Army at about 1,100. But from a strictly military viewpoint, the achievement of Vassilevsky's men was considerable. They successfully assaulted a heavily fortified city, whose garrison had been preparing for such a battle for many weeks. The massive Soviet superiority in artillery was used to the full, but nevertheless the city blocks still had to be taken one by one by infantrymen.

Even as the guns fell silent, the repercussions of the fall of Königsberg were beginning. Hitler was furious that the garrison had surrendered rather than fight to the last drop of blood, and the Wehrmacht report of 12 April reflected this:

After several days of attacks, Fortress Königsburg has been surrendered to the Bolshevists by the Fortress Commandant, General Lasch. Despite this, elements of the loyal garrison, broken into several battlegroups, continue to offer bitter resistance to the Bolshevists. As a consequence of his cowardly surrender to the enemy, General Lasch has been sentenced to death by hanging by a military court.[40]

Unable to reach Lasch, the vengeful authorities turned on his family. His wife and eldest daughter, who were in Denmark, were separated from Lasch's three small grandchildren and imprisoned. Fortunately for them, the local German commandant was more humane, and did everything he could to alleviate their plight for what remained of the war. Lasch's younger daughter was working at OKH, and was also arrested and held in Potsdam. Orders arrived for her removal to the infamous Gestapo headquarters on Prinz Albrecht Strasse in Berlin. Again, fortune intervened, this time when the prison superintendent refused to allow the transfer on the grounds that he had no female staff for such a move. Lasch's son-in-law, commanding a battalion in the frontline, was also recalled and arrested. He too survived his brief spell in captivity.

For General Müller, based in Pillau, the fall of Königsberg was a personal blow. The garrison had technically been part of his command, and although he had slavishly followed the Führer's instructions, demanding that the garrison fight on to the bitter end, he too was removed from office. The departure of this unpopular and singularly unsuccessful commander was greeted with relief amongst the formations under his command. After the war, he was tried for war crimes, and executed by the Greeks for atrocities committed under his command in Crete.

One of the more unusual survivors of the siege was Hans the hippo, who together with a deer, a badger and a donkey had lived through the bombardment and ground assault in the city zoo, or Tiergarten. Hans was found in a ditch in the Tiergarten, with several bullet wounds. Vladimir Petrovich Polonsky, a veterinary technician, took Hans under his care, and administered a terrifying regime of shredded vegetables, copious quantities of vodka (up to a literally staggering 4 litres a day) and frequent enemas. As a result of, or perhaps in spite of, this unusual treatment, Polonsky announced after about seven weeks that his patient had made a full recovery, and that he was now training the hippo to allow itself to be ridden around the zoo. Hans continued to live in the city for 30 years; his survival and subsequent prosperity contrasted starkly with other survivors of the siege, who faced a grim future at the hands of the Soviet occupiers.

CHAPTER 13
DANZIG

Danzig was German, Danzig remains German, and Danzig will henceforth remain German so long as the German people and the German Reich exist.

– Adolf Hitler[1]

Even as the Soviet rings around Heiligenbeil and Königsberg were closing, Rokossovsky's forces were seeking to complete their control of the Baltic coast. As has already been described, the powerful surge across Pomerania had almost completed this objective, but there remained the city of Danzig.

By the end of the war, Danzig was an important port, both for commerce and its shipyards. The neighbouring Polish city of Gdynia, or Gotenhafen as it had been renamed, was also of great value to the German war economy. Goebbels was delighted and relieved to note in his diary in November 1939 that the city had been comparatively unscathed during the brief German campaign against Poland, and that the shipyards in particular were in excellent condition.[2] The problem of the city's Polish population was settled by Albert Forster, Gauleiter of Danzig–West Prussia, in characteristic National Socialist fashion: those who could not demonstrate any claims on German nationality were summarily expelled and deported to the General Government.[3] The almost empty streets of Gotenhafen were then used to settle ethnic Germans from the Baltic states, brought 'home to the Reich' as part of the Molotov–Ribbentrop Pact. Now, as the rumble and thunder of the frontline approached the coast, the population of Danzig and Gotenhafen – hugely swollen by refugees from East Prussia and the Vistula valley – began to give thought to further flight.

Ever since Rokossovsky smashed 2nd Army's positions on the Narew in mid January, Weiss had struggled to rebuild a continuous frontline for his army. When the fighting reached the Vistula bend in the Thorn–Bromberg area, he was finally able to achieve this, establishing a fragile line. This was partly due to the arrival of reinforcements, such as 4th Panzer Division, from Courland and elsewhere, and partly due to Rokossovsky's diversion of forces towards Elbing. Hossbach's ultimately doomed attempt to break out from East Prussia towards Elbing further diverted the attentions of 2nd Belorussian Front, particularly Rokossovsky's air support. Nevertheless, the new frontline was flimsy in the extreme. Many divisions had lost much of their heavy equipment during their retreat, and others had been badly mauled in the initial Soviet assault. These losses meant that the lack of anti-tank firepower in German divisions was now critical, and the losses in personnel resulted in the divisions holding extended frontlines well beyond their strength. The 4th Panzer Division provided some welcome firepower, but the delay in bringing the division's original Panther tanks from Courland left it hamstrung, and despite his best intentions Weiss was unable to allow the division to concentrate its resources.

The biggest danger for 2nd Army lay on its flanks. The other units of Army Group Vistula proved unable to hold back the joint assault by 1st and 2nd Belorussian Fronts into Pomerania, thus creating a constant menace to Weiss' right flank. At the same time, the powerful forces of 2nd Shock Army, operating just to the west of the Vistula, constantly threatened to break through along the most direct route to Danzig. Throughout February, 2nd Army attempted to create mobile reserves – 4th SS-Polizei Panzergrenadier Division around Dirschau and Preussisch Stargard, and 4th and 7th Panzer Divisions further west – to deal with these twin dangers. But even if these divisions had been able to concentrate all of their strength, rather than having to loan out armour to their neighbouring infantry divisions, they would have lacked the punch to have a decisive effect. In any event, SS-Polizei was shuffled from one wing to the other in an ultimately futile attempt to shore up the line. The two Panzer divisions were able to halt the Red Army wherever they were committed, and their counter-attacks were often successful, but all too frequently such counter-attacks were abandoned as new crises erupted elsewhere.

The multiple breakthroughs to the Baltic coast in Pomerania dealt a further huge blow to Weiss. His army was now cut off from the rest of the fast-shrinking Reich. Some 7,000 tonnes of munitions and other supplies had built up around Stettin, destined for 2nd Army, but with the rail line now severed it would have to be shipped by sea. The bombing raids on Swinemünde killed mainly refugees, but they also disrupted the local rail network and damaged the port itself, making it an unsuitable point for the dispatch of supplies to the east. The supplies would have to travel to Lübeck and Stralsund. Such a move took time, and further time was lost while shipping was organized. In the meantime, 2nd Army had to survive on its almost exhausted stockpiles. For a brief time after the Soviet breakthrough to the coast, there was a particular moment of opportunity for the Red Army – with 2nd Army effectively without supplies, its ability to manoeuvre and deal with the permanent rupture of its western flank was greatly limited. If Rokossovsky's forces could move quickly enough,

The IS-2, photographed here in Berlin at the end of the war, was a powerful tank, but its 122mm gun had a slow rate of fire and limited penetrating power. Only 28 rounds of ammunition were carried, limiting its effectiveness.

The Il-2, known in the Soviet Union as *Sturmovik*, was almost invulnerable to small-arms fire and provided the Red Army with invaluable air support. Although its relative lack of manoeuvrability made it vulnerable in air-to-air combat, the weakness of the Luftwaffe in the closing months of the war meant that they were able to operate almost without fear of being attacked by German fighters.

The Polykarpov PO-2, known to the Germans as the 'Nähmaschine' (sewing machine) or 'UvD' (Unteroffizier von Dienst, or Duty NCO), did little damage in night raids, but was an immense nuisance. Its pilots would switch off their engines and glide during their bombing run; the small bombs thus often fell without warning.

The destroyed bridge at Nemmersdorf after the battle, late 1944, with a knocked-out Soviet tank.

Above: Two Panthers in Memel, photographed in December 1944.

Left: A 16-year-old is sworn into the Volkssturm in Insterburg, December 1944.

Volkssturm: a youth and an elderly man armed with Panzerfausts in a defensive position in April 1945.

Street-fighting in Königsberg, April 1945.

Above and left: Soviet artillery is photographed in action while the Soviet forces cautiously penetrate into Danzig, March 1945.

As the Red Army advanced into East Prussia in January–February 1945, refugees took to the frozen roads. Thousands perished in the cold, or when they were caught up in the fighting.

German refugees are seen here fleeing across the frozen Frisches Haff in February 1945.

T-34s and Soviet forces advancing towards Königsberg, February 1945.

German officers march into captivity after the surrender of Königsberg, April 1945.

his spearheads might reach Danzig and Gotenhafen before Weiss could pull back his western flank and protect the cities from the west. At the very least, the almost immobile German armour might be overrun in the relatively open ground west of the cities, before it could retreat into the girdle of hills and forests that lay just outside the suburbs.

The severance of land contact with the Reich also had serious consequences for the hundreds of thousands of refugees around Danzig and Gotenhafen. Some had endured the long journey from the furthest parts of East Prussia, and were reluctant to take to the road again, but faced with the imminent arrival of the Red Army, others headed west. Some successfully reached the Oder before Zhukov and Rokossovsky broke through to the Pomeranian coast, but large numbers found the route cut. Some, as already described, found themselves pressed back to the last coastal enclaves, while most simply turned and headed back east towards Danzig. The weather, which had intermittently allowed for a thaw, suddenly turned cold again, and the entire region was once more blanketed with a heavy snowfall. The roads around Danzig rapidly became choked – with snow, with retreating German frontline units, with the multitude of rear-area formations, and with thousands of exhausted, hopeless refugees.

Rokossovsky's memoirs predictably give a somewhat different account of the refugee problem:

> We were also terribly handicapped by refugees. The Goebbels' propaganda machine had hammered such slanders about the Soviet troops in the Germans' heads that at the first rumour of our advance people fled their homes in terror with their chattels, alone and in families. The Autobahns and byroads teemed with people, trudging to the west and to the east. The roads were, furthermore, littered with abandoned enemy equipment, and our troops had to make their way through the chaos.
>
> Soon, though, the refugees discovered that no-one molested them, that the Goebbels' propaganda was nothing but lies and, reassured, turned back to their homes, again crowding along the roads, this time in the opposite direction.[4]

Some Germans had prudently departed for the west before the railway lines were cut. On 22 January, Waltraud Foth learned from her sister, Annemarie Gerlach, that women with young children who had families in the west were permitted to depart immediately. Her husband Tom, who had been killed in Bialystok in 1944, had spoken to her as early as 1942 about what she should do if she and the children, Erika and Irmchen, had to flee their homes, as Annemarie Gerlach recorded:

'If you ever have to flee, fill the children's knapsacks with Coca-Cola chocolate, because you can last all day on one block.' (For years, he had saved the chocolate from his airman's rations and sent it home.) 'Take only the most essential things with you. Take a rucksack, and keep your hands free to hold onto the children.'

As the girls had grown a lot since then, Erika carried a small bag in addition to her knapsack and Irmchen had a small briefcase… Waltraud stitched valuable documents and photos into a linen pouch, which she always wore on her body. After packing, they all put on two sets of underwear and clothes. That very evening, we loaded all their things onto a sledge and went to the Oliva railway station. Although it was already dark, there was a lot of noise and turmoil there.

Drunks roared and staggered across the platform. After a long wait, a local train finally appeared and took us to Danzig. Waltraud had telephoned the wife of the railway chief … and had asked her to ask her husband how best to get from Danzig to Berlin. After speaking to her husband, Frau Steinke phoned back and said: 'My husband will wait for you at 0500 on Platform Three in Danzig.' As it was only 2200 when we reached Danzig, we went to the home of the Classings, our brother's parents-in-law, who lived opposite Danzig railway station.

… At 0430, we went to Danzig railway station. The scenes there were discouraging. Thousands of refugees streamed onto Platform Two and stormed an incoming passenger train. It wasn't possible to get aboard. We waited at the arranged place for the railway chief. When Herr Stenke finally came, he merely said, 'Please come with me.' He led us to a completely dark platform, which was sealed off by the SS. Here was a completely empty train. Herr Steinke opened a carriage door, saying, 'Please go aboard. The SS and Gestapo are using this train to take their women and children to safety!' Waltraud and the children went into a completely empty compartment. I helped them stow their luggage and left them… It wasn't long after, that the train set off. I waved to them for a long time.

Then I stood alone on the dark platform and stared after the train in which Waltraud and her two small girls were travelling into the unknown. Would I ever see them again?[5]

SS-Polizei had been driven north from Rummelsburg, but much of the division managed to regroup around Lauenburg. Standartenführer Harzer struggled to reorganize his division on the refugee-choked roads:

I decided on the appropriate use of the heavy flak guns and ordered their commander to withdraw from his positions on the west edge of the town when the other units of the division, including the rearguard, had passed through. As had been the case a few days before in Stolp, trains once more ran all night, carrying people and equipment towards

Danzig. By dawn on 10 March, there were only a few people to be seen in the town; it was now that there were the first signs of enemy activity, with Russian tank groups attempting to use the more northerly retreat road to try to outflank the division's rearguard. The refugee columns that were withdrawing on the neighbouring roads were recklessly overwhelmed, the defenceless people gunned down by tank guns. The result was wild panic. The flak batteries deployed once more and engaged the T-34s with good effect. Several tanks were set ablaze or left immobile.

… But in this action, the flak too had some casualties and lost some guns. I made contact with the Neustadt Kampfkommandant. He had a few flak batteries from the RAD [Reichsarbeitsdienst, or Reich Labour Service] and some local troops at his disposal, a real mishmash. I allotted him my own replacement battalion, as Neustadt would have to serve as a covering position for the division's rearguard. The rearguard fought bitterly all day on 10 March to hold off the numerically far stronger Russian tank forces.[6]

DANZIG–GOTENHAFEN

Unit headquarters are shown in their positions of 11 March

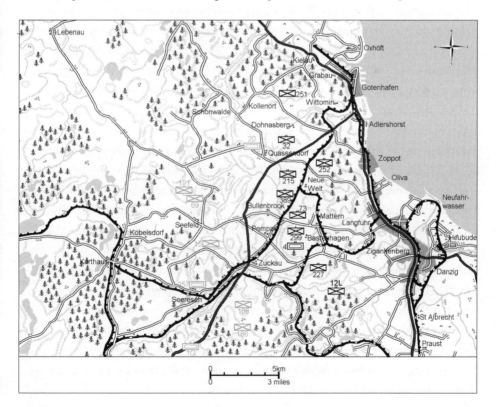

However, Rokossovsky's armies too had their difficulties. The drive to the Pomeranian coast was launched after a minimum period of preparation, and there hadn't been sufficient time to stockpile supplies to ensure the sort of continuation of advance that had occurred after the breakout from the Narew bridgeheads. Batov's 65th Army, like its neighbours, was showing signs of wear; he noted that none of his divisions had more than 40 per cent of their establishment strength, and rear-area units were ruthlessly stripped of personnel, who were transferred to the fighting formations.[7] One factor that worked hugely to the advantage of Rokossovsky's armies was the rapidly narrowing front. At the start of the drive into Pomerania, 2nd Belorussian Front held over 200km of frontline; now, it was reduced to less than 70km. Each army was responsible for less than 15km of front, allowing a concentration of force that the Germans simply couldn't match.

The sudden deterioration in the weather grounded much of Rokossovsky's aerial reconnaissance, and to a large extent the Red Army remained unaware of the supply crisis that had hit 2nd Army. Nevertheless, Rokossovsky was keen to destroy as much of 2nd Army as possible before it could take up positions that might turn the battle for Danzig into a major urban conflict. He urged his formations to keep up the momentum of their advance, particularly Panfilov's III Guards Tank Corps. After reaching the Baltic coast, Panfilov's tanks pressed east, overrunning attempts by the retreating debris of the German units to set up a defensive line. But although 19th Army made every effort to keep up with Panfilov's corps, the tanks were in danger of becoming isolated from their infantry support. For Rokossovsky's staff, the first priority was to drive to the Bay of Danzig from the west, aiming to reach the coast at Zoppot, between Danzig and Gotenhafen. This would break 2nd Army into two, and each city could then be reduced in turn. Tentatively, the timetable called for the drive to Zoppot to commence on 14 March. Heavy artillery would be moved to the coast as soon as possible in an attempt to neutralize the ability of German warships to intervene. Mikhail Katukov's 1st Guards Tank Army, temporarily assigned to Rokossovsky's Front from Zhukov's 1st Belorussian Front, and 19th Army would then secure Gotenhafen and the Putziger Nehrung, while 49th and 65th Armies reduced Danzig.

As with Königsberg, the Red Army was wary about assaulting what it regarded as a formidably fortified area. But unlike the East Prussian capital, Danzig's defences were relatively limited. A line of forested hills protected the city from the west, but Danzig did not have the chain of massive forts that surrounded Königsberg. Gotenhafen, too, had very limited defences, little more than the obstacles dug in the last few weeks. Nevertheless, both sides knew from bitter experience that urban warfare was always a potentially costly exercise.

The senior officers of 7th Panzer Division had already decided that such bloodshed was to be avoided. Generalleutnant Mauss, the division commander, had made no secret of his dislike of the Party during the fighting around Elbing, and with the memories of the division's time in the city of Memel still fresh, thoughts turned to the immediate future. With the agreement of General von Kessel, commander of VII Panzer Corps, Mauss created Corps-Group Mauss, consisting of his own division, 32nd Infantry Division, and 4th SS-Polizei Panzergrenadier Division. This structure effectively put all of the corps' units under his command, leaving only a few attached units and rear-area formations under corps command. The biggest advantage of this reorganization was that Mauss and the commanders of the other two divisions were now in regular and close contact, something that Hitler had tried to prevent for many years, insisting on a strict vertical line of command. Coordination between the divisions improved greatly as a result. Such willingness to bend the rules to circumvent Hitler's authority would have been unthinkable even a few months before.

During the siege of Memel, 7th Panzer Division had established a 'personnel office' in East Prussia, to which it had assigned, for example, tank crews for whom replacement vehicles were not available. This prevented the crews from being redeployed as infantry, and Mauss now resolved to do the same. Two officers were dispatched in early March to Gotenhafen to prepare for the embarkation of surplus division personnel, and to contact OKH to prepare for the complete withdrawal of the division. An inner staff operated within division headquarters, quietly making all the necessary arrangements. The first party of 190 men left for Swinemünde shortly after.

As they struggled east, the men of 7th Panzer Division became increasingly aware that there was no longer a coherent frontline. German units were trying to withdraw east, and the Soviet advance had degenerated into a host of spearheads. In these chaotic conditions, encounters could occur at any moment:

It was shortly before midday on 5 March. The fleeing columns slowly but tenaciously continued along the road to the east, towards Gotenhafen and Danzig.

There were two columns next to each other, the motorized vehicles and our tanks on the left, the horse-drawn wagons of the Wehrmacht and the civilian population on the right, but both heading in the same direction – eastwards. Occasionally, a horse-drawn wagon tried to make better progress by pulling into the motorized column, resulting in traffic jams which had to be cleared.

There was still snow, but at midday it began to thaw, it was already growing pleasantly warm. March!

... About two kilometres to our left, I saw a road running parallel, full of horse-drawn vehicles. They were therefore our own, not Russian, as they would have been motorized.

Then, on the other road, from the east, in the opposite direction to the column, Russian tanks drove up, and smashed through the column. We identified them as T-34/85s. The distance was too great, we heard nothing, only saw how the horses reared up, people ran to the sides, watched how the wagons were pushed and crushed by the tanks, how people fell from the wagons under machine-gun fire. This was how the Red Army did things – it was terrible!

We were really shocked, because we couldn't fire. We would just have endangered the civilians over there and of course over here by our own column, as the Russians would have fired back.

The tanks smashed through everything, crashing over the refugee wagons and heading west. Everything happened very quickly, and then the tank unit disappeared from view.

After this dreadful show our column doggedly continued. Suddenly I saw three soldiers, wearing earth-brown uniforms and civilian clothes, running amongst our vehicles. They carried Russian submachine-guns with drum magazines attached – a small scouting group! When they saw our tank, they disappeared between the vehicles to the south side, beyond the horse-drawn wagons.

Although I was not sure if these small, inconspicuous people were the enemy, Hans Kalb shouted:

'There! Look! Russians! How can they run amongst us like that, shoot them all, the damned dogs! Shoot!'

But he saw that the Russians had already taken cover on the other side. Then he said, 'It's come to this, that the Russians run around amongst us, and we can't do anything about it!'[8]

Although the retreating elements of 7th Panzer Division had sufficient fuel to remain mobile, other units were in a worse state. A group of 50 assault guns, newly arrived in Gotenhafen, was ordered to Neustadt, where it was to come under the command of 7th Panzer Division. The Hauptmann in charge of the unit presented himself to Mauss, who must have been delighted to receive such reinforcements; however, the assault guns were almost out of fuel, having been ordered to obtain fresh supplies from 7th Panzer Division. Angrily, Mauss ordered him to destroy the assault guns to prevent them falling into Soviet hands.

Meanwhile, more pointless orders emanated from Berlin. On 7 March, a message reached the frontline:

The Führer has ordered: whoever allows himself to be taken prisoner without being wounded or demonstrably fighting to the very end, loses all sense of honour. The brotherhood of decent and brave soldiers distances itself from him. His colleagues are responsible for him. All pay and supplies are forfeit. This is to be made known immediately.[9]

For the soldiers on the frontline, the reality was that they would go to almost any lengths to avoid becoming prisoners of the Red Army. Mauss decided not to pass the edict down the chain of command, a decision mirrored in many other divisions.

On 7 March, 4th Panzer Division was ordered to move with all speed to intercept Soviet forces advancing east along the Baltic coast. Roads choked with civilian traffic made rapid movement impossible, as did the crippling fuel shortage. Only diesel fuel was available in large quantities, and every diesel truck was soon towing up to four petrol-powered vehicles in a desperate attempt to keep the division mobile, and to preserve the precious stock of petrol for the division's tanks. Only the 4th Armoured Reconnaissance Battalion was able to move with ease – many of its armoured cars used diesel, and its personnel had located a stockpile of 17,000 litres of potato alcohol spirit. With minimal alterations, the battalion's petrol-powered tanks and half-tracks were able to use this as a petrol substitute.

The division's tanks and a battalion of Panzergrenadiers in half-tracks were loaded onto trains and slowly moved towards their new deployments, held up by large snowdrifts. Then a brief message arrived: Damerkow was in Soviet hands. Oberst Christern, the Panzer regiment commander, consulted his maps and found two villages bearing this name. Even more worryingly, one of them lay directly in the path of the train. Radio silence had been ordered to prevent the Red Army from detecting the redeployment of 4th Panzer Division, leaving Christern unable to ask for further information. Accompanied by Hans Schäufler, his signals officer, Christern proceeded towards Damerkow in his command vehicle. Some distance short of the village, they ran into Soviet troops, and were only saved by the swift arrival of three tanks from the train.

We gave a brief situation and location report by radio to 4th Panzer Division, which was no longer under radio silence; it was clear that the enemy was already in Damerkow.

The response was an 'urgent radio message': 'New situation. Soviet tanks attacking Karthaus. Immediate preparations for movement. Fight through to Karthaus immediately!'[10]

While 4th Panzer Division was struggling to move north to deal with the threat from the west, Batov's 65th Army drove forward swiftly through the area that the German division had just vacated, and thrust directly northeast towards Danzig and Gotenhafen.

The leading Soviet units were now east of 4th Panzer Division, between it and the ports on the coast. In the circumstances, despite the parlous fuel stocks, Christern had no alternative but to unload his vehicles from the train and set out for Karthaus by road. At first, the road was deserted, but the advancing vehicles soon came across refugees, some trying to head west and north, others heading in the opposite direction. Finally, Christern was forced to send his tanks across country, as the roads were completely choked, while he pressed on towards Karthaus with a small reconnaissance group.

Karthaus itself was in turmoil, with thousands of refugees milling about aimlessly. The local combat commandant, an elderly reservist Oberst, was relieved to hand over control to Christern. The energetic Panzer officer immediately deployed his reconnaissance vehicles as a defensive screen to the south of Karthaus, and rounded up all the officers and NCOs he could find amidst the tangle of rear-area formations. They were ordered to impose control over the roads, and the civilian traffic was directed into side-roads that ran north and east. The local telephone network was still functioning, allowing Christern to establish a local command network.

Bad news arrived by radio: the tanks that were following Christern had reached the village of Mooswalde, some 15km to the west of Karthaus, but were now completely out of fuel. Even more alarmingly, Soviet forces were reported to the east, between Karthaus and Danzig. Fortunately, a local man now came forward. He was the owner of a local garage, and he handed over four barrels of precious petrol to the army. Two half-tracks delivered them to the stranded tanks, which then resumed their journey.

The leading tanks reached Karthaus on 8 March, many running out of fuel as soon as they arrived. Oberst Christern had them dragged into defensive positions around the outskirts. A small group of tanks that was still mobile was dispatched east to Seeresen, where they surprised a Soviet unit and drove it out of the village. The tanks pushed on and secured Borkau, too, but could go no further without more fuel. A reconnaissance platoon continued east to Zuckau, where another group of Soviet soldiers had been spotted, and took the town in a swift surprise attack. But further operations were impossible, and the helpless vehicles stranded in the string of villages could only watch as further Soviet units bypassed them and continued northwards to Kobelsdorf and Seefeld.

The crush of refugees in Karthaus continued to build over the next day, as Schäufler recorded:

On the roads and tracks in and around Karthaus, there was complete pandemonium on 9 March. The terrified people could barely understand us. The people of West Prussia from the Tuchel, Konitz, and Berent areas wanted to take the direct road to Danzig and couldn't understand that this was no longer possible, and simply refused to understand about the proposed detour via Schönwalde. The refugees from East Prussia, who had already been on the road for six weeks and had travelled back and forth and had been resting in Karthaus, pushed on, as they had been told before, along the country roads towards Pomerania, because they never imagined in their dreams that this route had long been severed by the Red Army. And the poorest of the poor, those who had been driven back from Pomerania by the Soviets, those who had experienced terrors and had survived, turned mechanically towards the east, with ears that were deaf to everything.

The authorities and Party officials in the area, who should and had to give advice, usually took to the roads before everyone else. Aimless, leaderless and lost, the streams of refugees came together in the great German exodus in Karthaus, the junction of several routes outside the gates of Danzig.

Soviet ground-attack aircraft had hunted them. Mothers carried their dead children in their slack arms. Amongst the hastily gathered possessions on the horse-drawn carts were the shattered bodies of the dead and dying next to the wounded and sick. One could see from their faces that they had endured so much on the road. They had travelled through snowfalls and ice, crossing the frozen Frisches Haff under Soviet artillery fire. Many, very many had died en route, from the bombs and shells. Fear, sometimes madness, stared from their eyes.[11]

As the day progressed, Christern's impromptu 'traffic police' slowly brought order to the town, though more refugees continued to stream in from the south. Several vehicles from 7th Panzer Division that had reached the town set off northwards:

We drove along side-roads, only our tanks, nobody else. During the morning, we reached a wood, with spruce planted to either side. When we had all entered the wood, we stopped in a clearing.

The officers discussed matters. Hauptmann Kayser pointed at a map, and the other two nodded.

Hauptmann Kayser's penetrating voice called us together. 'Half-circle, move, gather round me!'

We swung ourselves down from the tanks and trudged across the clearing, and formed up.

'Come on, two ranks in a half-circle, come closer, I need to talk to you all!' When everyone was finally there, he began:

'Men, our frontline has collapsed. There is no longer a continuous defensive line, the Russians have broken through everywhere. There are no properly constituted defensive positions any more. Everything has broken up.

'Our only chance is to break through to the ports. There, a frontline can be established. I'm going to try to break through via side-roads. It is our only chance. The main roads are all choked up, and the columns there will be overrun by the Russians. So, we will drive wherever possible through woodland, in order to avoid being spotted by Russian aircraft.'

And then:

'Contrary to usual orders, we will drive close together. Complete radio silence! If the first vehicle breaks down, it must try to get out of the way. The next will take over the lead.

'Let's go, men! I'll lead! Absolute discipline! Prepare for combat!'

It was unusual to be spoken to in this manner by one's battalion commander. We kept silent. I knew that if Hauptmann Kayser did not succeed, it would be over for us.

But his confidence spread to us. If anyone could succeed, it would be him. It was good to stay united and press on when a senior officer led us in such a critical situation, as Generalleutnant Mauss had in February in Elbing.

And Hauptmann Kayser was, in every sense, a 'senior officer', like Major Brandes. One could see that he had foresight, and knew what he wanted.

And thus we set off through the wood.

Things went well, we drove quickly, but paused regularly to make sure everyone was still together … at midday there was a loud bang, and we saw that the Panther had turned its turret to the left and had fired.

We halted. Leutnant Schuster dismounted and went forward, then came back and clambered aboard. 'There was a Russian anti-tank gun to the left, quite close, but apparently not any more. It's been shot up!'

It was strange that it happened to be in the wood, operating alone. Its towing vehicle was smashed. We drove on quickly. The Russians had few radios, a bad oversight.

Perhaps we were just lucky.[12]

When they reached the new frontline that was assembling just inland from the ports along the coast, the tired tank crews had another surprise:

A group of four naval officers, with long, blue coats and large caps, reported to the infantry officers.

'I'm from the cruiser *Prinz Eugen*; I have been tasked with giving you fire support with our ship's guns…'

The gentlemen conferred, and then the naval officers sent a radio message from their vehicle. Fifteen minutes later, there was a fearful thunder and a huge crash. The detonations were right in front of our infantry. The shots were far too short.

The infantry leapt up and ran towards the rear as fast as they could. We also turned our tank – in case we needed to take cover.

After a further radio message from the sailors, the next fall of fire was much better, landing further forward near the enemy.[13]

In Karthaus, Major Tolke's battlegroup, consisting of some of 7th Panzer Division's tanks, a platoon from 4th Panzer Division's reconnaissance battalion, and infantry from 73rd Infantry Division, was gathered together and ordered to push down the road from Karthaus to Zuckau, along the route taken before by the leading elements of 4th Panzer Division. There was further fighting in Kobelsdorf, which had been retaken by the Red Army, but progress further east was impossible.

With the most direct route towards Danzig blocked, 4th Panzer Division was ordered to make a detour to the north, via Kobelsdorf, Lebenau and Schönwalde to Kollenort. Here, the division was to hold the high ground that formed the last defensive line outside Gotenhafen. Immediately, elements of the division that were still struggling to reach Karthaus were diverted to the new route; as they struggled along the snowy roads, they left a trail of abandoned trucks behind them, with every drop of fuel carefully siphoned off. Supplies, clothing, personal possessions and workshop equipment were all abandoned in an attempt to keep the fighting vehicles mobile. Meanwhile, after dispatching all of the remaining vehicles that still had fuel, Christern continued to hold Karthaus itself. Unless supplies arrived, however, Christern faced the prospect of having to abandon his stranded tanks. During the night of 9–10 March, Soviet units were close enough to the town to start broadcasting loudspeaker calls to the soldiers. By now, the Red Army was aware of the German supply problems, and the loudspeaker messages stressed again and again that the soldiers were surrounded, without fuel or ammunition, and should lay down their arms. Few if any followed the advice.

Early on 10 March, the leading elements of the division reported that they had passed through Lebenau and were heading towards Schönwalde. The heavy armour, on the other hand, was stranded in a series of small pockets stretching from Karthaus to Lebenau. A few cautious reconnaissance probes into Karthaus were beaten off, but an uneasy stillness lay over the now almost deserted town. The first elements of 4th Panzer Division finally reached Schönwalde at about 1715hrs, but reported that they had left 21 combat vehicles along the road from Lebenau. The following day, Soviet tanks attacked Schönwalde and were beaten off by a battalion of 4th Panzer Division's Panzergrenadiers, but the great bulk of the division remained stuck somewhere between Karthaus and Schönwalde. If they were to be spotted by Soviet reconnaissance, their destruction was certain.

Although Schönwalde remained firmly in German hands, alarming news reached Christern and his group in Karthaus that Soviet units had been spotted in Dohnasberg, between Schönwalde and the coastal cities. Dohnasberg was also significantly behind the ridgeline that had been designated as the new frontline. Even if 4th Panzer Division were to reach this line, there was the possibility that Soviet forces would reinforce the probe to Dohnasberg and outflank them.

Just as Christern and his men were giving up hope of escape, two half-tracks rattled into Karthaus, towing trailers heavily laden with fuel. In the chaos and confusion, they had somehow managed to make the journey from Danzig without being intercepted. Swiftly, the fuel was allotted to the tanks, and Christern's force set out along the roundabout route to Schönwalde, refuelling stranded units as they encountered them. The last company to take the route was part of the division's 33rd Panzergrenadier Regiment, and was overwhelmed when Soviet units caught up with it at Lebenau.

A little to the north, an entire battalion from the same regiment was encircled near Neustadt, together with elements of 7th Panzer Division's 7th Panzergrenadier Regiment. Completely out of fuel and almost out of ammunition, the mixed force was crushed. In Neustadt itself were parts of Harzer's SS-Polizei Panzergrenadier Division. Hauptsturmführer Dr Pichler, the medical officer with the division's replacement battalion, was with his unit when it took up positions on the western side of the town:

Between Lauenburg and Neustadt, the road was completely choked with refugees and military vehicles. The Russians caught up with this chaos and fired and literally rolled over it. Everyone who could still run fled in panic through Neustadt towards Rheda. The enemy's spearheads reached Neustadt during the evening hours of 10 March.

On 11 March, the Russians began their attack on the town. They launched a frontal attack with tanks and groups of infantry, but were beaten off almost everywhere. A heavy flak gun, manned by RAD crewmen, particularly distinguished itself, shooting up tanks. Our combat school's tank-destroyer teams knocked out several T-34s in close-quarters combat. The enemy then brought the town under heavy artillery fire and aerial bombardment. As the enemy moved to bypass Neustadt, we broke contact during the night without being noticed, evacuated Neustadt, and set off with other units towards Gotenhafen.

By dawn, the road at Rheda was once more completely choked with military and civilian vehicles. Wild firing broke out towards the rear at 1000. Bursts of machine-gun fire and tank shots repeatedly ripped through the massed, stationary column of vehicles, before Soviet tanks crushed them. There was no more thought of resistance. The drivers abandoned their vehicles, weapons and equipment lay discarded. Mothers grabbed their children, and everyone fled.

Cross-country vehicles attempted to make their way through meadows and fields, through front gardens and fences, running down everything that couldn't get out of their way in time and still ending up stuck in some obstacle or snowdrift. A wild, fleeing torrent poured in panic towards Gotenhafen, and Ivan followed with his tanks, firing shells and machine-gun bursts incessantly into this indescribable confusion.

At the same time, the airfield of Rahmel, to our left, was blown up. The fuel stores burned, and the hangars were blown into the air. The whole sky was black with smoke, and in the midst of the darkness were the flashes and flames of explosions. A dreadful scene. And, according to orders issued in Neustadt, we were meant to have set up a new defensive line at the Rahmel airfield – using fleeing, weaponless men, who no longer had any commanders, and who streamed on in panic towards Gotenhafen.

… Then, suddenly, our commander, the Knight's Cross holder Sturmbahnführer Auer, appeared on the road in the middle of all the chaos and, with his drawn pistol and the aid of a few junior officers and NCOs, hauled his men out of the mass of refugees. The abandoned vehicles were searched for weapons and ammunition, and the infantrymen re-equipped. The unlikely undertaking succeeded: after two hours, the replacement battalion was once more ready for action. It immediately took up position at the edge of the runway, amongst the ruins of the destroyed airfield.[14]

By the morning of 12 March, most of 4th Panzer Division had succeeded in reaching Schönwalde, where further fuel supplies were waiting. Hauptmann Lange, commanding a mixed group that included the remnants of 33rd Panzergrenadier Regiment and half the division's tanks, fought off mounting Soviet attacks, and once the last stragglers had arrived the village was abandoned, and the division withdrew to Kollenort. At about the same time, German infantry succeeded in clearing Soviet incursions around Dohnasberg and Quassendorf. Despite their losses, the retreating German units had succeeded in withdrawing to the defensive line to the west of Danzig and Gotenhafen. Material losses had been heavy, but most of the personnel had escaped.

The new defensive line lay perilously close to the coast. In addition to the shattered remnants of the retreating divisions, another division – 12th Luftwaffe Division – had been brought back from Courland. After suffering losses in the ongoing battles in the distant Baltic 'bridgehead', this division, made up of Luftwaffe personnel and therefore lacking experience of ground warfare, was below strength, but nevertheless it represented welcome reinforcements. Pantenius' 337th Volksgrenadier Division, at the southern end of 2nd Army's line, was now too weak to continue functioning as a division, and was disbanded. The remnants of Pantenius' regiment were still in the frontline, and were now assigned to 35th Infantry Division. Pantenius had previously encountered his new division commander, Generalleutnant Johann-Georg Richert, as an instructor before the war, and remembered him as an overly strict officer. He had distinguished himself as a frontline commander on the *Ostfront*, but Pantenius was not surprised that Richert did not regard the survivors of 337th Volksgrenadier Division as equal to the men of 35th Infantry Division, and it took several days of hard combat before the newcomers earned the respect of Richert and his staff.

Meanwhile, Berlin made further rearrangements to the chain of command. On 12 March, 2nd Army was detached from Army Group Vistula and returned to Army Group North, in order to bring all German forces in East and West Prussia under a unified command. Walter Weiss, who had commanded 2nd Army since February 1943, became the new commander of Army Group North, while Rendulic moved from command of Army Group North to Army Group Courland. Weiss' replacement in command of 2nd Army was Dietrich von Saucken, the East Prussian former commander of 4th Panzer Division and Panzer Corps *Grossdeutschland*, who had fought so hard to save the retreating forces of Nehring's wandering cauldron. He was summoned to Berlin and informed of his new appointment. Hitler finished the briefing by telling him that he would be subordinated to Gauleiter Albert Forster. To the surprise and consternation of all present, the aristocratic von Saucken gazed back disdainfully at the Führer before saying, 'I have no intention of placing myself under the orders of a Gauleiter'.

Such opposition to Hitler was unheard of, particularly as von Saucken also omitted the obligatory 'Mein Führer'. Guderian and the other senior officers waited for Hitler's inevitable rage. Instead, after staring at the general for a few moments, Hitler turned away. 'Very well, Saucken, keep the command to yourself,' he muttered.[15] Von Saucken left immediately for Danzig, arriving there by air on 13 March.

The German formations that managed to retreat to the new defensive line must have hoped for a few days' rest, but after a pause of barely 24 hours, Rokossovsky's armies launched their assault. Von Egloffstein of 7th Panzer Division found himself deployed in support of infantry to the south of Gotenhafen, in the heavily wooded hills. Despite armoured support, the infantry attack faltered when it ran into major resistance. The following day, von Egloffstein was wounded in the cheek during an artillery bombardment. He was evacuated on a motorcycle to a field hospital, which was full of casualties caused by the increasingly intense Soviet artillery bombardment.[16]

Dr Pichler, the medical officer of SS-Polizei's replacement battalion, recorded that the artillery bombardment of 12 March was the worst he had experienced in the war. Sturmbannführer Auer led his men in repeated counter-attacks to restore the frontline. Despite determined resistance, the ranks of the defenders were growing perilously thin:

One day, in an attempt to roll us up from the rear, the enemy infiltrated through our thin frontline during the night and took up positions in the houses and ruins near our battalion headquarters and aid post. From there, we came under fire at close range. The situation was desperate. Then, Sturmbannführer Auer took his clerk, messenger and radio operator, and whatever other men he could gather together, and with an assault gun and Panzerfausts cleared one point of resistance after another. He used the Panzerfausts to break up the walls behind which the Russians had sheltered. After two hours, the situation was restored.[17]

After its retreat to the coast, SS-Polizei was reinforced with a Luftwaffe battalion and two naval battalions. The division's own regiments, like those of other divisions in the line, received drafts from rear-area units, but all of these replacement units lacked the essential frontline experience. Nevertheless, the division was able to hold its sector, beating off repeated Soviet attacks. Everywhere along the line, Soviet forces pressed against the defenders, but particularly opposite Zoppot. The 4th Panzer Division, which had suffered substantial material losses during its retreat, had successfully concentrated its surviving elements around Kollenort, and was ordered south to Bastenhagen and Mattern.

On 13 March, as Soviet guns started to bombard Zoppot, Soviet forces began to put pressure on the defences west of Danzig, taking Pempau and threatening to push further east and northeast. The 4th Panzer Division immediately mounted a counterattack, retaking both Pempau and Bullenbrook. But the losses incurred during the retreat, together with the constant fighting since the division had arrived from Courland, had reduced its strength to a shadow of its establishment; by the end of the day, Betzel had only four Panthers and a single assault gun operational.[18] The workshops in the outskirts of Danzig toiled to return damaged vehicles to the frontline, but were constantly hamstrung by shortages of replacement parts, a problem that they partly alleviated by cannibalizing the more badly damaged vehicles. Early the following morning, Soviet forces renewed their attacks, once more taking the two villages. In bitter fighting, Bullenbrook was again recaptured, but Pempau remained in Soviet hands. Meanwhile, pressure grew on 389th Infantry Division a little to the north as the thrust towards Zoppot continued. The 4th Panzer Division was forced to release some of its tiny complement of tanks to support the hard-pressed infantry:

Shortly before the start of the move, a Panther had to be assigned to another battlegroup of the regiment, in whose sector Soviet 'Josef Stalin' tanks had been reported. During the move to its new area, the company lost two more Panthers, due to water contamination of their fuel. Just before evening, Oberleutnant Gerlach arrived in the operation area with only two Panthers and was ordered to accompany a fusilier battalion on a night attack on the village of Neue Welt and to destroy the enemy tanks that were reported in the area.

At 2000, the fusiliers set off. It was already completely dark. The attackers pressed on through heavy fire. One could clearly hear the sound of many tank guns firing.

Meanwhile it had become clear that no fewer than 24 enemy tanks, including eight 'Josef Stalins', had been counted in Neue Welt. And against this crushing superiority our only offering was an attack with two Panthers!

... When the fusiliers of 389th Infantry Division reached the village, they knocked out an enemy tank and an anti-tank gun with Panzerfausts, but then came under heavy fire, forcing them back. At this most unfortunate moment, Oberleutnant Gerlach's command vehicle broke down. The tanks had endured severe strains over the past weeks and had undergone too little maintenance. He had to send the Panther back with its crew to prevent its being lost permanently. With his reliable radioman, Unteroffizier Kupfer, he climbed aboard the last Panther ... all the other combat posts were occupied by old lags: gunner Unteroffizier Lang, loader Oberschütze Heinrich and driver Obergefreiter Bauer.

All alone, the Panther stalked along the railway line towards the village. Its engine ran quietly, so that its noise wouldn't be heard.

As an old 'tank fox', Gerlach knew only too well that he had to get off to a flying start if he was going to win this uneven fight. He was protected from enemy observation by a snowdrift. A goods wagon was on the railway line to his left, which meant that the tank's silhouette couldn't be viewed against the dawn horizon.

They were still about 400 metres from the village when the Panther ran into soft ground. It took all the driver's skill to keep it moving. But the inevitably louder engine noises meant that the Soviets were alerted and fired blindly at the direction from which the suspicious noises were coming, but without seeing or hitting the well-covered tank.

Gunner Lang opened fire at the muzzle flashes and with his first shot scored a direct hit on an assault gun, which burst into flames, setting the barn behind it alight and lighting up the area. Three more Soviet tanks that were securing the edge of the village were spotted in the lit-up area.

As the Panther was now under increasing and more purposeful fire, Gerlach drove so wide on the reverse slope that he could only see the enemy-occupied village with his periscope. Between the houses were two Soviet tanks, close together. Heavy artillery and mortar fire began to fall, as the enemy blazed away without attempting to conserve ammunition.

On 16 March, a second Panther, commanded by Oberfeldwebel Palm, the 'tank cracker', arrived at midday to provide support. During the afternoon this tank shot up two enemy tanks, including a Josef Stalin, knocked another Josef Stalin out of the fight, and knocked out a heavy assault gun. A few anti-tank guns were also destroyed.

The rest of the day and the following night passed. The Soviets didn't dare venture out from their cover. At dawn, they tried to attack further right with powerful infantry forces. Gerlach immediately drove to the endangered position.

Whilst he himself oversaw the engagement with the emerging enemy tanks, his radio officer used machine-gun fire to overcome the Soviet infantry.

In addition to driving back the attack of a Russian rifle company, the two German Panthers, from their excellent firing positions, knocked out five Josef Stalins, another heavy Soviet tank, three assault guns and a heavy anti-tank gun. The following day, 18 March, Gerlach was still holding the same positions in 389th Infantry Division's sector with his two Panthers. From a very favourable commanding position, they destroyed another Josef Stalin, two assault guns and two anti-tank guns, and set three other enemy tanks ablaze in a vicious fire duel.

The magnitude of the exertions and requirements of a three day and night battle of life and death can be measured by the fact that, during a conversation with the infantry regimental HQ, Gerlach, wide-awake in combat, immediately fell deeply asleep.

These three days of fighting saw 21 of the heaviest enemy tanks destroyed for no losses.[19]

Such accounts should be treated with caution. Ever since the first encounters between tanks in the Great War, tank crews have exaggerated the numbers of 'kills' scored, and verifying such figures is almost impossible if the 'killed' tanks are in ground held by the enemy. It is also highly likely that many of these kills were restored to combat within days or even hours. Nevertheless, the presence of a small group of 4th Panzer Division's fighting vehicles allowed the line to be held at Neue Welt, in the face of considerable opposition.

The deployment of Gerlach and his comrades left the rest of the division short of firepower, and on 16 March, after a powerful artillery bombardment, Batov's 65th Army pushed through Pempau and onto the high ground to the east of the village. In desperate fighting, 4th Panzer Division and its neighbours brought the Soviet advance to a halt, but a renewed drive by the Soviet forces, mainly from I and VIII Guards Tank Corps, drove the German defenders from Hill 165, the highest point of the ridge. Immediately, a battalion of Panzergrenadiers – in reality, barely a company of men – stormed the Soviet positions on the hill and recaptured it. The 4th Panzer Division was now functioning as part of General Felzmann's XXVII Corps, and received a string of orders that moved more and more of its diminishing strength to

389th Infantry Division's sector. In the past, Betzel had repeatedly complained about such dissipation of his division, and now, when its fighting strength was so reduced, these orders must have been even more unwelcome. Early on 18 March, Betzel moved his headquarters back to Oliva in preparation for moving the few remaining elements of his division out of the frontline, but at first light General Felzmann countermanded this. Hill 165 remained the focus of bitter fighting, and by the end of the day the frontline ran right across the hill, despite bloody attempts by both sides to secure complete control.

During the afternoon, Felzmann telephoned Betzel. He criticized the Panzer division for failing to retake the whole of Hill 165, pointing out that in contrast 389th Infantry Division had continued to hold its positions in the face of powerful armoured attacks. Betzel's angry response was terse and to the point: the reason that 389th Infantry Division had fared so well was because most of 4th Panzer Division had been subordinated to it. Betzel himself had been left with only two tanks.[20]

Danzig and Gotenhafen remained full of refugees and rear-area units. These units were now ordered to send their 'surplus' personnel to the frontline as casualty replacements. Many of these replacements had been transferred to rear-area units because they were not fit for frontline duty. Their fighting power was therefore very limited, and many frontline units, including 4th Panzer Division, attempted to create replacement drafts from their own ranks. For example, the division's artillery regiment disbanded several batteries that no longer had guns and created an infantry company, which was attached to one of the division's Panzergrenadier battalions. It was reasoned that at least the men were still within their own division, rather than being dispatched to 'foreign' units. One of the division's two tank battalions now handed over its last vehicles to the other battalion, and its personnel formed a tank-destroyer company.

Late on 18 March, a large force of bombers flew over Danzig, reducing much of the city to ruins. The historic Old Quarter was particularly badly hit, and casualties amongst the thousands of refugees crammed into the city were heavy. The following day, the bombers were back, doing further damage to the centre of Danzig. Meanwhile, the operation to evacuate civilians and wounded continued unabated. Kapitän Heinrich Schuldt had established two 'refugee camps' in large warehouses, allowing for coordination of food supplies to those waiting desperately for a ship out of the cities. Soviet aircraft bombarded Danzig and Gotenhafen constantly, but despite the claims of Rokossovsky and Batov in their memoirs, they had almost no effect on the Kriegsmarine warships operating just off the coast. The powerful guns of the old battleship *Schlesien*, the heavy cruiser *Prinz Eugen* and the light cruiser *Leipzig* continued to provide invaluable support to the hard-pressed troops struggling to hold the high ground outside the ports. Air attacks against civilian ships scored a few notable successes, but had no effect on the warships; to a large extent, the evacuation continued with little hindrance. Up to 30,000 people left the ports every day and were taken to comparative safety in the west.

Many of Danzig's residents chose not to leave. It had been a severe winter, with heavy snowfalls continuing into March. For some, infirmity or age made a long, hazardous journey unthinkable. Others did not believe the East Prussian refugees' reports of Soviet atrocities. A few felt that they would be quite safe in Danzig. Annemarie Gerlach, who had helped her sister leave Danzig with her two daughters before the city was cut off, was now working with the Red Cross, helping feed the refugees who waited desperately for an opportunity to leave, when she was asked if she wanted to depart:

> What should I decide? On the one hand, it was tempting to escape from the Danzig cauldron, which the Russians squeezed ever tighter, and to seek out Waltraud and the children in Eberswalde, but on the other hand, there was a letter at home from my sister-in-law Lotti, in which she wrote that she and my mother-in-law were en route for Danzig in a refugee column from East Prussia. I hesitated, but then decided to wait for them and to remain in Danzig. It was soon clear that this was the right choice, because only a few days later, Kurt's mother and sister arrived in Oliva.
>
> … When they arrived in Oliva, my mother-in-law's health was worrying. She had to be helped up the two steps of the house.[21]

Despite the battle-weariness of the German infantry, and despite their lack of armour and artillery, the defensive line continued to hold, though at a terrible cost. On 19 March, the battle for Hill 165 was finally settled. The Soviet VIII Guards Mechanized Corps committed some of its Josef Stalin tanks in support of elements of several rifle divisions, and after a fierce artillery bombardment the combined force drove the Germans from the eastern slopes. A planned counter-attack was abandoned due to lack of troops and tanks, triggering a further angry exchange between Betzel and his corps commander. The following day it was possible to prevent further penetrations, but on 21 March Soviet tanks and infantry attacked Bastenhagen from the south and west. Several flak guns supported by infantry had successfully defended the village the previous day, but were now driven off; some of the flak guns had to be abandoned as the German forces pulled back.

The shape of the Soviet thrust was now clear to the Germans, and in order to prevent any rearrangement of the defenders, Rokossovsky's army commanders kept up the pressure along the entire front. The 4th Panzer Division remained under constant attack, hamstrung by the transfer of troops to other divisions. Through difficult terrain, Soviet forces ground their way forward between Bastenhagen and Leesen. Although Mattern remained in German hands, a bulge developed in the line south of the village during 22 and 23 March. Much of 4th Panzer Division's artillery regiment was overrun, the gunners now fighting as infantry. Replacement drafts from rear-area units arrived constantly, and disappeared in the ferocity of battle – dead, wounded or simply slipped away in the confusion. One draft of reinforcements caused particular consternation:

> One day, 12th Panzergrenadier Regiment was also assigned a tank-destroyer company: 14 Hitler Youth from Danzig, the oldest of whom was about 15, equipped with bicycles and Panzerfausts. The kids tried to act grown up and were filled with the importance of their task. Naive earnestness shone from their childish faces. The grenadiers took them into their ranks, discreetly took away their Panzerfausts, and let them have a long sleep in the bunkers. Then they sent the kids home to their mothers, where they belonged.[22]

In some cases, parents prevented their children from being used in this manner. Horst Ponczek, who was 15, was ordered to report to the youth hostel in Bischofsberg in order to be enrolled in a tank-destroyer group. His father refused to allow him to go. After only brief service in the frontline, the group of Hitler Youth were evacuated by sea to Schleswig-Holstein, whereas Ponczek was left in Danzig.[23]

The key developments on 23 March were outside of 4th Panzer Division's sector. After further heavy artillery bombardment, the Soviet XI Guards Tank Corps battered its way onto the high ground at Dohnasberg. The 227th Infantry Division's adjutant, Major Windschügel, led a counter-attack, and briefly the vital ridgeline was retaken. In bitter fighting, Windschügel was killed shortly after being awarded the Knight's Cross for his actions, but Soviet forces had already bypassed the ridge. Exploiting a gap in the German lines, III Guards Tank Corps pushed on east, and a group of T-34s appeared on the shore just to the north of Zoppot. They were immediately brought under fire by the destroyer *Z 34*, which was about a kilometre off the coast. The ship's four 6in guns briefly drove the tanks off, but they returned in greater numbers and with infantry support. Zoppot was fully in Soviet hands by nightfall.

The first phase of Rokossovsky's plan to destroy the German pocket was complete. An earlier thrust had reached the Baltic to the north of the cities, cutting off the Kurische Nehrung, the narrow belt of dunes that stretched out to Hela, and now the main 'fortress area' held by 2nd Army was cut into two groups. The reduction of the fragments could now begin.

Generalleutnant Mauss had decided to avoid retreating into Gotenhafen. Instead, he intended to pull back to the Oxhöfter Kämpe, an area of high ground to the north of the city. Here, there was a stretch of coastline known locally as the Hexengrund ('witches' area'), sheltered by a high cliff, from where it would be possible to embark aboard military ferries; evacuation from this area would be easier than from the shelled and bombarded quays of Gotenhafen. The remnants of 7th Panzer Division, like 4th Panzer Division in the south, had been tied down by constant pressure along the frontline, preventing the division from being used to block the thrust to Zoppot. On 15 March, the division reported that it had only 12 tanks – eight Jg.Pz. IVs, a single Pz. IV and three Panthers, all of which were in need of repairs and not ready for combat. The division's anti-tank battalion had an additional four assault guns. Ranged against the division were Katukov's 1st Guards Tank Army and Romanovsky's 19th Army. The diary of Schorsch Zink, a tank gunner in vehicle 445, is typical of the division's experiences:

On 15 March, a counter-attack south of Kielau in woodland. We shoot up a Sherman and a Russian truck, destroy three anti-tank rifles, and a few infantry. At midday, we take a hit from a Russian 85mm anti-tank gun in our final drive, but luckily we four are unharmed. Leutnant Adam pulls us back a bit with his tank into cover, then a tractor hauls us to the workshops in Kielau, where we stay until 19 March, having a new final drive fitted.

On 20 March, our Jagdpanzer is once more ready for combat. We have to drive forward again and are subordinated to an SS unit, supporting their counter-attack on Volzendorf. There, we shoot up four enemy T-34/85s, a 122mm assault gun and engage several machine-gun nests and Russian infantry.

The following day, 21 March, we have to move to the woods northwest of Gotenhafen under heavy enemy pressure. The Russians press on to the Zoppot–Gotenhafen railway line. During the following night, almost an entire battalion of Latvian troops from 227th Infantry Regiment deserts to the enemy. The Russians drive on and reach Koliebken, close to the coast to the south of Adlershorst.

Our mission on 21 March: to hold this new position until 23 March. On this day, another T-34 falls victim to our good gun, as well as numerous infantry and a few machine-guns.

But we can only hold our position until the evening and at 0300 on 24 March we are to move to Wittomin. Unfortunately, we have to move through swampy ground and get stuck. We can't get out and in the darkness we must try to make a log road, but it is all in vain. Our Jagdpanzer sinks ever deeper into the ground, right up to the track decking. It's really hard for us, but we now have to blow up our 445, as we are already under fire from three sides.[24]

The 7th Panzer Division's staff continued with their multiple tasks – coordinating the remnants of VII Panzer Corps' three divisions, dealing with their own division and continuing their preparations for a seaborne evacuation. On 23 March, the day that Soviet forces seized Zoppot, Mauss made one of his regular trips to the frontline. Karl-Heinz Horn was a member of the signals troop with the division commander:

Our command half-track was dug in a little in order to protect the engine against shrapnel, but only at the front. The crew set up the radio sets. I stood with the general alongside the vehicle, with officers, Feldgendarmerie [Military Police] and messengers around us. Suddenly, a row of heavy-calibre shells impacted by the nearby road, from the northwest, a direction that had until now been quiet. Before the general could give any further orders, I was surrounded by dead men and the cries of the wounded. The general lay on the tracks of the vehicle and was still; he must have been very badly wounded, but he tried to move. First, I discovered that my crew had not been injured. They had their hands full [operating the radio sets] and were therefore protected from the effects of shrapnel, but the O3 [division signals officer], Leutnant Runkewitz, and the aides from Ic [division intelligence] who had accompanied the general, and several other officers were dead.

The last joint of my left middle finger was hanging loose, attached just by a shred, and I cut it off with a pocket knife and wrapped up the stump with my handkerchief. It was important to get help as quickly as possible for the wounded. I slipped down the steep rocky slope, as down below – a little above the shore – there were personnel bunkers dug into the hillside. Medics and other helpers hurried up. My injured finger was bandaged in the staff company bunker, and suddenly my comrades noticed that I was standing in a puddle of blood, the first time that we noticed the large wound in my back.[25]

Horn and other wounded were taken by ferry to the freighter *Goya*. The ship, its upper structure scarred by damage from Soviet air attacks, took them to Swinemünde. Mauss had a leg amputated above the knee, but survived the war; he eventually resumed his pre-war career as a dentist.

Generalleutnant Wilhelm Heun's 83rd Infantry Division was now fighting just to the north of the Soviet breakthrough to the coast, between 215th Infantry Division and the sea. The division's replacement battalion barely resembled a regular unit. Many of its personnel were former railway police, others rural police. Few were aged less than 40, but the 'old hares' of the division were impressed by their determination and endurance. But despite their undoubted courage, the battered divisions were slowly ground back to the edge of Gotenhafen. The diary of one of the infantrymen captured the desperate nature of the fighting:

25 March: Further enemy penetrations. Hauptmann Kleiber, an old, experienced, and reliable frontline soldier, leads a counter-attack with headquarters and rear-area personnel, which costs us 20 dead and 65 wounded. The regiment's engineer platoon is deployed in a moment of dire need and acquits itself well.

26 March: The roads are barely passable, blocked by barricades and shot-up vehicles. Electric cables lie tangled everywhere, and there is almost constant firing by snipers and heavy weapons. Houses are transformed into individual fortresses, and linked to each other by holes in their walls. Naval personnel from the demolished port facilities are deployed as infantry.[26]

Further south, 4th Panzer Division was subjected to the fiercest artillery bombardment yet. Soviet forces pushed forward again, and the last reserves were dispatched to Mattern. Leutnant Klaus Schiller was an officer in the division who had previously lost an arm. He was to be evacuated from the front, but volunteered to stay with his division; now, he was ordered to organize a tank-destroyer company from tankless crewmen:

Platoons and squads were swiftly arranged so that the bonds of old comrades remained intact. Supply vehicles brought us close to the positions we had been ordered to occupy. Despite everything, we sang the same songs we had always sung – at this moment!

Just before dusk, we took up positions in the trenches on either side of the Danzig road. In front of us was the village of Nenkau, with a hill in front of it. The company was organized in two platoons, led by battle-hardened NCOs. We separated after a final situation report. It has always seemed to me that the farewells on this day had a particular ring. The parting handshakes lasted a second longer than usual.

… At about midnight, we heard the Russians approaching. In the pauses of fire, we heard quite clearly their commands to their horses. The familiar sounds of heavy motors and the clatter of tank tracks had been audible for some time. These had to be the sounds of T-34s approaching us. Then the tracks clattered on the village road with loud rattles. The first tank would reach the houses soon.

The sky was lit up with explosions, the flashes of guns and the light of a few fires. In pairs, we crept forward in the shadows of trees and houses towards the noise.

... The approaching clatter of tracks stopped. We could clearly see a T-34 at the edge of the road, its gun turned away from us in search of a target. The steel colossus was thus a danger to only a few of us. Despite careful observation, we could see no Soviet infantry. So, onward!

We worked our way carefully closer to the steel mass. 50 metres, 40, 30 – and we were now in range. The armoured enemy was clearly silhouetted against the pale night sky.

The fiery tails of our Panzerfausts ripped through the darkness – two seconds, during which our hearts were still! And then a bright flash and a loud bang: direct hit!

A few cries, a hatch flew open, frightened men tumbled out and hobbled away into the night. We didn't shoot. The tank burst into flames and burned with oud explosions.

This was apparently an impressive, sudden greeting for the Soviets. They broke off their night attack. Instead, they let their guns and mortars speak for them. After a time, a frightening stillness suddenly returned.

At dawn, we saw the cause of this unusual silence: the fought-out, decimated infantry had abandoned their positions on the hill and in the village, and had not informed us of their retreat. That was obviously not good, but who amongst the exhausted, half-dead footsoldiers would have thought of it?

What were we to do now? If we too evacuated the small toehold, then contact between our first platoon and the Bavarian infantry unit would be lost. To take possession of the lost positions in front of the village with our black-uniformed men with only close-quarter weaponry would be a daring undertaking.

But we had already had to see so much in the previous weeks: the columns of fleeing families, trembling women, crying children; helpless people, that the Soviet tanks herded before them and pitilessly gunned down en masse on the roads to the coast, if they didn't get out of the way quickly enough. Should these poor victims of the war, whose hopes lay with us, be further disappointed? This thought made the decision easy.

A few of us worked our way forward through Soviet artillery fire. We already had two dead. Then we occupied the abandoned positions on the hill. We could only hold these forward bastions for a few hours, as the Soviets hugely outnumbered us. When we first became aware that there were no German troops to our right or left, we slowly withdrew before the enemy during the afternoon and formed up at the exit from the village. We were full of concern for our first platoon, with which we had lost contact at dawn.

Much later we learned that despite our counter-attack, which we launched partly on their account, they had been surrounded by the Soviets and were almost completely destroyed. Only a few escaped unharmed.[27]

Behind the frontline, Danzig and Gotenhafen were under constant artillery fire and air attack. Terrified refugees and thousands of wounded men still awaited evacuation. On 23 March, even as Soviet forces turned north from Zoppot to threaten Gotenhafen, and south towards Oliva, the whaler *Walter Rau* entered Gotenhafen harbour. The 13,700-tonne ship was swamped as thousands of people fought to get aboard. Eventually, 6,000 were taken onto the crowded decks, but many thousands more were still on the quayside. Smaller vessels and military ferries took as many as they could along the coast to Oxhöft, from where they could – hopefully – be evacuated at a later date.

The *Walter Rau* left Gotenhafen four hours after she arrived, the last large evacuation ship to enter the port. Dr Jesse, the ship's doctor, recorded the nightmare visions he experienced:

> Countless despairing people were on the pier, women and children, of whom the *Walter Rau* could take only a portion. The scenes when the ship departed were dreadful, with most of the unlucky ones thinking that this was their last chance.
>
> The conditions during the voyage to Copenhagen were in keeping with the unbelievable overcrowding aboard the ship, which had cabin space for only 300 people. No food supplies had been prepared, particularly no fresh milk. Almost all of the numerous newly borns who had come aboard died.
>
> As the ship was to have taken only healthy refugees aboard, the medical support available was completely inadequate. There was a single ship's nurse and two army medics for 6,000 people. Medical supplies, in particular analgesic drugs, were quickly exhausted. Surgical treatment for wounded people who had not yet received care was accordingly available for only a proportion of the unfortunates, particularly as there were inadequate helpers to carry people to the ship's medical bay on the upper deck.
>
> Refugees, women and children, the badly wounded and the dying, screaming people with head injuries and the dead, lay next to and on top of each other on the whaler's metal decks. Amongst them, some of the desperate indulged in wild sexual orgies.
>
> It was a gruesome, almost indescribable inferno.
>
> During the voyage to Copenhagen, we were attacked several times by aircraft. Consequently, there were repeated air raid alarms. The indifference and impassivity of the refugees, who had probably already endured much worse, in such a dangerous situation was striking.
>
> When the *Walter Rau* came into Copenhagen, she was swiftly unloaded so that she could return again.[28]

The relentless pressure around Danzig continued, made worse by the growing intensity of air attacks on the city itself. On 24 March, a particularly heavy series of attacks left almost the entire city ablaze; even the asphalt on the roads began to burn. But the Soviet aircraft dropped more than just munitions. Thousands of leaflets rained down on the exhausted defenders:

PROCLAMATION OF MARSHAL ROKOSSOVSKY TO THE GARRISONS OF DANZIG AND GOTENHAFEN!

Generals, officers and soldiers of the German 2nd Army!

Yesterday, 23 March, my troops took Zoppot and split the encircled fighting forces into two. The garrisons of Danzig and Gotenhafen are isolated from each other. Our artillery is bombarding the harbours and entry waters of Danzig and Gotenhafen. The ring of my troops grows steadily tighter.

In these circumstances, your resistance is senseless and will only result in your deaths, and the deaths of hundreds of thousands of women, children and elderly.

My proclamation:

1. End resistance immediately and surrender with white flags, as individuals, squads, platoons, companies or regiments.

2. I guarantee to all who surrender, their lives and retention of personal possessions. All officers and soldiers who do not put aside their weapons will be destroyed in the coming assault.

You will have to answer for all of the civilian victims.

Dated 24 March 1945

Commander of the troops of the 2nd Belorussian Front

Marshal of the Soviet Union

Rokossovsky[29]

This proclamation seems to have had little effect on most of the defenders.

The leading Soviet units were now only 2km from the quayside at Neufahrwasser, where several thousand refugees still waited. The Kriegsmarine had decided that the quay was now too dangerous for large vessels, and as they arrived the evacuation ships were directed to drop anchor in the approaches to Gotenhafen – it might be possible to enter the port at night, and in any event, military ferries could bring passengers out to the waiting ships. One of the ships was the 9,500-tonne *Ubena*, one of the liners that had spent most of the war serving as floating accommodation for German submarine crews in Pillau, and had been amongst the first to sail west with refugees at the commencement of *Hannibal*. Arthur Lankau, the captain of the *Ubena*, was known for his impatience, and early on 25 March he grew tired of waiting while Soviet aircraft launched repeated attacks on the ships. Instead, he ordered his ship to make for Neufahrwasser, and reached the quay as the morning mist was clearing. Soviet artillery fire had driven most of the waiting people into cover, but as the liner reached the pier thousands erupted from their hiding places. One of the first to come aboard the *Ubena* was Kapitän Heinrich Schuldt, the merchant navy officer responsible for those who had waited, expecting that the Russians would arrive before any more ships could come. After silently shaking the hand of the man who had risked his ship to save the last refugees waiting in the Neufahrwasser quay, he returned ashore to supervise loading. At first, everything proceeded with order and calm, but it wasn't long before Soviet artillery began to bombard the area. A salvo of rockets struck the quay, inflicting terrible casualties on those who were waiting. Order broke down as people desperately fought to get aboard. After four hours, the last of the waiting refugees had come aboard. Even as the *Ubena* drew away, a salvo of Soviet shells struck the quay exactly where she had been tied up. Kapitän Schuldt stayed in Neufahrwasser until nightfall, and then made his way to Hela in a small motorboat.

The *Ubena* moved slowly along the coast towards Gotenhafen. Kapitän Lankau reported to the naval authorities that he had 4,000 refugees aboard, but had space for another 1,000 wounded. Early on 26 March, Soviet artillery opened fire on the ships waiting for evacuees in the bay, and the *Ubena*, which had stopped to await the arrival of wounded men, immediately weighed anchor. The heavy cruiser *Prinz Eugen*, the pocket battleship *Lützow* and several smaller warships promptly returned fire, silencing the Soviet guns in a furious exchange of shells. The *Ubena* paused at Hela to take more wounded on board, and then sailed to Copenhagen in a convoy with five other ships. Lankau's vessel carried more than 5,500 refugees and wounded to safety. The *Ubena* made a total of 12 evacuation voyages, during which between 20 and 40 children were born. At Kapitän Lankau's suggestion, most of them were christened with the name of the ship that had saved their lives. In 1985, a container ship was built in Bremen and named *Ubena* in memory of Lankau's vessel. When the new ship was handed over to the Deutsche-Afrika-Linie, two of those wartime children, Karin-Ubena Osterwalder and Sabine-Ubena Gildemeister, were present to mark the occasion.[30]

On land, the bitter fighting continued. Soviet forces now pressed into Oliva, where the remnants of 389th Infantry Division fought on grimly in the face of powerful Soviet attacks, heavily supported by tanks. After the news of the loss of the *Wilhelm Gustloff* spread through Danzig and Gotenhafen, Annemarie Gerlach had decided not to risk escape by sea; her mother-in-law's poor health made such a voyage, with all its hardships, a risky undertaking. After a family friend joined the Gerlachs, the group numbered six: three young women, two elderly women and a child. Their house now became the frontline:

> Machine-guns rattled, shells crashed down, and our house shuddered. Outside, fierce fighting raged, and suddenly the Russians stormed forwards to our house with shrill shouts of 'Urra, Urra!'
>
> They set up an aid station in our kitchen. A table was dragged into the middle of the room, and wounded Russians brought in. At the start of the fighting, we had fled to the cellar, and heard from next door the painful groans of the wounded. From my work as a Red Cross nurse, I still had a bag with various dressings and medication, which I had taken into the cellar. At this moment, I didn't think that the enemy had come into our house, but rather that they were people who suffered and needed help. I quickly made my decision and went to the aid station, where I gave the medic sterile dressings and helped bandage the wounded. One Russian was particularly badly wounded. He had been shot in the head. I wanted to given him a painkiller to alleviate his pain, but first I had to swallow a tablet to show that it wasn't poison.
>
> When I returned to our cellar, I noticed that two Mongolians were following me – while I had been bandaging their comrades, they had been standing by the cellar door. Suddenly, one of them grabbed my wristwatch, and the other searched through my handbag. I couldn't believe it. They had watched while I helped their comrades, and had responded in such a low manner. Then I heard a scream. My sister-in-law had seen what was happening and called to the medical officer for help; he called the two brutes off. So there were also Russians who repaid humanity with humanity.[31]

Further south, the survivors of 4th Panzer Division were pushed back to Zikankenberg, on the edge of Danzig. As the division continued to shrink, some of its personnel were reassigned. After the tank regiment staff was disbanded, Oberst Christern was ordered to proceed to Danzig and thence by motorboat to Oxhöft, where he would replace the wounded Generalleutnant Mauss as commander of 7th Panzer Division. He asked Schäufler, his signals officer, to join him in his new assignment, but Schäufler decided to stay with his comrades in 4th Panzer Division.

> 'But come with me part of the way', he asked. I couldn't refuse my regiment commander this wish, when we had shared so many terrible experiences ... though with complete honesty I said that I had no desire to drive to Neufähr through the hail of Soviet shells landing on Danzig.

For the last time, our commander climbed into his 'Thunderwagon'. The radio was switched off. That too was unusual. But who were we now meant to communicate with by radio? The 35th Panzer Regiment had effectively ceased to exist a few hours ago.

Heaps of debris lay on the streets. There were fires all around. The city was almost deserted. Through the clouds of smoke, the façade of a church appeared before us, almost undamaged. The Oberst wanted to stop here. He climbed out and asked his driver and me to accompany him.

In the half-light, we entered the nave of the church, which had suffered little from the fighting. The Oberst looked around as if seeking something. Then a light laugh came from his battle-marked face. He told me with a silent look to take a seat on a pew. With his driver, he climbed the steep steps to the gallery.

I sat somewhat uncomfortably on the hard, brown old church pew and heard the rumble of war outside. Suddenly, I cried out. A completely alien sound drove the sounds of fighting from my stunned ears: the organ burst into life, overlaying the melodies of murder, making me completely forget the war. A strange, melancholy feeling filled me. The dark church suddenly seemed so bright to me.

Of course, I knew that the Oberst was a great enthusiast of music and played a few instruments. But this was the first time I heard him play an organ – and he played well. He slowly overlaid the thunder of battle with light-hearted sounds, which reminded me of the carefree days of peacetime. All woes sank away: war and destruction, death and cruelty. The wonderful sounds of the cheerful melodies made me think of a different future.

But would those of us damned by war see a new dawn? Would we ever experience a time when we did not have to kill to avoid being killed ourselves? These were questions to which no answers seemed to fit.

Today, I still don't know how long I listened and dreamed, before the Oberst patted me on the shoulder and brought me back to reality. His face was clear of worries.

Silently, we clambered back into the half-track. Gradually, the sounds of battle came back to me. The Oberst said a short farewell in the port at Neufähr, turned away quickly, and climbed into the waiting motorboat. He did not look back – and I forgot to salute him. He stared sunward, probably already thinking about his new command.

The sounds of the organ stayed with me a long time after, overlaying the war and misery and despair, as I drove back through the burning city to Zikankenberg, where the battle for Danzig still raged.[32]

Christern reached his new command on 27 March. Even as he took command, part of the division's sector came under fierce attack. Oberstleutnant Ehle rallied the remnants of his 7th Panzergrenadier Regiment and restored the frontline in a desperate counter-attack.

There was no respite for Christern's former comrades in and around Danzig. There was bitter fighting between Oliva and Langfuhr, where the city airport lay. The last available reserves – a solitary battalion of 7th Infantry Division's 62nd Grenadier Regiment – was thrown into the battle on 26 March to retake a key anti-tank ditch to the north of the airport, but further Soviet advances on either flank drove it back. By the end of the day, the regiment had taken heavy casualties, and was in danger of being isolated. The 4th Panzer Division also received reinforcements from 7th Infantry Division, but the line to the west of Danzig had to fall back as no fewer than 15 Soviet rifle divisions, supported by VIII Mechanized Corps, continued to batter the thinning ranks of 12th Luftwaffe Division, 4th Panzer Division and 252nd Infantry Division. By the end of the day, 4th Panzer Division had no tanks left operational.

Communications with higher command elements became almost impossible in Danzig, with artillery fire destroying telephone wires and radio sets failing due to damage or a shortage of batteries and spares. What remained of 252nd and 389th Infantry Divisions and 12th Luftwaffe Division voluntarily placed themselves under the control of 4th Panzer Division. Collectively, the four divisions probably numbered fewer than 10,000 men. Now that there was a new threat to the city from the north, Generalleutnant Betzel travelled to the Oliva Gate of Danzig during the afternoon of 27 March to organize a defensive line. It was increasingly dangerous to attempt any further evacuation by sea, and Betzel decided that the last battlegroup of 7th Infantry Division would attempt to hold the northern approach to Danzig, while the forces that had been driven back to Zigankenberg fell back through the blazing ruins and retreated behind the line of the River Mottlau, encouraging the remaining civilians to leave with them. While Betzel conferred with local officers, the area came under heavy artillery fire. Betzel was hit by shrapnel and killed; the commander of 33rd Panzergrenadier Regiment was badly wounded.

Control of 4th Panzer Division passed to Oberst Ernst-Wilhelm Hoffmann, formerly commander of 12th Panzergrenadier Regiment. The news spread rapidly, causing widespread consternation – Betzel had been a popular man with his troops, and his loss was a huge blow.

The one-armed Leutnant Schiller and his tank-destroyer company were now fighting in Danzig itself:

In the last few days of streetfighting, we had developed a very effective tank-destroyer tactic. The lofts had all been connected together for air defence reasons, and we used these as cover to approach the Soviet armoured spearheads. We positioned men with machine-pistols at the loft windows for protection. With our Panzerfausts, we hit out at the hatches of the armoured enemy. It was most unsettling for the Soviets to see a T-34 suddenly fly into the air. We used the enemy's confusion to creep away and to seek out a new target. In this way we forced the Soviets to advance very slowly and carefully. Every hour, every hard-fought day was so tremendously valuable to the refugees. There was no shortage of Panzerfausts. They could be picked up anywhere along the way. Food supplies unfortunately were not so plentiful.

After an operation behind a street barricade, we had dead and wounded. We promised over their graves that we would never forget them. We asked God to care for their families and for strength in this pitiless battle. We felt as if the deadly doubts in ourselves would stifle this last prayer.

Only when the old quarter of Danzig was completely ablaze and the bridges were breaking up did we pull back over the Vistula to the suburb of Heubude. For the first time in my life, and the last time, I saw from a burning and slowly collapsing bridge, the world-famous crane tower burning brightly. A heavy sense of despondency overwhelmed me. And yet, every saved life was a thousand times as valuable as all of these historic buildings put together.

… In Heubude, I met again all the comrades who had survived the hell of Danzig and were to some extent still in good health. A deep joy filled me. There was something peculiar about comradeship in war![33]

To the south of the cities, Soviet progress was slow. The relatively flat area between Dirschau and Danzig was crisscrossed by waterways, and the remnants of several German divisions fought on with grim determination. Army engineers destroyed many of the dykes, creating widespread flooding that rendered much of the area impassable. Fire support from the Kriegsmarine continued to play an important role; during one bombardment, a naval shell struck the headquarters of the Soviet 37th Guards Rifle Division, killing Major-General Rachimov and his commissar.[34] Pantenius and his regiment were now protecting the southern approaches to Danzig at St Albrecht:

The enemy attacked along the road and railway from Praust, with powerful artillery support and numerous tanks. Our regimental headquarters was at the southern end of the Herberge estate in the cellar of a solidly built house right next to the road, with communication to the two battalions in St Albrecht by radio and telephone, and with the division by a heavy motorized signals troop which was next to us in the estate, protected on all sides. Despite the murderous drumfire, which I had never experienced at such intensity in the entire war, the radio station remained operational, protected from shrapnel. It was impossible to dispatch messengers forward or back for hours at a time. Both battalions acquitted themselves outstandingly, fighting off repeated attacks on their positions in the village. The enemy couldn't target much in the village with his tanks. Hauptmann Ehlers, commander of 1st Battalion, was wounded for the second time and was later transferred to the field hospital, then via Hela to Schleswig-Holstein. Hauptmann Strohschneider took his place, giving up command of 2nd Battalion. I wanted the best officer for 1st Battalion, which was in the heart of the fighting. Behind us, the old quarter of Danzig was under constant bombardment, and was reduced to rubble, ablaze everywhere. The road to Ohra was under persistent artillery fire. The enemy forces opposite us were apparently from the 46th or 281st Rifle Divisions of 2nd Shock Army.[35]

Despite orders sent by Hitler directly to General Felzmann, there was no intention to make any sort of 'last stand' in Danzig. In any event, Felzmann had lost contact with his subordinate divisions, and Oberst Hoffmann, the new commander of 4th Panzer Division, had already received approval from the commander of 2nd Army, General von Saucken (who had himself once commanded 4th Panzer Division) for as orderly a withdrawal as possible. Neufahrwasser, from where the *Ubena* had lifted the last refugees, fell to the advancing Red Army on 28 March. The 62nd Grenadier Regiment was isolated and in danger of being cut off, but managed to escape across the Vistula to Heubude. Everywhere, German troops pulled back to and across the river. Soviet forces that followed close behind managed to secure a bridgehead around the chemical works near the dockyards. Late on 28 March, a counter-attack by 4th Panzer Division succeeded in retaking the area, though Soviet footholds on the eastern bank remained.

Gotenhafen, too, was under pressure. The Soviet III Guards Tank Corps had created the initial breakthrough to the coast, and now turned north alongside XI Guards Tank Corps. Two of 19th Army's rifle corps – I and XXVII – closed in from the northwest. Mixed battlegroups of VII Panzer Corps' exhausted and bled-out divisions continued to put up bitter resistance. Under heavy artillery fire, the last of the wounded and refugees were evacuated by sea. Many of those waiting had been reduced to a stunned impassivity by their ordeal, and had to be herded onto the ferries. Generally, the fighting withdrawal through Gotenhafen was carried out with precision – localized counter-attacks forced the Red Army back, and in the lull that followed, the German units retreated. The rearguard of 83rd Infantry Division, consisting of the division's replacement battalion and parts of 277th Grenadier Regiment, fell back to the port area, from where it was intended that the division's combat engineers would evacuate it in small boats. Under heavy fire, the engineers were unable to reach their comrades, a few of whom were able to swim to safety. The rest were forced to surrender.

Nevertheless, the bulk of the surviving troops abandoned Gotenhafen on 27 and 28 March. The 227th Infantry Division's staff were in the port area, and finally left late on 28 March. Their escape was almost prevented by their own side: the German battlecruiser *Gneisenau* had been laid up in Gotenhafen after being severely damaged in an air raid, and orders had been given for the ship to be sunk as a blockship in the port entrance. Even as 227th Infantry Division's staff attempted to leave the port in a motorboat, a tugboat pulled the *Gneisenau* into position to block the entrance. After a furious exchange, which at one point included the infantry personnel threatening the tugboat crew with machine-guns and Panzerfausts, the blockade of the port was delayed until early on 29 March, allowing the last few soldiers to escape.[36]

Shortly after, Generalleutnant Heun was ordered back to Germany to take command of the newly created Division *Schlageter*. What remained of 227th Infantry Division was now incorporated into 83rd Infantry Division, and 227th Infantry Division's former commander, Generalmajor Maximilian Wengler, was appointed Heun's replacement.

Johann Huber, whose Jg.Pz. IV had broken down during the fighting in Flötenstein, had been billeted in Gotenhafen while the vehicle was repaired. As he and his fellow crewmen prepared the vehicle for combat, the Soviet artillery bombardment continued around them. They had been out of combat for some time, so they needed to clean the barrel of the gun; Huber and his fellow crewman Bruno Kammer undertook the task:

I assemble the cleaning rod for the KWK [Kampfwagen-Kanone] and push the brush, which I have wrapped with a relatively clean rag, so that Bruno can pull it through the depressed barrel from the outside. The first pull-through of course results in a rusty brown rag. After a while we have to replace it with another, until the barrel is clean. When Bruno has pulled the rod through, he has to take it apart and pass it back to me. To do this, I have to get out of my gunner's seat. During one such manoeuvre, I am standing on the tank and waiting for Bruno, who is pulling the brush out of the barrel. He comes down the side of the tank, when suddenly I feel a strong gust of wind at my right ear, and almost at the same moment a shell passes the right drive wheel and strikes the cobbles 30 centimetres to the side of the tank. There's a clear, metallic clang – and – it's a dud! Bruno was two metres away, and the shell passed perhaps five centimetres from my ear. As I was looking along its line of travel, I see it strike and bounce away. It's a 76.2mm high-explosive shell. We stare at each other, thunderstruck, as it bounces 15, 20, 25 metres across the open ground and embeds itself in the sand. We stare at the round lying there, the thing is shining silver-bright, and then look each other in the eyes. Both of us know that once more we've come through. My knees feel weak. Even though it was a dud, the shell nearly took my head off. It missed by only five centimetres. Bruno is off. He runs over to the shell and wants to pick up the lucky thing that didn't go off. He picks it up in his hand and lifts it about 30 centimetres before he throws it away. It still doesn't go off. But he cries out, because he's burned his finger, as it was glowing hot. Meanwhile, I climb off the tank and go over to him, and mutter, 'You twit, do you really want to keep it?' We stand there, the two of us, a metre from the silver thing, unable to believe that it didn't go off.[37]

Even as the final battle for Gotenhafen began, Huber and his comrades left, their vehicle repaired just in time. Once more in the frontline, they had another lucky escape as they drove along the edge of a wood:

After 100 metres, there's a sudden shout, eerily magnified by the headset of the intercom: 'Tank!' Bruno, the driver, brakes. We stay there. Less than ten seconds. Then there's a tremendous blow. A bright flash blinds us. When I can think again, fractions of a second later, I look to the left, right, the front. The tank is fine. It was a hit that didn't penetrate. But Emil, the commander, shouts, 'Stalin, 50 metres to the right in the wood.' Bruno has already engaged reverse gear and drives back. Seconds of terror. I think to myself, this far again and we're away. Another 50 metres. We are exactly broadside on to him. What we can't see in the half-darkness of the tank, Emil describes to us: 'He can't turn his turret, there are trees in the way,' and then right after, 'Infantry, Russian infantry!' I ask over the intercom, 'Where?' 'To the right in the ditch, two metres,' and he's already pulled his head in. Machine-gun fire opens up, and we hear ricochets against the armour. Aaargh, we're right in the middle of things! What if a close-assault troop attacks and throws a hand grenade through a hatch! I mutter to Emil: 'Have a look out!' I check our hand grenades behind me in the fighting compartment. Our submachine-gun is there too. I take it and hold it.

We drive back blindly at full throttle. Bruno, the driver, lets the engine roar and steers by guesswork – he can only see the road in front of him, so he drives back as he guesses, because Emil isn't advising him. There is heavy rifle fire. Meanwhile, I throw our hand grenades, one after the other, to the left into the ditch, and then right into the wood. Bruno shouts, 'Right, right, they're in the ditch.' But the commander doesn't hear. When all the hand grenades are gone and we still need more, I pass him the flare pistol. It flashes through my head – I hope he doesn't fire it off in here, or we'll all go up! I push his arm high, so that he aims outside. Immediately, load the next shot and fire.

… After a further 100 metres, we halt. 'Engine off.' Silence. No more rifle fire. We puff out a breath, all of us knowing that once more we've made it.

… I get hold of myself first, and climb out of our tank – I want to see where the hit was. Nobody shoots at me. It's a real miracle that the shot didn't penetrate. It must have been on the sloping armour. As I work my way forward along the track decking, good grief, I go pale. The 122mm shot came from the right and struck at an oblique angle, punching a groove in the frontal plate, at least four centimetres deep and 70 centimetres long. The steel is dark grey, oxidized by the high energy of the impact. The traces of the copper ring of the shot are visible as two golden stripes along the furrow. Involuntarily, I reach out and touch them, and burn my finger, as the groove is still very hot from the impact. My knees shake. That was almost it. All four of us would have been dead but for a few centimetres – it was so close.[38]

With a couple of other armoured vehicles, Huber and his comrades helped reinforce the line at Grabau while Gotenhafen itself was evacuated. On 28 March, the defenders pulled back to the Oxhöfter Kämpe.

Throughout the last days of Danzig and Gotenhafen, Gauleiter Forster had been almost invisible. On 24 February, he visited Berlin, and enthusiastically agreed with the fantasists who continued to believe in final victory. On 21 March, his opinion was different, at least as far as his own Gau went; he wrote to Goebbels, describing the situation in Danzig and Gotenhafen as 'extraordinarily dramatic'. He wrote that the cities couldn't be held for long, and two days later, appeared in Berlin. After he had discussed matters with the Führer, his mood improved: 'He [Hitler] explained to me that he will save Danzig, and there is no need to despair.'[39]

The exact circumstances of Forster's final departure from Danzig are not clear. Even as the last refugees were scrambling aboard military ferries in Gotenhafen, a small steamer, the *Neufahrwasser*, passed the German torpedo boat *T 28*. The captain of the torpedo boat saw that the steamer had very few people aboard, and signalled the vessel, asking where it was going. The reply was startling: 'Gauleiter Forster is aboard, heading for Hela.' The torpedo boat's own decks were almost overflowing with refugees, and the *Neufahrwasser* was requested to come alongside and take off some of the passengers, but the steamer continued on its way. There was a brief radio conversation between the *T 28* and naval headquarters in Hela, and the torpedo boat brought her guns to bear on the *Neufahrwasser*, and ordered the steamer to heave to. The steamer stopped, and took aboard refugees, but apparently Forster himself was not aboard. Other accounts suggest that Forster left Danzig aboard a steamer named the *Zoppot*. He may have fled to the island of Bornholm, but was in Hela shortly afterwards. The military personnel treated him with almost open contempt:

> ... Forster, who had sought me out in the Hela bunker to have the situation outlined to him, said to me: 'There is really nothing more for me to do here, everything has been taken over by the military – I will ask the Führer to assign me to a special task in southern Germany.' General Specht [commander of XX Corps] was so angered by this that he said to the Gauleiter that there was still much for him to do here, to ensure that the escape route over the sea for as many refugees as possible to the west remained open.[40]

Shortly after, he cut a very different picture from the arrogant Nazi official of earlier years: 'He didn't speak a word, saw only suffering, and this broke the last of his strength. He accompanied two ferry voyages [to take refugees from the Vistula estuary to the waiting ships]. Then he collapsed and was taken west in a ship.'[41]

The battle for Danzig reached its climax. Much of the city was burning, and the defenders struggled to hold key positions – but only long enough for other units to retreat towards Heubude. It was no longer possible to arrange for seaborne evacuation of those who were still in the city, and as the remaining German troops fell back through the ruins, there was bitter fighting. On occasion, the Soviet infantry had to break into hastily fortified buildings via the basement, then fight their way up floor by floor while their supporting field guns continued to blast the defenders.

The staff of 203rd Infantry Division had been assigned to the garrison of 'Fortress Danzig', though the division no longer had any significant fighting units. It took command of a mixture of units – a single battlegroup from the division's remaining men, a group of naval personnel deployed as infantry, and Volkssturm – to defend the heart of Danzig. On 25 March, the division withdrew to the island of Holm, an area on the east bank of the loop of the Vistula that ran through the heart of the city, as Oberleutnant Hans Thieme, the division staff intelligence officer, recorded:

> We drove in a car – the blue Opel with the trusty Mayer as driver – with the IIa [division adjutant] in a fast drive along the short stretch of railway, then across the line to Hansa Square and the shipyards, across a bridge to Holm, and along to the southermost of the two bunkers. The short journey was sufficient to see the devastation brought about by the bombardment that had started that morning: there were ruined buildings everywhere, fallen telegraph wires, dead horses, abandoned civilian baggage. One saw barely any people, as they were probably in the various bunkers, such as the large, 3,000-man bunker in Hansa Square, and suffered badly from thirst and hunger.[42]

The staff of 203rd Infantry Division took up residence in a large bunker that had been designed as shelter for U-boat crews while they were in port. It was unsuitable as a fighting position, and on 27 March the headquarters personnel pulled back to a Luftwaffe bunker at the eastern end of Holm. Confused reports suggested that Soviet forces had crossed the Vistula and were fighting for the western parts of Holm, and Hauptmann Rietz, the division adjutant, was dispatched during the night to the northeast of the island to determine the situation there. An officer was sent back to the U-boat bunker to make contact with Oberst Grosser, who commanded the division's few remaining combatants:

We had come close to the bunker, our headquarters until yesterday afternoon, when we encountered a group of 20 to 30 people, soldiers with a few civilians, moving swiftly and silently, without a second to waste, heading past us. We had almost been passed by them, when I asked who they were and where they were going from one of the dark figures. 'Oberst Grosser's headquarters, redeploying!' Where is the Oberst? How fortunate that I had asked. The bunker had already been abandoned. We later learned that the 'redeployment' had been carried out so suddenly that a whole group of soldiers, not just the medics and wounded, fell into enemy hands, without knowing what was happening. This included a radio group from our division, whose leader, Unteroffizier König, later made an adventurous return to us.

I reported to the Oberst, whom I had never met before, a small, withdrawn, presentable officer in a camouflage jacket. I was to order him to retake and hold the northern part of the island, but had met him retreating. 'A counter-attack? Impossible! With what forces? The enemy is already too strong. The Marinekompanie *Bischoff* simply withdrew by ship without even informing me. There are only a few men under command of an Unteroffizier over there. But the Russians are already within 150 metres of the bunker. They are advancing quickly, the police battalion is shattered. The Volkssturm further south is a guard company of old men, and have only four rifles. I can't hold Holm with these forces. Tell the general that I couldn't wait for permission to redeploy my headquarters – we should be thankful that we managed to get out of the bunker. It was a savage fire!'[43]

Hans Schäufler was one of the last to withdraw through the devastated city:

This withdrawal from the burning, dying city created a dreadful spectacle. The retreating troops took the dead General Betzel back with them, lying in his command vehicle and covered with a Reich war-flag.

... By 29 March, the eastern part of the city of Danzig was already under attack. The last of the rearguard was able to break away from the enemy during the night of 29–30 March.

Late in the afternoon of 29 March, I was ordered to report to the new battalion headquarters with my radio crew in their half-track. The adjutant, Oberleutnant Grigat, would already be there, said the order.

The tracks ground laboriously along the roadway through the heaps of debris. The stretch of road to Heubude was, I remembered, about three kilometres long. I had marked the map with details of the route to the Vistula bridge, as we wanted to move swiftly through the city, which was under heavy fire. Here and there we came across small groups of scattered soldiers who had lost their way.

After a neck-breaking journey over remnants of walls, concrete beams, and shattered gables, attacked from the air, avoiding exploding rocket salvoes and constant artillery fire, we came to the end of a long column of vehicles.

We waited for a while with the patience expected of good soldiers in war. But the stay in this area was not comfortable. Shots from anti-tank guns rang out regularly from somewhere. All around, vehicles of every type were ablaze. Ammunition exploded like crazy. But nobody appeared anywhere. That made me thoughtful. Then I hopped up and sprang back to life – on, on! On to the head of the column. That was obviously risky and difficult – but it paid off in the end.

My first glance told me that almost all of the vehicles were unmanned. The crews had apparently made their way onward on foot, and had left their vehicles and cargoes in the middle of the roadway to annoy those who followed.

I determined that the Vistula bridge was only 300 metres away. My second glance told me that it was 300 metres of inconceivable horror: eviscerated corpses of horses; burned-out wrecks of goods vehicles; bomb craters a metre deep; dead, dead, dead – burned, smashed. And amongst the smoking trucks I saw a few patient drivers sitting at their steering wheels, staring with crazed eyes at the vehicle in front, waiting for it to move – but the vehicle ahead had only a dead driver.

It shook me. We had to get away from here! We clattered over mountains of rubble in our able half-track, drove through gardens and back yards and reached the bridge at precisely the same moment that a powerful Soviet bomber formation came overhead. What should we do?

We could all see it – and we were already so hardened against dangers of all kinds. The main point was, the bridge was still there! Nobody could say how long it would still be crossable, this only remaining solid crossing over the Vistula. So we dashed out, as it seemed wonderfully clear – and that was our lucky break.

We bumped through shell craters, rolled over concrete blocks – bombs burst to left and right, shaking our radio vehicle, as they exploded with ear-splitting crashes in the riverbed. Shrapnel drove against the armoured sides, fountains of water rose to the sky, and fell back onto us. It was a drive through hell. I stared out of the observation port with increasing fear, saw how the bridge was torn open by a bomb on one side, how it shuddered – but remained standing.

… And there on the far bank there were more burning vehicles, cadavers of horses, destroyed war supplies, the debris of war piled high, as far as the eye could see. Yet the wounded and the dead here were safe.

We rolled into a roadside ditch, as the concentration of the driver slipped. We bumped into a tree, pushed a vehicle in front of us, tipped it sideways, and reached open ground the other side of the bridge: thank God for our cross-country radio vehicle![44]

The bridges that crossed the 'Dead Vistula' in Danzig were vital for the escape of the German defenders. The Soviet 108th Rifle Division reached the river at 1600hrs on 29 March and seized one of the crossings, and a second bridge was secured shortly after. Batov himself entered Danzig the following day:

The Senate House, the former offices of the Deutsche Arbeitsfront, was barricaded. We managed to enter. There were Panzerfausts, submachine-guns and shellcases everywhere. Apparently, they had resisted here for a long time. But our troops had broken their resistance within two days of tough streetfighting. The German Panzerfausts gave us good service in the storming of the city, and later on the Oder.

In the main post office, we found great stacks of the fascist newspaper *Danziger Vorposten*. On the title page of the still damp copies, the headlines proclaimed Goebbels' boastful comments: 'We will never surrender! Danzig is an impregnable fortress!'[45]

Danzig, the city over which Germany had ostensibly gone to war in 1939, had been part of the Reich for less than six years. It now lay in ruins, and in the hands of the Red Army. It is difficult to calculate how many civilians remained; most of those who had wished to leave had done so. Forster's policy of allowing any Poles who could claim German ancestry to be regarded as Germans meant that several thousand residents of the city now proclaimed themselves as Poles. Many of them joined the Red Army as it celebrated its great victory, both in Danzig and Gotenhafen. In other cases, though, the Soviet forces treated them in the same manner as civilians who had fallen into their hands elsewhere. Rokossovsky's plan to reduce the 'fortresses' had succeeded, though the cost in lives was heavy. Nevertheless, 2nd Belorussian

Front could now start sending its forces west to prepare for the assault across the Oder and on towards Berlin.

At the end of March, there was finally a lull in the battle. As Soviet soldiers rejoiced amidst the ruins of Danzig, their German opponents took advantage of their first opportunity for several weeks to catch up on sleep:

> The soldiers of the Red Army noisily took possession of all of Danzig and celebrated their success with vodka and music. We heard the noise of their victory celebrations all night. The propaganda loudspeakers blared at us constantly from the other side of the harbour: 'Soldiers of the German 2nd Army! You are now in a trap, having to feed yourselves...' Then they played the Radetzky march, with many Red Army soldiers accompanying it by firing their guns in time with the music. Every now and then, this was followed by an announcement: 'Next, we bring you an organ concert. On the organ – Josef Stalin!' A bombardment of rockets no longer came as any surprise. Then we would hear the usual comments about a swift return home after the war and good treatment and retention of personal effects. They then threatened us with total destruction if we did not heed their words. A new propaganda trick was to play recordings of Marikka Röck singing for hours at a time, day and night, over the loudspeakers; they must have found a recording in Danzig, where the film *Woman of My Dreams* was being shown in the cinemas in January.
>
> On the harbour mole, directly opposite us, the flags of the Soviet Union and the Nationalkomitee Freies Deutschland were flying. That alone caused a lot of pain. But knowledge of the dreadful treatment and hatred endured by those left behind in Danzig reduced many to despair.[46]

CHAPTER 14
THE LAST COMMAND

In this grave hour, the Wehrmacht remembers its comrades who fell in battle. The dead remind us of their unconditional loyalty, obedience and discipline, to set against the countless wounds of the bleeding Fatherland.

– Grossadmiral Dönitz[1]

Following the capture of Danzig and Gotenhafen, Rokossovsky's 2nd Belorussian Front began to transfer its forces to the west. Their task in West Prussia was almost complete; all that remained was the reduction of the German bridgehead around Oxhöft. This would still leave German units in Hela, as well as the remnants of 2nd Army in the Vistula estuary, but these were of lesser concern to Rokossovsky. The forces in Hela were no threat, and could be left isolated. The rest of 2nd Army was also too weak to intervene, and could be reduced by Vassilevsky's 3rd Belorussian Front.

The 7th Panzer Division continued to hold the perimeter of the Oxhöft pocket, which had been declared as a 'fortress' by Hitler. This designation required the soldiers to defend the fortress to the last man, but both VII Panzer Corps and 2nd Army ignored such instructions. On 29 March, Huber happened to be near a radio set, tuned to a Berlin radio station:

Suddenly, the news is transmitted, and a Wehrmacht report. It is 1300. I haven't heard this for two months. We stop working and listen. It sounds grim. American armoured spearheads are in Ansbach, Würzburg, Hammelburg. There's fighting in Frankfurt. And then we raise our heads. When reporting the *Ostfront*, the speaker says:

'The garrison of the Danzig–Gotenhafen bridgehead, after a heroic fight for Führer, Volk und Vaterland [Führer, People and Fatherland], was overwhelmed by the enemy yesterday and killed to the last man. The German people thank these heroes for their self-sacrifice in battle against Bolshevism!'

The two of us stare at each other. We haven't listened to our own Wehrmacht report before! According to that, we are all now dead. But we're still very much alive, we're still here! OKW has given us up.[2]

The following day, Soviet artillery plastered the entire perimeter of the pocket with heavy artillery fire. The first attack came on 31 March, achieving a deep penetration in the northern part of the perimeter, held by the remnants of SS-Polizei Panzergrenadier Division. The 7th Panzer Division's precious tanks were committed to seal off the penetration, and at dawn on 1 April the division's last three Panther tanks, close to where Huber's Jg.Pz. IV was deployed, shot up four heavy Josef Stalin tanks. Two more Josef Stalins were knocked out at close range by another tank.

All day, Soviet shells passed overhead, but most of the bombardment was targeted at areas to the rear. On 2 April, the defenders prepared to face another tank attack. Huber hit and destroyed a Josef Stalin, and disabled a second, though repeated hits failed to set it alight. An infantry attack on the German positions followed, but as the infantry prepared to make a final surge into the German positions, the Soviet preparatory bombardment fell on the Soviet soldiers by mistake, and the attack was broken off.[3]

Christern and the staff of 7th Panzer Division had their plans for an evacuation of the pocket ready, but were worried that there would not be sufficient time to put them into effect: by the beginning of April, the pocket stretched along only 5km of coastline, and at most a little less than 4km inland. A determined push by the Red Army would surely overwhelm the exhausted, hungry men. Although there were occasional attempts to push in the perimeter, as Huber and his comrades experienced, the expected intense assault did not come. The reason became clear when 7th Panzer Division's intelligence officer intercepted a Soviet radio message; the Soviet artillery units complained that they had not received fresh supplies for two days. The reply from higher command was to the effect that the supply columns would arrive 'in two or three days', something that brought relief to the listening Germans. There was, therefore, a brief breathing space.

Nevertheless, the Soviet infantry in front of Huber's position infiltrated forward during the night, and by dawn on 3 April were only 80m away. Later the same day, Huber's crew agreed that they would keep watch on the Soviet lines while the men in a neighbouring vehicle took advantage of the lull in fighting to catch up on sleep:

> The long spell of endurance then makes us very tired, and we too want to doze. But they don't respond over the radio. They are all asleep. We try countless times, for a whole quarter of an hour. The others of our company, who are listening on the radio, are also aware that Michl Weber and his crew are asleep. Only 50 metres away, we should be able to call them. But Michl Weber's crew doesn't hear us. We can't exactly throw a hand grenade at them to wake them up! That would do the job, but we can't, as our riflemen are in their trenches in between. So how can we get their attention?

... As I have taken control of Penn's radio equipment over the recoil mechanism of the gun, I remain in my gunner's seat. Leutnant Meier climbs up, stands aloft and shouts loudly, his hands cupped around his mouth, over to the other tank. 'Michl,' he calls, once, twice. I tell him that he should come back in, and then I hear a short pop and he grabs at his belly. He immediately folds up. A belly shot! What did I tell him! I pull at his camouflage jacket and trousers. He has a puncture wound. All you can see is a small blue spot and a bit of blood at the entry wound. I turn him over and find no exit wound on his back, it's all clean. Thank God we haven't eaten all day, so there won't be any food in his bowel. He has a chance of pulling through. Now, in this mess, in this cauldron on the Oxhöfter Kämpe, it will be hard for him to endure this. There's nothing to bandage, the wound isn't really bleeding. I do his jacket and uniform up again and reach for the transmitter, and report our mishap. Battalion HQ agrees to take the wounded man from us at the northern entry to the Hexengrund. The other vehicles have heard, apart from Michl Weber, and are aware that we are now moving off.

All hell breaks loose when the Russians see us. We drive with our barrel depressed, so that we can fire quickly to the left if required, and then we move out of our hole. As Bruno drives backwards, Michl Weber's crew hears the sound of our engine and wakes up. Penn gives them a short summary, telling them what happened and that we are taking Leutnant Meier.[4]

Meier was handed over to the waiting medics, and Huber and his comrades headed back to the frontline with a new vehicle commander. As they approached their former position, their engine failed. Early on 4 April, a tractor hauled them back to the rear area, where they received a small supply of food and fresh water for the first time in several days. Rumours were circulating about an imminent withdrawal, and early in the afternoon Huber's crew was ordered to destroy their Jg.Pz. IV:

This is the end. I become melancholy. We will now have to blow it up, our splendid Jagdpanzer 39/IV, our excellent vehicle, that has protected us so often. No enemy shell ever penetrated it.

... I undertake its destruction, together with Penn. First, we get our personal possessions – wash-kits, messkits. We still have plenty of ammunition. Is that also to be blown up? I have a better idea. Our tank is here, in the Hexengrund, with its gun towards the enemy. Together with Penn, I decide that we will fire off most of the high-explosive rounds at Ivan. No sooner said than done. Elevate the barrel, Penn loads and I pull the trigger. One after another flies off – with this barrel elevation, they will go at least ten or 15 kilometres. Somewhere, they will have an effect. Then, when we still have ten rounds left, we stop firing. We must leave some, so that the tank blows up properly. I take the destruction charge and read its instructions. Everything is precisely described, and I read it out to Penn, who has to know what we are doing. There isn't much time to talk about this before we come under air attack. A group of Il-2s circles overhead, very low, spots us of course, and makes a large, wide turn towards us.

I've had enough of this shit. 'Get the machine-gun out, we're going to defend ourselves!' Penn removes the machine-gun from its ball socket on his side and passes it over to me. On the rear, on the engine decking, there is a support, and I put the MG-42 there and load. The first Russian ground-attack plane is already approaching and firing. I aim at the second, as the first is already overhead. We have prepared our machine-gun belt well, with every other round a tracer. This will have a big effect on the attacker's morale. I aim at his propeller hub, look up, correct aim from the tracer flight: now we're both shooting at each other, eye to eye, man to man. The 20mm shells fly past, over and to the side. That's fine by me, my finger remains on the trigger. It is of course an uneven fight, a machine-gun against eight 20mm cannon... He fires at our rear and our exhausts. When the first 20mm shells land behind us, I quickly pull my head in, as I don't want to get a burst in my face. After the Il-2 has passed, I give up. I conclude that there's no chance of my overcoming the Russian, and that I can do nothing to him with my machine-gun. These things are all armoured, and every shot bounces off.

The attack is over. They fly off. Now comes the end. Almost festively, we emerge. Penn places the destruction charge in the breech – I close it. Now out. We have 90 seconds to get clear. Not much happens, as we have fired off most of the high-explosive rounds and there's little fuel left. There's a dull explosion and the hatches fly open. There's little to see from the rear. There's no fire. We look at it sadly, as it's too dangerous to go close again. I feel really bad – now it's smashed, our tank 405.[5]

On the same day that Huber and his comrades had to destroy their tank, General von Saucken released the codeword *Walpurgisnacht* (the eve of Mayday, traditionally regarded as a night when witches meet in the Harz Mountains in Germany), authorizing the evacuation of the Oxhöft pocket. As darkness fell, a flotilla of 67 military ferries and small ships made their way to the makeshift landing stages. Some 30,000 refugees, most of them previously evacuated from Danzig and Gotenhafen just before the cities fell, were the first to leave, along with the last of the wounded. A little off the coast, the cruiser *Lützow*, three destroyers and several smaller warships stood ready to provide fire support.

The men of 7th Panzer Division waited patiently for their turn.

Late, at 0200, we finally move on. We receive instructions. In front of us is the coast, and we are to go down a steep slope to a landing vessel. Whatever, it's all the same. Orders are given to form a chain. Nobody is to let go of anyone else. It's very dark. There's only the firm grip of one hand on the next, one man to the next. Now forwards. After a while, it grows a little lighter – the sea is before us. And then we fall down. There's no more talk of holding hands – we roll, slip and slide down the steep coast. It must be quite high. It goes on and on, 30, 40 metres, then no further. There's not much to see, and we find ourselves in a ditch, with dune grass to left and right. Everyone is too busy looking after himself from the fall.

Suddenly, I find myself on a small beach. You can see the outline of the surf, a bright strip, quite close. Someone calls to us: 'On, up on the jetty, over here, on to the ferry.' Running, we cross a small two-metre-wide jetty in the darkness over the water to a dark space, the bow hatch of a ferry. Concentrating to make sure I don't fall from the jetty, I reach the hatch and go in. It goes a good metre down into the ferry. Then, further commands: back, towards the back! Everyone understands that they have to make space for those who are following.

Our ferry is only one third full. Then the engine is started. In the darkness inside, all you can see is the outline of the landing gangway against the moonless sky. Then there are churning noises, we move backwards, forwards, sideways, we can no longer tell the direction. The steady noise of a diesel engine. We are at sea, on the Bay of Danzig.[6]

The crews of the last four Jg.Pz. IVs, three Panthers and two assault guns – all that remained of 7th Panzer Division's armoured vehicles – left their engines running with the sump plugs removed, and silently made their way to the landing stage. The last ferry left at 0300hrs on 5 April, and as the eastern horizon began to show the first light of dawn, a party including General von Kessel, Generalmajor Wengler and Oberst Christern, the last men to leave, boarded a small naval motorboat. Not long after, delayed fuses detonated the last ammunition stores.

Von Saucken ordered the evacuation of the pocket without first securing approval from higher authorities. In the past, such behaviour would have earned him a court-martial. On this occasion, just hours after the evacuation had begun, orders arrived from Berlin authorizing the withdrawal.

Although this account appears in several memoirs and books, there is another version,[7] which describes how the corps commander called a conference of his division commanders. In this conference, Standartenführer Harzer took a leading role, pointing out that each day was costing his division 15 per cent casualties. As a result, it was agreed that an evacuation could not be delayed. The account states that preparations for the evacuation were made by Harzer's Chief of Staff, Hauptsturmführer Lutze, and that by dusk on 4 April no order for the evacuation had been received. Harzer and the other division commanders then took it upon themselves to begin the withdrawal without authority.

Few documents have survived to reveal the truth about this episode; given that many of the plans and discussions would have resulted in immediate court-martial, it is likely that few contemporaneous records, if any, were made. The account that credits Harzer and the staff of SS-Polizei with the evacuation seems at odds with the majority of the evidence. This account also states that a single company from 83rd Infantry Division was left behind, and had to fight alone on the Oxhöfter Kämpe all through 5 April. When boats arrived to evacuate it after nightfall, there were only five survivors.[8] The primary history of the 83rd Infantry Division, by contrast, makes no mention of such a finale to the fighting at Oxhöft, and it would be remarkable if this detailed work failed to mention such a dramatic event.[9] On balance, therefore, it seems likely that the 'majority version' of events is the correct one. General von Kessel was ordered back to Berlin to account for the 'premature' evacuation, but no action was taken against him.

German forces in East and West Prussia now held a small area of land, with their backs to the sea. These were disparate units – some from 2nd Army, some the remains of the units that had been evacuated from the Heiligenbeil pocket where 4th Army was destroyed, and some originally from 3rd Panzer Army. On 10 April, they were gathered together under a single command as Armee-Oberkommando Ostpreussen (AOK Ostpreussen; Army High Command East Prussia), commanded by General von Saucken. The former commander of 4th Panzer Division and Panzer Corps *Grossdeutschland*, who had been born in Fischhausen, would command all the remaining German forces in Prussia for what remained of the war.

Hela and its peninsula were isolated, with the only route in or out by sea. Although there was fighting on the Putziger Nehrung, Soviet forces made little determined effort to take the naval base. Shortly after the evacuation of Oxhöft, the Soviet 18th Rifle Division attempted to drive down the narrow strip, but was brought to a halt at the first anti-tank ditch that ran across the Nehrung. To the east of Danzig, the remnants of the units that had fought in and around Danzig continued to reorganize themselves as best they could, protected to the south by flooded land. The area was crossed by several arms of the Vistula – the river had changed its course many times over the centuries, the most important recent change being in 1840, when flooding resulted in a new, broad channel opening up near Schiewenhorst. The flat landscape, combined with the high water levels in the river as a result of the winter snows and rain, and the deliberate destruction of dykes by German Army engineers, brought about widespread flooding between Elbing and Danzig, making a Soviet attack from the south all but impossible. This small enclave, crowded with the remains of 2nd Army and tens of thousands of refugees, stretched to the Frische Nehrung, and thence to Pillau. Beyond Pillau, what remained of the divisions that had been driven into Samland by Cherniakovsky awaited the final Soviet onslaught. With Königsberg now in Soviet hands, such an attack would surely not be delayed for long.

Von Saucken's battered divisions had done their best to refill their ranks with stragglers and men from disbanded formations. Lorenz's *Grossdeutschland* had scoured Samland in search of armoured vehicles, and had managed to repair and salvage sufficient fighting vehicles to form a small battlegroup. But when the Soviet onslaught came, there could be no doubt about the outcome. The divisions in Samland existed more on paper than in reality. Although they still had regiments and battalions bearing the old numbers and names, these were shadows of their former strength – stragglers and rear-area personnel, Volkssturm and Hitler Youth, with a few veteran officers and NCOs amongst them. And even these veterans were at the end of their strength. Von Saucken made his views clear to his staff: the task of the remaining German forces

AOK OSTPREUSSEN

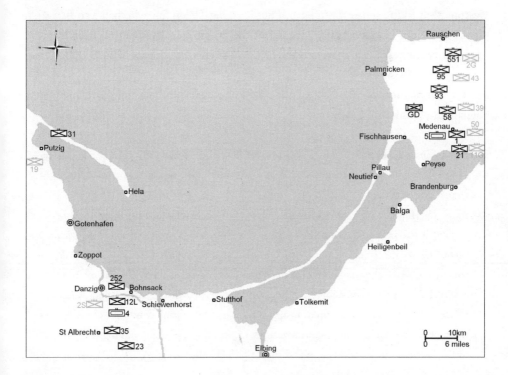

was to hold off the Red Army as long as possible, so that the thousands of refugees who still waited in Samland, the Vistula estuary and Hela would have a chance to escape.

After its heavy losses in and around Danzig, 4th Panzer Division rapidly absorbed soldiers from other units in order to replenish its strength. Although it was short of fighting vehicles – its Panzer regiment had only 15 tanks still capable of action – it remained one of the more powerful formations available to the German defenders in the Vistula estuary. Soviet units from 2nd Shock Army launched repeated attacks to the east of Danzig, and the German units there slowly fell back to the line of the Vistula and the '1840 channel'.

The Wehrmacht report that had disheartened Huber and the soldiers of 7th Panzer Division when it prematurely announced the destruction of the Oxhöft pocket, also had a depressing effect on 4th Panzer Division. The town of Würzburg, mentioned in the report as the scene of heavy fighting between American and German forces, was the home town of many of the division's men. One of the periodic reports produced by 4th Panzer Division's headquarters recorded that, despite its losses, the division was still in comparatively good shape.[10] Consequently, orders arrived from the Inspector-General of Armoured Forces in Berlin, to the effect that the division should be withdrawn from combat and shipped back to Germany as soon as possible. Once there, the orders continued, the division would receive new equipment and would be able to restore itself to full fighting strength. There can have been few who believed that such new equipment would actually appear, but the orders caused an enormous stir in the division: at the very least, there was the prospect of escape from the Vistula estuary, and return to Germany.

The sand dunes to the east of the 1840 channel were teeming with people, as Schäufler recorded:

Further inland, beyond the range of Soviet artillery, there was a great throng, a gathering of people who were almost impossible to understand. One could hear the languages of almost every country.

... The first I met were 32 British officers, prisoners of war who about four weeks previously had crossed the frontlines to us in the Heiderode area; they had behaved strictly according to the rules of war, with white flags and a formal parley. They told us convincingly that they had been liberated from German captivity by Red Army troops in Schlossberg – their expression was, they had been left by their guards – and were then going to be sent east to an unknown destination. They didn't trust this 'freedom', set themselves free again at an opportune moment, and through night and fog they crossed to the German lines. And they asked most politely and correctly, as is the English way, whether they could come and stay with us. If necessary, they stressed, without being asked, that they would be prepared to fight on the German side.

At the time, this offer had certainly given a huge lift to our greatly diminished morale. Of course, we readily accepted them, and gave them a fair share of food and cigarettes.

The situation at that time was so confused that the Englishmen had to stay in our regimental HQ for three days, before they could be sent to the rear. In this time, we achieved a good understanding with them, and became good friends. Now they were waiting, like hundreds of thousands of others, for a ship to the west.

… Somewhat detached from the 'ordinary folk' were the encampments of the aristocracy from Reval and Riga, with fur coats and heavy trunks and cases. They had fallen out with their former subjects, who were no longer so obedient in the new social structure.

In a hollow, a group of Polish women cowered, who appeared also to want to go west with us, perhaps because they had reason to fear the anger of their victorious compatriots. In any event, they were very taciturn, occasionally whispering softly to each other.

Here and there were groups of Russian volunteers, former soldiers of the Red Army who until now had chosen to fight on our side. In view of the approaching end, they had to decide quickly where they wanted to go. The situation for them was particularly tragic.

And all the hundreds of thousands, soldiers and civilians, West Prussians and East Prussians, Lithuanians, Estonians and Latvians, Pomeranians and Poles, English and French, they were all fed by our field kitchens, from appropriated cauldrons and even from dug-in bathtubs, and thanks to an astonishing degree of organization in this difficult situation, they were all well fed.

Admittedly, all the military horses of the infantry and also from the wagons of the refugees had been moved to the field kitchens and improvised cookhouses. We ate them without knowing whether we were eating crop or hoof, muzzle or tail. The support and feeding of all the people gathered in the Vistula valley was a masterful achievement.[11]

Amongst the thousands of civilians who had left Danzig with the retreating German soldiers was Renate Dannenberg, who was 25 years old. Wearily, she and her family trudged east, occasionally helped by passing soldiers and sometimes even receiving assistance from aid stations set up for the refugees. On 31 March, as they passed a church, they heard organ music, and ventured inside:

It was the most shocking thing that I experienced during our entire flight. Words can't express what I experienced at that time! Even now, I can see the scene clearly, every morning: a small village chapel, with white pews outside the door. A dim light streamed into the church through the stained glass windows. Wounded soldiers lay here on the straw, their bandages red with blood. And somewhere, someone played the organ – I can't remember now what it was that was being played. They weren't jubilant, uplifting tunes, but rather quiet melodies that flowed into each other, spreading calm and giving one a sense of peace, so that one could say from the depths of one's soul: 'Tell me Your will, Lord.'[12]

In the first few days of April, 2nd Shock Army made a determined attempt to drive northeast from a position south of Danzig, in order to prevent the German divisions facing Danzig itself from retreating over the 1840 channel. Pantenius and his soldiers were at the northern end of 35th Infantry Division's sector, and found themselves under constant attack. Matters were made worse by the presence of Soviet forces on the comparatively high ground to the southwest, from where they had clear line of sight through almost all the division's area. Pantenius was forced to relinquish the town of St Albrecht, but despite this the line continued to hold. Problems persisted between the personnel of 35th Infantry Division and the former Volksgrenadiers:

My relationship with the division commander, Generalleutnant Richert, had improved during and after the fighting for St Albrecht. He had probably convinced himself that something could be achieved with the new 109th Regiment (the former 690th Regiment); perhaps the replacement of the Chief of Staff (now Major Rehfeld) also played a role. It was only later that there was once more a difference of opinions, in the new positions near Reichenberg. It related to our field guns. Of the 12 light field guns, I had brought eight back with me, and had redeployed them. Now the division ordered that in view of the ammunition shortage – we had only 400 rounds – and to provide more 'trench fighters', I was to hand over half of the eight guns and redeploy their crews as infantry. I had deliberately taken some time to carry out the order. If the guns were taken away, I would never get them back, and the 400 rounds provided 50 per gun, which was sufficient to break up any infantry attack across the open ground anywhere along our front from the four firing points. With four guns, covering the entire frontage of the regiment was not possible. Besides, I had enough riflemen in the front, and therefore did not need the gun crews, who were hardly trained as infantrymen. The general had got the idea from somewhere, apparently from his aide-de-camp. In any case, he personally came forward, complained about orders not being followed, and took no heed of my objections. The four guns therefore had to be given up. There was no opportunity to prove who was right, as the enemy didn't make any energetic attacks. When they did make one attempt, the flooded ground constrained them to a dyke, at the western end of which we had an advance post, and at first a crisis developed. I happened to be right at the spot to stop four assault guns that were coming back from Gottswalde to rearm.

The guns had only armour-piercing rounds, no high-explosive rounds. But the Oberfeldwebel was very cooperative, and didn't stick to his orders, but immediately went into position and fired on the roughly company-strength enemy with armour-piercing rounds. The effect of the shells, partly by ricochets, was greater on morale than in casualties, and there were only two or three direct hits amongst them. The counter-attack I had organized with the company in that position, led by an energetic Leutnant, had the desired effect. The enemy pulled back off the dyke with considerable casualties, and didn't make any more attempts.[13]

To the surprise of many, the rumours about 4th Panzer Division's return to Germany suddenly came true: a group of 200 tank crewmen was to move to Hela immediately, from where it would be evacuated back to Schleswig-Holstein. Once there, the group would receive new armoured vehicles and would form the nucleus of a refreshed division. After much debate and argument, the officers of 4th Panzer Division decided to exploit this opportunity to save at least one group of men from surrender to the Soviet Union. Hauptmann Küspert, commander of one of 35th Panzer Regiment's tank battalions, was appointed commander of the small group, which was carefully selected from men who were either the last surviving sons of families, or had young families of their own. The disappointed men who were left behind waved their comrades goodbye, and returned to their own duties, comforting themselves that at least these men would escape the clutches of the Red Army.

Hela was now overflowing with refugees and evacuated soldiers. The tiny fishing village and neighbouring naval base had long ago run out of accommodation, and makeshift camps stretched along the dunes. Every day, ships continued to arrive to take away as many people as could be evacuated, running the gauntlet of air attack and the threat of submarines. Despite their plans, the Soviet forces had failed to make much impression on shipping movements using their shore-based artillery. But now that the entire western coastline of the Bay of Danzig was in Soviet hands, far more guns were able to open fire on both the ships and the Hela peninsula.

The *Moltkefels* was a 7,800-tonne freighter that had already completed several evacuation voyages, particularly in the second part of 1944 when she helped evacuate German troops from Finland. On 10 April, the ship approached Hela at first light, and promptly came under air attack. One of her escorts, little more than a large motor-boat, was hit and blown to pieces. As she entered the Bay of Danzig, the *Moltkefels* briefly ran aground, but by 0800hrs she was surrounded by small vessels ferrying refugees and wounded men to her. There was another air raid at 1100hrs, but no ships were hit and the loading continued until 1200hrs, when the *Moltkefels* was almost overflowing and could take aboard no more passengers. She was ordered, however, to remain in the bay until 1900hrs, when the next convoy would be leaving for the west. To the consternation of the ship's crew, the ship also took on board two large tanks full of petrol, which were surplus to requirements in Hela. At 1400hrs, the *Moltkefels* suddenly came under artillery fire. The shells landed right alongside, and the concussion damaged the freighter's engines.

Despite this damage, the ship could still manoeuvre, and when Soviet aircraft attacked again at 1600hrs the *Moltkefels* attempted to avoid the falling bombs by adopting a zigzag course. Moving slowly, she was hit three times and left dead in the water. The next bomber hit her again, setting the petrol tanks on her deck ablaze. In all, the *Moltkefels* was hit five times. Small boats rushed to her aid, but found it difficult to approach because of the inferno on her deck. The crew struggled for four hours to save their ship and the thousands of people aboard, as Henry Lange, the ship's second officer, recorded:

There were indescribable scenes. There was only one thing for us to do: to help save as many as possible.

We continued to pull wounded soldiers, who were still alive, from the hatches. Our third officer climbed down a rope from the bow into the smoke-filled hold below hatch two. But he had to return to safety when he was fired on by badly wounded men who had lost all hope of being rescued.

The front half of the ship was covered with smoking bodies, dead and wounded. Everywhere, wherever one turned – people. It was almost impossible to distinguish between the dead and those still alive.

There were flames wherever one looked: the superstructure, the bridge, and amidships.

We lowered anyone who still lived and cried out over the side to the ships that had gathered around the *Moltkefels* to save whoever could still be saved.

Not far from us, when the clouds of smoke allowed a glimpse, we could see the blazing hospital ship *Posen*.

The glowing, blazing funnel fell overboard, and the ammunition held ready at the flak mounts exploded. Shrapnel flew across the deck, wounding and maiming, killing here and there.

The burning oil poured from the bulkheads, across the deck and through the hatches.

Only the stern was not ablaze. From here, many people constantly leapt overboard into the Baltic.

There were still desperate refugees everywhere – women, with their small children clinging to them, their faces blackened by smoke, not injured, just distressed … a girl hurried across the deck, perhaps 12 or 13 years old, behind her mother. They had come from the ship's interior, risking a dash through the wall of flames, and were burning. The woman's hairpins were gone in a flash, and she had burns on her head and back. And the girl had suffered burns to her legs as she made her way up from the lower deck. A sailor dashed to help them. The girl still had the strength to climb down a scramble net and, when a sailor called to her, to let herself drop into the waiting arms of the helpers on a rescue boat. Two medics carried the badly injured mother down the gangway to a lighter that had tied up alongside the burning ship.[14]

Eventually, a tugboat pushed the stricken vessel aground, and the last survivors were taken off. The captain estimated that his ship had been carrying 2,700 refugees, 1,000 wounded and a crew of 300, including a large contingent of flak gunners. Of these, between 400 and 500 died in the inferno. The *Posen*, a small hospital ship that was hit in the same raid, was carrying 729 wounded and refugees. A little less than half of them died.

Engelhardt's evacuation ships continued their tireless work. Attacks from Soviet aircraft and the threat of submarines remained, but despite such dangers the fleet of ships, large and small, continued to shuttle between Pillau and Hela, and the ports of the west. On 15 April, the *Pretoria*, a 16,600-tonne liner, was moored off Hela awaiting a convoy for the west. She wore the distinctive livery of a hospital ship, but on this occasion she carried some 2,000 soldiers, not all of them wounded. They were mainly men from SS-Polizei and 7th Panzer Division, who had been evacuated from Oxhöft earlier in the month. As the morning light grew brighter, Soviet artillery along the Oxhöft coast opened fire on the ships near Hela. The destroyer *Z 34* promptly moved closer and silenced the guns. The next threat came from the air, at 0930hrs. The first attack was by a wave of fighters, seeking to silence the anti-aircraft defences of the ships. The bombers followed later and made their attack run, targeting the *Pretoria*. She suffered several near misses, which left small fires burning on her decks. These were quickly extinguished, and the crew soon satisfied themselves that the ship was not significantly damaged. At 1100hrs, there was a second bomber raid, again preceded by fighters. Once more, the *Pretoria* was the target, and once more she was left with numerous small fires. Again, the crew swiftly extinguished them.

In order to protect his ship, the captain moved the *Pretoria* closer to Hela's anti-aircraft guns. Johann Huber had just boarded an old steamer named *Charlotte Schröder*, which now moved away from Hela and waited for a convoy to form up:

The strong, ice-cold northeast wind blows steadily, and our steamer tosses at anchor in the high waves. The sea state must be between six and seven, according to the sailors above us on the quad flak mount, when we ask them. They remain at their posts, as we can expect air attack at any time… Ships gather around us. Picket boats, minesweepers move around us as guards, and then, at about 1500, the magic suddenly breaks loose. Over there, on another ship, the flak starts to fire and then ours joins in. The gun is only two metres above us. So we see, some distance from the tracers of our quad mount, a whole crowd of bombers flying up. They are in formation, and we hear their engines resonating. They are heavily loaded, Russian bombers flying in on the east wind. They are Douglas Bostons, twin-engined… Now the bombs start to fall from the bomb-bays, stick after stick, a heavy load, they are almost coming down on us. No, they're to one side. A quick glance around tells me that we are the smallest ship in the waiting convoy. We can hear the bombs falling and then howl after howl as they approach their target, a ship a few hundred metres from us, the *Pretoria*. The *Pretoria* is the biggest ship in our convoy, about 16,000 tonnes, white, beautifully white, with a large red cross on her – she's a hospital ship. The bastards are aiming right for her, without any regard for the Articles of War. The bombs tumbling down – the squadron has now moved on – confirm our suspicions. What will happen? Now they hit – in the water! The whole load drops into the sea. All off target. Hooray! The water spouts rise high, 60 or 80 metres, all behind the *Pretoria*'s stern. But the last bomb hits her stern. It explodes, and the ship burns. Smoke swiftly envelops her. What will happen now? The beautiful ship turns immediately into the wind, the crew run frantically hither and thither – and actually put the fire out in ten minutes. The fire is out! Thank God, we say to each other.[15]

The bomb left 11 dead and 24 wounded, but the ship was still able to get under way. At 1730hrs, she left in a convoy with four other ships. Although she was taking in water, her crew laboured with the ship's pumps to keep her afloat. The *Pretoria* survived the war, having evacuated a total of more than 35,000 people, and was taken over by the British under the name *Empire Doon*. She was converted into a troop carrier, and in 1949 renamed the *Empire Orwell*. For a brief time, she served as a ship carrying pilgrims on the Hajj from Asia to Saudi Arabia under the name *Gunung Djati*. In 1973, she became a troopship again, as part of the Indonesian navy, and was renamed *Tanjung Pandang*, before finally being sold to Taiwan for scrap in 1987, the last surviving ship of Engelhardt's evacuation fleet.

In Samland, 5th Panzer Division's commander, General Hoffmann-Schönborn, was wounded near Metgethen on 9 April, and Oberst Herzog, who had commanded the division during the retreat to Königsberg and the subsequent breakout, resumed command. At this stage, a draft order appeared, which later caused a great deal of controversy. The order, codenamed *York*, appeared to suggest that 5th Panzer Division should break through Russian lines to the north, and then attempt to escape westwards in small groups. The intention, it seems, was to prevent the isolation and destruction of the division in the Peyse peninsula – if it found itself cut off here, it would try to reach the German lines north of Pillau. In any event, the order was not put into effect, but the movements of some of the division's elements in the coming days appeared to be contrary to the instructions of higher commands.

Although 24th Panzer Division had suffered catastrophic losses trying to reach Balga, a few thousand men, many from the division's rear-area units, had succeeded in reaching Samland. On 5 April, the division received orders to arrange for a party of 250 'specialists' to be sent back to Germany, ostensibly to form the core of a new division. This group was carefully selected, much in the way that 4th Panzer Division's officers chose the men who formed Group *Küspert*, and dispatched to Hela; from there, the men travelled west aboard the *Ganther* on 19 April. By a variety of means, an additional 500 men from the division were transferred to Germany, many nominated as advance

THE PILLAU AND PEYSE PENINSULAS

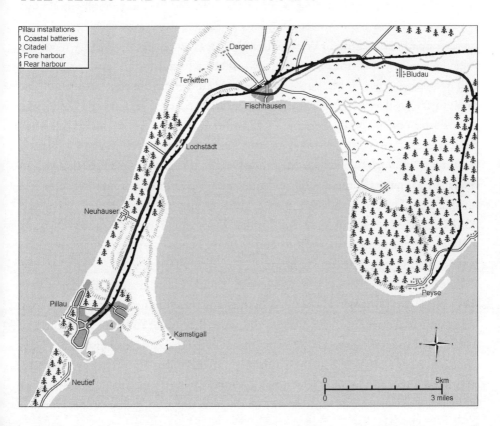

parties to prepare for the complete withdrawal of the division. It was even possible to arrange a Luftwaffe plane to collect the wounded Generalmajor von Nostitz-Wallwitz from Neutief and take him to the west. The rest of the division was deployed as infantry, to face the final Soviet assault.

On 12 April, Vassilevsky's air forces dropped thousands of leaflets on the German troops facing 3rd Belorussian Front in Samland. The message was the same as in previous leaflets: the situation was hopeless, the Germans should lay down their weapons, and there was a promise of good treatment and a swift return home after the war. The response, too, was the same – resistance.

Another important event on that day was the death of the US President, Franklin Roosevelt. He had been unwell for many months, but his death still came as a shock. In Germany, Goebbels and others greeted the news with jubilation: here was definitive proof that the events of the reign of Frederick the Great were about to be repeated. Now, surely, the western Allies would join Germany in the great fight against the Bolshevik menace. It wasn't just the Nazi diehards who hoped for a new upsurge in German fortunes; a soldier in 35th Panzer Regiment recorded in his diary that 'This must be the great turning point of the war.'[16] But even though the doubts Churchill had held about Soviet intentions in Europe were now receiving a slightly more sympathetic hearing in Washington, there was no prospect of history repeating itself. Unlike Frederick the Great, there would be no escape for Hitler.

The following day, 3rd Belorussian Front started its final drive into Samland. The preliminary artillery bombardment and air attacks stretched far into the hinterland. At the southern end of the German line, 21st Infantry Division was outflanked when Soviet forces advanced swiftly to Heydekrug, forcing both this division and 1st Infantry Division to its north to pull back their line. Despite the heavy pressure, both divisions managed to maintain their front and prevent a Soviet breakthrough, though at a terrible cost. The commanders of three regiments from the two German divisions – 43rd Grenadier Regiment and 22nd Fusilier Regiment from 1st Infantry Division, and 45th Grenadier Regiment from 21st Infantry Division – were killed or mortally wounded during the first day's fighting.

The 5th Panzer Division, together with 505th Heavy Panzer Battalion, still deployed about 20 tanks. Hamstrung by fuel and ammunition shortages, the tank crews and artillerymen of the division did what they could to help the infantry of 1st and 21st Infantry Divisions. Reinforcements in the shape of elements of 28th Jäger Division were committed to the frontline, but the relentless pressure continued. The 32nd Infantry Division, which had been reforming in the Hela peninsula, was also rushed to Pillau. As it made its way up the Nehrung road, it came under constant air attack. Many of its men were killed or wounded before the division even reached Samland.

Further north, Soviet infantry and armour smashed through the lines of 93rd Infantry Division. Behind the infantry was a group of ten Tiger tanks from 511th Heavy Panzer Battalion, and these moved immediately into action. Their swift intervention brought the Soviet advance to an abrupt halt, and 93rd Infantry Division was able to recover most of its positions. Further north, 2nd Guards Army attacked 95th Infantry Division and 551st Volksgrenadier Division with rather more success – XII Guards Tank Corps broke through the lines of both divisions and swiftly advanced. A small group of Hetzer tank-hunters from 511th Heavy Panzer Battalion attempted in vain to intercept the Soviet drive, which reached Palmnicken in the evening. The 95th Infantry Division was reduced to a single regiment, and 551st Volksgrenadier Division was encircled in and around Rauschen. Generalleutnant Siegfried Verhein, the division commander, and General Rolf Wuthmann, commander of IX Corps, were taken prisoner.

With the northern part of the German line in Samland swept away, the Soviet 2nd Guards Army turned south. Even if the southern part of the front should continue to hold, it was now threatened with being enveloped from the rear. What remained of 95th Infantry Division fell back to Palmnicken, on the west coast of Samland. Isolated in its little enclave, the men fought on in the town until 16 April, when small groups attempted to make their way south towards Pillau. Generalmajor Joachim-Friedrich Lang, the division commander, was one of the last to be killed as the groups were overwhelmed. In the path of the advancing Soviet forces were the battlegroups built around the surviving personnel of *Grossdeutschland*; none was stronger than 150 men, and they had few heavy weapons. Hauptmann Mackert's group deployed immediately to the rear of 58th Infantry Division, and Oberleutnant Pohl's group, made up mainly of former tank crews, took up positions to the rear of 1st Infantry Division. Mackert and his men attempted to launch a counter-attack late on 13 April to recover lost ground:

My attack lane ran from the trench west of Norgau to Hill 60, where I had contact with a Panzer-Fusilier battalion. To the right of the trench across Hill 63 ran the attack lanes of 5th and 7th Companies. During the night our attack got to within almost 50 metres of the first houses of Norgau. However, since we had just one light machine-gun and no other heavy weapons to support us, we were unable to evict the Soviets from their entrenched positions in the houses in spite of the use of Panzerfausts. My company (6th Company) advanced with élan, which was especially spurred on by the screams of women being tormented in the town. But we were unable to enter; the men were halted in front of the town by heavy mortar and machine-gun fire. By going around the large bog west of the town, however, 5th and 7th Companies were able to enter the first houses of Norgau. They could not hold out there for long, however; enemy tanks forced them to give up and withdraw to their starting positions.[17]

Despite this failure, the Soviet advance was, for the moment, brought to a halt. Low cloud on 14 April provided welcome relief from Soviet air attacks, but a few bombs still fell on Pillau, where refugees and wounded continued to wait for a ship to take them to safety. Some 60,000 had been evacuated from the beleaguered port in the first two weeks of the month. For the 20,000 who remained, the only route of escape was by military ferry to the Frische Nehrung, and thence down the coast to the Vistula estuary. Through much of March, Engelhardt had ordered his fleet to concentrate on evacuating refugees from Danzig and Gotenhafen, and it was only after the fall of the two cities that major ships were sent once more to Pillau. The first significant convoy had appeared on 10 April, with four ships ranging from the *Adele Traber* at slightly more than 2,500 tonnes to the diminutive 127-tonne *Nautik*. Soviet air attacks failed to score any hits, but shrapnel from a near miss left the *Herkules* with a leak. After making emergency repairs, the ships left port again that night with its companions, taking 6,500 refugees, 2,350 wounded and 400 soldiers with them.[18]

On 12 April, the *Vale* arrived in Pillau, bringing desperately needed munitions, but was unable to unload during daylight because of Soviet artillery fire. During the following night, the supplies were taken ashore, at least in part by slave labourers from the prison camp that lay immediately outside the old naval fortress in Pillau. The following morning, Soviet bombers struck while the ship was taking wounded men aboard. Three bombs struck the *Vale*, and she was left powerless and drifting. The wind blew her aground, where she was abandoned. A total of 250 wounded men died in the stricken ship. Two other ships, the *Weserstein* and *Wiegand*, also came under attack on the same day, this time from bombers. The *Weserstein* took several hits and quickly sank. *Wiegand* was hit once before she had taken any passengers aboard. The bomb penetrated her deck and lodged in her interior, but failed to explode. It wasn't possible to remove the bomb or defuse it, and after a brief discussion the captain ordered that the presence of the bomb was to be kept secret. The ship took aboard 2,800 refugees and sailed west, making an uneventful journey to Rendsburg, near Kiel.[19]

After Danzig and Gotenhafen had fallen, Hela remained full of refugees, with more being brought constantly from Schiewenhorst. On 16 April the *Goya* arrived, having completed her fourth evacuation voyage. To date, she had taken nearly 20,000 people west, and as the waiting refugees and soldiers gazed at the 5,230-tonne ship, with her striking polygonal camouflage pattern, many wondered whether she would be the last large vessel. The *Goya* was much newer than many of the other ships in the evacuation fleet, having been completed in 1942. For much of the war, she had been used by U-boat crews for target practice, being hunted and attacked with dummy torpedoes. Now, at first light, she came under aerial attack. One bomb struck her, causing damage to her superstructure and destroying her submarine and mine detection gear.

Dozens of small boats ferried passengers out to the *Goya* and the smaller ships that had arrived with her. Amongst those who went aboard were the personnel of Group *Küspert*, the carefully selected soldiers who were officially returning to north Germany to receive new tanks, but in reality were using the only escape route from the Red Army. Meanwhile, air attacks continued, inflicting heavy casualties on those who waited on the crowded quay. Three near misses riddled the small *Kurisches Haff*, which was relaying passengers to the *Goya*, with shrapnel, and swamped her with a wave that swept refugees from her crowded deck into the sea. Nevertheless, the loading continued, and by the evening roughly 7,000 people were aboard the *Goya*.

The convoy that set off consisted of the *Goya, Merkator, Kronenfels* and *Aegir*, escorted by two vessels, the *M 256* and *M 328*. The *Goya* was capable of running at 18 knots, but the other ships were far slower, and the convoy was restricted to a maximum speed of only 9 knots. At 2200hrs, flares rose into the night sky from the *M 328*: a lookout had spotted a shadow, possibly a Soviet torpedo boat or even a submarine. The captain of the *Goya* ordered lifejackets to be donned, but there were only 1,500 aboard, and several worried passengers attempted to purchase lifejackets with jewellery.

At 2230hrs, the convoy hove to. The *Kronenfels* had developed mechanical problems. The two escorts worriedly crisscrossed between their charges, but after only 20 minutes, the crew of the *Kronenfels* reported that they had successfully repaired the problem. Once more the convoy headed west.

The original destination of the ships had been Swinemünde, but at 2300hrs a signal was received redirecting the convoy to Copenhagen. For the crews of the ships, this news was greeted with relief: the danger of mines was far less in Danish waters. But a much greater danger was already waiting. The Soviet submarine *L 3* had been awarded 'Guards' status for previous successes, and its commander, Captain Third Class Vladimir Konovalov, was anxious to improve on his last attempt – on 31 January he had fired torpedoes at the liner *Cap Arcona* without scoring any hits. At 2352hrs, he opened fire on the largest ship in the convoy.

Jochen Hannemann was one of the personnel of Group *Küspert* aboard the ship:

We men of 35th Panzer Regiment were amidships in the lower decks. Everywhere, in the gangways, cabins and holds, women, children, wounded and soldiers stood, sat and lay. One could hardly move about. It was hot and the air was very stale. Again and again, I worked my way to the upper deck to breathe fresh air. That probably saved my life.

The night was crystal clear and the sea was calm. It was cold and sharp outside. Shortly before midnight, when I was once more on deck, there were two dull explosions. The ship rocked. Enormous spouts of water flew into the black sky and fell back onto the deck. Then the lights went out. There was a terrible panic inside the *Goya*. Everyone rushed for the exits. There were terrible scenes at the stairwells on the lower decks. A fight for life or death began. What happened inside the ship is probably beyond anyone's experiences. It must have been terrible, appalling. The water surged and rushed through the enormous holes left by the torpedoes. The ship broke apart amidships and sank very quickly. The din of the waters closing on the wreck was terrible.

When I could no longer stay on the ship, I jumped over the railing into the icy Baltic. An enormous wave broke over me. Suddenly a life-raft drifted past, which had apparently been washed off the *Goya* as the waters broke over her. I was able to climb aboard. Later a whole crowd of people grabbed at the raft.

Desperately we fought with the waves in the ice-cold water for two hours. We were completely exhausted when a navy ship came and took us aboard.[20]

The first torpedo struck the *Goya* near the bow, the second amidships. All power was lost immediately, and the ship was plunged into darkness, as the account above shows. The lower holds were packed with wounded, cared for by two nurses and a few volunteers. Hundreds of them perished in the first seconds. The ship began to list to starboard and the bow sank rapidly.

The steward of the *Goya* was accompanied by his wife. He had previously tried to send her to safety aboard the *Wilhelm Gustloff*, and she had survived the sinking of the ship, returning to Gotenhafen in one of the rescue ships. On this current voyage, she had steadfastly refused to leave the rail of the ship and go inside. This probably saved her life; she and her husband leapt into the dark waters within seconds of the ship being hit, and swam as best they could to get away from the *Goya* before she went down.

There were dreadful scenes on deck. One survivor described how a young woman wrapped one arm around the legs of a man in a Party uniform, who was attempting to climb over the railing and jump into the sea, and pulled him back. With her other arm, she clung to the lifeless body of her newborn baby – in the rush, she had dropped the child, and before she could recover it, the stampeding mass of people had trampled the baby to death. Now, she cried out to the Party official, 'You – you are murderers – and the Führer – where is he now – he should see my dead child!' Another recalled a small girl, clinging to the railing, crying out for her mother.

Just before midnight, only seven minutes after she had been hit, the *Goya* broke in two and disappeared below the waves. It is impossible to calculate how many people leapt from the ship before she sank, but most of those aboard the *Goya* went down with her. The water temperature at that time of year was only 3ºC, and the air temperature was a chilly 6ºC. The two escorts with the convoy were themselves carrying large numbers of refugees and wounded. Before they could even consider rescuing those adrift on the sea, they had to deal with the threat from the Soviet submarine. After a quick attack with depth-charges, the *M 328* returned to the scene and the crew laboriously brought about 160 people aboard. Nine of these were either already dead, or died shortly after. Throughout the entire rescue operation, the warship's submarine detection system continued to warn that Konovalov's submarine was still close by. The *M 256* and *Aegir* also did what they could to rescue survivors. At about midday on 17 April, over 11 hours after the *Goya* disappeared beneath the waves, a patrol boat found a life-raft with four survivors, the last to be rescued.

Only 183 of those aboard survived, including just seven men from Group *Küspert*. With more than 6,000 people killed by the torpedo explosions or drowned in the cold Baltic waters, the sinking of the *Goya* remains the greatest loss of life at sea in history.[21] Captain Third Class Vladimir Konovalov was awarded the title 'Hero of the Soviet Union' for his achievement. His submarine remained in service until 1971, when it was broken up. The conning tower formed part of a war memorial in the Latvian port of Liepaja, known during the German occupation as Libau. In 1995, it was moved to Moscow, where it remains on display in Victory Park.

In Samland, the fighting continued. With the end of the war clearly only a matter of weeks away, Soviet tactics changed, perhaps in an attempt to keep casualties in their armies to a minimum. Whenever advancing Soviet forces encountered significant resistance, they pulled back and hammered the area with air and artillery attacks before resuming their advance. In the face of this fire, even veterans simply gave up and slipped away to the rear. On 15 April, the curved line of exhausted infantry units in the southern part of Samland began to collapse under the onslaught, and Generalleutnant Henning von Thadden, who had taken command of 1st Infantry Division after the successful breakout from Königsberg, ordered a withdrawal to a new defensive line, about 4km to the west of Fischhausen. The division headquarters moved into the town itself, which was now under heavy artillery bombardment. A salvo of Katyusha rockets struck the buildings occupied by von Thadden and his staff towards the end of the day; the division commander and adjutant were badly wounded. Von Thadden was swiftly evacuated to Pillau, from where he was taken aboard one of the last ships to Denmark, where he died in May. The division, reduced to a single battalion, now came under the command of Major Egon Overbeck.

The Soviet push to Fischhausen threatened to pinch off a large group of German units in the Peyse peninsula. Fischhausen itself was choked with vehicles as the front overran the rear-area units, and constant explosions from artillery shells and bombs reduced everything to chaos. Hauptmann Kraus, commander of one of 5th Panzer Division's Panzergrenadier battalions, led a counter-attack late on 14 April to restore the front between 58th and 93rd Infantry Divisions. Almost out of ammunition, he lost contact both with his own division and the infantry divisions he was supporting. On 15 April, with order completely breaking down, Kraus led his remaining 20 men south into the Peyse peninsula. Hauptmann Nökel, commander of one of the division's Panzer battalions, had reported on 13 April that his tanks had shot up 30 enemy vehicles, but the following day he recorded in his diary:

Air attacks as never before. The front didn't look like it could hold much longer. I had to move tanks from the right flank to the left, west of Powayen. The Russians had to be prevented from cutting into our rear. The redeployment was very difficult; wherever the tanks were withdrawn, the infantry disappeared. Despite our shooting up 30 enemy tanks, our front pulled back ever further to the southwest. During the night, our resourceful Feldwebel was able to obtain supplies. We still had ten tanks and two Tigers available in the evening. Repaired tanks continued to emerge from the workshop, or we would have long since burned out.[22]

The following day, things got worse:

No more orders reached us, I/31 was no longer in touch. We fought from positions south of Powayen. At midday, we still had six or seven tanks available; all the Tigers in our sector were blown up. There were constant air attacks, no contact with anyone by radio. I was in complete despair. During the night, I received orders that I was to take command of the regiment.[23]

The 5th Panzer Division's rear-area units were in the woodland of the Peyse peninsula, and the fighting elements of the division now fell back through this area. Some accounts suggest that corps headquarters ordered Nökel to retreat towards Pillau, and that he ignored this order; it is more likely that he simply did not receive the order in the prevailing chaos.[24] In Peyse, Major von Wilmsdorf, who had commanded the division's Panther tank battalion, had organized a flotilla of six boats to take wounded men to Pillau. Late on 15 April, the boats failed to return from their run to the seaport. Later, it transpired that von Wilmsdorf, Oberst Hoppe – who had previously commanded the Panzer regiment – and 35 other members of the regiment had taken the boats and travelled on from Pillau to the island of Bornholm, without permission from higher authorities. It is as clear a sign as any that even elite formations like 5th Panzer Division were disintegrating under the unrelenting pressure and the proximity of total defeat.

Other units, too, were crumbling and breaking up. Elements of *Grossdeutschland* were holding the defensive line north of Pillau:

While I was with the neighbouring battalion (a Panzer-Fusilier battalion), the Ivans began pounding our positions with barrage fire (mortars and Stalin organs). With the greatest effort I managed to regain my command post, which consisted of an anti-tank hole. During this barrage I suddenly saw the neighbouring battalion fleeing to the rear through my 1st Platoon's trench. My platoon leader was still trying to halt the soldiers, but he was simply overwhelmed by the panic caused by the barrage and the resulting heavy casualties. My company was also caught up in this panic. My attempts to hold the company together with threats failed. The people preferred to let themselves be shot down rather than remain in the positions. I cannot explain what caused this panic, especially since the Ivans had not attacked yet. In any event, my company headquarters squad leader, a runner, two radio operators and I found ourselves all alone. Only a squad leader with a light machine-gun reported in from the next hole. Meanwhile I saw that the 5th and 7th Companies were running away from Hill 63. A machine-gun manned by a Feldwebel and an officer was still firing from Hill 60. When the battalion began to run I sent the following radio message to battalion, I had no telephone link: 'Company running, please stop and send back; Russians not attacking.' But I soon saw that the people were not fleeing in the direction of the battalion command post. In the meantime the Ivans emerged from their entrenchments and moved toward us. I then transmitted the following radio message: 'Russians attacking, cannot hold position with three men, request further orders.' Enciphering and deciphering took a great deal of time, and in spite of our defensive fire the Ivans were much nearer. I had to decide for myself now, especially since we had to cover an open stretch of 100 metres if we were to retreat. Then I ordered the squad leader with the machine-gun to provide covering fire for our withdrawal. After the headquarters squad and I had reached the trench we provided covering fire for the squad leader to retire.

In this way we reached the battalion command post without loss. There I met the leader of my 1st Platoon. Of the rest of the company I saw nothing. A three-barrelled anti-aircraft gun was in position near the battalion command post. It opened fire when the Russians drew near, and the Ivans fled in panic. Soon afterwards came the order to reoccupy Hill 63 together with a tank that had arrived in the meantime. We formed an assault team from the available officers, what was left of the battalion and part of 8th Company for the attack on the hill.

Halfway there we suddenly came under heavy mortar fire which seriously wounded my platoon leader and me. One officer was killed, others escaped with minor wounds. My runner and another officer helped bring me back to the command post and from there I was transported to the medical clearing station in Dargen.[25]

The remnants of 1st and 58th Infantry Divisions fought desperately to hold the eastern part of Fischhausen, which was subjected to devastating artillery and aerial bombardment on 16 April, reducing it to ruins. The last Hetzer tank-destroyers of 5th Panzer Division's Panzerjäger battalion fought alongside the defenders, and were destroyed or abandoned; their crews retreated on foot into the Peyse peninsula. The remnants of 1st Infantry Division fell back to the west, forming up around Lochstädt. By the end of the day, Fischhausen was in Soviet hands, and the Peyse peninsula was isolated.

The reduction of the Peyse pocket now began. There appears to have been little or no coordination and control of the defenders; what resistance there was depended entirely on resourceful junior officers organizing whatever groups of men were at hand. The relationship between 5th Panzer Division's commander, Oberst Herzog, and General Matzky, commander of XXVI Corps, had been poor from the outset, and when Matzky ordered Herzog to launch a counter-attack late on 16 April to restore the situation at Fischhausen, the Panzer division commander simply ignored it. What remained of his division was almost completely out of ammunition, and that afternoon, he sent the last radio message to be transmitted by his headquarters: 'Division is cut off in Peyse. Do not expect further restoration of communications. All the best! Herzog.'[26]

The intention of this signal, it seems, was to give permission to the remaining elements of the division to escape as best they could. Matzky attempted to countermand Herzog's orders, and gave instructions that an attack was to be launched on Fischhausen, regardless of the ammunition situation. Yet it took six hours for this order to be received by the troops on the ground. Rumours had already reached Matzky's headquarters about the unauthorized escape of the small contingent of 5th Panzer Division's personnel by sea, and this last order from Herzog caused much alarm.

Wild charges of treason and cowardice were thrown about. The 28th Jäger Division was ordered to take command of the defence of the Peyse peninsula, and Matzky ordered that a search be made for Herzog and his Chief of Staff. Herzog had previously dispatched his intelligence officer, Hauptmann Tilse, to Matzky's headquarters in a vain attempt to make clear the futility of launching further attacks, and Tilse now travelled on to von Saucken's headquarters to explain the division's conduct: 'General von Saucken wanted to know exactly what was happening with 5th Panzer Division. After I had given him a detailed report, he said, "Anyone who speaks ill of the division, will have to deal with me! Please tell everyone that."'[27]

During the night, small boats ferried as many men as they could across the bay that separated Pillau from Peyse. The remaining gunners from 116th Artillery Regiment withdrew to the coast. Here, they found a single small boat:

As it began to grow dark, we gathered together. Major Baumann had some news for us. 'If you are in agreement, meine Herren, I will go with this single motorboat from Peyse to Pillau under cover of darkness, and will seek out the naval commandant there, to request that he sends any landing boats that are available to take aboard all the men here, and to carry them over to Peyse.'

It was very hard to reach agreement on this, with many understandably bitter words of suspicion being spoken aloud, that Baumann wanted to escape from this mess in such a dishonest way. But those who knew Baumann, knew the absolute reliability of this outstanding officer. We succeeded in convincing our comrades. Herr Baumann shook hands with us all and gave his word of honour that if he was unable to procure boats, he would return in the motorboat to go into captivity with us. Completely exhausted – more than 48 hours on my feet – I now lay down in the bunker next to our gun and hoped that I would awake when it was necessary.

I was awoken in the middle of the night; boats were here and we were to gather as inconspicuously as possible, and go to the landing stage in small groups. One of my comrades – I think it was Emil Marburger – and I decided to fire off the last shells, so that the enemy wouldn't notice the unavoidable noise of our departure. Once we had done this, and we had removed the firing pins and bolts, which we took with us to throw into the water, we packed our things and were the last to walk away from our gun.

It was about 1,200 metres to the landing stage. The embarkation proceeded quickly. The brave sailors had sent six boats, each capable of carrying 200 to 300 soldiers. The crossing to Pillau took about two hours, during which our old tormenting spirits, the 'Crows' [another nickname for the Polykarpov biplanes], attempted to hinder us with their flares and bombs. Five of our boats reached Pillau at dawn, but the sixth was missing.

Several days later, when we were fighting on the Nehrung, I learned that this missing boat had headed directly for Neutief.[28]

The 5th Panzer Division's Chief of Staff, Major von Knyphausen, withdrew onto a jetty near Peyse, from where he succeeded in signalling to a small fishing boat. Once aboard, von Knyphausen learned that the Feldgendarmerie were seeking him, presumably in response to Matzky's orders, and rather than face arrest von Knyphausen boarded a dredger that was being towed west. He eventually reached safety in Copenhagen.

On 17 April, those who were left had to face the prospect of Soviet captivity:

The total of assembled officers, NCOs and soldiers who had gathered in the extensive pine woodland of the Peyse peninsula, the last refuge of 5th Panzer Division, could not be estimated. The Frisches Haff was in our rear. A report circulated that Russian anti-tank guns had sunk the last three ferries from the Kamstigall stage, running to Pillau, south of Fischhausen. The men had clung to this last possibility of escape and it seems unlikely that any of them made it back to the coast. Our hope was now finally buried. Some tried, nevertheless. But there were no boards, vehicle tyres or empty drums to be found. The way over the Haff without such aids was impossible. A young Leutnant from our regiment made the attempt regardless, but didn't survive – the water was still too cold.

Night fell over the Peyse woods. Everyone waited for the arrivals of Russians with uncertainty. We heard the engine noises of heavy enemy tanks, which seemed really close. Now it was time to discard items of equipment that were dispensable for the road ahead. All superfluous clothing, equipment and weapons went into the ground, and radio equipment was destroyed.

At first light on 17 April, there was no more firing. There was an unnatural calm. We faced this sudden silence and the uncertainty of what lay ahead.

We heard loud voices from the naval arsenal. There were repeated shouts of 'Assemble! Everyone assemble!' Word went around that the Russians had ordered us all to go to Peyse. There, they would be able to assess the total number of German soldiers present. We trotted across the heath land in no particular order to Peyse. Wherever possible for us to do it without being seen, Soldbuchs [the German armed forces pay and identity book], shoulder boards, awards and documents were ground into the sand. Russian soldiers approached us, shouting 'Dawai, Dawai [Go on, go on].' They treated us correctly. The Russian officers carefully watched with their field glasses as we approached. First, the officers were separated from the NCOs and soldiers. It took a good hour before we were told what was happening. All units of the division were represented here. They sat in the sand along the long hill before Peyse and contemplated the last destructive days, and the end of the once-triumphant and battle-proven 5th Panzer Division.[29]

Even in this last, bitter moment of defeat, some attempted to escape. Three men from 5th Panzer Division's 116th Artillery Regiment hid in a bunker as the Soviet units advanced into the peninsula, and then attempted to escape overland. Only one of them, Hauptwachmeister Kolbe, succeeded; after several weeks disguised as a deaf-and-dumb Pole, he reached the Oder and crossed into Mecklenburg. He was very much the exception – Oberst Herzog and about 2,000 men from 5th Panzer Division and 28th Jäger Division went into captivity.

The only part of Samland that remained in German hands was the narrow stretch of dunes and woodland that ran down to Pillau. A series of positions had been constructed across the peninsula, and these were now subjected to the full weight of the Soviet assault. The first position ran from Tenkitten, and came under heavy bombardment on 17 April. The trenches and anti-tank ditches rapidly collapsed under the barrage, but the defenders – a mixture of men from *Grossdeutschland*, 1st and 93rd Infantry Divisions and 551st Volksgrenadier Division – held on grimly. Casualties mounted steadily, reaching a figure of more than 8,000 per day, a heavy price to pay for such a short frontline. There was no longer any question of formal units with proper chains of command. Officers gathered together what men they could, replacing their losses with stragglers. After four days of bitter fighting, the 'Tenkitten Position' was abandoned, and the defenders withdrew to the next line at Lochstädt. Elements of 1st Infantry Division had gathered behind this line, and provided welcome reinforcements, but the now-familiar Soviet tactic of probing until defences were located, and then withdrawing while the massive firepower of Soviet artillery and aviation was brought to bear, was once more used to devastating effect.

On 20 April, the Führer's birthday, the Soviet Air Force subjected Pillau to its heaviest attack yet. Whenever the bombers were not overhead, Soviet artillery battered the town, which was still full of refugees and wounded. As darkness fell, military ferries resumed their tireless shuttle to Neutief, and on 21 April rain and low clouds kept the Soviet bombers away. Barely a building was standing in the town; those people who remained, cowered in the cellars.

By the end of 23 April, the 'Lochstädt Position' was no longer tenable, despite supporting fire from naval batteries in Lochstädt itself. During the night the Germans retreated south to the line at Neuhäuser, but the Soviets were close behind. Even as the defenders took up their positions, they found that parts of the line had already been overrun. Naval batteries along the Baltic coast, and further south in Neutief, provided fire support, but late on 24 April the Neuhäuser line was abandoned, with the defenders pulling back to Pillau itself.

Soviet spearheads had actually reached the town earlier during the day, but elements of 83rd Infantry Division had just been deployed in the town. Led by the division commander, Generalmajor Wengler, the small battlegroups successfully held off the Soviet forces, despite heavy casualties. By the end of the day, Wengler and many of his men were dead. Nevertheless, another vital day had been bought, and as darkness fell the military ferries began the final evacuation of Pillau. Two small ships, the tugboat *Adler* and coastal oil tanker *Kolk*, were the last major vessels to leave the rear harbour at 2300hrs, under fire from Soviet tanks that had penetrated into the port area. The coastal batteries at the North Mole and Kamstigall fired until their ammunition was exhausted, and were then abandoned. Fighting raged at close quarters in all parts of Pillau, while Soviet artillery shells rained down on the two harbours – and despite this fighting, the evacuation continued. Gretel Dost, the nurse from Königsberg, had spent her days since arriving in Pillau working in one of the many ad hoc hospitals. Now, with the last 7,000 wounded, she was evacuated to Neutief, with the sky lit up by Soviet tracer rounds and parachute flares.

At 0300hrs on the morning of 25 April, Korvettenkapitän Schön, the naval officer in charge of the port, received orders to abandon his position in the citadel and make his way to the rear harbour. With his small group of 80 men, he made the hazardous journey through the devastated town, only to find the harbour empty. At 0400hrs, as Soviet tanks cautiously edged forward, the small company quietly moved back through the ruins to the fore-harbour, where they found a single military ferry. Together with the last 800 defenders, Schön and his men were taken across the channel to Neutief.

In the last few days, about 30,000 German soldiers, many of them wounded, had been evacuated, together with the last of the refugees. About 8,000 men were killed in the fighting in Pillau itself. When the Red Army finally took possession of Pillau on 25 April, they found an empty, dead town. Under the toughest of circumstances, the Kriegsmarine and army ferries had carried out an exemplary evacuation.

For the men who were lifted out of Pillau even as the Red Army occupied the ruins, the ordeal was not over. Soviet infantry had already been ferried across to the Frische Nehrung, and threatened to cut off Neutief and the large group of soldiers gathered in the area. Fortunately, help was close by. The 4th Panzer Division's 4th Armoured Reconnaissance Battalion had been sent east to the Nehrung for just such an eventuality. Pressing forward through the exhausted columns of soldiers and refugees who had been evacuated from Pillau, the half-tracks and light Lynx tanks of the reconnaissance battalion arrived just as further Soviet landings were taking place, about 7km south of Neutief. In a short, fierce action, the battalion shot up and destroyed several landing craft, and the surviving Soviet units withdrew. The remaining 12 tanks of 4th Panzer Division, together with a battery of artillery and what remained of 12th Panzergrenadier Regiment, were formed into a new battlegroup to support the defences on the Nehrung, but right at its tip, around Neutief, fierce fighting continued. Generalmajor Henke, whose engineers had helped reinforce the Nehrung road and who had improvised the *Sea Snake* to evacuate Balga, fought to the bitter end in Neutief. He and many of the 2,000 men with him died when, their ammunition exhausted, the defenders were overwhelmed late on 25 April. Other German units that had been nearby, and were also in danger of being isolated, were able to fight their way south in the general confusion, linking up with the new defensive line being erected by 4th Armoured Reconnaissance Battalion and other units. Their task was now to defend a series of pre-constructed defences that stretched across the Nehrung, in order to buy time for the evacuation of those in the Vistula estuary.

Despite the bitterness of the fighting in Samland, the last battles of AOK Ostpreussen were little more than a sideshow. On 16 April, the Red Army launched its assault on the German defences to the east of Berlin. For three days, the huge drive made little progress, despite heavy casualties on both sides. Yet on 19 April, with ammunition and fuel running out, the German lines gave way and the tide of Soviet armour poured west towards Berlin. The first Soviet artillery shells landed on the German capital on 20 April, and four days later, as Vassilevsky's troops reached the outskirts of Pillau, the 1st Belorussian and 1st Ukrainian Fronts completed the encirclement of the German capital.

The shattered German units trapped in the city put up bitter resistance, but the outcome was inevitable. Hitler committed suicide on 30 April, and at 0600hrs on 2 May, General Helmuth Weidling, commander of the remaining German forces in Berlin, surrendered. Hitler had declared Grossadmiral Karl Dönitz as his successor; Göring had been out of favour for some time, and Hitler placed the blame for the arrival of the Red Army squarely at the door of the army. On 1 May, Dönitz issued a proclamation to what remained of Germany's forces. It opened with a eulogy to Hitler, but then continued:

> The Führer has nominated me as his successor as head of state and supreme commander of the Wehrmacht. I assume command of all parts of the Wehrmacht with the intention

to continue the fight against Bolshevism until the fighting men and hundreds of thousands of families in the German Baltic are saved from enslavement or destruction.

I must continue the fight against the British and Americans as long and as hard as required if they hinder the continuation of the fight against Bolshevism.

The situation requires further unreserved efforts of you, who have already achieved so many historic feats and who now long for an end to the war. I require discipline and obedience. Only through unconditional execution of my orders will chaos and collapse be avoided. Any who turn their back on their duty and thus allow German women and children to face death or enslavement are cowards and traitors.[30]

There were still many tens of thousands of civilians in the remaining German enclaves held by AOK Ostpreussen. Since the loss of the *Goya*, naval traffic to and from Hela had rapidly dwindled. On 28 April, the first major convoy since the disaster set out for the west, consisting of the tireless *Ubena*, the *Ganther*, the *Westpreussen* and the *Nautik*. They carried some 10,000 people to safety on the same day that Vizeadmiral August Thiele arrived to take up his new post as Admiral for the Eastern Baltic. He found that the tiny peninsula of land stretching out to Hela was now home to some 200,000 souls, including two Gauleiters – both Koch and Forster were in Hela, cautiously watching each other and events in the west. Both feared the wrath of Hitler if they were to leave prematurely, but both kept vessels close at hand for their eventual escape.

Erich Koch left Hela aboard the icebreaker *Ostpreussen* on about 27 April, making first for the island of Rügen and then travelling on to Copenhagen. Here, he contacted Obergruppenführer Werner Best, the senior German civilian authority in Denmark. Koch requested that he should be given an appointment as an inspector of the refugees who had been brought to Denmark from East Prussia. Unable to come to any arrangement with Best, he travelled on to Flensburg, where with the Gauleiter of Schleswig-Holstein he asked Dönitz to provide a submarine so that they could escape to South America. Given the enormous pressures on Dönitz at the time – attempting to keep Engelhardt's evacuation going whilst trying to bring about a ceasefire in the west and holding off the Red Army in the east – such a request was unsurprisingly rejected out of hand. At this stage, Koch decided to adopt a new identity to escape capture by the western Allies. He changed his name to Major Rolf Berger, shaved off his Hitler-like moustache, and took to wearing glasses. Under this identity, he was taken into British custody and placed in a camp near Hasenmoor. Meanwhile, learning that his rival had left Hela, Forster too departed for the west.

Most of the refugees and soldiers from shattered units who had reached Hela spent the days and nights in the forested dunes of the Putziger Nehrung, where hot food was delivered daily from special kitchens set up in Hela itself. Although many refugees complained bitterly about being forced to live amongst the dunes, in ad hoc shacks and bunkers, they soon discovered that the dense pine woodland provided far better protection from air attack than the increasingly ruined buildings of Hela. In order to try to keep casualties from air attacks to a minimum, refugees and soldiers were only called to the two harbours immediately prior to boarding. Despite this, Soviet aircraft frequently inflicted casualties on those queuing for ferries to take them out to the waiting ships. Food continued to be available in plentiful amounts: numerous herds of cattle had been driven into the Vistula estuary, which was also full of horses abandoned by military units and refugee columns. These animals were slaughtered daily, and served together with potatoes and vegetables taken by ferry to Hela. Only bread remained in short supply.

Thiele sent a signal to Engelhardt on 29 April: 'Due to the almost complete cessation of convoy traffic from Hela, 200,000 people have accumulated in a short time. Inevitably, this is creating signs of general collapse. Request urgent dispatch of substantial shipping for evacuation.'[31]

The decline in shipping traffic was not due to the loss of the *Goya*, or even due to the threat of Soviet attacks. The ports along the north German coast and in Denmark had a large number of ships present, but most of the larger vessels were no longer seaworthy. Many had sustained damage from Soviet air attacks, and others had developed mechanical problems. Given the chaotic state of the Reich, it was almost impossible to obtain replacement parts. Even more desperate was the fuel shortage. Fuel oil and coal stocks in the ports were effectively exhausted, with the result that even the ships that did not require repairs were unable to make major journeys.

Despite this situation, some maritime movements continued. Close to the southern end of the Frische Nehrung was the concentration camp of Stutthof, which had been created originally as an internment camp after the fall of Poland in 1939. It is impossible to know how many prisoners were taken to Stutthof, as those who were designated for immediate execution were not registered in the camp records. More than 120,000 prisoners were registered; of these, more than 60,000 died, many of malnutrition or disease, others as a result of mistreatment or execution, particularly after the gassing of inmates began in June 1944. In January 1945, with Soviet troops approaching Elbing, several hundred prisoners were marched into the freezing waters of the Baltic and gunned down by their guards. Others were dispatched on a forced march, intending to head for Lauenburg. After days of marching along frozen roads through deep snow, an ordeal that resulted in the deaths of several thousand prisoners, the survivors found themselves back in Stutthof.

Günter Emmanuel Baltuttis, who had served with one of the *Hermann Göring* divisions before being wounded and evacuated, passed the camp as he walked away from the Nehrung:

> At that time, I was not aware that there was a concentration camp here, although I had learned about other camps far earlier in my parents' house. We were to be sent to Danzig the following day. In the meantime, I tried to get a glimpse of the camp, whose guards seemed less attentive than before. So I strolled across the camp road, and nobody took any notice of me... Some Jewish women spoke to me and asked for some bread. Unfortunately, I had to tell them that I couldn't help them, as I had no food. They were in poor physical shape, but their eyes were unnaturally bright, as I had often seen with those who were dying. They asked me if the war was over, and I replied that they would have to wait for a few months more before they had survived everything. They asked me my name, which I gave them. I hoped constantly that the ghastly encounter would end. In an open-topped cage, there were tree-trunks, on which a Russian prisoner of war was working with a small hatchet. The man looked pitiful, seeming to be just skin and bones, his thin jacket and trousers hanging off him and giving him the appearance of a living scarecrow. When I sharply asked a sentry what this nonsense meant, he replied to me that the prisoner was being punished. Mockingly, I asked whether this meant that he had been sentenced to death, in other words. The guard just shrugged his shoulders. At least he didn't continue driving the Russian on. 'Destruction through work' was the dehumanizing slogan of an ideology that even the Bolsheviks rarely achieved. These camps were appallingly shameful for us, and gave shocking meaning to my grandfather's words, that we would have to answer for our deeds.[32]

Von Saucken was anxious to have the survivors in the camp evacuated as soon as possible. A second contingent of prisoners was marched into the sea and gunned down, and a larger group was loaded onto barges. These were towed out to sea on 29 April, and took three days to reach Neustadt Bay, close to the city of Lübeck. Without any food or water, and clad only in their ragged camp clothing, many died during the journey. They arrived in the bay in time to be caught up in the last great tragedy of the war in the Baltic.

One of the ships unable to continue as part of Engelhardt's evacuation fleet was the 27,500-tonne liner *Cap Arcona*. The ship completed three evacuation voyages, taking 26,000 people to safety. On two occasions, Soviet submarines tried unsuccessfully to torpedo her. After completing her last trip, she was unable to return to Hela: her turbines had developed serious problems, as had several boilers. Replacement parts were unavailable, but her crew and the shipyard crews in Copenhagen did the best they could. However, it was clear that the ship would risk complete breakdown if she were to attempt another run to the Bay of Danzig. Instead, she was ordered to proceed to Neustadt Bay, where, along with the freighter *Thielbek*, the *Cap Arcona* was forced to accept thousands of concentration camp prisoners, despite the objections of the ships' captains. The purpose of this shipment remains unclear. Some ships had been used to transport concentration camp prisoners to Sweden, but before the prisoners went aboard an SS contingent removed all life-rafts and lifejackets. It is possible – perhaps even probable – that the intention was to take the fully loaded *Cap Arcona* out to sea and sink her, to prevent the prisoners from being rescued by the approaching British.

When the Stutthof barges arrived, an attempt was made to put their occupants aboard the *Cap Arcona*, but there wasn't room. Instead, the barges were run aground, and the prisoners staggered into Neustadt. Many were rounded up and put in the nearby sports stadium; others were shot by the SS.

British armoured units had reached Lübeck on 2 May, and their arrival in Neustadt was imminent. General George Roberts, commander of the British 11th Armoured Division, was informed by local Red Cross officials in Lübeck that several thousand concentration camp prisoners were aboard the ships in Neustadt Bay. Although he passed this information up to higher commands, its further dissemination would take time. British aerial reconnaissance had spotted the accumulation of ships in the western Baltic, and there were persistent rumours at the time that the SS was planning to evacuate personnel to Norway, with the intention of continuing the war from Scandinavia. On 3 May, the RAF's 2nd Tactical Air Force issued an order to 83 Group to attack enemy shipping in the coastal waters of Lübeck and Neustadt. Typhoon fighter-bombers from five RAF squadrons, armed with 20mm cannon and rockets, attacked the *Cap Arcona* and *Thielbek*, and the nearby empty liner *Deutschland*. All three ships were left ablaze. Many of the concentration camp prisoners who had managed to get into the water lacked the strength to swim to safety. Some who reached the shore were promptly shot by the SS. The *Cap Arcona* slowly capsized and eventually drifted ashore. Corpses continued to be washed ashore for many years, the last occasion being 1971. The *Thielbek*, which was also hit during the RAF attack, sank within 15 minutes.

The total number of those who died aboard the ships is not precisely recorded. It is estimated that nearly 5,600 died aboard the *Cap Arcona*; this number includes several who were machine-gunned in the water by the RAF aircraft.[33] A further 2,400 died aboard the *Thielbek*.

In the first three days of May, a total of 32 ships were sunk in the western Baltic by the RAF. In addition, air raids on Kiel accounted for the heavy cruiser *Admiral Hipper*. These losses were particularly significant, because they mainly involved ships at sea – in other words, many of the few remaining seaworthy vessels available. Engelhardt's evacuation fleet, already hamstrung by fuel shortages and mechanical problems, was now critically reduced.

Grossadmiral Dönitz was determined to reduce bloodshed to a minimum for whatever remained of the war. Orders were issued to give up Hamburg and Lübeck without a fight. Generaladmiral Hans-Georg von Friedeburg had been the commander of Germany's submarine forces, and now replaced Dönitz as commander of the Kriegsmarine. Together with the recently promoted General Kinzel, who had formerly commanded 337th Volksgrenadier Division, von Friedeburg was to open negotiations with the British forces in northern Germany. Generalfeldmarschall Kesselring, Commander-in-Chief in the west, was to make arrangements for a ceasefire for troops on the western front, but should avoid making commitments on behalf of other sectors. It was Dönitz's intention that Army Groups Centre, South and Southeast should be free to continue fighting, and would ultimately be able to retreat to the west where they could surrender to the western Allies.

On 2 May, von Friedeburg and the newly appointed Reichsminister Graf von Schwerin-Krosigk met near Kiel to discuss how best to proceed. Dönitz instructed them to open talks with Field Marshal Montgomery, to explore the possibility of arranging a surrender in northern Germany, whilst attempting to secure British promises that they would not interfere with the ongoing evacuation of soldiers and civilians across the Baltic.

Back on the Frische Nehrung, the war was still raging in earnest. The defenders in the flooded Vistula estuary faced no major attacks, but were constantly harassed by artillery and mortar fire. Pantenius' regiment remained in the frontline until 2 May, when it was pulled back with a view to being redeployed on the Frische Nehrung. Pantenius was disgusted when all but a minimum number of radio sets were removed from his men:

Apparently, this was to prevent the troops from learning of the initiation of talks for a partial surrender, for fear that this would unsettle them or result in a breakdown of discipline, in other words they would be tempted to abandon their positions without orders and gather at the landing stages at Schiewenhorst and Nickelswalde. I regarded these measures as unnecessary and rather harmful. Discipline in all units and formations was faultless, and nobody had taken to their heels without orders.[34]

As 35th Infantry Division was withdrawn from the frontline and gathered east of Schiewenhorst, Generalleutnant Richert called his officers together to tell them of Hitler's death.

> He ended with the words: 'I am deeply shaken.' We felt less shaken than freed from a nightmare, and now there existed the prospect of being able to break off the fighting here in the Bay of Danzig, which had once served a purpose but was now senseless, and perhaps we could still be evacuated. We knew nothing officially about the relevant planning of AOK Ostpreussen. Wild rumours, that the British had allied with us to fight against the Russians and consequently would fetch us out of here, were actually believed. Hope rose like never before. We only learned after the surrender and our departure on 9 May that the Russians on the other side had similar fears.[35]

On the Frische Nehrung, the Soviet 11th Army had established a pontoon bridge from Pillau across the straits to Neutief, and was now ferrying tanks and other heavy equipment south. Although 11th Army now had elements of five divisions deployed on the narrow Nehrung, it was impossible for them to do anything other than smash their way south, reverting to the successful tactics used in the advance to Pillau: as soon as the Soviet soldiers encountered resistance, they fell back and the area was subjected to a ferocious artillery bombardment. Prior to 1939, a series of defensive positions had been prepared along the Nehrung, but these had anticipated an attack from Poland, advancing towards Pillau. Nevertheless, these obstacles were bitterly contested by the retreating Germans. The 4th Panzer Division's remaining 12 tanks, together with the vehicles of the reconnaissance battalion, continued to put up tough resistance, helping the fragments of several divisions to hold the line. Repeated Soviet attempts to bypass the line by effecting amphibious landings further south were in vain.

Engelhardt and his staff had laboured long hours to track down every last drop of fuel and sack of coal, and had dispatched as many ships as they could to the east. Escorted by a mixture of torpedo boats and destroyers, a flotilla of 12 merchant ships was dispatched to Hela, and a further five to Libau. In addition, a fleet of smaller boats accompanied the ships – every man who could be brought west before the inevitable final surrender, would be one man fewer to fall into Soviet captivity. The first vessels, the 4,500-tonne *Sachsenwald* and the much smaller 1,900-tonne *Weserstrom*, reached Hela on 2 May. The *Sachsenwald* took aboard 5,500 wounded soldiers, with another 300 refugees and 400 army medical personnel going aboard the *Weserstrom*, and headed west. They had barely enough fuel to reach Copenhagen.

On 3 May, Dönitz's staff sent a signal to AOK Ostpreussen:

The changed military situation in the Reich requires the urgent evacuation of numerous troops from East and West Prussia as well as Courland.

Combat operations by the army in East Prussia and Army Group Courland are to reflect this requirement.

Personnel with light infantry weapons are to be embarked for return. All other materiel, including horses, is to be left behind and destroyed. Army Group Courland is given operational freedom to pull back the frontline to the planned bridgeheads at the ports of Windau and Libau.

The Kriegsmarine will dispatch all available transports to East Prussia and Courland.[36]

On 4 May, von Friedeburg reported back to Dönitz. Montgomery's demands were that Holland and Denmark were to be included in the surrender. No ships were to be scuttled, but in return, the British would not interfere with ongoing evacuations. Whilst the British would accept the surrender of individuals and small groups making their way to the west, larger units, such as 3rd Panzer Army and 21st Army, currently facing Rokossovsky's forces north of Berlin, were expected to surrender to the Red Army. Nor would Montgomery give any guarantees for the welfare of civilians in Mecklenburg: this area was to be in the Soviet sector after the war, and responsibility for the civilians would lie with the Soviet Union. In the circumstances, this was as good a deal as Dönitz could expect, and the ceasefire document was signed that evening, coming into effect at 0800hrs on 5 May. Immediately after the document was signed, von Friedeburg flew to Rheims to meet General Eisenhower and arrange a ceasefire for all German forces facing the Americans.

AOK Ostpreussen fought on. The Soviet 11th Army had advanced to within 10km of the western end of the Frische Nehrung. Almost all the remaining civilians in the Vistula estuary had been evacuated, and now it was the turn of the soldiers to be moved to Hela. Leaving only a small battlegroup, including the division's remaining tanks, 4th Panzer Division began to cross to the Putziger Nehrung, to await ships to the west.

There were 180,000 men, mainly soldiers, gathered in and near Hela. Some civilians remained. Many of the residents of the small fishing communities of the Putziger Nehrung preferred to stay, hoping that the occupying Soviet and Polish forces would allow them to resume their trade, and large numbers of civilians, exhausted by their long flight to Hela, could not contemplate any further journeys. As ships approached Hela on 5 May, many attempted to push through the cordons thrown up by the military police at the quaysides, but generally order and discipline continued to hold. The same day, another flotilla of vessels left Copenhagen for Hela. Near Bornholm, a British bomber squadron appeared. Nervously, the German seamen waited for attack, but none came. Montgomery had passed instructions to all British forces not to interfere with the evacuation.

This order, of course, did not apply to the Soviet forces on the Pomeranian coast. A group of Soviet patrol boats attempted to intercept the convoy to the east of Bornholm, but withdrew after a brief exchange of fire, leaving one patrol boat burning and dead in the water. The German vessels continued running east at full speed. They reached Hela late on 5 May, and loading continued through the night. Early the following morning, the vessels left for Copenhagen, carrying 43,000 passengers. Meanwhile, ferries continued to bring people to Hela from the Vistula estuary; a little more than 13,000 arrived on 5 May, including 910 wounded and the last 270 refugees. During the return voyage to Copenhagen, the ships passed the location of the previous morning's brief gun-battle with the Soviet gunboats. The boat that had been crippled was still afloat, and the passing German ships spotted four Soviet sailors aboard the wreck, waving frantically. The torpedo boat *T 28* went alongside and took them aboard, probably the last Soviet personnel to become German prisoners in World War II.

In Rheims, the German delegation met Eisenhower's staff for discussions. Generaloberst Jodl was under instructions to try to persuade the Americans to delay a final ceasefire in the east as long as possible, so that Engelhardt's ships would be able to rescue more men from Courland and Hela. Engelhardt's staff estimated that they needed an additional three or four days – given this time, and provided fuel could be found, all of the men in Hela and the Vistula estuary, and all of those in Courland, could still be brought west. Jodl cited communications difficulties, requesting that the Germans be given 48 hours to contact all of their units prior to a universal surrender. The Americans insisted on a general surrender of all German forces, not just those in the west: there was to be no question of German forces being permitted to continue operations in the east. All ships would have to be surrendered to whichever Allied power had control of the area in which the vessels were at the time of the surrender. Shortly after midnight on the night of 6–7 May, Jodl advised Dönitz that Eisenhower had issued an ultimatum for immediate surrender. If these terms were not accepted, the war would be prosecuted to the end. Jodl was given just 30 minutes to make up his mind. His message to Dönitz continued:

I see no alternative other than chaos or signing. I request immediate confirmation by radio whether I have permission to sign the surrender document. It will come into effect immediately. Hostilities will cease on 9 May, 0000 hours.[37]

Permission was granted in a signal at 0130hrs, and an hour later Jodl signed the surrender document. At the same time, Dönitz issued orders to all German forces facing the Red Army to move as fast as they could to the west, so that they could surrender to the western Allies. Dönitz also ensured that Engelhardt was kept informed of developments in the negotiations. All of Engelhardt's staff, and all of the ships answerable to him, had been aware that the end of the war was only a few days away. Now, the timescale was mere hours. Speed was of the essence. Three destroyers and two torpedo boats that arrived in Copenhagen, laden with troops from Hela, wished to discharge their passengers as fast as possible so that they could head back east for one last run. Aware that the quaysides were overflowing with refugees and soldiers who had not been relocated, the destroyers made for the *Ubena*, which was lying empty at anchor, unable to take part in any further evacuation voyages due to mechanical problems. Kapitän Lankau of the *Ubena* quickly realized what was needed, and his crew allowed the destroyers to transfer their soldiers to the empty liner. Within seven hours, the transfer was complete, and the warships were free to head out to sea again.[38]

In the Vistula estuary, only the remnants of six German infantry divisions remained in the frontline, reinforced by the last tanks of 4th Panzer Division. Even at this late stage, the ships arriving in Hela continued to bring munitions to keep von Saucken's troops operational; on 6 May, 230 tonnes of ammunition arrived aboard freighters, which were rapidly unloaded at the same time as soldiers clambered aboard for the return voyage. On 7 May, von Saucken sent sealed orders to all commanders down to regimental level. These were only to be opened when expressly ordered. The officers who received the documents had mixed feelings. Did they contain final instructions for the last-minute evacuation of AOK Ostpreussen, or did they give instructions for a final surrender?

Troops gathered in the two small harbours in Hela on 8 May, a sunny, warm spring day. The first ships, a small group of destroyers and torpedo boats, appeared at 1840hrs. Shortly after, a few larger merchant vessels arrived. Every last inch of space was put to use, and astonishing numbers of men were squeezed in. The torpedo boat *T 28*, with a displacement of less than 1,300 tonnes, left port with 1,237 soldiers aboard, and the similar-sized *T 33* managed to pack in almost 2,000 men. Given the circumstances, it is difficult to know for certain exactly how many men were lifted out of Hela on the last days of the war. In the final hours, all of the ferries that had been active between the Vistula estuary and Hela left with the last large ships, and some estimates suggest that this convoy managed to evacuate perhaps as many as 65,000 men.[39] Despite this remarkable achievement, at least 60,000 were left behind. Amongst them was Dietrich von Saucken, their commander, who was awarded the highest award available in the Reich, the Knight's Cross with Oak Leaves, Crossed Swords and Diamonds. Dönitz dispatched an aircraft to bring him to safety; few can have been surprised when von Saucken had several wounded men loaded onto the plane in his place, and sent it back to the west.

After the last ships had left Hela, there was unrest amongst the soldiers who remained. Hearing of this, von Saucken had himself driven to the gathered soldiers. He stood up on the back seat of his open-top Volkswagen and addressed them: 'We must compose ourselves. There are no more ships, and none are expected. Now, when we have to go into Russian captivity, we must do so with dignity and the knowledge that we did our duty to the very end.'[40]

The troops silently filed away, back to their bunkers, to await the end of the war. Just before midnight, three torpedo boats suddenly arrived in the naval harbour. Several hundred soldiers, who had thought their last hope of escape had gone, rushed aboard, and the vessels headed out to sea, determined to get as far west as possible before daybreak.

Two of the vessels to depart from Hela for the west late on 8 May were the small tankers *Julius Rütgers*, with a displacement of 854 tonnes, carrying about 400 soldiers and crew, and the even smaller, 517-tonne *Lieselotte Friedrich* with a further 300. Accompanied by two artillery barges, also heavily laden, the vessels made their slow but steady way west through the night. Only the crew on watch on the bridges of the vessels marked the moment when the war officially came to an end. Briefly, the officers aboard the *Julius Rütgers* considered whether they should now switch on their navigation lights, but decided to continue with their wartime blackout until they were further west. Shortly after sunrise on 9 May, lookouts spotted aircraft approaching, and a group of Soviet torpedo-bombers made a low-level attack. For the aircrews and the men on the four ships, it was as if the war had not ended: a cloud of anti-aircraft fire rose up to meet the planes, which launched torpedoes and raked the ships with bursts of machine-gun fire. The *Julius Rütgers* turned hard to port as the torpedoes raced in, and avoided being hit, but the *Lieselotte Friedrich* was less fortunate. Struck by a single torpedo, she began to sink immediately. The other three vessels successfully rescued all those aboard, including about a dozen who had been wounded in the Soviet attack. Captain Grewe immediately gave up his cabin to the small group of medics aboard.

As the tanker and two barges continued towards Kiel, Grewe kept a close eye on his diminishing stock of coal. Would there be sufficient to reach his destination? By early morning on 10 May, it seemed that they would be safe, but suddenly, the engine gave a splutter and stopped. The ship's compass had ceased working before they left Hela, and Grewe and his crew anxiously debated whether they were sufficiently far to the west, or whether the coastline to their south was in Soviet hands. Fortunately for the men aboard, the debate proved to be little more than academic. The drifting ship was spotted by a tugboat, which towed them into Kiel Bay.

The 1,400-tonne passenger ship *Rugard*, which was the very last major vessel to leave Hela, had served as the headquarters of the Kriegsmarine's 9th Security Division. The ship left Hela with about 1,300 soldiers, with a small group of the division's patrol boats, at 2100hrs on 8 May. In order to avoid being captured by Soviet forces, the small group ran close to the Swedish coast, and at first it seemed that they would succeed. Late on 9 May, four fast-moving gunboats were spotted astern, closing rapidly. The patrol boats accompanying the *Rugard* were some distance ahead, and the Soviet gunboats closed rapidly with the passenger ship. A message was shouted across from one of the gunboats, demanding that the *Rugard* turn back immediately. When the *Rugard* responded by increasing her speed, the Soviet vessels launched torpedoes, which narrowly missed.

The *Rugard* was armed with a single 75mm gun, originally from France, of World War I vintage. The weapon was mounted astern, and the gun crew now opened fire on the Soviet gunboats. The first shot narrowly missed, but the next two both struck their target, leaving a gunboat ablaze. The other three Soviet vessels broke off their attack and turned to help their stricken comrade, and the *Rugard* was able to make good her escape, bringing to an end the last surface combat at sea in the European theatre. The former passenger ship, together with the 1,300 soldiers aboard, reached Kiel Bay early on 10 May.

Hela was not the only point of departure in the eastern Baltic during the closing hours of the war. A fleet of 175 vessels, ranging from small freighters to motorboats, attempted to rescue as many men as possible from Courland before the final surrender. Following a process similar to that used by 4th Panzer Division to determine who would form Group *Küspert*, most of the German divisions in Courland dispatched groups of men – fathers, last surviving sons – to the ports of Windau and Libau to go aboard the waiting ships. As soldiers streamed aboard a German torpedo boat, the ship's captain was stopped by an army Hauptmann, who gave him a list of names. These, he explained, were the names and addresses of his men, who were unable to leave Courland. Would the ship's captain ensure that their families learned that they were still alive, even if they were to go into Soviet captivity? The ship's captain asked the Hauptmann if he wished to stay aboard the torpedo boat – it would be easy to squeeze in one more person. In the same spirit that Dietrich von Saucken declined to be evacuated by air from Hela, the Hauptmann shook his head. His place, he explained, was with his men, even though, as a father of three, he would have qualified for membership of the group nominated by his division.[41]

In five convoys, the armada of small vessels left Courland for the west. They saved 23,000 men of Army Group Courland from Soviet captivity. The very last convoy, with

11,300 men aboard, came under Soviet air attack on 9 May when it refused to turn back to port. Many men were killed by machine-gun fire from the planes, but no ships were lost. Almost all of them reached the coast of Schleswig-Holstein on 11 May, but three small ferries were unable to make the long journey, heading instead to Sweden. Behind them, nearly 200,000 officers and men of Army Group Courland began the long march into captivity.

Back in the Vistula estuary, fighting had continued throughout the last day of the war. Along the western perimeter of the German pocket, there were exchanges of artillery fire, and at the base of the Frische Nehrung, 4th Panzer Division's remaining tanks prepared to defend the last defensive line. Hans Schäufler listened to a foreign radio report on 7 May, where he learned that German unconditional surrender had been arranged. Together with the last 50 men of 35th Panzer Regiment, he waited and hoped for a last-minute route to safety:

When a blood-red sun rose from the Baltic on 8 May, it showed us clearly and unmistakably, that over us, the last German soldiers on the Frische Nehrung, judgement had fallen – the warships in the Vistula estuary had steamed away under cover of darkness. For us, they had always given a little hope.

A beautiful May day developed around us. But in our hearts there was despair. A light easterly wind played with the treetops, but the wind smelled of fire and blood, of death and corpses, of gunsmoke and decay. We felt ourselves to be so unspeakably forgotten and abandoned, even by our enemies, who barely shot at us now. The front grew steadily quieter. The Nehrung, the bank of the Vistula, had become very empty overnight.[42]

Later that afternoon, Schäufler was ordered to go to the Vistula landing stages, but there were no boats available to take him or the men accompanying him. As they waited, word spread that the final surrender would take place at midnight. Two vessels were moored a short distance from the shore:

One of the two ships lay closer to our eastern bank. The survivors of 4th Armoured Reconnaissance Battalion were loaded aboard. I succeeded without difficulty in taking my 28 men aboard. I had express orders to accompany the men. But on the bank here was still the radio-half-track that had been assigned to us by the signals battalion, with four men. The radio sets were still working, and provided contact with Group *Grigat*, the last handful of men of 35th Panzer Regiment.

The commander of 4th Armoured Reconnaissance Battalion, Major von Gaupp, told me several times to come aboard. The four radio operators were still in their positions.

Undecided, I stood on the bank. But then I returned to the radio crew. I felt ashamed that I had only thought of myself, and had thought to leave them to their fate.

The driver, Obergefreiter Eckstein, was busy with the machine-gun and said to me a little distractedly, with damp eyes, 'Herr Oberleutnant, I don't know what I would have done if you had left us alone here. I don't think I could have borne this last disappointment after everything else.'

At 1820, the last vessel left the Vistula estuary, terribly overladen. Soldiers clung to anything like clusters of grapes. And they waved to us, the ones left behind. It was hard – and yet I watched the two ships for a long time with a lightening heart. The two had reached the far side of the Vistula with their cargoes. Now, they set off for home. They were probably safe!

A whistling in our headsets startled us. A radio message. We swiftly decoded it. 'Destroy vehicle and radio set. You are relieved of your oath of allegiance. Find a way to escape. Ceasefire in effect from midnight. End.' We confirmed. Over and out. Deathly silence from the ether. These few words struck us like hammer blows.[43]

At 1900hrs, Schäufler and his four companions found a lifeboat. They still had radio contact with the group from 4th Armoured Reconnaissance Battalion, who were now aboard two military ferries in Hela. If they could reach Hela, the ferries promised to take them in tow. But they would have to cross nearly 30km of water to reach Hela, and it was likely that the ferries would have left long before they could get there. A motorboat passed them, with only a few soldiers aboard, but despite their requests for help, the crew ignored them and continued towards the Bay of Danzig. Then another opportunity arose:

It was growing dark, and our courage had failed, when a small motorboat came up. A major stood on deck and waved me over. He quietly asked me if I could manage a motorboat on the Baltic. I didn't have the slightest idea of serious or recreational seafaring, I was a landlubber through and through. But I couldn't, I mustn't say that to this man, who had been sent to me from heaven at this last moment. I therefore screwed up my courage and looked him straight in the eye. 'Jawohl, Herr Major, I can!' By way of confirmation, I pointed at the Russian prismatic compass on my wrist, which looked thoroughly nautical.

Before the good man knew how it happened, my four radio men were aboard. All five of us had suddenly understood that this was our last chance to cheat fate, that we must seize it quickly before it could slip away.

It was 2145 when we left the Vistula estuary, heading for Hela. It began to grow properly dark. The first 'night owls' were already in the sky and dropping parachute flares, and also occasional bombs.

Our motorboat, named the *Zander*, actually had only five berths. With 15 men, it was overladen. But that didn't bother anyone. The sea was flat. The small, approximately six-metre little ship sprang from wave to wave like an excited foal. The first men became seasick.

… From far away, we could see the explosions of shells and bombs – isolated ones behind us on the Vistula, substantially more frequently ahead of us on the Hela peninsula… Parachute flares hung over the water.

At 2310 we briefly ran aground. A small, barely noticeable sandbar stretched out to sea in front of us. We felt it more than saw it. It must be the Putziger Nehrung. We had actually only wanted to cross to here. But it was so unnaturally still here, so uninviting, that we left it to move out into the wider bay at Hela, and to see the other side. We travelled further and further.

Then a new day dawned. It was 9 May, 0130. Behind us lay Hela, ceasefire and surrender. Before us stretched the wide, open Baltic… Our boat was small and clearly not built for a journey on the open sea. But we wanted to take our chance, our one and only, to escape Soviet imprisonment. Perhaps heaven had a say.

We therefore made a unanimous decision: escape over the Baltic.[44]

Others were less fortunate. Pantenius and his men remained in their positions, and about three hours before the final surrender received word that they could open the sealed orders that had been distributed. The orders read: 'Today at 2300 German Summer Time, AOK Hela surrenders unconditionally to the Soviet armed forces. The commander thanks all soldiers, NCOs and officers for their proven courage. Our fight is over. Von Saucken.'[45]

Pantenius made sure that his battalion and company commanders were made aware of this message. All heavy weapons were thrown into the Vistula, and preparations began for the following day. Like many other units, Pantenius' regiment had ignored the instruction to slaughter all of their horses, and now prepared horse-drawn supply wagons, one for every hundred men, as well as three complete field kitchens and fodder for the horses.

As the night drew on, the officers gathered together to await events. Some discussed the possibility of escape overland. Even allowing for night marches of 20km, they estimated that it would take between two and three weeks to reach the Oder. At best, they calculated, the chances of success were no better than one in ten. And even if they should reach the Oder, what would they find beyond the river? And when should they make the attempt? It was surely impossible to try now, while the frontline was still heavily manned, and any attempt to escape once the march into captivity had begun would invite retaliation against the rest of the regiment.

With such discussions, they whiled away the dark hours, while Soviet artillery continued to make occasional bombardments of the landing stages; even though a ceasefire was officially in effect, the Red Army was keen to ensure that as few Germans as possible escaped.

News of the surrender gradually filtered down through the ranks. One soldier of 4th Panzer Division recorded in his diary, with the typical humour of soldiers of all nationalities, and of all eras: 'I can scarcely believe it, but it is true. And in a few hours we would have had the Russians by the throat, just as we had successfully beaten them off before so often and for so long!'[46]

As the ceasefire came into effect, Grossadmiral Dönitz issued the last Wehrmacht communiqué of the war:

> In East Prussia, German divisions were still bravely defending the Vistula estuary and the western part of the Frische Nehrung yesterday, with 7th Division particularly recognized for its contribution. The commander, General von Saucken, in recognition of the exemplary conduct of his soldiers, is awarded the Knight's Cross with Oak Leaves, Crossed Swords and Diamonds.
>
> As an advanced bulwark, our armies in Courland, under the tried and tested command of Generaloberst Günther, tied down superior Soviet rifle and armoured formations for many months and distinguished themselves in six great battles. They refused any premature surrender. Only the wounded and fathers of many children were transported in full order by aircraft that still left for the west. Staffs and officers remained with their troops. At midnight, in accordance with the agreed arrangements, all activity on the German side ceased.
>
> The defenders of Breslau, who stood firm against Soviet attacks for over two months, succumbed to the enemy's superiority at the last moment after a heroic struggle.
>
> On the southeast and eastern fronts, from Brünn to the Elbe, all higher commands have been ordered to bring fighting to an end. A Czech uprising – involving all of Bohemia and Moravia – may endanger the execution of the ceasefire arrangements.
>
> The High Command has not yet received reports about the situation with Army Groups Löhr, Rendulic and Schörner.
>
> Far from the Fatherland, the defenders of the Atlantic Wall, the troops in Norway, and the garrisons of the Aegean Islands have maintained the honour of German soldiers with obedience and discipline.
>
> Weapons fell silent on all fronts at midnight. On the orders of the Grossadmiral, the Wehrmacht has brought to an end its hopeless fight. The six years of honourable conflict are thus at an end. These brought us major victories, but also heavy defeats. In the end, the German Wehrmacht has conceded to overwhelming superiority.

The German soldier, faithful to his oath, will be remembered forever for his best endeavours for his people. The homeland supported him with all its power under the heaviest blows. The unique conduct of the front and homeland will find its final expression in the judgement of history.

The enemy cannot gainsay the conduct and suffering of German soldiers on water, on land and in the air. Every soldier can thus lay down his weapons with honour and pride and, in the hardest hour of our times, go with courage and confidence to work for the eternal life of our people.

In this grave hour, the Wehrmacht remembers its comrades who fell in battle. The dead remind us of their unconditional loyalty, obedience and discipline, to set against the countless wounds of the bleeding Fatherland.[47]

CHAPTER 15
THE LONG ROAD HOME

To ravage, to slaughter, to usurp under false titles, they call empire; and where they make a desert, they call it peace.

– Tacitus[1]

Many German soldiers had succeeded in escaping the final surrender in Hela and the Vistula estuary, and were already in Germany. Others, like Hans Schäufler, managed to find a way to leave at the very last moment, and now faced a difficult journey. Schäufler's small motorboat encountered two other boats, one of them carrying Oberst Hoffmann, 4th Panzer Division's last commander. One of the three boats had developed engine trouble, and was abandoned; the other two, the *Seeadler* and *Zander*, continued together:

> At about 1000, we saw a large cloud of smoke behind us. Then we saw a large convoy majestically sailing westwards. We were sure that they were the last transport ships from Courland or Hela. We wanted to join them.
>
> At 1030, the *Seeadler* developed clutch trouble, bringing us all to a halt. It turned out that the driveshaft was broken. We therefore took the large boat in tow, and made for the convoy. The *Zander* could now only travel at half-speed. And we could see that, with this huge disadvantage, it would take us three days to reach Kiel – assuming that all went well. Our 65-PS engine chugged away laboriously but bravely. We reached about a kilometre south of the convoy's route, anxious that we might not effect an encounter.
>
> At about 1300, grey clouds suddenly welled up over the Baltic. A bad storm blew up. The *Zander* shook like mad, up and down, and the *Seeadler* tossed in its wake. We learned very quickly how to manoeuvre and steer. Our course unfortunately shifted to the northwest, as we had to cut through the ever larger waves perpendicularly, as we quickly discovered.
>
> The convoy passed us by. We failed to keep pace with it. We had wanted so much to transfer the men on the *Seeadler* to a larger ship. We could have joined the convoy and safely accompanied it westwards.[2]

It was actually a major stroke of good fortune for the German soldiers that they failed to link up with the convoy. The ships were from the Soviet Red Banner Fleet, on their way to take control of the German Baltic ports in what was to become the Soviet occupation zone.

The storm that swept the southeast Baltic swamped a number of small vessels that German soldiers were using in an attempt to escape. A wooden barge, carrying much of 4th Panzer Division's combat engineer battalion, broke up and sank. There was only one survivor.[3] Schäufler and his companions were forced to abandon the *Seeadler*, and crowd aboard the *Zander*. Later that day, as the storm finally slackened, the boat approached the Swedish coast. A Swedish police boat approached them, and indicated that they should make for shore, but one of the men aboard the Swedish boat, younger than his colleagues, signalled behind their backs that the Germans should turn away from the coast. After a brief debate, they turned back to the open sea.

Carefully preserving their precious fuel, Schäufler and his companions travelled south and west. Finally, on 13 May, they reached the Schleswig-Holstein coast:

In the distance a small church tower peeped from between tall trees across the water. We saw people on the shore. We turned our boat in this direction. If necessary we would have jumped into the water and swum the last stretch, so impatient we had become.

As the *Zander* swiftly approached land, I involuntarily thought back: five days, five nights, two unforgettable, dreadful nights and two hopeless grey days somewhere between West Prussia and Sweden; water, nothing but bubbly, greedy water that devoured so many; then Sweden, the first glimmer of light; and then Denmark. Only consuming uncertainty first, then preoccupied hopes. And now Germany: freedom; peace; a future and life!

Through carelessness, we ran aground close to the shore. That snatched me back out of my dreams. A fisherman, who had apparently seen our impatience in our faces, swiftly rowed over to us. With a pole he helped us to free the *Zander*. I jumped into his boat, put my arms around his neck. I waded the last stretch of shallow water to land.

It was precisely 1816 when I felt solid ground under my feet. I had thus fulfilled my promise given in extremity, and had in the end brought this boat with 22 men on board over the Baltic. I wanted to celebrate, I wanted to cry and felt like sobbing. No shots, no trenches, no shattered trees: peace!

At first, in my overwhelming joy, I simply couldn't see why the many people on the shore were not laughing with us, were not joyful, why they looked at us with questioning glances and anxious faces. And then gradually I saw the truth: in their eyes, we soldiers were just the flotsam of a lost war, sons of other parents, not their own, for whom they longingly waited here.

In small groups we came ashore, shook hands without many words, wished each other luck for a swift homecoming and a new start. Only my radio crew waited for me in a fisherman's house.

Under the pretext of asking the name of the town of our disembarkation, I crept away, because tears ran down my face with the release of terrible tensions. I wanted to be completely alone for a few minutes.

When that had passed, I involuntarily asked: actually, why did we fight? Why did we have to endure everything? For what purpose were so many magnificent young men killed? Why? Why? Why? Where was there any sense in this?

A world collapsed like a house of cards for me. Or was this world, that they had taught us to believe in, only a deception?

A mountain of questions piled up inside me. I couldn't find a single answer.[4]

The village where they came ashore was Heiligenhafen, close to Kiel. Schäufler was advised to surrender to the local British authorities, and was taken to the town of Plön, where Montgomery's headquarters was based. He underwent a brief interrogation, and rapidly realized that his interrogators already knew most of the circumstances of his escape from the Vistula estuary, leaving him to conclude that other officers from the *Zander* must already be in British custody. The treatment he received after the interrogation was exceedingly agreeable, and he joined Oberst Hoffman and other German officers for breakfast:

Porridge and fresh milk, eggs with bacon, black tea and real coffee, white bread, butter and marmalade, sausages and ham – after six years' purgatory we felt we were in paradise. We ate with satisfaction, and we ate well. We shouldn't have done so. For my part, I could not digest all that rich food. I spewed like a drain. I choked for hours.

After they had offered us this and that, and had gathered around us and listened with astonishment and had marvelled at our adventurous escape, they told us that we were free to come and go as we wished. But where could one go in a prison surrounded by thick walls and a dozen guards in every nook and cranny?

Oberst Hoffman reached agreement after a long discussion with a senior English officer that an official vehicle with a military police driver would be freely placed at our disposal. They told us in passing that we were termed 'internees', not prisoners of war, and that we were free to move around within the internment area of Schleswig-Holstein. That was nevertheless a good start.[5]

As they toured the countryside, Hoffman and his fellow officers rounded up the survivors of the division. One of the few moments of unpleasantness related to the legacy of the destruction of the *Cap Arcona*; the British authorities insisted that the German prisoners bury the bodies that were washed ashore every day, and refused to accept any argument that the British had contributed to the tragedy. Hoffman refused to allow the men of his old division to be used in this way, and ultimately authorities from Hamburg arrived and took charge. Hoffman, Schäufler and the other survivors of 4th Panzer Division were moved to Bujendorf, closer to Lübeck. Food was limited, both for the soldiers and the thousands of civilians packed into the countryside, and widespread looting made matters worse. In order to help restore and maintain order, the British allowed Hoffman's men to form an unofficial police, and pairs of officers stood guard over barns and herds, armed with homemade cudgels. In return, the farmers gave them food, which they shared with their comrades.

Another group of soldiers who were in British custody in Schleswig-Holstein were the survivors of 24th Panzer Division. The division was officially dissolved after a last parade in Samland on 6 April, when contingents were dispatched back to Germany to form the core of a new division, while the rest remained in East Prussia to fight as infantry. By the end of April 1945, about 1,000 men from the division had concentrated around the town of Eckenförde, where they surrendered to the British 11th Armoured Division. Generalmajor von Nostitz-Wallwitz, still recovering from the wounds he suffered during the final days of the Heiligenbeil pocket, had rejoined his comrades, who were relieved and delighted at the warm relationship that they rapidly established with the British. Like 4th Panzer Division, the officers of 24th Panzer Division were allowed to form a police force, but towards the end of May the general became suddenly unwell. He had an internal abscess as a result of his wounds, and despite the efforts of the British medical services, he died on 31 May. In a deeply emotional ceremony, he was buried in Eckenförde with full military honours the following day. His son, who had been born in January, was baptized as part of the same ceremony.

> The last war grave at which we all gathered was on a hill with a clear view of the Baltic, and a coastline reminiscent of the division's homeland, East Prussia. To the southwest, the view was over a beautiful German landscape, across lakes, woods and fields, which had endured none of the horrors of this war. In this happy landscape, the division's road came to an end.[6]

Unlike 4th and 24th Panzer Divisions, almost all of 7th Panzer Division was evacuated in an controlled manner before the end of the war. The ships carrying Johann Huber and his comrades reached Swinemünde on 17 April. They travelled by train to a cluster of villages north of Berlin, close to Neustrelitz. Here, they watched American bombers heading for Berlin on 20 April, Hitler's birthday, and a few days later they were organized as infantry companies. Slowly, the rumble of the frontline to the east grew louder, and on 28 April Huber and the others formed up for parade, expecting to be ordered to the front. To their surprise, their company commander failed to appear, and when they went to find him they discovered that he had fled during the night. Hauptmann Thaler, a decorated officer from division headquarters, arrived and took command. The company marched towards the front, struggling against the stream of rear-area units and stragglers heading in the opposite direction, and first spotted the advancing spearheads of the Red Army on 30 April. They immediately broke off contact and retreated, determined to reach the lines of the western Allies rather than surrender to the Soviets. On 3 May, they crossed into territory controlled by the US Army, and were taken prisoner, together with most of 3rd Panzer Army.

Conditions for the men of 7th Panzer Division were rather different from those experienced by the men of 4th and 24th Panzer Divisions. The soldiers could understand the need for them to sleep in the open – there were tens of thousands of men surrendering every day, and it was impossible to find accommodation for them all – but the lack of food caused considerable resentment. At first, the officers were allowed to remain with their men, but after an incident in which the officers attempted to set up a court-martial for two soldiers who refused to obey orders, the Americans segregated the officers from the other ranks. Although the food supply slowly improved, the men remained weak from hunger, sometimes attempting to break out from the prison camp in search of food, and then creeping back in again.

The problem with food was widespread, and the men who broke out of the camps usually found that the local civilian population was almost as badly off as they were. For most of the war, German agriculture had relied on foreign labour, much of it from prisoners of war, to keep the farms functioning, and Germany had forcibly imported millions of tons of food. Now, with the labour pool removed and no imports appearing, hunger was widespread. Furthermore, the flight from the Red Army meant that there were about 17 million more people in the western parts of Germany, mainly civilians but including three million soldiers, than the western Allies had anticipated. Aware that the harvest in Germany would be poor in 1945, the western Allies feared a famine in the winter of 1945/46, and attempted to stockpile food in anticipation, thus making the shortages during 1945 worse. Finally, the devastation of German industry meant that Germany had no opportunity to purchase food abroad; countries such as Denmark and the Netherlands were in a position to sell food to Germany towards the end of 1945, but funds to make the purchases were not available. It could be argued that the western Allies should have contributed funds for such purchases, but in the case of the European powers they had pressing needs of their own, and for much of 1945 the USA remained locked in a war in the Pacific.

Other aspects of imprisonment by the Americans also caused considerable resentment to the Germans. When Huber and his companions were transported to Sülstorf, several men were robbed of their wallets, watches and medals by American soldiers. The prisoners protested in vain to US officers about the thefts.[7] Not long after, Huber and his fellow prisoners were handed over to the British, and he noted that their treatment improved markedly.

There has been much debate about how many German prisoners died in captivity in the hands of the western Allies. After the war, the Maschke Commission was established in Germany to investigate this issue. In 1974, it reported that by the end of the war some 940,000 men were held by the French, 3.64 million by the British and 3.1 million by the Americans. About 25,000 German prisoners died while in French custody; some were killed when they were made to clear wartime minefields, while others suffered considerably from malnutrition. Photographs of emaciated German prisoners in French captivity appeared in American newspapers late in 1945, but the reports failed to mention the widespread hunger of Germans in American custody. The Maschke Commission found that about 5,000 German prisoners died whilst being held by the Americans, compared with 1,300 deaths in British custody. The death rates were therefore markedly different for the three Western Allies: 2.7 per cent for the French, 0.16 per cent for the Americans, and 0.04 per cent for the British. Under the terms of the Geneva Convention, the western Allies were required to provide the same rations for prisoners of war as they provided for their own men, and to release their captives as soon as possible after the end of the war. In order to avoid falling foul of this, Germans held in the west were reclassified as disarmed combatants, thus removing any obligations under the Geneva Convention. Many have condemned this policy as a cynical act, while others have defended it, on the grounds that it would have been impossible to provide such rations for so many people, and in any event, with the war over, they were no longer 'prisoners of war'.

The British had a distinctly different attitude to captured Germans from their American and French allies. At first, it was official policy for German prisoners to be held in camps close to the stores that had been set up for their captured weapons; Churchill intended to keep his options open, and he and Montgomery had some sympathy for the pleas from Dönitz for an alliance against the Soviet occupation of Eastern Europe. In particular, there were concerns that if the USA moved significant numbers of troops to the Pacific for the ongoing war against Japan, the British might be left exposed to the potential threat posed by the Red Army in eastern Germany.

In such circumstances, it was reasoned, it would be prudent to ensure that help in the form of rearmed German units was close at hand. Montgomery gave express orders that captured German weapons were not to be destroyed, on the grounds that 'they might be needed for any reason'.[8]

The Americans strongly disapproved of Churchill's dalliance with the Dönitz government. Few Americans – General George S. Patton was an exception – shared his view, and although President Truman was rather more cautious with respect to Stalin than Roosevelt, Churchill's telegram to Truman on 12 May, warning that an 'iron curtain' was descending across Europe, made little impact. On 18 May, Dönitz and his ministers were arrested and subjected to humiliating strip-searches. Some committed suicide, including Generaladmiral von Friedeburg, who had replaced Dönitz as commander of the Kriegsmarine; he had been tearful and depressed throughout the last few days, and this was one dishonour too many. Most were robbed of medals, watches, rings and other valuables. General Kinzel, the former commander of 337th Volksgrenadier Division, had been separated from his wife for many years, and was openly living with his lover Erika von Aschoff. He remained at liberty until 24 June, when he was ordered to report to a British internment camp. He and his lover drove to a nearby lake, where their bodies were found shortly after. He had left a suicide note with his landlady, describing where they could be found.

As the year progressed, many of the hundreds of thousands of soldiers in the prison camps were slowly released. Some were made to work in Britain, France, Belgium and the Netherlands as part of Germany's reparations, but the majority were soon free. They travelled to their homes to find their cities lying in ruins. Many of their families had been killed or left homeless by air raids. For the men whose home towns and villages lay in the Soviet occupation sector, there was great reluctance to enter the jurisdiction of the old enemy, not least because many soldiers who did so were promptly rounded up by the Soviets. And for the men from Silesia, Pomerania and Prussia, there was no question of returning home. Their homelands would soon cease to be German.

On 4 September, the remaining officers of 24th Panzer Division paraded one last time. The address to them speaks much about the close camaraderie that had held them together through so many tough moments:

Meine Herren!

First, we should remember our last division commander, General von Nostitz-Wallwitz, whom we laid down to his final rest here in Eckenförde on 1 June. As a result of serious wounds which he received at the end of March in East Prussia, he died here three weeks after the final collapse, when he and we all had come to believe that he was healed. With unwavering loyalty and concern for our welfare, he led the division through the battles of the last seven months of the war, which one can without exaggeration regard as the toughest of the entire war. In earlier years, he stood in our ranks as a regimental commander and shared good days and bad with us. It was his task to lead us through not only the heaviest of the fighting, but also through the greatest mental strains – the collapse of everything – holding the honour of the division high and pure. It was not granted to him to bring forth the attacking spirit of the old, determined regiments in a major attack, fully equipped, supported by all modern weapons. It fell to him frequently to mobilize the reserves of morale in the division in constant changes in the front, in often desperate situations, faced with unachievable orders, with inadequate forces and inadequate support.

The ranks of the old riders grew thinner and thinner, and the men of the rifle squadrons had to take up the heavy weapons, the artillery, the tanks and supply formations, so that they could give their advice to the young replacements from the homeland. And constantly at the last moment, faced with the pressure of enemy attacks, the division would order: 'Attack!' And it was done! With our general at our front, without any personal protection.

… we want to recall our fallen comrades from the old 1st Cavalry Brigade, 1st Cavalry Division and 24th Panzer Division.

Their blood that they spilt

Must never be for nothing

And will never be forgotten!

They all gave their lives in the spirit of the tradition of the German cavalry. We can set no memorial in metal and stone for them today, but our hearts will be their living memorial. Every day and in everything we do, we will have before our eyes our debt to our fallen comrades, and we will find our way through the difficult times to the future.

… Never let dull despair or apathy gain ground in our ranks. We want to hold before our eyes the final conduct in battle of the division, a successful attack by the oldest senior NCOs, Schirrmeister and Functioner [technical NCO posts] on the Haff coast on 27 March, when all other soldiers had given up and sat in their trenches. On this day we proclaimed: 'The old horsemen's spirit lives on!'[9]

However much the German prisoners in the west may have resented their treatment, they were all glad not to be prisoners of the Soviet Union. As has already been described, Hans Jürgen Pantenius and his men spent their last night of freedom discussing all manner of subjects, including fanciful ideas of escaping west overland. Soviet gunners sporadically bombarded the landing stages to the rear of Pantenius' regiment, but fell silent at about 0300hrs:

In the morning, as I had still not received any orders from the division, I made my way alone on foot towards division headquarters. The headquarters was on the western shore by Schiewenhorst, apparently in the Kronenhof estate. In any event, I didn't get far. I unexpectedly came across a crowd of about 50 freed Russian workers, escorted by three or four soldiers, who immediately encircled me and started shouting loudly. One of the Russians, who spoke good German, came close to me and muttered to me that I should remain quite calm and leave my pistol holstered. One of their leaders had had a brother killed by the Germans, hence their anger. I followed the advice. Now the soldiers approached. Their first authoritative act was not to take my pistol, but my watch, which was swiftly removed, and only then was the pistol taken. One spoke in broken German, saying that he had nothing against we frontline soldiers, but had plenty against the SS. But there weren't any of them for far and wide in this area. Then they let me go on, and continued on their way. There was no point in my continuing alone to division headquarters, and I returned to the regiment, where nobody had noticed what had just passed.

A short time later, a delegation led by the division adjutant arrived from headquarters, and he told me personally where, when and how weapons were to be handed over. It would have been appropriate to have received a last greeting from the division commander, as he didn't appear himself.

The assembly and handover area was close by. The regiment assembled, still about 800 men strong. After a short speech, in which I thanked them for their earlier achievements and acknowledged their constant bearing and discipline, I relieved them of their military oath in accordance with instructions from the division, and set them free as individuals to make use of any promising opportunities to escape, but at the same time warned them against any rash or thoughtless undertakings, particularly here in the encirclement on the Binnennehrung. I advised them further that during the march into captivity, it would be in the interests of everyone to continue to follow the instructions of officers and NCOs, as they had done before. Besides, the Russians should not find a disorderly rabble, but disciplined troops, as they had been before. Finally, we had not given up our positions, but were following the orders from the highest level for an overall surrender; this was a difference that gave some hope that the Russians would release those laying down their arms now in the foreseeable future. Of course, this last hope was naive and in vain. The only difference was that our transportation and march into captivity was to some extent easy-going and without liberties or trickery.

After the final parade, the soldiers laid their rifles, submachine-guns and light machine-guns in neat rows. The officers were officially allowed to keep their pistols for now.[10]

As they began their march into captivity, accompanied by an agreeably friendly Soviet captain, Pantenius and his men received a surprising insight into the brittle nature of the alliance that had defeated Germany:

> Next, we marched south to the village of Gross Zünder in 23rd Infantry Division's old sector. Marching columns of Russian infantry, constantly overtaken by motorized artillery of every type, passed us in the opposite direction. I asked the captain why these deployments were still occurring close to the coast, as we were no longer opposing them. He merely replied briefly that these were precautionary measures, as one couldn't know whether the British had now combined with our troops in the west to attack the Russians and would carry out landings here in the Bay of Danzig. The Russians no longer had much regard for a friendly and trustful relationship with the Western Allies.[11]

In Hela, General von Saucken had held final negotiations with the Soviet authorities. A fluent Russian speaker, von Saucken was able to ensure that his men would be permitted to take their supply wagons with them into captivity. He then stood at the base of the Putziger Nehrung with his staff, as the soldiers of his command marched past. Eleven other generals went into captivity with him.

The men from Hela marched south through the ruins of Gotenhafen and Danzig. Here, they encountered some of the German civilians who had stayed in the ruined city. Marching in step, the soldiers sang the songs with which they had passed many long marches during the war. Many threw their rations to the watching civilians. Some shouted out that they would be free soon, and that everyone could look forward to better times.

Much of 4th Panzer Division had been evacuated to Hela, to await ships to the west, but other elements remained on the mainland. Most of 12th Panzergrenadier Regiment was still near the base of the Frische Nehrung as the war came to a close. Oberleutnant Manfred Nase, who commanded one of the regiment's companies, went into captivity with his men:

> We reached Elbing on 11 May. We marched into the town singing; it left a dreadful impression on us. We saw no men, no elderly. The defenceless women and girls had lost all that they had once possessed: their belongings, their homes, their menfolk and their womanhood; and they stood crying in the ruins and displayed their misfortunes to us.
>
> … We marched on towards Braunsberg the following day. Our march out of Elbing was a moving demonstration. We sang louder and our crisp marching echoed defiantly from the broken walls. Girls and women with tears streaming down their faces brought

us the first blooms of spring to bind in little posies. For the last time in its history, 12th Panzergrenadier Regiment marched as a single unit. It helped us to forget our comfortless position when comrades in front of us, to either side, and behind us, marched in step, sang the same song. It would have been very different if we had been alone.

Again and again we were harassed, mainly by troops from Soviet rear-area formations, who all wanted their share from us. Watches, boots, awards and medals, these were the most sought-after souvenirs. We had to keep the gunners from the self-propelled guns in the middle ranks, as their black Panzer uniforms attracted particular interest.

… [In Braunsberg, while] the long column waited at the gates of the barracks of the former 21st Infantry Regiment, the officers were ordered to the front of the column. There were a few quick handshakes and good wishes. In the main barracks, we had a further opportunity to say goodbye through the wire fence and to show how tightly we had been welded together by the years of struggle, officers, NCOs and soldiers of 4th Panzer Division. Perhaps we had never been so clearly aware of this as we were now, when we were separated at the whim of the enemy.[12]

As they marched into captivity, the men of 4th Panzer Division consoled themselves that at least some of their comrades, the handpicked men of Group *Küspert*, had escaped Soviet captivity. The loss of the *Goya* was not made public in Germany until after the war, and the men who surrendered to the Soviet Union did not learn of the disaster until their eventual return to Germany.

Another group of German soldiers was about to discover that they, too, were destined for Soviet captivity. Many Germans had ended the war in Sweden, men such as Erich Steinbach, a veteran of 4th Panzer Division. He left Hela with the last convoy in the final hours of the war, but the small submarine-hunter carrying him to safety was ordered to take in tow a ferry damaged by a sudden Soviet air attack the morning after the end of hostilities. Caught up in the same storm that nearly swamped Hans Schäufler and his comrades, the submarine-hunter wallowed through the heavy seas, until its propeller became entangled with the hawser connecting it to the ferry. The following day, a Swedish destroyer offered to help them, and towed them to the port of Ystad. Here, about 20 small German vessels had gathered, and their occupants were transported to a camp near the Norwegian border. Swedish officers repeatedly assured them that in no circumstances would they be handed over to the Soviet Union. Along with about 2,600 other German soldiers, Steinbach and his comrades settled down to life in the internment camp, receiving good rations and buying newspapers and clothing with the money they received in return for labouring at the new airfield nearby.

On 2 June, a diplomatic note was passed to the Swedish Foreign Minister, requesting that Latvians and Estonians who had served in the German armed forces, and any Wehrmacht personnel who had escaped to Sweden from the *Ostfront*, should be handed over to the Soviet Union. The issue was discussed in the Swedish government, but some members of the government subsequently claimed that the issue of the German prisoners was not stated clearly, and that they were under the impression that the soldiers would be handed over to a commission formed by all of the Allied powers. A treaty that confirmed the transfer, and also included a trade agreement between the two nations, was signed.

The first inkling that Steinbach and the others in the internment camps had of this turn of events was in the form of rumours that circulated widely in November 1945. On 10 November, they were alarmed to find that they could no longer purchase newspapers. On 18 November, the guards were reinforced, and two days later a guard told the prisoners that they would be handed over to the Soviet authorities at the end of the month.[13]

News about the transfer of the Estonians, Latvians and Germans to the Soviet Union was greeted with dismay throughout Sweden. Many newspapers carried strident headlines questioning the decision, stating that the honour of the Swedish nation was at stake. Representations were made to the Swedish Foreign Minister by the Swedish church and army, and a letter was sent to the King of Sweden on behalf of the officers and NCOs of two Swedish regiments involved in the prisoner transfer, making clear the deep sense of shame and outrage felt by the Swedish troops involved. Several hundred Swedish officers handed in their resignations in disgust, and railway workers went on strike. Nevertheless, the Swedish government stood by its decision. Whatever the arguments about honour might be, there was a large element of *Realpolitik* involved. Ultimately, Sweden was a small nation, faced by demands from an immensely powerful neighbour. But in view of the protests from the army, police units were deployed in place of soldiers.

As predicted, it was on 30 November, when the Swedish military marched into the camp at 0500, led by the 200 men in blue uniforms. The soldiers encircled each barrack block and separated us from each other – and from our officers. Further united action was thus no longer possible. Every barrack block had a triple encirclement, each of at least a company in strength. The inner ring was formed by the giant fellows in blue police uniforms. Breaking through at any point was impossible.

There was general turmoil. Many comrades mutilated themselves by striking their legs with rocks or hacking off toes or fingers. They were gripped by hysteria. My old comrade from 6th Company cut off two of the toes on his right foot. A few cut their wrists. Others slashed their bodies. It was dreadful. The Swedish medics silently carried those who had hurt themselves to the waiting medical tent or even to the hospital in Udevalla. We were parted from some of our comrades from our company in this manner.[14]

A Soviet ship, the *Kuban*, arrived in the Swedish port of Trelleborg, and the former soldiers of the Wehrmacht were taken aboard. Some German soldiers hanged themselves rather than become prisoners of the Soviet Union. All those who sought to avoid transfer by self-harm were treated in hospital, and transferred to the Soviet Union the following year.

The *Kuban* took the Germans to Libau. In 1946, they were dispersed to a number of different camps. Erich Steinbach went to Riga:

> There, we were put to work building a phosphate factory. They told us loud and clear that when the work was complete, we would be sent home immediately. It was another lie. We were sent to a camp in the Donetz basin to a new worksite. From there, I was released after four years. I came home shortly before Christmas 1949. It was the best Christmas present of my life.[15]

Bodo Kleine, who surrendered with the rest of 367th Infantry Division in Königsberg, was marched out of the city with several hundred other officers, along the road running east on the shores of the Pregel. Those who were unable to keep up – through exhaustion, hunger, thirst or wounds – were summarily shot by their guards. The marching column repeatedly encountered Soviet rear-area units heading in the opposite direction, and on most occasions the Soviet soldiers attempted to rob the Germans of boots, belts and any remaining valuables. Sometimes, but not always, the guards with the column intervened to stop the thefts.

On the day that the war came to an end, Kleine was in a large prison camp just outside the town of Insterburg, established in a nearby stud farm. The Germans listened to the Soviet celebrations, and wondered whether they would now be allowed to return home:

> We, the losers, who had so far survived the war unscathed, returned to our wooden beds and were nonetheless delighted that this damned war was over. Naturally, we thought that we would shortly be able to return to our homeland and the war would thus finally be laid to rest. Today, when I recall that day, I must still say that the surrender gave me a sense of release, because I had been able to survive this war without injury.[16]

A few days later, a group of about 2,000 German officers was assembled and marched to the railway station. Here, they boarded a long train of cattle-trucks. Many hoped that the train would take them west; instead, after waiting for several hours, they were taken in the opposite direction. The long, slow journey, with inadequate food and water, took a heavy toll on the prisoners, some of whom died and were unceremoniously dragged from the wagons by the Soviet guards whenever the train stopped to take on coal and water. After a week, Kleine and his comrades learned that they had passed the city of Gorki, to the east of Moscow. Finally, they disembarked in Kazan, and were marched to a nearby camp. Here, they joined other officers, many of whom had been held captive since the German defeat at Stalingrad.

Most German prisoners in Soviet captivity were put to work. Pantenius was sent to a camp near Minsk, where he worked on reconstruction tasks until 1949. Kleine found that the work routine in the camp near Kazan was tough, but not overly so, until later in 1945. One of the prisoners gave the others a speech praising Stalin, and called upon his fellow inmates to join the Bund Deutscher Offiziere (Federation of German Officers, a part of the NKFD). Although some officers signed up for membership, many did not. Those who refused were sent off to a hard-labour camp in the forest.[17] In this new camp, there were no rest days, even when Christmas 1945 approached:

At the beginning of December 1945, our camp received a supply of pale wheat flour. In the meantime, the camp bakery had been made ready, so that bread could now be baked within the camp. We now received pale bread, of course not proper white bread, as we had known in our own homes, but nevertheless excellent-tasting pale bread that was not as damp as the other black Russian bread. The kitchen personnel continuously kept back a portion of this pale flour so that they could bake us cakes at Christmas, which was now not far off. Thus 24th December, Holy Evening, came. As on every other day, we had to make our trip to the forest. On our return to the camp, we received our evening meal at 1900. We each were given our portion of soup, which was rather better than usual, a shot of Kaschka porridge [made using a local wild herb that the work details collected on their way back to the camp] and in addition to the normal 200 grams of bread, a small pale cake of about 500 grams. What joy! Finally, we had a satisfying meal, which on this Holy Evening seemed like a gift from heaven. Then we sang Christmas carols, and a slight, young Leutnant, who had a wonderful voice, sang solo 'Softly falls the snow' and 'Lo, how a rose e'er blooming'. Then, in place of candles, we lit our bunker with wooden torches, which burned brightly, and many comrades gave each other presents they had prepared. After everyone had finished his Christmas cake, we lay back on our wooden bunks, alone with our thoughts of our homeland and our relatives, who had no idea that we were forced to live here in deepest Russia in such dreadful subhuman conditions. For the Stalingrad prisoners, this was already the third Christmas behind the wire.

... On the first day of Christmas we once more had the usual dreadful food, a thin oat soup and five small potatoes which had already started to rot because of the frost. A young Flak-Leutnant named Harms, from Schleswig, found that three of his five potatoes were rotten, and despite his great hunger they were inedible. He then sat in the bunker on his bunk with the metal ration-can that served as his meal dish.

Hunched up, he said through his tears, 'I wish that today, the first day of Christmas, if I could have just one Christmas present, it would be to sit in my grandmother's pigsty by the feeding trough and for once eat enough pigswill to fill me up.' Just how dreadful our life was, cannot be understood by anyone who has not experienced it.[18]

Occasionally, there were medical inspections of the camps. The purpose of these was obvious to all involved – the prisoners were classified into groups to determine whether they were fit for all forms of work, fit for light duties only or completely unfit for work. With his weight reduced by poor nutrition to only 45kg, Kleine was classified as fit for light work, and attached to the camp kitchen, where he had the opportunity to get occasional extra rations. As soon as his weight had begun to recover, he was once more assigned to general work duties. In June 1946 he was moved to a different camp, where the work routine was as hard as ever. Failure to achieve daily work targets resulted in threats of punishment, including transfer to hard-labour camps. For the former Wehrmacht soldiers, toiling hard with inadequate rations, the concept of other camps having even tougher conditions was almost unimaginable. Occasionally, though, contact between the prisoners and their guards was cordial and productive, as Kleine discovered when he was ordered to help load goods onto a riverboat in Kazan. One of the guards, who spoke good German, told Kleine that he was merely on leave in Kazan, and was actually stationed in Germany. When he learned that his garrison was close to where Kleine's parents lived, he volunteered to take a letter to them. Written on a scrap of paper with a pencil stub, this note was the first news his parents received of his capture and subsequent survival.[19]

Like many prisoners, Kleine was moved from one camp to another every few months. Although some had better accommodation, the harsh working conditions and inadequate rations took their toll. It should be remembered, however, that much of western Russia, the Ukraine and Belarus had been left devastated by the war. The huge casualties sustained by the Soviet Union, and the continuing absence of so many men in the armies of occupation, would ensure that it would be many years before Soviet harvests reached pre-war levels, and whilst food supplies for prisoners were very poor, civilians only did marginally better.

The price that the Soviet Union paid for its victory was enormous. More than 20 million civilians and 8.6 million soldiers were dead, a further 25 million people were homeless, and about one-third of the Soviet Union's pre-war wealth had been spent on the war. There was an understandable desire to use German prisoners to try to repair some of the damage that the war had done. The death rate amongst Germans held by the Soviet Union was far higher than in the west – German estimates suggest that about 3,349,000 Germans were taken prisoner by the Red Army, and of these, about 1.4 million, or a fraction over 40 per cent, did not return to Germany. However dreadful this rate may be, it is actually lower than the death rate of Soviet prisoners in German hands during the war.

Occasionally, prisoners were required to carry out work that gave them opportunities for a small degree of revenge:

> Once, we were taken to a railway station close to Vyasma, where there was a train loaded with electric motors and weaving machines, booty from Germany. We had to unload them. In the familiar, customary Russian manner, we chucked the heavy electric motors off the wagons with crowbars, with the result that if one motor landed on another, the cast-iron casing would split or break into fragments. When it came to unloading the weaving machines, one of the prisoners suggested that we should remove the shuttles from the machines and throw them into the field next to the railway line, which we then did. Consequently, the weaving machines brought here from Germany were completely useless, as where would anyone wanting to use them obtain a replacement shuttle? Our behaviour showed that we prisoners of war remained uncooperative and hostile to the Russians, and sought opportunities to do damage to the Russians whenever we could. In any case, this is hardly surprising, given how the Russians treated us.[20]

In 1948, US attitudes to German prisoners changed, and the US government put considerable pressure on countries holding German prisoners to release them as soon as possible. Kleine and his comrades learned of this from a Soviet radio announcement in a factory where they were working, but not all would be allowed to return home. The Soviet authorities detained many tens of thousands after convicting them of a variety of 'war crimes'. In many cases, these crimes were little more than excuses for keeping them in captivity. For example, a Luftwaffe officer was sentenced to hard labour by a war crimes court when he was found guilty of destroying Soviet state property – the property in question being the Soviet aircraft that he had shot down during the war.

Generalfeldmarschall von Kleist was sentenced to ten years' imprisonment after being charged with 'having alienated through mildness and kindness the people of the Soviet Union'.[21] Von Kleist died in captivity in October 1954; he had only been allowed to write a single postcard to his family every month, and only during the last seven months of his life. The continued detention of these men caused much bitterness in Germany, particularly as there was little or no notification to their families about whether they were still alive. Many parents, wives and children of former Wehrmacht personnel waited with diminishing hope as the years passed. Some prisoners were executed after their trials. Generalleutnant von Rappard, whose 7th Infantry Division put up stubborn resistance in the lower Vistula valley, and Generalleutnant Richert, who commanded 35th Infantry Division, were amongst the generals who went into captivity after the final surrender of AOK Ostpreussen. Von Rappard was convicted of ordering the execution of captured partisans in the Veliki Luki area, and was hanged in the same area in February 1946. Richert had commanded 286th Security Division in Belarus, where he was heavily involved in anti-partisan operations, and he was hanged in Minsk in the same month.

For the German civilians who remained in East and West Prussia, life was extremely tough. Almost all German men had already left, either because they were in the Wehrmacht or because they were forcibly enrolled into the Volkssturm. Those who remained were usually rounded up and dispatched to the Soviet Union as forced labour. Many of them died, either during the march to the east or during captivity. As no official records were kept of the numbers of German civilians forced to work by the Soviets, it is impossible to calculate how many were involved, or how many died. Life was even harder for the women in the occupied lands. Most, from young girls to elderly women, were subjected to repeated rapes, which continued for several months after the end of the fighting.

After the fall of Königsberg, many of the remaining civilians were marched out of the city, not least because however hard it would be for the Soviets to feed them in the countryside, it would be even harder in the ruins of the former East Prussian capital. Erika Morgenstern, her younger sister and her mother were in one such march:

> It was already evening when an endless, long column of women, children, the elderly and the sick marched out of the city of the dead. Again and again, I stumbled over the body of someone lying on the ground, not knowing whether they had died some time ago or had collapsed during the march. In front of us and behind us, we repeatedly heard screams from women as they were dragged out of the ranks to be raped. To do this, the Russians shone torches into their faces, as it was now completely dark. Many had a clever form of lighting; they had a bulb in the red Soviet star on the front of their hats, with a switch in

their pocket. This made them seem especially dreadful, like devils. My mother, too, was illuminated in this manner; and in my terrible fear, with my body shaking, I began to scream awfully every time. The Russians would then leave her alone.[22]

This tactic protected her mother for a time, particularly when there were easier targets available, but eventually, during an overnight stop, her mother too was taken away and raped.

Slowly, order began to return to the ruins of Königsberg. Work-parties of civilians were organized to clear rubble, in exchange for minimal rations. Starvation rapidly became a major problem, and as the year went on there were reports of cannibalism amongst the diminishing population. The Morgenstern family was put to work on a farm. If a woman was unable to work, neither she nor her family received food, and what rations they did receive were completely inadequate. After a long day of labouring in the fields, the women had to try to forage for food in the fields at night, aware that if the Soviet guards spotted them, they risked being shot. The children spent the days searching for wild herbs and berries with which to supplement their diets. Medical care was almost non-existent, and anything other than the most trivial illness was often fatal to the malnourished victims.

Hans von Lehndorff was marched out of Königsberg with several other men, and late on 16 April he slipped away from his guards. He was recaptured almost immediately, and taken to Rauschen. One by one, the prisoners were interrogated. Von Lehndorff was asked why he had never joined the Party; a youth who was in the group was asked how many Soviet prisoners of war he had shot during Hitler Youth training. Another man, who had served in the police, simply did not return from his interrogation. After the interrogation, von Lehndorff was told that he was free to go, and cautiously set off, expecting to be re-arrested at any moment. One night, he and his elderly companion encountered two men from 5th Panzer Division who were attempting to evade capture. They shared their meagre food supplies, and the two soldiers disappeared into the darkness. A short while later, von Lehndorff was captured by another Soviet band, and marched back to Königsberg. While he was in a prison camp, a former acquaintance recognized him as a doctor, and he was transferred to the camp 'hospital'. Dysentery broke out in the camp on 28 April, and the first deaths occurred the same day as the weakest and most malnourished rapidly succumbed. Finally, in June, von Lehndorff's old friend Doktora was able to arrange his release. He joined her in an ad hoc hospital that had been set up in the relatively intact local government finance building, but not long after the hospital staff were given one day's notice to leave by the Russians. They were forced to give up the building, and move their 1,500 patients to another hospital. Food continued to be desperately scarce, and when he foraged in the ruins of former hospitals and military medical units for medical supplies, von Lehndorff repeatedly came across the corpses of those who had died during the siege.

The privations and suffering began to wear down even the strongest, as von Lehndorff found:

> On Wednesday, Doktora came to see me in the operating theatre. She wanted me to look at her neck, on which she had a very itchy patch. I found a whole host of lice, which had firmly established themselves in her hair. When I told her, she collapsed. I worked hard to calm her, while Dr Rausch helped me to cut her hair and clear the area. She rallied again, but remained altered, leaving me feeling helpless.[23]

The following morning, she took an overdose of sleeping tablets, and died a day later. Water and electrical supplies, destroyed during the fighting, remained non-existent, and the survivors had to find water wherever they could. Von Lehndorff found children playing in a pool of foul water, and tried to dissuade them from entering it; to his horror, the children replied, 'Oh, whatever, it's all the same how we die. Nobody's going to get out of here alive.'[24]

At the end of July, von Lehndorff found himself weakening, becoming short of breath on minimal exertion. Although he regarded this as unremarkable – his nutrition was as poor as that of most Germans in Königsberg – his colleagues admitted him to the hospital, where he made a slow recovery over the next few weeks. Others who worked with him were less fortunate. Several sickened with typhus, spread by the widespread body lice, and many died. Von Lehndorff did not recover his strength until October. As summer turned to autumn, there were repeated rumours that Swedish ships were going to come to the shattered city to evacuate those who were still alive. Such rumours fed on themselves, and there were reports that the Red Cross had already established a camp in Pillau. Believing that escape was close at hand, many sold their last warm clothing for scraps of food; but no ships came.

A few days later, von Lehndorff received an alarming warning: he was to be arrested the following day. Such arrests were commonplace, and often resulted in deportation to the Soviet Union. He slipped away from the hospital, intending to head south to his family home. When he reached the village of Ponarien, he was overjoyed to find some old friends. One of them told him about what had happened in the village:

The Russians came on 23 January [1945]. Of course, they took everything we had and pursued the women, but otherwise the first three weeks went by reasonably. Then the commissars came and gathered together all the people in the area and interrogated us, and took the younger people with them back to Russia. The Gräfin [countess] (my mother-in-law) had stayed here, and at first was treated fairly well. She was often even able to protect the young girls. Then she had to clean rooms for the Russians. But she did that too. But carrying things along the roads was too much for her. When she had to do that, she immediately became ill. Near Reichau, she refused to go any further, and she was put up against a small wall and shot. Someone found the backrest of a carriage that was lying in the ditch and wrote on it, 'Here lies the Gräfin from Ponarien.'[25]

Von Lehndorff travelled on to Grasnitz, and to his great delight found his aunt there. She was now living in what had been the gardener's cottage, and with the other locals worked for the new Polish landlords, receiving food in return for labouring in the fields. Cautious about drawing too much attention to himself, von Lehndorff kept a low profile. In January 1946, he realized that the authorities were increasingly aware of his presence, and as he did not have any documentation allowing him to be in the area, he decided that it was time to leave. He moved to the hospital in Osterode, where he stayed for three days, but was then arrested. He was told that he was accused of holding political meetings; the only 'meetings' he had held, other than as a doctor, were several trips to local villages to help with evangelical services. A day after his arrest, he managed to escape and returned briefly to his aunt's house in Grasnitz, and then went on to Ponarien. Many of those he had met when he passed this way during the autumn were gone; Poles were moving into the area in ever-greater numbers, and German families were simply deported to make room for them. He learned that his mother and brother had been shot by the Russians the previous winter, together with 16 others, as they all attempted to flee to the west. Although there were many Russians and Poles in the area, there was still a substantial German community, and von Lehndorff was able to secure permission from the local Soviet commandant to stay.

Although life was comparatively comfortable for the remaining Germans, provided they kept a low profile, there were still moments of terror. In March 1946, von Lehndorff and a young woman were returning to Brausen when two Soviet men on horseback accosted them. They struck von Lehndorff, and took the woman away with them to rape her; she returned to the village later. In May, von Lehndorff returned to Grasnitz to visit his aunt, only to find that she had been arrested and taken to Allenstein. Relations with the remaining Soviet forces and the rapidly growing Polish population were complex. On the one hand, the Soviets behaved with the arrogance of conquerors, taking whatever they wanted, but on the other hand, when the Soviet presence began to diminish late in 1946 von Lehndorff noted that life in the countryside for the remaining Germans became tougher. Many Poles were friendly and helpful, while others – particularly those who had moved to the area from former Polish areas that were now to be annexed by the Soviet Union – were prone to be hostile and rapacious.

Life in Danzig, too, was difficult for those who had either deliberately chosen to stay, or had been unable to leave before the city fell. Annemarie Gerlach, who had watched her sister leave the city on one of the last trains, was still in Danzig with her friend Ruth Augstein, and they faced constant advances from the Russians:

> A Russian wanted to force Ruth and me to go with him. When we refused, he pointed his submachine-gun at us. By this point, it was all the same to me. I looked at him and said, 'Shoot, then!' He must have understood me, stared at me speechlessly, and went away. We thus learned that one shouldn't show fear in front of the Russians, but should somehow impress them with our cold-bloodedness.[26]

Others were less fortunate. Reinhold Jahnke, an elderly man, took his family from the village of Buschkau to Danzig as the Soviet encirclement of the city grew tighter, but returned to his home after the fall of the city. In one building, they found seven civilians who had been shot. A 15-year-old girl, who had survived, described how she and the other women had been repeatedly raped. At one stage during his travels, Jahnke was held in a barn with other civilians:

> There was also a woman in this barn who had to give birth ... the child came dead into this world. After the child was born, this woman was raped about 25 times in the presence of more than 100 people. I was about ten metres from the scene and saw it all. The women standing there could also see it clearly, and then attempted to hide. After these rapes, the woman died.[27]

Poles arrived in Danzig and Gotenhafen within days of the end of the war. Many were former residents of the Polish lands in the east, which were to be handed over to the Soviet Union. Their attitude to the Germans in the cities was mixed. Some were hostile, vocally expressing a desire for revenge on the Germans, while others took advantage of the situation in which the Germans now found themselves, selling food and other essentials to the Germans at vastly inflated prices. But many discovered that despite the horrors of the first few days after the arrival of the Red Army, many Soviet soldiers were kind and sympathetic. Annemarie Gerlach was surprised by one encounter with a Soviet officer: 'He pulled an amulet from his pocket with the words, "I too Christian. But so long as I soldier of Father Stalin, I carry amulet in pocket. When I am home again, I carry it again on my chest."'[28]

The Poles forced many Germans to work in the cities, clearing ruins or burying the dead. Others were sent on long marches by the Soviet authorities, with many being deported to the Soviet Union where they worked as forced labourers. Annemarie Kleist, who was 21, was one of several women rounded up at the end of March 1945:

On Sunday 7th April, we departed from Danzig for Graudenz. We had very little baggage with us, but it was still hard to keep up with the march. Whoever couldn't keep going, sat at the roadside. The Russians encouraged them, saying 'Dawai, dawai', but if this wasn't effective, the exhausted people were executed with a single shot to the back of the head. They drove us on mercilessly. We spent the nights in empty barns or houses, which were often partly destroyed, in Hohenstein and Rauden, and on the third day reached Graudenz. We were given warm soup once a day.

We were kept in the prison in Graudenz, 40 women in each single-man cell. Once more, we were interrogated and sorted. Once a day, we had to walk around the compound with our hands behind our backs, and were not allowed to speak to each other. On 17 April, we were loaded in groups of 40 into cattle-trucks, where we lay in two rows of 20 on the bare boards. We were packed in like sardines. In this manner, about 2,200 innocent people, women and also children and the elderly, were dispatched to the Urals in an endless freight train.[29]

The train reached Camp 1090 in Kazakhstan on 6 May. The Germans were put to work laying a new railway line to the nearby nickel mines. About 20 died in the first month. Most remained in captivity for three years before they were transported back to Germany.

Gertrud Synofzik and her daughter Brunhilde fled from their home in East Prussia in late January 1945, and were overtaken by Soviet spearheads near Bischofstein. In April 1945, the 15-year-old Brunhilde was separated from her mother, and dispatched via Insterburg to the Soviet Union. She remained in a labour camp until the autumn, when an international commission visited the camp.

One day, a foreign commission appeared in our camp and asked us if we had all willingly come to Russia to help with reconstruction. Two women replied to the gentlemen that the Russian GPU [part of the NKVD] had herded us all together in our homeland like cattle, had loaded us into cattle-trucks in Insterburg, and shipped us here. After the commission left the camp, there was much agitation amongst the Russian guards, and in the days that followed, there was a big change in the camp and in the hospital. All of those in the hospital were selected, including me, and loaded aboard a train that was to carry us home. The transport consisted of people from many camps.

On 5 October, we reached Frankfurt an der Oder. There, we were deloused and received three days' food. We went on the following day, through Berlin to Richtenburg.[30]

Many of the Poles who moved into East and West Prussia took over the abandoned German farms. In some cases, the fields had already been sown the previous winter, and provided that there was sufficient labour to hand – if necessary, gathered together by force – it was possible to get a reasonable harvest. But in other cases, large tracts of land were left untended. There were many reasons for this: a shortage of seed, insufficient manpower and a lack of local knowledge meant that the Poles often did not know which crops would grow best in which fields. Consequently, food remained scarce, and it was inevitable that the dwindling number of German residents were classed as the lowest priority.

The fate of the Germans in Silesia, Pomerania and Prussia was settled when the victorious Allies met in Potsdam in the summer of 1945. The location was chosen because Berlin had suffered too much damage to host such a conference. All parties attended with grave doubts about the 'other side'. Spies such as Kim Philby and Donald Maclean ensured that Stalin was fully aware of British talks with the Germans before the end of the war, and that Montgomery had ordered that German troops in Schleswig-Holstein should be held alongside their weapons, in case there should be a need for them. President Truman had little interest in a continued American involvement in Europe, but was wary of the Soviet Union gaining too much power. And for Churchill, the war in Europe was merely the latest stage in the long history of the continent. Even before the conflict was over, he had turned his thoughts to the shape of post-war Europe. The question of Poland's borders featured strongly in his mind.

After a few preliminary skirmishes that made clear the divisions between the former allies, the conference began in earnest when the three leaders arrived on 16 July. The British delegation was in a curious limbo; the post-war election had been held, but with so many soldiers deployed around the world, the count was not yet complete. It remained to be seen whether Churchill, who started the conference as the British Prime Minister, would still hold that post at the end of the conference.

The conference lasted until 2 August, and the issue of the territory to be handed over to Poland constantly recurred. In the end, the British and Americans accepted the Soviet position, and Pomerania, Silesia, West Prussia and the southern half of East

Prussia were transferred from Germany to Poland. For the Poles, the acquisition of this land was vital, as Poland had lost so much territory to the Soviet Union in the east. Churchill complained that the Poles had already established authorities to run these provinces before the Potsdam Conference, but Stalin countered by saying that the Germans had already effectively fled from these areas, and the only significant population remaining was Polish. Churchill returned to London part way through the conference, to learn that he had lost the general election. Clement Attlee replaced him, and took his place at Potsdam. Churchill later wrote that had he returned to Potsdam, he would have fought to prevent the transfer of all of Silesia to Poland. Given how little he achieved prior to leaving the conference, and the fact that the Soviet Union was physically in possession of the territory in question, such assertions are doubtful at best.

The northern half of East Prussia was to become Soviet territory. This had already been agreed in principle in Yalta, and Stalin now insisted that there was no deviation from this. The Soviet people, he maintained, deserved something for their huge sacrifices, and the Soviet Union had need of a Baltic port that was free from ice in the winter. Whatever the rights of the Soviet Union to reparations or compensation, this justification of the Soviet annexation of Königsberg was simply not valid. The Soviet Union already had access to the Baltic ports in Estonia, Latvia and Lithuania, which were effectively free of ice, and although Königsberg did have a port, it could only be reached by a dredged channel across the Frisches Haff – which, as had been seen during the fighting in early 1945, often froze during the winter.

There was no question of repeating the unsatisfactory state of affairs left after World War I. If necessary, civilian populations would have to move so that no country was left with large 'foreign' minorities. When discussing the shape of post-war Europe, Churchill had made his views clear to the House of Commons in 1944:

> Expulsion is the method which, insofar as we have been able to see, will be the most satisfactory and lasting. There will be no mixture of populations to cause endless trouble … A clean sweep will be made. I am not alarmed by these transferences, which are more possible in modern conditions.[31]

The agreement signed by the Allies at Potsdam stated:

> The Three Governments, having considered the question in all its aspects, recognize that the transfer to Germany of German populations, or elements thereof, remaining in Poland, Czechoslovakia and Hungary, will have to be undertaken. They agree that any transfers that take place should be effected in an orderly and humane manner.[32]

The reality of how this 'orderly and humane' transfer would be carried out became clear almost immediately. Christel Janza learned in August that the remaining German population would be expelled from Danzig. Before the order came into effect, she and her family sold all their belongings and purchased tickets to Stettin. They left the ruins of their beloved Danzig behind them on 16 August, but the overcrowded train suddenly came to a halt near Lauenburg. On the railway embankment, several Polish youths waited watchfully for night. The terrified Germans aboard the train waited too, but suddenly a goods train drew alongside, heading west. Many surged aboard to escape certain attack.

The goods train was loaded high with heavy machinery, but those who had loaded it knew little about the line to the west, and as the train passed under a low bridge, some of the heavy machinery was knocked onto the passengers. Several were killed, others badly injured. But their ordeal did not come to an end when they left Poland. Trying to reach Hamburg, the family of ten travelled on through Mecklenburg. At one stop, several Russians boarded the train and robbed the refugees of what few belongings they still had.[33]

Annemarie Gerlach was still in the house in Oliva that she shared with her friend Ruth Augstein and her sister-in-law, Lotti. They learned that the Polish Red Cross was organizing transport to Germany, and Ruth, her mother and her daughter left first. When they returned to their home, they found that their house had been stripped of their few remaining possessions. They then went to stay with a Jewish woman who had somehow survived the war, but shortly after they learned that the final transport to Germany would be leaving shortly, and managed to board the train:

After two days, we reached Schneidemühl. We remained stationary in a freight station for several hours. Then the locomotive set off again and we went on westwards, directly into a glowing red evening sky. This gave us new hope. But a long, difficult journey remained before us. We were underway for a total of five days and nights. We drove through devastated, abandoned villages, past unharvested fields. From our train, we saw Russian trucks driving along the country roads. They were loaded high with German sewing machines, German sofas, armchairs and pianos, which the Russians had gathered for their own homes.

From time to time, a Russian boarded our train. When we spotted them, we all screamed so loud that they took the very next opportunity to get off.

At the Polish–German border, we had to board open goods-wagons without sides. Anyone who wanted to avoid the risk of falling off had to try to get a place in the middle of the wagon, and we succeeded in doing so after much shuffling about.

On the evening of the fifth day, we rolled into Berlin.[34]

From Berlin, Gerlach travelled on to Prestin. Here, to her great joy, she found Waltraud Foth and her children, who had left Danzig on one of the last trains to escape to the west before Rokossovsky's armies cut the rail links across Pomerania. The reunited family faced several difficult years in the Russian Zone, until they were able to move to the west in 1955.

The two parts of East Prussia – the Polish region in the south, and the Soviet region in the north – were also to be cleared of their German inhabitants. The remaining German community in Rosenberg, where von Lehndorff was now working, was aware of the stories of robbery of trains on their way to Germany, and consequently many were reluctant to make the journey. His aunt, who had spent several months under arrest without charge, was able to join him in November 1946, and travelled west on a scheduled train. In May 1947, there were reports that Germans were to be gathered in a camp in Deutsch-Eylau, and transported from there back to Germany. One of von Lehndorff's friends was not technically eligible to join those leaving, but he and others succeeded in smuggling her aboard a train. After he returned to Rosenberg, three Polish militiamen told him that it was time for him, too, to leave. With other Germans, he was taken to Deutsch-Eylau.

> Before we finally left for the railway station, something remarkable happened. We all had to form up more or less in rows and columns, about 400 people, and then the district administrator asked me to speak a few words on his behalf to the crowd. A little alarmed, I asked what he had in mind. He said that he wished to explain that the manner in which we had been treated was not dishonest, but official policy. The Germans had also treated the Poles like this. We therefore had to endure this now, even though individuals were perhaps not guilty of anything. I therefore walked to the front and said: 'My dear compatriots, listen to me! This is the district administrator, who regrets that we have to leave our homeland in this manner. But he can't change things, as our people did the same to the Poles in the past, and that is unfortunately true. But we thank him for the nice soup that we received here in the camp, and ask him to ensure that the next transport will be well treated in this manner. And now let us hope that we will actually get to Germany.'[35]

The train journey west took several days. As they rolled across Poland, the East Prussians saw the same scenes everywhere: damaged cities and towns, abandoned fields. Eventually, they crossed the German–Polish border to the east of Dresden. Von Lehndorff stayed in the transit camp to which they were taken for several weeks, helping treat severely malnourished patients who had been brought there from captivity in the Soviet Union. When all of his friends had left the camp, he too departed, travelling to Berlin where he was reunited with his family.

In 1948, Erika Morgenstern, her sister, and her mother were informed that they were to be sent back to Germany. The following day, a huge Soviet truck appeared:

I had never seen such a big vehicle, and it made a dreadful noise. The wheels were nearly as big as me. I remembered German military vehicles well, and they were far smaller than this iron machine, which had been built for a Siberian winter. The driver, a Russian solder, dropped the back flap and signalled to us to climb aboard. Everyone immediately pushed, thrust and shoved like mad, but nobody could get in. It was simply too high. It was only now that the children were lifted up and pushed aboard. It was still not possible for the women to climb into the truck. Then my mother had the idea of climbing onto the rear wheel, but she couldn't get high enough without help. So the women helped each other, first onto the wheel, and then into the truck. It wasn't possible any other way.

As the vehicle set off with an ear-splitting roar from the engine, dear Frau Mayer waved to us with sorrowful laughter, and I can only hope that she was on the next transport with her children. The journey took us through Kaimen. All along the route through the countryside, we were bombarded with stones by Russian children, whose families had already been settled in the area. Our mothers protected us, but we constantly felt the stones strike us.[36]

The process continued throughout the parts of Eastern Europe with large German populations – East and West Prussia, Pomerania, Silesia, and parts of Hungary and Czechoslovakia – for several years. But decades later, when the Iron Curtain ceased to exist, tiny German communities were found to have survived this sustained period of 'ethnic cleansing'.

Gretel Dost, who was amongst the last civilians to escape from Pillau before the town fell, made her way down the Frische Nehrung to the Vistula estuary, from where she was evacuated first to Hela, and then to Denmark. She was aboard one of the ships in the very last convoys to carry civilians to safety in the west, and the war ended while she was still at sea. She was eventually put on a train back to Germany. At the border, British officers checked to ensure that no major Nazi officials were attempting to pass themselves off as ordinary refugees, and interviewed all the German refugees aboard the train. In Germany, she met a British soldier, whom she married. When her first child was born, she remembered what she had promised herself one memorable day at school in Friedrichstein, and named her child Marion. Several years later, she learned that Marion Dönhoff had written about her old homeland and her own escape to the west, and was able to meet the former Gräfin again, more than two decades after their first meeting.

The Soviet soldiers who had been involved in the great battles were also anxious to go home. The opening years of the war showed all of the weaknesses of the rigid Soviet system, in which individuals were discouraged from showing any initiative. As the war progressed, command and decision-making within the army became increasingly flexible, and consequently, at least within the ranks of the army, there was a widespread feeling that the post-war Soviet Union should be more open and liberal. Soldiers who had witnessed the horrors of the concentration camps were not slow to draw parallels with Soviet labour camps. Such views were widespread, but there was little appetite for serious political change. Nevertheless, despite their very modest nature, almost none of the demands for change from the frontline resulted in any change of policy. With its war-fighting task done, the army was to return to its pre-war subservience. Stalin had no intention of creating any structure that might threaten his own hold on power. All parts of Soviet society, civilian as well as military, would be kept firmly in their place.

It was inevitable that it would take time for the huge numbers of Soviet men to be demobilized and sent home. In the meantime, many were put to work as labourers, as the Soviet Union attempted to bring order to the devastated territory it had acquired. Discipline amongst the troops, particularly the rear-area elements, remained a problem, and now that the war was over there were serious concerns that rape, looting and other crimes would have a detrimental effect on the reputation of the Soviet Union. In June 1945, Zhukov issued orders that troops would be confined to base unless they were specifically sent out on duty. Anyone, including officers, seen entering a private house without authorization faced punishment. Although these measures seemed to improve discipline – at least, the frontline units reported a considerable improvement – the Soviet authorities became increasingly alarmed by the effect on the Red Army's soldiers of exposure to capitalism. Many soldiers were amazed at the wealth of farms in Poland compared to their homes; when they heard from prisoners that the western half of Europe made Poland look like a devastated wasteland, it was inevitable that they would begin to question the entire basis of communism. It was decided, therefore, that the veterans would be returned home as soon as possible, and would be replaced by fresh recruits.

In June 1945, the first Soviet troops were demobilized. At first, priority was given to those aged over 30. All troops being sent home were required to attend special discussions with their political commissars, where the weaknesses of the apparently rich capitalist system were emphasized. Soldiers were also made aware of the need to respect military discipline and not to talk about anything that might be regarded as a military secret. There was to be no discussion about the hardships at the front, the high casualty rates, the punishment battalions, the atrocities. All soldiers were required to sign documents that bound them to remain silent.

For the first trainloads of homecoming veterans, there were ceremonies organized by local branches of the Communist Party. The families who had waited years for their menfolk thronged the railway platforms, as the veterans stepped a little uncertainly off the trains, every step taking them a little further from the brutal simplicity of army life. As the months passed, and more and more veterans came home, the public welcomes became less effusive, though for the individuals and their families they remained just as emotional. But it wasn't just a question of a nation that had already celebrated the end of the war, and had already held homecoming celebrations. Stalin wished to ensure that any celebration of the great victory should reflect his leading part. The glory was to be his alone. Even the men left crippled by the war – one estimate puts their number in 1946 at 2.75 million[37]– were swept aside. They had been promised help, and the best medical care available, but many were left to beg on the streets of Moscow. In 1947, Stalin ordered them to be cleared from his capital, and they were transported to a camp near Lake Ladoga, where many of them died.

Isaak Kobylyanskiy and his gunners finished the war in Pillau. The officers continued to hold training sessions on gunnery, which most of the men regarded as a bit of a joke – these lessons merely told them how to do the job they had so effectively performed for several years. Work parties were dispatched into the Samland countryside to tend the fields, a welcome change for the soldiers, even if the labour was hard. And, of course, there were the compulsory lectures on politics and foreign affairs. Despite this, the soldiers had time on their hands, and like idle soldiers of all armies, they soon established their own illicit brewery and distillery. Kobylyanskiy found that the spare time also created friction with one of his superior officers. After yet another argument in late July, Kobylyanskiy requested a transfer, and to his astonishment his request was granted, and he was dispatched to a reserve unit in a small town called Kozelsk. He spent four months kicking his heels here before he was demobilized in January 1946 and allowed to go home to Kiev, to a joyous reunion with his family, and particularly with his beloved childhood sweetheart Vera. He resumed his long-interrupted studies, but found Stalin's increasing anti-Semitism blighted his prospects, and those of all other Soviet Jews. It was only after Stalin's death in 1953 that his chances of success improved.

Soviet soldiers who had been held captive by the Germans, and had survived the appalling conditions in which they were kept, were universally treated as 'contaminated', in that they had been exposed to western capitalism. All were processed through dozens of specially constructed camps, and many were held for several years. But the worst treatment was reserved for those who had chosen to change sides. Tens of thousands of former Soviet soldiers, with varying degrees of enthusiasm, had served in the Wehrmacht, ranging from *Hiwis* (Hilfwilliger, or volunteers) who tended the horses and drove supply vehicles, to men who formed the ranks of Andrei Vlasov's Russian Liberation Army and fought, however briefly, against the Red Army. Many of these men had only volunteered in order to escape almost certain death in prison camps, but they now faced a grim fate. Labelled as traitors, they were lucky if they received ten years' hard labour. Many, including all of their leaders, were executed.

The commanders who had played their parts in the great events of early 1945 also went their various ways. Konstantin Rokossovsky's 2nd Belorussian Front had torn through 2nd Army, then isolated 4th Army with its back to the Frisches Haff, and finally took Gotenhafen and Danzig. He moved his armies to the lower Oder, where they drove west in April and May. In the last days of the war, his spearheads linked up with Montgomery's forces advancing from Hamburg. He asked for information about his British opposite number, and appeared to be mystified by what he was told about the field marshal's ascetic habits: 'He doesn't smoke and doesn't like women. What the devil does he do all day?'[38]

Once the war with Germany was over, Stalin reappraised the use to which he would put his half-Polish marshal. Rokossovsky's 2nd Belorussian Front now became the Northern Group of Forces, and he remained as their commander. In 1949, his Polish credentials were used to have him appointed Polish Defence Minister. He subsequently became Deputy Chairman of the Council of Ministers in Warsaw, but struggled to be accepted by the Poles, who regarded him as a tool of the Soviet Union. Rather bitterly, Rokossovsky once complained that he was treated as a Pole in Russia, and as a Russian in Poland. The distrust of the Poles appears to have been justified. He played a major role in the suppression of dissent in Poland, ordering the creation of army labour battalions. All those regarded as unreliable – individuals who showed dissent, former members of the wartime British-backed Polish resistance, even Poles who happened to have family members living in the west – were dispatched to these battalions, through whose ranks some 200,000 Poles were processed. In 1956, when Poles in Poznan protested against the ongoing Soviet occupation of their country, he ordered military force to be used, resulting in the deaths of more than 70 civilians. Later in the same year, however, Nikita Khrushchev refused to authorize the further use of force against liberal elements in Poland, and Rokossovsky lost his appointments in Warsaw. He returned to the Soviet Union, holding a variety of posts until he retired in 1962. He died in 1968, and is buried in the Kremlin Wall Necropolis.

General Bagramian, who oversaw the drive to Memel and ended the war as commander of 3rd Belorussian Front, remained in the Baltic states after the war, directing operations against anti-Soviet partisans. He played a major role in writing the official Soviet military history of World War II. He was also centrally involved in negotiations with North Vietnam in 1967, ensuring a steady supply of Soviet equipment and expertise to fuel the communist effort in the Vietnam War. He retired the following year, and died in 1982, the last surviving Front commander from the war years. He, too, is buried in the Kremlin Wall.

Conrad Engelhardt, who supervised the evacuation of so many people, civilians and soldiers alike, went into British captivity with his staff at the end of the war. His achievement was extraordinary by any standard. Despite negligible air cover, and over waters patrolled by Soviet submarines, he and his subordinates ran an operation that brought more than two million people to the west. Despite the loss of life aboard the *Goya*, *Cap Arcona*, *Thielbek*, *Wilhelm Gustloff*, *Steuben* and other ships, the overall casualty rate was astonishingly low, at less than 0.5 per cent. Engelhardt himself expressed surprise at the minimal intervention of the Soviet fleet. Only its submarines and a few torpedo boats played any significant part, and there was no attempt by the Red Banner Fleet's larger vessels to put to sea. The speed with which the entire fleet sailed at the end of the war in order to secure the Baltic ports suggests that the ships were perfectly seaworthy. Was the inaction of the fleet due to fear that the German warships in the Baltic might sink them? Or was it more a political calculation? Stalin was very aware that Germans were fleeing to the west, and that the conduct of the Red Army did much to bring this flight about. It is conceivable that Stalin wanted the flight to continue, so that the residual post-war German population in territories that were to cease being part of Germany was reduced as much as possible.

Engelhardt's main regret was that fuel shortages had placed such constraints on the last days of the operation. It had been his intention to save the last 60,000 men of AOK Ostpreussen and as many as possible of the 200,000 men of Army Group Courland who went into Soviet captivity at the end of the war. He was released from captivity in December 1946. In 1965, he joined the Forschungsstelle Ostsee (Baltic Sea Research Institute), an academic research institute. Amongst his co-workers was Heinz Schön, who had served as a crewman on the *Wilhelm Gustloff*, and after the ship was sunk transferred to the *General San Martin*. Schön became one of the leading authorities on the Baltic evacuation, writing extensively on the subject. He attributed his own experiences in his works to the pseudonymous Peter Schiller. Engelhardt died in Lüneberg in October 1973.

THE BALTIC EVACUATION PORTS

With numbers of people evacuated

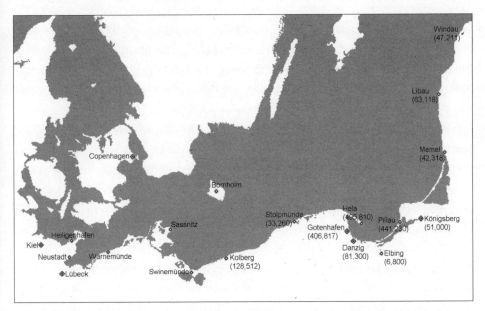

Albert Forster, Gauleiter of Danzig–West Prussia, left Hela accompanied by Gauamtsleiter Professor Grossmann, who had been involved in the euthanasia of people with mental and physical disabilities. They arrived in the small town of Grömitz, near Lübeck, in early May 1945. From there, he travelled to Hamburg, where he was arrested. He was placed in an internment camp in Fallingbostel, and on 12 August 1946 the British extradited him to Poland. He was taken to Danzig in September, where trials relating to the concentration camp in Stutthof had started earlier in the year.

On 5 April 1948, after many delays, Forster's trial began. His charges were multiple:

Membership of the National Socialist Party, which had conducted a war of aggression and conquest and had perpetrated crimes against the population of Poland and the Free City of Danzig.

Reducing the status and rights of Poles in the Free State of Danzig before the war.

Involvement, either of his own volition or on orders, in the mass murder of the Polish intelligentsia and of Jews.

Involvement in the propaganda relating to the so-called Bromberg Massacre, resulting in revenge killings of Poles.

The persecution of the Polish community by illegal restraints on movement, mass deportations, discrimination, involvement in the illegal transfer of Polish children

447

from their families to German families, and the destruction of Polish culture and religious practice.

Despite their best efforts, the prosecutors failed to establish any clear link between Forster and Stutthof, and consequently no direct charges relating to the concentration camp were made against him. Forster's defence, like that of so many accused with war crimes during that time, was that he had simply followed instructions from Berlin, and had attempted to reduce their impact wherever possible. On 29 April, he received the inevitable verdict: he was found guilty, and condemned to death. His Polish-appointed lawyers declined to enter a plea for mitigation, on the grounds that 'Forster's crimes and his guilt are so great that mitigation doesn't come into question'.[39]

In the months that followed, Forster wrote many letters, and a whole series of documents that looked at, amongst other matters, foreign relations before the war. He maintained that until 1939, Hitler had been a good neighbour to the Poles, and that the tension between Poland and Germany was primarily due to British machinations. In June 1951, he was removed from the prison in Danzig by the Polish secret police, and it is unknown where he spent the next few months. There were suggestions that he was held by the Soviets, and attempted to avoid the death sentence by helping to write a detailed history of the Nazi Party. At some stage, he returned to Danzig, and was taken from there to Warsaw at the end of February 1952, where he was hanged. His death was not publicized, giving rise to rumours for several years that he was still alive.

After being released from the internment camp near Hasenmoor, the former Gauleiter, Reichsverteidigungskommissar and Reichskommissar Erich Koch remained in the area, living with other refugees under the name of Major Rolf Berger and continuing to escape recognition. He was aware that he was sought on charges of war crimes. Generaloberst Jodl and others had told their interrogators that Koch was personally responsible for many of the mass executions in the Ukraine, and that the Reichskommissar had repeatedly exceeded his authority. Whilst there can be little doubt of Koch's personal responsibility for many crimes in the east, there was at least an element of blame-passing. While he remained in hiding he was a convenient scapegoat for others, who tried to reduce their own personal culpability by testifying that Koch had a greater degree of blame than was actually the case. The personal rivalries of National Socialist politics that had played such a large part in Koch's life also came into play, as old enemies took this opportunity to settle scores. And while rumours abounded for years of secret networks that helped former high-ranking officials of the SS to escape, particularly to South America, the rivalries and enmities of Koch's past ensured that any such escape route was closed to him.

Of the 42 Gauleiters in post at the end of the war, one died in combat, 12 committed suicide, three died of unknown causes and one was executed by the SS. All but four of the rest were arrested, and their treatment varied greatly. Seven were convicted of capital crimes and – like Albert Forster – executed. Others were released after brief periods of detention. Koch must have known that his role in the east, regardless of exaggeration or scapegoating by others, would prevent him from being treated leniently.

Unfortunately for Koch, his past was waiting to catch up with him. He had been unable to establish a detailed background for his new identity, which was suspicious enough, but when he attended a meeting of refugees he couldn't resist the temptation to speak to the assembled people. He was even nominated for election as a representative of the refugees, at which point he was recognized. On 24 May 1949, after two years of successfully evading detection, he was arrested by the British occupation forces.

Koch was taken to Bielefeld, and held there while the case against him was prepared. In June 1949, the Polish government requested his extradition, followed by the Soviet Union in August. There were demands – particularly from East Prussian refugees – for him to face justice in Germany, but the chorus of those wanting him to be extradited grew ever louder. Marion Dönhoff, who was now working as a journalist in Hamburg, wrote an article describing the forcible removal of Poles from their land and their use as slave labour, and the mass executions, particularly of Jews, and summarized both points of view:

> Not since 1945 has any extradition been as well justified as this, and nobody deserves the certain death sentence that awaits him in the east – something that is no longer possible in our penal system – as much as Erich Koch does a thousand times over … [but] this criminal, who has the deaths of countless Germans in the east on his conscience, should face a German court.[40]

The reality of the situation, however, was that if Koch were to be tried in Germany, he would only face charges relating to membership of the National Socialist Party. He might have had responsibility for the fate of the East Prussian refugees, but it would be almost impossible to formulate a legal charge relating to this. It was therefore highly likely that he would face, at most, ten years' imprisonment. In any event, it had been Allied policy since 1943 that German war criminals would face justice after the war in the countries where they had committed their crimes. Consequently, in late 1949 the

British decided that he should be extradited to Poland, where he would face far more serious charges. It is not entirely clear why extradition to Poland was favoured over extradition to the Soviet Union, though it seems likely that the order of the extradition requests, together with better-quality documentary evidence submitted by the Poles, played a major part in the decision.

Despite a hunger strike, Koch was handed over to the Poles in January 1950, and taken to Warsaw. Here he stayed in prison for nine years, awaiting trial. The Poles were anxious to ensure that Koch's trial should be as detailed and faultless as possible, and further delays were the consequence of Koch's own determination to explore every legal option for postponement, including several adjournments due to his apparent ill-health.

The trial finally began on 20 October 1958. The main charges against Koch related to his time as the senior civil authority in Bialystock and Zichenau, or Ciechanow as the town was now known. He was accused of involvement, either on his own initiative or in cooperation with others, of planning, preparation and execution of crimes that contravened the human rights of the citizens of these areas. The charge sheet listed details of executions, both of individuals and of groups, the use of extermination camps, forced labour and mass deportations. None of the charges related to activities in the Ukraine; the Polish court decided that it had no jurisdiction over these, and only submitted evidence of crimes in Soviet territory insofar as this evidence shed light on Koch's conduct in Polish territory.

After so many years of using every legal option to avoid coming to trial, it was inevitable that Koch would defend himself energetically. He claimed that the true culprit was Heinrich Himmler, and that nobody had dared to do so much to oppose the will of the Reichsführer-SS as Koch had done. His legal team took a slightly different route, accepting that while Koch bore some personal responsibility, he – like so many of those who had appeared at Nuremburg – was merely following the instructions of his superiors. In any event, it was argued, it would be inhumane for Koch to face a death sentence, after such a long incarceration.

The court came to its judgement in March 1959. It concluded that mass murder was an indispensable part of Hitler's plans for a New Order in Europe, and that by being part of the machinery by which these plans were to be implemented, Koch was directly implicated. It was concluded that, contrary to his own evidence, he had been in a position to exert considerable influence on how the SS and police operated within his domain, and that he had done little, if anything, to prevent crimes against the civilian population. He was sentenced to death.

Koch continued to fight on. He explored every possible avenue to avoid sentence being carried out, and as the years dragged by it became clear that the Polish authorities could see little point in executing this relic of a previous era. In December 1970, the German chancellor Willy Brandt visited Warsaw, and the Poles suggested to his delegation that they might wish to take Koch back to Germany with them. The startled diplomats ignored the offer, and shortly afterwards Koch's sentence was formally commuted to life imprisonment.

The months after the guns fell silent gradually grew into years, and the refugees who had fled East Prussia slowly found new homes. In most parts of Germany, they were received with sympathy – the one area where there was widespread hostility towards them was, ironically, Bavaria, the part of Germany that had been the homeland of the greatest number of Nazi leaders. The former homeland of the Prussians was lost to Germany forever. On 4 July 1946, the city of Königsberg, originally named after King Ottokar the Golden, was renamed Kaliningrad, in honour of the Chairman of the Presidium of the Supreme Soviet, Mikhail Kalinin. As the shattered city slowly recovered, some of its original roads remained in use, but in other areas the devastation was so complete that even the street plans of the new city were different. Few buildings had survived the fighting intact. One of them, the former police headquarters, which had housed the East Prussian headquarters of the Gestapo, became the location of the local branch of the KGB. Kaliningrad became the home of the Soviet Baltic Fleet, and was consequently closed to foreigners throughout the years of the Cold War.

Almost every town and village in East Prussia was given a new name. The Soviet Union gained the northern half of the province, and many places were renamed by the people who were settled there, in memory of their previous homes. Other towns received new names on direct instruction from the Soviet authorities. Insterburg was renamed Chernyakovsk in honour of the man who commanded the 3rd Belorussian Front during the closing months of the war, and who died on the outskirts of Königsberg. To the south, many towns had substantial Polish populations before the war, and in these cases Polish versions of their names were already in existence. Yet there were still places where names were appointed by the dour bureaucrats of officialdom. Rastenburg was known to its Polish population as Rasternbork, but instead it was named Ketrzyn in honour of the Polish historian Wojciech Ketrzynski. Elbing became Elblag, and Gotenhafen was once more Gdynia. Danzig had for almost all of its history been known by the same name, regardless of whether it was under Polish or Prussian control, but in a conscious effort to break the link with the past, the city was renamed Gdansk.

Josef Stalin, the last of those three leaders who met in Yalta in 1945 to remain in power, retreated into a world of increasing paranoia. In March 1953, Stalin collapsed after dinner and died. He was replaced, briefly, as Soviet leader by Lavrenti Beria, the former head of the NKVD, who was deposed in June and executed shortly afterwards. His replacement was Nikita Sergeyevich Khrushchev.

Germany was slowly rising from the ashes of defeat. One of the aspirations of the Potsdam Conference was that the occupation zones held by the British, Americans, French and Soviets would eventually be reunified into a new Germany. Khrushchev, however, appeared to be completely against reunification, and the two Germanys – the Federal Republic of Germany (FRG) in the west and the German Democratic Republic (GDR) in the east – became the focus of the Cold War. In 1955, a high-level conference was held in Geneva, in an attempt to improve relationships. German reunification was on the agenda, but the Soviet Union was only prepared to discuss this if Germany would be guaranteed to be a neutral state.

Another topic that was discussed, albeit briefly, was the status of the remaining Germans in Soviet captivity. These men, the Soviet delegation insisted, were not prisoners of war, but convicted war criminals. There was, officially at least, no question of their early release. In private, Khrushchev had other views. Normalization of relations between the Soviet Union and the FRG would do much to bring to an end the ongoing speculation about German reunification, as it would cement the existence of the two Germanys. Consequently, at almost the same time that the Soviet delegation was telling the representatives of the western powers in Geneva that there would be no early release, Soviet diplomats advised Walter Ulbricht, First Secretary of the GDR's ruling Sozialistische Einheitspartei Deutschlands (SED; Socialist Unity Party of Germany), that the remaining prisoners could be released in return for normalization of diplomatic relations with the Federal Republic.

It was against this background that Konrad Adenauer, the West German Chancellor, visited Moscow in September 1955. Adenauer was a leading figure in the German Centre Party until it was abolished by the Nazis, and although Hitler occasionally expressed admiration for him, there was no question of his being given any official post. After the war, he established a new political party, the Christlich Demokratische Union Deutschlands (CDU; Christian Democratic Union of Germany), and went on to become the first Chancellor of West Germany. He now travelled to Moscow, with the fate of the remaining prisoners firmly on his agenda.

Both Khrushchev and Adenauer were aware of the momentous nature of the visit. When detailed discussions began, the issue of the remaining prisoners immediately came up. Relations between the two countries, Adenauer stated, could not be normal while so many German citizens remained in Soviet captivity. The Soviets at first rejected the German approach; Nikolai Bulganin, Khrushchev's loyal ally and Prime Minister, refused to accept that the captive Germans were prisoners of war, insisting that all of them had been convicted of war crimes. In frustration, Adenauer briefly considered abandoning the talks, but too much was at stake. Carlo Schmid, one of the German delegation, resumed discussions. Every man, woman and child in Germany, he said, was behind Adenauer in his desire to bring the captives home.

The debate continued at the traditional evening banquet in St George's Hall in the Kremlin. Bulganin and Khrushchev flanked Adenauer, and there were several animated exchanges between the three; at one point, the two Soviet leaders seemed to be arguing passionately across Adenauer. Then, suddenly, Bulganin smiled and told Adenauer that the prisoners could be released if normal relations were established between the two countries.

It had been Adenauer's intention to hold out for reunification of Germany on his own terms in exchange for normalization of relations, but it was clear that this was not achievable. The following morning, Adenauer agreed to the establishment of full relations with the Soviet Union. Bulganin promised him that before his plane had returned to Germany, the first steps to release the remaining Germans would have been taken.

Whatever doubts that Adenauer may have had about whether he had secured a fair deal, most of West Germany rejoiced after his return. Shortly after, the first prisoners arrived, brought by train from the depths of the Soviet Union to a crossing point on the border between the two Germanys, and from there to a special transit camp in Friedland. A total of 9,262 prisoners came home, including about 3,000 civilians. Contrary to Bulganin's claim, many of the civilians had never been charged or convicted of any crime. The great majority of them chose to be released to the FRG, even those whose homes were in the GDR. For those whose homes were no longer part of Germany, the only homecoming was to a new land. One such veteran was Alfred Jaedtke, who had commanded 5th Panzer Division's armoured battlegroup during the last months of the war. Shortly after his release, he joined the ranks of the new West German army, the Bundeswehr, ultimately rising to the rank of Oberstleutnant. His former commander, Hans-Georg Herzog, was aboard one of the last trains that brought the prisoners out of the Soviet Union, and died shortly after his release.

One of the very last to be released was Dietrich von Saucken, the man who commanded the last German army in Prussia. Like his men, he had endured harsh conditions during his long imprisonment, spending several spells in solitary confinement. He emerged unbroken, and a defiant opponent of the Soviet Union, an attitude that he did not attempt to hide during his captivity. Despite his hardships, he was comparatively fortunate. Of the 12 generals who surrendered with him, two – Generalleutnant von Rappard and Generalleutnant Richert – were executed. Another two were seriously ill, and died within months of their release. Six others died in captivity; the recorded dates of their deaths are almost all in 1955, just a few months before the final release. Indeed, the recorded dates of death of many German prisoners are 1955, and it seems likely that many of them had died earlier, but the precise dates had not been recorded. It was only when release became imminent that a date had to be recorded.

Erich Koch remained unrepentant to the very end. He continued to insist that he had done everything in his power to save the people of East Prussia, and that his trips to Berlin and elsewhere during the dark days of early 1945 were not motivated by self-preservation, but by his desire to obtain permission and resources for mass evacuation. In November 1986, this last surviving major figure of the closing months of the war in Prussia died in a hospital in the Polish town of Olsztyn, a town that had once been called Allenstein.

For the soldiers of both sides, the post-war years brought mixed fortunes. Many wrote extensively about their experiences, and several veterans' associations grew up in both the Soviet Union and Germany, allowing them to share their memories, remember their lost comrades, and relive their past triumphs and disasters. But East Prussia, the land described by Marion Dönhoff and Erika Morgenstern, in which they fought their terrible war, is gone forever. The idyllic rural landscape, with its wide skies, dark forests and orderly little villages, will be preserved only in the memories of those who lived there. Their old homeland has changed – as has the rest of Europe. But as exiles, they have not lived through the change, and thus have preserved the memory of their lost Heimat, unblemished and untainted.

NOTES

PREFACE

1   William Shakespeare, *Henry IV Part II*, Act IV, Scene 1

INTRODUCTION

1.   Interview with Hans Frank recorded on 3 October 1939, EC 344-16, subsequently Exhibit USA 297 at the Nuremburg War Trials
2.   M. Dönhoff, *Namen die keiner mehr nennt*, p.7
3.   'Üb' immer treu und Rechlichkeit bis an dein kühles Grab', quoted in G. MacDonogh, *Prussia*, p.110
4.   D. Schenk, *Hitlers Mann in Danzig*, p.74
5.   H. Rauschning, *Men of Chaos*, p.105
6.   Ibid., p.98
7.   K. Dieckert and H. Grossmann, *Der Kampf um Ostpreussen*, pp.41–42
8.   Schmundt's diaries, quoted in *Nazi Conspiracy and Aggression*, pp.390–400
9.   Adolf Hitler, quoted in U. Saft, *Krieg im Osten*, p.9
10. S. Kudryashov, *Diplomatic Prelude: Stalin, the Allies and Poland*, quoted in R. Davies, *Rising 44*, p.145
11. Dmitrov's diary, quoted in S. Sebag Montefiore, *Stalin: The Court of the Red Tsar*, p.318
12. V. Molotov, quoted in Saft, p.9
13. Schmundt's diaries, quoted in A. Clark, *Barbarossa*, p.25
14. Hitler, quoted in Schenk, pp.120–21
15. Schenk, pp.132–33
16. Ibid., p.155
17. Ibid., p.172
18. Ibid., pp.169–70
19. Ibid., pp.152–54
20. E. von Manstein, *Lost Victories*, pp.180–81
21. R. Meindl, *Ostpreussens Gauleiter*, pp.311–12
22. Bundesarchiv Berlin, R6/70, p17, quoted in Meindl, p.338
23. Oberkommando der Wehrmacht (OKW) order, 25 July 1941, quoted in Clark, p.152
24. OKW order, 16 September 1941, signed by Generalfeldmarschall Keitel, Exhibit RF 1432, 389-PS at the Nuremburg War Trials
25. Soviet report quoted in C. Merridale, *Ivan's War*, p.123
26. Ibid., p.124
27. German intelligence report, quoted in Merridale, p.122
28. W. Warlimont, *Vortragsnotiz Leningrad*, Bundesarchiv/Militärarchiv, RW 4/v.578, Bl. 144–146
29. E. Ziemke, *Stalingrad to Berlin: The German Defeat in the East*, p.316
30. I. Ehrenburg, originally published in *Krasnaya Zvezda* newspaper in 1942, quoted in A-M. de Zayas, *Nemesis at Potsdam*, pp.6546, 201; see also E. Kern (ed.), *Verheimlichte Dokumente*, pp.260–61, 353–55

CHAPTER 1

1. Goebbels' speech in the Sportpalast, Berlin, 18 February 1943
2. H.J. Pantenius, *Letzte Schlacht an der Ostfront*, pp.41–43
3. Ibid., p.43
4. P. Bamm, *The Invisible Flag*, p.154
5. H. von Luck, *Panzer Commander*, p.249
6. J. Neumann, *Die 4. Panzer Division 1943–1945*, p.501
7. R. Meindl, *Ostpreussens Gauleiter*, pp.416–17
8. K. Dieckert and H. Grossmann, *Die Kampf um Ostpreussen*, p.31
9. Diary of Goebbels, quoted in Meindl, pp.421–22
10. Meindl, p.425
11. Ibid., pp.426–27
12. Ibid., p.435
13. S. Sebag Montefiore, *Stalin: The Court of the Red Tsar*, p.225
14. I. Kobylyanskiy, *From Stalingrad to Pillau*, p.8
15. Ibid., p.15
16. S. Zaloga and L. Ness, *Red Army Handbook, 1939–1945*
17. P. Batov, *From the Volga to the Oder*, pp.24–25
18. H. Schäufler, *So lebten sie und so starben sie*, p.233
19. Sebag Montefiore, pp.483–84

CHAPTER 2

1. E. Hadamovsky, *Weltgeschichte im Sturmschritt*, p.344
2. Quoted in J. Erickson, *The Road to Berlin*, p.225
3. The 1st Baltic Front deployed Petr Malyshev's Fourth Shock Army in the north, and Ivan Chistiakov's 6th Guards Army facing Kursenai a little further south. Immediately to Chistiakov's south was 43rd Army, commanded by Beloborodov. As a second echelon, Bagramian had 51st Army, 5th Guards Tank Army and the independent III Guards Mechanized Corps. This second echelon, particularly 51st Army and the tanks of 5th Guards Tank Army, would be fed into the gap that would develop as 6th Guards Army advanced west and 43rd Army pushed southwest. The 2nd Guards Army, setting off from a start-line a little further south, would drive southwest in order to sweep behind Tauroggen. To the south of Bagramian's front was Cherniakhovsky's 3rd Baltic Front, and 39th Army, commanded by Nikolai Erastovich Berzarin, would form the southern part of the drive towards the Baltic, ideally linking up with 2nd Guards Army in the Tauroggen area, surrounding the German forces before they could retreat.
4. J. Huber, *So war es wirklich*, pp.50–53
5. Ibid., pp.68–69
6. Ibid., pp.71–72
7. Ibid., p.72
8. Ibid., pp.72–78
9. R. Meindl, *Ostpreussens Gauleiter*, p.433
10. Huber, pp.80–81
11. H. Spaeter, *The History of the Panzerkorps Grossdeutschland*, p.413
12. A.D. von Plato, *Die Geschichte der 5 Panzer Division*, p.363
13. I. Kobylyanskiy, *From Stalingrad to Pillau*, p.224
14. In addition to 4th Panzer Division, 12th and 14th Panzer Divisions were to be used, as well as 11th, 87th and 126th Infantry Divisions

15. Spaeter, p.414
16. Ibid., p.417
17. K. Dieckert and H. Grossmann, *Die Kampf um Ostpreussen*, p.53
18. B. von Egloffstein, W. Hegen and J. Huber, *Y Rothenburg*, pp.41–43
19. Ibid., pp.44–45
20. Huber, p.97
21. H. Schön, *Ostsee 45*, p.63
22. Ibid., pp.47–48, 57–59

CHAPTER 3

1. A. Solzhenitsyn, *The Gulag Archipelago 1918–1956*
2. H. Fleischer (ed.), *Combat History of Sturmgeschütz Brigade 276*, pp.66–68
3. The Soviet units involved were Lieutenant-General Ivan Ilich Liudnikov's 39th Army, particularly XCIV Rifle Corps, reinforced by 266th Tank Brigade. Liudnikov had just replaced Berzarin as army commander.
4. Hitler, quoted in K. Dieckert and H. Grossmann, *Die Kampf um Ostpreussen*, p.63
5. A. Regenitter, *Knight Gunner*, p.20
6. Ibid., p.21
7. These were 25th Guards Tank Brigade and 4th Rifle Regiment.
8. H. Spaeter, *The History of the Panzerkorps Grossdeutschland*, II, pp.437–39
9. A.D. von Plato, *Die Geschichte der 5 Panzer Division*, p.367
10. G.K. Koschorrek, *Vergiss die Zeit der Dornen nicht*, pp.435–36
11. Jaedtke, quoted in von Plato, p.367
12. A-M. de Zayas, *Nemesis at Potsdam: The Expulsion of the Germans from the East*, pp.63–64
13. T. Hinz, *Nemmersdorf: Neue Aspekte eines Verbrechens*
14. Solzhenitsyn, p.21
15. Y. Aronov, quoted in C. Merridale, *Ivan's War*, p.260
16. Intercepted field post quoted in Merridale, p.261
17. Jaedtke, quoted in von Plato, p.370

CHAPTER 4

1. Adolf Hitler
2. R. Tiemann, *Geschichte der 83 Infanterie Division*, p.282
3. J. Huber, *So war es wirklich*, p.110
4. E. Morgenstern, *Überleben war schwerer als sterben*, pp.54–55
5. M. Mackinnon, *The Naked Years: Growing up in Nazi Germany*, pp.147–48
6. M. Dönhoff, *Namen die keiner mehr nennt*, p.21
7. H. Schäufler, *Panzer an der Weichsel*, pp.19–20
8. Huber, pp.113–14
9. E. Kieser, *Danziger Bucht 1945*, p.11
10. G.E. Baltuttis, *Auf verlorenem Posten*, p.13
11. Ibid., pp.53–54
12. Ibid., pp.84–85
13. H.J. Pantenius, *Letzte Schlacht an der Ostfront*, pp.54–55
14. O. Lasch, *So fiel Königsberg*, p.24
15. Ibid., p.27

16. Ibid., p.31

17. Quoted in H. Fleischer (ed.), *Combat History of Sturmgeschütz-Brigade 276*, p.70

18. A.D. von Plato, *Die Geschichte der 5 Panzer Division*, p.372

19. B. Kleine, *Bevor die Erinnerung verblasst*, pp.68–69

20. Quoted in Kieser, p.12

21. H. Ahlfen, *Der Kampf um Schlesien 1944–45*, p.39

22. Quoted in Kieser, p.13

23. H. Guderian, *Panzer Leader*, p.387

24. Quoted in Guderian, p388

25. Lieutenant B. Tartakovskiy, quoted in Glantz, p.38

26. Colonel A Smirnov, quoted in Glantz, pp.28–29

27. Abt. Fremde Heere Ost (1), 81/45 gKdos, 5/1/1945, quoted in D. Glantz, *Art of War Symposium 1986*, p.285

28. I. Ehrenburg, leaflet distributed to Red Army, October 1944

29. C. Merridale, *Ivan's War*, p.261

30. *Pis'ma fronta i na front*, quoted in Merridale, p.262

31. Von Plato, pp.372–73

CHAPTER 5

1. Adolf Hitler, on the eve of the German invasion of the Soviet Union, 1941

2. J. Huber, *So war es wirklich*, p.121

3. D. Glantz, *Art of War Symposium 1986*, pp.297–300, 502–11

4. 39th, 21st, 5th, 28th, 2nd Guards and 31st Armies, with 2nd Guards Army a little to the rear.

5. 50th, 49th, 3rd, 48th and 65th Armies

6. 47th Army

7. A. Gruber, *Das Infanterie-Regiment 213*, p.325

8. H.J. Pantenius, *Letzte Schlacht an der Ostfront*, p.77

9. Ibid., p.81

10. Ibid., pp.81–84

11. C. Duffy, *Red Storm on the Reich*, p.83

12. Pantenius, p.85

13. H. Spaeter, *The History of the Panzerkorps Grossdeutschland*, p.182

14. Duffy, p.86

15. Most of 39th Army in the north, 5th and 28th Army in the centre, and parts of 2nd Guards Army in the south

16. 11th Guards Army, I Tank Corps and II Guards Tank Corps. Cherniakhovsky intended to commit them sequentially – first would be II Guards Tank Corps, then I Tank Corp, and finally – probably on about the fifth day of the assault – 11th Guards Army.

17. P. Batov, *From the Volga to the Oder*, pp.358–59

18. I. Fediuninsky, quoted in B. von Egloffstein, W. Hegen and J. Huber, *Y Rothenburg*, p.70

19. S.N. Borshchev, *The Campaigns of 46th Rifle Division between the Vistula and the Elbe*, p.204, quoted in von Egloffstein et al., p.94

20. Von Egloffstein, et al., p.94

21. Ibid., pp.96–102

22. O. Heidkämper, quoted in von Egloffstein et al., p.109

CHAPTER 6

1. K. Cherniakhovsky, quoted in A.D. von Plato, *Die Geschichte der 5 Panzer Division*, pp.372–73
2. Jaedthe, quoted in von Plato, pp.374–75
3. Von Plato, pp.375–76
4. H. von Lehndorff, *Ostpreussisches Tagebuch*, p.18
5. H. Schön, *Ostsee 45*, pp.257–58
6. Ibid., pp.259–60
7. Jaedthe, quoted in von Plato, p.377
8. Ibid., p.380
9. Ibid., p.382
10. Von Lehndorff, pp.22–24
11. O. Lasch, *So fiel Königsberg*, p.36
12. Ibid., p.37
13. I. Kobylyanskiy, *From Stalingrad to Pillau*, pp.135–36
14. E. Morgenstern, *Überleben war schwerer als sterben*, pp.61–62
15. Ibid., pp.64–65
16. Major Schaper, 367th Infantry Division, quoted in Lasch, pp.49–51
17. K. Dieckert, quoted in Lasch, p.52
18. Morgenstern, pp.67–69
19. L. Kopolev, *No jail for thought*, quoted in C. Merridale, *Ivan's War*, p.263
20. L. Rabichev, quoted in Merridale, p.268
21. Merridale, p.277
22. K. Rokossovsky, *A Soldier's Duty*, pp.288–89
23. Kobylyanskiy, p.145
24. Ibid., p146

CHAPTER 7

1. Quoted in E. Kieser, *Danziger Bucht 1945*, p.54
2. J. Huber, *So war es wirklich*, pp.144–45
3. Ibid., pp.150–51
4. Ibid., pp.156–58
5. G.E. Baltuttis, *Auf verlorenem Posten*, p.111
6. Ibid., p.118
7. 3rd, 48th, 2nd Shock and 5th Guards Tank Armies
8. H. Schäufler, *Panzer an der Weichsel*, pp.24–25
9. Ibid., pp.25–26
10. Quoted in Huber, pp.163–67
11. M. Dönhoff, *Namen die keiner mehr nennt*, p.17
12. Ibid., p.20
13. Ibid., pp.28–29
14. Ibid., pp.32–34
15. Ibid., pp.13–15
16. XLII Rifle Corps
17. H.-W. Horn, quoted in B. von Egloffstein, W. Hegen and J. Huber, *Y Rothenburg*, p.137
18. Huber, p.171

19. Kieser, p.56
20. CXVI Rifle Corps
21. P. Batov, *From the Vistula to the Oder*, p.362
22. Ibid., p.364
23. U. Saft, *Krieg im Osten*, pp.246–50
24. G. Eismann, *Heeresgruppe Weichsel*, p.62, quoted in H.J. Pantenius, *Letze Schlacht an der Ostfront*, p.133
25. P. Hausser, *Soldaten wie andere auch*, p.68, quoted in Pantenius, p.134
26. Pantenius, pp.126–27
27. 160th, 162nd and 165th Rifle Divisions, 76th Guards Rifle Division and 1st Guards Mechanized Brigade
28. Pantenius, pp.135–42
29. Saft, p.251
30. M. Domarus, *Hitler – Reden und Proklamationen 1932–1945*, p.1117, quoted in D. Schenk, *Hitlers Mann in Danzig*, p.256
31. Pantenius, pp.153–55
32. Huber, pp.177–79
33. Kieser, pp.61–62
34. Von Egloffstein et al., p.141
35. R. Poensgen, quoted in Schäufler, pp.31–40
36. J. Neumann, *Die 4. Panzer Division*, p.631

CHAPTER 8

1. K. Tippelskirch, quoted in K. Diekert and H. Grossmann, *Der Kampf um Ostpreussen*, p.115
2. E. Kieser, *Danziger Bucht 1945*, p.24
3. Ibid., pp.31–34
4. Ibid., pp.40–44
5. Ibid., pp.45–46
6. B. Kleine, *Bevor die Erinnerung verblasst*, p.71
7. G.E. Baltuttis, *Auf verlorenem Posten*, pp.121–24
8. Kleine, p.74
9. Ibid., p.78
10. Baltuttis, pp.132–33
11. Ibid., pp.144–46
12. F. von Senger und Etterlin, *Die 24 Panzer Division*, pp.289–90
13. Dieckert and Grossmann, p.116
14. R. Meindl, *Ostpreussens Gauleiter*, p.443
15. Quoted in J. Thorwald, *Es begann an der Weichsel*, pp.166–67
16. Von Senger und Etterlin, p.291
17. Kieser, p.70
18. Baltuttis, p.162
19. Ibid., p.164

CHAPTER 9

1. M. Dönhoff, *Namen die keiner mehr nennt*, p.15
2. H. Schön, *Ostsee 45*, pp.74–76

3. E. Kieser, *Danziger Bucht 1945*, pp.115–18
4. Ibid., p.118
5. Schön, pp.86–88
6. Kieser, p.125
7. Schön, pp.94–95
8. Kieser, pp.127–28
9. Ibid., pp.168–69
10. Peter Schiller, quoted in Schön
11. Schön, p.286
12. Ibid., pp.100–235
13. Ibid., p.243
14. Ibid., pp.263–68
15. Ibid., pp.268–69
16. Ibid., pp.270–71
17. Ibid., pp.299–301
18. Ibid., pp.308–09

CHAPTER 10

1. Stalin, quoted in S. Sebag Montefiore, *Stalin: The Court of the Red Tsar*, p.494
2. Churchill, quoted in J. Erickson, *The Road to Berlin*, p.477
3. Churchill, quoted in Sebag Montefiore, p.490
4. Churchill, quoted in Erickson, p.497
5. Stalin, quoted in Sebag Montefiore, p.494
6. H. Spaeter, *The History of the Panzerkorps Grossdeutschland*, vol. 3, p.199
7. A.S. Zavyalov and T.E. Kalyadin, *The West Prussian-Pomeranian Operation*, p.38, available online at: http://elibrary.ru/cit_title_items.asp?titid=7789
8. P. Oberhuber, quoted in H. Schäufler, *So lebten und so starben sie*, pp.251–52
9. J. Neumann, *Die 4. Panzer Division*, vol. 2, p.641
10. H. Schäufler, *Panzer an der Weichsel*, p.43
11. S. Borstchev, *From the Narew to the Elbe*, p.208
12. J. Huber, *So war es wirklich*, p.174
13. Ibid., pp.185–86
14. Zavyalov and Kalyadin, pp.57–58
15. R. Hufnagel, quoted in B. von Egloffstein, W. Hegen and J. Huber, *Y Rothenburg*, pp.149–50
16. Ibid., pp.150–51
17. Huber, pp.196–203
18. Zavyalov and Kalyadin, p.56
19. Zavyalov and Kalyadin, p.90
20. Neumann, p.660
21. Schäufler, pp.253–54
22. R. Tiemann, *Geschichte der 83 Infanterie Division*, p.293
23. Zavyalov and Kalyadin, pp.62–67
24. U. Saft, *Krieg im Osten*, p.224
25. Ibid., pp.216–29
26. H.J. Pantenius, *Letzte Schlacht an der Ostfront*, p.186
27. Zavyalov and Kalyadin, p.100

28. Ibid., p.116
29. K. Rokossovsky, *A Soldier's Duty*, p.300
30. Huber, pp.246–50
31. Von Egloffstein, quoted in von Egloffstein et al., p.179
32. W. Haupt, *Als die Rote Armee nach Deutschland kam*, p.92
33. Zavyalov and Kalyadin, pp.134–35
34. Rokossovsky, p.304
35. F. Husemann, *Die gute Glaubens waren*, p.489
36. Ibid., pp.610–13
37. Kompanieführer Hieneck, quoted in Husemann, p.615
38. Husemann, pp.498–99
39. Schäufler, pp.46–52
40. P. Poralla, *Unvergänglicher Schmerz*, p.223
41. Tiemann, p.308
42. Schön, *Ostsee 45*, pp.321–22

CHAPTER 11

1. H. Schäufler, *Panzer an der Weichsel*, p.20
2. E. Kieser, *Danziger Bucht 1945*, p.88
3. Ibid., pp.89–91
4. Ibid., pp.94–96, 107–08
5. Ibid., pp.99–100
6. G.E. Baltuttis, *Auf verlorenem Posten*, pp.180–91, 196–98
7. B. Kleine, *Bevor die Erinnerung verblasst*, pp.81–82
8. H. Spaeter, *The History of the Panzerkorps Grossdeutschland*, pp.255–56
9. Baltuttis, pp.199–200
10. Ibid., pp.203–05
11. F. von Senger und Etterlin, *Die 24 Panzer Division*, p.292
12. K. Dieckert and H. Grossmann, *Der Kampf um Ostpreussen*, p.128
13. Ibid., p.145
14. P. Bamm, *The Invisible Flag*, pp.169–73
15. Ibid., pp.183–84
16. Von Senger und Etterlin, p.295
17. Ibid., p.296
18. C. Duffy, *Red Storm on the Reich*, p.206
19. W. Haupt, *Als die Rote Armee nach Deutschland kam*, p.32

CHAPTER 12

1. O. Lasch, *So fiel Königsberg*, p.64
2. Ibid., pp.57–59
3. Ibid., p.65
4. Ibid., p.66
5. H. von Lehndorff, *Osspreussisches Tagebuch*, p.35
6. K. Dieckert and H. Grossmann, *Die Kampf um Ostpreussen*, p.158
7. A.D. von Plato, *Die Geschichte der 5 Panzer Division*, pp.383–84

8. Lasch, p.68
9. Ibid., p.69
10. Jaedtke, quoted in von Plato, p.386
11. Lasch, pp.70–71
12. Jaedtke, quoted in von Plato, p.387
13. Ibid., p.388
14. I. Kobylyanskiy, *From Stalingrad to Pillau*, pp.137–38
15. Ibid., pp.138–39
16. Lasch, pp.74–75
17. E. Kieser, *Danziger Bucht 1945*, pp.256–57
18. Lasch, p.82
19. Ibid., pp.83–84
20. Ibid., pp.84–85
21. Kobylyanskiy, pp.147–48
22. Dröger, quoted in Lasch, p.88
23. J. Erickson, *The Road to Berlin*, p.545
24. Von Plato, p.394
25. Dröger, quoted in Lasch, pp.88–89
26. B. Kleine, *Bevor die Erinnerung verblasst*, p.88
27. Lasch, pp.92–94
28. Kobylyanskiy, pp.148–49
29. Lasch, pp.96–101
30. Kleine, pp.88–89
31. Kobylyanskiy, pp.150–51
32. Ibid., pp.152–53
33. Lasch, p.101
34. Ibid., pp.115–16
35. Kleine, pp.103–04
36. Von Lehndorff, pp.67–69
37. E. Morgenstern, *Überleben war schwerer als sterben*, pp.83–84
38. Kieser, p.259
39. J. Szilowski, *Königsberg 1945*, p.80
40. U. Saft, *Krieg im Osten*, p.495

CHAPTER 13

1. Hitler's speech in Danzig on 19 September 1939, quoted in D. Schenk, *Hitlers Mann in Danzig*, p.137
2. Schenk, p.152
3. The *Generalgouvernement* was the authority in control of those parts of Poland that had not been formally annexed by Germany.
4. K. Rokossovsky, *A Soldier's Duty*, p.308
5. P. Poralla, *Unvergänglicher Schmerz*, pp.17–18
6. Quoted in F. Husemann, *Die guten Glaubens waren*, pp.499–500
7. P. Batov, *From the Volga to the Oder*, p.371
8. B. von Egloffstein, W. Hegen and J. Huber, *Y Rothenburg*, pp.214–15
9. Order from Generalfeldmarschall Keitel, quoted in von Egloffstein et al., p.220
10. H. Schäufler, *Panzer an der Weichsel*, pp.60–63

11. Ibid., pp.65–66
12. Von Egloffstein et al., pp.230–31
13. Ibid., p.240
14. F. Husemann, *Die gute Glaubens waren*, pp.502–503, 508
15. G. Boldt, *Die letzten Tage der Reichskanzlei*, p.81, quoted in A. Beevor, *Berlin: The Downfall 1945*, p.121
16. Von Egloffstein et al., pp.244–45
17. Husemann, p.509
18. J. Neumann, *Die 4. Panzer Division 1943–1945*, p.690
19. Schäufler, pp.82–84
20. Neumann, p.696
21. Poralla, p.19
22. Schäufler, p.85
23. Poralla, p.170
24. Von Egloffstein et al., pp.255–57
25. Ibid., pp.259–60
26. R. Tiemann, *Geschichte der 83 Infanterie Division*, p.317
27. Schäufler, pp.90–97
28. H. Schön, *Ostsee 1945*, p.381
29. Schäufler, p.100
30. Poralla, p.369
31. Ibid., pp.21–22
32. Schäufler, pp.101–03
33. Ibid., p.98
34. Batov, p.371
35. H.J. Pantenius, *Letzte Schlacht an der Ostfront*, p.252
36. Ibid., p.240
37. J. Huber, *So war es wirklich*, pp.283–84
38. Ibid., pp.292–93
39. Schenk, p.262
40. Poralla, p.181
41. J. Thorwald, *Es begann an der Weichsel*, quoted in Schenk, p.262
42. Poralla, p.339
43. Ibid., pp.340–41
44. Schäufler, pp.105–08
45. Batov, p.375
46. Schäufler, pp.111–12

CHAPTER 14

1. Grossadmiral Dönitz, the last Wehrmacht communiqué, quoted in P.E. Schramm, *Kriegstagebuch der Oberkommando der Wehrmacht 1944–1945*, Part II, pp.1281–82
2. J. Huber, *So war es wirklich*, pp.304–05
3. Ibid., pp.317–19
4. Ibid., p.325
5. Ibid., pp.328–29
6. Ibid., p.331
7. F. Husemann, *Die guten Glaubens waren*, pp.527–31

8. Ibid., p.531
9. R. Tiemann, *Geschichte der 83 Infanterie Division*
10. J. Neumann, *Die 4. Panzer Division 1943–1945*, p.719
11. H. Schäufler, *Panzer an der Weichsel*, pp.119–21
12. P. Poralla, *Unvergänglicher Schmerz*, pp.45–46
13. H.J. Pantenius, *Letzte Schlacht an der Ostfront*, p.271
14. H. Schön, *Ostsee 1945*, p.415
15. Huber, p.346
16. Neumann, p.720
17. H. Spaeter, *The History of the Panzerkorps Grossdeutschland*, vol III, pp.454–55
18. H. Schön, *Ostsee 45*, p.488
19. Ibid., p.489
20. Schäufler, pp.126–27
21. Schön, pp.463–83
22. A.D. von Plato, *Die Geschichte der 5 Panzer Division*, p.396
23. Ibid., p.397
24. K. Dieckert and H. Grossmann, *Die Kampf um Ostpreussen*, pp.190–91
25. Spaeter, pp.456–57
26. Von Plato, p.399
27. Tilse, quoted in von Plato, pp.399–400
28. Von Plato, pp.401–02
29. Ibid., p.400
30. Schön, p.583
31. Ibid., p.510
32. G. Baltuttis, *Auf verlorenem Posten*, pp.208–09
33. Schön, p.688
34. Pantenius, p.292
35. Ibid., p.293
36. *Kriegstagebuch Oberkommando der Wehrmacht Volume IV*, p.1472, quoted in Pantenius, p.294
37. Quoted in Schön, p.606
38. Schön, p.608
39. Ibid., p.613
40. Quoted in Pantenius, p.305
41. Schön, p.627
42. Schäufler, p.143
43. Ibid., pp.144–45
44. Ibid., pp.145–47
45. Pantenius, p.306
46. Neumann, pp.728–29
47. Grossadmiral Dönitz, the last Wehrmacht communiqué, quoted in Schramm, pp.1281–82

CHAPTER 15

1. Tacitus, *Agricola*, Chapter 30
2. H. Schäufler, *Panzer an der Weichsel*, p.149
3. J. Neumann, *Die 4. Panzer Division 1943–1945*, p.729
4. Schäufler, pp.163–65

5. Ibid., p.171
6. F. von Senger und Etterlin, *Die 24 Panzer Division*, p.298
7. J. Huber, *So war es wirklich*, pp.404–05
8. C. Whiting, *Finale at Flensburg*, p.153
9. Von Senger und Etterlin, pp.318–19
10. H.J. Pantenius, *Letzte Schlacht an der Ostfront*, p.309
11. Ibid., pp.309–10
12. Quoted in Schäufler, pp.184–85
13. Schäufler, p.194
14. Quoted in Schäufler, pp.195–96
15. Ibid., p.199
16. B. Kleine, *Bevor die Erinnerung verblasst*, p.110
17. Ibid., pp.121–22
18. Ibid., pp.136–37
19. Ibid., p.158
20. Ibid., p.191
21. C. Barnett, *Hitler's Generals*, p.260
22. E. Morgenstern, *Überleben war schwerer als sterben*, pp.85–86
23. H. von Lehndorff, *Ostpreussisches Tagebuch*, pp.159–61
24. Ibid., p.164
25. Ibid., p.189
26. P. Poralla, *Unvergänglicher Schmerz*, p.23
27. Ibid., pp.98–99
28. Ibid., p.24
29. Ibid., pp.103–04
30. Ibid., pp.113–15
31. Churchill in a speech to House of Commons, 15 December 1944
32. Potsdam Agreement 1945, Section XII
33. Poralla, pp.15–16
34. Ibid., pp.28–29
35. Von Lehndorff, pp.301–02
36. Morgenstern, pp.296–97
37. Quoted in C. Merridale, *Ivan's War*, p.313
38. Quoted in Whiting, p.49
39. Quoted in D. Schenk, *Hitlers Mann in Danzig*, p.276
40. M. Dönhoff, 'Der Henker von Ostpreussen', published in *Die Zeit*, 11 November 1949, quoted in R. Meindl, *Ostpreussens Gauleiter*, p.474

BIBLIOGRAPHY

BOOKS IN ENGLISH

Bamm, P., *The Invisible Flag*, Signet Books, 1958

Barnett, C., *Hitler's Generals*, Grove Weidenfeld, 1989

Batov, P., *From the Volga to the Oder*, Deutscher Militärverlag, 1965

Beevor, A., *Berlin: The Downfall 1945*, Viking, 2002

Clark, A., *Barbarossa*, Papermac, 1985

Davies, R., *Rising 44*, Macmillan, 2003

Duffy, C., *Red Storm on the Reich*, Castle Books, 1991

Erickson, J., *The Road to Berlin*, Cassell Military Paperbacks, 2004

Fleischer, H. (ed), *Combat History of Sturmgeschütz Brigade 276*, Fedorowicz (Canada), 2000

Glantz, D., *Art of War Symposium 1986*, self-published

Glantz, D., *Red Army Officers Speak!*, self-published

Guderian, H., *Panzer Leader*, Penguin Classics, 2000

Kobylyanskiy, I., *From Stalingrad to Pillau*, University Press of Kansas, 2008

von Luck, H., *Panzer Commander*, Cassell Military Paperbacks, 2002

MacDonogh, G., *Prussia*, Sinclair-Stevenson, 1994

Mackinnon, M., *The Naked Years: Growing up in Nazi Germany*, Chatto and Windus, 1987

von Manstein, E., *Lost Victories*, Presidio Press, 1982

Merridale, C., *Ivan's War*, Faber and Faber, 2005

Rauschning, H., *Men of Chaos*, Putnam's Sons, New York, 1942

Regenitter, A., *Knight Gunner*, Shelf Books, 2000

Rokossovsky, K., *A Soldier's Duty*, Spantech and Lancer, 1985

Sebag Montefiore, S., *Stalin: The Court of the Red Tsar*, Phoenix, 2004

Solzhenitsyn, A., *The Gulag Archipelago 1918–1956*, Harper Collins, 1974

Spaeter, H., *The History of the Panzerkorps Grossdeutschland*, Fedorowicz, 1995

Szilowski, J., *Königsberg 1945*, Polish edition by 'Militaria', Warsaw, 2005

Whiting, C., *Finale at Flensburg*, Leo Cooper, 1973

Zaloga, S. and L. Ness, *Red Army Handbook, 1939–1945*, Sutton Publishing, 1998

De Zayas, A.-M., *Nemesis at Potsdam: The Expulsion of the Germans from the East*, Lincoln and London 1988

Ziemke, E., *Stalingrad to Berlin: The German Defeat in the East*, Dorset Press, 1986

BOOKS IN GERMAN

Ahlfen, H., *Der Kampf um Schlesien 1944–45*, Motor Buch Verlag, 1998

Baltuttis, G.E., *Auf verlorenem Posten*, Rautemberg, 2006

Dieckert, K. and H. Grossmann, *Der Kampf um Ostpreussen*, Motor Buch Verlag, 2002

Dönhoff, M., *Namen die keiner mehr nennt*, Diederichs Eugen, 2004

von Egloffstein, B., W. Hegen and J. Huber, *Y Rothenburg*, self-published, 1994

Gruber, A., *Das Infanterie-Regiment 213*, Selbstverlag der Kameradschaft des Ehemalige Infanterie-Regiments 213, 1963

Hadamovsky, E., *Weltgeschichte im Sturmschritt*, Eher, 1939

Haupt, W., *Als die Rote Armee nach Deutschland kam*, Podzun-Pallas Verlag, 1970

Hinz, T., *Nemmersdorf: Neue Aspekte eines Verbrechens*, Junge Freiheit Verlag, 1997

Huber, J., *So war es wirklich*, self-published, 1994

Husemann, F., *Die guten Glaubens waren*, Nation Europa Verlag, 1999

Kern, E. (ed.), *Verheimlichte Dokumente*, FZ- Verlag, 1988

Kieser, E., *Danziger Bucht 1945*, Bechtle, 1978

Kleine, B., *Bevor die Erinnerung verblasst*, Helios, 2004

Koschorrek, G.K., *Vergiss die Zeit der Dornen nicht*, Fleschig, 2005

Lasch, O., *So fiel Königsberg*, Motor Buch Verlag, 2002

von Lehndorff, H., *Ostpreussisches Tagebuch*, Biederstein, 1973

von Manstein, E., *Verlorene Siege*, Athenaum-Verlag, 1955

Meindl, R., *Ostpreussens Gauleiter*, Fibre Verlag, 2007

Morgenstern, E., *Überleben war schwerer als sterben*, Herbig, 2004

Neumann, J., *Die 4. Panzer Division 1943–1945*, self-published, 1989

Pantenius, H.J., *Letzte Schlacht an der Ostfront*, Mittler, 2002

von Plato, A.D., *Die Geschichte der 5 Panzer Division*, Walhalla und Praetoria Verlag, 1978

Poralla, P, *Unvergänglicher Schmerz*, Hogast, Freiburg im Breisgau, 1987

Saft, U., *Krieg im Osten*, Militarbuchverlag, 2002

Schäufler, H., *Panzer an der Weichsel*, Motor Buch Verlag, 1979

Schäufler, H., *So lebten sie und so starbten sie*, Kameradschaft Ehemalige Panzer-Regiment 35 eV, 1968

Schenk, D., *Hitlers Mann in Danzig*, Dietz, 2000

Schön, H., *Ostsee 45*, Motor Buch Verlag, 1983

Schramm, P.E., *Kriegstagebuch der Oberkommando der Wehrmacht 1944–1945*, Manfred Pawlak, 1982

von Senger und Etterlin, F., *Die 24 Panzer Division*, Dörfler

Tiemann, R., *Geschichte der 83 Infanterie Division*, Bad Neuheim, 1960

INDEX

Adam, Leutnant 351
Adele Traber, German ship 388
Adenauer, Konrad 452–3
Adler, German tugboat 398
Admiral Hipper, German heavy cruiser 227, 404
Admiral Scheer, German pocket battleship 218, 282
Aegir, German ship 389, 391
agricultural collectives, Soviet Union 41
Alexander Nevsky (Eisenstein) 40
Alexeyev, Dmitri Fedorovich 129
Allenburg 214, 275
Allenstein 107, 110, 175, 205, 280, 435, 454
   evacuations 199–201
     Soviet atrocities 159
     women's prison 200
Aminde, Hildegard 200, 280
Andros, German freighter 235
Anisimov, Major-General 260
Antonov, General Alexei Innokentovich 238
Ardennes offensive vii, 101, 114, 211, 238
Arnhem operation vii, 96
Arnim, Oberstleutnant von 184–5
Arras counter-attack, France (1940) 23–4
Aschoff, Erika von 422
Attlee, Clement 439
Auer, Sturmbahnführer 342, 344–5
Auerstedt, Battle of (1806) 2
Augstein, Ruth 436, 440
Austria 2, 8

Bagramian, General Ivan Khristoforovich 47–8, 71, 151,
   166, 285, 286, 446
Bagration, Operation 20, 26, 33, 34, 42, 43, 51, 79, 85, 96,
   135, 166, 309
   planning phase 44, 45
Balaton, Lake oilfields 212
Balga peninsula 290–1, 385, 399
Baltic Evacuation Ports 447
Baltic Sea Research Institute 446
Baltic States 18, 19
   occupation and annexation by Soviet Union 11–12,
     40, 47
Baltuttis, Günter Emanuel 103, 104, 165, 202–4, 206–7,
   216, 282, 286, 402
Bamm, Peter 289–90
Barbarossa, Operation 24
Batov, General Pavel Ivanovich 42, 127–8, 132, 178, 179,
   188, 242, 334, 337, 347, 348, 369
Baumann, Major 395
Bavaria 451
Bechler, Major Bernhard 261
Becker, Karl 200
Belorussia 97
   population in Poland 4
Beloborodov, General Afansii 48, 61, 327
Belov, Pavel Alexeyevich 244
Bendig, Alice 190, 191

Beria, Lavrenti 451–2
Berlin 100, 238
   assault on 44, 45, 242
   encirclement 399
Berzarin, General 179
Best, Obergruppenführer Werner 400
Bethke, Willi 10
Betzel, General Clemens 33, 65–6, 67, 76, 167, 191–5,
   244–6, 254, 345, 348, 349, 360, 367
Bialystok 14, 15
Bix, Hermann 271–3
Blanc, Fregattenkapitän Adalbert von 222
Blaskowitz, Johannes 11
Blattner, Hauptsturmführer 270
Blitzkrieg principles 23
Blondmin 191–5
Blume, Major 205
Bock, General Fedor von 12
Bogdanov, Semen 244
Bogoliubov, Aleksandr Nikolaevich 243
Böhm, Hauptmann 215
Böhme, Oberführer Horst 322, 323
Boldin, Ivan 164, 279
Borissov, Captain 42–3, 129
Bormann, Martin 36
Borshchev, General Semen Nikolaevich 133–4
Brandenburg 2
Brandes, Major Ernst 132, 170, 172, 248, 249, 340
Brandt, Willy 451
Braumandl, Richard 52, 54, 56, 57, 58
Bredow, Landrat von 143
Breese, Battlegroup 60
Breitenstein breakthrough, Soviet 136, 140–1
Brest-Litovsk 11
Britain 236, 418
   attitudes to German POWs 421–2
British Army
   11th Armoured Division 403, 419
   Arnhem operation vii, 96
   Fall of France (1940) 23–4
Brody, Ukraine 20
Bromberg 10, 184, 329
   'Bloody Sunday massacre' (1939) 184
   garrison breakout 186
Budapest 105, 109, 123
   siege and surrender 240–1
Budyonni, Marshal Semyon 38
Bulganin, Nikolai 452–3
Bulgaria's declaration of war against Germany 104
Bund Deutscher Offizier (Federation of German Offers,
   part of NKFD) 429
Bundeswehr, German 453
Burech, Dr 143
Burgdorf, General 134–5
Burgner, Obergefreiter Alfred 229–30, 232
Burkersdorf, Battle of (1762) 2
Busse, General Theodore 121
Butkov, General Vasily Vasilevich 135

Kröhne, Major Wilhelm 129, 135
Kroll, Heinz 307
Kronenfels, German ship 389
Krosigk, General Ernst-Anton von 79
Krottingen 60, 70
Kryakhov, Major 249
Krylov, Nikolai 93–4
Krylov, Vladimir 227
Kuban, Soviet ship 428
Kuckuck, Eva 144–5, 146, 275
Kuhlwilm, Hauptmann 282
Kühn, Rittmeister 69–70
Kühnek, Major 176, 190
Kurisches Haff, German ship 389
Kursk, Battle of (1943) 18, 109
Küspert, Hauptmann 191, 192, 193, 194–5, 381
KV-2, Russian tank 245

L 3, Soviet submarine 389, 390, 391
Lancaster bombers 235
Landsov, Lieutenant-Colonel 297
Lang, Generalmajor Joachim-Friedrich 387
Lange, Hauptmann 343
Lange, Henry 382–3
Lankau, Arthur 356, 357
Lasch, General Otto 106–7, 117, 149–50, 151, 156, 216,
  293–4, 296–7, 303, 304, 305, 306–7, 308–9, 310, 311,
  314, 315, 317, 321
  Nazi persecution 324, 327–8
Latvia 12, 26, 40, 47
Lauchert, Oberst Meinrad von 62, 63
Laza, Hauptmann 215
leaflet drops, Soviet 386
League of Nations 46
Ledebur, Oberst Freihur von 288
Lehndorff, Hans Graf von 144, 149, 294–5, 325–6, 433–6,
  441–2
Leipzig, German light cruiser 348
Lenin 4, 39
Leningrad 45
  German Army plans for occupation 17–18
  German retreat from 28
Leonhardt, Korvettenkapitän 222, 223
Leser, Oberbürgermeister 189–90
Lewinski, Major 317, 318, 323
Libau (Liepaja) 64, 68, 75
Licht, Hauptmann 51
Lieselotte Friedrich, German tanker 409
Lippert, Oberst Rolf 64
Lithuania 11, 12, 26, 40, 47, 78
  annexation of Memelland 46
Lodz 124
Lorenz, Generalmajor 216, 283, 292, 377
Lötzen fortress loss 207–8
Löwe, German torpedo boat 225–6, 227
Lowicz 10
'Lublin Committee' 237, 239
Luchinsky, General Alexander Alexandrovich 85
Luck, Hans von 30–1
Lüdecke, General der Pioniere Otto 181, 182
Luftwaffe, German 23, 24, 33, 34, 308, 386
  aerial reconnaissance *Ostfront* 111
  field divisions 33
  New Year's Day attack, Ardennes (1945) 101–2

Luftwaffe units
  12th Division 343
Luoke 54–8, 59, 61
Lüttwitz, Oberleutnant Smilo Freiherr von 121, 299
Lutze, Hauptsturmführer 376
Lützow, German pocket battleship 71, 190, 282, 357, 374
Lynx, German light tank 246

M 256, German minesweeper 389, 391
M 328, German minesweeper 389, 391
Mackert, Hauptmann 387–8
Maclean, Donald 438
Maidanek extermination camp 92
Maisky, Ivan 9
Makarenkov, Lieutenant 263
Malenkov, Georgi 44
Malotka, Hauptmann 300
Manstein, Erich von 14
Marienburg 257–8
Marinesko, Alexander 225, 226, 230, 234
Mars, Operation, Soviet 45
Marshall, General George 238
Maschke Commission 421
Masuria province 3–4
Masurian Lakes 106, 116, 117, 118
Matzky, General 78, 81, 126, 127, 139, 141, 201, 394, 395,
  396
Mauss, Generalleutnant Karl 177, 190, 335, 336, 337, 340,
  351, 352, 358
Me 163 Komet, German fighter 103
Me 262 Schwalbe, German fighter 103
Meier, Leutnant 373
Memel bridgehead 6, 46–76, 97, 98, 151, 156, 164, 166, 228,
  250, 296, 335, 446
Memelland Germans 46–7
  Lithuanian annexation 46
Merkator, German ship 389
Metgethen, Soviet atrocities 300
Meyer-Schewe, Major 261
Mikosch, General Hans 156
Minsk 309
Mischke, Emil 213–15, 280, 281
Mischke, Frau 214, 215
Molotov, Vyacheslav 9, 19, 44
Molotov–Ribbentrop Pact (1939) 40, 47, 236, 329
  Polish Protocol (Article II) 9, 40
Moltkefels, German freighter 381–3
'Mongols' (German propaganda term) 326
Montgomery, Field Marshal Bernard 44, 96, 237, 404, 406,
  407, 418, 421, 422, 438, 445
Morgenstern, Erika 98, 152, 157–8, 326–7, 432–3, 442,
  454
Moscow 17
  Battle of 41, 65
  conference (1944) 239
Mosquito fighter-bombers 235
Müller, General Friedrich Wilhelm 277, 279, 290, 292, 306,
  308–9, 315, 317, 328
  appointed commander of 4th Army 211
Müller, Generalleutnant Vincenz 309
Müller, Leutnant 55, 72, 73
Müller, Major 274
Müller-Rochholz, Hauptmann Friedrich 122
Mummert, Oberst Werner 82